HISTORICAL DICTIONARY OF NIGER

AFRICAN HISTORICAL DICTIONARIES
Edited by Jon Woronoff

1. *Cameroon,* by Victor T. LeVine and Roger P. Nye. 1974. Out of print. See No. 48.
2. *The Congo,* 2nd ed., by Virginia Thompson and Richard Adloff. 1984.
3. *Swaziland,* by John J. Grotpeter. 1975.
4. *The Gambia,* 2nd ed., by Harry A. Gailey. 1987.
5. *Botswana,* by Richard P. Stevens. 1975. Out of print. See No. 44.
6. *Somalia,* by Margaret F. Castagno. 1975.
7. *Benin [Dahomey],* 2nd ed., by Samuel Decalo. 1987. Out of print. See No. 61.
8. *Burundi,* by Warren Weinstein. 1976.
9. *Togo,* 2nd ed., by Samuel Decalo. 1987.
10. *Lesotho,* by Gordon Haliburton. 1977.
11. *Mali,* 2nd ed., by Pascal James Imperato. 1986.
12. *Sierra Leone,* by Cyril Patrick Foray. 1977.
13. *Chad,* 2nd ed., by Samuel Decalo. 1987.
14. *Upper Volta,* by Daniel Miles McFarland. 1978.
15. *Tanzania,* by Laura S. Kurtz. 1978.
16. *Guinea,* 3rd ed., by Thomas O'Toole with Ibrahima Bah-Lalya. 1995.
17. *Sudan,* by John Voll. 1978. Out of print. See No. 53.
18. *Rhodesia/Zimbabwe,* by R. Kent Rasmussen. 1979. Out of print. See No. 46.
19. *Zambia,* by John J. Grotpeter. 1979.
20. *Niger,* 2nd ed., by Samuel Decalo. 1989.
21. *Equatorial Guinea,* 2nd ed., by Max Liniger-Goumaz. 1988.
22. *Guinea-Bissau,* 2nd ed., by Richard Lobban and Joshua Forrest. 1988.
23. *Senegal,* by Lucie G. Colvin. 1981. Out of print. See No. 65.
24. *Morocco,* by William Spencer. 1980.
25. *Malawi,* by Cynthia A. Crosby. 1980. Out of print. See No. 54.
26. *Angola,* by Phyllis Martin. 1980. Out of print. See No. 52.
27. *The Central African Republic,* by Pierre Kalck. 1980. Out of print. See No. 51.
28. *Algeria,* by Alf Andrew Heggoy. 1981. Out of print. See No. 66.
29. *Kenya,* by Bethwell A. Ogot. 1981.
30. *Gabon,* by David E. Gardinier. 1981. Out of print. See No. 58.
31. *Mauritania,* by Alfred G. Gerteiny. 1981. Out of print. See No. 68.

32. *Ethiopia,* by Chris Prouty and Eugene Rosenfeld. 1981. Out of print. See No. 56.
33. *Libya,* 2nd ed., by Ronald Bruce St John. 1991.
34. *Mauritius,* by Lindsay Rivire. 1982. Out of print. See No. 49.
35. *Western Sahara,* by Tony Hodges. 1982. Out of print. See No. 55.
36. *Egypt,* by Joan Wucher King. 1984. Out of print. See No. 67.
37. *South Africa,* by Christopher Saunders. 1983.
38. *Liberia,* by D. Elwood Dunn and Svend E. Holsoe. 1985.
39. *Ghana,* by Daniel Miles McFarland. 1985. Out of print. See No. 63.
40. *Nigeria,* by Anthony Oyewole. 1987.
41. *Côte d'Ivoire (The Ivory Coast),* 2nd ed., by Robert J. Mundt. 1995.
42. *Cape Verde,* 2nd ed., by Richard Lobban and Marilyn Halter. 1988. Out of print. See No. 62.
43. *Zaire,* by F. Scott Bobb. 1988.
44. *Botswana,* by Fred Morton, Andrew Murray, and Jeff Ramsay. 1989.
45. *Tunisia,* by Kenneth J. Perkins. 1989.
46. *Zimbabwe,* 2nd ed., by R. Kent Rasmussen and Steven L. Rubert. 1990.
47. *Mozambique,* by Mario Azevedo. 1991.
48. *Cameroon,* 2nd ed., by Mark W. DeLancey and H. Mbella Mokeba. 1990.
49. *Mauritius,* 2nd ed., by Sydney Selvon. 1991.
50. *Madagascar,* by Maureen Covell. 1995.
51. *The Central African Republic,* 2nd ed., by Pierre Kalck; translated by Thomas O'Toole. 1992.
52. *Angola,* 2nd ed., by Susan H. Broadhead. 1992.
53. *Sudan,* 2nd ed., by Carolyn Fluehr-Lobban, Richard A. Lobban, Jr., and John Obert Voll. 1992.
54. *Malawi,* 2nd ed., by Cynthia A. Crosby. 1993.
55. *Western Sahara,* 2nd ed., by Anthony Pazzanita and Tony Hodges. 1994.
56. *Ethiopia and Eritrea,* 2nd ed., by Chris Prouty and Eugene Rosenfeld. 1994.
57. *Namibia,* by John J. Grotpeter. 1994.
58. *Gabon,* 2nd ed., by David Gardinier. 1994.
59. *Comoro Islands,* by Martin Ottenheimer and Harriet Ottenheimer. 1994.
60. *Rwanda,* by Learthen Dorsey. 1994.
61. *Benin,* 3rd ed., by Samuel Decalo. 1995.
62. *Republic of Cape Verde,* 3rd ed., by Richard Lobban and Marlene Lopes. 1995.
63. *Ghana,* 2nd ed., by David Owusu-Ansah and Daniel Miles McFarland. 1995.

64. *Uganda,* by M. Louise Pirouet. 1995.
65. *Senegal,* 2nd ed., by Andrew F. Clark and Lucie Colvin Phillips. 1994.
66. *Algeria,* 2nd ed., by Phillip Chiviges Naylor and Alf Andrew Heggoy. 1994.
67. *Egypt,* by Arthur Goldschmidt, Jr. 1994.
68. *Mauritania,* by Anthony G. Pazzanita. 1996.
69. *Togo,* 3rd ed., by Samuel Decalo. 1996.
70. *Congo,* 3rd ed., by Samuel Decalo, Virginia Thompson, and Richard Adloff. 1996.
71. *Mali,* 3rd ed., by Pascal James Imperato. 1996.
72. *Niger,* 3rd ed., by Samuel Decalo. 1997.

HISTORICAL DICTIONARY OF NIGER

Third Edition

by
Samuel Decalo

African Historical Dictionaries, No. 72

The Scarecrow Press, Inc.
Lanham, Md., and London
1997

SCARECROW PRESS, INC.

Published in the United States of America
by Scarecrow Press, Inc.
4720 Boston Way
Lanham, Maryland 20706

4 Pleydell Gardens, Folkestone
Kent CT20 2DN, England

British Cataloguing-in-Publication Information Available

Library of Congress Cataloging-in-Publication Data

Decalo, Samuel
Historical dictionary of Niger / by Samuel Decalo. — 3rd ed.
p. cm. — (African historical dictionaries ; no. 20)
Includes bibliographical references.
ISBN 0-8108-3136-8 (cloth : alk. paper)
1. Niger—History—Dictionaries. I. Title. II. Series.
DT547.5.D4 1997
966.26′033—dc20 95-52222
CIP

ISBN 0-8108-3136-8 (cloth: alk. paper)

♾ ™ The paper used in this publication meets the minimum requirements of American National Standard for Information Sciences—Permanence of Paper for Printed Library Materials, ANSI Z39.48—1984.
Manufactured in the United States of America.

For Roma, Ruth, and Niv

Contents

Editor's Foreword

While realizing the difficulties, Niger was among the African countries that could approach independence with relatively high expectations. The new state was rather large, covering a big chunk of West Africa, yet had a comparatively small population. Politically, it was united around a single party directed by one of the more promising leaders, Hamani Diori. Although its economy was quite backward, it was lucky enough to have huge reserves of uranium which could finance its development. Yet, as it turned out, Niger has not done particularly well. The civilian regime failed the tests of leadership and, because of uranium wealth, that of probity, while the economy faltered once the price of uranium fell. Successive military regimes were equally dismal failures, and the recent post-democratization civilian governments have not been able to provide new directions.

This means that Niger can now be grouped with the relative failures although by no means the worst. Its leadership is weak, incapable of solving the many nagging problems, and not even certain to hold the country together as ethnic and religious frictions grow. There are no real prospects of economic progress or even paying off its debts. The only positive sign is that the latest governments have been elected by the people rather than imposed on them, and democracy may give them a better chance of sorting out any difference and charting a new, if painful, way forward. This is essential for the Nigeriens. It is also important for the rest of Africa, since ethnic groups spill over the frontiers, and this centrally located country has seven neighboring states.

This is the third edition of the *Historical Dictionary of Niger*. Like its predecessors, it was written by Samuel Decalo, who has followed events very closely over the years and summed them up for us periodically. Dr. Decalo is one of the foremost authorities on West Africa, and especially its military and Francophone regimes, and has written a number of significant books on the subject. He has also written the Benin, Chad, Congo, and Togo volumes in this series. He is currently Professor of Political Science at the University of Natal, South Africa, and Visiting Professor at the University of Florida in Gainesville.

Jon Woronoff
Series Editor

Recent Political Chronology

Jan. 13, 1899	Infamous Voulet-Chanoine Mission leaves for Zinder.
July 29, 1899	Battle of Tirmini and defeat of Damagaram. Occupation of Zinder the next day.
Sept. 15, 1899	Sultan Amadou of Damagaram killed in Roumji, avenging the murder of Cazemajou.
July 23, 1900	Territoire Militaire de Zinder established.
June 22, 1910	Territoire Militaire du Niger established.
Jan. 1, 1911	Zinder designated as capital.
Dec. 7, 1915	Tibesti, recently conquered and pacified, attached to the Kaouar cercle of Niger.
Dec. 13, 1916	Siege of Agadez by Tuareg troops led by Kaocen.
Mar. 3, 1917	Siege of Agadez finally lifted by French reinforcements from Zinder.
Oct. 13, 1922	Colonie du Niger established.
Aug. 1926	Niamey designated capital of the colony.
Nov. 11, 1929	Tibesti detached from Niger and attached to Chad.
May 20, 1957	After territorial elections in which Djibo Bakary's UDN is victorious, a council of government is set up under his leadership.
Sept. 28, 1958	Referendum in all French Africa; Bakary's call for a "no" vote defeated in Niger.
Dec. 14, 1958	Legislative elections in which the PPN emerges victorious, defeating Bakary's SAWABA.
Oct. 18, 1959	SAWABA banned.
Aug. 3, 1960	Proclamation of independence.
Dec. 3, 1963	Incidents along the Dahomey border, origin of the Lété Island border dispute.
Dec. 13, 1963	Arrest of Captain Diallo and others for a mutiny plot.
Sept.–Oct. 1964	SAWABA guerrillas attack Niger frontier posts.
Jan. 1965	Reconciliation with Dahomey at Yamassoukro, Côte d'Ivoire.
Apr. 13, 1965	Grenade attack on President Diori by SAWABA.
May 16–25, 1965	Ikhia Zodi and Captain Diallo sentenced to death. Trial of sixty-five people accused of involvement with SAWABA's guerrilla drive.

Nov. 23, 1965	Major government shuffle and purge of elements suspected of being disloyal. Dispatch on diplomatic assignments of key cabinet ministers.
Feb. 17, 1969	Francophone conference in Niamey decides to set up a common organization.
Aug. 1970	Onset of the Sahel drought.
Jan. 4, 1973	Breaking off of diplomatic relations with Israel.
Mar. 9, 1974	Treaty of Defense and Security with Libya.
Apr. 15, 1974	Coup d'état of Lieutenant Colonel Kountché deposes President Hamani Diori.
Apr. 17, 1974	Formation of an all-military provisional government.
June 8, 1974	First shuffle in Kountché's military cabinet, as a result of internal splits and tensions.
Dec. 1974	Commission of inquiry implicates most members of former president Hamani Diori's cabinet of embezzlement and other fiscal irregularities.
Mar. 15, 1976	Attempted coup by former ministers Bayeré and Sidi.
Apr. 21, 1976	Key leaders of the March 15 conspiracy executed.
Apr. 15, 1979	Decree proclaiming the establishment in Niger of a "Development Society."
Feb. 5, 1980	Five-Year Plan (1979–83) published.
Mar. 18, 1980	First meeting of the high-powered committee charged with outlining the details of Niger's Development Society.
Jan. 13, 1981	Libyan embassy closed down after its transformation into a People's Bureau.
Feb. 25, 1981	Uranium Road inaugurated.
Apr. 14, 1981	Anou Ararêh thermal complex inaugurated.
Apr. 14, 1982	New National Assembly inaugurated.
Jan. 1, 1983	Kountché promoted to general.
Jan. 1983	More than a hundred thousand Nigeriens expelled from Nigeria.
Jan. 24, 1983	A dual executive established with the appointment of a prime minister.
Nov. 15, 1983	New, largely civilian cabinet set up with Hamid Algabid as prime minister.
Apr. 4, 1984	Bakary and Diori released from house arrest.
May 15, 1984	Mamane Oumarou, former prime minister, appointed president of the Conseil National de Développement.
Nov. 14, 1984	Diplomatic relations with Libya resumed.
Nov. 16, 1984	Decision reached to privatize partially up to twenty enterprises of the fifty-four in the parastatal sector in light of their heavy deficits and budgetary squeezes.

	Though some are privatized, unionist opposition keeps most intact, with the public sector expanding over the next decade.
Dec. 3, 1984	Niger's public debt rescheduled as global uranium glut leads fall in uranium earnings, causing major budget squeezes.
Feb. 1985	The UNCC privatized.
May 29, 1985	Commando group intercepted prior to an attack on Tchin Tabaraden.
June 5, 1985	Anticorruption drive initiated after major embezzlements discovered in several state agencies.
June 23, 1985	Hamani Diori rearrested in connection with the attempted raid on Tchin Tabaraden by his son.
Dec. 31, 1986	President Kountché rushed to a hospital in Paris after suffering a heart attack.
Feb. 16, 1987	Kountché hospitalized in Paris for treatment of a brain ailment. Speculation mounts about the succession issue.
Nov. 10, 1987	President Kountché dies in Paris of brain tumor.
Nov. 14, 1987	Chief of Staff General Ali Saibou, nominated by the Supreme Military Council, is sworn in as Kountché's successor, as Colonel Moumouni, head of an opposing Djerma clan, is sidelined and later appointed ambassador to the U.N.
Aug. 22, 1988	Twenty-eight plotters of the 1983 coup are tried in camera, and four death sentences are handed down. Those acquitted, however, are rearrested after the verdict, on General Saibou's orders. The executions are to plague Saibou after democratization.
Sept. 1988	France's economic disengagement from Africa most visible in Niger, where figures reveal 82 percent of entrepreneurs deserted the country between 1985 and 1987.
Nov. 13, 1988	Saibou announces the first legislative and presidential elections since 1974 will be held on December 10, 1989, after a constitutional referendum on September 24, 1989.
Apr. 23, 1989	Former president Hamani Diori, released by Ali Saibou, dies in Rabat, Morocco.
May 17, 1989	Presidential and legislative elections announced for December. Saibou, elected president of the MNSD, Niger's single political party, will be the sole presidential candidate.

Sept. 24, 1989	New constitution ratified by referendum, with alleged 95.08 percent participation and 99.28 percent approval rate.
Nov. 2, 1989	List of the ninety-three approved candidates for the legislature published.
Dec. 1, 1989	Two hundred employees laid off as Niger's development bank, the BDRN, is formally declared bankrupt.
Dec. 10, 1989	First presidential and legislative elections in nineteen years take place, allegedly with over 99 percent electoral ratification of the candidates.
Feb. 8–12, 1990	Large demonstrations by students in Niamey, aggravated over scholarship cuts and restricted hiring by the civil service; they clash with the police, resulting in twenty deaths and the closure of schools and the university. Debate about the responsibility for the student deaths is to reverberate throughout the 1990s.
Feb. 16, 1990	Renewed student riots.
Apr. 1990	Major cutbacks announced in Niger's foreign diplomatic representation, in allowances to members of the government, and in official use of water, electricity, and phones.
May 6, 1990	A Tuareg attack on Tchin Tabaraden, aimed at stealing arms, is quelled. In the ensuing "pacifications," security forces massacre either 66 (government figures), 600 to 700 (humanitarian organizations' estimates), or 1,500 (Tuareg claims) people. In retrospect the event marks the onset of a full-scale Tuareg rebellion in Niger.
May 1, 1990	USTN calls for a multiparty system, a demand rejected by Saibou as premature.
June 11–12, 1990	General strike called by the USTN, expressly forbidden by the regime, a success. Saibou retreats on June 15, pledging to revise the constitution to allow for political pluralism.
July–Nov. 1990	Social unrest widens in Niger, including the country's longest (five-day) union strike to date in September, over multipartyism and resistance to the repercussions of a Structural Adjustment Plan freezing civil service hiring and salaries. The SAP is not fully implemented as of the 1990s.
Nov. 15, 1990	Saibou announces a multiparty system is to be implemented.
Nov. 16, 1990	Students demonstrate for the trial of those responsible for the February shootings of students, and for

	payment of registration fees; the threat of a general strike again is voiced.
Nov. 20, 1990	A fundamentalist Muslim party, pledged to create a truly Muslim society, is the first to register.
Feb. 8, 1991	The CCCE cancels 21.1 billion CFA francs of Niger's debt.
Feb. 26, 1991	University of Niamey again closed down after students riot, demanding punishment of those responsible for the previous year's killings of students.
Mar. 1, 1991	Tuareg attack travelers in the north.
Mar. 10, 1991	Fifteen new political parties register. The MNSD, after an extraordinary congress, declares itself a "simple party" with Saibou "above politics." The armed forces also formally "disengage" from commitment to the MNSD.
Mar. 12, 1991	Virtually all of Niger's debt to foreign banks ($107 million) assumed by the World Bank.
Mar. 23, 1991	Peaceful demonstrations in Niamey over the MNSD's arrogating to itself the organization of a National Conference to thrash out details of the new political order.
Mar. 31, 1991	The government caves in to USTN demands and lifts the austerity measures in effect since May 1990; the USTN cancels a general strike scheduled for April 3.
May 1991	Military executions of innocent Tuareg in neighboring Mali, where unrest has been intermittent, highlights the spread of the "Tuareg problem" in the region.
July 12, 1991	General Saibou resigns as president of the MNSD.
July 29, 1991	The National Conference convenes with 1,204 delegates. André Salifou, one of Niger's most famous scholars, is elected conference president. He later is elected head of the HCR, the provisional parliament.
Aug. 9, 1991	The National Conference suspends the existing constitution, and indicts General Saibou, the inspector general of the army, the interior minister and the prefect of Tahoua as culpable for the February 1990 student deaths.
Sept. 1, 1991	One hundred Tuareg, armed with rocket and grenade launchers, destroy a border checkpoint, symbolically erasing their division between Mali and Niger, which dates from colonial times.
Sept. 3, 1991	Niger's army chief of staff and his deputy are

	dismissed for their responsibility in the Tuareg massacres after the 1990 Tchin Tabaraden incident.
Sept. 30, 1991	Gendarmerie headquarters stormed and ransacked by army soldiers over the arrest of one of their officers.
Oct. 11, 1991	The National Conference, despite some dissent, decides to keep Saibou as interim head of state. Revelations surface of massive fiscal improprieties of his predecessor, General Kountché.
Oct. 12, 1991	Amadou Cheiffou, a political newcomer, is elected by the National Conference as interim prime minister until the scheduled 1993 elections.
Oct. 19, 1991	Two retired senior officers are placed under arrest for their role in the execution of Major Sani Souna Sido after his attempted coup in 1976.
Oct. 21, 1991	Armed Tuareg attack on In Gall.
Oct. 31, 1991	Niger's worst bout of interethnic fighting sees a hundred Fulani hacked to death by Hausa over a grazing incident 300 miles east of Niamey.
Nov. 3, 1991	The National Conference, originally scheduled to last forty days, winds up after a three-month conclave.
Nov. 14, 1991	The interim government announces draconian austerity measures to cope with Niger's parlous economic straits.
Dec. 20, 1991	Details on a rent freeze coupled with a 4–8 percent "solidarity tax" on salaries is published.
Jan. 8, 1992	Following continued raids, Niger for the first time admits the existence of a Tuareg "rebellion" as opposed to "armed banditry" in its northern regions, and calls for negotiations. The rebel FLAA demands the withdrawal of government troops first.
Jan. 22, 1992	Tuareg attack on tourists on the Arlit–Agadez road.
Jan. 28, 1992	Niger's 1988 census is published, indicating a population of 7.2 million, nearly half below the age of fifteen. By 1995 there are 8.8 million Nigeriens, with a projected 21.3 million for the year 2025.
Feb. 28, 1992	Mutiny of Niger troops in Niamey over nonpayment of their salaries for two months. Two other mutinies take place, quelled by loyalist troops and a strike of unionists.
Mar. 10, 1992	The Garde Républicaine is dismantled.
Mar. 23, 1992	Prime Minister Cheiffou dissolves his transitional government, claiming it was unable to surmount its ethnic divisions or cope with the country's economic problems. New cabinet formed on March 27.

Apr. 3, 1992	Niger's 1992 budget is decided upon, balanced at 27 percent less than that of 1991.
May 15, 1992	Truce agreed upon by the Tuareg FLAA and the government.
July 21–22, 1992	Two Tuareg assaults in northern Niger.
July 1992	Students strike over four-month arrears in their grants, culminating in taking hostage the minister of education.
July 20, 1992	Clashes with animists in Zinder take place, as Muslim fundamentalists claim debauchery has caused the rains not to come on time.
July 31, 1992	Niger recognizes Taiwan after the latter offers $50 million in aid; the People's Republic of China suspends relations.
Aug. 8, 1992	Fulani-Songhay ethnic clashes east of Niamey.
Aug. 24, 1992	Two-day strike by more than eight hundred customs workers over back pay.
Aug. 27, 1992	In a crackdown in the north, the army arrests 186 Tuareg supporters in Aïr, including several politicians. Another Tuareg appeal to the U.N. on their plight.
Sept. 9, 1992	Tuareg attack on convoy escorting civilians near Agadez.
Oct. 2, 1992	Segments of the north declared "zones of protection" and placed under military administration.
Oct. 29, 1992	FLAA attacks In Gall.
Dec. 26, 1992	Referendum approves Niger's new constitution.
Feb. 7, 1993	Another Tuareg attack in the north, raising the number of their hostages to fifty.
Feb. 14, 1993	Niger's first free legislative elections since independence take place. The anti-MNSD nine-party coalition gains fifty of the eighty-three seats.
Feb. 27, Mar. 13, 1993	First round of the presidential elections give Mamadou Tandja of the MNSD the lead with 34.22 percent of the vote *vis* Mahamane Ousmane of the CDS coalition with 26.59 percent.
Mar. 6, 1993	Police strike over their conditions of service; later unions join in over a three-months pay backlog.
Mar. 27, 1993	After several deals with other candidates Mahamane Ousmane wins the second round of the presidential elections, to become president, marking the ascendance to power of the country's Hausa majority.
Apr. 13, 1993	Djermakoy Adamou Moumouni is elected president of the National Assembly, part of a deal with Ousmane under which he withdrew his presidential candidacy. The MNSD protests the unconstitutionality of

	the election. The results are overturned by the Supreme Court; he is nevertheless reelected.
Apr. 17, 1993	Mahamadou Issoufou is appointed by Ousmane as prime minister. Gaining 15.9 percent in the first round of the presidential elections, he had withdrawn from the second ballot in favor of Ousmane.
Apr. 29, 1993	Three thousand students demonstrate in Niamey as a warning to the government not to contemplate cutting their grants or restricting the civil service's hiring from their ranks.
May 18, 1993	Youths sets fire to the headquarters of four political parties over the government's May 3 decision to close down all schools for the remainder of the year.
Apr. 1994	Muslim fundamentalists, proselytizing animists, clash with police, leaving ten dead.
Apr. 17, 1994	Three key politicians—Tandja, Salifou, and Issoufou Assoumane—briefly arrested after violent demonstrations in Niamey against Ousmane's government.
May 3, 1994	Customs officers go on four-day strike, the third in two years.
May 12, 1994	A new liberation front announces its formation, this time grouping the Kanuri and Toubou of the southeast near Lake Chad.
May 18, 1994	Violent student demonstrations in Niamey over stipends.
June 1, 1994	Civil service goes on strike over austerity measures.
June 22, 1994	Renewed peace talks in Paris between the government and Tuareg rebel leaders.
July 25, 1994	Niger's 39,000 civil servants suspend their strike to allow negotiations with the government to take place.
Aug. 12, 1994	Tuareg assault on government troops.
Aug. 16, 1994	Tuareg attempt to disrupt electricity supplies to Niger's uranium mines.
Sept. 28, 1994	Prime Minister Issoufou resigns to join the opposition, claiming his powers were being whittled down by the president. Minister of Commerce Souley Abdoulaye becomes prime minister.
Oct. 9, 1994	Fragile peace agreement negotiated with the Tuareg rebel groups after negotiations in Burkina Faso.
Oct. 16, 1994	Souley Abdoulaye ousted by a vote of "no confidence" in an Assembly now dominated by the opposition.
Oct. 26, 1994	Ignoring contrary advice from France, President Ousmane announces new parliamentary elections for December 31, 1994.

Jan. 12, 1995	Parliamentary elections, conducted amid massive apathy and low turnout, reflect the new balance of power, with the coalition forged by Tandja's MNSD gaining an edge over Ousmane.
Feb. 7, 1995	Ignoring the MNSD's parliamentary ascendance and its choice for the post, President Ousmane appoints Amadou Cisse as prime minister.
Feb. 20, 1995	Amadou Cisse is ousted by a vote of censure before he can present a cabinet.
Feb. 21, 1995	President Ousmane is forced to appoint MNSD secretary general Hama Amadou as prime minister. The new cabinet includes no one from Ousmane's political alliance.
Mar. 13, 1995	Attack in southeast Niger by the new Toubou-Kanuri liberation movement leaves eighteen dead.
Apr. 15, 1995	Peace accord signed between a Tuareg umbrella group and the government of Niger, formally marking the end of the Tuareg revolt. Clashes with dissident groups nevertheless continue.
July 6, 1995	The Ousmane-Amadou tug-of-war continues to paralyze governance.
Dec. 10, 1995	Niger reluctantly signs a Structural Adjustment letter of intent.
Jan. 27, 1996	Coup d'etat by Col. Mainassara to end the "absurd, irrational and personalized" executive paralysis. The first coup in Francophone Africa to oust a newly civilianized regime leads to global condemnation and suspension of aid.
Feb. 1, 1996	The junta appoints a transitional civilian cabinet, pledging elections later in 1996. Ousmane and Amadou, released by the military, accept their dismissal and appeal for a restoration of foreign aid. France, but not other donors, relents on March 6th. A 30 percent civil service paycut is rescinded when the unions threaten strikes.
April 1–7, 1996	Six hundred junta-appointed delegates codify a new constitution in a Democratic Renewal Forum conclave. A new peace accord with the Tuareg is signed, but periodic clashes occur with the Toubou near Lake Chad.
May 12, 1996	The new constitution is ratified by referendum, though 64.9 percent of the electorate, and more in Niamey, abstain. Mainassara (now General), Tandja, and Moumouni, all military officers, as well as Ousmane and Issoufou to contest the Presidential elections.
May 19, 1996	Ban on parties lifted, with parliamentary elections slated for late 1996.

Acronyms and Abbreviations

AANL	Association d'Amitié Nigéro-Libyenne
ABN	Autorité du Basin du Niger
ACCTF	Agence de Coopération Culturelle et Technique des Pays Francophones
AEF	Afrique Equatoriale Française
AFC	Alliance des Forces du Changement
AFN	Association des Femmes du Niger
AIN	Association Islamique du Niger
AMM	Affaires Militaires Musulmanes
ANDP	Alliance Nigérienne pour la Démocratie et le Progrès
AOF	Afrique Occidentale Française
ARCN	Association des Radio-Clubs du Niger
ARLA	Armée Révolutionnaire de Libération de l'Azawad
ARLN	Armée Révolutionnaire de Libération du Nord Niger
ASECNA	Agence pour la Sécurité de la Navigation Aérienne
BALINEX	Banque Arabe Libyenne Nigérienne pour le Commerce Extérieur et le Développement
BCC	Banque du Crédit et du Commerce
BCEAO	Banque Centrale des Etats de l'Afrique de l'Ouest
BCL	Bureau de Coordination et de Liaison
BCN	Banque Commerciale du Niger
BDRN	Banque de Développement de la République du Niger
BIAO	Banque Internationale pour l'Afrique Occidentale
BICIN	Banque Internationale pour le Commerce et l'Industrie du Niger
BID	Banque Islamique du Développement
BIN	Banque Islamique du Niger
BIPN	Banque Internationale pour le Niger
BNA	Bloc Nigérien d'Action
BRANIGER	Brasseries du Niger
BUREMI	Bureau des Mines
C.A.	Convention Africaine
CAA	Conseil Africain d'Arachide
CBLT	Commission du Bassin du Lac Tchad

CCCE	Caisse Centrale de Coopération Economique
CCD	Commission Consultative Départementale
CCFOM	Caisse Centrale de la France d'Outre-Mer
CDC	Caisse des Dépôts et Consignations
CDS	Convention Démocratique et Sociale
CEA	Commission Exécutive d'Arrondissement
CEM	Commission Exécutive Municipale
CFA	Communauté Financière Africaine
CFAO	Companie Française de l'Afrique Occidentale
CFDT	Compagnie Française pour le Développement des Fibres Textiles
CFN	Commission du Fleuve Niger
CLD	Conseils Locaux du Développement
CMS	Conseil Militaire Supérieur
CNCA	Caisse Nationale de Crédit Agricole
CND	Conseil National de Développement
CNRS	Centre National de la Recherche Scientifique
CNRSH	Centre National de Recherches en Sciences Humaines
COMINAK	Compagnie Minière d'Akouta
CONOCO	Continental Oil Company
COPRO-NIGER	Société Nationale de Commerce et de Production du Niger
COTEDEP	Comité Technique Départemental
CPCT	Caisse de Prêt aux Collectivités Territoriales
CRA	Coordination de la Résistance Armée
CRD	Conseils Régionaux du Développement
CRDTO	Centre Régional de Documentation pour la Tradition Orale
CSLTN	Confédération des Syndicats Libres de Travailleurs du Niger
CSON	Conseil Supérieur d'Orientation Nationale
CSPPN	Caisse de Stabilisation des Prix des Produits du Niger
CVD	Conseils Villageois de Développement
ECOWAS	Economic Community of West African States
EDF	European Development Fund
EMAIR	Ecole Minière de l'Aïr
ENA	Ecole Nationale d'Administration
FAC	Fonds d'Aide et de Coopération
FDAPR	Fonds de Dotation pour l'Amélioration de la Productivité Rurale
FDN	Forces Démocratiques Nigériennes
FDR	Front pour la Démocratique Renouveau
FDU	Front Démocratique Uni
FEANF	Fédération des Etudiants de l'Afrique Noire en France
FED	Fonds Européen de Développement

FIAA	Front Islamique Arabe de l'Azawad
FIDES	Fonds d'Investissement pour le Développement Economique et Sociale des Territoires d'Outre-Mer
FIPMEN	Fond d'Intervention en Faveur des Petites et Moyennes Entreprises Nigériennes
FLAA	Front de Libération de l'Aïr et de l'Azawad
FLT	Front de Libération de Temust
FNI	Fonds National d'Investissement
FNN	Front Nigérien National
FOI	Front Oumma Islamique
FPLA	Front Populaire de Libération de l'Azawad
FPLN	Front Populaire pour la Libération du Niger
FPLS	Front Populaire de Libération du Sahara
G.R.	Garde Républicaine
HCR	Haut Conseil de la République
IFAN	Institut Français d'Afrique Noire
IMF	International Monetary Fund
INDRAP	Institut National de Recherche Pédagogique
ING	Institut National de Géstion
INRA	Institut National de la Recherche Agronomique
IOM	Indépendants d'Outre-Mer
IPDR	Institut Pratique de Développement Rural
MFUA	Mouvement des Fronts Unifiés de l'Azawad
MNSD	Movement National de la Société de Développement
MOUNCORE	Mouvement Nigérien de Comités Révolutionnaires
MPA	Mouvement Populaire de l'Azawad
MPLA	Mouvement Populaire pour la Libération de l'Azawad
MRLN	Mouvement Révolutionnaire pour la Libération Nationale
MSA	Mouvement Socialiste Africain
NIGELEC	Société Nigérienne d'Electricité
NIGERTOUR	Société Nigérienne pour le Développement du Tourisme et l'Hôtellerie
NITEX	Société Nigérienne des Textiles
NITRA	Niger Transit
OCAMM	Organisation Commune Africaine, Malgache et Mauritienne
OCBN	Organisation Commune Bénin-Niger des Chemins de Fer et des Transports
OCDN	Organisation Commune Dahomey-Niger des Chemins de Fer et des Transports
OCRS	Organisation Commune des Régions Sahariennes
OFEDES	Office des Eaux du Sous-sol
OLANI	Office du Lait du Niger
ONAHA	Office National des Aménagements Hydro-Agricoles
ONAREM	Office National des Recherches et Exploitation Minière

ONERSOL	Office de l'Energie Solaire
ONPPC	Office Nigérien des Produits Pharmaceutiques et Chimiques
OPVN	Office des Produits Vivrers du Niger
ORA	Organisation de la Résistance Armée
ORTN	Office de Radiodiffusion-Télévision du Niger
PINE	Parti Indépendant du Niger-Est
PNDS	Parti Nigérien pour la Démocratie et le Socialisme
PPN	Parti Progressiste Nigérien
PRLPN	Parti Républicain pour les Libertés et le Progrès du Niger
PSDN	Parti Social-Démocrate Nigérien
PUND	Parti pour l'Unité Nationale et la Démocratie
RDA	Rassemblement Démocratique Africain
RDFN	Rassemblement Démocratique de Femmes du Niger
RINI	Riz du Niger
SAPELAC	Société Africaine des Piles Electriques
SCIMPEXNI	Syndicat des Commerçants, Importateurs et Exportateurs du Niger
SDN	Société de Développement du Niger
SEPANI	Société d'Exploitation des Produits d'Arachide du Niger
SHN	Société des Huileries du Niger
SIAM	Société Industrielle et Alimentaire de Magaria
SICONIGER	Société Industrielle et Commerciale du Niger
SMD	Société des Mines du Djado
SMDN	Société Minière du Dahomey-Niger
SMDR	Société Mutuelle de Développement Rural
SMPR	Société Mutuelle de Production Rurale
SMTT	Société Minière de Tassa N'Taghalgué
SNC	Société Nigérienne de Cimenterie
SNCF	Société Nigérienne de Collecte des Cuirs et Peaux
SNGTN	Société Nationale des Grands Travaux du Niger
SNH	Société Nigérienne d'Hôtellerie
SNTFM	Société Nigérienne des Transports Fluviaux et Maritimes
SNTN	Société Nationale des Transports Nigériens
SOGANI	Société des Gaz Industriels du Niger
SOMAIR	Société Minière d'Aïr
SONAL	Société Nigéro-Arabe-Libyenne
SONARA	Société Nigérienne de Commercialisation de l'Arachide
SONERAN	Société Nigérienne d'Exploitation des Ressources Animales
SONIA	Société Nigérienne d'Alimentation

SONIBANQUE	Société Nigérienne de Banque
SONICA	Société Nigérienne de Crédit Automobile
SONICERAM	Société Nigérienne de Céramique
SONICHAR	Société Nigérienne du Charbon d'Anou Araren
SONIDEP	Société Nigérienne de Produits Pétroliers
SONIFAME	Société Nigérienne de Fabrications Métalliques
SONIPRIM	Société Nigérienne des Primeurs
SONITA	Société Nigérienne des Transports Aériens
SONITAN	Société Nigérienne de Tannerie
SONITEXTIL	Société Nouvelle Nigérienne des Textiles
SOTRAMIL	Société de Transformation du Mil
SP	Société de Prevoyance
SPCN	Société de Produits Chimiques du Niger
SPEIN	Syndicat Patronal des Entreprises et Industries du Niger
SPMC	Syndicat des Petits et Moyens Commerçants du Niger
SST	Société des Salines de Tidekelt
STN	Société Nigérienne de Télévision
SYNAPEMEIN	Syndicat National des Petites et Moyennes Entreprises et Industries Nigériennes
SYNTRACOM	Syndicat National des Transporteurs et Commerçants
SYNTRAMIN	Syndicat des Travailleurs des Mines du Niger
UCFA	Union pour la Communauté Franco-Africaine
UDFP	Union Démocratique des Forces Progressistes
UDFR	Union Démocratique des Forces Révolutionnaires
UDN	Union Démocratique Nigérienne
UDP	Union pour la Démocratie et le Progrès
UDPS	Union pour la Démocratie et le Progrès Social
UFDP	Union des Forces pour la Démocratie et le Progrès
UFN	Union des Femmes du Niger
UNCC	Union Nigérienne de Crédit et de Coopération
UNDP	United Nations Development Plan
UNE	Union des Nigériens de l'Est
UNIS	Union Nigérienne des Indépendants et Sympathisants
UNTN	Union Nationale des Travailleurs du Niger
UPDP	Union des Patriotes Démocratiques et Progressistes
UPN	Union Progressiste Nigérienne
URANIGER	Office National de Recherches, d'Exploitation et de Commercialisation de l'Uranium du Niger
USN	Union des Scolaires Nigériens
USTN	Union des Syndicats des Travailleurs du Niger

Tables

Table 1: Population by Département, 1990

Niamey	1,818,000
Zinder	1,467,000
Maradi	1,415,000
Tahoua	1,373,000
Dosso	982,000
Diffa	227,000
Agadez	189,000

Table 2: Principal Agricultural Crops, 1991*

Millet	1,853,000
Sorghum	472,000
Pulses	387,000
Manioc	216,000
Sugar	140,000
Rice	71,000

*In tons

Table 3: Uranium Production, 1988–95, and Selected Prior Years*

1971	410	1992	2,504
1977	1,441	1993	2,500
1980	4,300	1994	2,504
1988	2,970	1995	2,878
1989	2,962		
1990	2,831		
1991	2,777		

*In tons

Table 4: Gross Domestic Product Growth and External Debt, 1989–93

	1989	1990	1991	1992	1993
GDP Growth (in %)	−6.5	2.2	1.0	-0-	-0-
External Debt (in millions)	$1,588	$1,824	$1,622	$1,711	$1,812
External Debt Service Ratio (in %)	32.2	24.8	30.1	14.2	15.0

Table 5: Breakdown of 1991 Gross Domestic Product

Agriculture and Livestock	35.2%
Services	35.2%
Industry	14.8%
Mining	8.7%
Manufacturing	6.1%

Table 6: Exports, 1992

Product		Destination	
Uranium	$190*	France	73.7%
Livestock	38	Algeria	8.6%
Peas	6	Canada	3.8%
		Côte d'Ivoire	3.6%

*In millions

Table 7: Imports, 1992.

Type		Origin	
Consumer Goods	$130*	France	21.7%
Raw Materials/Equipment	71	U.K.	10.6%
Cereals	22	Côte d'Ivoire	7.8%
Petroleum	20	Taiwan	3.7%

*In millions

Table 8: Imports/Exports and Balance of Trade, 1987–92

Year	Imports	Exports	Balance	Exports as % of Imports
1988	443.9	411.9	−31.9	92.79
1989	369.6	311.0	−61.4	84.14
1990	337.5	303.4	−58.6	89.89
1991	273.3	283.9	+10.6	103.87
1992	331.1	283.1	−50.0	85.50

Note: The "improved" balance of trade in 1991 was due to Niger's lack of funds, which put a lid on imports

Table 9: Recent Budgets

1985	$88.060*
1986	105.575
1987	123.331
1988	140.445
1989	138.547
1990	167.640
1991	132.105
1992	106.800
1993	108.320

*In millions of dollars

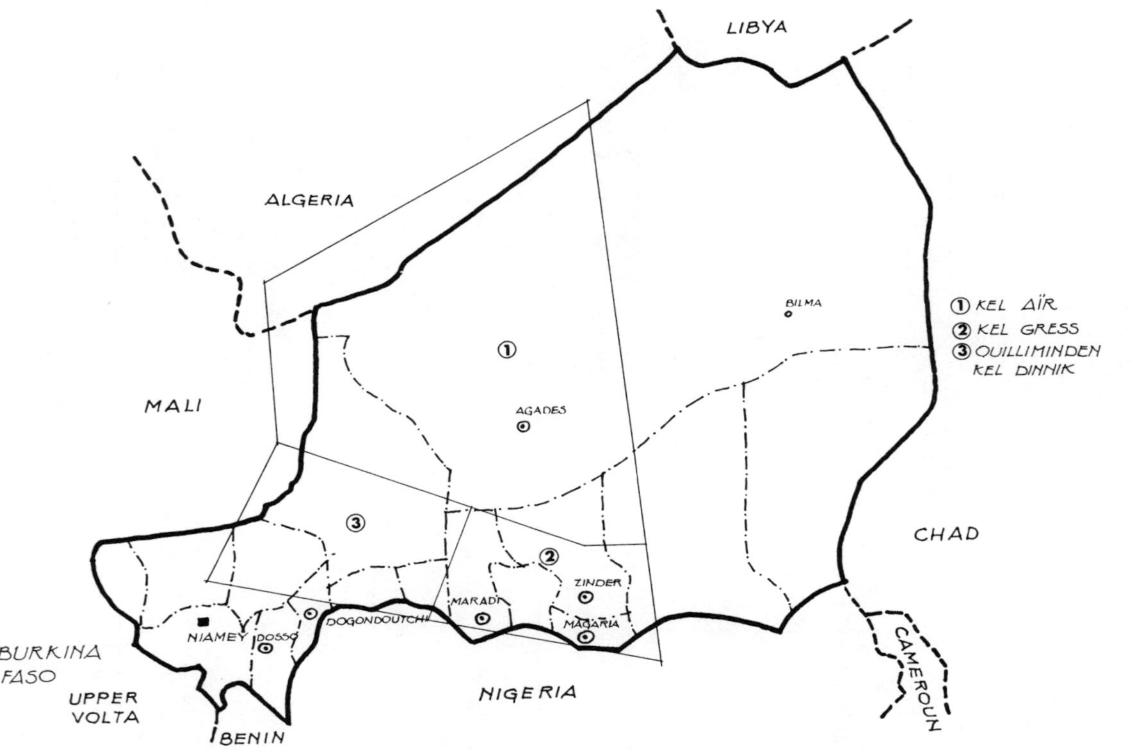

Niger: Nomadization areas of major Tuareg confederations

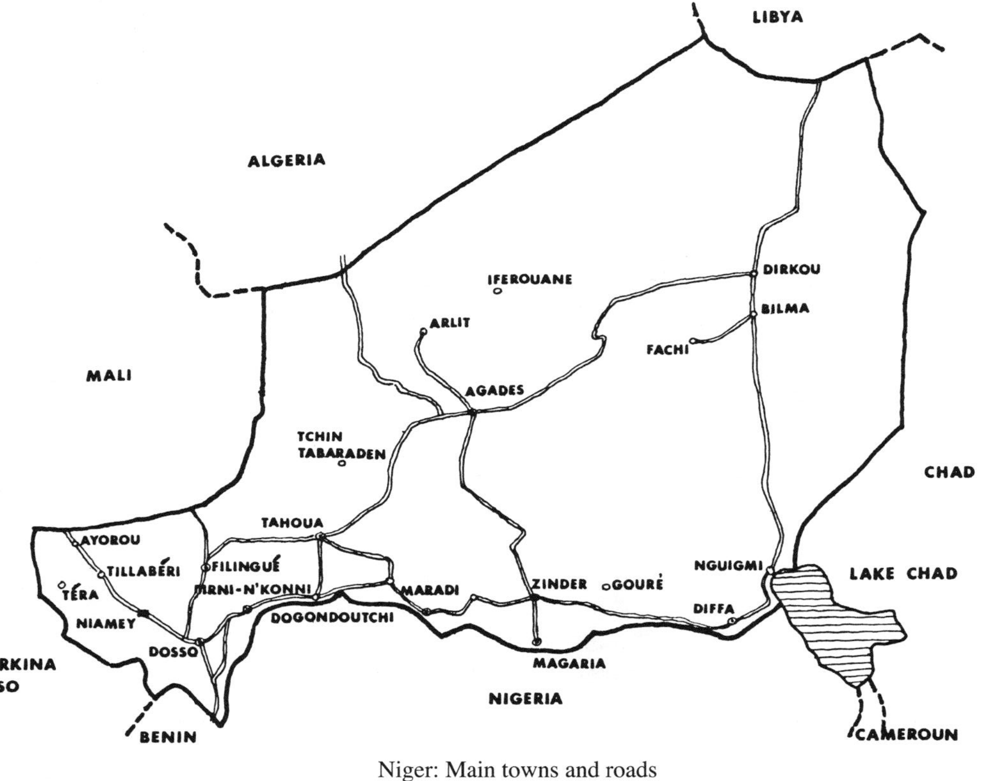

Niger: Main towns and roads

Introduction

Niger is the second largest state in West Africa, and one of only three in that region that are landlocked. It stretches over an expanse of 1.267 million sq km—twice the size of France—encompassing a segment of the Sahara Desert that constitutes roughly two-thirds of its own territory. In the south the country includes a fertile strip bordering the Niger River that, due to its 592-km course in Niger, gives the country its name. Africa's tenth largest country, at its last census (1988) Niger had a population of 7.2 million people, nearly 50 percent below the age of fifteen, largely concentrated in the southern third of the country. The north is very sparsely populated; the northeast, in particular, is uninhabitable.

Relief and Climate

Except for its northern regions, Niger is a relatively flat country with monotonous topographical features, numerous depressions, and a very harsh climate. It has three distinct climatic regions: (1) The intensely cultivated south, and especially the fertile Niger River region, with a mean altitude of 300–350 meters above sea level and with a Sahelian climate with one rainy season between June and October (preceded in June by violent tornadoes). (2) The arid transitional center of the country, suitable for nomadic pastoralists raising cattle, and with a sharply lower rainfall. This region is usually divided into the South Sahel belt, which receives between 350 and 750 mm of rainfall, permitting three to four months of agriculture in a region including Niamey, and the North Sahel belt (which includes Agadez), with a maximum of 350 mm of rainfall, in which true agriculture is impossible except in oases. Finally, (3) the desert expanses where there is little rainfall, and which include Ténéré and Bilma.

It is essentially only in the first area, comprising roughly 120,000 sq km—or some 10 percent of Niger's total territory—that intensive and/or regular agricultural activity is possible. The Sahel belts, marginally self-sufficient in good years, suffer tremendously in periods of drought. The overall population density of Niger, 5.2 people per sq km, reflects both the higher density in the south (60 per sq km) and the relative absence of populations in the desert areas of the north.

Niger is one of the hottest countries in the world. Niamey's temperature range is 47° F–114° F; Tillabéry's annual average maximum is 106° F, and in Aïr the range is from −23° F to 122° F in the shade. The country's wildlife, much decimated, includes small numbers of elephants, giraffes, hippos, and (in the W Park) lions, buffalo, and antelopes.

In terms of relief, the ruggedly beautiful Aïr mountains in the north are an extension of the Algerian Ahaggar Mountains, and include the core north-south 80,000–sq km Aïr massif (with an altitude of 700–800 meters), bisected by numerous ravines (*koris*) and punctuated by a north-south line of volcanic crests, as well as other isolated outcroppings. The northernmost of these includes Niger's highest elevation, the 2,300-meter-high Mont Gréboun. In the northeast a series of high plateaus form a bridge between Chad's Tibesti (until 1929 governed by Niger) and Algeria's Ahaggar massifs. These include the plateaus of Djado, Tchigai, and Manguéni. On each side of Aïr extend the Saharan sand lowlands. In the west is found the Talak Desert, which includes in its northern segment the Temesna region, where fossilized river valleys filled with shifting sand dunes flow south, and in the south the Azaoua region. In the east stretches the huge (400,000-sq-km) Ténéré Desert, with its large ergs interrupted only by the remote Kaouar oases to which caravans from Agadez (in Aïr) still trek for their salt output. Fossilized river valleys (*dallol*) "flow" from Aïr southward into the Niger River. Once filled with water, these tributaries of the Niger (and the drainage system of Aïr), some 5,000 to 6,000 years ago enabled the desert north to support large populations of pastoralists, hunters, and fishermen, as stunningly revealed in ancient cave drawings of rivers and wildlife.

In the east Niger includes 2560 sq. km. of Lake Chad, which in times of intense drought (as in 1970s and 1980s) greatly contracts (being essentially very shallow), allowing a dry crossing to Nigeria and Chad. Part of the frontier in this area (for 150 km) is formed by the Komadugu-Yobe river system (dry 1974–84), which flows from the west into the lake. In the south the Niger River—ninth longest in the world, and Africa's third largest—flows for 592 miles through Niger, from the rapids of Labezanga on the Malian frontier to Gaya on the Nigerian border. It receives several tributaries on its right side, notably the Goroul, Sirba, Tapoa, and Makrou. Its left bank is joined by the dry fossilized valleys that once drained the northern regions.

The landlocked country is bordered on the south by the long frontier with Nigeria and by Benin, on the west by Burkina Faso and Mali, on the north by Algeria and Libya (which claims a strip of land in the northeast), and on the east by Chad. Though caravans do travel in the east-west direction, communications are mostly along the north-south axis and along the southern road system connecting Zinder, Maradi, and Niamey with Mali. The southward route is utilized for the evacuation of all of Niger's exports and for the importation of the country's needs, via

Cotonou in Benin or the Nigerian ports. Niamey itself is some 2,500 km from Algiers, 2,000 km from Dakar, and 1,000 km from Cotonou, the nearest Atlantic port.

Population

Most of Niger's population of 7.1 million people (1988 estimate) resides in the southern départements, with those of Zinder (1.6 million), Niamey (1.7 million), Tahoua (1.2 million), Maradi (1.1. million), and Dosso (759,000) being the most populous. By contrast, in the huge Agadez département only 120,000 people are to be found.

Most of the people are from one of five basic ethnic groups. Just over half the population is Hausa, to be found in a broad arc north of the Nigerian border and in the key départements of Zinder and Maradi. Slightly less than one quarter of the population is of Djerma-Songhay ethnicity, usually residing west of the Hausa in a belt stretching into Mali. The Fulani of Niger number roughly 600,000 people and are scattered in small concentrations in the south center of the country. In the extreme east are found the Beri Beri (or Kanuri) and Manga, while the Tuareg (and their former slaves), comprising 11 percent (750,000) of the population, nomadize the vast expanse of Agadez département and central Niger, north of the Hausa-Fulani and Djerma-Songhay belt but at times in their close proximity.

The slow sedentation of society in Niger has lowered the country's nomadic groups to 20 percent of the total population and raised urbanization levels to 16 percent. Niamey, one of Africa's newest capital cities, was virtually nonexistent prior to the twentieth century. Even in 1976 it had a modest population of 160,000. Today, the modern nerve center of the country has over 400,000 people. Zinder and Maradi, both important economic centers in the heart of Niger's peanut-growing belt, until recently were closely tied for second place, with a population of around 40,000 each. In the late 1970s Zinder's population spurted, and currently stands at 90,000; Maradi's is 72,000. In fourth place is Tahoua with 45,000 people. In the far north, the ancient Agadez (until the 1990 Tuareg rebellion a magnet for tourists wishing to explore Aïr's spectacular scenery), prime city of the Sahara, has an estimated population of 30,000, while nearby the newly erected "uranium city" of Arlit has a population of 16,000. It should be noted, however, that at times of drought the transient population of some of these urban centers swells considerably.

Economy

Regarded until the 1970s as one of the world's least-endowed countries, and to this day one of the world's ten poorest (according to the World Bank), Niger's prospects were dramatically transformed by the discovery in Aïr of large deposits of uranium. By the early 1980s Niger had become the world's fifth (or possibly sixth) exporter of uranium. Since then other mineral resources have been discovered and some exploited, leading to the 1978 assessment by EEC Commissioner for Development Claude Cheysson that Niger was about to enter the economic takeoff stage with "stupefying" prospects for the future. Though one cannot exaggerate the degree to which state royalties from uranium exports transformed the utterly depressed Nigerien socioeconomic context, already by the early 1980s the prediction had to be drastically scaled down. In the face of a global glut in uranium and depressed prices, the role of uranium royalties in state finances plummeted to insignificance, and a fiscally overextended Niger was forced into a vicious bout of belt-tightening with little relief on the horizon. Today, producing only 3,000 tons of uranium a year, Niger has become the world's second largest exporter of the mineral (after Canada), though royalties account for less of 10 percent of state revenues. Other minerals beneath the Saharan sands that seemed to offer great promise in the 1980s (such as vast coal deposits) have likewise not delivered on expectations, though the country in 1995 was counting heavily on favorable feasibility studies on the exploitation of its gold fields.

Of the traditional subsistence crops, millet holds pride of place in Niger. Being Francophone Africa's prime millet producer, Niger plants fully 55 percent of its arable land with this crop, leading to harvests of up to one million tons. Except in times of extreme drought, around 10,000 tons is available for export, usually to Nigeria. Niger's second largest subsistence crop is sorghum, with production prior to the recent drought around 300,000 tons.

Until the exploitation of Niger's mineral wealth, the country's exports were primarily peanuts (constituting up to 85 percent of total exports) and cattle. Exports of both were severely depressed by the Sahel drought (peanut exports dropped to zero), which also brought widespread famine to many areas of Niger and a complex pattern of population movement. Roughly half a million people migrated into Nigeria, while a similar number—mostly Tuareg—flocked into Niger from the harder-hit Mali. Niger has no other significant agricultural exports, and of minerals only cassiterite, in very modest quantities (100–135 tons), was exported. Small quantities of natron from the Kaouar oases also find their way south to Nigeria, though most of this low-cost, high-volume commodity is consumed locally, and even in poorer communities commercial salt is replacing local natron. Niger also produces small amounts of gypsum and limestone in Ader-Doutchi and Malbaza, respectively.

The 1970s were essentially the years when Niger's extractive industry came of age. By 1980 the country was the West's fifth-largest uranium exporter, based on its rich Aïr mines. Whole new cities, facilities, and roads (and even the carving out of a separate arrondissement) have been created as a result of Niger's newly exploited uranium wealth. And with the exploitation of some of the richest mines in the world, other known deposits of minerals came under production. The best examples are the huge coal reserves at Anou Araren producing electricity for the uranium plants, and the over 250 million tons of iron ore near Say, hitherto regarded as uneconomic for exploitation. Traces of copper, lignite, zinc, chrome, molybdenum, oil, titanium, and phosphates (especially in the west near Burkina Faso) are also being further investigated, though attention has focused in the mid-1990s on gold.

The Precolonial Era

Prior to the arrival of French influence and control in the area, Niger was the meeting ground of Songhay and Bornu power exerted from the east and west, respectively, and later Tuareg and renascent Fulani power from the north and south.

Until the collapse of the Songhay Empire in Gao (Mali) at the end of the sixteenth century, parts of Niger, including Aïr, were under Songhay control. With the defeat of Gao to musket-bearing troops from Morocco, Aïr fell temporarily under the control of Bornu. The eastern provinces of Songhay—most currently in Niger—retained their independence but soon disintegrated into a series of small chiefdoms, easy prey to assaults from both north and south.

In the east Bornu's weakening hegemony over the territory was first challenged by the coalescing Sultanate of Damagaram, based in Zinder, which emerged as a powerful factor in east Niger, and later by renascent Fulani power in the south. The latter displaced certain Hausa groups northward, and much of the history of southern Niger in the nineteenth century is the story of a tug-of-war between these two ethnic groups along a frontier coinciding with the current Niger-Nigeria border.

The Tuareg, arriving in the eleventh century in Aïr and strengthened by further waves from the north (many coming from Ahaggar), created a population pressure in the north resulting in the migration of various clans (*kel*) southward, to clash with established sedentary groups. From this were born the persistent sedentary-versus-nomadic clashes of central and southern Niger that affected many Djerma, Songhay, Maouri, and Hausa settlements, and remain as fearful memories to many to this day.

The Colonial Era

With the entry of French explorers, and then military force, in the region, the various ethnic groups reacted differently. To the Tuareg—many of whom had been converted to the Sanusiya sect—the French were infidel conquerors threatening their culture, way of life, and military dominance over sedentary groups in the area, and thus had to be expelled. The concomitant Franco-Tuareg wars, fiercely fought and inadequately documented, greatly decimated most Tuareg confederations and in particular whole warrior castes. The Toubou in the Kaouar region similarly suffered devastation.

To the Djerma-Songhay, however, the French were much sought after allies who could assist them in stemming the inexorable dual pressures from north and south: the Tuareg and the Fulani. The Djerma, in particular, were from the outset avid Francophiles and joined in the French military "pacification" (colonial conquest) of the area. Their most enthusiastic ally was the chief of Dosso, Aouta, France's *grand ami,* whose descendant—former colonel Djermakoy Amadou Moumouni—is an important political leader in Niger today, though Dosso's colonial role has not been forgotten or forgiven by many groups, including Djerma, to this day. The Hausa were, on the other hand, alienated to some extent by France's refusal to assist them in regaining their territories lost to the Fulani in the south (what was to become north Nigeria) and by the abolition in 1906 of their Damagaram sultanate.

Sporadic revolts broke out among the four ethnic groups. It was not until 1922 that a civilian-headed Colonie du Niger was set up; some areas of the vast territory were not secure until the 1940s, and one (desert) region was under military administration until after the Second World War. Indeed, so distant and alien was central government from certain areas that until the 1990s, when disrupted due to the spread of the rebellions in northern Niger, the traditional Kaouar *azalay* had to be escorted by a military detachment, to protect it from marauders. The rebellions in north Niger brought back "colonial"-style military administration in "zones of protection," where all civilian transport is escorted by armed contingents.

Independence

Historically one of French Africa's most traditional and underdeveloped Muslim territories, Niger paradoxically nearly emerged at independence under a militantly radical regime. As elsewhere in Francophone Africa, the post–Second World War evolution of indigenous parties in Niger was a complex process full of splits and mergers that finally resulted in the ascendance of the RDA-affiliated Parti Progrèssiste Nigérien. Just prior to independence, however, the dominant power in Niger was the neo-Marxist MSA (later SAWABA) leader Djibo Bakary, who was Hamani Diori's cousin and had forged together a delicate coalition of Hausa chiefs from the east, militant unionists, and some conservative Djerma nobility, cemented by the temporary benevolent support of the local French administration. The coalition promptly collapsed, however, when Djibo Bakary appealed for a "no" vote in the 1958 de Gaulle referendum, which antagonized most of his supporting groups. Bakary's position on the referendum lost him the support of the administration (who then did everything they could to defeat him), and of the Hausa chiefs who feared that if the French were alienated and left Niger this would "unleash" renewed bouts of the Tuareg assaults of the past. Since politics in Niger had all along been very much an elite activity, and under the tight control of the country's powerful chiefs, Bakary's loss of support from these two groups brought about his defeat in the referendum, and shortly later in the subsequent territorial elections. The PPN, under Hamani Diori, and now with support of the French, emerged victorious and shortly later banned the SAWABA party and established a one-party system that lasted until the 1974 coup d'état. An amateurish attempted coup in 1963, a guerrilla assault on border posts, and a grenade attack on Diori brought about further repression and the consolidation of PPN rule.

The PPN had always been an extremely small and tightly controlled elite party, totally moribund insofar as internal party life was concerned (it had had no party congress for fifteen years prior to the coup), and under a remarkably stable politburo whose composition hardly changed in eighteen years and which did not include a single Hausa or Fulani. Actually the party of the west and under tight Djerma-Songhay control, real power revolved around a triad of leaders: Hamani Diori, Diamballa Yansambou Maiga, and the prolific author and Assembly president (much admired abroad but detested at home) Boubou Hama.

Though non-Songhay-Djerma members were freely integrated into the cabinet (preventing the growth of clear-cut regionalist resentments), cabinet shuffles were extremely infrequent, with some ministers setting African records for longevity in office. And the National Assembly, also virtually frozen in terms of its incumbent membership, was composed of most of the traditional leaders of the country's various ethnic groups, whether from the east or west. Modern elements were locked out of this array of power. Many had to be content with remaining mute in the higher echelons of the administration or going abroad as international civil servants.

For years cited as the paragon of stability in a continent beset by turmoil and coups, and even cited as a "model" of fusion of traditional and modern authority, Niger's leadership started losing control rapidly in the 1970s, and especially with the onset of the Sahel drought. Increasingly challenged by student upheavals and impossible unionist demands, suffering from widespread public cynicism and loss of support due to corruption that had been long tolerated at the highest levels of the government, and finally, unnecessarily antagonizing the military hierarchy by assaults on its corporate autonomy, the Diori regime collapsed in April 1974. The immediate background of the coup was the widespread revulsion with the Sahel drought famine-relief fiascoes (where grain from abroad was diverted from drought regions and sold on the black market), though many other factors played a role in shifting the army to attack the presidency. In the aftermath of the coup, revelations of major and routine fiscal improprieties at all levels of the regime brought about the imprisonment of many of the political giants of the past as well as their traditional chiefly allies. Of the civilian politicians, most were eventually freed; Diori was rearrested, however, due to his son's efforts to foment a Tuareg revolt on his behalf.

The regime that came to power in April 1974 was greeted with considerable rejoicing in urban centers. The particular emphasis Kountché placed on alleviating the worst ravages of the drought (including the distribution of free seed, crackdowns on profiteering on foodstuffs, and so on) gained him considerable goodwill and support. Yet the military regime was unable to capitalize on its early popular support. It rapidly fell afoul of students, unionists, and mercantile groups (for different reasons) and SAWABA elements (including Djibo Bakary) who were allowed to return from exile abroad were also in due time to be rearrested. More importantly, the army started developing internal fissures. As elsewhere where the military came to power, personal ambitions, competitions, and animosities within the officer corps led to internal mutinies and attempted coups. Three of these were quite serious, and resulted in the truncation of much of the senior officer hierarchy, which had coalesced to seize power. Though military rule was greatly stabilized by massive infusions of state royalties from uranium exports and the patronage this allowed, by 1980 virtually every one of the original military junta core was either in disgrace or dead, consequent to coup attempts against Kountché.

The prime characteristic of Kountché's progressively civilianized regime was the retention of real political power in his own hands, and in a nonideological management style developing the infrastructure of the country with the benefit of Niger's new mineral wealth. Kountché's acerbic personality, authoritarian style, and conservative outlook rankled and antagonized many in Niger, however. Notwithstanding the massive transformation of the country during the 1977–80 boom years, he was more feared than respected.

With the collapse of global market prices for uranium in the 1980s, Niger was faced with a major fiscal squeeze. Construction activities in particular were seriously curtailed; wastage of resources on Niger's largely unprofitable public sector could no longer be sustained, and many state enterprises were privatized or closed down. Development funds dried up; new mining projects—some in advanced stages—were shelved indefinitely. A renewal of drought conditions further highlighted how, despite Niger's mineral riches (productive or not), most of the masses lived an inherently precarious existence. Simultaneous with the drought and the economic squeeze, the glaring corruption that had slowly seeped into the highest levels of government and administration began to focus discontent against the regime, as did the continued Djerma political hegemony in the country. Kountché's death (of a brain tumor) in Paris in November 1987 spared him the onus of dealing with the societal turmoil that was building up. It was left to his successor to preside over the return to civilian legitimacy, and to the new, post-1993 civilian leadership to witness and cope with the apparent unraveling of Niger itself.

The Saibou Interregnum and the Travails of Contemporary Niger

The Djerma general, Ali Saibou (also originating from Kountché's home village), was allegedly the choice of the military junta governing Niger to succeed Kountché, who had, in reality, completely emasculated collective rule. With the only other credible military alternative far away as prefect of Zinder (Colonel Moumouni), Saibou's "election" by the military's high council was a foregone conclusion. (He later distanced Moumouni even further from the center of power by appointing him ambassador to the United Nations.)

There then followed the institutionalization of the Nigerien movement for a developing society party (MNSD, which paradoxically Moumouni had assisted in creating), a new constitution, and in December 1989 Niger's first (single-party) parliamentary and presidential elections in nineteen years, which technically conferred upon Saibou civilian legitimacy.

These efforts at gaining a veneer of legitimacy were totally in vain. Throughout Africa winds of change were blowing, and military and autocratic rule was under pressure. Barely two months after the elections, large student demonstrations erupted in Niamey. The unrest was over cuts in scholarships and grants and restrictions on civil service hiring of university graduates—part of a Structural Adjustment Program the regime had been forced to acquiesce to. Unmindful of the fact that old strong-arm tactics of military rule were no longer the norm in Africa, the security forces blocked the demonstration, shooting into the crowds and leaving some twenty students dead. On May 6 a Tuareg assault on Tchin Tabaraden took place, aimed at stealing arms. Again the security forces overreacted with impunity, massacring two hundred Tuareg they encountered in the region.

In retrospect, these twin incidents in 1990 spelled the end of military rule in Niger, and much more. The February killings of students fueled the revolt of civil society, already straining under austerity programs and aware of winds of change in neighboring Benin and elsewhere. The Tuareg massacre triggered the full-scale Tuareg revolt, simmering in neighboring countries, which is still going on in Niger today. More importantly, the political vacuum that developed in a Niamey bereft of funds, and with legitimacy eroding rapidly, was to usher in other fissiparous manifestations severely taxing the very existence of the state to this day—a "liberation" movement in the remote Lake Chad region grouping Toubou and Kanuri, including refugees from civil unrest in Chad; religious strife as fundamentalist Muslims clash with animist groups; interethnic confrontations in various parts of the country, pitting different groups against one another, and so on. Most of these problems continue to beset Niger, a country transformed virtually overnight into one of Africa's most unstable.

Ongoing student demonstrations after the February 1990 killings, and calls for the placing on trial of those culpable of giving the orders to fire, meshed with constant union strikes and unrest over an uncertain future and the progressive backlogs in workers' pay by a bankrupt regime. By November Niger was politically seething, gripped by intermittent strikes and virtually ungovernable. When the USTN trade union confederation called for a general strike in support of multipartyism, Saibou had no choice but to capitulate. Possibly indicative of things yet to come, the first party to emerge was a fundamentalist Muslim one that has not, however, played a significant role to date, due to the greater polarizing effect of ethnicity in Niger. By March 1991 there were fifteen new parties, including the MNSD—from which Saibou had resigned in order to play an apolitical role as president.

On July 29, 1991, a National Conference convened to debate the future political landscape of the country. Including over 1,200 delegates from all walks of society—including the government and armed forces—it was scheduled for forty days but lasted three months. The conference elected as its head and as subsequent president of the interim legislature the noted Nigerien scholar André Salifou. Apart from agreeing on basic structural issues (including a dual executive) left to a constitutional committee to codify and present to a referendum, the conference heard evidence of fiscal improprieties during Kountché's administration (his infamous aide, "Bonkano," was given immunity to testify), and several retired officers at the fore of the decision to execute the leader of the 1976 coup attempt were arrested. The conference also summarily dismissed the army's chief of staff and his deputy, as well as several other key military and civilian personnel deemed guilty of the brutal reprisals against both Aïr's Tuareg and the February 1990 student demonstrations. Saibou's admission of ultimate responsibility was accepted at face value but, despite some opposition, he was retained as interim titular head of state. To his credit, he relinquished any political role and remained virtually invisible until replaced by a civilian president.

These gestures appeased few groups, though they ushered in multiparty civilian rule and a period of remarkable social discipline. Social unrest rapidly reemerged, however, indeed increased, as the austerity measures necessitated by Niger's acute financial situation affected all. Pay arrears of more than five months by an empty Treasury triggered constant urban unrest as students and trade unionists mounted wildcat strikes. Even the police, armed forces, and customs officers went unpaid, though their "strikes" (or mutinies) tended to be more rapidly settled. Nor did the imminent return to civilian rule stabilize the political elite. Intense ethnic polarization took hold in a country hitherto artificially united by the iron grip of military rule. Cheiffou's cabinet was so ethnically deadlocked by past grievances and in anticipation of civilian rule that barely five months after it was inaugurated it had to be dissolved in favor of a new realignment. And the onset of politicking, organizing long-atrophied political networks, and establishing regional paramountcy by aspiring elites inevitably worsened interethnic relations, adding to grievances that burst out in uncontrolled strife in several localities.

Nor did the Tuareg rebellion abate. Indeed, it gathered further momentum, linking up with similar seething Tuareg grievances in neighboring Mali and Algeria, where it had been periodically manifest and more brutally suppressed. By 1994 there were eight independent guerrilla movements that, though marshaling barely 2,000 warriors (some equipped with rocket and grenade launchers) were operating virtually at will as near as 200 miles from the capital. They were coordinated by a team in Paris, and sent communiqués and representations to the United Nations; Niger finally had to "upgrade" their activities from "banditry" to rebellion. Though some more intemperate voices were raised for an independent Tuareg desert state, or a federal arrangement with Niger, the main demand has been a laissez-faire cultural and political decentralization of Tuareg regions, coupled with greater attention to their marginalized political and economic situation, and integration of their warriors into the armed forces. The rebellion, which showed few signs of abatement, was only contained—first by a series of truces and finally by a peace accord (in April 1995) brokered by France and Burkina Faso.

On February 14, 1993, Niger's first free elections since independence took place, and witnessed the slim victory of a broad alliance of nine parties united to prevent a victory by the "old" MNSD party (now ranged behind retired colonel Tandja, onetime strongman of the military regime, and Saibou aide, Hama Amadou. Two weeks later the first round of the presidential elections took place, in which Tandja emerged the front-ranker with 34.22 percent of the vote, followed in second place by the Hausa Mahamane Ousmane of the CDS, with 26.59 percent. In the maneuverings prior to the second round Ousmane struck various deals with influential Djerma leaders, including Djermakoy Adamou Moumouni, who tightly controlled his Dosso fiefdom, and when the vote was in eased out Tandja.

The elections saw the rise for the first time of the numerically dominant Hausa, hitherto locked out of political supremacy by the Songhay-Djerma in Niger. The victory was assured in part by the support tendered by the Dosso branch of the Djerma (rewarded when their Djermakoy was elected president of the Assembly), themselves shunted from paramountcy among the Djerma-Songhay by historically competitive branches further west, traditionally the mainstay of Kountché's, Saibou's, and now Tandja's political machine. Some of the same fissures that had appeared in the transitional government of Cheiffou rapidly surfaced in the government set up by the new prime minister, Mahamadou Issoufou (another first-round presidential candidate who swung his electoral following behind Ousmane in exchange for the post). Frustrated by what he regarded as presidential monopolization of power, and unable to come to grips with Niger's most pressing problems, Issoufou tendered his resignation in September 1994 and joined the opposition. His desertion from the president's party alliance swung the parliamentary balance in favor of the opposition (centered around the MNSD) and saw the ouster of his successor in the next month by a vote of "no confidence."

Rather than seek an accommodation with the various parliamentary groups, as counseled by France, Ousmane tried his luck at the polls by calling a new parliamentary election. In the subsequent apathetic turnout, the MNSD-headed opposition coalition gained a majority, forcing Ousmane (after a try to split the alliance by a maverick appointment as premier) to cohabit with an opposition prime minister, Hama Amadou, secretary general of the MNSD.

Niger is at a very momentous crossroads. It has managed a relatively smooth transition to civilian rule, remarkable for retaining the loyalty of the armed forces, which had been at the helm of the country for nineteen uninterrupted and unchallenged years, and that of the ethnic group (Songhay-Djerma) that technically reigned supreme since independence. But the country is beset by equally momentous problems. Its corporal integrity can still be challenged in the north by renascent Tuareg nationalism (despite the peace accord of 1995), while peripheral groups in the equally unruly southeast also lay claim to the resources of the state.

The country's ethnic groups—not many by African standards, and hitherto quiescent—have been drawn into conflict even as a possible religious polarization seeps in. And at the root of all this, but certainly a precondition for any resolution of these many strains, is the fact that the country is economically bankrupt, thrown back to reliance on its agricultural crops, which are susceptible in this part of the continent to intermittent droughts. Living from hand to mouth, virtually a pauper despite "forgiveness" of various loans and despite new development aid, Niger does not have enough funds to cope with its day-to-day administration, let alone to meet the new demands for relief or the escalating security threats on its peripheries. Trimming the budget, the bloated civil service, or the unprofitable state sector (which could generate some fiscal relief and is demanded by outside donors) is politically suicidal in Niger, which is why the government has resisted implementation of structural adjustment programs. It is a foreclosed option in a country whose very marginal and now largely agrarian economy (after the uranium boom) offers no upward mobility or regular paid employment except through the civil service to urban groups and especially college graduates. And even not abiding by IMF/ World Bank conditions for standby credits (which rob the country of desperately needed funds) cannot secure a stabilization of a society that has been in nearly constant turmoil. During one five-month period in 1993 there was a daily strike of three-hours duration. Constant student involvement in demonstrations, the participation of teachers in wildcat or USTN strikes, coupled with the bankruptcy of the entire educational establishment, so disrupted one academic year that the regime declared the year null and void—only to have to rescind the decree when faced by even uglier strikes.

Whether Niger manages to turn the corner, to attain at least a modest degree of stability and a measure of economic upturn, or continues to limp along as West Africa's most unstable country has yet to be seen. Certainly the country has many things going for it; but conversely, it faces a multitude of extremely severe challenges, some of which exist only in the Sahel belt, and others having to do with the fact that the bottom line is that Niger is one of the poorest of countries on the continent.

Mid-1996 Update

Within months of the forced political "cohabitation" of President Mahamane Ousmane and Prime Minister Hama Amadou, it was clear Niger was in for a period of acute executive instability. For apart from their different ethnic, regional, and political origins and clienteles—with Ousmane regarding Amadou with contempt and as little more than a front man for the military—the two men were incompatible in terms of character and temperament. With political coexistence impossible, a state of tension, conflict, jockeying for supremacy, and executive paralysis became the norm. This made decision making very difficult, delaying the implementation of much-needed political and economic reforms (such as privatization and agreement on a Structural Adjustment Plan), while politicizing the civil service and further polarizing society at large.

The instability in Niamey, and the preoccupation of the leadership with their internal squabbles also meant that the delicate cease-fire with the Tuareg and the increasing tensions in the (Kanuri/Toubou) Far East were not accorded full attention. Soon the tediously brokered peace with the Tuareg began to unravel as several armed groups renounced it on the grounds of the nonimplementation of Niamey's promises, while the intermittent clashes in the vicinity of Lake Chad continued unabated.

It was within this context that, on January 27, 1996, Chief of Staff Colonel (later General) Barre Mainassara mounted his coup d'etat, justifying it as "a lesser evil" than the civilian political stalemate. Precisely what might subsequently have transpired, had there not been the changed global context, cannot really be assessed. It is clear, however, that Mainassara had not anticipated the immensity of the negative global reaction and the suspension of aid his action triggered. With Niger dependent upon foreign aid even for balancing its budget, suspension of aid immediately made Niamey incapable of meeting the State payroll, forcing the junta to declare a 30 percent cut in salaries (and 40 percent for cabinet ministers), only to have to backtrack on this when the trade unions threatened a massive general strike.

Due to these domestic and external pressures, Mainassara rapidly moved to appoint a transitional civilian cabinet, replacing the initially largely military one and leading France—that was in the process of reassessing its policy—to recommence fiscal subventions. Further momentum toward "normalization" was provided in April when the junta convened a conclave of civil society to codify a new constitution that would prevent the emergence of the kinds of anomalies the previous one allowed. The constitution was ratified in a national referendum that saw, however, massive abstentions (nearly three-quarters of the electorate), setting the stage for civilianization later that year, when both presidential and parliamentary elections were scheduled to take place. Though it is likely that Niger will have recivilianized herself by the end of 1996, its "detour," once again, through military rule powerfully underscores the extreme political and economic fragility of the new order in Niamey.

The Dictionary

-A-

ABAGANA MOLI (1910–). Long-term Kanuri head of the Nomadic Guard of the Bilma district, responsible for the security of the entire region and the salt caravans. A well-known figure, he retired from the service in 1975 and until the mid-1980s served as a private guide and interpreter.

ABALAK. Small village 590 km from Niamey, and 150 km from Tahoua, on the main route to Agadez. It possesses scenic charm and is also somewhat unusual in the region because it is a producer of fish—fresh, dried, and smoked—from an artificial lake.

ABALAMMA. *See* DALLOL MAOURI.

ABARA. Name of the distinctively shaped pirogues of the Sorkawa.

ABARCHI, DANDI (Lieutenant Colonel). Former member of the Supreme Military Council under General Kountché, and one of the senior officers in the Niger military. When Kountché died in 1987, his successor, General Saibou, dispatched some of Kountché's allies on diplomatic postings. Abarchi was appointed ambassador to Senegal, and in January 1991 was shifted to become ambassador to Benin. After the onset of civilian rule, Abarchi returned to Niger and retired from military service.

ABARI EMINAMI (1910?–). Chief of the village of Dirkou and of the Kouar canton since 1943. Belonging to the traditional ruling family of Kouar, Abari Eminami's fief includes the seven key settlements and some 2,000 people.

ABBATOIR FRIGORIFIQUE DE NIAMEY. Niamey's refrigerated slaughterhouse and meat-processing plant. First opened in 1959 and shut down for some time prior to its reopening in 1967, the plant was expanded in 1971 and again in the late 1980s, when it was also renovated. Its staff of around a hundred includes several Europeans. Originally capitalized at 247 million CFA francs, since doubled, the plant can process 40,000 head of cattle and produce up to 5,000 tons of fresh and 4,000 tons of frozen meat per year.

ABDOU DAN GALLOU (1934–). Educator. Born in Konni in 1934 and trained as a teacher, Abdou Dan Gallou shifted to a political career in 1964 and was elected to the National Assembly as a PPN deputy in October 1965. He served in the Assembly until 1974, becoming also its secretary. Following the 1974 coup he reentered the teaching profession and recently retired.

ABDOU HASSA, AHMED (1948–). Former minister of waters and the environment. Graduating in 1973 in Ouagadougou as a rural hydraulic engineer, Abdou Hassa first served as head of a hydraulics section carrying out inventories of Niger's water resources (1973–75) and then between 1975 and 1980 as Niger's director of hydraulics. In 1980 he took up the post in Ouagadougou as secretary general of the Comité Inter-Africain d'Etudes Hydrauliques, serving until 1991, when he returned to Niamey. After the National Conference he was appointed to the transitional cabinet, serving as minister of waters and the environment until April 1993.

ABDOU MOUMOUNI DIOFFO UNIVERSITY. New name, adopted in mid-1991, for the University of Niamey. Abdou Moumouni Dioffo, a distinguished Nigerien scientist, was rector of the university for several years prior to his death in April 1991. *See also* MOUMOUNI, ABDOU DIOFFO.

ABDOU SIDIKOU (1927–73). Former secretary of state for foreign affairs. Born in 1927 in Kouré (near Niamey) where he was chef de canton, and educated locally as well as at the Ecole William Ponty (Dakar), Abdou Sidikou continued his education at Dakar's and Paris's Faculty of Medicine, graduating from the latter in 1956. He served his internship at the Hôpitaux de la Seine (1956–57) and continued specialization in serology, biology, and bacteriology, returning to Niger to become chief pharmacist at Niamey Hospital (1957–59). In 1959 he was brought into the government as cabinet director of the minister of health, and in 1962 moved into the diplomatic world when he was appointed ambassador to the U.S., U.N., and Canada. In September 1964 he was shifted to head his country's embassy to West Germany, Benelux, Austria, Scandinavia, and the EEC, and in November 1965 returned to Niamey to become secretary general of foreign affairs. On April 14, 1967, he was promoted to secretary of state for foreign affairs. In January 1970 he was shifted, for health reasons, and appointed secretary of state attached to the presidency. He was throughout also Niger's inspector of pharmacies. Abdou Sidikou died on July 26, 1973.

ABDOUILMISA, ELHADJ. Interim minister of mines in the transitional cabinet between March 1990 and September 1991.

ABDOULAYE, KHAMED. Former cabinet minister and currently secretary general of the Parti pour l'Unité Nationale et la Démocratie (PUND). A well-known Tuareg leader from the Tchin Tabaraden area, Abdoulaye was director of Radio Niamey until September 23, 1985, when he was brought into General Kountché's cabinet as secretary of state for the interior. He subsequently served as minister of communications, and in December 1989 was shifted to head the Ministry of Civil Service and Labor. After the brutal February 1990 dispersal of striking students in Niamey, Abdoulaye was moved to head the Ministry of National Education, serving until the new National Conference government was set up in September 1991. He was involved, directly or indirectly, with the Tuareg unrest in his region, and on September 2, 1992, was arrested in the military sweep of Tuareg dissident leaders, though he was released shortly thereafter.

ABDOULAYE, MOHAMED. Former minister of state enterprises. A civil administrator by profession, and a Tuareg leader, Abdoulaye joined the cabinet in May 1989 but was dropped from it at the end of the year. He played an indeterminate role in supporting what became the Tuareg revolt in north Niger. In March 1992 he was appointed interim secretary of state in charge of administrative reform, serving until the new government was set up in April 1993.

ABDOULAYE, SOULEY (1965–). President of the National Assembly and briefly prime minister of Niger. Abdoulaye joined the cabinet in the new April 1993 civilian government of Prime Minister Mahamadou Issoufou as minister of commerce, transport, and communications. When Issoufou grew disenchanted with what he viewed as President Ousmane's usurpation of governmental powers and tendered his resignation to join the opposition on September 28, 1994, Abdoulaye was appointed prime minister in his stead. The parliamentary balance of power had swung to the opposition, however, and Abdoulaye was defeated in a "no confidence" vote on October 16,1994, even before having lined up a new cabinet. After the new legislative elections held to resolve the crisis, Abdoulaye submitted his resignation, and on February 8, 1995, was elected president of the National Assembly.

ABDOULLAHI, MOHAMED. Leader of a small, post-1991 political party, the Union pour la Démocratie et le Progrès Social (UDPS-Amana), which is part of the AFC coalition and secured one seat in the National Assembly. *See also* POLITICAL PARTIES.

ABDOULMOUMINE, MOHAMED. Head of the Armée Révolutionnaire de la Libération du Nord-Niger (ARLN), one of the fronts that sprang up to oust Nigerien control of Aïr. He is supported by Libya.

ABDOURAHMANE, SOLI. Magistrate, and General Saibou's first minister of justice. He served in that post between November 1987 and December 1989.

ABDOUSALE, TANKARI (1914–). Longtime deputy to the National Assembly. Born in 1914 in Bouza, and a local notable, Abdousale was a civil servant by profession. In March 1957 he was elected deputy to the Territorial Assembly from Madaoua on the **Mouvement Socialiste Africain** ticket (later the Parti du Regroupement Africain). He remained deputy at the National Assembly (switching to the PPN) until the 1974 coup d'état. He was also the Assembly's longtime president of the Social Affairs and Labor Committee, and secretary of the Assembly's bureau, and is currently in retirement.

ABOUBAKAR, ABDOU. General Saibou's first minister of civil service and labor. Aboubakar joined the cabinet in that capacity as a political newcomer in November 1987, serving until May 1989.

ABOUBAKAR, SHEIK EL-HADJ. Spiritual leader of Niger's Nyassite Islamic sect. He resides in Kioto, near Dosso, and is married to one of the daughters of Nyass, founder of the sect in Kaolack in Senegal.

ADA, MAHAMANE. Interim secretary of state in charge of primary education between March 1992 and April 1993.

ADAMOU, ABOUBAKAR (1948–). University professor and interim cabinet minister. Born in 1948, and educated at home and in France, where he obtained in 1976 a doctorate in geography from the University of Lyons, he then joined the University of Niamey, serving also in a variety of second-echelon capacities within the Ministry of Education. In March 1990, after the student demonstrations and their brutal dispersal by the armed forces, General Saibou called him in to serve as his new minister of higher education, in an effort to appease students. He served in the capacity until the new National Conference government was formed in September 1991.

ADAMOU, ALHERY (1939–). Former mayor of Tahoua, Niger's fourth largest city. Born in Niamey on March 23, 1939, and a civil administrator by profession, Adamou holds degrees from both the local school of administration (ENA) and the IIAP of the University of Paris. He was appointed mayor of Tahoua in May 1971, and was shifted to other administrative duties in 1976. He is currently in retirement.

ADAMOU, YAHAYA (1935–). Former director of civil service. Born in 1935 in Birni–N'Konni, and a civil administrator by profession, Adamou served as state inspector between March 1966 and July 1970, and as director of the civil service between 1970 and his retirement in 1993.

ADAMUSAWA. Hausa name for the resident merchants from the Ghadames area. The term is also often used to refer to any person originating from north of Aïr. *See also* GHADAMSI.

ADDOU, ADAM. Former prefect of Agadez. An instructor by training, Addou joined the administration in 1970 and was appointed subprefect of the new mining district of Arlit in 1971. In 1973 he was promoted to the key post of prefect of Niger's vast northern Agadez département. In 1977 he was shifted to become director general of the Office des Eaux du Sous-Sol.

ADEMANION, FELICIEN. Physician. Dr. Ademanion briefly served also as director of public health, from January to September 1968.

ADER. A mostly arid, windswept region with permanently eroded soil, occupying much of the Tessaoua département. In prehistoric days heavily wooded, fertile, and full of big game, the area has remnants of some very ancient settlements. The region's history has always been tightly intertwined with that of Aïr and Azawak. Until the sixteenth century it was controlled by both Gobir and Bornu (at a time when Agadez controlled only Azawak). Ader was then conquered between 1674 and 1724 by Aggaba—son of the then-sultan of Agadez—who gave the region its name (*ader*-"foot"). Aggaba established his capital at **Birni-n-Ader** south of Tamaské. Only the **Magorawa** successfully resisted his conquest, which made the entire region a tributary of Aïr. The administration and tax collection in the area was delegated to three **Lisawan** chiefs on a territorial basis.

Because of its crossroad location, Ader faced continuous encroachments in succeeding decades, especially by the Ouilliminden, and friction with **Kebi** in the south. This continued right up to the French conquest in the nineteenth century. By 1865 the original Tuareg chiefdom in Ader (which eventually encompassed the Magorawa) had capitulated to these pressures. The political center had shifted much earlier (c. 1738) to the canton if Illela. Currently Ader's large population is composed of **Azna** heavily intermixed with Tuareg and other groups. In 1900 it was estimated that the region's population was only 10,000. Today estimates are around 560,000, of whom 400,000 are Hausa (mostly Azna), 55,000 Tuareg, and the rest Fulani and other seminomadic groups. Ader's Hausa constitute fully 25 percent of all the Hausa in Niger. During the dry season sandy tornadoes sweep the bleak, inhospitable area, while the harmattan blows amid violent electrical storms.

ADERAWA. A term referring to the inhabitants of **Ader.**

ADJI, BOUKARY (1940–). Economist, banker, and former cabinet minister. Born in 1940 in Tamout, and educated both locally and in Dakar, Senegal, and in France in economics and banking, Adji joined the Niger Development Bank (BDRN) as an administrator, and between 1973 and 1975 was deputy director of Niamey branch of the Banque Centrale des Etats de l'Afrique de l'Ouest (BCEAO). In 1975 he was promoted to director, serving until 1983. In that year he joined General Saibou's cabinet as minister of finance, in which capacity he served until November 1987. Since then he has rejoined the BCEAO.

ADMINISTRATIVE ORGANIZATION. Among the last territories conquered by France in Africa (1897), the region currently the Republic of Niger was designated on July 23, 1900, the Territoire Militaire de Zinder, and attached to the Colonie du Haut-Sénégal-Niger, which stretched from today's Mali through Burkina Faso into Chad. On June 22, 1910, the territory was designated the Territoire Militaire du Niger, into which was included the **cercle** of Gao, which was later (June 21, 1911) returned to the Timbuktu (Mali) region and the Territoire was directly attached to the AOF federation. On October 13, 1922, the area was finally designated a "colony" (i.e., coming under civil administration) as the Colonie du Niger. During this period the capital shifted a number of times, from Sorbo-Haoussa (until 1903) to Niamey (1903–11), to Zinder (1911–26), and back to Niamey (in 1926).

The July 1922 administrative organization of Niger included nine cercles—Agadez, Dosso, Gouré, Maradi, N'Guigmi, Niamey, Tahoua, Tillabéry, and Zinder—each with a Comité de Notables. The cercles were in turn composed of twenty-seven subdivisions. This administrative organization lasted until independence; the internal breakdown was as follows:

Cercles	*Subdivisions*
Agadez	Bilma, Agadez
Dosso	Dosso, Dogondoutchi
Gouré	Gouré, Mainé-Soroa
Maradi	Maradi, Dakoro, Tessaoua
N'Guigmi	N'Guigmi
Niamey	Niamey, Niamey-Centrale, Boboyé, Filinqué, Say
Tahoua	Tahoua, Tahoua-Nomade, Birni-N'Konni, Madaoua
Tillabéry	Tillabéry, Djermaganda, Téra
Zinder	Zinder, Zinder-Centrale, Magaria, Tanout

The N'Guigmi and Agadez cercles were administered by a military bureaucracy until December 31, 1946, with the Bilma subdivision remaining under military rule for another decade.

At various times parts of other colonies have been administratively lumped into the territory of the Niger colony. Apart from the previously noted Gao cercle, between 1932 and 1947 two regions of Upper Volta (which disappeared as a separate colony)—Dori and Fada N'Gourma—were attached to Niger, as was a border region of Dahomey, while all of Tibesti (now in Chad) was also part of the Niger colony until 1930.

The cercles, whose number increased to sixteen, were replaced on January 1, 1961, by thirty-one circonscriptions—several with internal subdivisions. Following the Réforme Administrative of 1964 (effective October 1, 1965), these were regrouped into seven départements and thirty-two arrondissements, the number of which has inched upward to the thirty-eight of today with the creation of new units, and specifically the 1969 creation of the uranium center of Arlit and the 1972 split of the Maradi and the 1973 split of the Tassaoua arrondissements each into two separate units. With the explosive urban growth in Niamey, in 1992 the headquarters of the département of Niamey was transferred to Tillabéry, with Niamey itself removed from the new département. The départements and their internal divisions are as follows:

Départements	*Arrondissements*
Tillabéry	Filingué, Ouallum, Kosso, Say, Téra, Tillabéry; postes administratifs in Abala, Ayorou, Banibangou, Bankilaré, Gothéye
Dosso	Dosso, Boboyé, Dogondoutchi, Gaya, Loga; postes administratifs in Dioundiou, Falmey
Tahoua	Tahoua, Birni-N'Konni, Bouza, Illela, Keita, Madaoua, Tchin Tabaraden; postes administratifs in Tillia, Abalak, Dogueraoua, Bagaraoua
Maradi	Madaroumfa, Guidan-Roumji, Dakoro, Mayahi, Tessaoua, Agyé; postes administratifs in Gazaoua, Tibiri

Zinder	Mirria, Gouré, Magaria, Matameyé, Tanout; postes administratif in Damagaram-Takaya
Diffa	Diffa, Mainé-Soroa, N'Guigmi; postes administratifs in Goudoumaria, N'Gourti, Tourmour
Agadez	Agadez, Arlit, Bilma; postes administratifs in Iférouane, In Gall

The country also has eleven communes (or urban centers) though only four—Niamey, Zinder, Maradi, Tahoua—are fully autonomous (*see* COMMUNE). Originally, the 1964 Administrative Reform specified dotting the country with 120 communes, but the project was never implemented. On each administrative level there is a consultative and executive body. *See* COMMISSION CONSULTATIVE DEPARTEMENTALE *for the départements;* COUNSEIL D'ARRONDISSEMENT *for the arrondissements; and* CONSEIL MUNICIPAL *for the communes.*

AFASTO OUEST. Site of uranium deposits originally scheduled to be exploited in 1986 jointly by ONAREM and Nigeria (16 percent). The global glut in uranium of the 1980s postponed implementation of the project.

AFFAIRES MILITAIRES MUSULMANES (AMM). Elite, Muslim-affairs intelligence-gathering unit (in which many top scholars worked) set up by the French colonial administration. The AMM's creation was motivated by France's fears of a renascent militant Islam spreading into Niger from the north. The unit was disbanded in 1962.

AFRIQUE OCCIDENTALE FRANCAISE (AOF). French West Africa—one of France's two colonial federations, encompassing the territories of Ivory Coast, Niger, Upper Volta, Mauritania, Senegal, French Sudan, Guinea, and Dahomey. Established between 1895 and 1905, after the Second World War the AOF was headed by a governor general in Dakar, Senegal, who was responsible for the federation to the minister of colonies in Paris. The governor general was assisted in Dakar by a Council of Government with consultative authority, composed of five delegates from each of the federated territories. Each colony also had its own governor responsible to the governor general in Dakar, and a territorial assembly with limited powers.

AG AHMADOU, MOHAMMED. Former president Kountché's personal chef de cabinet and advisor. A Tuareg of considerable traditional status, Ag Ahmadou was linked to the attempted coup of March

1976, but was nevertheless integrated into the presidential office. In 1982 he defected to Libya in order to organize dissident Niger Tuareg at the behest of Qaddafi, part of a project to revive pan-Tuareg subnationalism in the Sahel states. The defection of someone so close to the president was a considerable embarrassment to the regime. He has also been linked with the 1990 Tuareg assault on Tchin Tabaraden, which (after Nigerien military reprisals) marked the onset of the current Tuareg rebellion in Niger.

AG BOULA, GHISSA. Top Tuareg chieftain, head of the Front de la Libération de l'Aïr et l'Azawad (FLAA), one of several groups in armed rebellion against rule by Niamey in the 1990s. Also vice-president of the Coordination de la Résistance Armée. He was caught and arrested in south Algeria in September 1992, but was soon released.

AG GHALI, IYAD. Secretary general of the *Movement Populaire pour la Libération de l'Azawad* (MPLA), one of the liberation fronts operating in northern Niger, with headquarters in Mali.

AGADA, NAGOGO (1919–75). *Serkin* ("chief") Gobir, veteran politician, and former financial officer of the National Assembly. Born in Tibiri in 1919 and of the main chiefly lineage, Agada was educated at an agricultural school in Tarna, Maradi. He then commenced working as an agricultural technician in Maradi (1940–45), Tarna (1945–46), Magaria (1946–52), and then in Kolo (1953–58). In 1958 he was elected to the National Assembly and was reelected throughout the Diori era until the 1974 coup d'état. Earlier, in 1963, he had succeeded to the post of serkin Gobir (at Tibiri), thus becoming one of the most important traditional Hausa leaders in the country.

AGADEZ. A historically important Tuareg town, capital of Aïr, major center of Niger's tourism until the 1990 Tuareg rebellion, and also the name of Niger's northern département. Founded in 1430, the town's name possibly comes from *Takadest*—"place of congregation of visitors." The city prospered and developed at the expense of other regional centers, becoming also a major slave market and caravan stop in the sixteenth century by virtue of its location at the fringe of the Sahara Desert. At its height the town had a population of 30,000, though **Heinrich Barth** found it (in 1850) a decrepit city of ruins and memories of fewer than 7,000 people. By that time its caravan importance had been ceded to **Iférouane** further north. Around 1495–97 Mohamed Askia, the Songhay ruler, probably passed through Agadez on his way to Mecca with a retinue of a thousand people, from whom the town's Songhay-speaking population allegedly descends. In 1500 the entire area was subjugated to Songhay with its capital at Gao. *See* AGADEZ, SULTANATE OF.

The town and countryside are dominated by the famed sixteenth-century mosque (actually rebuilt in the mid–nineteenth century) and its Sudanese-style eighty-eight-foot spiked minaret. The market square in the center of the town is flanked by houses ornamented with various embossed motifs and terraces with openwork balustrades. In this extremely picturesque town, the sultan's original palace is currently the Hôtel de l'Aïr, having been confiscated after the 1916 Tuareg uprising. The famed gold or silver filigree cross of Agadez circulates throughout Africa from this area, though artisans produce the item in coastal cities as well.

Until the discovery of uranium in the area, Agadez had a small population of 7,100, an increase over the 3,000 people resident there in 1926. With the development of Niger's extractive industry the town's population jumped to 27,000, and with the influx to the city of former-nomads-turned-refugees from the Sahel drought, the population swelled even more to the 105,000 recorded in 1975. Many from the influx left the area with the abatement of the drought.

The département of Agadez covers an area of 700,000 sq km and has a normal population of around 68,300, giving it a population density of 0.1 per sq km. The population is composed of Tuareg, Hausa, Fulani, Kanuri, Arab, and Toubou. The département is divided into the arrondissements of Agadez, Arlit, and Bilma and the postes administratifs of Iférouane and In Gall. The département borders Algeria and Libya, the latter having claimed a large slice of its north on the basis of the (invalid and never ratified) 1935 **Mussolini-Laval Boundary Agreement.** The département is the lucrative center of Niger's uranium and cassiterite mines, and a magnetic attraction for tourists from afar. It has an international airport, renovated and modernized in 1990, though the Tuareg rebellion that year rapidly put an end to an anticipated major tourist boom.

The town is 465 km from Zinder (via Tanout), a route practical except during the July–September rainy season when it is often impassable. The Agadez–Bilma 700-km route is always hazardous, while the Agadez–Tamanrasset (Algeria) 1,000-km trans-Saharan track is passable only between October and June and then only in officially sponsored convoys accompanied by security units. The other routes in the region include the previously sandy Agadez–Tahoua "Uranium Road" currently completely paved due to its importance; the stunningly picturesque—though very rugged—track to Iférouane, much used (between November and May) by venturesome tourists; and the routes to In Gall and the salt pans at Teguidda-n'Tesemt. All these routes, including those reaching to within 200 km of Niamey, are today hazardous due to the Tuareg rebellion that broke out in 1990. Both individual travelers and those escorted by armed contingents have been attacked by heavily armed Tuareg bands.

AGADEZ, SULTANATE OF. The history of the Tuareg Sultanate of Agadez is partly recorded in the invaluable *Chronicles of Agadez*. The sultanate developed as an important caravan stop at the edge of the Sahara Desert, a crossroad on the routes to the Hausa in the south, Tibesti and Bornu in the east, and Gao in the west. According to widely recounted tradition—disputed by some scholars—the original Tuareg clans in Aïr, constantly at war and unable to select a ruler from among themselves, sent a deputation to the Ottoman court (in reality to Fezzan, north of Aïr, in today's Libya) requesting the appointment of a king. The sultan could not find a legitimate son ready to go to Aïr and instead sent **Younous,** his son by a slave-concubine, who arrived in Aïr with a large retinue. Hence the origin of the low status of the sultans of Agadez. Since the original initiative came from the **Itesen**, the sultan was immediately recognized as supreme by them, as well as by the Kel Gress (then in Aïr) and the Kel Owey; later other clans accepted suzerainty.

In 1424 Younous was deposed by his nephew Ag Hassan, who himself was overthrown by his brother Alissaoua in 1430. The latter was the one who chose Agadez (actually Tagadest, or Eguédech) as the permanent capital of the sultanate. At the outset, the sultanate was largely nomadic but eventually settled first at **Tadeliza,** then **Tin Chaman**—actually just outside Agadez—and finally Agadez. The sultan rules over those clans which accept his authority but in reality has never had much power, except in arbitration. Many sultans have in the past been overthrown at will. Most power is concentrated in the hands of the **anastafidet**—the supreme chief of the Kel Owey, and the second most important leader in Aïr after the sultan—though with the onset of the colonial era the sultans slowly increased their power base.

There are four principal trade routes leading out of Agadez. These include (1) the route west to In Gall and on to Timbuktu; (2) the eastern route to Bilma, Tibesti, and Kufra; (3) north to Tamanrasset and Touat; and (4) south to Damergou, Damagaram, and Nigeria. A percentage on all commodities passing through Aïr traditionally belonged to the sultan (as well as part of the **azalay** trade), a fact that made most sultans quite wealthy. Among the sultan's prime duties were leading the prayers for rains, upholding the faith, arbitrating clan disputes, and organizing wars (with armies fielded by the various confederations), though traditionally only his sons headed the forces. Notwithstanding the sultan's authority, even in his own capital his direct rule was restricted only to the black population (though it did extend to In Gall and Teguidda-n-Tesemt), with the bulk of the population of Agadez—that claim descent from the religious **Ineslemen** clan—not paying tribute.

In the sixteenth century, Agadez became a major mercantile center and slave depot, even though it lost its autonomy first to **Gao** and then to Bornu. Under Sultan Mohammed el-Moubarak (1654–87), an expansion to the south occurred, into **Ader,** but in succeeding decades the sultanate fell into rapid decay. The trade routes (especially the Gao–Agadez route, paralyzed by the fall of the Gao Empire) collapsed in importance, or shifted away from Agadez, Iférouane successfully challenging Agadez for the Tripoli–Kano route. Instability in the sultanate's lineage also brought a decline in the importance of Agadez, as coups, depositions, and murders came in rapid succession. In 1740 the town was sacked by the Kel Owey, marking its final decline. Also around this time, **Assodé** disappeared. With the rise of the salt trade into greater prominence, Agadez regained some of its former importance but never became again the powerful state it had once been. The legends of its grandeur, however, no doubt much inflated, continued to circulate. When visited by Heinrich Barth in 1850, the town was in an advanced state of ruin. The Great Mosque of Agadez, a major landmark, was built in 1844 and its minaret, which once fell down, in 1847. The base of the minaret is thirty square feet, and rests on four pilasters inside the mosque, with the (mud) tower rising more than eighty-five feet with a spiral to the top, dominating the entire landscape.

In the process of conquering Aïr, the French deposed the ruling sultan of Agadez—Othman ben-Abdel Qadr—in 1907, imposing in his stead Ibrahim ed-Dasouqy, who was himself deposed by the French and exiled to Konni. The next sultan—**Tegama**—ruled until 1916 when he joined in the general upheaval against French colonial rule that year. *See* KOACEN REVOLT. After breaking the long siege of Agadez, the French went on a brutal rampage that saw the execution of hundreds of religious and civil leaders. Tegama himself was murdered, and Ibrahim ed-Dasouqy was reappointed sultan. On his death Umar was elevated to the sultanship, reigning until the 1960s. By tradition the sultan, descending from the Younous lineage, is designated by the five major tribes of the area under the chairmanship of the Itesen. *See also* AGADEZ.

AGALAK. Volcanic range of peaks in the Aïr massif.

AGENCE DE COOPERATION CULTURELLE ET TECHNIQUE DES PAYS FRANCOPHONES (ACCTF). Organization encompassing most French-speaking states of the world, it was conceived on February 17, 1969, and formally founded in Niamey on March 20,

1970. Containing twenty-one member states, the principal contributors of the ACCTF's 1971 budget of 9 million French francs were France (45 percent), Canada (33 percent), and Belgium (12 percent). Its first executive secretary was Canada's Jean-Marc Leger. Niger's former president Hamani Diori was a principal figure in motivating the creation of the organization.

AGGABA, SULTAN OF AIR (r. 1687–1721). Son of the reigning sultan in Agadez, Aggaba imposed, with **Lisawan** help, a Tuareg chiefdom in **Ader,** which he conquered in what is still referred to as *yakin Aggaba* (''the war of Aggaba"). Only the Magorawa successfully resisted his invasion of the region. In 1687 he succeeded his father as sultan in Agadez and further expanded Aïr's dominions. Deposed by his brother in 1721, Aggaba took refuge in Ader, which he had set out to conquer thirty-seven years previously.

AGRAM. Another name for **Fachi.**

AGRAMMA DAJI (1905–). Head of the Fachi canton, which includes the village of Fachi in the Ténéré Desert. Agramma Daji holds the allegiance of a thousand residents and of the itinerant merchants of the area.

AGUELLAL. Small village near Iférouane in Aïr. Originally (at the beginning of the twentieth century) just a mosque and center for religious study, Aguellal slowly became a small village with a sedentary secular population. The drought in the 1970s brought to its wells refugee groups, swelling its population even more.

AHMADOU DAN BASSA (1878–1950). Last independent sultan of Damagaram. Born in 1878, and the younger brother of **Ahmadou Mai Roumji,** who was killed by the French in 1899, Dan Bassa ascended the throne on his brother's death. From the outset, however, he was under pressure from his court to resist the French, while the latter were seriously contemplating abolishing outright the sultanate. Persistent rumors of **Sanusiya** contacts with Damagaram, problems in tax collection, and Dan Bassa's alleged indecisiveness further drove wedges between the sultan and the French. Finally, in 1906, a plot was uncovered—since verified to have been fabricated by a courtier, **Bellama**—and the sultan was deposed and exiled to Dahomey and Ivory Coast for ten years. **Malam Yaro,** his trusted aide and strong pro-French ally, was also implicated in the plot, and exiled to Paris. The ambitious Bellama was elevated to the sultanship and ruled between 1906 and 1923. Ahmadou Dan Bassa, who had all along protested his innocence, was returned to Niger in 1922 when it had become clear that the alleged plot was a fake. The legitimate lineage was restored to the throne on February 27, 1923, under Mustapha.

AHMADOU MAI ROUMJI (?–1899). Sultan of Damagaram at the time of the French conquest. One of **Tanimoun**'s sons, Ahmadou ascended the throne in 1893. A courageous warrior, he extended Damagaram's dominions in the direction of Kano. He reigned during a very troubled period, when Zinder was being threatened by both **Rabah** in the east and the French in the west. Ahmadou was especially uneasy about the intentions of the **Mission du Haut-Soudan,** which visited his court, and he was later personally held accountable by the French for the murder of Captain **Cazamajou** by an anti-French court faction. Following France's invasion of Damagaram and the defeat of the latter's armies at the Battle of **Tirmini,** Ahmadou escaped into the countryside. He was pursued by the French and killed at the village of Roumji on September 16, 1899, hence the place of his death (Roumji) is traditionally added to his name.

AHMET ANKRIMI (1905–). Head of the Gounda clan of the **Teda** in the Agadez-Bilma region. His father was a celebrated slave raider. The Gounda clan, one of the largest, encompasses about a thousand people organized into six subclans.

AIR. Mountainous massif in northern Niger in the Agadez département of which the administrative capital is also Agadez. It was widely known until the twentieth century under its Hausa name of Abzin. Geologically the upper basin of the fossilized valley of **Azawak,** Aïr is largely a Precambrian granite massif with previous volcanic activity. Some 400 km from north to south, 100 to 200 km from east to west, and peppered with fertile valleys and hidden oases of great beauty, Aïr encompasses some 61,000 sq km between the desert plains of Azawak and **Ténéré** and provides pasturage for animals as well as adequate water in its subterranean water table to form oases. Aïr receives an average rainfall of 169 mm per year (1940–70), with the highest ever recorded being 288 mm, and the lowest ever recorded (in 1970) being 40 mm. During the Sahel drought of the 1970s, which hit Aïr very hard, rainfall averaged (between 1969 and 1974) only 73 mm, and only in 1974 did it rise somewhat to 136 mm.

With peaks rising to 1,800, Aïr is currently populated by some 80,000 nomadic and seminomadic Hausa, Tuareg, and other ethnic groups (*see* AGADEZ). The region has salt pans of considerable regional importance in In Gall and Teguidda-n 'Tesemt, cassiterite at El Mecki and elsewhere, uranium in several localities (with the earliest to be exploited at Arlit), coal in the south, and several other minerals in what is Niger's mining center and until the mid-1980s its prime source of foreign revenue. Occupied by France in 1904, and center of a major Tuareg uprising during the First World War, Aïr has been settled since prehistoric times, when its ecology was much more hospitable. Relics from this early period are continually discovered (*see* ARCHAEOLOGY; CAVE ART).

Visited by Ibn Batuta in the middle of the fourteenth century, Aïr's earliest known inhabitants were probably Hausa. These were chased out to the south (to become the Azna, Gobirawa, etc.) commencing with the eleventh century by successive waves of Tuareg confederations coming out of what is today Libya. The **Bella** and **Buzu** in Aïr and elsewhere are descendants of Hausa captives of the Tuareg. Among the first clans to arrive in Aïr were the Sandal and the Kel Gress, later the Kel Owey. In internecine fighting among these three, the Sandal were nearly annihilated as a separate clan (some remnants, the Lisawan, remain). Most of the Kel Gress were chased out of Aïr by the Kel Owey in the middle of the eighteenth century to settle north of Gobir in the Madaoua area where they are still to be found. The Kel Owey remained more or less in control of Aïr. Other clans later arrived, some continuing on south. Thus, from the Ahaggar Mountains (Algeria) came the Kel Ferouane, Kel Fadey, and the Ouilliminden. The Sandal (also Issandalan) who came to Aïr in the twelfth century, and among whom the **Itesen** were the most important component, founded **Assodé** as their capital, the latter becoming the oldest city in Aïr. It was also the Sandal who sparked the foundation of the Sultanate of Agadez (*see* AGADEZ, SULTANATE OF) prior to their clashes with the Kel Gress and Kel Owey.

With the collapse of Assodé the principal center in Aïr became Tadeliza, then Tin Chaman, and finally Agadez. The fact that a number of important trans-Saharan routes crisscrossed Aïr gave the area much of its importance from the sixteenth through the eighteenth centuries. These were the Gao–Tibesti–Kufra and Tripoli–Kano route in particular. With the Aïr towns at the edge of the Sahara Desert, they acquired prominence as important caravan stops just before, or at the conclusion, of the difficult desert crossing.

Aïr repelled an assault from the Bornu Empire around 1450 but was conquered by the Gao Empire in 1515. After the fall of the Songhay Empire, Bornu gained dominance over the area, loosely controlling it between 1600 and 1750. Prior to the 1970s swell in the population of Aïr with the influx of refugees from the Sahel drought from further north and west (Mali and Algeria), the Tuareg population of Aïr was composed of (1) the **Kel Owey,** around 6,000, residing in the most mountainous regions and in the east; and (2) the **Kel Tamat**—including the

Ikazkazan—found west of the former group in strength of around 4,800. These groups are under the direct authority of the **anastafidet,** the leader of the Kel Owey, the true power wielder in Aïr though only second most important traditional Tuareg leader, after the sultan of Agadez. The other groups in the region include (3) the **Kel Ferouane** (6,000) found west of the massif, south toward Damergou, and also in the vicinity of Agadez.

Drought-triggered population dislocations during the 1970s altered these figures—at times quite dramatically—and increased Aïr's sedentary population; however, no new demographic estimates have been published. Most of the Tuareg in Aïr who are pastoralists are not under the rule of the anastafidet and are collectively known as the Kel Amenokal.

Until the Tuareg rebellion in the 1990s, Aïr was one of Niger's major tourist attractions with its stunning desert scenery, Tuareg oases, and historic relics. The Agadez–Iférouane–Igoulaf–Timia–El Mecki–Agadez route is an unforgettable basic staple for the venturesome, with the difficult track passing through some of the wildest and most spectacular Saharan scenery.

AIR NIGER. Niger's domestic airline. Formed on February 10, 1966, and capitalized at 28 million CFA francs, with the state holding 55.5 percent of the equity, the airline possesses one Fokker and two DC6 planes. The airline has two international routes serving Nigeria and Libya, but concentrates on linking up Niamey with Zinder, Tahoua, Maradi, Agadez, and Arlit. Its turnover in 1980 was 1,300 million CFA francs, when it flew 27,778 passengers (up from 7,061 in 1975), 1,550 tons of freight (333 in 1975), and 70 tons of mail (49 in 1975). Except briefly for passenger traffic, these figures remained static, or declined, during the 1980s. In 1984 Air Niger sharply curtailed its operations due to fiscal and maintenance problems. By 1988 even flights on the popular Agadez route were cut back (due to the state's parlous finances) to one flight a week, with all but five seats reserved in advance for mining personnel and their families in Arlit.

AISSATA, MOUMOUNI. Former secretary of state in General Saibou's cabinet. Aissata started off as secretary of state for public health in Saibou's first cabinet in November 1987, and subsequently was transferred to duties relating to the promotion of women and social issues. She remained in that capacity until September 1991 when she was replaced by an appointment of the interim National Conference government.

AJO OMO SAHKI KPARAPO. Yoruba sociocultural association in Niamey. The most vibrant and active of all such groups, the twenty-five-year-old organization encompasses more than 250 members who meet every Friday evening at the yard of the *Oga Yoruba* (''chief of the Yoruba") or *Baba Egbe* (''father" of the association), as their respected leader is called. Actually a branch of a federation uniting all originating from Sahki and Igboho abroad, the association make decisions binding on all members, passes sanctions against those regarded as acting against the common good, serves as a mutual-help association, and provides cultural and social activities. There are similar associations in Niamey for several of the town's other resident non-indigenous ethnic groups. *See also* YORUBA.

AKASA. Tamasheq for the June/July–September rainy season and cooler weather. For cultivators this is a period of intensive farm work, while for the nomads the *akasa* marks the onset of the livestock trek to the northern salt pans (*see* CURE SALEE).

AKOKAN. Niger's second "uranium city," 265 km from Agadez, near **Arlit,** and home base of the labor force working the **Akouta** mines of COMINAK. Erected in the middle of the arid region, Akokan housed some 29,000 people in the early 1980s, and has a hotel, sports center, and cultural hall. Cutbacks in uranium production since the mid-1980s, and the departure of many expatriates, have eroded the glitter of what was supposed to be a labor magnet for the region, and the town's population has declined. The Tuareg rebellion in Aïr has also made life hazardous in the entire region, and some foreign technicians have either departed or repatriated their families, to Niamey or France. *See also* URANIUM.

AKOUTA. Second major site of uranium ore to be exploited in Aïr. In 1970 an agreement was signed between the government of Niger and the Japanese Overseas Uranium Resources Development Company Ltd. (OURD)—which groups twenty firms—for the exploitation of the site, 10 km southwest of Arlit, Niger's original uranium center. In 1974 the larger Compagnie Minière d'Akouta (COMINAK) was created. The first ore from the mine was processed in 1977. By 1982 the company employed 2,000 workers in Akouta, lodged in the new city of **Akokan.** With the development of a global uranium glut in the mid-1980s, which has not abated, production has declined and many projects have been shelved indefinitely. *See also* URANIUM.

AL. Definite article that precedes many Arabic names.

AL-MUKHTAR AL-KUNTI (1729–1811). Also known as Sidi al-Mukhtar ibn Ahmed ibn Abi Bakr al-Kunti. Kunta Islamic scholar who brought together the highly splinterized Kunta people and allied them with the Berber. A devout theologian and leader of the Quadriya sect, his prestige was phenomenal. He also checked the rampaging Tuareg marauders by bringing them under his spiritual authority. *See also* KUNTA.

AL-SIDI, ABD-AL-RAHMAN (1596–1656?). Chronicler of the Songhay Empire. Of noble Timbuktu birth, he wrote the *Tarikh al-Sudan,* the seminal Songhay history (1650), which was not discovered until 1853 by the German explorer Heinrich Barth.

ALAJERI. A Hauka cult spin-off among the **Kurfey** of Niger that sprang up in the 1930s before being banned by the French colonial administration. *See also* HAUKA.

ALASSANE, MUSTAPHA (1940–). One of Niger's prime cinematographers. Born in Djougou (north Benin) in 1940 of Niger parents, Alassane was educated locally and in Niamey. He studied painting and design in a lycée and worked also in these fields at the local museum. There he was befriended by **Jean Rouch**, and his ambitions shifted to cinematography. His first film—*Aouré*—was a documentary on marriage. One of his other early films received a prize at the world Festival of Black Arts in Dakar. He has received some fiscal support from UNESCO and from the former president of Niger's National Assembly, Boubou Hama. In 1968 he made his first full-length movie on Niger proper, and has followed this up with half a dozen others.

ALFA MAHAMAN DIOBO. *See* DIOBO, ALFA MOHAMED.

ALGABID, HAMID (1941–). Former long-term prime minister of Niger. Born in Tanout, and a lawyer by profession, Algabid is an important Tuareg chief. He studied at the University of Abidjan and at IIAP in Paris where got his law degree. On his return to Niamey he was appointed head of a department in the Ministry of External Finance under Hamani Diori (1971–73), and was promoted by General Kountché to secretary general of finance (1973–79). He was concurrently administrator of first the ECOWAS Central Bank (1975–76) and later of the Islamic Development Bank (1976–79). In September 1979 he was integrated into Kountché's cabinet as secretary of state for foreign affairs, and in February 1981 as minister delegate of commerce. In November 1983 he was appointed prime minister. Despite his top position, his powers were quite limited, being essentially a managerial technocrat. Since he posed no threat to the paranoid Kountché, he retained his post until the latter's death. Kountché's successor, General Saibou, retained him as prime minister until 1989, when Algabid reassumed an administrative career.

ALGABIT AG MOHA (1902–). Major Tuareg chief, local chef de canton, and head of the Kel Gress, in which capacity he received tribute and "taxes" from loyal kinsmen as far away as Kano and Sokoto in Nigeria. Born in Tanout in 1902, Algabit originally supported the **Bloc Nigérien d'Action** and was elected on its ticket to the Territorial Assembly (1952–57) as deputy from Madaoua. Between March and November 1958, he represented Madaoua as a PRA deputy, joining in the swing to the **Parti Progressiste Nigérien** in that year. He remained a member of Niger's National Assembly until the coup d'état of 1974.

ALHAJI. One who has performed the **hajj**. Since the honorific title carries with it the connotation of piety, and commands respect in Muslim countries, pilgrims who have performed the hajj are in great demand to officiate at various ceremonies, lead prayers, or teach Koranic schools. Not all, however, who call themselves Alhaji have really carried out the requisite pilgrimage. The plural is *Alhazai*.

ALI, MARIAMA. Former minister of social welfare and women's affairs. Ali served as minister for the duration of the first civilian government of Niger, between April 1993 and its collapse at the end of 1994.

ALICHINA, IDRISSA (1957–). Deputy director of statistics. Born in 1957 and educated in demographic statistics at universities in Togo, France, and Belgium, after completing his studies in 1985 he was appointed to his current post.

ALIDJI, SIDI MAHAMANE (1923–). Administrator and government accountant. Born in 1923 in Timbuktu (Mali), where he was secretary general of the local RDA youth branch (1947–50) as well as of the RDA branch in Diré (also in Mali), Alidji worked between 1951 and 1954 as a trade union leader and a bank employee. He also served between 1947 and 1955 as an administrator of the CFAO. In 1944 he transferred to Niger as assistant accountant at the Treasury, moving in 1959 to become an attaché in Minister of Interior Diamballa Yansambou Maiga's cabinet. Occupying a series of senior posts in the accounting service of the Ministry of Interior, he went into retirement in the mid-1980s.

ALIDOU, BARKIRE (1925–). Former minister of justice and one of the powerful leaders of the PPN party prior to the coup d'état of 1974.

Of Djerma origin, Alidou was born in 1925 in Niamey, where he was also educated (1933–47). He continued his studies at the Teachers Training College at Katibougou, Mali, and after military service (1947–48) he taught in Mali for several years (1948–58). In 1959 he returned to Niger and was appointed chef de cabinet of the minister of interior. In 1962 he was further promoted to become secretary general for national defense and director of national defense. In 1965 he dropped his security responsibilities when he attained full ministerial rank as minister of the economy, trade, and industry. He then moved to head the Ministry of Justice in 1970, a post he held until the April 1974 coup d'état. During the years 1952–74 his career was strongly advanced by his being the first vice-president of the Veterans Association (Office des Anciens Combattants et Victimes de Guerre)—a powerful pressure group—and president of the Association Amicale de Niamey. His early affiliation with the RDA, and the PPN, brought him membership on the latter's political bureau in 1956, as well as the post of PPN treasurer (the same year), both of which he retained right through the 1974 upheaval; as such, more than for his ministerial duties, Alidou was one of a small group of politicians who were the ultimate source of power in Niger.

ALKALAWA. Capital of **Gobir** that was destroyed in 1804 by the Fulani jihad with a total dispersal of its population. Alkalawa was located ten kilometers northwest of Sabon Birni, both now in Nigeria. In 1815 the site was abandoned in favor of **Kadaye.** *See also* GOBIRAWA.

ALKALY, AMADOU (1929–). Administrator. Born in Say in 1929 and trained in France at the IHEOM and EPS, Alkaly served as head of the Office of Exchange (1963) before becoming an administrator of the Société Nigérienne de Produits Céramiques (SONICERAM). In 1968 he was appointed deputy secretary general of the Société Nigérienne de Cimeterie (SNC) in Malbaza, and in 1970 he became cabinet director of the minister of finance. After the 1974 coup d'état Alkaly's personal property was confiscated by the military regime, on the grounds of its having been obtained through fiscal fraud and embezzlement. He has since been involved in private business.

ALKASSOUM, AL BAYHAKI. Secretary general of the **Association Islamique du Niger** since its foundation in 1974. Alkassoum had previously been the director of the *medersa* in Say, and just prior to his appointment as head of the first Arab-French high school in Niger. In 1979 he was also appointed director of Arabic education in the Ministry of Education. He is a Tuareg of Kel Aghlal origins (a nomadic clan) and a specialist in Islamic studies.

ALLAKAYE, JOSEPH SEYDOU. Editor of the influential Niamey weekly *Le Sahel.*

ALLIANCE DES FORCES DU CHANGEMENT (AFC). One of the two broad coalitions of disparate political parties that emerged with the onset of competitive politics and civilian rule in Niger in 1991. (The other revolves around a "retooled" MNSD party, stemming from the Saibou military era.) The AFC was created by nine parties, shut out from power under military rule, to prevent at all costs the electoral reemergence of the Old Guard Songhay-Djerma dominance of the previous era. Some of these did not gain any representation in the 1993 parliamentary elections, and one deserted the AFC in 1994. At the core of the AFC is Mahamane Ousmane, currently president of Niger, and much of the formerly politically disenfranchised Hausa elite, whose merchants have been major contributors to Ousmane's own political candidacy and political formation. Among the nine-party coalition was Ousmane's own CDS party; the Dosso Djerma ANDP party of **Djermakoy Adamou Moumouni,** shut out of an alliance with the western Songhay-Djerma MNSD due to historic competition; and the PNDS party (also Hausa) of **Mahamadou Issoufou.** The coalition gained in the February 1993 elections an absolute majority of fifty of the eighty-three seats of the National Assembly and formed Niger's first freely elected government. The coalition was not very stable, however; originally including the PNDS party of Mahamadou Issoufou, the latter's resignation in 1994 as prime minister led to a parliamentary crisis and new legislative elections. The new elections narrowly tilted the balance in favor of the MNSD-led alliance that since February 1995 constitutes the government of Niger. The original partners of the AFC were the CDS, ANDP, PNDS, PPN, PSDN, UDP, UDPS, PUND, PRLPN. *See also* POLITICAL PARTIES.

ALLIANCE NIGERIENNE POUR LA DEMOCRATIE ET LE PROGRES (ANDP–Zaman Lahiya). The political formation of **Djermakoy Adamou Moumouni** that has a stranglehold over the Djerma of Dosso, of which he is titular head. Because of historic intra-Djerma competition stemming from colonial days, and because of Moumouni's own advancement having been shunted aside by the antecedent Kountché and Saibou military regimes (elements of which are found in the MNSD party), Moumouni has joined the largely Hausa parties of the AFC coalition, in support of the presidency of **Mahamane Ousmane**. He was rewarded for his support with several cabinet positions in the 1993–94 government, and he himself was appointed president of the National Assembly. The bolting from the AFC coalition of the PNDS and Prime Minister Issoufou in 1994 triggered new elections and the parliamentary ouster in February of the AFC government in favor of one led by the MNSD coalition.

ALMOU, ALKA. Political leader of the Parti Républicain pour les Libertés et le Progrès du Niger (PRLPN-Nakowa), a small post-1991 party, part of the AFC alliance, though it failed to secure representation in the 1993 parliamentary elections.

ALOU, SAHIDOU (1940–). Former cabinet minister. Born in Tillabéry on May 14, 1940, Alou was educated in Madaoua, Gaya, and Niamey (1946–60) before continuing his studies at the universities of Dijon and Paris (1961–66), obtaining diplomas in sociology and law. He then served through 1974 as director of press of the Niger Information Service, and with the rise of the Kountché military regime was appointed director general of information and editor of *Sahel-Hebdo*. He rejoined the cabinet after Kountché's death in November 1987 as General Ali Saibou's minister of information, serving until May 1989.

ALOU BADAROU, HIMADOU (1910–). Former top PPN party administrator and official in the Niamey district. Born in 1910 in Tourikoueyé (Téra), and of Songhay ethnicity, Alou Badarou served as the longtime (1956–74) propaganda secretary of the PPN. In 1960 he was appointed administrative head of the Niamey cercle, and in 1963 delegated administrator to the Niamey municipal commune. In 1966 he vacated both municipal posts to become president of one of the judicial divisions of the Cour de Sûrété de l'Etat, and state inspector attached to the presidency. During the entire Diori presidency he was one of the inner circle of party officials who ruled Niger and was purged after the 1974 coup.

ALZOUMA, TIECOURA. Diplomat. Former first counselor at Niger's embassy in France and delegate to UNESCO, Alzouma returned to Niamey in 1964 to head the Administrative and Consular Affairs section of the Foreign Ministry. On August 22, 1964, he was appointed ambassador to Ghana, remaining in that post through 1974. He has since been rotated to other diplomatic appointments and has served as head of a division in the Ministry of Foreign Affairs in Niamey.

AMADOU, ABOUBAKAR SANDA. Sultan of Zinder. Installed in office in January 1980 at the death of his father, the previous sultan, Amadou is thus one of the most important traditional leaders of Niger. He was still in office in 1995.

AMADOU, HAMA (1948–). Prime minister of Niger since February 1995, and secretary general of the MNSD political party. A Fulani, born in 1948 at Youri near Niamey, Amadou was educated locally and trained as a customs inspector. He entered the customs service and served as regional inspector of Zinder and Maradi (1971–74). He then undertook further studies at Niger's School of Administration (ENA), following which he was appointed assistant prefect of Agadez (1978–80) and secretary general of the prefecture of Zinder (1980–82). After further studies at the Institute of International Administration in Paris he returned to a posting as subprefect of Tahoua. In 1984 he was appointed director of Niger's national radio and television services, and in 1985 he joined General Kountché's presidential staff as his cabinet director. After Kountché's death he continued in this capacity under General Saibou.

In 1988 Saibou advised him of his intention to replace him, soliciting his preferences for a new post. Amadou indicated a desire to take over NIGELEC (Niger's electricity company) and engaged in an unsuccessful conspiracy to have the latter's head, Adamou Mayaki, denounced by his subordinates. Saibou discovered the power gambit and chose to ignore it, appointing Amadou in July 1988 as minister of information. The affair, and Amadou's advancement rather than sanction, drove a wedge between Saibou and a number of intellectuals supporting him. With the institutionalization of the MNSD, Amadou was elected to the party's executive bureau as secretary general, and in December 1989 he resigned from the cabinet to concentrate on party activities. Shortly thereafter competitive politics returned to Niger, and Amadou is credited with reviving and transforming the MNSD into a regular political party and with its strong showing in the 1993 parliamentary elections. When the AFC government fell in 1994, Amadou was the party's choice for the prime ministership, but President Ousmane declared new legislative elections. The MNSD-led coalition emerged with a majority, and in due course Ousmane was forced to appoint him as prime minister.

AMADOU, HASSANE (1931–). Civil administrator. Born in Garemdikieye, near Dosso, on January 15, 1931, Amadou was trained as a medical orderly. In his early years he served as deputy treasurer of the Syndicat des Infirmiers du Niger and PPN secretary general for Dosso. With these credentials he secured entry to the National Assembly and was elected on the PPN ticket in March 1957. He remained deputy until the 1974 coup d'état. There he served as second vice-president of the Assembly (February 1958+), rapporteur of the Assembly's Publications Committee, and AOF grand councillor from Niamey (December 1958–April 1959). He also was, at one stage or another concurrent with his membership in the Assembly, an administrator of Air Niger, vice-president of the Société Minière d'Aïr (SOMAIR), deputy secretary general of the CGTA of Niger, member of the OCRS High Commission, and member of the Constitutional Panel of the Supreme

Court (November 1967–1974). Since the 1974 coup d'état he has been involved in administrative duties.

AMADOU, IDRISSA (Lieutenant). Key conspirator in the 1983 attempted coup against Kountché. Amadou's role was central to the conspiracy since he was at the time commander of the Garde Républicaine and Kountché's personal security aide. After the collapse of the conspiracy, Amadou fled to Europe.

AMADOU, KOUNTIE (1924–). Early opposition leader. Born in Fendou on July 17, 1924, and a civil administrator by training, Amadou was a member of the UPN, later BNA, and was elected on its ticket to the Territorial Assembly to represent Niamey. He served in that capacity between 1952 and 1957. In March 1957 he was elected on the PPN ticket from Filingué, but was dropped from the Assembly and the party in 1964 in the widescale purge of former opposition members. Since 1966 he has been a civil administrator with the municipal administration of Niamey.

AMADOU ANGOH (1933–). Former chef du cabinet of the minister of public health. Born in 1933 in Dogondoutchi and by profession a nurse, Amadou Angoh was appointed chef du cabinet of the minister of public health on October 1, 1966. He was later shifted to fill a similar position with the minister of posts, remaining in office until the 1974 coup d'état.

AMAJEGH. *See* IMAJEREN.

AMARYAL BORI. "The wife of Bori," that is, the one possessed by the spirits in the Bori ritual. *See also* BORI.

AMBOUTA, KARIMOU (1949–). Agronomist. Born in 1949, Ambouta received a degree from the University of Nancy in France as an agronomical engineer. He currently serves at the University of Niamey as head of the social sciences division, and has undertaken a variety of studies in the country.

AMENOKAL. Tuareg title of suzerains of both large Tuareg political units and of countries. Usually applied to the chiefs of the large Tuareg confederations.

AMGHID. *See* AMRID.

AMINA, JOSEPH (1928–). Former diplomat. Born in Tanout on October 28, 1928, Amina obtained his education at home and in France studying at, among others, Niamey's national administration school (ENA) and at the Geneva Institute of Higher Studies. Between 1948 and 1960 he occupied a variety of posts in the ministries of Interior, Finance, and Civil Service. In February 1961 he was sent as attaché to Niger's embassy in Cotonou, Dahomey. In April 1962 he was repatriated to Niamey, joining the central administration staff, but in August 1964 he was again sent abroad, as first secretary at the embassy to Nigeria. In June he was appointed councillor at the embassy to the U.S., a post he held until 1974, when he was reattached to the Ministry of Foreign Affairs in Niamey. He was recently retired.

AMRAR. Tuareg title, in certain tribes and clans, equivalent to the Arab *Sheik,* referring both to leadership of a clan and to age.

AMRID. Singular of **Imrad**.

AMSA, ISSA (Lieutenant Colonel). Former cabinet minister. Amsa joined Saibou's government as minister of posts after the latter's accession to power in November 1987. Following the February 1990 student strikes and their bloody suppression he was shifted to head the Ministry of National Education, serving until January 1991. He was retained in Saibou's cabinet, though without portfolio, until the National Conference government of September 1991.

ANAGOMBA. Name by which the Wodaabe are called by outsiders. *See also* BORORO; WODAABE.

ANAKO, MOHAMAD. Rebel Tuareg leader who founded in January 1994 the Front Patriotique pour la Libération du Sahara (FPLS), which is currently part of the Coordination de la Résistance Armée (CRA). *See also* TUAREG REBELLIONS.

ANASTAFIDET. Head of the **Kel Owey** Tuareg, once resident in **Assodé** but since the 1920s in Agadez. He is the most powerful individual in Aïr, though he cedes primacy of status to the sultan of Agadez (*see* AGADEZ, SULTANATE OF). Of noble birth, the anastafidet is elected for three years and is subject to annual recall by the Kel Tafidet and Kel Azanieres. The Ikazkazan—junior clan of the confederation—have little voice in his selection. Usually reelected to office, between 1875 and 1925 only six individuals occupied the exalted post. The anastafidet's symbol of office is the confederation's drum.

ANEY. Small oasis 89 km from **Bilma** and traditional residence of the sultan of Kaouar, who is always of **Toubou** origin. *See also* KAOUAR.

ANGLO-FRENCH TREATIES (1890–1906). Of the various Anglo-French treaties that demarcated the borders of the colony of Niger, the following are the most important:

Treaty of 1890, which delineated the Say–Baroua Line (a straight line between the two localities) as the boundary separating the British and French spheres of influence. The haste with which the line was accepted by France was indicative of the latter's gross overestimation of the extent to which British influence was to be found south of it. This cost France the populated centers of Nigeria, including the former Bornu Empire itself, while pushing its own dominions to the edge of the Sahel belt. More intensive and careful exploration of the region revealed the weakness of Great Britain's presence in the area, and the nonviability of the agreed-to boundaries, leading to demands for border revisions. (Great Britain's vast claims over the area were based on Heinrich Barth's explorations and included claims over Ader, Aïr, Gobir, Maradi, and Tessaoua.)

Treaty of 1892, in which Great Britain renounced its claims to Aïr, Gobir, and stipulated a hundred-mile zone around Sokoto as an integral part of the future colony of Nigeria. The French agreed to these provisions in order to have their claim to Aïr and Agadez legitimated, losing in essence all the Hausa border towns except for Zinder. In light of the fact that without the existing wells in these border towns little east-west traffic was possible, another border revision treaty was signed.

Treaty of 1904 and 1906, a "package-deal" treaty that involved contested areas outside Niger-Nigeria, indeed, some non-African ones. The treaty shifted south the British boundaries, to within sixty miles of Sokoto (or just south of British boundaries, to within sixty miles of Sokoto (or just south of Birni-N'Konni and Maradi), conforming somewhat more to traditional boundaries in the area and placing under French jurisdiction the border towns and their wells. Still, complaints were voiced that though the centers of the small kingdoms in the area (Maouri, Konni, Damagaram, Gobir) had been allocated to France, their peripheral dominions ended up in Nigeria.

ANOU ARAREN. Site of extensive coal deposits 50 km northwest of Agadez. Reserves are estimated at over 10 million tons. Discovered in 1964 during prospecting for **uranium**, in 1976 SONICHAR was set up to exploit the coal deposits and convert them into electric energy to serve the uranium mines. A thermal complex on the site was inaugurated on April 14, 1981; at the time it had an electricity output of 16,000 kw, with a second plant scheduled to enter into production. The slowdown of the Niger economy, starting in the early 1980s, and the costliness of extracting coal from Anou Araren, has aborted early expectations that the deposits could serve as yet another focal point of Niger's industrial transformation.

ANOU MAQQAREN. Site of ancient cave drawings and rock paintings from ca. 515 B.C., located 10 km west of the track cutting through the Kori d'Anou Maqqaren, some 37 km southeast of Arlit in Aïr.

AOUMI, MAHAMANE MALLAM. Magistrate, former minister of justice and current president of Niger's Supreme Court. Aoumi served as minister of justice in General Kountché's cabinet from December 1977 to September 1979, when he returned to magisterial duties. As president of the Supreme Court he was responsible for annulling **Djermakoy Adamou Moumouni**'s first (April 1993) appointment by President Ousmane as president of the National Assembly.

AOUTA, ABDOU. Djermakoy of Dosso since 1962.

AOUTA, DJERMAKOY (1846?–1912). **Djermakoy** of Dosso who formed the original de facto alliance with the French at the time of their occupation of Niger. As such the djermakoy, and the Djerma in general, received preferential treatment; in turn the djermakoy's cavalry helped subdue several recalcitrant regions, and later helped quell revolts in the Dosso hinterland during 1905 and 1906. On Aouta's death he was succeeded by Seydou, his nephew.

ARABE, BALLA. *See* BALLA ARABE, CHAWEY.

ARABS. Unlike in neighboring Chad, there are not many Arab clans in Niger. Only approximately 5,000 people are known to exist, composed of a fraction of the **Ouled Sliman** who penetrated Niger in 1923, some Shoa Arabs resident since 1910, and a few groups of Kanemi Arabs (from Chad's Kanem region) who arrived in Niger after 1950. Most of these clans are found in the Tintouma area.

ARBRE DU TENERE. The **Ténéré** Desert's best-known landmark until 1973. A lone, straggly tree—the only one in a vast area the size of France—in the middle of the sandy dunes, marking the vitally important oasis (of the same name) for all trans-Ténéré traffic. L'arbre du Ténéré was found three-days' travel from Agadez in the direction of the oases of Bilma and Fachi, 270 km east of Agadez. The tree was uprooted accidentally by a truck in 1973.

ARCHAEOLOGY. Possibly not as profuse with prehistoric relics and sites as neighboring Chad, Niger nevertheless is extremely rich in prehistoric remains, including cave engravings and fossil remnants. They are found mostly in Aïr—which in prehistoric days had a much wetter climate and was home to large populations—though the region did not yield its treasure until 1938, and the major sites were not discovered until after 1946. Indeed, a large number of sites peppered with cave drawings were only discovered in 1960 by the Mission Berliét-Ténéré in the Ténéré Desert. The latter was also climatologically much more hospitable in prehistoric days, having had profuse vegetation and being crisscrossed by rivers. Many remains of former human habitation have been found, including pottery and fishhooks. In Aïr at least five thousand cave engravings are known to exist with scores also in the Kaouar district. In the southern regions there is practically no cave art but, instead, numerous invaluable ancient village sites have been located. One of these is close to Niamey, and another some 15 km north-northwest of the town. Many archaeological sites have also been found along the Niger River, especially of *domborei kware* (in Djerma) or *tombo* (in Hausa), both terms denoting "place of inhabitants of the past." In the Filingué region, for example, many such sites of ancient villages have yielded much pottery and jewelry of historic interest. In the Dosso and W area of the Niger River ancient Gourmantché villages have been excavated, and at Rosi—15 km southwest of Birni N'Gaouré—scientists have investigated a fifteenth-century village. *See also* CAVE ART.

AREWA. Region of the Dallol Maouri with its indigenous capital—at the time of the French conquest—at Matankari, 15 km north of Dogondoutchi, the current administrative headquarters. The origin of the name *Arewa* is unclear, with two theories being proposed: that it comes from the word *arèoun* (''north" in Hausa), or from *Ari* (the name of the son of the sultan of Bornu, Kaloumbou), with *Arewa* meaning "the people of Ari." The population of Arewa, formerly a part of the Kingdom of Bornu, was formed out of the marriage of Ari with a local woman. The first recorded chief of the region was Akazama, son of Ari. According to tradition the original inhabitants were the Goubé, organized along religious, and not political, lines. The Maouri conquered the area from them in the seventeenth century and set up their capital 25 km south of Bagagi, named after their founder, Matankari. In the next century Bornu established its suzerainty over the area. *See also* DALLOL MAOURI; MAOURI.

ARFAI BOGERMI (1885?–1960). Chief of Séguédine, and in his day the prime entrepreneur in the entire canton. Arfai Bogermi left his home village of Emi Tchouma in 1940, and settled in Séguédine (then badly devastated by bandits), some 100 km to the north. Through his efforts the village revived and commerce recommenced. By 1943 the **azalays** once again began to call upon Séguédine, and in return for his initiative the French administration recognized Arfai Bogermi as chief of Séguédine. The village salt pans are widely recognized as producing the best-quality **natron** in the entire Kaouar.

ARGOUNGOU. Capital of the **Kebi** Kingdom.

ARIEGE. Site of uranium ore deposits in the Arlit concession. Discovered in 1976, the site has known reserves of 10,000 tons. *See also* ARLIT; SOCIETE MINIERE D'AIR.

ARIMI, MAMADOU (1926–). Veteran National Assembly deputy. Born in 1926 in Dewa-N'Guigmi, Arimi was first elected to the Territorial Assembly in 1958 as deputy from N'Guigmi. He served in the Assembly for the next sixteen years until the 1974 coup d'état. Between April 1959 and January 1961 he was also Niger's representative to the senate of the French Community, and he has also been secretary of the Niger Assembly's Administrative Bureau.

ARIWAN. The most basic Tuareg social unit, the individual nomadic camp. The term is usually applied to the **Kel Owey** though other clans have similar names for the individual extended-family unit.

ARLETTE. Site of one of the uranium deposits in the Arlit franchise. With known reserves of 10,000 tons, the site was the first to be exploited. *See also* ARLIT; SOCIETE MINIERE D'AIR.

ARLIT. Nearly equidistant from the Atlantic and the Mediterranean, 250 km northwest of Agadez, and 850 km northeast of Niamey, Arlit is Niger's first "uranium town." In the middle of dry and barren desert country in Aïr, the town is a totally artificial creation. It was founded in the 1960s to cater to the needs of the mines nearby and their workers. Arlit rapidly expanded to encompass in 1971 a resident population of 3,512. By the early 1980s it had developed into a vibrant town of 30,000, though with the decline of Niger's economy and of uranium production the population soon dropped until by 1989 Arlit had only 20,000 residents. Even then the town was Niger's seventh largest. The Tuareg rebellion in Aïr in the 1990s has seen a further desertion of workers from the once booming town, and especially of European entrepreneurs and families of expatriate specialists working on the concession.

An Arlit arrondissement of 194,000 sq km (and a 1971 population of 7,896) was created in April 1969, carved out of the existing Agadez arrondissement. The erection of new mining towns in the area (such as **Akokan**) further increased the arrondissement's population, though these have suffered more from the population erosions than Arlit. Evacuation of the region's uranium ore is by truck (along the Uranium Road, and then across Niger's main east-west paved artery) to Parakou in Benin (1,600 km away) where it joins Benin's OCBN railroad to the Atlantic Ocean port of Cotonou. Nearly 40 percent of the mine workers and townspeople in Arlit are Tuareg, despite the inclination to continue their seminomadic life. *See also* ARLETTE; ARIEGE; ARTOIS.

ARMA. Name of the much-intermarried descendants of the Moroccan conquerors (1591) of the Songhay Empire. Most are found in Mali, though descendants have made their way down the Niger River to Niger.

ARMED FORCES. Niger's armed forces, whose creation was decreed on July 28, 1960, were composed, as of 1995, of 5,300 troops: 5,200 in the army and 100 in the air force. This is a large increase from the figures of 1978, when the uranium boom saw a progressive augmentation of Niger's security forces. The figures reflect both increases due to the Tuareg rebellion of the 1990s and the entry into the regular army of the disbanded Presidential Guard of the days of generals Kountché and Saibou.

The army has one company of paratroopers and one squadron of armor stationed in Niamey. Army headquarters is in Niamey (camps are located at either extremity of the city, at Gamkelle and Yantala), with garrisons (of one company each) in Agadez, Zinder, Madawelé, N'Guigmi, and Tahoua. Recently a significant percentage of Niger's military has been shifted to the northern regions. In addition to the regular military, Niger has paramilitary forces that include 2,500 men in the Republican Guard, a national police force of 1,500, and 1,400 gendarmes; the latter two branches were also augmented in recent years due to the Tuareg crisis. The police have their national headquarters in Niamey, with separate brigades in Zinder, Maradi, Agadez, and Tahoua.

Set up with French military and technical assistance out of three former companies of troops in the French colonial armies, and originally in part officered and staffed by French personnel, the armed forces also benefited at the outset by the presence in Niamey of the French Fourth RIAOM regiment (of some 1,000 soldiers) with other bases in Zinder, Bilaro, and Agadez. At the beginning there were only ten Nigerien officers, of low rank, in the armed forces, but promotions and a rapid pace of Africanization after 1963 achieved a fast transformation of the force. Official defense allocations have fluctuated over the years, in the vicinity of 9 percent of the national budget. In the austerity of the 1990s they declined to 5–6 percent, despite the military threat in the north. (Niger has, however, received military replenishments from France to cope with the Tuareg crisis.) Moreover, several départements have funds indirectly scheduled for security purposes, and during Niger's 1991 National Conference details were revealed of additional large unbudgeted sums having been diverted to the armed forces during General Kountché's administration.

In the 1970s international treaties brought about a diversification of military aid, including assistance from Libya (1972) and West Germany (1973). Though the French military presence effectively ended on March 1, 1965, some 250 officers and men remained in Niger right up to the 1974 coup d'état. At that time, the new military regime promptly asked for the repatriation of all French troops from Niger; the main reasons for the demand were (*a*) the notoriously poor relations between the French commanders and Nigerien officers, especially Kountché, (*b*) claims by Kountché that the French force had not been neutral just prior to the coup, and (*c*) fears of possible French action in support of a Diori comeback. The Kountché regime benefited from the expulsion of French troops, since they left behind 500 million CFA francs worth of equipment. Since then, relations with France have been smoothed over and a more modest French military presence has been reestablished in Niger.

At independence the embryonic Niger armed forces were commanded by Major Damba Mainassara, followed by Major Balla Arabe. In 1973 the latter was replaced by Major Seyni Kountché, despite knowledge that he was not politically reliable. Following Kountché's 1974 coup d'état, leadership of the armed forces shifted to Major Ali Saibou, who had brought his regiment from Agadez to buttress the coup in Niamey. Ever suspicious of all possible threats from officers surrounding him, Kountché tried to sideline Saibou from command of the armed forces as early as 1975, when he dismissed him from the cabinet (for which he was clearly unsuitable) and appointed him to head a parastatal enterprise. Saibou's pledge to remain loyal throughout Kountché's administration and blunt request to be retired from the army if he could not command it, won the heart of Kountché, and Saibou remained at the head of the armed forces for the duration of the Kountché era.

When Saibou succeeded Kountché on the latter's death, command of the armed forces passed to Colonel Toumba Boubacar. The latter's implication (together with the deputy commander of the force) in both the bloody suppression of the February 1990 student demonstrations and the Tuareg massacres the same year brought about their dismissal by the National Conference in 1991. In their place were appointed Colonel Issa Maazou as chief of staff and Major Abou Oumarou as deputy chief of staff. With the rise of the Hama Amadou government in 1995 Lieutenant Colonel Ibrahim Baré Mainassara was briefly appointed chief of staff (later, Lieutenant Colonel Mahamane Korohou assumed command), with Colonel Youssouffa Maiga becoming commander of the gendarmerie.

The armed forces are organized in four infantry battalions, and apart from the paratroop company and armored-car squadron, also have a camel corps and small ancillary units, for a total of 5,200 troops. There is also a hundred-man air force that was doubled in size by 1986, when it was equipped with four combat aircraft, ten transport planes, five helicopters, and several light planes. With the onset of fiscal austerity the air force was trimmed back to its original size, since several of the aircraft were no longer operational.

The paramilitary force was 5,700-strong under Kountché, who had greatly augmented it. The police, for example, doubled in number, and the paramilitary used to have a large (1,000-man) elite Presidential Guard regiment (increased from its Diori-era 120-man complement). Responsible for, inter alia, protecting the presidency, but also used as a force of social repression, the Presidential Guard was for a long time headed by a cousin of Kountché, was specially trained by Morocco, and had several Moroccan officers seconded to it. A pillar of the regime between 1974 and 1992, it was disbanded on March 10, 1992, in accord with the 1991 resolution of the National Conference in 1991. Its personnel were distributed between the regular armed forces and the Republican Guard. Currently all paramilitary forces number 5,300 men.

During the civilian era, the army was disaffected with the Diori regime and with the tasks it had been given over the years. These included (in particular) tax collection and police duties in the rural areas, both duties greatly reducing the force's popularity in the countryside. Moreover, during the tenure of Noma Kaka as minister of defense, civil/military relations greatly deteriorated. In 1970, President Hamani Diori personally took over the portfolio, passing it over to Leopold Kaziendé in 1972. Following the coup d'état one of the very first actions of the military regime was to raise all salaries throughout the country and crack down on hoarding and profiteering in grains. Despite its initial popularity, and its role in spearheading the development of Niger with royalties from the uranium boom, the military regime remained unpopular in Niger, especially with the onset of austerity in the mid-1980s and because of the regime's inability to pull the country out of its recession. Its conservative bias and Djerma-Songhay political hegemony also antagonized the "disenfranchised" Hausa east and students in the urban centers. Internal tensions within the officer corps triggered five major attempted coups during the military era; several of the executions of plotters (and liquidations, as revealed during the National Conference) have not been popular in all quarters, however.

Though the armed forces have shown remarkable equanimity in regard to their removal from the seat of power with civilianization in Niger, they have been susceptible to the same bread-and-butter issues and pay gripes over the regimen of fiscal austerity in Niamey that have afflicted civilian society. Several mutinies have erupted over the nonpayment on time of their salaries, which have remained quite low. In 1992, for example, the pay of new recruits was 2,400 CFA francs (less than $10) a month, while junior officers received only 24,000.

More importantly, morale has plummeted in the forces that are now patrolling the vast Aïr region against Tuareg marauders (*see* TUAREG REBELLION), without the fiscal backup this effort requires or a steady supply of arms and transport, which the government cannot provide. The armed forces have thus on several occasions taken the easy way out via mass arrests or reprisals against civilians, something that might have been possible under military rule but that comes under immediate scrutiny by the current civilian government, and this has caused considerable grumbling.

ARMEE REVOLUTIONNAIRE DE LIBERATION DE L'AZAWAD (ARLA). One of several Tuareg armed groups fighting a liberation war in **Azawak** against the armed forces of Niger. *See* TUAREG REBELLION. The ARLA was originally part of the Mouvement Populaire pour la Libération de l'Azawad (MPLA) but seceded in June 1993, together with three other movements, after the MPLA signed peace accords in Mali. In 1992 it joined with two other movements to form the Mouvement des Fronts Unifiés de l'Azawad (MFUA), and in 1993 it joined in the more all-encompassing Coordination de la Résistance Armée (CRA).

ARMEE REVOLUTIONNAIRE DE LIBERATION DU NORD NIGER (ARLN). One of several Tuareg armed groups fighting a liberation war in northern Niger against the armed forces of Niger. *See* TUAREG REBELLION. Its geographical sphere of operations is contested by a second group, the Front Patriotique de Libération du Sahara (FPLS). Led by Mohamed Abdoulmoumine, in 1993 the ARLN joined the more all-encompassing group, the Coordination de la Résistance Armée (CRA).

ARNI. Site, 4 km southwest of **Arlit**, where uranium ore deposits were discovered, falling within the concession area of the **Société Minière**

de Tassa N'Taghalgué. Production began on the site in 1982, with exploitable reserves estimated at 20,000 tons, but the global uranium glut that developed soon thereafter terminated efforts to exploit fully the site's resources.

AROUA. Common divination method whereby marks on the sand are interpreted by a qualified diviner.

AROUNA, IDRISSA (Major). Former minister of interior. An infantry captain before the 1974 coup d'état, Arouna was first appointed minister of labor and civil service, and several months later also took over the interior portfolio (from President Kountché). Originally considered a key Kountché aide, he rapidly fell into disfavor when he tried to assert himself vis-à-vis the latter. In July 1975 he was downgraded to the Ministry of Education, a post he lost in September 1978 when he was dropped from the cabinet altogether. In 1979 he was dispatched abroad as ambassador to the People's Republic of China, and in 1982 was given another posting overseas.

ARRONDISSEMENTS. Local administrative units into which Niger has been divided since the **Réforme Administrative** of 1964 (effective October 1, 1965). Replacing the former subdivisions and circonscriptions, there were originally 32 arrondissements grouped into 7 départements and covering 150 lower-level communes. Since then the number of arrondissements has increased. In 1969 the Arlit unit was carved out of the Agadez arrondissement to satisfy the needs of Niger's uranium north, and in 1972 the Maradi arrondissement was split into 2; the following year Tessaoua was also split into 2, resulting in the current 35 arrondissements.

Each arrondissement is administered by a sous-préfet assisted by a **Counseil d'Arrondissement,** elected by universal franchise, and sends two representatives to the higher **Commission Consultative Départmentale**. For the complete lists of the arrondissements and the départements in which they belong, *see* ADMINISTRATIVE ORGANIZATION.

ARTOIS. Recently discovered uranium ore deposit site in the Arlit concession. Depth soundings and preliminary exploration have suggested some 25,000 tons of reserves. *See also* ARLIT; SOCIETE MINIERE D'AIR.

ARWA. *See* AROUA.

ASBN. *See* AIR.

ASKIA. Songhay dynasty established in **Gao** in 1493 when one of Sonni Ali's lieutenants, a Soninke warrior named Mohammed Touré, usurped power from Sonni Barrou, the legitimate successor. There were eight subsequent Askias before the dynasty collapsed. The new dynasty expanded the power of the empire into Aïr and ruled between 1493 and 1591, when the Moroccan invasion from the north destroyed it (*see* TONDIBI, BATTLE OF). The southern part of the empire continued on as an independent unit (*see* DENDI) under a legitimate Askia lineage, but slowly disintegrated into a series of small states.

ASKIA, MOHAMED (1951–). High-level civil administrator. Born in 1951 and educated in economics and finance in France, Askia served for several years as head of Niger's mixed-economy sector, later to move to become head of finance with the regional branch of the Banque Ouest Africaine de Développement, based in Lomé, Togo.

ASNA. *See* AZNA.

ASSAMAKA. Border village on the Agadez–Tamanrasset (Algeria) route. Some 460 km from Agadez, the village has a plentiful supply of water (though of high sulfur content), making it a staple stop on the trans-Saharan route.

ASSANE, IDE (1940–). Diplomat. Born in Saké on August 14, 1940, and by training a teacher, Assané joined the Foreign Ministry in 1960 and served as secretary at the Niger embassy to the Ivory Coast (1963–66) and at the consulate in Kano, Nigeria (1966). Following specialized studies abroad, he returned to Niamey to become head of the Materials and Personnel Department of the Ministry of Foreign Affairs (July 1968), a post he held through 1973. At that date he was shifted to head the Bureau of Cultural Affairs and Documentation within the ministry.

ASSANE, SIDO. *See* HASSANE, SIDO.

ASSAO (1850?–1910). **Kaura** of Maradi in the critical period of its history and a strong figure comparable to **Dan Kassawa** and **Dan Baskore**. Son of a Fulani father from Mobiraya (near Sokoto), and a simple trader at the outset, Assao profited from the period of upheaval during which King Majingawa fled to Tessaoua, to become named kaura of Maradi. Widely detested by many, he became a maker and breaker of kings. Appointed by Nabo (1892–94), Assao died in 1910 after being poisoned by one of his wives. *See also* MARADI.

ASSEMBLEE CONSTITUANTE. Constituent Assembly of Niger, created temporarily in December 1958 out of the **Assemblée Territoriale**, following the **SAWABA** party's electoral defeat, to adopt the constitution of February 25, 1959, which it did (by 44 votes to 8) before dissolving itself. The body was dissolved on March 12, 1959, at which time it was transformed into the Assemblée Législative.

ASSEMBLEE LEGISLATIVE. Created on March 12, 1959, as the successor to the **Assemblée Constituante** of December 1958, and the predecessor of Independent Niger's Assemblée Nationale of July 29, 1960.

ASSEMBLEE NATIONALE. Niger's national assembly proclaimed on July 29, 1960, with the dissolution of the former **Assemblée Législative**. Since independence there have been three elections, with the PPN party winning all the seats. In 1960 the assembly had sixty deputies, though the number was reduced to fifty for the August 21, 1965, elections, and the same number were elected on October 22, 1970. In the latter election, the last prior to the 1974 coup d'état, thirty-three incumbents were reelected—many of whose tenure dated from the 1960 elections. Elected at the same time as the president of the republic, the Assembly was largely neglected in the decision-making process and was dissolved after the coup.

ASSEMBLEE NATIONALE. Niger's current legislature, elected in the country's first competitive elections since 1960. Comprised of eighty-three deputies, there have been two elections to date: in 1993, resulting in a government led by the AFC coalition of parties, and in late 1994, after the previous year's parliamentary crisis, resulting in a government of the MNSD coalition.

ASSEMBLEE TERRITORIALE. Successor to the **Conseil Général**, which it replaced in February 1952. In line with changes throughout France's AOF and AEF the Assemblée Territoriale possessed wider powers. Still elected by a **double electoral college**, of its fifty deputies fifteen were elected by the first (European) and thirty-five by the second (African) college. In the March 1952 elections the UNIS party captured thirty-four of the thirty-five African seats and one of the European seats.

In December 1958—following the electoral defeat of the SAWABA party—the organ transformed itself into the **Assemblée Constituante** in order to ratify the constitution of February 25, 1959, and on March 12, 1959, it became the Assemblée Législative. Among the presidents of the Assembly, successors to Moumouni Aouta, Djermakoy of Dosso, were Georges Mahaman Condat and Malick N'Diaye. The Assembly elected two councillors to the French Republic and three to the French Union as well as five councillors to the AOF Grand Council in Dakar, Senegal.

ASSIMILATION POLICY. Theoretical underlying tenet of French colonial policy in Africa, which assumed the gradual cultural assimilation of colonial populations. The status of the assimilé or évolué was granted to colonial subjects who acquired the accoutrements of French civilization—including language, dress, customs, education, and religion—or who had served with distinction in the French colonial armies or civil service. The status conferred the right to petition for French citizenship, a process so cumbersome that in the entire AOF barely two thousand Africans acquired it. The advantages of being classified an évolué and attaining citizenship included voting rights, falling under French civil and penal codes (instead of customary law), and freedom from the **indigénat** code and from **corvée** labor. The basic assumption of the assimilation policy was the unquestioned superiority of French culture and its suitability for all populations. When this tenet proved to be unrealistic and the end result unattainable, colonial philosophy shifted to the concept of association—the development of close cultural, economic, and political cooperation between France and its overseas territories. *See also* INDIGENAT.

ASSIMILE. Colonial subject who had assimilated the basic ingredients of French culture and mannerisms (or had served with distinction in the French colonial armies or civil service). *See also* ASSIMILATION POLICY.

ASSOCIATION DAHO-TOGO. Mutual-aid and cultural association grouping all those in Niamey (mostly merchants and civil servants) from the coastal areas, except for the Yoruba who had their own organization (*see* AJO OMO SAHKI KPARAPO). The association no longer exists, for it collapsed with the expulsion of the Dahomans in 1964–65 from Niger (*see* DAHOMEY-NIGER BOUNDARY DISPUTE). It had been mostly involved in sponsoring cultural activities and helping members with loans and other assistance. The organization was actively supported during the colonial era by the French administration, which regarded it as a grouping of favorably disposed, modern, and progressive elements, a fact that rankled the local population and added to the grudges harbored against Dahomans.

ASSOCIATION D'AMITIE NIGERO-LIBYENNE (AANL). The Libya-Niger Friendship Association. Founded on March 8, 1972—some time before Niger's diplomatic break with Israel—in order to promote greater Nigerien amity for Libya and Arab positions, the organization was headed by a Libyan Muslim leader—Sheikh m. Subhi—and was involved in various cultural, religious, and pro-Libyan propaganda activities. Since the 1974 coup had distinct anti-Libyan overtones (*see* LIBYA), the AANL was moribund till 1976 and has had a checkered history since, mirroring the ups and downs of Niger-Libya relations.

ASSOCIATION DES FEMMES. A 1956 alliance of Niamey's women, organized by the town's four **magajiyas**. The association was superseded at the end of 1958 by the wider **Union des Femmes du Niger**, which the magajiyas also set up.

ASSOCIATION DES FEMMES DU NIGER (AFN). Successor to the **Union des Femmes du Niger**, created on September 21, 1975, in Niamey. More highly structured than the UFN, it has a national bureau of thirty-three members elected by a congress of all members. At the level of each département there is a vice-president of the association and a bureau of some twenty members. Branches exist also at unions and in government divisions. The honorary president of the AFN was for a long time President Kountché wife, Mintou Kountché.

ASSOCIATION DES RADIO CLUBS DU NIGER (ARCN). *See* EDUCATION.

ASSOCIATION ISLAMIQUE DU NIGER (AIN). Religious organization set up by General Kountché on August 15, 1974, four months after he seized power, to group together Niger's various local Muslim organizations and religious leaders. The AIN then took its place alongside similar organizations set up by the regime grouping women and youth (the *samariya*) to participate in debates on local development issues. The AIN's first meeting took place in September 1974 under its then-president Oumar Ismail, son of a venerated marabout who had taught in Say, the Islamic center in Niger, and Vice-President (elected in 1976) El Hadj Mustapha Moussa, son of Malam Moussa, one of the principal marabouts in Aïr after the Second World War. The AIN's secretary general was Al Bayhaki Alkassoum, a Tuareg, previously the director of the Say *medersa* and at the time principal of the first Arab-French high school in the country. The AIN benefited from important Libyan largess.

Though the association grouped all Muslim elements in the country and had important Fulani, Hausa, Djerma, and Tuareg membership, primarily Arab or Arabized elements (a small minority in Niger) percolated to the top posts in the association, causing much internal acrimony and friction. Other points of internal division, common in such organizations elsewhere, were personality disputes and the fact that neither Nyassites (*see* NYASSISM) nor Wahhabites have been represented. Both of the latter two sects, making serious inroads in parts of Africa including north Nigeria, to which many Nigeriens are attracted, have been viewed as beyond the pale by mainstream Muslim leaders in Niger and have been largely discriminated against. Nyassites (of whom there are more in Niger than Wahhabites, both being minority sects, however) in general tend to avoid organizational structures, but in Niger they have been actively excluded. This has rankled since **Sheik El-Hadj Aboubakar** is married to one of the daughters of Nyass himself, and many Hausa and (to a lesser extent) Djerma Muslims are drawn to the sect.

ASSODE. Former capital of **Aïr** and one of the most ancient known cities in that region. Established around A.D. 880 by the head of the **Isandalen** Tuareg clan. The site—completely deserted since 1917—still has the ruins of some two hundred houses and a mosque originally built over ten centuries previously. Assodé's decline is linked with the creation of the Sultanate of **Agadez** by 1405 and its rise to prominence. Originally the headquarters of the powerful **anastafidet**—supreme chief of the Kel Owey—whose relocation to Agadez in 1917 sounded the death knell of the city. Destroyed during internecine fighting between the Kel Gress and Kel Owey, the ruins lie 216 km from Agadez on one of the routes to Algeria.

ASSOUMANE, ISSOUFOU. Minister of mines and energy in the February 1995 cabinet of Prime Minister Hama Amadou. The leader of the UDFD party, Assoumane was briefly imprisoned on April 17, 1994, following violent demonstrations in downtown Niamey, in which he and other leaders called for the establishment of a parallel government.

ATAKORA. Mountain range mostly in northwestern Benin and northeastern Togo. The Atakora ends in Niger between Say and Gaya, where it is traversed by the Niger River (between Kartachi and Boumba), which traces a sinuous W outline, giving the name for the **Parc National du W.**

ATTIMOU, IBRAHIM (1934–). Former secretary general of the Ministry of Interior. Born in Agadez in 1934 of Hausa ethnicity to the Muslim minister and secretary in the qadi, Attimou was educated in Agadez (1942–48) and at the Teachers Training School in Tahoua (1948–53). Between 1953 and 1958 he was a teacher in Magaria and

Tanout before going to France (IHEOM) for further studies (1959–61). Upon his return to Niger he was appointed deputy commissioner of the Tillabéry district (1961–62), head of the central subdivision of Zinder (1962–64), and commissioner of Maradi district (1964–66). In 1966 he was appointed prefect of the Maradi region, in 1970 prefect of Zinder, and in 1972 prefect of the Dosso region. In 1974 he was named the new secretary general of interior, a post he held until 1977 when he returned to other administrative duties in the parastatal sector.

AUTORITE DU BASSIN DU NIGER (ABN). Interstate organization of which Niger is a member, charged with coordinating the development of the Niger River basin.

AUTORITE DU LIPTAKO-GOURMA. Interstate authority created in 1971 and headquartered in Ouagadougou (Burkina Faso). The organization covers the frontier areas of Niger, Burkina Faso, and Mali, with a territory of 470,000 sq km and a population of 5 million people. If developed to the full extent of its potential—one of the stated goals of the Autorité—the region could produce enough food to feed all of Africa. The area is also rich in minerals, including reserves of 20 million tons each of manganese and phosphates and 60 million tons of calcium, but requires an extensive communications infrastructure for the exploitation of these ores. A 1973 FED grant was a step in this direction, aimed at paving the Mopti (Mali)–Ouagadougou–Koupela–Fada–Niamey segments prior to a Mopti–Gao and Gao–Niamey project. There are also hopes for a Timbuktu–Niamey canal and for the extension of the Abidjan–Niger railroad (which links Abidjan with Ouagadougou) to the manganese deposits of Tambao in Burkina Faso. Finding external financing for all these projects has been extremely difficult, and most have remained merely in their planning stages. The first interministerial meeting of the authority was held June 2–3, 1971.

AYARGA, KARADJI. Interim minister of hydraulics between May 1989 and September 1991, when a National Conference–designated cabinet took over.

AYOROU. Small but important Songhay town of 3,500 people on the Niger River near the border of Mali, 30 km west beyond Tillabéry and 210 km from Niamey. Its picturesque Sunday afternoon market draws many nomadic clans, including Tuareg, and canoes from Mali. The market, the town's setting on the Niger River, its tourist facilities, and the wildlife (especially giraffes and hippos) along the scenic drive from Niamey have made Ayorou a regular staple of the Niger tourist industry. Ayorou is important historically, since after Sonni Basou was toppled by Mohammed Touré in 1493 he withdrew to Ayorou and reigned over a small kingdom there (*see* DENDI; SONGHAY EMPIRE). Ayorou is administratively in the Tillabéry arrondissement of Niamey.

AZALAY. The huge annual or semiannual salt caravans plying the Ténéré Desert between the oases of Bilma and Fachi, and Agadez. (In Mali, the Tuareg use the term to refer to the important caravan to Taoudeni.) Among the Hausa called *taglem* or *tagalem*, the caravans are always prey to raid by groups of marauders up to several hundred strong. The azalay usually travel in October and November and in March and April, bringing food and other commodities to the desert oases, as well as for their entire round-trip, returning with the salt cakes produced in Kaouar. In the colonial period they were accompanied by a strong French military escort. In 1904 that year's azalay was plundered in front of Bilma's walls by 200 **Ouled Sliman** from Borkou, Chad, while the 1906 azalay was destroyed at Fachi. The latter caravan numbered 20,000 camels. No caravans plied the route between 1916 and 1924 due to generally unsettled conditions. The 1948 azalay numbered 8,000 camels, with the average caravan in the precolonial era composed of 10,000 camels stretching in a file 25 km in length. At the head of the azalay rides the representative of the amenokal of Aïr, followed by the camels of each Tuareg drum group.

The round-trip across the Ténéré takes about three weeks. Previously all azalay were exclusively Tuareg (and specifically Kel Gress), but since the onset of the colonial era the Hausa have also become deeply involved. The Toubou participate only to a minimal extent, not being trusted in the salt oases where reliability and long-term credit are important, while the Fulani have never had an affinity for camels or caravanning. In recent decades the profitability of the azalay has declined as trucks have begun to link the Agadez–Kaouar routes. On the other hand, post-1973 increases in gasoline prices have somewhat reversed this trend, since salt is a heavy and cheap commodity, sensitive to fluctuations in transport costs. With the onset of the Tuareg rebellion in the north in 1990, however, they have virtually ceased plying their ancient routes. *See also* NATRON.

AZAWAD. Tuareg term for the Azawak which has become much more common recently with the Tuareg rebellion in the area. *See also* AZAWAK.

AZAWAK. Vast area between the Ader plateau of south Niger and the valleys of Aïr, or more specifically the dry sandy plateau north of

Tahoua, between Ader, the Tiguidit fault, Talak in the north, and Ménaka to the west. Composed of sand dunes at its center, the Saharan Ténéré in Tamesna in the north, and the sandstone plateau of Tagama in the northeast, Azawak in prehistoric times was part of a drainage system for the Ahaggar Mountains (now in Algeria) and Aïr, and extended to the south via the Dallol Bosso, which joined the Niger River at Boumba just before the current W National Park.

AZBIN. Hausa name for **Aïr**.

AZELIK. Political center of Aïr before the foundation of Agadez. Seventeen miles northeast of Teguidda-n'Tesemt, it is referred to by oral tradition as the oldest settlement in the area, ruling over a population including the Igdalen, the oldest settled clan in the area. The rise of the **Agadez** Sultanate brought about clashes with Azelik in which a stalemate developed. One surprise attack, however, finally succeeded, and all residents of Azelik were killed except (according to tradition) one boy and one girl. They settled at Teguidda-n'Tesemt where some Azelik workers were established at the salt pans, perpetuating the clan though now under Agadez suzerainty. According to some traditions the ancestors of Azelik come from Fès. Uranium ore deposits have been discovered in the area.

AZNA. A term used by the Fulani to denote all non-Muslims in the Hausa areas, and synonymous in Niger with animists. Possibly a contraction of *Abzinawa* (''people of Abzin" or "Aïr"), the Azna are Hausa (according to some, a mix of Tyenga and Songhay) chased out of Aïr by the first Tuareg waves in the eleventh century. Disorganized politically (as opposed to the Gobirawa, also chased out), they have retained their traditional religious rites, the most important of which is the **Bori** cult. Found in a wide arc in the **Dallol Maouri** and in general from Madaoua to Birni-N'Konni, they were later colonized by the Gobirawa and strenuously resisted the Fulani jihad of Othman Dan Fodio and Islamic incursions. Some of their strongholds are **Darey**, Lugu (a village famed for its religious rites), and Birni-N'Konni. *See also* MAOURI.

AZU. Title of one of the important chiefs of Maradi. The first holder of the post, from Kano (capital of one of the seven Hausa states) was given command over the Maradi market by the sarkin of Katsina; later a Katsinawa dignitary was appointed sovereign of the region and the two split up the area between them. A descendant of the original azu still lives in the town of Maradi today.

-B-

BA, ABDOUSSALAM (1939–). Physicist specializing in solar energy and an international administrator. Born on February 11, 1939, Ba was trained in physics at the University of Niamey except for a year (1973–74) at the University of Pennsylvania's Solar Energy Utilization and Energy Conversion unit. He has served as an electronics technician and researcher with ONERSOL (1968–81) before becoming its deputy director in 1981. In 1986 he became project director of the West African Economic Community and director general of the region's solar energy center.

BA, BOUBAKAR (1935–). Educator and former rector of the University of Niamey. Born in Upper Volta (Diapaga) on December 29, 1935, and educated in Diapaga, Fada N'Gourma, and Niamey (through 1951), Ba completed his studies at the Lycée Van Vollenhoven (Dakar, Senegal), the Institut des Hautes Etudes (Dakar), and the Lycée Hoche (Versailles, France) before entering the elitist Lycée Louis le Grand (Paris, 1955–56) and the Ecole Normale Supérieure (Paris, 1956–59), obtaining a mathematics diploma. He continued his studies in mathematics at the Fondation Thiers, CNRS (1959–61), at Princeton University (1961–62), and again at the CNRS (1962–64), obtaining a doctor of science degree in 1965. Between 1965 and 1968, lecturer at Dakar's Faculty of Science, Ba then served as professor of mathematics at the University of Madagascar (1969–71) and in 1971 came to Niger to assume the post of director of what was to become the University of Niamey. In September 1973 he was appointed rector of the university, serving for two terms of office before joining the university's health sciences faculty. Ba has published several scholarly papers.

BABA N'GULBI. "The Big River" in Hausa; name of the Niger River.

BABULE. Same as **Hauka**.

BACHARD, ISSOUFOU (1946–). UNCC civil administrator. Born on October, 19, 1946, in Zinder, after local studies he proceeded to Paris where he first (1971) obtained a degree in cooperative studies before joining EPHE (1971–73). He continued his studies in Turin, Italy (obtaining a personnel management diploma), and at Canada's Sherbrooke University. On his return to Niamey he joined the UNCC in a variety of posts as staffing officer and as secretary general of the Interim National Bureau (1973–75). In 1976 he was promoted to head of the cooperative animation division, and has since occupied similar increasingly important posts in the UNCC.

BADAMASSI, ANOU MAHAMANE. Former interim minister of finance. A former secretary general to the presidency, Badamassi served as minister of finance between January and September 1991, when the National Conference civilian government took over.

BADEGUISHERI. Important village on the Birni-N'Konni–Tahoua route that is a major center, producing and marketing millet.

BADERI, MAHAMANE LAOUAL (1934–). Civil administrator. Born in 1934 in Konni, Baderi served for several years as the chef de cabinet of the minister of civil service before being reassigned to a variety of posts in the Niger prefectural system. He has been deputy prefect of Diffa; deputy prefect of Dosso, and deputy prefect of Magaria, serving also between 1968 and 1974 as head of the General Administration Office in the Ministry of Interior. He currently serves in another capacity in the same Ministry.

BAGNA, AISSATA. Former minister of social development, from November 1991 until March 1992.

BAGUBE. Singular of **Gubawa**.

BAIDOU, IBRAHIM. Minister of justice in the new MNSD-led government of February 25, 1995.

BAKARY, DJIBO (1922–). Former secretary general of the PPN and head of the banned SAWABA party, first mayor of Niamey (1956), first vice-president of the colonial Executive Council of Niger, and contemporary political leader of the small UDFP party. Born in 1922, Bakary, who is a cousin of **Hamani Diori**, was educated locally and at Dakar's Ecole William Ponty (to 1942). A teacher by training, Bakary entered political life at the end of the Second World War, becoming secretary general of the then-new PPN party, and a leading figure in the interterritorial RDA movement. Extremely active as a politician, journalist, and trade unionist, Bakary was one of the top militants in the RDA's struggle with the administration in Ivory Coast (1949–50) but devoted his attention fully to Niger after 1950. His active support for peanut farmers in west Niger gradually assisted his electoral aspirations. When the RDA broke with the French Communist party (following Ivory Coast's Houphouët-Boigny's lead), Bakary refused to follow suit and was expelled from the party. The local

PPN then promptly split into two factions, with Bakary's renamed the Union Démocratique Nigérienne (UDN) and based mostly on his unionist support in west Niger.

In the 1956 elections for the French National Assembly, Bakary ran against Hamani Diori; despite active French manipulations in the latter's favor, Bakary nearly beat him. In that year's municipal elections the UDN won ten seats to the PPN's thirteen and the BNA's four, and an alliance of the UDN and the BNA made Bakary Niamey's first mayor. The two parties later fused to become the Niger branch of the interterritorial **Mouvement Socialiste Africain**, which was founded in 1957 by Senegal's Lamine Gueye and backed by France's SFIO. In the 1957 Territorial Assembly elections the MSA scored a dramatic success, gaining forty-one seats to the PPN's nineteen, and Bakary was appointed vice-president of the Executive Council (a post normally becoming the premiership with the grant of full internal autonomy). The next year the MSA joined the new interterritorial PRA party of Senegal's Leopold Sédar Senghor, and changed its name to SAWABA ("freedom"). In the September 1958 referendum regarding the future status of French Africa, the party campaigned strongly for a "no" vote (and for immediate independence) but was massively deserted by many of the country's chiefs, who swung the electorate against the party. Though having benefited for some time from the support of the French administration (according to some scholars, to a very considerable degree), the loss of this support practically sealed the fate of Bakary and the SAWABA government.

The party was badly trounced, while the former BNA faction (led by the djermakoy of Dosso) deserted Bakary to join the PPN party. In the December 1958 elections the PPN—under a temporary new name, UCFA—unseated the SAWABA, gaining fifty-four seats to the latter's four. In October SAWABA was banned, most of its leaders arrested, and Bakary was exiled. Establishing himself in Bamako, Mali, Bakary made several efforts to topple the Diori regime. In 1963–64 an attempted coup d'état followed by a guerrilla attack on Nigerien border posts caused considerable unrest in Niamey, though the attack was sophomoric. Bakary was allowed to return to Niger only after the 1974 coup d'état. Then ailing, he had to pledge to the military regime to refrain from political activities. This pledge was not kept, for soon afterward Bakary and several other members of his old SAWABA party were implicated in the attempted coup of Major Sani Souna Sido. Bakary was arrested and imprisoned until April 1984. He was held in the isolated garrison of N'Guigmi near Lake Chad.

After his release Bakary remained out of politics until the onset of the National Conference in 1991. Though by now seventy-three, he founded a new political party, the Union Démocratique des Forces

Progressistes (UDFP-SAWABA), but with only a segment of his lieutenants, the others forming "another" SAWABA party, the Union Démocratique de Forces Révolutionnaires (UDFR-SAWABA). Bakary contested the presidential and legislative elections of 1993. His personal candidacy garnered only 1.68 percent of the vote, and the party likewise. Largely shunned by the AFC alliance, he threw his lot behind the MNSD, in whose coalition his party is a member. The second SAWABA party is aligned with the AFC.

BAKO, MAHAMANE SANI (1951–). Former minister of foreign affairs. Born on April 25, 1951, at Tessaoua, and educated at the University of Benin in Lomé, Togo (1971–74), Bako then proceeded to the University of Abidjan (1974–75), where he studied law and international relations, and to the University of Yaoundé, Cameroon. He joined Niamey's Ministry of Foreign Affairs' U.N. desk in 1976 and the next year was promoted to director of the Division of International Organization in the same ministry. In January 1979 he again moved up, to assume the post of assistant secretary general of the ministry and in October became the secretary general. In September 1981 he was brought into General Kountché's staff as his cabinet director, and on September 23, 1985, moved into the cabinet as foreign minister after the incumbent, **Ide Oumarou**, was elected secretary general of the Organization of African Unity. After General Saibou's accession to the presidency, he was retained in his old post for a year, but in September 1988 Bako was dispatched as ambassador to Belgium. He returned to head the Ministry of Foreign Affairs in May 1989. He stayed in that office until the civilian National Conference government was set up in September 1991, when he was attached to the Foreign Office in Niamey.

BAKO, MOUSSA (1938–). High commissioner of the Kandadji Dam Authority, with full ministerial rank, and former minister of rural development. Born in Agadez in 1938, and educated locally and abroad as a bridge engineer with a diploma in mathematics, Bako served between September 1965 and April 1967 as head of public works for west Niger. In September 1967 he became director of public works and urban affairs in the Ministry of Public Works in Niamey. After the 1974 coup he was brought into the cabinet as secretary of state and later minister of public works, shifting in 1976 to head the Ministry of Rural Development. In June 1980 he was appointed to his current post.

BAKO, NOUHOU (Lieutenant Colonel). Inspector general of the Nigerien armed forces, appointed in February 1995 by the new MNSD government of Hama Amadou.

BALABILI. One of Bilma's oldest quarters, some 200 meters south of the center of the settlement. Balabili is a venerated graveyard today, marking the site of the massacre in the eighteenth century of over two hundred townspeople during an attack by Arab marauders from Ouadai (Chad). Remnants of the old mosque, ruined in the attack, are still visible. *See also* BILMA.

BALEYARA. Djerma village 96 km north of Niamey on the route to Filingué. Of interest to tourists because of its charm and local color, Baleyara has a very important Sunday market that brings into the village large numbers of Fulani nomads and their cattle.

BALLA ARABE, CHAWEY (Colonel) (1925–). Former chief of staff of the Niger armed forces. Born on July 25, 1925, in Niamey, and the son of a soldier, Balla Arabe was educated in Zinder and then at a military school in Saint-Louis, Senegal, going on to the Saint-Maxient (France) NCO-training school. He then (1946) served with the French colonial forces in Madagascar (to 1949) and in a number of other colonies including Algeria (1956–57), rising up through the ranks. Repatriated in 1962, he was appointed chief of staff of the newly created Niger armed forces, though at the time he was only the third-ranking officer in the hierarchy. Since 1967, commander of the ground forces, Balla Arabe was replaced by Lieutenant Colonel **Kountché** in 1972, and appointed special chief of staff to the presidency. The shuffle, allegedly due to President Diori's fear of disloyalties in the armed forces, paradoxically placed at their head the one officer who for some time had been discontented with the domestic policies of the regime, and led to the coup d'état of 1974. Balla Arabe was imprisoned after the coup and not released (and retired from the army) until April 1978. He has since been involved in very profitable trucking operations between Maradi and Kano, Nigeria.

BALMA. Bilma's **natron**, as it is called in Hausa.

BANA TOURMI. Legendary Gobirawa chief under whom they first arrived at Bilma in the seventh century.

BANAKOYE, MARIAMA. Minister of the civil service and labor of the new civilian government, serving between November 1991 and April 1993.

BANDIERE, ALI. Magistrate and General Saibou's last minister of justice. Bandieré was brought into the cabinet in December 1989 and served until the new civilian National Conference government took over in September 1991.

BANK OF AFRICA–NIGER (BOA). New bank, established in late 1993 to acquire the assets of the Nigeria International Bank–Niamey. Capitalized at 1,000 million CFA francs, it is owned by African Financial Holding (35 percent) and Bank of Africa–Benin (35 percent).

BANKS. In the 1980s Niger had the following banks: Banque Internationale pour le Niger (BIPN); Banque Arabe Libyenne Nigérienne pour le Commerce Extérieur et le Développement (BALINEX); Citibank Niger; Banque du Commerce et du Crédit (BCC); Banque Internationale pour le Commerce et l'Industrie du Niger (BICIN); Banque Massraf Faycal al-Islami-Niger; Banque de Développement de la République du Niger (BDRN); Caisse Nationale de Crédit Agricole (CNCA); Crédit du Niger; and Union Nigérienne de Crédit et de Coopération (UNCC). Other financial establishments at the time included: Société Nigérienne de Crédit Automobile (SONICA); Caisse de Prêts aux Collectivités Territoriales (CPCT); Caisse Nationale d'Epargne (CNE); Fonds de Garantie des Petites et Moyennes Entreprises nigériennes (FIPMEN); and Société Islamique d'Investissement du Niger. Of note is that banking facilities are very limited, with at most only twenty-seven branches of all institutions in the entire country, one-third of these in the capital.

With the onset in the mid-1980s of a major fiscal squeeze, several of these banks collapsed—in the case of the state organs, the government being unable to sustain the deficits any longer. The ones that closed their doors included BICIN, BDRN, BCC, FIPMEN, SONICA, and BIN. BALINEX was also on the verge of closure but was rescued in March 1992 by the infusion of 746 million CFA francs from Libya. Several other private banks closed their doors, finding banking operations in Niger not profitable. In 1992 the following banks existed in the country; Bank of Commerce and Credit (BCC); Banque Arabe Libyenne Nigérienne pour le Commerce Extérieur et le Développement (BALINEX); Banque Meridien BIAO Niger; Crédit du Niger; Nigeria International Bank; Société Nigérienne de Banque (SONIBANK).

From 1993 through 1995 several major consolidations and changes took place on Niger's banking scene. Among these could be noted the 1994 establishment of the Bank of Africa–Niger, taking over the assets of the Nigeria International Bank–Niamey. Also in 1994 the former BALINEX became a private bank, coequally owned by Libyan and Nigerien interests and now trading under the name Banque Commerciale du Niger (BCN). The Banque Massraf Faycal al-Islami entered a period of restructuring in 1994, to reemerge as the Banque Islamique du Niger. And the Nigerian Trust Bank opened its doors, taking over the assets and liabilities of the defunct Bank of Commerce and Credit.

BANQUE ARABE LIBYENNE NIGERIENNE POUR LE COMMERCE EXTERIEUR ET LE DEVELOPPEMENT (BALINEX). Niamey-based bank, established under this name in 1978 in partnership between the Libyan Arab Foreign Bank (49 percent equity) and the Republic of Niger, and capitalized at 1,000 million CFA francs. Though it has funded several development projects, expectations that Libyan money would play a major role have not been actualized. By the late-1980s illiquid, the bank was spared the fate of several other financial institutions in Niger that collapsed, when on March 17, 1992, Libya pumped an additional 746 million CFA francs into its operations. In 1994 BALINEX became a private bank, coequally owned by Libyan and Nigerien interests and trading under the name Banque Commerciale du Niger (BCN). Its capitalization was augmented to 5,000 million CFA francs.

BANQUE CENTRALE DES ETATS DE L'AFRIQUE DE L'OUEST (BCEAO). Francophone Africa's central bank for the former AOF colonies and Togo. (There is a separate structure for the AEF territories, Madagascar, and Cameroon). The bank has branches in the member countries and was established in its present state in 1958. For a long time headquartered in Paris, the BCEAO responded to pressures that it relocate to Africa, and did so in 1974 when it shifted to Dakar, Senegal. It is currently headed by Mamadou Diop. The BCEAO regularly publishes some invaluable statistical compilations on member states, including data not obtainable elsewhere.

BANQUE COMMERCIALE DU NIGER (BCN). Post-1994 name of the restructured **Banque Arabe Libyenne Nigérienne pour le Commerce Extérieur et le Développement**.

BANQUE DE DEVELOPPEMENT DE LA REPUBLIQUE DU NIGER (BDRN). National Development Bank created on May 29, 1961, and inaugurated on November 8, 1961, with technical assistance from the Société Tunisienne de Banque, and with **Crédit du Niger** as a major shareholder. **Boubou Hama** served until 1974 as its director general. In 1984 the BDRN had a capitalization of 2,500 million CFA francs (compared to 450 million in 1961). With parastatal and state organs in the majority the BDRN was, until 1978, the only public bank in the country. Progressively mismanaged, and suffering from the illiquidity of the parastatal sector to which most of its loans had been made, in 1989 the bank was rescued from bankruptcy with new state and external funds. At the time it had 44 billion CFA francs of unpaid debts, including, it was revealed in 1991, some 468.5 million amassed by the Kountché family. It limped along for a few months until September 1990, when it entered into liquidation.

BANQUE DU CREDIT ET DU COMMERCE (BCC). Private bank in Niamey, capitalized at 400 million CFA francs, and headed by director general Jawed Sultan. The bank was one of the casualties of the banking crisis in Niger and went under in 1990. In 1992 its assets and liabilities were taken over by the Nigerian Trust Bank (NTB).

BANQUE INTERNATIONALE POUR L'AFRIQUE OCCIDENTALE (BIAO). Established on December 26, 1979, with 2.2 billion CFA francs in capital, BIAO has branches in Niamey, Maradi, Zinder, Tahoua, and Arlit. Shares were originally held by the Banque de Paris and six individual investors. Starting in the late 1980s the ailing bank experienced several name changes, and was taken over in 1992 by the Meridien Group, being known for some time as Banque Meridien BIAO Niger S.A. It still trades, however, as the BIAO.

BANQUE INTERNATIONALE POUR LE COMMERCE ET L'INDUSTRIE DU NIGER (BICIN). With headquarters in Niamey, BICIN was the fully owned subsidiary of the Banque Nationale de Paris. Officially inaugurated on December 12, 1979, with 600 million CFA francs in capital, later augmented to one billion, the bank went bankrupt in 1988 and was not rescued by its parent company.

BANQUE ISLAMIQUE DU NIGER (BIN). Formerly the **Banque Massraf Faycal al-Islami-Niger**.

BANQUE MASSRAF FAYCAL AL-ISLAMI-NIGER. Islamic bank formed in February 1983 with 1.75 billion CFA francs in capitalization, 49 percent of which was from Nigerien private sources. Bad loans, Niger's dramatic economic downturn, and mismanagement twice brought the bank to the brink of collapse, and it finally stopped operations in February 1992 when it was closed down. In 1994 its operations were revived, after restructuring, and it is now operating as the Banque Islamique du Niger.

BANQUE MERIDIEN BIAO NIGER S.A. Private bank, successor to the previous BIAO, with headquarters in Niamey. Principal shareholders are the Meridien International Bank (83.62 percent) and private Nigerien interests (16.36 percent). The bank's director general is Mahamane Mallam Anou. The bank is, however, still known as the **Banque Internationale pour l'Afrique Occidentale**.

BARAOU, LAOUALI. Minister of equipment and transport in the National Conference government, serving between November 1991 and September 1992.

BARCOUGNE, COURMO. *See* COURMO, BARCOUGNE.

BARE MAINASSARA, IBRAHIM (Lieutenant Colonel). Briefly chief of staff of the Niger armed forces, former cabinet minister and diplomat. Baré was brought into General Saibou's government in November 1987 when the latter succeeded General Kountché, but being part of a liberal military clique he was shunted from the center of Niamey politics, as were several other officers. He was appointed ambassador to France in 1989, a post he occupied for two years. When he returned he rejoined the officer corps, and in February 1995 was named acting chief of staff by the new MNSD-led government of Hama Amadou, but was replaced by Lieutenant Colonel Korohou a few months later.

BARKA ALAFOU (?–1876). Important **Toubou** chief of the Kecherda clan who, allied with the Tuareg of the Koutous, soundly defeated the **Ouled Sliman** in 1845. The latter, who had displaced the Toubou in Tibesti (now in Chad), had continually harassed neighboring regions and disrupted the **azalay** trade by attacks on the Kaouar oases. Barka Alafou died in a round of fighting that erupted in 1876.

BARMA MUSTAPHA, Sultan (1923–50) of Damagaram. First sultan, of the legitimate lineage, since the reestablishment of **Damagaram** in 1923. Barma Mustapha was a strong supporter of France in the Second World War. *See also* DAMAGARAM; ZINDER.

BARMOU. Small village north of Tahoua in **Ader** which has Niger's biggest cattle market. The second biggest market is Zinder, though it is dwarfed by the large collection centers of northern Nigeria.

BARMOU, SALAOU. Minister of posts and telecommunications between November 1983 and September 1985.

BARTH, HEINRICH (1821–61). Famous German explorer. Born in February 1821 and educated in the classics and linguistics, Barth toured North Africa from Tangier to Egypt between 1845 and 1847 and went up the Nile as far as Wadi Halfa, publishing accounts of his explorations. Following his return to Germany he was invited by the British government (at the suggestion of expedition leader James Richardson) to join the forthcoming expedition into Central Africa. The expedition started from Tripoli in 1850. After Richardson's death in 1851, Barth assumed leadership, reaching the capital of Bornu in April 1851. He later mounted expeditions to neighboring areas, including Aïr and Zinder, returning to England in 1855. In 1857–58 he published five volumes on the regions he explored. The wealth of data provided by Barth, including detailed linguistic studies, made him the greatest of the nineteenth-century explorers of the western Sudan. In April 1990 the German government announced that it would further honor Barth by donating 18.89 million CFA francs to construct a German pavilion in the Zinder museum as homage to Barth. The museum specializes in the colonial history of Niger.

BATTLE OF TIRMINI (1899). *See* TIRMINI, BATTLE OF.

BATTLE OF TONDIBI (1592). *See* TONDIBI, BATTLE OF.

BAWA, MUHAMADU. Serkin Gobir. A descendant of Serkin Gobir Barari, who defeated the Zamfaras in the mid–eighteenth century, Bawa has been a member of the Nigerien parliament and the local chief of a small village in the Rima River valley bordering the Niger River. He was enthroned Serkin Gobir in 1975 and currently resides in Sabon Birni.

BAY AL-KUNTI, SAYKH (1865–1929). Important religious leader. His full name is Sidi Muhamad bin Sidi Umar bin Sidi Muhamad bin Sidi l'Mukhtar al-Wafi. He was born in 1865, and after the death of his father, Bay al-Kunti, became spiritual leader and head of the **Azawak Kunta**. Living in Adrar-n-Ifoghas and with a **zawaya** at Télia, Bay al-Kunta had an immense influence in the Tahoua region and was one of the most important religious leaders in the Sahel. Many French reports refer to his semiascetic maraboutic life in the wilderness, and the huge numbers of Tuareg who came to consult with him or to ask for prayers or amulets. The authorities ignored him, however, or considered him an enemy of France, though he always counseled against anti-French activities and was especially opposed to the Tuareg uprising under **Kaocen** in 1916.

BAYERE, MOUSSA (Major) (1936–76). Key conspirator in the March 15, 1976, attempted coup d'état. A Hausa born in Filingué on February 7, 1936, during the Diori era Bayeré was director of materials and housing on secondment from the army. Following the 1974 coup, Bayeré, a captain, was integrated into the cabinet as minister of public works, transport, and urban affairs. On November 30, 1974, he was reshuffled to head the Ministry of Rural Economy. He was totally dropped from the cabinet on February 21, 1976, shortly before the attempted putsch, in which Bayeré was the driving force. (When arrested he had on his body three kilograms of amulets and charms to help him in his assault.) Blinded by utter hatred of Kountché, Bayeré's motives in the conspiracy were purely personal. The other conspirators wished power; he desired solely Kountché's death. In his trial he reiterated his belief that Kountché was the devil incarnate. Sentenced to death for his role in the attempted coup, Bayeré was executed on April 21, 1976.

BAZABAS, BERNARD. Senior technical councillor. Bazabas served his entire career in the Ministry of Public Works, Mines, and Urban Affairs as technical councillor and consultant. He has also been Niger's representative on the Trans-Saharan Committee, and between March 1966 and his recent retirement was director of the Solar Energy Office.

BAZOUM, MOHAMED. Niger's foreign minister, and coleader of the PNDS political party. A member of the MNSD, Bazoum rose to prominence when he joined the first National Conference government in November 1991 as minister of cooperation, normally part of the Foreign Affairs portfolio. He lost his post in April 1993 when the AFC postelection cabinet was formed, but was reappointed minister of foreign affairs in February 1995 when the MNSD formed the government following new elections. He is the coleader of the PNDS, which is headed by **Mahamadou Issoufou.**

BEIDARI, HAMIDOU. Head pharmacist of Niger, Beidari is also head pharmacist at Niamey Hospital and chief inspector of pharmacies.

BEIDARI, MAMADOU (Lieutenant Colonel). Former minister of labor and the civil service, General Saibou's right-hand man and for a long time a pillar of the military regime. A strict and efficient technocrat, Beidari—who at the time was quartermaster general of the armed forces—was initially brought into Kountché's cabinet to streamline the parastatal sector. In October 1985 he was shifted from the Ministry for Public Enterprises to his current post, remaining one of only two military officers in the cabinet. After Kountché's death it was Beidari who, somewhat prematurely but effectively, formally nominated Saibou as Kountché's successor in a conclave of the army's CMS, preventing a possible coalescence of sentiment behind Djermakoy Adamou Moumouni or some other military candidate. He was then promptly appointed to Saibou's cabinet as minister of finance. Widely detested in the north, especially in Tuareg regions, because of his rough style of military administration, Beidari's official role in the government was downgraded when he lost the Finance Ministry, remaining without portfolio. He was finally dropped from the cabinet in May 1989, and appointed, like other military officers, to a diplomatic posting—in his case as ambassador to Cameroon. He returned to Niger in 1992 and is retired.

BEIDOU, BAGNA (Colonel). Key member of the former Saibou military regime, part of a hard-line faction at the summit of power, Saibou's last minister delegate for defense, and one of the officers whose tough policies triggered the Tuareg rebellion. During Kountché's heyday Beidou was one of his few confidants, who pressed for summary execution of all leaders of coup attempts. He continued serving General Saibou as minister delegate for defense but in 1989 was posted to Tahoua as prefect. In that capacity Beidou was linked to the brutal repression of the Tuareg in Aïr after their 1990 armed assault on Tchin Tabaraden. During testimony given at the 1991 National Conference it was further revealed that Beidou was responsible for the execution of the death sentence against Major Sani Souna Sido, leader of a coup attempt in 1976, and that the latter was, moreover, in reality casually murdered. For his role in both events Beidou, by now retired from the armed forces, was arrested in October 1991 and placed on trial.

BELLA. In Songhay, the slaves of the Tuareg. The equivalent term in Hausa is *Buzu*, and in Tamasheq, *Iklan*.

BELLAMA (1858–1953). Originator of the intrigues in Damagaram in the first decade of the twentieth century that misled the French to depose Sultan Ahmadou, elevating Bellama to the throne. Born in 1858 and of Sara ethnicity (the dominant group in southern Chad), captured as a youth and sold as slave in Bornu (by a Baguirmi expedition), Bellama was acquired by Sultan Tanimoun and became his confidant. A eunuch, he was in charge of all sensitive and delicate court matters. Internal jealousies and competitions provoked him to complain continually—to the already suspicious French authorities—of the misdeeds of the sultan, revealing to them, in 1906, details of an alleged anti-French plot. The reigning Sultan Ahmadou was consequently deposed and exiled and the title Serkin Damagaram abolished. Bellama was entrusted to serve as chef de cercle over the former sultanate. By 1921, however, it was quite clear that the plot had been fictional and concocted by him, and he was dismissed. Bellama died thirty-two years later, on October 18, 1953.

BELLO, BOUBAKAR. Muslim religious leader. One of the leading members of the **Association Islamique du Niger**, Bello has been counselor on Islamic affairs attached to General Kountché's presidential office. Bello comes from a maraboutic family.

BEMBELLO, HAROUNA (1932–). Former minister of development, currently vice-president of the West African Development Bank. Born in Yatakala (Téra district) in 1932, Bembello was educated in Téra and Niamey, following which he attended the Ecole Normale at Katibougou (Mali) and the Ecole William Ponty in Dakar, Senegal. In 1953 he entered the Faculty of Science at the University of Dakar, and in 1955 the National Veterinary School at Toulouse, France, obtaining a doctor of veterinary medicine degree. Niger's first such degreed individual, Bembello returned to Niger in 1960 to become Niamey's director of animal husbandry. In 1962 he was moved to become deputy head of that service for Niger, and the following year was appointed director of animal husbandry of Niger. He served in that capacity until 1970, and also as an administrator of SONERAN. In 1970 he was brought into the cabinet as secretary of state for rural economy, and in August 1971 was shifted to head the Ministry of Development and Cooperation. At the time the opinion in Niamey circles was that Bembello's extensive veterinary competencies were being greatly wasted in these political appointments though his administrative talents were recognized. Following the 1974 coup d'état Bembello was placed under arrest for over a year, but was granted clemency and released in August 1975. Since January 1976 he has been serving as vice-president of the West African Development Bank.

BERI BERI. Name by which the **Kanuri** of East Niger are known.

BILMA. Arrondissement encompassing 260,000 sq km and some 8,000 people, mostly **Toubou**, the headquarters of which is the village of the same name, which has a population of 1,800 and is the most important settlement in the Ténéré Desert. The village has extensive **natron** salt pans (called *balma* by the Hausa) and is important because of the 500 to 800 tons it exports annually. Bilma is actually the principal and biggest oasis of ten such salt-pan sites in the **Kaouar**, and also has large date plantations and plentiful water. Found on the main historic Fezzan–Tibesti–Bornu route, Bilma (as also **Fachi**) has for a long time been a **Kanuri**-populated island in the desert. Natron extraction plummeted in the modern era, though until the Tuareg rebellion of the 1990s it was still the principal economic activity of the population. In 1907 15,000 camels (*see* AZALAY) came to Bilma to transport some 1,600 tons of salt, bringing into the community meat and cereals. By 1929 only 9,094 camels were involved in the azalay that evacuated 727 tons of salt. The natron itself is of very poor quality, especially compared to that of Amadror in the north, but is still widely used for human and animal consumption. Trade in natron declined in profitability in the 1970s due to cheap imports from Nigeria and the cost of the long and hazardous Ténéré crossing.

Half a kilometer from Bilma is Balabili, an old quarter and now a venerated graveyard marking the spot where Bilma's population was massacred in the eighteenth century by Arab marauders from Ouadai, Chad. Separated from Agadez and the Aïr massif by the Ténéré, Bilma is one of the most remote spots in the world, and as such has been featured in *National Geographic* reports. Surrounded by sand dunes, it has been and still is used as a natural prison. The salt-extracting community has lived there for centuries. Natron is mined by the same age-old methods, via oblong pits dug in the ground which are filled with water into which salty soil is scattered. The salt separates from the soil and floats to the top. Scooped up and pressed into mounds of different sizes and dried in the sun, two kinds of salt cakes are produced: one for animal and another for human consumption. The latter are round, ten-inch-diameter cakes.

The round-trip across the Ténéré by the azalay takes three weeks from Agadez, and all food and fodder must be carried from Agadez since none exists in Bilma. The caravans are now headed by Hausa (who broke the Tuareg monopoly of the past), but never by Toubou or Fulani. In the nineteenth century, Bilma was very much a slave town, with the masters living in Kalala near the salt pits themselves, which was raided so frequently that the residents finally moved in within Bilma's walls. The salt pans are 2 km northwest of the town and are the scene of hectic activity when the azalay season arrives. The pans are divided into concessions held by various ethnic groups. Until the arrival of the Tuareg in the area the Kanuri—original inhabitants of Kaouar—held most of the plots. With the Tuareg domination of the trade established, other groups have been given concessions until today most have a plot, though the biggest and best are owned by a few powerful families.

BILO, SOUMANA. Minister of water supplies and the environment in the first AFC civilian cabinet, between April 1993 and October 1994.

BIR ALALI. A Senousi **zawaya** founded in 1898 deep in Kanem (Chad) by Sidi Muhamad al-Barrani—an important Senousi leader. The outpost changed hands a number of times during the French occupation of the area, and finally fell to the French in January 1902 when a force of 600 was necessary to wrest it from the defenders. Still, on December 4, 1902, Bir Alali fell to a combined force of 3,000 Ouled Sliman, Toubou, and Tuareg, many coming all the way from Niger for the assault. The next day, after bitter hand-to-hand fighting, the zawaya was regained by the French, and the Niger clans retreated to their homes.

BIRNI. In Hausa, "city." The plural is *birane*. The term actually signifies a walled city.

BIRNI-LALLE. For two centuries the capital of the **Gobirawa** before the relocation to **Alkalawa**. The name, in Hausa, means "citadel of well-being." *See also* GOBIR.

BIRNI-N-ADER. Former capital of **Ader** after its eighteenth-century conquest by **Aggaba**, who set up his administration in Birni-n-Ader but was later (around 1738) forced to relocate due to the incessant assaults against it by various groups in the area. At the time (after Aggaba's death), Illela was founded as the new capital.

BIRNI N'GAOURE. Small though key village 107 km east of Niamey on the Zinder road. Situated in the Dallol Bosso, its population is mostly Djerma and Songhay.

BIRNI-N'KONNI. Important Niger border town of 13,000, and arrondissement with a population of 146,000 in the Tahoua département. Birni-N'Konni is 422 km east of Niamey and 95 km from Sokoto in Nigeria. Its big Wednesday market is a major commercial magnet for the entire area. The region is the bastion of Hausa animism (*see* AZNA) in Niger, with the principal centers being Birni-N'Konni itself, Safo, and Houdel in the Maradi region, Fissatao in Gobir, and Gazaoua and Korgom south of Tessaoua. A reunion of traditional fetishists can bring thousands of participants into Birni-N'Konni, as it indeed does from time to time. The town was crushed in very bloody battles during the Fulani jihad in the eighteenth century, and was later brutally sacked by the Voulet-Chanoine mission (*see* MISSION AFRIQUE CENTRALE).

BIRNI N'KOUNIA. Gobirawa capital following the destruction of Dakourawa by Fulani armies. The center was also sacked in 1823 and the new Gobirawa capital was established in Gao n'Gazo.

BLOC NIGERIEN D'ACTION (BNA). Successor political party to the **Union Nigérienne des Indépendants et Sympathisants**. Set up in 1955 as a traditionalist, chiefly, and anti-RDA party following the split in UNIS that left Dr. **Francis Borrey** and **Ikhia Zodi** in control of the remaining elements. Shortly later the BNA joined in an alliance with the Union Progrèssiste Nigérienne, which had been unable to link up with the PPN, and the Condat-Seydou electoral ticket obtained 127,000 votes to the 83,000 of the PPN. Late in November 1956 the party merged with **Djibo Bakary**'s Union Démocratique Nigèrienne (which on November 19 had set up an MSA branch in Niger); the joint party was later to be called SAWABA. The BNA was all along strong in traditional Hausa areas. *See also* POLITICAL PARTIES.

BOBOY. Djerma name for the Dallol Bosso in the Dosso region.

BOGU. Working songs aimed at giving rhythm to cultivators in the fields. From the Djerma term for the collective labor obligation a farmer could invoke by declaring a *bogu* on his plot of land.

BOKAYE. Traditional healers, referred to by diviners (madiba), who also sell traditional medicines, treatments, amulets, aphrodisiacs, and sundry other items. They carry an aura of the supernatural but in grave cases suggest their patients visit modern clinics or hospitals.

"BONKANO." Popular name in Niamey for Lieutenant Amadou Oumarou, who masterminded the 1983 attempted coup d'état. *See* OUMAROU, AMADOU.

BORI. Ritual spirit cult, mostly prevalent among the **Azna** Hausa in the southern areas. Possession rites of the kind prevalent also among the Songhay (holey) and elsewhere (voodoo in Haiti; candomblé in Brazil; zar in Ethiopia), Bori is a ceremony by which the gods intervene directly in human affairs by possessing the body of initiated women. Most Bori members are either divorced women or prostitutes, though many women join to appease the gods for an illness visited on them or for infertility. They are led by the **magajiya** or the iya, queen of Bori, leader of the prostitutes and a powerful figure (though not an initiate herself), who lives in Maradi. During the rites that take place at least once a month in which the serkin Bori (''chiefs of Bori," usually men) officiate, dancing leading to frenzy and hysteria are conducive to the possession by Bori of one of the initiates. Bori refers in Hausa specifically to the state of possession. There are differences between the cult as practiced in the countryside and in such larger centers as Birni-N'Konni.

BORNU EMPIRE. *See* KANEM-BORNU EMPIRE.

BORORO. Nomadic Fulani herders. Also called *Wodaabe* (''the rejected") and by outsiders *Anagomba*, their origin is in the Katsina area (the small Sultanate of Kazaoure), whence they immigrated to Tahoua and Damergou commencing around 1850. Similar to the Bororo in Chad, Niger's tribesmen are less affected by Islam and are much more nomadic. Bororo are also to be found in Nigeria and in Cameroon. According to some traditions the Bororo were sedentary Hausa in the fourteenth and fifteenth centuries who, once united under one chief, shifted to a nomadic life at his death. Other accounts refer to them as those Fulani who refused to accept Islam when the faith was introduced in Sokoto early in the nineteenth century, and thus became distinct from other groups and clans.

BORREY, FRANCIS (1904–76). Colonial administrator, surgeon, and early political leader in Niger. Born in Besançon, France, on April 8, 1904, and a physician and surgeon by profession, Dr. Borrey was director general of the Centre d'Etudes et d'Information des Problèmes Urbains dans les Zones Arides (PROHUZA). In 1946 he entered the political sphere when he competed in the French National Assembly elections from Niger, and placed second after Hamani Diori. Originally a cofounder of the PPN, Borrey later became a prominent leader of the UNIS party and dominated its activities until 1955, when the party split over his insistence that it affiliate with the IOM. Since the bulk of the membership followed the dissidents—led by Mayaki and Seydou—his faction fared poorly in the subsequent elections and eventually changed its name to the FDN. Borrey served as IOM councillor from Niger at the French National Assembly and president of its Social Affairs Committee (1947–53). In 1952 he was the IOM assembly faction vice-president and also served as future Ivory Coast president Houphouët-Boigny's technical councillor, as well as minister of health in the French government of 1959. A former technical councillor also in Hamani Diori's 1959 cabinet (and just prior to that district officer in Zinder), Dr. Borrey was appointed Niger's representative to France's Social and Economic Council and Niger's deputy delegate to UNESCO. After Niger's independence Dr. Borrey served as representative of French Polynesia at the Social and Economic Council (1964–66), played a role in the administration of the New Hebrides, and was later integrated into the French cabinet first as minister of agriculture, then of national education.

BORRORODJI. "People of the bush," another name for **Bororo**, or **Wodaube**, nomadic Fulani herders.

BOUBACAR, TOUMBA (Colonel). Former chief of staff of the Niger armed forces. Boubacar, a career soldier, undertook prompt and loyal action in October 1983, defusing the attempted coup of Lieutenant **Amadou Oumarou**, and rescuing then-colonel Saibou, who had been captured by the plotters. In September 1985 Boubacar was brought into Kountché's cabinet as minister of youth and sports. Boubacar, also vice-president of the National Development Council (CND), was brought into this key ministry (which controlled the country's **samaria**) after administrative inquiries into general mismanagement under its previous minister. Promoted also within the armed forces by Kountché to deputy chief of staff in 1984, and by General Saibou to succeed him as chief of staff when he assumed the presidency in 1987, Boubacar was summarily dismissed by the National Conference in September 1991 over his handling of the Tuareg crisis of 1990 that developed into a full-fledged rebellion.

BOUBE, IDRISSA (1938–76). Former director of the Sûrété Nationale, which in March 1976 joined in the attempted coup of Major Moussa Bayeré. Prior to the attempt Boubé had been the Sûrété's deputy head (1967–73) and head since shortly before the Kountché takeover. His support for the Bayeré conspiracy cost Boubé his life; sentenced to death in court martial, he was executed in April 1976.

BOUBE, ISSA (1930–). Former civil administrator. Born in 1930 in Birni-N'Konni and educated locally, Boubé joined the administration and was attached to the presidential office (1959–60) as head of protocol. He later served with the Ministry of Information and in 1961 was sent on a special mission to Saudi Arabia. From 1962 he was counsellor to the Supreme Court and head of the Protocol Department in the Ministry of Foreign Affairs. After the 1974 coup d'état his property was confiscated on the grounds that it had been obtained by fraudulent means. He is currently involved in commerce.

BOUBON. Small fishing village in the Niger River some 23 km from Niamey on the road to Mali. It is a very popular weekend congregation point for the capital's expatriate community.

BOUBOU, HAMA. *See* HAMA, BOUBOU.

BOUDE, GADO (1944–). Educator and former minister of education. Born in 1944 and educated in France in history and archaeology, Boudé joined the Niamey branch of CNRS in 1969 as a lecturer, serving until 1973. He then joined INTSH as head of its archueological division and in 1979 was nominated head of IRSH. He has written several books and is widely respected in Niamey. Boudé was brought into the transitional civilian government in March 1992 as minister of education, serving in that capacity until April 1993.

BOUDOUMA. From *Boudou* (''high grass") and ma (''men"), or from Boulou, a Kanembu ancestor. The Boudouma are a Yedina subgroup more widely found in neighboring Chad, that occupies the islands and archipelagos of Lake Chad (and hence their designation as "men of the tall grass"). In 1964 it was estimated that there were 135,000 Boudouma in the N'Guigmi circonscription; their number is higher today, but unknown. Together with the **Kanuri**, with whom they are in close geographical proximity, the Boudouma make up 5.5 percent of the population.

BOUKAR, AMADOU (1929–). Civil administrator. Born in 1929 in Gouré, Boukar was educated at home and in Paris (IHEOM) in administration. He then served in a variety of administrative posts including as Niger representative to the African Bank of Development. Between 1966 and 1971 he also was director of external financing in the Ministry of Finance. Following the 1974 coup he was reassigned a division in the Ministry of Finance. He is currently retired.

BOUKAR, MAINA MOUSSA. Former minister of state enterprises, brought into the cabinet from his prior position as a senior aide of Prime Minister Algabid in September 1985. He left the cabinet two years later, being assigned to the Ministry of Interior.

BOUKARI, BAOUA (1933–). Mayor of Maradi. Born in 1933 in Zinder of Hausa nobility and an instructor by profession, Boukari was elected deputy to the National Assembly in June 1959 and served as an administrator of SAPELAC. He remained deputy until July 1969 and then was appointed mayor of Maradi, a post he held until 1984, when he returned to commercial activities.

BOUKARI, MAHAMANE. Former minister delegate to General Saibou, responsible for administrative reform. He held this position between May 1989 and September 1991.

BOUKARY, SIDI. High-level administrator in the Ministry of Civil Service. Early in 1966 Boukary was appointed head of the Personnel Division in the ministry and served between 1967 and 1970 as director of the civil service of Niger. Since 1970 he has continued to function in other high-level positions in the ministry.

BOUKARY, WASSALKE. Senior civil administrator and former minister of finance. A former treasurer-general of Niger, Boukary was brought in 1988 into Prime Minister Algabid's staff as director of the prime minister's office and secretary of state in charge of the budget. A few months later, in November 1989, he was appointed minister of finance. He left the cabinet in January 1991, rejoining the treasurer general's office.

BOUKARY MAIGARI, AMADOU (1934–). Administrator. Born in 1934 in Niamey, Boukary Maigari served for five years as the cabinet director of the Ministry of Education (1963–68) before being attached to the Ministry of Interior as technical consultant. Since 1974 he has been with the Ministry of Education in a similar capacity.

BOUKOUKI. Quarter in the outskirts of the city of Niamey where many newcomers settle in woven straw huts. The animal population of the quarter is much larger than the human population.

BOULAMA, ISSA MAMADOU. *See* ISSA, BOULAMA MAMADOU.

BOULAMA, MAHAMANE. Former interim secretary of state for agriculture, between March 1990 and September 1991, when the transitional civilian government took over.

BOUREIMA, ABDALLAH. Briefly minister of finance and planning in the first civilian government of post-1990 Niger. He served in the post between April 1993 and October 1994, when the AFC government fell.

BOUREIMA, MALIKI (Captain). Commander of the unit involved in the brutal reprisals against Tuareg after the 1990 Tchin Tabaraden assault. Boureima was arrested in October 1991 for direct responsibility in utilizing indiscriminate force, directly triggering the subsequent full-scale **Tuareg rebellion**. Army mutineers in February 1992 called for him to be released (which he ultimately was), arguing he was being made a scapegoat for direct orders given from higher up in the military command. His release was also supported by the new chief of staff in order to boost the morale of Nigerien forces in the north, though it led to the resignation of the minister of trade, **Mohamed Moussa**, then negotiating with the Tuareg rebel leaders.

BOUZA. Arrondissement in the Tahoua département with a population of 94,000 (in 1994) and headquarters in the small town of the same name. The latter is some 50 km north of Madaoua on the Madaoua–Tahoua road. Its population is 3,300.

BOUZOU. *See* BUZU.

BOZO. A small tribe of fishermen on the Niger River, numbering some 20,000. Descendants of the Soninke who migrated southeast to the river after the fall of the Ghanata Empire, most Bozo are still found in the Mopti region of Mali, though some have filtered down the river to Niger. Famed fishermen, using the most modern techniques, the Bozo are widely renowned as masters of the river.

BRAH, MAHAMANE. Former cabinet minister. Brah joined the Kountché cabinet in September 1979 as minister of rural development. He was shifted in February 1981 to head the Ministry of Planning, and in July 1983 again, this time to head the Ministry of Posts and Communications. He was dropped from the cabinet in November 1983 and a few months later became the executive secretary general of the Interstate Committee for the Combat of Drought in the Sahel, better known under its French acronym, CILSS.

BRAOUIA. *See* TEDA.

BRASSERIES DU NIGER (BRANIGER). Created in Niamey in 1963 by SOBRADO (Société des Brasseries du Dahomey) to manufacture beer, juices, soft drinks, and ice cream. BRANIGER commenced operations in June 1964 with a capitalization of 300 million CFA francs, of which 59 percent is held by SOGEPAL and 20 percent by BRADUNI. The company's capacity has since been increased to 80,000 tons and its capitalization to 550 million CFA francs. In 1970 BRANIGER was Niger's eighth largest enterprise in terms of turnover, though its relative weight has declined with the mining boom in Aïr. In the 1980s the company was producing, inter alia, 80,000 hectoliters of beer, had a turnover of 1,500 million CFA francs, and employed 75 workers.

BUDE N'DAJI. Major ritual celebrations in Birni-N'Konni and Massalata—**azna** areas of importance—which attract large delegations from various Hausa communities, including Kano, Zaria, and Katsina, as priests unite to offer ritual sacrifices to the Dogoua spirit and others.

BUREAU DE COORDINATION ET DE LIAISON (BCL). Niger's security police, presidents Kountché's and Saibou's prime prop against domestic subversion.

BUREAU DES MINES (BUREMI). Government organ established in 1975 to handle mining and geological research (pinpointing priorities and centralizing the grant of concessions) and also as a watchdog over Niger's mineral resources.

BUZU. Equivalent, in Hausa, to the Songhay *Bella*, that is, Tuareg slaves.

-C-

CAISSE CENTRALE DE COOPERATION ECONOMIQUE (CCCE). Official French agency through which French governmental aid to Francophone Africa is channeled, banked, and administered. Successor to the Caisse Centrale de la France d'Outre-Mer (CCFOM). Between 1960 and 1971 the sum of 7,945 million CFA francs were disbursed to Niger, with credits usually transferred to the BDRN. Among projects assisted are the BDRN itself, SOMAIR, and Crédit du Niger. In April 1975, a long-term loan of 4.5 million French francs was granted to augment the capital of the Compagnie Minière d'Akouta.

CAISSE CENTRALE DE LA FRANCE D'OUTRE-MER (CCFOM). *See* CAISSE CENTRALE DE COOPERATION ECONOMIQUE (CCCE).

CAISSE DE PRETS AUX COLLECTIVITES TERRITORIALES (CPCT). Banking organ, 90 percent owned by Niger's collective movement. Founded in 1964 under director general Albora Naba, with 1.4 billion CFA francs in capitalization. The CPCT is the leading banking agency for the collective movement.

CAISSE DE STABILISATION DES PRIX DES PRODUITS DU NIGER (CSPPN). Price stabilization office for Niger's agricultural crops, the CSPPN guarantees prices to farmers and ensures that no major vacillations develop from year to year.

CAISSE DES DEPOTS ET CONSIGNATIONS (CDC). Official French agency that serves as banker, administrator, and manager of Francophone Africa's pension, national security, and other social-welfare programs.

CAISSE NATIONALE DE CREDIT AGRICOLE (CNCA). Founded on September 20, 1967, under the Ministry of Finance, with original capitalization of 67 million CFA francs (later raised to 650 million), the CNCA is a banking organ that offers low-interest agricultural credit, including assistance for stockbreeding purposes and rural artisanal projects. The CNCA is based in Niamey and has branches in Dosso, Tahoua, Maradi, and Zinder. It took over the operations formerly conducted by the UNCC but encountered the same problems that had seriously jeopardized the latter's economic viability: very low repayment rates and high default percentages, even though loans by the CNCA were in theory given not to individuals but to cooperatives. The CNCA is also in charge of the commercialization of peanuts, rice, and cotton. It relies heavily on BDRN for short-term credit. In September 1970 when the S.P. and SMDR were dissolved the CNCA took over all their operations. Following the 1974 coup d'état, investigations into the CNCA substantiated criticism levied against it all along. Of all its loans, more than 80 percent had benefited not farmers but civil servants, and it had financed everything possible except agriculture. The CNCA was virtually bankrupt in 1989, but continued being sustained by the government.

CAMP CAZEMAJOU. Important military camp in Zinder, named after the French soldier and explorer (*see* CAZEMAJOU) assassinated in Zinder in 1898. In 1961, following independence, the camp was renamed Camp Tanimoun, after one of Zinder's most illustrious kings.

CAMP LAZARET. *See* LAZARET.

CAMP TANIMOUN. *See* CAMP CAZEMAJOU.

CAMPEMENT DE LA TAPOA. Main camp in the **Parc National du W.** Located just inside the park on a cliff overlooking the **Tapoa** River, the camp boasts attractive thatch-roofed bungalows with all facilities at very low rates. The Tapoa camp is a popular tourist site even though the park is quite modest in terms of wildlife and scenery.

CARAVAN ROUTES. Several major caravan routes cross Niger, both east to west and north to south. Of the former, the **azalay** route linking Agadez with Kaouar (including Bilma and Fachi) is still important and allows for the evacuation of Kaouar's natron, though competition from trucks has recently reduced the profitability for caravans, and the Tuareg rebellion in the 1990s has curtailed them severely. The classical western route linking In Gall and Teguidda-n'Tesemt with Gao is no longer of any importance, though in former centuries it was a major trade artery. The north-south routes have similarly ossified, though there are still caravans plying the routes from Tahoua through the Aïr massif to Algeria and Libya. Prior to the colonial era, important caravan routes from the north, most passing via Agadez, terminated at Zinder, the capital of Damagaram, which benefited greatly from this fact. These routes, traversing both Damagaram and Damergou, gave rise to many caravan stops that flourished in the seventeenth through nineteenth centuries. The ancient Garamantian route (Tripoli–Fezzan–Bornu), which was the mainstay of Kanem and Bornu until the nineteenth century, also benefited Niger towns, since caravans needed to stop in Kaouar, and at times branched off westward. The collapse of the route in the nineteenth century (due to security problems) led to a major shift in caravan routes to the east, resulting in a decline in many of the Niger centers along its southern end.

With the onset of the colonial era most of the northern caravan trails were rapidly eclipsed in importance by other modes of travel and commerce. The principal ones had been (all from or via Agadez): (1) west to In Gall and on to Timbuktu (Mali); (2) east to Bilma and on via Tibesti to Koufra (Libya) and northward; (3) north to Tamanrasset and Touat (Algeria); and (4) southward to Zinder and Nigeria via Damergou and Damagaram, usually coming from Tripoli with the ultimate destination of Kano. Trade from Zinder destined for the north included slaves, skins, and ostrich feathers (in great demand in Europe).The Tripoli trade brought south mostly guns and steel. The bulk of the slave trade from the Niger area was directed to the southern coast, however, and the trans-Saharan slave trade tended to be of non-Niger origin. The Zinder–Tripoli route was so profitable that important communities of merchants from Ghadames (an oasis south of Tripoli) established themselves all along it until the onset of the colonial era. Commercially, the Tripoli–Ghadames–Aïr–Zinder–Kano route (taking from seventy to ninety days to traverse) was the most important one in the nineteenth century. Even at the turn of the twentieth century large caravans used it. In August 1904, for example, eight thousand camels passed along this route. Changing patterns of trade shifted the terminus from Zinder to Kano (and Katsina), and other changes in caravan stops occurred from time to time. Toubou-Tuareg quarrels continually disrupted the caravan trade, and in the second decade of the twentieth century caravanning became increasingly unprofitable due to the loss (to Great Britain) of such southern terminals as Kano and Katsina, and to competitive prices of the same commodities arriving across the Atlantic and shipped north by rail. Today only limited local trade and the azalays ply the desert routes.

CASSITERITE. Tin dioxide, one of the principal minerals for the production of tin, found mostly in El Mecki mountain and in Tarroundji and Timia south of Aïr. The El Mecki deposits and sites produce fully 60 percent of Niger's output. Total production in 1960 was 76.8 tons; in 1971, 125.9 tons; and 38 tons in 1990. Production could be increased if a more automated system was adopted, at the cost of some 300 million CFA francs. The first explorations commenced right after the Second World War, and the ore was first discovered at Tarroundji. The Société Minière du Dahomey-Niger (SMDN), formed to exploit the concessions, encountered major difficulties including water shortages and the problem of evacuating the ore to the coast. Nevertheless regular production commenced in 1950 with the entire output sold to a smelting firm in northern Nigeria. In 1964 the Niger government took over 75 percent of the shares of the SMDN (renamed the Société Minière du Niger). In 1966 two other sites were discovered in the vicinity of Zinder with excellent conditions for exploitation.

CATTLE. Niger is an important stockbreeding country, second in Africa after Mali, with 4.5 million head of cattle, 8.5 million sheep and goats, and 400,000 camels. The above (1971) estimates were reduced by some 15 percent by the Sahel drought. Niger's prime export market for cattle is Nigeria. Herders took cattle on the hoof all the way to Lagos right through the 1960s, the ravages of the tsetse fly–infested areas notwithstanding. Only in the mid-1960s and 1970s did truck transport become prevalent and economical. The official cattle exports are only a bare fraction of the country's true exports of cattle. Throughout the 1960s, for example, registered annual exports varied between 52,000 and 59,000 head, though real exports were conservatively estimated at around 170,000 per year. The slaughterhouses have been able to export only very small tonnages of processed meat due to the reluctance of herders to sell their cattle to the state, preferring to use traditional markets that pay higher prices. When the Nigerian meat market collapsed during the civil war, alternate sales were made to Ivory Coast, Ghana, and the Middle East, but these were essentially minimal quantities. SONERAN was given the monopoly over meat sales in October 1968.

CAVE ART. Most of Niger's prehistoric art is found in the desert north, an area formerly humid and thickly vegetated. Two areas of profusion of rock engravings and cave art are found in Aïr and in the Djado-Kaouar region of the Ténéré. A total of over 5,000 sites are known, making Niger, together with Chad, among the most archaeologically interesting countries in Africa. *See also* ARCHAEOLOGY.

CAZEMAJOU, MARIUS GABRIEL (Captain) (1864–98). French colonial officer. Born in Marseilles on December 10, 1864, and commissioned in the army in 1886 (becoming a captain in 1889), Cazemajou first served in Indochina and Tunisia before being dispatched to West Africa in 1896. Head of the Mission du Haut-Soudan sent to contact the Sudanese slave raider Rabih Fadl Allah (or, as usually referred to, Rabah), in order to negotiate some form of agreement allowing contiguity of the French possessions in West and Equatorial Africa (threatened by Rabah's conquests). On his way to Rabah's court, Cazemajou stayed three weeks in Damagaram and was murdered there by a faction fearing that a Franco-Rabah link would free the latter to attack Zinder. Subsequently the Mission Afrique Centrale was mounted to punish Zinder and avenge Cazemajou's death, leading to the occupation of Damagaram in 1899. Cazemajou was honored when the main garrison camp in Zinder was named after him. Following independence the camp was renamed after one of Zinder's most illustrious kings.

CENSUSES. Niger's first census, conducted in 1977, revealed that the country's population stood at 5,121,000 people, with projections of 6,265,000 in 1985; 8,370,000 in 1995; and 9,796,000 in the year 2000. Niger's urban population, it was estimated, would grow to 982,000 in 1985, and more dramatically to 2,182,000 in 2000. These projections assumed the 1977 demographic growth rate of 2.33 percent would rise to 3.19 in 1995.

The second census, the latest to date, took place in 1988 (results were published at the end of January 1992). It revealed that the country's population had grown at a significantly faster pace than projected (at a rate of 3.3 percent) to 7.25 million people, of whom 49.5 percent were below the age of 15. Life expectancy in 1988 was now up to 47 years, and infant mortality rates had dropped to the still-high 140 per 1,000 births. The percentages of the country's population by ethnic groups was: Hausa, 53 percent; Djerma-Songhay, 22 percent; Tuareg, 10.4 percent; Fulani, 9 percent; and Kanuri, 4.4 percent. New projections based on the 1988 census point at an accelerated population growth over the next three decades, tripling to 22 million by the year 2018. At these levels, keeping in mind the general barrenness of much of the country, population pressures will become a major constraint; moreover, given the fiscal pauperization of a country that in previous decades was able to tap mineral resources, the burgeoning population augured poorly for future public finances.

Among other data contained in the census report was that fully 85 percent of the population still lived in rural areas; that women got married at the age of 16½, compared to men at the age of 23½; and that female fertility stood at an average of 7 births.

CENTRAL AFRICAN MISSION. *See* MISSION AFRIQUE CENTRALE.

CENTRE D'ENSEIGNEMENT SUPERIEUR. Precursor to the University of Niamey. Originally opened with only a sciences section, in October 1971, today the university has faculties of medicine, agronomy, literature, and pedagogy. The center was transformed into a university on June 7, 1973. In 1976 it had a budget of 420 million CFA francs, a 75 percent increase over the 1975 budget. By 1988 this figure had doubled again. *See also* UNIVERSITE DE NIAMEY.

CENTRE NATIONAL DE RECHERCHES EN SCIENCES HUMAINES (CNRSH). Successor (since 1964) of the Institut Français d'Afrique Noire (IFAN) set up in Senegal in 1938 and in each one of France's colonies subsequently, in Niger in 1944. The CNRSH inherited the functions of IFAN and conducted basic research, mostly in the humanities but also in the sciences and social sciences. The CNRSH published the invaluable Etudes Nigériennes series (through a linkup in Paris) of which some sixty volumes have already been published, many of which contain material practically impossible to find elsewhere. The center's staff stands at thirty researchers under **Diouldé Laya**. The **Musée National** is also nominally the responsibility of the CNRSH. With the creation of the Université de Niamey in 1974 the CNRSH was attached to it as the Human Sciences Research Institute.

CENTRE REGIONAL AGRO-HYDRO-METEOROLOGIQUE DES PAYS DU SAHEL. Niamey-based agency set up in 1979 to reinforce meteorological services in the Sahel region and to study rainfall patterns with the view of attempting to predict weather cycles.

CENTRE REGIONAL DE DOCUMENTATION POUR LA TRADITION ORALE (CRDTO). Niamey-based center collecting oral history, especially in the Songhay-Djerma areas.

CERCLE. Early administrative units into which Niger was divided, further separated into subdivisions. In 1922, for example, the territory had nine cercles (Agadez, Dosso, Gouré, Maradi, N'Guigmi, Niamey, Tahoua, Tillabéry, and Zinder) and twenty-seven subdivisions. In each cercle a **Conseil de Notables** was elected, meeting once or twice a year as a deliberative organ on matters of taxation and administration. The number of cercles went up over the years, reaching sixteen at independence. The colonial cercles were disbanded on January 1, 1961, when the country was divided into thirty-one temporary **circonscriptions**, sixteen of which were the former cercles. Following the 1964 **Réforme Administrative**, which became effective on October 1, 1965, the divisions were regrouped into seven départements (equivalent to the old cercles) and (originally) thirty-two arrondissements (replacing the subdivisions). *See also* ADMINISTRATIVE ORGANIZATION.

CHAAFI, LIMAN. Rebel Tuareg leader of the Front Populaire pour la Libération du Niger (FPLN), with headquarters in Libya, which mounted the first assault against Tchin Tabaraden (in 1982) with the help of **Hamani Diori**'s son, Abdoulaye. Chaafi was also one of the secondary instigators of the March 1976 coup d'état against Kountché in Niger. He has intermittently used a base in Mauritania.

CHADELIA. Minor Islamic order in Niger. Founded by the Sufi Abou Hassan Chadli (b. 1196), the order was quite popular in the Maghrib, and especially Algeria, where it had numerous **zawayas**. It still has some adherents in Niger.

CHAFEI, MOHAMED ABD-AL. Muslim leader. A member of the Tuareg Kel Aghlal clan from the Tahoua area, Chafei was in the 1970s and early 1980s a presidential councillor on religious affairs attached to General Kountché's office, and a leading member of the Association Islamique du Niger.

CHAFFANI, LAOUAL. Interim minister of economics and planning between November 1991 and April 1993, when a new government emerged.

CHAIBOU, ABACHE. Former minister of higher education under General Kountché, and MNSD deputy to the National Assembly in 1989.

CHAIBOU, OUSMANE (1948–). Educator. Chaibou studied mathematics at Dakar University, graduating in 1980, and is currently attached to the University of Niamey's Pedagogical School.

CHAIBOU, SALEY. Briefly minister of youth under General Saibou, serving between May and December 1989.

CHAMBRE DE COMMERCE, D'AGRICULTURE ET D'INDUSTRIE DU NIGER. Set up by parliamentary statute in June 1964, the chamber of forty members and twenty associates is elected by a college of heads of industrial and commercial firms. It is composed of twenty-three members from the commercial sphere, twenty-two from industry and transport, and fifteen from agriculture. Members are reelected to four-year terms of office. Expenditures of the chamber are financed by a small tax on all transactions in Niger. For purposes of operation the country is divided into three regions: Niamey, Maradi, and Zinder. The longtime (since 1965) president of the chamber (from Niamey) has been Jacques Nignon, director of COPRO-NIGER. A reorganization after the 1974 coup d'état increased its membership to eighty full members and forty associates.

CHAMCHOUM, NABIH. Important merchant. Of Maghribi origin, Chamchoum came to the Zinder-Magaria region from Kano in the 1930s, attracted by the area's peanut potential. Establishing a local network of purchasing agents he became one of the most important peanut purchasers in the area despite the competition from the big French companies (which tried to undercut him), other private dealers, and finally Niger state agencies. By 1973 he had survived all attempts to nationalize fully this sector of agrarian marketing and was one of only two nonexpatriates purchasing peanuts in Magaria. Despite his advanced age Chamchoum is still a very powerful economic force in the peanut belt of Niger, and served as an important member of the Social and Economic Council of Niger until it was banned in 1974.

CHANOINE, JULIEN (Captain) (1870–1899). The vain, egotistical, and ruthless leader of the ill-fated **Mission Afrique Centrale**. Born in Paris to a military family on December 18, 1870, Chanoine was commissioned and dispatched to Upper Volta. There he won several citations for his campaigns against the Mossi, and he was reassigned to Niger to avenge the murder of Captain **Cazemajou** and the collapse of his **Mission du Haut-Soudan**. For the brutal swath of destruction under the Voulet-Chanoine leadership, *see* MISSION AFRIQUE CENTRALE.

CHARDON, AMOUKI (Lieutenant Colonel). One of General Saibou's closest cronies, confidant, and manager of the Presidential Palace during his reign.

CHECHE. Turban cloth with which the Tuareg wrap their heads.

CHEIFFOU, AMADOU (1942–). Former interim prime minister of Niger and long-time director general of Air Niger. Born in 1942 in Kornaka and educated locally, at the University of Dakar (1961–66), and Toulouse (1966–67) as an engineer, he then proceeded to Toulouse's School of Civil Aviation, graduating in 1969 as a civil aviation engineer. Cheiffou then served in a variety of capacities with ASECNA, as commander of Niamey airport (1970–75), deputy director general of ASECNA in Dakar (1975–85), and West Africa's representative to OACI in Dakar (1985–91). A militant socialist in his student days, he became a champion of competitive elections and gained entry to the National Conference in 1991. Though a political newcomer, he was surprisingly selected by the National Conference over six other competing candidates to be Niger's interim prime minister during the fifteen-month transitional period (November 1, 1991, to January 31, 1993) leading to elections and a new government. Cheiffou dissolved the cabinet he inherited from the National Conference after only five months, citing its paralysis along ethnic lines, internal political intrigues, and animosities, and appointed a new cabinet.

CHEMIDOUR. Religious capital of Kaouar. A **Sanusiya zawaya** was set up in Chemidour in 1865 by a Marzouk missionary, and the center thrived, spreading the Sanusiya message in all directions. The original mosque is in ruins, and the village is very small.

CHIBO, CHIEF. Head of the **Soudié**, or **Kurfey,** village of Chikal, who in the winter of 1925 (at Toudou Anza) and in 1926 (in his home village) initiated the Hauka cult that greatly disturbed the French administration and brought about its suppression. Still, by 1927 the cult was to be found in all Kurfey villages, expressing deep-seated anti-French sentiments. The incredible popularity of the cult so alarmed the French that a major effort was mounted to stamp it out, and harsh punitive expeditions were sent to all villages practicing it. Chibo himself was exiled to Upper Volta and Ivory Coast for nine years. *See also* HAUKA.

CHIEFS OF STAFF. Since their creation, the Niger armed forces have had eight chiefs of staff, four of these during the current civilian era: 1960–63, Major Damba Mainassara; 1963–73, Major Balla Arabe; 1973–74, Major Seyni Kountché; 1974–87, Major Ali Saibou; 1987–91, Colonel Toumba Boubacar; 1991–95, Colonel Mazou Issa; 1995, Lieutenant Colonial Ibrahim Baré Mainassara; 1995–, Lieutenant Colonel Mahamane Korohou. *See also* ARMED FORCES.

CHIKAL. Home village of **Chief Chibo,** where the **Hauka** cult was initiated. Despite intense French reprisals, and Chibo's forced exile to Upper Volta and Ivory Coast, in Chikal the cult survived into the 1940s; elsewhere it was more or less rooted out by the late 1930s.

CHIRFA. Small oasis some 8 km from **Djado,** populated exclusively by **Toubou** nomads. Chirfa is the site of a long-deserted and ruined French Foreign Legion fort that is half-submerged in the shifting sands. Not far away is a particularly striking area of moonlike rocky landscape.

CHRISTIANITY. There are very few Christians in Niger, the dominant religions being Islam (up to 85 percent) and animism. Accurate figures are not available. One 1992 estimate noted the total number of Christians in the country was 0.5 percent of the population, with Catholics at 18,000 and Protestants at 8,000—figures that do not compute properly. *See also* RELIGION.

CHRONIQUES D'AGADEZ. Important historical records of the dynasty of the sultans of Aïr, resident in Agadez. They contain some very ancient manuscripts, chronologies and king lists, and a brief history of the sultanate, all written and rewritten over the ages. The material comprises around seventy pages of texts and is much cited in the scholarly literature.

CHUDEAU, RENE (1864–1921). Geologist and explorer. Attracted to the Sahara quite by accident, Chudeau commenced a voyage from

Algiers that took him through Iférouane in Niger to Chad. He later was to publish the account of his explorations. He followed this exploit with another trip from Mauritania (1908–12) and later Mali and Algeria (1912). He was neither a civil servant nor sponsored by the government, and his last years were very hard. Chudeau died of malnutrition in 1921.

CIRCONSCRIPTION. Temporary post-independence administrative unit for the colonial **subdivisions.** Effective between January 1, 1962, and October 1, 1965, there were thirty-one circonscriptions, sixteen of which had been the colonial **cercles.** *See* ADMINISTRATIVE ORGANIZATION. Following the 1964 Réforme Administrative the circonscriptions were regrouped into seven départements and (originally) thirty-two arrondissements. Each circonscription had a **Conseil de Circonscription** that later became the **Conseil d'Arrondissement.**

CIROMA. In the precolonial **Damagaram** hierarchy, the commander of the armies, chosen from the brothers and nephews of the reigning sultan. With a personal tribute from a number of outlying villages, the ciroma was usually a very important official in the court.

CISSE, ABDOU SALAMI. *Alfaize* (''leader'') of Say since 1956.

CISSE, ALDIOUMA MAHAMADOU (1935–). Administrator. Born on August 19, 1935, in Mainé-Soroa, and a graduate of IHEOM and IDEP (France), Cisse joined the administration and served as deputy prefect of Tahoua and as government commissioner of SOTRAMIL in Zinder. In 1970 he became state inspector attached to the presidency. Between 1975 and his recent retirement Cisse was head of a division in the Ministry of Interior.

CISSE, AMADOU (1938–). Director of rural development at the Ministry of Rural Economy since 1970. Born in Say in 1938, and by training a rural development engineer, Cisse joined the Ministry of Rural Development in 1967 as deputy director of rural development. Prior to that he had served for several years as secretary general of Maradi's mayoral office.

CISSE, AMADOU (1948–). Engineer and, briefly, prime minister of Niger. Of Fulani origin and born in Niamey, Cisse graduated in 1975 from the Paris Ecole Nationale des Ponts et Chaussées as an engineer. He then worked for several years in Paris serving bridges and roads. In 1979 he returned to Niger to take over the Department of Public Works. In 1982 he was sent to the World Bank to represent Niger, and the following year assumed a post in that agency responsible for transport projects in Benin, Côte d'Ivoire, Chad, and Guinea-Bissau. With the onset of competitive party politics in Niger, Cisse joined the MNSD. In 1995, after the legislative elections attending the fall of the AFC government in 1994, the MNSD emerged as the largest party in the legislature and expected to have its secretary general, Hama Amadou, appointed as prime minister. President Ousmane instead chose Cisse in February 1995; however, he was promptly faced by a vote of censure in parliament and was ousted.

CISSE, BOUBACAR (1909–). Politician and senior civil administrator. Born in Say in 1909, and an administrator by training, Cisse was elected to Niamey's municipal council in December 1956, serving on it until January 1959. In March 1957 he was also elected PPN deputy to the Territorial Assembly, and was reelected in both 1958 and 1965. Prior to his retirement in the mid-1980s he also served as the administrator of the Société Nigérienne de Produits Céramiques (SONICERAM) and of the SMDR, as well as director general (since 1964) of CNGTN and president (since 1971) of the Syndicat Patronal des Entreprises et Industries du Niger (SPEIN), the employers' union of Niger.

CISSE, OMAR (1945–). Administrator and poet. Born in 1945 Cisse works with the Belgian airline SABENA as a freight agent, having been trained in Pointe Noire (Brazzaville) and Le Bourget (Paris). He writes poetry on the side and has had some of his work published, including two volumes of poetry.

CITIBANK S.A. NIGER. Subsidiary of the U.S. bank, inaugurated in Niamey on January 21, 1980.

CIVIL SERVICE. The civil service of Niger was quite modest at independence, and heavily staffed with nonnationals, especially Dahomeans, Senegalese, Malians, and Upper Voltans. The bulk of the Dahomeans (estimates vary from 850 to 1,300) were forcibly repatriated in 1964 following the Lété Island dispute between Niger and Dahomey (now Benin). Progressive Nigerienization since has likewise reduced the role of nonnationals in the civil service.

In 1974 of a total of 36,000 salaried workers in the country, fully 20,000 were in the civil service. With the boom in state revenues consequent to the coming on-stream of uranium exports, numerous new state enterprises were set up in Niger, with the regular civil service also expanding. Those in one way or another on the public payroll (civil service and parastatal workers) were estimated in 1984 at 51,000, with considerably more working in the state enterprises. Since then Niger's major economic slump and dire fiscal straits triggered the military regime of General Saibou to prune selectively the state payroll and freeze new recruitment, as well as to commence the closure of privatization of state enterprises whose deficits could no longer be sustained. As the number of state employees declined, unrest grew in the country, especially after Saibou agreed on a Structural Adjustment Program (not implemented) that would have entailed even harsher budgetary (and hence employment) cuts. All these have been strenuously resisted by the country's trade union movement and later—when the government announced that it would no longer automatically hire graduates from the University of Niamey—by students in general.

For the past few years the civil service has remained stable at around 39,000 employees. Neither the transitional government nor the duly elected civilian regime that replaced it have been able to make much headway in reducing the government payroll, which cannot be met from Niger's limited resources. This has resulted in perennial pay backlogs of up to six months (though more commonly of two or three months), which keeps unrest alive in urban centers, even as overseas donors press for greater employment cuts as a precondition of bailing out the country's parlous finances.

COLONIE DU HAUT-SENEGAL-NIGER. Designation of a vast area stretching from French Sudan (Mali) to contemporary Chad, which included within it the **Territoire Militaire du Niger,** which later became the **Colonie du Niger.** On December 4, 1920, Haut-Sénégal-Niger came to an end with the creation of the separate constituent colonies. *See also* ADMINISTRATIVE ORGANIZATION.

COLONIE DU NIGER. Successor designation of the (1900) **Territoire Militaire Autonome de Zinder,** the 1910 Territoire Militaire du Niger, and the short-lived Colonie du Haut-Sénégal-Niger. It was formed July–October 1922, and included at the time the nine cercles of Agadez, Dosso, Gouré, Maradi, N'Guigmi, Niamey, Tahoua, Tillabéry, and Zinder, and twenty-seven subdivisions. The original capital of the colony was Zinder (1911–26)—previously it had been Sorbo-Haoussa (to 1903) and Niamey (1903) before shifting back, in 1926, to Niamey. *See also* ADMINISTRATIVE ORGANIZATION.

COMINAK. *See* COMPAGNIE MINIERE D'AKOUTA.

COMITE TECHNIQUE DEPARTEMENTAL (COTEDEP). Created by decree on August 7, 1971, the COTEDEPs were committees at the département level presided over by the prefect and including his deputies and the heads of the various services and semipublic and cooperative organizations. The committee's responsibility was to coordinate the various activities of the département, to organize its economic development, and to develop all projects handed down to it by the central government. The committees continued to operate during the Kountché regime until replaced in 1983 by new agencies.

COMMISSION CONSULTATIVE D'ARRONDISSEMENT. *See* CONSEIL D'ARRONDISSEMENT.

COMMISSION CONSULTATIVE DEPARTEMENTALE (CCD). Consultative organs on the département level, tendering advice to the prefect and acting as his channel of communications with the lower levels of the administration. Composed of the prefect, the subprefects, mayors, and two elected members from each of the département's **Counseil d'Arrondissement.** Unlike the latter body the CCD did not have a separate executive committee. The commissions continued operating until replaced in 1983 by new structures.

COMMISSION DU BASSIN DU LAC TCHAD (CBLT). Interstate organ for the joint development and protection of the Lake Chad basin, covering 200,000 sq km. The commission was founded on May 22, 1964, when a convention was signed following five meetings between March 1962 and April 1964. The participating states are Chad, Cameroon, Niger, and Nigeria, which pledged that they would act to prevent policies or action likely to pollute the lake or drain its waters, and would act to promote cooperation on projects affecting the basin. The commission is composed of eight delegates, two from each state, with a secretariat in Ndjamena, Chad, and meets at least once a year.

COMMISSION DU FLEUVE NIGER (CFN). Interstate organization of all states through which the Niger River flows, aimed at improving navigation and riverain communications, and at developing the areas through which the river flows. The founding treaty of the organization was signed November 23–25, 1964, in Niamey. Participating states are Niger, Nigeria, Burkina Faso, Chad, Mali, Guinea, and Ivory Coast, with Benin and Cameroon having been present at the discussions but absent from the signing ceremony. The CFN is supposed to meet at least once a year in order to define its annual budget and decide on projects that need to be executed or explored. It has not been meeting regularly, however.

COMMISSION EXECUTIVE D'ARRONDISSEMENT. *See* CONSEIL D'ARRONDISSEMENT.

COMMISSION EXECUTIVE MUNICIPALE. *See* CONSEIL MUNICIPAL.

C[OMMUNAUTE] F[INANCIERE] A[FRICAINE] FRANC. Common currency of the Communauté Financière Africaine—that is, all former colonial territories of the French West African Federation (AOF) and the French Equatorial Federation (AEF), except for those states which have since left the union (Guinea, Mali, Mauritania, Madagascar). Included are also Togo and Cameroon, former mandates but administered by France not much differently from the colonies in the two federations. Established in 1946 as the Colonies Françaises d'Afrique franc, the currency's name (though not the abbreviation) was changed in 1962. The CFA franc is fully backed and guaranteed by France (preventing its collapse) and pegged at a fixed rate to the French franc, indirectly making it a hard currency. In the late 1960s, persistent Francophone African demands led to the 1974 relocation of the central bank of the monetary union—the BCEAO—to Dakar, and the creation of fiscal reserves in Africa rather than France. In 1994, shortly after the death of Côte d'Ivoire's President Houphouët-Boigny, the fixed exchange rate of the CFA franc vis-à-vis the French franc was devalued by 50 percent from its original fifty-to-one ratio.

COMMUNAUTE FRANCAISE. Free association of autonomous republics set up with the adoption by France of the constitution of the Fifth Republic. Within the community, which included its former colonies, France retained jurisdiction over the fields of foreign affairs, defense, external communications, and fiscal and monetary matters. The structures originally set up for the community included an executive (the French president) and Executive Council (all heads of associated republics plus the minister of community affairs) and a Senate with representation from all the territories in accord with their relative populations. Early in 1960 an amendment to the French constitution was passed allowing associated republics to attain the full independence while remaining in the community.

COMMUNE. Local urban units of which Niger has eleven: Niamey, Zinder, Maradi, Tahoua, Agadez, Dosso, Dogondoutchi, Birni-N'Konni, Tessaoua, Filingué, and Tibiri, though only the first four are "communes en plein exercice" (fully autonomous consequent to their ability to raise their own budgets). The other seven were declared communes by decree on December 21, 1972, effective October 1, 1973. Each commune is governed by a mayor and assisted by municipal councils. The mayors are functionally equivalent to the sous-préfets.

Originally it had been hoped to dot Niger with 120 rural communes, but the project was never truly started.

COMMUNICATIONS. Niger is landlocked, undeveloped, far from the coast, and has wide population dispersals; thus inadequate internal communications and external import/export linkages have always been a major constraint to development in Niger, which until the late-1970s had barely 300 miles of paved roads. Several principal railroads, none of which is fully satisfactory, are used, or could be used, for Niger's foreign trade. These include:

1) The Nigerian railroad system, which terminates at two localities 125 and 262 km from major Niger towns. The routes tend to be heavily used by importers and exporters for they are the least costly. Thus 80 percent of Niger's peanuts have been dispatched from Zinder to Kano, and on to Apapa on the coast, the remainder going via Benin. The route is, however, not fully satisfactory, for Niger's peanut season coincides with Nigeria's and the latter's crop receives priority on the railroad. Moreover, the massive delays at Nigeria's ports have made the import of goods from overseas via Nigeria extremely hazardous.

2) The Régie Abidjan–Niger that links Côte d'Ivoire's Abidjan port with Ouagadougou in Burkina Faso, which is 590 km from Niamey. The route could be quite useful except that the Ouagadougou–Niamey section, plied by heavy trucks, is frequently in a state of disrepair, while the railroad itself has slowly deteriorated from its once-healthy state. There have been numerous discussions about prolonging the rail terminus to Dori (which would make economical the exploitation and export of Burkina Faso's Tambao manganese mines), from which the remaining 260 km to Niamey could be paved or laid with tracks at a later date. Prospects of this option have blown hot and cold over the past two decades; the cost would be immense, there are no global donors available, and the World Bank itself has consistently viewed railroads as uneconomical options for Africa.

3) The Algerian railroad system that now terminates near Colomb-Béchar (at Adabla). There have been some exploratory talks regarding its extension to Gao (Mali) and thence to Niamey, though the project appears even less economical. In the fall of 1977 a trucking link was established between the Algerian Colomb-Béchar terminus and Kano, Nigeria, with the massive port congestion in Nigeria (and the added costs on goods this created) making shipping of goods from Europe over the trans-Saharan route economical again, but this lasted only temporarily.

4) The Dakar–Niger railroad, linking Senegal with Mali and ending at Koulikoro (Mali), just beyond Bamako. Its extension has been discussed on several occasions, though the entire project is likewise tentative.

5) The OCBN and **Opération Hirondelle.** The OCBN route links Niamey via Dosso and Gaya to Parakou in Benin by regular truck schedules, and from Parakou by railroad to the port of Cotonou. The route is extensively used by Niger, especially for its imports, as well as for the evacuation of some of its mineral output (uranium, for instance). The Benin railroad, however, was in the 1970s and 1980s in a state of acute disrepair, requiring expensive renovations and the purchase of new rolling stock, something Benin was reluctant to undertake due to its own acute fiscal straits, and because the railway has always been of much lesser importance to Benin. The railbed was improved, however, and some new (mostly passenger) rolling stock was purchased in the mid-1980s when Niger threatened to divert her transit trade to other routes, but the route is still not fully satisfactory. The extension of the OCBN railroad north into Niger has been envisaged for over five decades, but poor relations between the two countries since independence blocked any development on this project. In the early 1980s prospects of actualizing the extension suddenly looked brighter as several portions of the route were surveyed in detail and preparatory work initiated. It is this extention that is most likely to be undertaken, since the bulk of Niger's imports utilize this route, but Niger's economic slump in the mid-1980s put a brake on efforts to seek definitive financing.

COMPAGNIE FRANCAISE POUR LE DEVELOPPEMENT DES FIBRES TEXTILES (CFDT). Private French-owned company with three cotton ginneries in Madaoua (erected in 1967), Maradi (1968), and Saya-Gay (1970), with a total capacity (in 1973) of 15,000 tons per year. The CFDT has a total investment of 276 million CFA francs and employs some fifty people, including a number of Europeans. In 1973 the company produced 3,450 tons of cotton grain and 1,280 tons of cotton fiber, the figures having fallen significantly due to poor cotton harvests consequent to the Sahel drought. The creation of the CFDT spurred Niger's cotton industry (*see* COTTON); the company, together with the UNCC, has a total monopoly over the purchase of Niger's cotton harvest.

COMPAGNIE MINIERE D'AKOUTA (COMINAK). Founded on June 12, 1974, by the Niger government, the French atomic energy commission (CEA), a Japanese consortium (Overseas Uranium Resources Development Ltd.), and a Spanish company to exploit uranium concessions in the **Akouta** region. The mines, 10 km west of **Arlit,** were targeted to yield 2,000 tons of processed ore by 1980. Capitalized with 35 billion CFA francs to exploit the ore field discovered in 1966–67 by the CEA (and more precisely pinpointed 1970–73),

COMINAK is the second such uranium company (after SOMAIR) to be established in Niger. Its plant opened in 1978, with further buildings completed in the 1980s. Estimated reserves should suffice for the production of 25,000 tons of processed ore. Of the COMINAK shares, ONAREM owns 31 percent, the CEA 34 percent, the OURD 25 percent, and the Spanish Empresa Nacional del Uranio S.A. 10 percent. The company imports all its supplies via Cotonou, Benin. It employs some 2,000 workers in a new city, **Akokan,** which developed into an urban center of 7,000 people by 1984, before slowly declining as the global uranium glut forced Niger to cut production.

COMPAGNIE TRANSAFRICAINE. Trucking company created on August 1, 1961, and transformed on November 4, 1964, into the mixed-economy company **Société Nationale des Transports Nigériens.** Formerly an expatriate company with a quasi monopoly over various aspects of hauling in Niger, the new company has acquired this dominance as well.

CONDAT, GEORGES MAHAMAN (1924–). Diplomat and former ambassador to the United States and to the United Nations. Born in Maradi on October 23, 1924, of mixed Fulani-French origin, Condat was educated at the Ecole William Ponty in Dakar. An early PPN figure, Condat deserted the party in 1946 (with Harou Kouka) to form the splinter movement PINE, which later merged with UNIS (*see* POLITICAL PARTIES). He won election to the French National Assembly in 1948 with strong support from the French administration, defeating Djibo Bakary, then the PPN delegate. In 1951 he was re-elected to Paris, defeating Hamani Diori, and served there through 1956. In that year Condat was elected to the Territorial Assembly and served as its president (1956–58). Earlier, in 1953, he had split with UNIS to set up a new party—UPN—largely because of his desire for a more conciliatory posture vis-à-vis the PPN. He joined the UNIS successor party (BNA) when it was formed. After the victory at the polls of the PPN, Condat was shifted to diplomatic duties. He was first appointed delegate to Dahomey (1961–62) and was later appointed ambassador to West Germany, Benelux, and the EEC (1962–64). Upon repatriation to Niamey in 1964, he was made director of administrative and consular affairs in the Foreign Ministry, serving in that capacity until 1970. In July of 1970 Condat was named ambassador to the U.S. and Canada and permanent representative to the U.N. In 1972 he returned to Africa to take up the position of deputy secretary general of the Peanut Council, with headquarters in Lagos, Nigeria.

CONFEDERATION DES SYNDICATS LIBRES DES TRAVAILLEURS DU NIGER (CSLTN). Breakaway confederation of trade union affiliates formerly grouped within the USTN. The CSLTN was formed in 1993 with four of the USTN's thirty-five affiliates.

CONFERENCE NATIONALE. The National Conference of 1991 that presided over the redistribution of power that saw the reemergence of civilian rule in Niger. General Saibou had tried earlier to divert social rumblings for an end to military rule by institutionalizing the MNSD into a party (formerly it had been a "movement"), enacting a new constitution, and holding legislative (one-party) elections. The example of the ouster of military rule in neighboring Benin and elsewhere, however, and the spread of multipartyism (especially in Côte d'Ivoire) made such half-hearted gestures untenable—especially in light of the ongoing economic slump afflicting Niger, which was causing constant social unrest, and the twin crises of 1990 that would not go away: the brutal suppression of the February 1990 student demonstrations in Niamey and the massacre of Tuaregs following the same year's Tchin Tabaraden assault. When the UNST trade union flexed its muscles and threatened a general strike unless a national convention was convened, Saibou had no choice but to acquiesce.

The National Conference opened on July 29, 1991, with the participation of 1,204 delegates from all walks of life, including 24 political parties (newly emerging), 69 mass organizations, students, religious leaders, the government (100 delegates), the armed forces, and others. Though the government disproportionately packed the Conference in its favor, this had little effect on the outcome.

The Conference elected **André Salifou,** a noted history professor, as Conference president, and on July 31 declared itself sovereign; on August 9 it suspended Saibou's recently enacted constitution. It decided to retain Saibou as interim head of state (despite opposition; Saibou had in the meantime admitted "ultimate" responsibility for the brutalities against the Tuareg and students), though it dismissed the key officers (including the chief of staff and his deputy) who were directly responsible for the events. It also had arrested the retired colonel responsible for the liquidation of Major Sani Souna Sido after the latter's abortive coup bid in 1975, and bound the security forces to Salifou directly.

On August 14 a thirty-man commission on crimes and political abuses was elected under the chairmanship of Mamane Abou, leader of a human rights organization. It was charged inter alia with investigating 185 instances of embezzlement during the 1959–91 period. It was before this commission that "**Bonkano**" revealed stunning details about misrule under General Kountché—having been given personal immunity for his own monumental thefts. Originally scheduled to last for forty days, the Conference continued deliberations for three months, setting up a fifteen-month interim government and legislature from its membership, to resign after the holding of legislative and presidential elections. What was noteworthy in Niger was that despite a couple of pay-related mutinies by armed units, continued social unrest linked to the state of the economy, and the political instability of the successor civilian regime, the armed forces accepted their subordination to civilian leadership without demur, and indeed, even before the convening of the Conference, distanced themselves politically from the MNSD.

CONSEIL D'ARRONDISSEMENT. Deliberative (until 1972, and since then executive) body at the arrondissement level, which replaced the previous Conseil de Circonscription. Elected by the local population for five years, the conseil had the competence to decide on local taxes, and possessed certain other decision-making powers. Composed of the arrondissement's sous-préfet and the elected members, the counseil sent two delegates to the higher **Commission Consultative Départementale.** Until 1964 the counseil had an executive called Commision Exécutive d'Arrondissement, composed of the sous-préfet and between one and five of the elected members. In the 1964 drive for administrative decentralization the CEA was replaced by a Commission Consultative d'Arrondissement with somewhat wider powers. The latter executed the policies adopted by the Conseil d'Arrondissement and administered the arrondissement and the local budget. New structures replaced the conseils in 1983.

CONSEIL DE CIRCONSCRIPTION. Local administrative council on the circonscription level. *See* CONSEIL D'ARRONDISSEMENT.

CONSEIL DE L'ENTENTE. Regional organization encompassing Ivory Coast, Niger, Benin, Upper Volta (now Burkina Faso) and Togo, created on May 29, 1959, as Ivory Coast President Houphouët-Boigny's countermove to the projected Mali Federation. The Council of the Entente theoretically provides for freedom of movement across state boundaries, coordination of policies in the fields of judicial, communications, fiscal, economic, and developmental matters, and has a solidarity fund aimed at fiscal redistribution of accumulated funds in favor of the weaker members. Many of the goals of the council have not been fulfilled, for a variety of reasons. Niger's President Hamani Diori played an important role in the Conseil de l'Entente, as Houphouët-Boigny's trusted ally and lieutenant.

CONSEIL DE NOTABLES. Largely deliberative organ set up in all of Niger's cercles in 1912. Under the local commandant de cercle, the council met once or twice a year to discuss local taxes, local administration, and so on, and included the most important chiefs and notables of the area, as well as some évolués.

CONSEIL ECONOMIQUE ET SOCIAL. An advisory council with recommendatory authority over legislation in the social and economic areas. Established by decree in 1971, and meeting for the first time on May 10, 1971, the council was abolished after the 1974 coup d'état. Its members included former foreign minister Barcougne Courmo, the deputy director of the BDRN Gabou Abou, the director of the UNCC Ahmed Mouddour, Professor Dan Dicko Dan Koulodo of the local university, the influential merchant Nabih Chamchoum, and several expatriates.

CONSEIL GENERAL. Niger's first colonial territorial assembly. Set up by decree on October 25, 1946, in Niger as well as in the other colonies of France, the first local elections (in two stages) took place on December 15, 1946, and January 5, 1947. The **double electoral college** elected ten councillors from the first college and twenty from the second. The first president of the council was the Djermakoy of Dosso, Moumouni Aouta. On February 6, 1952, the General Council was transformed into the Assemblée Territoriale.

CONSEIL MILITAIRE SUPERIEUR (CMS). The Supreme Military Council that theoretically ruled Niger from General Kountché's 1974 coup d'état until the May 1989 election of a CSON by the new single party of Niger under General Saibou. Originally headed by Kountché, it had as vice-president Major Sani Souna Sido until he was purged in 1975. Most of the original members of the CMS were purged, demoted, imprisoned, or sent on diplomatic assignments abroad, several being implicated in attempted coups, plots, or corruption. In theory the CMS reached a consensus about Kountché's successor (Saibou), but in reality the body that for a long time had played no real political role was faced with Saibou's nomination (from a clique of officers supportive of the latter), and they meekly ratified it. After the 1989 "civilianization" of Niger, the CMS was disbanded as the supreme authority of the country.

CONSEIL MUNICIPAL. Municipal council with similar administrative powers and responsibilities as the **Counseil d'Arrondissement.** Composed of the mayor and elected members, the municipal council has an executive arm called the Commission Exécutive Municipale (CEM), which includes the mayor and several of the elected members.

The counseil sends two delegates to the higher **Commission Consultative Départementale.**

CONSEIL NATIONAL DE DEVELOPPEMENT (CND). The highest bureau of the Niger Development Society, an epistemological, ideological, and structural innovation of the 1980s, lauded (and derided) as Niger's noncapitalist, nonsocialist approach to development. The CND developed out of a 1978–79 attempt by General **Kountché** to inject some structured purpose and ideology into his rather drab pragmatic administration, which had come under fire from a variety of directions. With the declaration that Niger needed no imported ideologies since it was a developing society, the quest was announced for the structural underpinnings of such an organism. Ultimately a system of hierarchically organized Development agencies was ratified in which primacy was granted to the local samaria and the cooperatives. At the top of the hierarchy stood the national-level Conseil National de Développement, which became also the first deliberative assembly since the 1974 coup d'état. The CND was composed of 150 delegates elected from the 7 départements of Niger, and included the entire CSM and other military representatives via the prefects, who were all officers. The function of the CND—whose first meeting took place in November 1983—was to propose to the cabinet fundamental development options. It was regarded as an agency of greater importance than the cabinet, with the leadership of the CND entrusted to the hands of the former prime minister, **Mamane Oumarou**.

Elections for the CND took place by "consensus voting" in July 1983, with the ballot box being bypassed because of the illiteracy of the masses and their "traditional" mentality. The basic unit of the hierarchy was the village CND, followed by the local (canton), subregional, regional, and ultimately the national CND. After the death of Kountché and the rise to power of General Saibou, the MNSD "movement," of which the CND was an integral part, was institutionalized as a political party in a further attempt to legitimate the regime through "national elections." The entire structural hierarchy disappeared with the transformation of the MNSD into a "normal" party with the onset of competitive civilian politics.

CONSEIL NATIONAL POUR LA MISE EN PLACE DE LA SOCIETE DE DEVELOPPEMENT. Consultative organ established with great fanfare in March 1980, charged with submitting recommendations on a noncapitalist, nonsocialist structural setup for the Niger Société de Développement. *See* CONSEIL NATIONAL DE DEVELOPPEMENT; SOCIETE DE DEVELOPPEMENT.

CONSEIL SUPERIEUR D'ORIENTATION NATIONALE (CSON). Agency formally set up by General Saibou in May 1989 as the top level of the newly institutionalized single political party of Niger (hitherto a "movement")—the MNSD—replacing the original Conseil Supérieur Militaire. Saibou was both the president of the CSON and, after the elections of 1989 in which he ran as the sole candidate of the sole new political party, of Niger. The CSON, composed of 67 civilian and military members, was elected by a 750-man constituent congress of the MNSD on May 17, 1989. It had a 14-man executive organ—the Bureau Exécutif Nationale—which included 6 cabinet members and 8 without specific portfolios. The council was in place until 1991.

CONSEILS LOCAUX DU DEVELOPPEMENT (CLD). Second level of the new Development Society structure adopted in Niger. Composed of the canton-level samaria leadership and its cooperative movement presided by the canton chief and with the representation of other elements including the military. The council numbered twenty to thirty members. *See* CONSEIL NATIONAL DE DEVELOPPEMENT; SOCIETE DE DEVELOPPEMENT.

CONSEILS REGIONAUX DU DEVELOPPEMENT (CRD). Regional-level organs of the Development Society structure adopted by Niger. The sixteen-to-thirty member structures included regional-level cooperative-movement representation as well as heads of the samaria movement at the regional level, plus the département prefects. *See* CONSEIL NATIONAL DE DEVELOPPEMENT; SOCIETE DE DEVELOPPEMENT.

CONSEILS SOUS-REGIONAUX DE DEVELOPPEMENT (CSRD). Intermediate-level Development Society organs set up at the canton level under the presidency of the canton chief. Comprising between twelve and thirty members, the CSRD included samaria and cooperative-movement representation *See* CONSEIL NATIONAL DE DEVELOPPEMENT; SOCIETE DE DEVELOPPEMENT.

CONSEILS VILLAGEOIS DE DEVELOPPEMENT (CVD). Basic unit of the Development Society structure adopted by Niger and in place until 1990. Presided over by the village chiefs—allegedly in all nine thousand villages of Niger—the CVD ranged in number from six to sixteen members and included samaria and cooperative-movement delegates. *See* CONSEIL NATIONAL DE DEVELOPPEMENT; SOCIETE DE DEVELOPPEMENT.

CONSTITUTIONS. Niger has had four constitutions and one major constitutional revision:

(1) The constitution of February 25, 1959, ratified by the **Assemblée Constituante.** The constitution set up a quasi-parliamentary system with a president of the council (or P.M.) with executive powers invested by an Assembly to whom he was responsible. The assembly, elected for five years, was composed of sixty deputies.

(2) The constitution of November 8, 1960, ratified by the National Assembly, set up a presidential system in which the executive president was to be elected by universal franchise simultaneously with deputies for the Assembly who, as before, were elected for five years. The constitution also transferred to the Niger government powers hitherto lodged in the French Community, including Defense, foreign affairs, and currency matters. The constitution further provided that cabinet members could not also be members of the Assembly.

(3) The constitutional reform of September 7, 1965, disassociated the election of the president of the republic from the elections of the Assembly, and specified that deputies would be elected on the basis of national lists.

(4) The constitution of September 24, 1989, allegedly ratified by 99.28 percent of those who voted, and 95.08 percent of the total electorate. The constitution saw the reemergence of party politics via a single governmental party headed by General Saibou—the recently institutionalized MNSD—and a National Assembly elected for the first time since the onset of military rule in 1974. The constitution was short-lived since shortly later came the demonstrations that ushered in civilian rule. It was specifically abrogated by the **Conference Nationale** in 1991 (with the National Assembly dissolved in favor of an interim HCR, elected from the Conference's membership), which in due course codified a new constitution.

(5) The constitution of December 26, 1992, enacted on January 22, 1993. The constitution was ratified by 89.79 percent of those who voted *vis* 10.21 percent who rejected it. Of Niger's total population at the time, 3.9 million were entitled to vote, 2.7 million registered to vote, and 2.2 million actually voted. The constitution set up a dual executive with a head of state (elected for five years in two electoral rounds, and reelectable only once) who names a head of government responsible to an eighty-three man National Assembly elected by proportional representation. A supreme court and a council are specifically charged with ensuring freedom of speech.

CONVENTION AFRICAINE (C.A.). Interterritorial African political movement, sponsored by Senegal's president, Leopold Sédar Senghor, and successor movement to his Indépendants d'Outre-Mer. The party had several territorial branches in French Africa. In Niger the UNIS party became affiliated with the C.A. on February 24, 1957, under its new name, **Forces Démocratiques Nigériennes.**

CONVENTION DEMOCRATIQUE ET SOCIALE (CDS-Rahama). Current president **Mahamane Ousmane's** largely Zinder-Tahoua-based, Hausa political party, heavily supported financially by some of the major Hausa merchants of that city. Set up in 1991 after political parties were allowed to emerge, the CDS was a key partner in the nine-party coalition that aimed to block a possible reemergence to power of the "old regime" via a restructured MNSD party. The coalition, the AFC, was successful in the country's first new elections and formed the government. A secession of one of the partners in 1994 resulted in Ousmane's decision to call for new elections, however, and in these the MNSD emerged with a small majority to form the government of February 1995.

COORDINATION DE LA RESISTANCE ARMEE (CRA). Early coordinating group of several of Niger's Tuareg liberation movements. *See* TUAREG REBELLION. The CRA was formed on September 11, 1993, by **Mano Dayak** and groups the Front de Libération Temust (FLT), Front Patriotique de la Libération du Sahara (FPLS), Armée Révolutionnaire de Libération du Nord Niger (ARLN), and the Front de Libération de l'Aïr et l'Azawad (FLAA), the last having been the first to form. The president of the FLAA, Ghissa Ag Boula, was the vice-president of the CRA. The CRA gave way, in 1995, to the Organisation de la Résistance Armée (also headed by Ghissa Ag Boula), which in April 1995 signed a peace agreement with the Niger government.

COPRO-NIGER. *See* SOCIETE NATIONALE DE COMMERCE ET DE PRODUCTION DU NIGER.

CORVEE. Forced labor for purposes of infrastructure building and porterage exacted in Francophone Africa until the end of the Second World War as part of the **indigénat** code applicable to the non-**assimilé** population. In Niger large numbers of farmers in the south were impressed for the construction of the Savé section of the Parakou–Cotonou railway in Dahomey and for the construction of two government residences in Niamey in the 1930s.

COTTON. Cotton is cultivated only in selected areas in Niger, specifically in the **gulbis,** in the valleys of Ader-Doutchi-Maggia, and on the lower Dallol Maouri. Originally a minor crop in Niger, cotton has been produced only since 1956, when the Compagnie Française pour le Développement des Fibres Textiles (CFDT) began promoting it. Commencing from 112 tons in 1956, cotton harvests went up to 10,000 tons before plummeting with the onset of the Sahel drought in the 1970s, to revive in the 1980s. The purchase of the cotton harvest is allowed only to the CFDT and the UNCC, with the price (for the highest purity) set at 37 CFA francs per kilo in the mid-1970s.

COULIBALI, OUMAROU (Major). Former cabinet minister. Coulibali was appointed by General Saibou to head the Ministry of Public Works and Housing between November 1987 and May 1989. He subsequently reverted to military duties.

COUP D'ETAT OF DECEMBER 3, 1963 (attempted). Little-publicized mutiny and attempt at sedition that was a prelude to a coup attempt. The key figures were Captain **Hassan A. Diallo,** who was arrested on December 3, 1963, then released and arrested again on December 13, and **Ikhia Zodi,** at the time the minister of defense, who lost his post over the affair and was imprisoned. The coup attempt had its origins in the tug-of-war between the PPN and the **SAWABA** opposition.

COUP D'ETAT OF APRIL 15, 1974. Led by the chief of staff of two years, Colonel Seyni Kountché, the 1:00 A.M. coup had the almost total support of the armed forces. The only unit to resist, spurred on by President Diori's wife, Aisa, was the Tuareg Presidential Guard. Aisa Diori was one of the few victims of the coup. The army had developed throughout the years a variety of grudges against the regime. Used all along to enforce highly unpopular tax collection, the army was also vividly aware of the effects of the drought in the countryside—relief for which ministers sold on the black market for personal profit—and the discrimination against certain groups in the government and the countryside. In like manner the mutual-defense treaty signed with Libya shortly before the actual coup was deeply resented (according to many observers, this was the prime cause of the coup), as were Diori's efforts to harness the army for political tasks. Paradoxically, President Diori had been forewarned, as early as 1973, that Kountché was unreliable, but had nevertheless promoted him to chief of staff. The officially stated reasons for the coup were slightly different: (1) widescale corruption, (2) the absence of democracy in Niger, and (3) the government's overinvolvement in foreign affairs to the detriment of domestic concerns. Many observers believed that France played a role in the coup, angry at Diori's attempts to draw into Niger's uranium industry non-French commercial interests. On the other hand, the resident French military mission was expelled immediately after the coup. Following the coup most government agencies were abolished, and most high government officials were placed under house arrest subject to charges being levied against them. The military regime also immediately opened up grain-distribution centers in Zinder, Maradi, Konni, and N'Guigmi, and began expeditiously to move goods destined for drought relief but bottlenecked all the way to the Atlantic ports. Large amounts of peanut seeds were also distributed, even though it was known that farmers would consume them rather than plant them. Support for the coup was immediate from most circles, including Niger's exiled opposition groups who were reinvited back to Niamey on condition that they would avoid political activity.

At first mostly military, the regime slowly civilianized until on February 21, 1976, a government shuffle resulted in a majority of civilian appointments, most untainted by the former regime. During the first year the government's stress was on drought relief and on preventing hoarding, which was being practiced on a gigantic scale. Internal competitions within the armed forces resulted in at least five major challenges to Kountché's leadership.

COUP OF AUGUST 1975 (attempted). Conspiracy aimed at overthrowing the military regime of **Kountché** in favor of a civilian military clique. The conspiracy was headed by the vice-president of the Supreme Military Council, Major Sani Souna Sido, allegedly in coordination with the recently returned SAWABA leader, Djibo Bakary, and with the involvement of a variety of individuals, including Maitourare. The coup was nipped at the bud, and some of the key conspirators died in prison, while others were not freed until 1983. Sani Souna Sido was officially executed for his role, but at the 1991 National Conference it was revealed that he was in reality murdered.

COUP OF MARCH 15, 1976 (attempted). An attempted coup against the Kountché military regime that lasted a few hours. In the uprising—which resulted in the capture by rebels of the radio station, the army headquarters, and a few other installations—the regime stated that eight government soldiers were killed. Outside observers put the total killed in very fierce fighting at over fifty. An attack on the Presidential Palace was repulsed. The uprising was led by Captain **Muhamad Sidi** and Major **Moussa Bayeré.** Arms were brought into Niger from Libya via the latter's diplomatic pouch (allegedly without the knowledge of Libyan authorities) and transported by trucks of the COPRONIGER company at the orders of former director **Ahmed Mouddour.** Most of the plotters were Hausa, and there were a variety of personal motives behind the assault. A court-martial after the attempted putsch issued a number of harsh sentences, including twenty-eight of life imprisonment and nine death sentences. The key leaders were executed on April 21, 1976. They included Mouddour, Bayeré, Sidi, former chief of general intelligence Idrissa Boubé, and Issaka Dan Koussou.

COUP OF OCTOBER 5, 1983 (attempted). Carefully organized coup attempt during President **Kountché**'s absence abroad, masterminded by his own crony and security adviser, chef de cabinet of the prime minister, Lieutenant Amadou Oumarou, nicknamed "Bonkano," who was also in charge of security in the presidency. Among those involved, apparently solely for reasons of self-advancement, were Lieutenant Idrissa Amadou (commander of the Presidential Guard) and Major Amadou Seydou (commander of the Niamey garrison). The coup attempt collapsed when officers loyal to Kountché questioned the orders aimed at their entrapment. Most of those involved escaped the country, including Bonkano, immensely rich from his control of the portals of the presidential office. In 1991, granted personal immunity for his misdeeds, he returned to Niger to testify before a committee of the National Conference investigating corrupt practices in Niger.

COUR DE SURETE DE L'ETAT. Formed in April 1964 as a court for crimes against the state and, specifically, plots and attempted coups. The impetus for its creation was the revelation of the Diallo plot (*see* **DIALLO, HASSAN A.**). In June 1964 the court became a cour martiale empowered to judge, in accord with specific procedures, flagrant antistate activities. The president of the Cour de Sûrété was Boubacar Diallo, who had been aware of the Diallo plot. Among cases heard by the court was that of Amadou Diop—the grenade attack on Diori—in which the death sentence was meted out, and of some eighty political prisoners from Tahoua and Agadez, sentenced to life imprisonment in connection with the SAWABA uprising.

COUR MARTIALE. *See* COUR DE SURETE DE L'ETAT.

COUR SUPREME. Court of last resort, not to be confused with the **Haute Cour de Justice,** which was a section of the Cour Suprême. Abolished after the May 1974 coup d'état, the Supreme Court's long-term president was Ousman Bassarou Diallo, and it had four specific chambers: civil affairs, constitutional affairs, audit matters, and the Haute Cour de Justice. The Cour Suprême reemerged with the constitutionalization of the Saibou regime in 1989 under Mamadou Malam Awami, and was reconstituted by the National Conference in 1991 and the subsequent constitution of 1993, charged specifically with ensuring freedom of speech in Niger.

COURMO, BARCOUGNE (1916–). Former cabinet minister and early secretary general of the PPN ruling party of President Hamani Diori. Born in 1916 in Say and of Djerma ethnic origins, Courmo has been one of the inner circle of PPN politicians and cabinet ministers ruling Niger. Educated in Niamey and at the Ecole William Ponty in Dakar, Senegal (1933–36), he continued his studies in Paris before returning to Niamey to become an administrator in the local treasury, where he was to work for the next seventeen years. Between 1946 and 1955 the secretary general of the PPN, Courmo by 1953 had become head of the Equipment Department of the Treasury and in 1956 transferred to become personnel manager of the Ministry of Public Works. In 1958 also briefly deputy prefect of the Madaoua district, he became minister of finance after the fall of the Djibo Bakary government the same year. In 1963 his ministry was enlarged to include economic affairs, and he served in those capacities as a key minister until 1965. At that date he was shifted to head the **Conseil Economique et Social,** serving as its president until 1972, and as political secretary of the PPN politburo. Despite his status in the party Courmo manifested his basic disloyalty when he hastily and opportunistically acted in support of a clumsy and very amateurish aborted coup leading to his immediate purge from the PPN. He became one of only two members of that body ever dropped. He has served also on a number of other administrative boards, including that of the Banque de Développement du Niger, and between 1959 and 1963 was president of the OCDN. He is currently in retirement.

COURTEYES. *See* KURTEY.

CREDIT DU NIGER. Opening in 1958 and by 1970 Niger's sixth largest enterprise, Crédit du Niger is headquartered in Niamey and has a capitalization of 220 million CFA francs, of which the government holds 45.45 percent of the shares, the CCCE 27.27 percent, the BDRN (since dissolved) 18.18, and the BCEAO 9.1 percent. Crédit du Niger offers specialized loans for the purchase of such durable goods as houses. It is periodically rocked by allegations of fiscal irregularities, and in 1985 President Kountché revealed that embezzlement of over 319 million CFA francs had been discovered in the accounts of Crédit du Niger. The regime has periodically had to cover some of these losses, to the detriment of efforts at budget balancing. In the 1990s the bank was struggling to survive.

CURE SALEE. Annual Tuareg cattle trek to the northern salt pans west of Agadez and in the In Gall area, where the salt needs of the cattle are satisfied. Known also as *tenekert,* the trek is especially traditional to the Ouilliminden Kel Dinnik and involves a migration of over 400 km.

CURRENCY. French currency was introduced with some difficulty in Niger. In Damagaram **Maria Theresa dollars** and cowrie shells were the common currency, some remaining in circulation to this day. The caravans from the north commonly imported shells in cases of 30,000, and the dollar—not used in Austria since 1854, though over 2 million were minted between 1891 and 1896—was much sought after. The rate of exchange fluctuated around 5,000 cowrie shells per dollar in 1890. With the introduction of the French currency, native preference remained for the dollar. The 5-franc piece was exchangeable in 1902 in Zinder at the rate of 4,000 cowries. Coins were always more valued than paper money, and a 5-franc bill was commonly exchanged for a 2-franc coin. Only in the 1920s did the French franc become more prevalent in Niger, though right up to 1945 other currencies circulated alongside it.

CYRILLE, GABRIEL (Captain). Promoted from lieutenant shortly after the 1974 coup d'état, Cyrille was brought into the cabinet of Kountché as minister of public works. Shifted to head the Ministry of Posts, Telecommunications, and Information, he was also appointed chairman of the Special Committee of Inquiry into the financial abuses of the Diori regime. The committee issued a large number of stiff penalties against many individuals who occupied office under Diori. Some time after the committee ended its investigations, Cyrille was purged from all offices (March 3, 1975) for "being a threat to the state," due to his ethnic biases in these cases. President Kountché also announced that Cyrille had used his position as chairman of the committee to wreak vengeance, resulting in abuses of justice. He remained in prison until released in 1987 by General Saibou after the death of Kountché, when he was appointed head of NIGELEC, Niger's electricity company, in part compensation for his lengthy incarceration.

-D-

DAGRA, MAMDOU. Interim cabinet minister. A political newcomer, Dagra was originally appointed minister of education in December 1989, but was shifted to head the Ministry of Civil Service after the brutally dispersed student demonstrations of February 1990. He remained in that ministry until a government selected by the National Conference took over in September 1991.

DAHOMEANS (*now* Beninois). Until the **Dahomey-Niger boundary dispute** large numbers of Dahomeans resided in Niger—mostly in Niamey—working in the civil service, in the private sector (where the expatriate community valued their services highly), and as private traders.

In the last role they dominated large sectors of local trade, especially the import of tropical produce into Niger (mostly from the Dahomean coast). The trade in bananas, mangoes, oranges, and pineapples (imported by truck from the Savé-Bohicon area) was for a long time dominated by Dahomeans who parceled out their sale to Djerma and Maouri traders. Likewise, the sale of peanut oil, a staple, and other such commodities were practically monopolized by Dahomean women (both Fon and Yoruba). In the administration many of the top officials were Dahomean, having been brought in during the colonial area, causing frustrations among local aspirants for civil service posts. Many anti-Dahomean incidents erupted in Niamey starting in 1956, but in all cases the government frowned on the outbursts. When the Dahomey-Niger dispute arose, however, the government—in an immensely popular move—expelled all Dahomeans in the civil service, and some others in the private sector joined in the exodus. For quite some time this expulsion caused utter administrative chaos in Niamey since the regime had not been aware of the degree to which it had been dependent upon Dahomean trained personnel and traders. The French expatriate community was solidly against the expulsions since Dahomeans were universally regarded as trustworthy and hard workers. Estimates of those expelled range from 6,000 to 20,000, but it was likely about 16,000. Of these about 1,000 had been with the civil service.

DAHOMEY-NIGER BOUNDARY DISPUTE. A boundary dispute, outstanding since 1960, which erupted in November 1963. Involving the question of ownership of the half-submerged Niger River island of Lété (between Gaya and Malanville, between 1 and 2 km wide by 15 km long), the crisis resulted in the dispatch of troops by Niger and Dahomey to the area and the sealing of the international border. Other by-products of the clash were the disruption of **Opération Hirondelle** and the expulsion of **Dahomeans** working in Niger. The conflict, dormant for quite some years, had other causes: the takeover by the military in Dahomey and the toppling of Diori's good friend, Hubert Maga. The dispute was finally resolved on January 15, 1965, by President Felix Houphouët-Boigny of Ivory Coast.

DAKORO. Arrondissement in the Maradi département encompassing 130,000 people (of whom 14,500 are nomads) and centered around the village of Dakoro, the administrative capital, which has a population of 2,500 and is 128 km from Maradi.

DAKOURAWA. Capital of the **Gobirawa** after the fall of **Kadaye** to Fulani armies. Dakourawa, 35 km southwest of Madaoua, was also destroyed by the Fulani, and the Gobirawa capital was shifted to **Birni**

n'Kounia. Dakourawa was resurrected as the Gobirawa capital in 1831 at the time of the anti-Fulaṇi rebellion, but was destroyed again in 1835.

DALLOL. Fulani term equivalent to the Hausa **Gulbi.** Fossilized valleys, usually very fertile, of which the two principal are Dallol Bosso and Dallol Maouri. In wetter prehistoric times these were major affluents of the Niger River, which drained the entire northern regions of Niger up to and including Aïr (especially the Bosso) and into Ahaggar (Algeria). *See also* DALLOL BOSSO; DALLOL MAOURI.

DALLOL BOSSO. Called Boboy by the local Djerma, Dallol Bosso is a large fossilized valley (*see* DALLOL) in the Dosso arrondissement—one of two major ones in Niger—which in prehistoric times drained Aïr. Called a variety of names along its various segments (including Azawak in the plains of the same name), the Dallol Bosso is a dry valley, 300 km length and between 5 and 15 km width, whose western "bank" is a major geological fault.

DALLOL FOGA. *See* DALLOL MAOURI.

DALLOL MAOURI. One of Niger's two major fossilized valleys, which in wetter prehistoric times drained the entire region to the north. The Dallol Maouri (*see* DALLOL) runs from Matankari to south of Gaya. (For the political history of the area, *see* AREWA.) In theory a basin that extends up to the Tidjeddi fault (50 km south of Agadez), it is in reality a series of different affluent basins (Abalcmma, Kcita, Badeguicheri) joined by the Dallol Foga around 20 km north of Gaya, and joining the Niger River around Dole. The Dallol has some water in its lower course.

DAMAGARAM. Powerful precolonial state centered around **Zinder** and encompassing the current southeastern corner of Niger. With a population of 400,000 in the mid–nineteenth century, the kingdom included Hausa (its major component) as well as Tuareg, Fulani, Kanuri, Arab, and Toubou groups. Starting as a vassal to the **Kanem-Bornu Empire,** Damagaram eventually controlled eighteen chieftainships and emerged as the dominant power north of Kano. Part of its importance was consequent to its developing into the southern terminus for the caravan trails coming in from Fezzan. There are several explanations of the origin of Damagaram's name, which may be Kanuri. At the time of the French conquest the state covered some 70,000 sq km and had a king list of twenty-six since its founder, Mallam. Sultans could usually only be brothers and sons of the preceding ruler. The sultan's family was extremely large. In 1851 the sultan had 300 wives and 150 children; even in 1906 the ruler's wives numbered 81. Two of the most important officials in the kingdom were the **ciroma**—chief of staff—and the **yakudima**—the heir apparent.

The Damagaram armies included powerful units of Tuareg who had traditionally been allowed to reside peacefully outside Zinder's walls, and this cavalry had been decisive in several battles. For a major, well-planned campaign the Damagaram army could field five thousand horsemen and thirty thousand infantry as well as up to a dozen cannon, locally produced. (This production was a Zinder specialty; not even the infinitely more powerful Kanem-Bornu to the east possessed either the skills or any operational cannon.) In its drive to expand, the Damagaram kingdom first absorbed the old kingdom of Myrria, then the **Sossebaki** states, at which time the capital was transferred to Zinder. Encouraging Tuareg traders to settle outside the town's walls, Zinder became a regular stop on the Tripoli–Kano route and greatly benefited from this. It remained independent of Fulani control during the Fulani jihad and even lent assistance to other Hausa elements driven out of their lands, helping found Maradi.

With the onset of the colonial era Damagaram was threatened by both **Rabah** in the east and the French in the west. When the French mission headed by Captain **Cazemajou** visited Zinder on its way to Rabah, mistrust of the intentions of these two anti-Damagaram forces led to the murder of Cazemajou. *See* MISSION DU HAUT-SOUDAN. France's eventual retaliation brought about the conquest of the kingdom. In the process of defining the new frontiers of Niger many of Damagaram's dependencies were ceded to the British (Nigeria), and Damagaram's traditional access to the Kano market was cut. In 1906 a court intrigue led to the false imprisonment of the reigning sultan and the elevation of one of his aides. The legitimate lineage was restored only in 1923. *See also* ZINDER.

DAMAGARAM, SULTANS OF. Mallam, 1731–46; Baba dan Mallam, 1746–57; Tanimoun Babami, 1757–75; Assaf dan Tanimoun, 1775–82; Abaza dan Tanimoun, 1782–87; Mallam Babou Saba, 1787–90; Daouda dan Tanimoun, 1790–99; Ahmadou dan Tanimoun, 1799–1812; Suleyman, 1812–22; Ibrahim, 1822–41; Tanimoun, 1841–43; Ibrahim, 1843–51; Mahamane Kace, 1851; Tanimoun, 1851–84; Abba Gato, 1884; Suleyman dan Ausa, 1884–93; Ahmadou mai Roumji, 1893–99; Ahmadou dan Bassa, 1899–1906; Barma Mustapha, 1923–50; Oumarou Sanda, 1950–.

DAMANA. The rainy season, in Hausa.

DAMERGOU. Region immediately northwest of **Damagaram.** With the onset of the colonial era the area was administered from **Djadjidouna,**

at the time a major caravan stop on the Tripoli–Zinder–Kano route. A vast, monotonous pastureland plateau, Damergou used to be dominated by the **Imouzourag** Tuareg, who protected sedentary groups in return for payment in kind against predatory attacks by the Kel Owey, who traditionally led all caravans through the region. These two Tuareg groups continually clashed in the area in the nineteenth century, leading to the intervention of the French. Solicited by each for military help against the other, France promised assistance to the group that would provide the most mounts for the expedition then being prepared against **Rabah** in Chad. The Kel Owey, the only ones with camels (due to their role in the caravan trade), donated two hundred mounts, and the subsequent battle of Tanami saw the defeat and dispersal of the Imouzourag. The anastafidet of the Kel Owey was then appointed head of Damergou. In due time the abolition of slavery in the area brought about the collapse of the economy. The name *Damergou* comes from "the country of meat," because of the Hausa hunters who were its original inhabitants. Damergou is a geographical entity; no protostate ever developed in the region, which remained one of scattered millet-growing villages, sovereign to, and under the protection of, Tuareg clans.

DAN BASKORE. Serkin Maradi, 1858–79. Serkin Maradi, and one of its most important kings. Son of Maroua (1825–35), Dan Baskore ruled at a time of Maradi's apogee. He was the last of the Dan Kasawa successors to mount truly serious expeditions at Katsina aimed at reconquering the area from the Fulani. Of his eighty battles in that direction one reached within 8 km of Katsina in a campaign that included a force of ten thousand from Maradi, Gobir, Damagaram, and the Tuareg Kel Owey. Under him Maradi prospered greatly and built walls, becoming a birni. *See also* MARADI.

DAN BASSA, AHMADOU *See* AHMADOU DAN BASSA.

DAN BOUZOUA, MAHAMANE (1933–). Labor inspector. Born in 1933 in Tanout to the Kanuri chef de canton, and educated locally, in France (IHEOM), and in Geneva (at the International Institute for Higher Studies), Dan Bouzoua worked as a health official (1950–53) and commercial clerk (1953–57) before joining the National Assembly as deputy in 1957. He was not reelected in the subsequent elections and after completing his education abroad became labor inspector in the Niamey region, a post he held until retiring from the civil service.

DAN BOUZOUA, MUSTAPHA. Secretary of state in charge of primary and secondary education between November 1991 and March 1992.

DAN DOBI, MAHAMANE (1923–). Author and former cabinet minister. Born in 1923 in Guécheme in the Dogondoutchi district, and of Maouri chiefly origins (he was the chef de canton of Fakassaka), Dan Dobi studied in Dogondoutchi, Konni, and Niamey before going to the Ecole William Ponty in Dakar, Senegal, where he graduated in 1942. He then joined the police force in Niamey (1942–45), and served as an administrative official in Téra, Conakry, Niamey, and Konni (1948–57) before being elected to the Territorial Assembly in 1957. It was during this period that he wrote his widely acclaimed play, *Kabrin Kabra* (1958). In the Assembly he joined the PPN party and was reelected through 1965. In the party he became the deputy secretary general of the political bureau and hence key man in the ruling circle. He served in the latter capacity between 1957 and 1974. In 1959 Dan Dobi served also as senator to the French Community, and in 1960 he was appointed president of the Société Nationale des Transports Nigériens (SNTN), in which he served until the 1974 coup. In 1965 he was integrated into Diori's cabinet as minister of justice; in 1970 he served for two months as minister of health before being shifted to head the Ministry of Urban Affairs and Transport (which was split from the Ministry of Works) and later the Ministry of Rural Economy (1972–74). Following the 1974 coup Dan Dobi was found guilty of embezzlement of 26 million CFA francs and of fiscal fraud of 12 million CFA francs. He was imprisoned until April 1978. He is currently retired.

DAN FODIO, OTHMAN (1754–1817). Fulani itinerant preacher and famed scholar from the kingdom of Gobir—popularly known as the Shehu—who triggered the Fulani jihad of 1804, destroying Hausa power. After religious studies in Agadez Dan Fodio returned to his hometown of Degel, where he acquired renown for his piety. He was called upon to tutor the king's son at the court, where he had the chance to observe the alleged deviations from Koranic prescriptions. The call for a jihad was in part aimed at purifying Islam in the region and in part a response to the anti-Fulani policies of Gobir, initiated in particular by Dan Fodio's pupil once he ascended to the throne. Between 1804 and 1817 all the Hausa monarchs were overthrown, and Fulani power expanded into former non-Hausa areas. After the conquests the new Fulani Empire was divided into a western wing with its capital in Gwandu, and an eastern wing centered at Sokoto. The Shehu himself returned to his religious studies.

DAN KASSAWA (?–1831). True founder of the Katsina successor Hausa state of Maradi. After the Hausa expulsion from Katsina by the Fulani, and the suicide of the exiled Serkin Magajin Halidou, Dan Kassawa was selected as his successor. After two years in Zinder

Dan Kassawa and his followers settled at Gafai on the Damagaram border. After ten years there, during which Dan Kassawa's strength was augmented by new refugees from the Fulani, an assault was mounted against Maradi—a former Katsina province—after its local population revolted against its Fulani masters. Maradi then became the center of Hausa resistance against the Fulani in Katsina. By the time Dan Kassawa died, the town was totally entrenched.

DAN KOULODO, DAN DICKO (1934–). Scientist and currently secretary general of the Agence de Coopération Culturelle et Technique in Brussels. Born in 1934 in Maradi of Hausa ethnic origin and the son of the serkin Katsina, Dan Koulodo was educated in Maradi, Niamey, and at the Lycée Vollenhoven, Dakar, Senegal. After attending the academies of Dakar (1953–54), Montpellier (1954–58), and the Collège d'Agde (1959), at which he studied science, he graduated with a doctoral degree in organic structural chemistry. He then joined the faculty of the University of Montpellier (1959–61) and the Center for Higher Studies, Abidjan (1961–68). While in the Ivory Coast he also taught at the Ecole Nationale Supérieure des Travaux Publics (1963–68). He remained in Abidjan, at the newly created Université d'Abidjan, through 1971 before returning to Niamey to teach at the new Université de Niamey and to assume the post of vice-president of the Conseil Economique et Social. In August 1972 he was brought into the cabinet as minister of education and after the 1974 coup d'état he was sent abroad to head the Agence de Coopération Culturelle et Technique des Pays Francophones (ACCT). Dan Koulodo is the author of several scientific articles.

DANDA, MAHAMADOU. Minister of animal and water resources under General Saibou, serving between November 1987 and May 1989.

DANDAWA. Name by which the Djerma are known among the Hausa.

DANGI. Basic clan unit among the Hausa.

DANN-INNA, CHAIBOU. Secretary general of the Ministry of National Education. Dann-Inna was briefly seized by rampaging students in the July 1992 riots over their arrears in scholarly grants.

DAOUEL, AKOLI. *See* DAWEL, AKOLI.

DAR AL MAAL AL ISLAM. *See* MASSRAF FAYCAL AL ISLAMI.

DARA. Popular West African game.

DAREY. One of the most important, though small, chiefdoms in **Ader** prior to the conquest of the region by **Aggaba.** Possibly of Gobir origins, founded in the sixteenth century, and organized along the lines of Gobir, Darey's oral history refers to 333 chiefs prior to the Aggaba conquests. Darey's population traces its origins, like many other groups, to Arabia, and local scarifications are of the Gobirawa kind. Until it fell to the Tuareg, Darey controlled several local principalities, including Follakam. Darey was also the name of the chiefdom's principal village of some 3,000 people, ruins of which are still visible. The village was very brutally destroyed by Aggaba and later reconstituted some distance away, though much of the population drifted west to the Dallol Maouri.

DARGOL. Small Songhay kingdom that became a major center of anti-Moroccan resistance after the 1591 Battle of Tondibi (*see* TONDIBI). Later, in the eighteenth and nineteenth centuries, Dargol had a series of violent confrontations with both Fulani and Tuareg invaders. The kingdom was centered around the town of the same name, which today has a population of around 5,000 and is located in the Téra arrondissement in the Niamey département. *See also* DENDI.

DARKOYE, ATTAHER. Former long-term cabinet minister. Darkoye, at the time secretary general for national education since November 1983, was brought into General Kountché's cabinet as minister of hydrology in September 1985, serving until 1987, when he was replaced after General Saibou came to power. He was recalled by Saibou May 1989 to assume the key post of minister of interior, serving until December 1989.

DAWEL, AKOLI. Tuareg political leader. A member of the National Conference, and its HCR, on January 7, 1992, he was named by interim prime minister Cheiffou as special emissary in Aïr in an attempt to resolve the Tuareg crisis. *See* TUAREG REBELLION. In September 1992 he was arrested in the roundup of suspected Tuareg rebellion sympathizers by the Nigerien armed forces in Agadez, and was only released after protests in the National Assembly. He is president of the Union pour la Démocratie et Progrès Social (UDPS) political party based in Agadez, as well as leader of the Parti pour l'Unité Nationale et al Démocratie (PUND), which secured three seats in the 1995 parliamentary elections. Dawel supports the Tuareg federal cause.

DAYAK, MANO. One of the key leaders of the Tuareg rebellion in Aïr, and specifically of the Front de Libération de Temust (FLT), of which he is a leader. Dayak, who has written a book delineating Tuareg grievances against Niamey—leading to a rebuttal in a book by the HCR's interim president, **André Salifou**—is a spokesman of the Tuareg in Paris, and vice-president of the **Coordination de la Résistance Armée,** formed in 1993.

DAZA. A branch of the **Toubou** found both in northern Chad and in northeastern Niger. They call themselves *Dazagada* ("those who speak Dazaga"). The other Toubou branch, the Teda (or Tedagada), speak a very similar dialect, both of which are related to Kanuri. The Daza are found in Chad in Ennedi and Borkou, and in Niger in Manga and Kaouar. They are divided into numerous small clans, the total population of which is hard to estimate but is placed at around 20,000. Some non-Nigerien elements filtered in from Chad after the ouster there of former president Hissene Habre, and they have either sold their arms or joined newly formed liberation movements in the region.

DELANNE, RENE. Former secretary general of the Niger National Assembly, of the UNTN, and of several other agencies, all from September 25, 1960, until the coup of 1974, and a key and loyal second-echelon personal aide of former president Diori. Between 1956 and 1971 Delanne was the social affairs secretary of the political bureau of the PPN, tracing his power from this appointment. Though he was to be a key personality in the Diori regime, Delanne sided with his UNTT lieutenants in demanding major pay raises—rejected by the government—and was consequently purged from his PPN posts, becoming one of only two politburo members the PPN ever dropped, losing his post in 1971. Since Delanne—who is of mixed parentage—was extremely visible in all the posts he occupied, he was one of the most detested members of the Diori regime and was immediately arrested after the 1974 coup d'état, not to be released until the mid-1980s.

DELEI, MAHAMA (1890–1971). Former chief of Djado. Of local origins, Delei assumed his functions as chief of Djado (including the oases of Chirfa and Djaba) in 1930, but was suspended from his duties by the French between 1935 and 1944. During this period direct French military rule was exercised over the region. His traditional supremacy was not recognized until 1944 when Delei was reinstated.

DENDI. Both a geographical term referring to the country beyond Koulou and a Songhay province. At the time of the **Askias** the area included the Niger River valley below Goungia; it slowly began to refer more narrowly to the most southern segment and especially to the sinuous W region of the Niger. Also, the term was used to refer to the almost totally

Songhay population of this region, which has retained a dialect much more similar to the Songhay of **Gao** than to the Djerma. Currently there are nearly 40,000 Songhay in the Dosso arrondissement, with an additional 25,000 further south, in neighboring Benin's Nikki region.

Dendi became the last remnant of independent Songhay after the Moroccan invasion and conquest of Gao, and the **Battle of Tondibi.** They are based in Loulami, since disappeared, and accept the rule of Askia Nouha; a total break with Gao occurred in the seventeenth century, and several attempts were mounted to liberate the ancient empire's core. The frontiers with the Moroccans eventually stabilized in the vicinity of the contemporary Niger-Mali borders (between Tillabéry and Ansongo). The new dynasty in Dendi continued its Askia titles and traditions for some time. Eventually Dendi disintegrated into five or six smaller kingdoms, each with a genuine Askia descendant at its head. Among these states are Téra, Garoul, and Dargol.

DEPARTEMENTS. Administrative regions into which Niger is divided, replacing the colonial **cercles,** effective October 1, 1965. There were originally 7 départements, 32 arrondissements, and some 150 communes. The number of arrondissements and communes has increased somewhat over the years, with the former's numbers currently standing at 35. Each département is headed by a préfet appointed by the minister of interior, and is assisted in his duties by a **Commission Consultative Départementale** formed of the sous-préfets and members appointed by the local Conseils d'Arrondissements. *See also* ADMINISTRATIVE ORGANIZATION.

DEREMCHAKA. Arab-Berber people who penetrated **Azawak** in the eighteenth and nineteenth centuries, migrating toward Tahoua and Koureya. For a long time in southern Algeria (in the Touat Aoulef oasis and at In Salah) before migrating south, they eventually became assimilated with the Tuareg, becoming in effect the Kel Ahaggar. Rejected by the sultan of Agadez in their attempts to settle in Aïr, they mounted various battles with the Kel Owey. The Kel Ahaggar raided Agadez a number of times and fought both with and against the Kel Dinnik. In 1894 a very bloody battle occurred near Tahoua, and as a consequence the Kel Ahaggar finally retreated northward greatly weakened, while the Kel Dinnik, also much decimated, were left in a weak position vis-à-vis the Kel Gress in the region.

DEVELOPMENT PLANS. Niger has had seven development plans, all requiring considerable foreign financial involvement, but all either had to be downscaled in midpoint or failed to attain their targets. The sixth plan, for 1979–83, was one of the most ambitious, being predicated on the continuation of substantial uranium exports and revenues, and the end of the Sahel drought of the 1970s that put to shambles the previous development plan. The 1979–83 plan had to be revised, however, due to the onset of another drought in the Sahel, and to grossly declining uranium receipts—a completely unforeseen eventuality. Total anticipated expenditures had been targeted at 730,223 million CFA francs with a 53 percent (384,493 million) contribution from the public sector and the remainder from private sources. The major emphasis was, as in previous plans, on attaining self-sufficiency in food production. Public-sector contributions were targeted in the following sectors: rural development (116,450 million CFA francs); mines and industry (70,206 million); human resource development (84,847 million); communications (67,762 million); administrative infrastructure (26,266 million); and commerce and tourism (19,962 million). The seventh plan, for the ten-year period 1981–90, based on lower projected domestic revenues, and with most contributions scheduled to come from external sources, also had to be revised as Niger's finances deteriorated further. It projected a two-stage program of investments, with those by 1985 (not attained) of 520,000 million CFA francs.

DEVELOPMENT SOCIETY. *See* CONSEIL NATIONAL DU DEVELOPPEMENT.

DIADO, AMADOU (1940–). Journalist. Born in 1940 in Dalway, Diado obtained primary education in Say and agricultural training in Kola, becoming an agrarian instructor. In 1963 he began his career as a writer and journalist and shortly thereafter went to Tunisia for training in journalism. In 1966 he attended journalism school in Paris, returning to Niamey, where he joined the staff of *Le Niger* as a journalist and poet. In 1980 he was integrated into the Foreign Ministry and appointed first secretary of the Niger embassy in Paris. He served there until 1984, subsequently remaining in Paris in a private capacity.

DIALLO, ABDOULAYE AMADOU (1924–). Diplomat and educator. Born in Debéré-Talata and educated in Mali at the Teachers College of Katibougou, Diallo worked as a teacher and headmaster between 1947 and 1958. In 1958 he assumed the post of chef de cabinet of the minister of education, and in 1961 he became director of the cabinet. He remained in that post until 1968. During these years he also served as secretary for external relations of UNTN. In 1968 he was appointed commissioner general for development, and in 1972 he was appointed ambassador to the U.S. and the U.N. serving until 1974. In May 1976 Diallo was appointed ambassador to Egypt, and since 1984 has been in Niamey in retirement.

DIALLO, ALTINE AIDIO (1915–). Early National Assembly delegate. Born in 1915 in Lamordé Torodi, and an agent of the central administration, Diallo became a PPN party organizer in Niamey and in March 1957 gained entry into the National Assembly. Reelected through 1964, Diallo served as president of the Public Works Committee of the Assembly, and also a delegate of the Niamey SMDR and member of the CNCA. In 1964 he was dropped from his PPN seat but continued his administrative career in the Ministry of Interior until his retirement.

DIALLO, BOUBACAR ALI (1906–65). Former cabinet minister. Born on February 6, 1906, in Niamey, and a chef de canton and secretary general of the Association des Chefs Coutumiers du Niger, Diallo was elected to the Territorial Assembly in March 1952 on the UNIS list. Serving concurrently as councillor to the AOF Grand Council in Dakar (1952–57), he was reelected to the Assembly in December 1958 as the UCFA (later PPN) deputy from Niamey and was appointed minister of health (December 18, 1958 to December 31, 1960). He was subsequently appointed minister of justice (1961–62) and minister of labor and social affairs. At the time also president of the Cour de Sûrété de l'Etat, he was dropped from all his positions in September 1964 for involvement in the military plot of that year by withholding information he possessed about it (*see* ZODI, IKHIA). He died of fever in prison on May 11, 1965.

DIALLO, BOULI ALI (1948–). Educator and currently government spokeswoman and minister of national education. Born in 1948 and trained in microbiology at the University of Dakar, Senegal, Diallo completed her doctorate in biology in France at the University of Montpellier (1975), following which she returned to teach at the University of Niamey. With the liberal reforms in Niger she commenced a political career, and after the rise of the February 1995 government dominated by the MNSD she was named to her current posts.

DIALLO, CHEIK OUSMANE (1943–). Journalist and international administrator. Born on February 5, 1943, in Tougouri, Burkina Faso, and educated in Burkina Faso, Mali, Togo, and France, he secured a law degree and a diploma in journalism. Between 1968 and 1971 he served as head of the documentation service of the Supreme Council of Sport in Africa, following which he became assistant director of publications at the Organization of African Unity. More recently he has been director of linguistic and historical studies in Niamey, secretary general of the OAU cabinet, and currently serves as director general of the Pan-African News Agency.

DIALLO, DAOUDA. General Kountché's longest-serving cabinet minister (twelve years). Diallo joined Kountché's cabinet in September 1979 as foreign minister; in November 1983 was appointed minister of information, serving for two years; and continued in Kountché's cabinet until the latter's death. He was dropped from the cabinet with the rise of General Saibou, and appointed head of a parastatal company.

DIALLO, HAROUNA MATIENGA (1944–). Meteorological engineer. Born in 1944 in Gabikané, a village in the Téra district, Diallo was trained as a meteorologist at Saint Louis University in the U.S., continuing at Florida State University (1965–69; 1970–71). Since 1971, when he returned home, he has been Niger's chief meteorological officer and permanent representative of Niger to the World Meteorological Association.

DIALLO, HASSAN A. (Captain). Former military officer. One of the two key instigators of the 1963 attempted coup d'état by the SAWABA party (*see* COUP D'ETAT OF DECEMBER 3, 1963). Arrested on December 3, 1963, Diallo was released under the strong protests of his colleagues in the army. He was rearrested on December 13 following a cabinet shuffle that saw the eclipse of one of his protectors, Minister of Defense **Ikhia Zodi.** In 1964 came a series of guerrilla attacks on border posts; in 1965, cashiered from the army, Diallo was condemned to death for his earlier role in the SAWABA plot. Granted clemency in 1969, he was released from prison in 1971.

DIALLO, MOCTAR. Former minister in charge of relations with parliament and government spokesman in Niger's first postmilitary cabinet. He served in that capacity between April 1993 and the fall of the AFC government in September 1994.

DIALLO, OUMAR BACHIR (1934–). Former minister of public works and former secretary general of the Ministry of Development, Mines, and Water Resources, and a geological engineer. Born on June 9, 1934, in Gouré, Diallo was educated in Filingué, Maradi, and Niamey before going on to Dakar's Lycée Van Vollenhoven (1953–55) and the University of Dakar (1955–58), where he graduated in science. Diallo continued higher studies at the University of Nancy (France) and in Niamey (through 1962), obtaining an engineering diploma in applied geology and mineral prospecting. He then worked with the French Bureau of Mining (1962–66) in France, Upper Volta (Burkina Faso), Niger, and Ivory Coast, before returning home to an appointment as deputy director of mines, later director of mines. In 1967 he assumed the post of secretary general of the inter-African Comité d'Etudes

Hydrauliques. In 1967 he became codirector of the U.N. Mining Research Project for Niger, and in 1974 was appointed secretary general of the Ministry of Development, Mines, and Water Resources. Diallo held this post until 1980 when he was brought into Kountché's cabinet as minister of public works, transport, and urban affairs. Shifted in July 1982 to head the Ministry of Mines and Industry, he was dropped from the cabinet in November 1983 to be appointed chairman of the Société Concessionaire de la Route Tahoua–Arlit (CONCERTA).

DIALLO, OUSMAN BASSAROU (1908–). Former president of the Supreme Court and key PPN member. One of former president Diori's oldest friends and most intimate allies, Diallo was born in 1908 in Ganki-Bassarou to the traditional head of a Fulani tribe. He was educated in Say and in Ouagadougou, Upper Volta (Burkina Faso), completing his secondary education in 1928. He then entered the civil service as a simple clerk serving in various postings, including Filingué, Gaya, Say, and Agadez (1928–44). He participated in the Bamako founding congress (1946) of the interterritorial Rassemblement Démocratique Africain, following which he helped finance both the nascent PPN party (which was a section of the RDA) and Hamani Diori's first electoral campaign. In 1958 he joined the Ministry of Public Works, Mines, and Water Resources as chef de cabinet of the minister. In 1962 he left that post to become president of the Supreme Court, where he served until the 1974 coup d'état, and was concurrently also president of the Constitutional Council. In the mid-1960s he served on several parastatal boards, including as president of Crédit du Niger. He has been a key PPN figure since its foundation, serving as the party's first vice-president of the political bureau (until 1974). A colorful figure in Niamey, Diallo is an ardent horseman and has been president of the local Société Hippique.

DIALLO, SAMBO IBRAHIMA (1927–). Former civil administrator, prefect and director of customs. Born around 1927 in Gongongou, near Dori, Upper Volta (Burkina Faso), and educated locally and in France (IHEOM, EPS) as an administrator, Diallo has worked as an officer of SONARA and head of Niger's External Commerce Department (1950–59). In October 1961 he joined the staff of the minister of industry and commerce as his chef de cabinet, serving until July 1962. In May 1966 Diallo was appointed prefect of Tahoua, and in 1970 he became director of customs, a post he held until his retirement in 1987.

DIALLO, SORY MAMADOU (Lieutenant Colonel). Former minister of interior. Originally appointed minister of justice at the time of the 1974 coup d'état and then a captain, Diallo was shifted to head the

Ministry of Public Works, Labor, and Posts in 1975, and in March 1976 became minister of civil service, labor, and commerce. Later the same year he was appointed minister of interior. He was part of the core army faction sustaining the Kountché regime, and was widely regarded as the number two man in the army. Despite this he was slowly eased out of prominence. In September 1979 he was demoted to the Ministry of Posts, and in February 1981 he was dropped altogether from the cabinet. Apart from friction and disagreements on fundamental issues, Diallo's popularity in the urban areas tended to threaten Kountché's self-image. In 1984 he was retired from the armed forces.

DIAMBALLA, MAIGA YANSAMBOU. *See* MAIGA, DIAMBALLA YANSAMBOU.

DIAWARRA, IDRISS (1941–). Psychologist. Born on May 23, 1941, Diawarra did his graduate studies at the University of Paris, where he obtained a doctorate in psychology. On his return to Niamey he joined the Pedagogical School of the University of Niamey. He has written especially about problems of divorce in Niger.

DIFFA. Northern département bordering Chad and Libya, encompassing a vast territory of 155,000 sq km and a population of 145,000, most of whom are Manga, Mobeur, Kanembu, Fulani, Toubou, Arab, and Boudouma. Total density of population is less than 0.9 per sq km. The town of Diffa, headquarters of the département, is 140 km from N'Guigmi and has a population of 1,200. It is situated on the Komadugu-Yobe River and has a big Sunday market of regional importance. The département includes the arrondissements of Diffa, Mainé-Soroa, and N'Guigmi and the postes administratifs of Goudoumaria, N'Gourti, and Toumour. Internal routes in the département are very sandy and poor, passable (between Diffa and N'Guigmi, for example) only during the dry season. Diffa is also the name of an arrondissement in the same département with a population of 48,000 people. Since 1993 the region has been troubled by the emergence of a "liberation front," mostly of Toubou warriors, who have carried out several assaults.

DILLALI. Also sometimes called *dillani.* Widely used Hausa name for middlemen who arrange (for a specific commission) the sale or purchase of cattle and other livestock during market days. The fee varies from market to market, but in the 1970s it was between 25 and 50 CFA francs for a sheep or goat and between 150 and 250 CFA francs per head of cattle.

DIOBO, ALFA MOHAMED (1768–1840). Fulani ruler and founder of Say. Born around 1768 in Macina and trained as a marabout, Diobo first settled in Gao, then in Zinder and Dargol. He was there widely acclaimed as a great saint by the Kado, Kurtey, and Wago. He drifted then to the immediate vicinity of contemporary Niamey, where he lived for seven years, finally moving to Say and establishing it as a holy city. Diobo greatly consolidated the town as the center of Islamic learning and of the **Quadriya** sect for which it became renowned from Gao to Gaya. As a Fulani island in Djerma country, Say also attracted many new Fulani immigrants who bolstered its position in the region. One of his followers, Boubakar Loudoudji, settled in Dallol Bosso and helped the Fulani conquest of the area in which Diobo was also involved. By the time Diobo died, Say was solidly established as the center of Islamic purity uncontaminated by pre-Islamic beliefs and ritual. As it was founded and settled essentially by voluntary converts to the faith, it was able to maintain this reputation and held an importance far out of proportion to its actual size. After Diobo's death in 1840 his sons succeeded him as rulers of Say; the current chief of Say, Abdousalam, is a direct descendant of Diobo.

DIOP, MUSTAPHA. Cinematographer. Diop's first film was titled *Synapse* (1971), and among his later films was *Médicin de Gafiné* (1986).

DIORI, ABDOULAYE. International entrepreneur and commercial agent. Son of former president **Hamani Diori,** Abdoulaye Diori was linked with at least one Libyan effort to destabilize the regime of Kountché in the late 1970s, as a consequence of which his father was kept under tighter house arrest and not released until 1984. In 1985 he was involved in the attempted Tuareg commando raid on Tchin Tabaraden, following which his father was rearrested.

DIORI, AISSA (1928–74). President Diori's wife, killed in the 1974 coup d'état when she tried to fight off the assaulting force. During her husband's administration, she personally amassed a large fortune, including quality buildings in Niamey, and was greatly detested especially in the more militant student circles where she was allegedly referred to as "The Austrian" (after Marie Antoinette). Of Fulani origin, she was the mother of six.

DIORI, HAMANI (1916–89). Former president of Niger, toppled in the 1974 coup d'état. Born on June 6, 1916, in Soudouré (near Niamey) and of Djerma ethnic origin, Diori was educated locally (studying under Boubou Hama, whence their long friendship and alliance), in Porto Novo, Dahomey (Benin), and at Senegal's Ecole William Ponty. His father, Sidibe Hamani, was one of those who welcomed the arrival of the French in Niger and joined the French colonial civil service as a public health official, becoming later an infirmary worker.

In 1936 Diori returned to Niger and worked as a teacher in Niamey and Maradi (1936–38) and at the ENFOM (where he taught Djerma and Hausa) between 1938 and 1946. One time Hamalli disciple of Tierno Boukar Salif Tall (d. 1940), Diori was cofounder, with Boubou Hama of the RDA section in Niger, the PPN, and became one of Houphouët-Boigny's closest lieutenants. (Indeed, after independence whenever the latter was attacked internationally, it was usually Diori, and Radio Niger, who sprang to his defense.)

Diori was elected to the French National Assembly in 1946 but was defeated in his bid for reelection in 1951 when the PPN split into two factions and the French administration decided to support that of **Djibo Bakary,** Diori's cousin (*see* POLITICAL PARTIES). Diori returned to teaching as director of a school in Niamey (1951–58) and was finally reelected to the French National Assembly in 1956, narrowly defeating Bakary despite strong support for the latter on the part of the administration. In 1957 he joined the Niger Territorial Assembly for the first time as deputy from Zinder and the same year became municipal councillor of Niamey. In Paris he was elected deputy speaker of the French Assembly. In 1958, following the referendum regarding the future of the French colonial empire, and after Bakary's unsuccessful plea for a "no" vote, Diori found himself president of the Ministerial Council and prime minister (1958–60).

In November 1960 the changes in Niger's constitution made Diori president of the Republic. From 1960 to 1963 his own minister of foreign and defense affairs, and in 1965 again of foreign affairs, Diori was much sought after internationally as a mediator in African disputes. Indeed, his mild and gentle manner made him an agreeable compromise candidate in many instances, and he served for seven years as president of the Entente (1967–74) and in 1966 was also chairman of OCAM (to 1967). In 1973 Diori was nominated chairman of the West African Community (CEAO). Always much more popular abroad than at home, Diori's attention was frequently on the international arena where he could score minor triumphs rather than on the domestic front where Niger's awesome problems continually acted as restraints on development.

In the 1970s, having survived several amateur plots and coup attempts by the banned SAWABA party and its leader, Djibo Bakary, Diori began to run afoul of major strata in society as a consequence of the mismanagement of world drought aid pouring into Niger (*see*

DROUGHTS) and his toleration of corruption in high places. As the regime grew totally out of touch with the masses Diori was toppled with ease by the 1974 coup d'état. Most of the ministers of the cabinet, he himself, and many other public officials were arrested and imprisoned subject to inquiries into their behavior while in office.

Though the military regime was not so punitive of corrupt practices as it had stated it would be, many of Diori's associates, and the political and ethnic giants of the country during his era, were indicted for embezzlement, corruption, misuse of funds, mismanagement, and a host of other offenses. Included was Diori's original mentor and lifelong ally, Boubou Hama. Diori remained under close house arrest in Zinder, despite poor health, advanced age, and near-total blindness. His terms of confinement were twice eased (and indeed he was twice temporarily released) only to be reimposed subsequent to his son's activities—with Libyan aid and Tuareg assistance—on his behalf. Diori was rearrested in mid-1985 after the attempted Tuareg raid on the Tchin Tabaraden armory masterminded by Abdoulaye Diori. He was finally freed by General Saibou after Kountché's death and went to live in Rabat, Morocco, where he died on April 23, 1989.

DIRKOU. Oasis at the foot of the Kaouar cliffs. Though currently virtually deserted, the oasis was historically quite important. A military outpost guards entry and exit from Algeria and Libya. Several rock engravings from prehistoric times are to be found in the cliffs behind the oasis.

DJADJIDOUNA. Small village in Damergou that was once an important stop on the trans-Saharan Tripoli–Zinder–Kano caravan route. As evidence of Djadjidouna's past commercial importance, an extensive **Ghadamsi** trading community was resident there (larger than that in Zinder itself) and there was an important Sanusiya lodge (zawaya) in the area. The French established a customs post in the village for the salt caravans that brought in up to 20,000 loads per year. With the decline in caravan trade, the village plummeted in importance, and its Ghadamsi community dispersed, many going to Kano.

DJADO. Small, currently extremely dilapidated village, mostly in ruins, some 330 km north of Bilma, populated mostly by Toubou. Located on a mountaintop, and formerly an important caravan stop and Turkish garrison town, Djado was totally razed by the Tuareg just prior to the French conquest of the region, following which most of the population took refuge in Tadjéré. Even with the pacification of the area by the French, the region suffered from repeated razzias (in 1911 and 1912, for instance), most sweeping to include Djado. Important frescoes were discovered in the area (1960–61) by the Mission Berliet-Ténéré. Some 7 km from Djado is **Chirfa** with its very picturesque deserted Foreign Legion fort and moonlike landscape. In 1974 a concession that included Djado was granted for uranium prospecting. Djado's **ksar** is much photographed by tourists.

DJAMBALA, ISSAKA. General Saibou's secretary of state for foreign affairs between December 1989 and September 1991, when a new interim government was created in the aftermath of the National Conference.

DJERMA (*also* Dyerma, Zerma, Zarma). For all practical purposes a branch of the Songhay, the Djerma are found along the Niger River valley from Mali (Djenné, Hombori) to Gaya in Niger and in small numbers in the Nikki-Kandi area of Benin. A wide array of oral traditions offer disparate accounts of the origin of the Djerma, the most common referring to their Malinke and Sarakollé origins from Mali whence they migrated southward. Their main towns in Niger are Niamey, Dosso, and Ouallam. They were strongly Islamized in the tenth century, and this was further reinforced by the Fulani in the eighteenth and nineteenth centuries. In the seventeenth century the Djerma peacefully settled the **Dallol Bosso** valley—called Boboy by them—occupied previously by the Kallé, with whom they freely intermarried. In the eighteenth century they moved to the area of Dosso and allied with is original inhabitants to fight the Maouri of the Dallol Raffi. Under pressure from the Tuareg to the north, the Djerma also soon faced the jihad of Othman dan Fadio and his Fulani armies, who occupied some of the most fertile Djerma lands and were not pushed back until around 1870. The French arrived in the immediate areas of the Djerma in 1898 at a time when the **djermakoy** of Dosso had acquired preeminence over the other Djerma chieftains (*see* DJERMAKOY; DOSSO, KINGDOM OF). From the outset an intimate link was established between the new colonizing power and the Djerma, with the latter among France's most ardent supporters in the new colony. In 1906 Djermakoy Auta helped the French put down several rebellions in the new colony, including the one fomented by the blind marabout, Seydou. As a consequence of this de facto alliance, the status of the djermakoy of Dosso, and indeed of the Djerma as a group, was elevated in the new colony.

Aggressive and aristocratic, the Djerma usually shun manual labor. Historically a loose confederation of clans and small village-states, the Djerma developed a feeling of deeper affinity only with the wars against the Fulani and the pressure from the Tuareg. Never organized into an extensive state or kingdom, the Dosso chieftainship was their largest and most prestigious polity. Due to the poor lands that they currently cultivate, many have migrated seeking work to Ghana and Ivory Coast. The Djerma language is spoken in Niger by some one million people and is part of the Songhay-Djerma group of the Nilo-Saharan family of languages. Together with the Songhay the Djerma, according to the latest census (in 1988), made up a bloc of 1.6 million, or 22 percent of the population of Niger, though they are a minority in that constellation. In most countries where they have settled (such as Benin, Ivory Coast, and Ghana) the Djerma have acquired a reputation for hard work and honesty. Djerma-Songhay political dominance in Niger (through the occupation of the presidency) came to an end with the onset of the civilian elections in 1993, which saw the rise of President Ousmane and a cabinet composed of members of a variety of ethnic groups. The second parliamentary elections (of 1995) saw a comeback of the MNSD, dominated by Songhay-Djerma, but the cabinet is unlike that of Saibou's days, when sixteen of twenty-two ministers were Songhay-Djerma.

DJERMAGANDA. Area north of Niamey on the eastern bank of the Niger River, a bastion of non-Islamized Songhay and Djerma.

DJERMAKOY. Head of the **Djerma.** There are several such chiefs, but the title usually refers to the leader of the Djerma of the Dosso region, who acquired prominence over all the other chiefs and other Djerma groups (*see* DOSSO, DJERMAKOY OF). In Dosso the djermakoy is chosen and enthroned by the **sandi** representing the indigenous pre-Djerma population—a personality of almost equal importance and an individual who is always consulted on important matters. The djermakoy is always selected from the Auta family. The djermakoy's cavalry, the *dogarey,* is very colorful and still very popular among the masses though increasingly used only for ceremonial occasions. Since the advent of national politics the djermakoy of Dosso has been an extremely powerful figure and one of the most important traditional leaders in Niger

DJERMAKOY ISSOUFOU, SAIDOU (1920–). Former politician, diplomat, and international administrator. Born on July 10, 1920, and **djermakoy of Dosso,** Issoufou Saidou had a distinguished career. He served as a counselor of the French Union (1947), member of the Grand Council of the AOF in Dakar, Senegal (1952–57), member of the French senate in Paris (1957), vice-president of the Council of Ministers of Niger (1957–58), and minister of justice (1958–59). In 1960 he was briefly attached to Hamani Diori's presidential office, and then was sent for a year to represent Niger at the U.N. On his return in 1963 he again put in two years as minister of justice (1963–65) and then joined the United Nations until his retirement as under secretary for trusteeship matters (1967–72), under secretary general for economic and social affairs (1973–78), and secretary general for technical cooperation (1978–86).

DJI, MOUKE. Minister of higher education in the February 1995 MNSD-dominated government.

DJIBO, AMADOU. Minister of youth, sports, and culture between January 1983, when he joined Kountché's cabinet, and September 1985.

DJIBO, YACOUBA (1923–68). Former minister of defense. Born in Téra in February 1923, and educated locally and at the Ecole William Ponty in Senegal, Djibo worked initially as a schoolteacher prior to becoming involved in politics. He was elected in December 1958 as UCFA (later PPN) deputy to the National Assembly and on January 3, 1959, joined Diori's cabinet as minister of stockbreeding. On December 31, 1960, he was shifted to head the Ministry of Rural Economy and on June 26, 1963, he was appointed minister of defense, serving in that capacity through 1965. Forced out of the cabinet on suspicion of being basically disloyal to the PPN (since he had rallied to the party only in 1958) after the 1965 **SAWABA** disturbances, Djibo was appointed ambassador to Belgium and the EEC. Djibo died in a car crash in Niamey on August 3, 1968.

DJINGARAYE, BANAKOYE. Last director general of Niger's development bank (BDRN), which went bankrupt and closed down in 1990.

DJINN. Among the Songhay the djinn are local spirits, protectors of villages or small localities, to whom offerings are made. According to mythology the djinn were the first inhabitants of the earth but became invisible when people were created. They continue, however, to inhabit inanimate objects, such as trees, rocks, rivers, and mountains.

DOBI, MAMANE (Lieutenant Colonel). Senior military officer, currently retired, and minister of Defense. When he was a major, Dobi was president of the State Security Court, which in 1989 tried the plotters of the 1983 attempted coup. Regarded as a liberal, he was nevertheless dismissed in 1991 from the army (where he was deputy chief of staff) by the National Conference, together with the chief of staff of the force, over the military's brutal suppression of the 1990 student disturbances in Niamey, and over the brutal massacres of Tuaregs in Aïr after an assault in Tchin Tabaraden, also in 1990. After Niger's second parliamentary elections he joined the MNSD-dominated government as minister of Defense.

DOCUMENTATION CENTERS IN NIGER. Apart from regional archival centers, some of which possess much untapped material, the following are Niger's main documentation centers and libraries: the National Archives, located behind the Ministry of Planning, containing basic legislative material on Niger and the AOF; the BRDN documentation library (currently closed with the bank in liquidation), containing 1,000 monographs and 20 periodicals; the University of Niamey library, opposite the old Muslim cemetery, containing some 20,000 volumes, with periodicals stored within faculties; the American Cultural Center library, containing 2,500 books and carrying 40 periodicals; the Franco-Nigerian Cultural Center library, opposite the Musée Nationale, with 26,000 books and 140 periodicals, significantly greater than any in Niger; the Libyan Cultural Center, containing 20,000 works; the AGRHYMET (Agrometeorological and Hydrological) Center library (opposite the university), containing some 2,500 scientific publications; the Niger River Commission Center library (near Maison d'Afrique), containing 6,500 works; the Directorate of Fairs and Expositions documentation center (opposite the SONORA building), with 450 works and 30 periodicals); the National School of Administration, 21,000 books and 50 periodicals; the INRA Center, 3,500 books and 60 periodicals on agronomical topics; the IRSH Center (behind the National Press), 15,000 books and 180 periodicals; the Ministry of Economic Affairs library, 15,000 works; the Ministry of Planning library, 5,000 works; the Office for the Promotion of Nigerian Enterprise library (in the building formerly used by the BRDN), 400 books and 25 periodicals; the ONERSOL Center library, 100 books and 15 periodicals primarily on solar energy; and the UNDP Center library, some 1,500 reports.

DODO, AISSATOU DAMBO. Minister of social development and the promotion of women in the February 1995 MNSD-dominated government.

DODO, BOUKARY (1932–). Diplomat. Born in 1932 in N'Guigmi and an educator by profession, Dodo has diplomas from schools in Mali (Sévare) and the Institute for Higher Studies in Geneva. He was appointed consul of Niger to Kano, Nigeria, in October 1965 and in 1971 was made ambassador to Algeria. Since 1980 he has been integrated within the Foreign Ministry in Niamey.

DOGAREY. The very popular cavalry of the **djermakoy of Dosso,** resplendent in their colorful tunics. The *dogarey* is used nowadays only on ceremonial occasions.

DOGONDOUTCHI. Important though small town of 13,000 people some 140 km northeast of Dosso (237 km from Niamey) in **Arewa,** of which it is the major center. The area is essentially Maouri country and center of the Bori cult, whose possession dances traditionally take place between April and June. Following the French occupation Dogondoutchi became the regional French headquarters, prompting the serkin Arewa to relocate there from his previous capital at Matankari. Dogondoutchi has an important regional market and is also the name of the arrondissement of which the town is the headquarters. The short Dogondoutchi–Matankari stretch of road is very picturesque.

DOMBOREI KWARE. Djerma for remnants of ancient villages, of great interest to archaeologists. *See also* ARCHAEOLOGY.

DOSSO. Département encompassing 40,754 sq km, a population of 730,000, and a density of 14 per sq km. The administrative capital is in the important town of the same name, which has around 12,000 people. Most of the people in the region are Djerma with minorities of Maouri, Hausa, Fulani, and Gobirawa. Dosso was founded in the eighteenth century after a period of population dislocations consequent to a tug-of-war with the Tuareg and is dominated by its white palace. It is 139 km east of Niamey. Its name derives from *do-so,* a spirit. Once an important Islamic center, Dosso is the traditional headquarters of the **djermakoy of Dosso,** the most important Djerma leader. Most of the population of the town claims chiefly descent and hence is "forbidden" to work, pay taxes or engage in commerce, living off the generosity of the djermakoy who receives a variety of gifts from his commoner subjects. The département has five arrondissements: Dosso, Boboyé, Dogondoutchi, Gaya, and Laga; and two postes administratifs: Dioundiou and Fadmey. *See also* DOSSO, KINGDOM OF.

DOSSO, DJERMAKOYS OF. The founder of the dynasty of the djermakoys of Dosso was Boukar, though eleven chiefs were to succeed him before Djermakoy Kossom truly founded the state of Dosso. Subsequent djermakoys have been: Kossom, 1856–65; Abdou, 1865–90; Alfa Atta, 1890–97; Attikou, 1897–1902; Auta, 1902–13; Moussa, 1913–24; Seydou, 1924–38; Moumouni Seydou, 1938–. Among the Djerma each clan has a djermakoy. The one from Dosso became supreme among all the djermakoy because of his noble descent and his fierce resistance to the Fulani. Eventually all the Djerma clans began to pay homage to Dosso even as the latter progressively became Islamized and fell under the sway of the amirou of Gando. In the Fulani wars of 1820–66 Dosso lost its independence, which was resurrected in the 1890s. In the contemporary era the djermakoy of Dosso is one of Niger's most important political figures and has played an important role in the evolution of national politics in Niger.

DOSSO, KINGDOM OF. Corresponding more or less with the département of Dosso, the Dosso kingdom was a Djerma chieftainship that became preeminent among the other Djerma clans because of the noble origin of its leadership and resistance to the Fulani during the invasions. Eventually Islamized and falling under the control of the amirou of Gando, Dosso did not regain its independence until the 1890s. The kingdom was not fully established as such until 1855, when Djermakoy Kossom united under his leadership all the eastern Djerma. On his death in 1865 he left behind a small kingdom stretching from Tibbo and Beri in the north to Gafiadey in the south and Bankadey and Tombokware in the east. He was succeeded (*see* DOSSO, DJERMAKOYS OF) by Abdou and Alfa Atta, and during the reign of Attikou the area became part of the French colony of Niger.

DOUASSOU, MADOUGOU. Administrator and former mayor of Zinder. Between 1968 and 1971 Douassou was sous-préfet of Mainé-Soroa. In 1971 he became mayor of Zinder, serving until 1975; he was then integrated into the Ministry of Interior serving in a wide array of capacities.

DOUBLE ELECTORAL COLLEGE. Electoral system set up by the French in their colonial territories in September 1945 under which territorial representatives were elected from two separate electoral colleges: one composed of metropolitan citizens and the other of Africans satisfying certain lower criteria. The system drastically discriminated against the electoral power of the African populations and was abolished in 1956.

DOUTCHI. *See* DOGONDOUTCHI.

DROUGHTS. Niger has been periodically ravaged by devastating droughts and famines affecting diverse regions of the country but usually Damergou, Damagaram, and Aïr. Until the major Sahel drought in 1968–74, the 1913–14 **Ka Kalaba** famine had been the most vicious in living memory. The drought of the 1970s, however, surpassed the earlier one quite easily. Droughts and famines in the twentieth century have included one in 1902—coinciding with the French occupation of the country—that saw many Hausa relocate to the Sokoto region in Nigeria; the 1913–14 famine that decimated the country; the 1919 drought that hit Djermaganda; the 1920–21 drought that affected all of southern Niger along the Nigeria border; and the 1930–31 drought in the western part of the country (in Djerma areas)—with the last two triggering major migrations from Ader (the hardest hit) to Nigeria. The recent series of Sahel droughts commenced in 1968, with progressively less rainfall each succeeding year. In 1972 there was a major migration south of ethnic groups and cattle normally resident in the areas affected as the Sahara gradually expanded southward into the Sahel. Rainfall in Agadez in 1970 was 40 mm; in 1972, 74 mm, contrasted with the thirty-year average for the city of 164 mm per year. Forty-four food and seed distribution centers were established in Aïr to assist the local population to survive the worst drought to hit Niger. Each center was headed by a committee of government officials and local notables entrusted with the equitable distribution of ration cards. Much of the grain intended for the stricken populations was not delivered, however, due to embezzlement in the cities in the south by government officials. The Tuareg of Aïr—the hardest-hit region and ethnic group—were forced to give up their nomadic patterns and congregate around boreholes southeast of Agadez, where aid was also given, and lost around 95 percent of their cattle. The town and region of Agadez greatly swelled consequent to this southward migration of refugees, and the population of Agadez itself (normally 20,000) jumped to 105,000 in 1972.

Complaints of corruption, hoarding, and speculation with grain intended for the north were often heard; indeed, one motivation of the 1974 coup was disgust with the Diori regime's callous attitude and toleration of the abuses in grain distribution. Certainly the complaints were valid, and much of the relief donated by the outside world never reached its intended recipients. Numerous examples have been cited, including forty new vehicles flown into Niamey specially at great cost to assist in grain distribution that were harnessed by politicians to act as Niamey taxis, and the storage in Zinder of 3,000 tons of grain in anticipation of even higher prices. At the height of the drought nearly 500,000 refugees from Mali (mostly Tuareg) entered Niger seeking relief. At the same time, however, some 500,000 Nigeriens had moved into Nigeria for the same reason. *See also* LAZARET.

In the mid-1980s another drought afflicted Niger. In 1985—as during the mid-1970s—**Lake Chad** shrank so much in size that it no longer extended into Niger territory, and the Niger River itself was nearly dry at Niamey—reaching its lowest levels since 1922. Though the Kountché regime's main post-1974 economic emphasis was on making Niger self-sufficient in food in case of future droughts—an effort that paid handsome dividends and gained the regime many accolades—by 1984 the country was again on its knees. It had not needed foreign aid as the dry spell expanded over much of the country in the early 1980s; by 1985, however, almost the entire population was living on food aid from abroad, with over 500,000 people totally displaced by the drought. The onset of good rains later that year allowed the country to become self-sufficient once again.

DUMI. Among the Songhay, the extended family unit. It encompasses all descendants from a common founder. Members are the **hama,** as in *si hama,* "descendants of Si."

DUPUIS YACOUBA, HENRI. *See* YACOUBA, HENRI DUPUIS.

DYA (*also* Za). Songhay dynasty established around the year 690, and ruling for some six hundred years, with the foundation of Koukya (also Goungia), the pre-Islamic capital of the Songhay. The twenty-first dya of the dynasty, in the mid–fifteenth century, revolted against the suzerainty of the Mali Empire and took office as Sonni, or Si. (The Songhay had become Muslim with the conversion of the fifteenth dya, Kosoy, at which time the center of the kingdom shifted to Gao.) Though the lineage of the kingdom remained intact, future kings were known under the new prefix, Si, or Sonni. In 1493 one of the lieutenants of Sonni Ali—one of the kingdom's greatest rulers and true founder of the **Songhay Empire**—seized power and set up the **Askia** dynasty, which itself was to be shattered with the invasion from the north of Moroccan armies in the waning years of the sixteenth century. *See also* ASKIA; SONGHAY; SONGHAY EMPIRE.

-E-

ECOLE MINIERE DE L'AIR. "Hands-on" mining school set up in 1975 in Aïr by the various mining companies in order to assist in the training of local engineers and technical staff, and as part of the mining companies' pledge to bring about a localization of staff—to the 50 percent level by 1983. The goal was not attained; indeed, by 1983 only 52 Nigeriens had graduated from the school, even as the number of mining expatriates in the cantry went up.

ECOLE NATIONALE D'ADMINISTRATION (ENA). Niger's national school of administration was set up in Niamey in 1963 to train administrative staff for the state; in 1973–74 it had a record student body of 392.

ECOLE WILLIAM PONTY. Prestigious lycée initially on Gorée Island off Dakar, Senegal, to which the creation of Francophone Africa's elite were usually admitted. Later, at Sebikotané, much of Niger's current elite attended the lycée: **Abdou Sidikou, Djibo**

Bakary, Harouna Bembello, Georges Mahaman Condat, Barcougne Courmo, Mahamane Dan Dobi, Hamani Diori, Yacouba Djibo, Pierre Foulan, Amadou Gaoh, Boubou Hama, Ibra Kabo, Noma Kaka, Garba Katambe, Leopold Kaziendé, Abderahmane Keita, Harou Kouka, Mai Maigana, Amadou Mossi.

EDUCATION. School enrollment rates have always been low in Niger, a function of the country's great distances, isolation of the northern part of its population, the economic weaknesses of the economy, and resistance to sending girls to schools. In 1927 the barely established educational network counted only 700 pupils in all the country, and this figure was modestly increased to 1,629 by 1942. Even in 1958, shortly before independence, the rate of school attendance had not risen above 2.5 percent, though it was to jump dramatically to 7.7 percent under the new Niger regime, which placed more emphasis on education. Standing at that percentage in 1968, the total of children enrolled in primary school amounted then to 77,300 (boys, 68 percent; girls, 32 percent), an increase of 556 percent over the past decade. Secondary education, lagging even more in the country, reached barely 4,100 in 1968, though this was practically a doubling of registrants from the figures of only four years previously (1964: 2,015 students). In 1968 there were also 167 students studying abroad in colleges or universities. By 1980 the rate of school attendance had gone up dramatically to 23 percent (*vis* 13 percent in 1976, itself nearly double the 1968 rate). In that year there were 230,000 primary school pupils (*vis* 139,000 in 1976), 29,607 were in secondary schools, 2,452 at the Université de Niamey, and 3,691 in various professional schools.

One educational experiment for which Niger became widely known and cited was the use of educational television. Begun in 1965 with only 80 students, by 1967 the program eventually encompassed 800 students tied in to a closed-circuit television. Though only 167 finished their courses of study, when the project was terminated in 1971 it was considered a technical success. The next phase, for some time seriously considered, would have involved an expansion of the program to include some 80 to 85 percent of all pupils in the country. The immense cost of the program prevented its implementation.

Scholarization rates increased dramatically in the 1970s but began decreasing in the 1980s as sending children for an education was deemed as less important than maintaining household incomes via their labor in light of the drought in that decade. Later, the spectacle of a regime curtailing government employment, in which over half of salaried employees find positions, further discouraged education. One should also note that many children go to Koranic schools, which deliver a modicum of general education mixed with religious training. Still, by 1989 there had been a dramatic improvement, especially as compared to the data at independence. The following are the country's scholarization rates for 1992, by départements (of interest is the fact that, compared to 1988 the rates have gone down for Dosso, Maradi, Tillabéry, and Zinder, and, despite increases, especially for Diffa, for the country as whole as well, from the earlier 36.37 to 35.46 percent): Agadez, 45 percent; Diffa, 35 percent; Dosso, 25 percent; Maradi, 20 percent; Niamey, 89 percent; Tahoua, 23 percent; Tillabéry, 25 percent; Zinder, 21 percent. The average for the entire country in 1992 stood at 35.46 percent.

EFFAD, EMOUD. Minister of industry in the first regular civilian government, between April 1993 and the October 1994 parliamentary crisis.

EFFEUY AHMED. Rocky outcropping in the eastern part of the Isseretagen massif in Aïr, site of numerous important wall engravings from ca. 515 B.C. *See* ARCHAEOLOGY.

EGUEDECH. Tuareg name for Agadez.

EGUEREW N'EGUEREW. Name of the Niger River (''River of Rivers") in Tamasheq from which, according to some scholars, the name of Niger is derived.

EL BECK, ADAM. Political newcomer and interim minister of youth appointed at the conclusion of the 1991 National Conference. El Beck served between November 1991 and March 1992.

EL MECKI. Aïr volcanic peak, 113 km north of Agadez, where **cassiterite** deposits are currently being exploited by the SMDN. The immediate vicinity of El Mecki is very scenic and is part of the tourist circuit in Aïr.

ELECTIONS, PARLIAMENTARY, OF FEBRUARY 1993. The elections of February 1993 were the first competitive and free elections of Niger since independence. Though a large number of parties initially emerged after political liberalization, considerable consolidation resulted ultimately in only 12 parties fielding some 600 candidates for the 83 seats at the new National Assembly. The consolidation resulted in two core electoral compacts emerging. With only minor realignments, they remain the political coalitions to this day. One, the Alliance des

Forces du Changement (AFC)—whose main plank was to prevent the Old Guard (former military) from a comeback via the polls, and which won a majority (50) of the 83 seats—and a restructured Mouvement National pour la Société de Développement (MNSD)—which had been the sole political party during the military era, and which won 29 seats. (Despite emerging from the elections with the largest single bloc of seats, the MNSD could find no other major partner willing to join in a government with them, and hence the AFC, a coalition of 9 much smaller parties, formed the government.) In the presidential elections the AFC coalition supported **Mahamane Ousmane,** one of the two front-runners on the first ballot, and the latter subsequently beat the MNSD candidate, **Mamadou Tandja,** a former military officer, despite his better showing on the first ballot. Ousmane's party (the CDS), is an important part of the AFC coalition, which subsequently lost its parliamentary control when one of its constituent parties (headed by the prime minister, Mahamadou Issoufou) bolted, claiming Ousmane was usurping too much power. Rather than attempting to appease the opposition, or attempting to broaden his coalition to include the MNSD opposition, Ousmane decided to call a new election, which saw the MNSD gain the upper hand and form the new government of February 1995.

The elections of 1993 were contested by the following parties (those which secured deputies have the number of their seats noted):

ALLIANCE DES FORCES DU CHANGEMENT

Convention Démocratique et Sociale (CDS), 22 seats (Mahamane Ousmane's party).

Parti Nigérien pour la Démocratie et le Socialisme (PNDS), 12 seats (Mahamadou Issoufou's party).

Alliance Nigérienne pour la Démocratie et le Progrès (ANDP), 11 seats (Djermakoy Adamou Moumouni's party).

Parti pour l'Unité Démocratique (PUND), 3 seats (Akoli Dawel's Tuareg party).

Parti Progrèssiste Nigérienne (PPN), 2 seats (remnants of Hamani Diori's party).

Union Démocratique des Forces Progrèssistes (UDFP), 2 seats.

Parti Social-Démocrate Nigérien (PSDN), 1 seat.

Union pour la Démocratie et la Progrès (UPDP).

Parti Républicaine pour les Libertés et le Progrès au Niger (PRLN).

THE OPPOSITION

Mouvement National pour la Société de Développement (MNSD), 29 seats (Hama Amadou's party).

Union des Forces Populaires pour la Démocratie et le Progrès (UDFP), 2 seats (Djibo Bakary's party).

ELECTIONS, PARLIAMENTARY, OF JANUARY 1995. The elections took place after the fall, in late 1994, of the preceding government, following the desertion from the ruling AFC coalition of the Parti Nigérien pour la Démocratie et le Socialisme (PNDS), headed by the then prime minister, Mahamadou Issoufou. In contrast to the 1993 vote, the 1995 election was marked by apathy, with only a 35 percent voter turnout, though fully 774 candidates contested the 83 seats. There were no major electoral swings in the vote, but the fact that the balance of power between the two electoral alliances (AFC and MNSD) had shifted in favor of the MNSD was confirmed when the latter won 43 of the 83 seats. In due course President Ousmane was forced to call on MNSD secretary general Hama Amadou to form the next government.

ELECTIONS, PRESIDENTIAL, OF FEBRUARY 23, AND MARCH 20, 1993. These were Niger's first free competitive presidential elections, conducted in two rounds. Of note is that the National Conference decreed that the three individuals previously holding top office could not seek the presidency (former head of state General Ali Saibou; HCR president André Salifou; and interim prime minister Amadou Cheiffou). In the first round, on February 27, the full slate of presidential aspirants presented themselves:

Candidate and Party	Percent of Votes
Mamadou Tandja (MNSD)	34.22
Mahamane Ousmane (CDS)	26.59
Mahamadou Issoufou (PNDS)	15.92
Djermakoy Adamou Moumouni (ANDP)	15.24
Illa Kané (UPDP)	2.55
Oumarou Youssoufou Garba (PPN)	1.99
Kazelma Oumar Taya (PSDN)	1.82
Djibo Bakary (UDFP)	1.68

Prior to the second round, in which only the top two candidates could compete, there was a great amount of politicking for the vote of those candidates who could not run. Ousmane, representing the nine-party coalition trying to prevent the "old" MNSD from coming back to power electorally (under a former military officer, Mamadou Tandja, to boot), pledged the two most important political leaders, Mahamadou Issoufou and Djermakoy Adamou Moumouni, the prime ministership and presidency of the National Assembly in the new government. They delivered the vote, and indeed assumed the positions promised to them. (The Supreme Court invalidated Moumouni's appointment, but he was subsequently reelected).

In the second round, on March 20, 1993, the vote was divided between the two candidates: Mahamane Ousmane, 54.8 percent, and Mamadou Tandja, 45.2 percent.

ERG. Geological term for desert regions of large sand dunes.

ESPALLARGAS, JEAN. French civil administrator. Espallargas served as deputy director, later director, of the cabinet of the French governor of Niger between 1942 and 1946 and in a variety of other administrative positions (in Madaoua, 1943–45; Birni-N'Konni, 1946–48; Zinder, 1949–50; N'Guigmi, 1951–52; Filingué, 1958–59). Director of political and administrative affairs just prior to independence (1956–57; 1959–60), he was retained for some time after independence as cabinet director of the minister of interior (1960–70).

ETTEBEL. War drum, symbol of political power among the Tuareg, and especially the Ouilliminden.

ETUDES NIGERIENNES. Irregularly published but extremely valuable series of monographs on Niger, issued since 1953 by the **Centre National de Recherches en Sciences Humaines** and corresponding bodies in Paris, where the actual printing and distribution is primarily done. Some fifty volumes have been published to date; many of the earlier ones are out of print. Mostly in the humanities and social sciences, the studies are invaluable to the serious student of Niger.

EUROPEAN DEVELOPMENT FUND (EDF). *See* FONDS EUROPEEN DE DEVELOPPEMENT.

EUROPEAN ECONOMIC COMMUNITY (EEC). Consequent to the Yaoundé conventions of 1963 and 1969, Niger has been an associate member of the EEC (now the European Union), receiving preferential tariff treatments for commodity exports and partaking of the community's technical assistance fund, the **Fonds Européen de Développement.**

EVOLUE. *See* ASSIMILATION POLICY; ASSIMILE; INDIGENAT.

-F-

FACHI. Remote oasis in the Middle of the desert in **Kaouar.** Called *Agram* by the Toubou and Kanuri of the area, Fachi is its Hausa-Tuareg name. The settlement is inhabited by roughly 1,200 people, mostly Kanuri, and is 200 km west of Bilma and 400 km east of

Agadez. Extremely isolated, Fachi has on numerous occasions been pillaged by marauding bands, including one major assault in 1911 by a combined force of Toubou, Tuareg, and Ouled Sliman. It is fortified by an eight-to-ten-meter-tall wall made out of **natron**—which in this area is more prevalent than stone—and has extensive salt pans, though they are not quite so large as those of Bilma. Fachi has abundant subterranean water and palm trees and date groves, though it depends for everything else upon the **azalay** caravans.

FADAMA. Hausa name for the **Dallol Maouri,** also known as the Dallol Raffi.

FAKARA. Meaning literally "desert," Fakara is the vast arid plateau between the Niger River and the Dallol Basso that has a mean elevation of 250 meters.

FALLAKAM. Small chiefdom in Ader that owed allegiance to **Darey** before being crushed and dispersed by the Tuareg victories of **Aggaba.** Reestablishing its chiefdom at Sehia, the village was brutally massacred by the Voulet-Chanoine ravages of 1899 (*see* MISSION AFRIQUE CENTRALE). Considered indigenous to Ader, most of the population is currently dispersed among other villages further to the south.

FEDERATION DES ETUDIANTS DE L'AFRIQUE NOIRE EN FRANCE (FEANF). Militant union of Francophone Africa's students in France, with branches in most university cities. Several of Niger's current intellectuals and professionals played a role in the FEANF during their student days.

FETISHISM. Throughout southern, and non-Muslim, areas in Niger there are numerous fetishist or spirit cults, the principal ones being the **Bori** initiation and possession rites among the Hausa and the **holey** among the Songhay.

FEZZAN–BORNU TRAIL. One of the oldest trans-Saharan caravan trails connecting Fezzan (in southern Libya) via the Kaouar with Bornu. Though the trail has seen vacillations in traffic over the centuries, it was the most popular route until the 1820s when it suffered from unsettled conditions at both terminals. This eroded its general security by increased banditry, especially by the Toubou and Tuareg, and shifted the caravan patterns east and west of the traditional route.

FIHROUN (1885?–1916). **Amenokal** of the Ouilliminden who raised an anti-French revolt in 1914. Assuming leadership of the confederation in October 1902, Fihroun accepted French suzerainty but schemed to achieve independence. His clashes with the Kunta—traditional enemies of the Tuareg—brought greater French intervention, and finally Fihroun rebelled against the colonial authority. Having joined in the Grand Sanusi's call for a jihad in Fezzan in 1914, Fihroun was arrested in October of the same year, condemned to ten years imprisonment and twenty years exile and exiled to Timbuktu. Through flattery he succeeded in having himself transferred to Gao and from there escaped on February 13, 1916, declaring a jihad on the French infidel. He then marched on Filingué, placing the outpost under siege. His assault coincided with the drought of 1914 and its aftereffects. Had he succeeded in the battle the entire Dallol Bosso, the granary of Niger, would have been his. The assault was, however, badly organized and failed disastrously. His force was decimated by superior firepower of the French, and Fihroun himself died on June 25, 1916, some 150 km east of Menaka. Only six months later all of Aïr was to burst out in revolt under the leadership of another Tuareg chieftain, **Kaocen.**

FILINGUE. Important and historic Hausa town, 187 km from Niamey and 256 km from Tahoua, with a population of nearly 10,000, up from 7,051 in 1970. Also an arrondissement within the Niamey département with a population of 250,000. On the right side of the Dallol Boboy, at the foot of the fault, Filingué is the site of a major convergence of several ethnic groups. A very picturesque town (though with few tourist amenities), its huge Sunday market brings into town large camel and cattle herds and Tuareg, Hausa, Fulani, and Djerma traders.

FONA. Great Tuareg warrior chief. Dissident chief of the Kel Tafidet, Fona succeeded in imposing himself over all the Kel Owey of the east, and personally participated in all the anti-French campaigns in Aïr, Damergou, and Tibesti. One of **Kaocen**'s prime lieutenants, he directed resistance in Tibesti, remaining in Tripolitania after the collapse of the Agadez siege. He later (1918) participated in the sacking of Fachi. He was finally caught and imprisoned in Kano, Nigeria, then shipped off to Zinder, dying in prison in Niamey.

FONDS D'AIDE ET DE COOPERATION (FAC). French financial and technical-assistance development fund, the successor, after the independence of Francophone Africa, of the **Fonds d'Investissement pour le Développement Economique et Social des Territoires d'Outre-Mer.** During the period 1980–1987, Niger received from FAC annually between 20 and 60 million French francs, for a grand total of 269,296,000 French francs.

FONDS DE DOTATION POUR L'AMELIORATION DE LA PRODUCTIVITE RURALE (FDAPR). State organ, created in September 1973, to spur and assist Niger's rural economy. With headquarters in Niamey, the FDAPR had a board with representatives from the Ministries of Finance, Rural Economy, Economic Affairs, and Development and Cooperation, and the director of the UNCC.

FONDS D'INTERVENTION EN FAVEUR DES PETITES ET MOYENNES ENTREPRISES NIGERIENNES (FIPMEN). Fully state-owned innovative bank, set up to assist small- and medium-sized Nigerian enterprises. Under Director General Ibrahim Beidari the bank has been profitable.

FONDS D'INVESTISSEMENT POUR LE DEVELOPPEMENT ECONOMIQUE ET SOCIAL DES TERRITOIRES D'OUTRE-MER (FIDES). Established on April 30, 1946, and the precursor of the contemporary **Fonds d'Aide et de Coopération,** FIDES was the development fund that dispensed development capital to the French colonial territories following the Second World War. Between 1949 and 1960 some $26 million was granted to Niger, mostly for projects to increase food production and spur export commodities.

FONDS EUROPEEN DE DEVELOPPEMENT (FED). The European Development Fund is an agency of the European Community, with which most of Africa is associated. The FED dispenses the community's economic and technical assistance to member and associate states. Niger has received funds totaling 31,291 million ECUs for the first FED program, 30,371 million ECUs for the second, and 23,500 million ECUs for the third (1970–74) program. Between 1974 and 1984 Niger received 76,815 million ECUs, plus a share of the regional allocations of 87,372 ECUs.

FONDS NATIONAL D'INVESTISSEMENT (FNI). National investment fund, first of its kind in Francophone Africa. Set up by the Niger government in 1969 to replace all other previous development funds and the state's equipment budget. Contributions come from foreign sources (especially France) and from uranium receipts, and are used for general development purposes. Reaching 21 billion CFA francs in 1978, the FNI has been a major force for the socioeconomic development of Niger. In the 1980s contributions from abroad as well as local allocations plummeted in light of the global recession and Niger's tight economic straits.

FORCES DEMOCRATIQUES NIGERIENNES (FDN). The name of the territorial section in Niger of the Convention Africaine interterritorial party. The FDN was essentially the post–February 24, 1957, name of the UNIS party, by then badly truncated by desertions. *See also* POLITICAL PARTIES.

FOULANI, PIERRE (1939–). Professor at the University of Niamey. Born in Zaziatou, near Dogondoutchi, in 1939, and educated in Zinder, Tahoua, and at the Ecole William Ponty in Senegal (1957–60), Foulani continued his higher education at Abidjan's Centre d'Enseignement Supérieur, obtaining a number of certificates in physics and chemistry. He then taught for one year (1963–64) at the Ecole Normale in Zinder before going to the University of Bordeaux (1964–70), where he obtained his D.Sc. in chemistry (1967) and D.Sc. in physics (1970). Between 1967 and 1970 he also served as an engineer with the CNRS in Bordeaux and between 1970 and 1971 as principal engineer at Grenoble's Center for Nuclear Studies. Since 1971 he has served as professor of physics, and in 1972 also assumed the directorship of the School of Science at the University of Niamey. In the 1980s he was promoted and serves as dean of the Faculty of Sciences and vice-rector of the university. He has published a number of scholarly papers and also serves on the Franco-Niger Commission on Uranium and on the Inter-Ministerial Technical Committee on Uranium.

FOUMAKOYE, GADO (1950–). Academic and former minister of mines. Born in 1950 and holding a degree in chemistry from a French university, Foumakoye teaches at the Pedagogical School of the University of Niamey. In April 1993 he was appointed minister of mines and served until the government fell after the October parliamentary crisis.

FRANC ZONE. Monetary-transaction association formed by most of the territories previously ruled by France, including the Communauté Financière Africaine. National or regional currencies (such as the CFA franc) are pegged to the French franc, guaranteed by France, and freely convertible into other hard currencies. Transfers within the franc zone, which is under French fiscal control, are free.

FRENCH OCCUPATION. The first European explorers of what later became Niger were **Heinrich Barth** and Edward Vogel, who during 1853–55 went from Niger to Chad via Say, Sokoto, Zinder, Gouré, and Kouka (Bornu). In 1870 Gustav Nachtigal, also on his way to Chad, passed along the classic Fezzan–Bornu route touching on Bilma and N'Guigmi in Niger, and in 1891–92 Lieutenant Colonel Monteil crossed the Niger at Say going as far as Bilma via Sokoto and N'Guigmi. Following these first exploratory visits, in December 1897 a thirty-seven-man mission was sent to the court of Damagaram at Zinder, and onward to Chad, led by Captain Cazemajou. Originally well received, Cazamajou was later assassinated by a court faction fearing France's real intentions, and the column retreated. Following that debacle, the infamous Voulet-Chanoine mission was dispatched primarily to punish Damagaram and to explore further the Niger-Chad territories. Its unintended swath of destruction even prior to arrival in Damagaram was terminated by the death of the two officers. The column—under new command—attacked Zinder to avenge Cazemajou's death, killing Sultan Ahmadou in Roumji on September 13, 1899. Consequently the Third Military Territory was set up to encompass the area of Sabon-Haoussa up to Zinder.

In 1901 Agadez was conquered with a force of seventy troops, and other areas began to feel the French presence. In adjudicating various interclan and interethnic disputes that the French encountered (especially among the Tuareg), the French helped those groups willing to assist them in their push toward Chad and in the impending battle with Rabah. A decisive battle with the Kel Gress ensued in Damergou, following which many of the latter clan migrated to Chad. Several of these clans continued east all the way to Sudan before trickling back to Niger fully thirty years later. The French authority among the Tuareg was also disputed in numerous instances and led to several violent revolts, including those of **Fihroun** and of **Kaocen.** In the south periodic anti-French resentments erupted both in the form of localized revolts and in the form of various religious or quasi-religious cults. *See also* REBELLIONS.

FRENCH UNION. Structure established under the French constitution of October 1946 allowing a measure of representation to French colonial territories in the decision-making process in Paris. The French Union was composed of metropolitan France and her territories, which were classified as Overseas Territories, Overseas Departments, Associated Territories, Protectorates, and Associated States. The mainland African colonies fell under the Overseas Territories heading. The union had a president (the president of France), a High Council, and an Assembly in which deputies from all the various territories participated. The provisions also included African representation in the two houses of the French parliament and in the economic council. In 1945 one deputy to the National Assembly was allocated to Niger, and on November 10, 1946, Hamani Diori won the seat. On April 1, 1948, a second seat was allocated to the colony, and shortly thereafter Georges Mahaman Condat won it.

FRENCH WEST AFRICA. *See* AFRIQUE OCCIDENTALE FRANCAISE.

FRENCH WEST AFRICA, GOVERNORS OF (1895–1959):

1895–1900	J. B. Chandié
1900–1902	N. E. Ballay
1902–8	E. N. Roume
1908–16	W. Merlaud-Ponty
1916–17	M. F. Clozel
1917–18	J. Van Vollenhoven
1918–19	G. L. Angoulvant
1919–23	M. H. Merlin
1923–30	J. G. Carde
1930–36	J. Brevié
1936–40	J. M. de Coppet
1940	L. H. Cayla
1940–43	P. F. Boisson
1943–46	P. C. Cournarie
1946–48	R. V. Barthez
1948–51	P. L. Bechard
1951–56	B. Cornut-Gentille
1956–58	G. Cusin
1958–59	P. A. Messmer

FRONT DE LIBERATION DE L'AIR ET DE L'AZAWAD (FLAA). Originally a broad Tuareg liberation front, from which several splinter groups seceded in June 1993, namely the ARLN and the FLT. The front is the only one claiming to represent both Aïr and Azawak. Headed by Ghissa ag Boula, who is also vice-president of the rebel coordinating group, the Coordination de la Résistance Armée (CRA), the FLAA has between 400 and 800 men, some heavily armed with matériel from remnants of Hissene Habre's army after the latter was ousted in Chad. The FLAA operates on a minimalist platform of the ouster of Nigerien armed forces and the establishment of a decentralized federal system in Niger. Its external sponsor is Algeria.

FRONT DE LIBERATION DE TEMUST (FLT). Tuareg liberation movement operating in the Temust region, until June 1993 part of the FLAA. Headed by **Mano Dayak,** the FLT is not part of the **Coordination de la Résistance Armée,** which was set up on September 1993 and chaired by Dayak, who is its spokesman in Paris.

FRONT DEMOCRATIQUE NIGERIENE (FDN-Mountounchi). Political party set up in January 1995 as a result of the merger of the Parti Progressiste Nigérien with another small party. It continued being led by the former's Oumarou Youssoufou Garba as chairman, with Mohamad Mudur as its secretary general.

FRONT DEMOCRATIQUE UNI (FDU). Short-lived grouping in the late 1980s of some of the main forces opposing General Saibou's regime in Niger. The front disbanded with the democratizations of 1991.

FRONT ISLAMIQUE ARABE DE L'AZAWAD (FIAA). Distinct from the other largely Tuareg liberation fronts, the FIAA groups the Arab clans into a liberation movement in Azawak, operating parallel to their Tuareg counterparts of the FPLA. The FIAA has fundamentalist religious goals as well. The front was one of the several splinter groups to secede from the MPLA after the latter signed peace accords in Mali.

FRONT NIGERIEN NATIONAL (FNN). Political party set up in February 1993 by Fulani leaders who believe their community continues to be marginalized in Niger, being bypassed by the liberalizations of the 1990s. The party is headed by Secretary General Salifou Sadikou.

FRONT OUMMA ISLAMIQUE (FOI). Moribund Islamic fundamentalist party. Fundamentalist Islam has gained strength in Niger as in neighboring countries, and Muslim/animist clashes have taken place in various regions. In November 1990 several Muslim leaders announced they would register the FOI as a political party. Internal divisions within the Muslim community and tactical political considerations have prevented the party from playing a role to date.

FRONT PATRIOTIQUE DE LIBERATION DU SAHARA (FPLS). Tuareg liberation army, comprising some two hundred warriors claiming sovereignty over the Niger's Saharan regions. Headed by Mohamad Anako, the front was created in January 1994, and its sphere of operations is the same as those of the Armée Révolutionnaire de Libération du Nord Niger (ARLN).

FRONT POPULAIRE DE LIBERATION DE L'AZAWAD (FPLA). Tuareg liberation movement in Azawak, until 1991 part of the MPLA. After the latter entered into negotiations for peace in Mali, it declared its autonomous existence.

FRONT POPULAIRE POUR LA LIBERATION DU NIGER (FPLN). Organization set up with the aim of overthrowing the Kountché regime in Niger. Headed by **Hamani Diori**'s son, **Abdoulaye Diori,** and Khamed Moussa (former cabinet director of the Ministry of Defense), the FPLN recruited mostly disgruntled Tuareg and was involved in several raids in Niger in the mid-1980s, and especially on May 29, 1985. Based in Tripoli, Libya, it had a coordinating office in

Tamanrasset in Algeria. Abdoulaye Diori's efforts on behalf of his father resulted in the latter's being imprisoned anew. Several of the key leaders of the FPLN in the 1990s joined in the Tuareg uprising. *See also* TUAREG REBELLION.

FRONT POUR LA DEMOCRATIQUE RENOUVEAU (FDR). New rebel movement that emerged in southeast Niger in March 1995. Operating near Lake Chad, and composed of Toubou, Shoa Arabs, and Kanuri, the movement is armed by remnants from Hissene Habre's army, encamped in the region since 1990 when the latter was ousted from power in Chad. The force of possibly two hundred people has carried out a number of assaults on nearby villages. It has not yet issued any specific manifesto.

FULANI. Large ethnic group known in English and Hausa under this name, as *Peul* in French, *Fellata* in Kanuri, *Fula* in Senegal and Guinea, *Fulbe* or *Ful Be* (their own name, with *Pullo* being the singular), and at times as *Bororo*. The Fulani are a mostly Muslim (*see* BORORO) people estimated at over sixteen million (according to some scholars, many more) scattered throughout West and Equatorial Africa, but found in larger numbers especially in northern Nigeria, Niger, Mali, Guinea, Senegal, and Cameroon. Their language is Fulfulde, which exists in several dialects. As cattle-owning, nomadic groups, they are known as Bororo, or *Bororoje* (which refers to their red, long-horned zebu cattle) in the Chad-Niger-Cameroon area, where they speak the purest Fulfulde and are least affected by Islam. This group is also sometimes referred to as *Wodabe* or *Wodaabe* Bororo, the former word meaning "People of Taboos."

Coming from the west with their cattle, the Fulani were not united until the rise of Othman Dan Fodio in the nineteenth century. Their distant and even recent past and origins have always been clouded with mystery, but many scholars have assumed an Ethiopian, and a few have posited a possibly Jewish, origin. They rose to prominence in north Nigeria under Othman Dan Fodio, supplanting the various Hausa principalities long established there. In February 1804 a jihad was declared against all the enemies of Islam, and by 1810 four of the seven Hausa states—Katsina, Kano, Zaria, and Daura—had fallen to the Fulani armies, and Sokoto, the city from which the new empire was to be ruled, had been founded. At the same time segments of the Bornu Empire to the east, already aged and crumbling, were detached from it, and constant pressure was exerted upon unconquered or refugee states, such as Maradi and Damagaram in Niger. (Indeed, much of the history of Maradi, after the restoration of Hausa rule there, has been the military tug-of-war with Fulani Katsina.) Othman Dan

Fodio (a preacher born in Gobir and brought up strictly in the Maliki rite) died in 1817 and was succeeded by Bello.

Niger's 1988 census placed the number of Fulani in Niger at about 650,000, constituting 9 percent of the country's population. Many of these, especially along the Niger River, have become totally sedentary and have picked up the local language and the Hausa practice of the **Bori** cult. Most Fulani migrated to Niger (from north Nigeria) during the colonial era.

FULBE. *See* FULANI.

FULFULDE. Language of the **Fulani.**

-G-

GADJO, MAITOURARE MOHAMMADOU (1926–). Personal assistant of former president Diori. Born in October 1926 in Djoulgoua (in the Gouré district) and trained as an administrative secretary, Gadjo became deputy director of President Diori's presidential office cabinet in January 1959, losing his post only with the eruption of the 1974 coup d'état. Prior to 1959 he served on the staff of the French governor's personal cabinet. Gadjo also occupied a variety of other positions delegated to him by Diori. In March 1962 he assumed the post of counselor to the Supreme Court, and he has also been deputy director of SONARA, and director of economic affairs of SEPANI between 1971 and 1974. Accused of fraud and embezzlement after the 1974 coup, Gadjo's personal property was confiscated. Shortly thereafter he was arrested for complicity in the plot against Kountché by Major **Sani Souna Sido.** He was still in prison in 1995.

GADO, ABDOU (1930–). Former director of the Banque de Développement de la République du Niger (BDRN). Born in 1930 in Madaoua and educated in Madaoua, Maradi, and Niamey, Gado joined the Treasury of Niger in 1948 after completing secondary school. Eleven years later, at independence, he attended a two-year advanced training course in external treasury services, following which he was appointed treasury inspector and, also in 1961, head of the cashiers service at the BDRN. In 1966 he was promoted to inspector at BDRN, and in 1969 director of the bank, a post he held until the April 1974 coup d'état. During 1973–74 he also served as president of the Administrative Council of SICONIGER.

GADO, BOUBE (1944–). Archaeologist. Born in 1944 and educated in Dakar and in Paris where he secured his Ph.D. in 1978, Gado is attached to IRSH in Niamey. He has written several books on the archaeology and oral traditions of Niger.

GADO, SABO (1928–). Longtime deputy and traditional leader. Born in 1928 in Mayahi and by training a farmer, Gado was a local chef de canton before being elected to the National Assembly in 1958. He remained deputy until the 1974 coup d'état. In 1965 he also became the Assembly's third vice-president.

GAFAI. Temporary (1810–20) capital of the Katsinawa after their defeat and expulsion by the Fulani in 1807. On the border between Damagaram and Maradi (then a former Katsina province under Fulani rule), Gafai was abandoned in favor of Maradi once Fulani rule was terminated by a popular upheaval in that center.

GALADIMA. In the pre-Fulani Hausa Katsina, and in the successor Hausa state of Maradi, head of the royal palace household, holding the same rank as the **kaura.** Usually a eunuch. Also, the senior civil administrator and supervisor of territories south of the Karaduwa River, including the vassal states of Maska, Gwari, and Kogo. The title is also to be found in several non-Hausa areas, including in Chad.

GALLE, ETIENNE PAUL (1936–). Educator. Born on August 20, 1936, and having studied literature at the universities of Ouagadougou and Abidjan, Gallé teaches English and English poetry at the University of Niamey.

GAMKALLE. Niamey quarter (originally a small suburban village) at the eastern extremity of the city, and site of a military camp. It is mostly (90 percent) populated by Djerma, and Niamey's abbatoir is located in the quarter.

GANDA, OUMAROU (1935–81). One of Niger's greatest cinematographers and actors. Born in 1935, Ganda was assisted in his career by **Jean Pierre Rouch.** Two of Ganda's films—*Wazzou Polygame* (1972) and *Cabascabo* (1969)—have in particular been acclaimed, the latter being a Cannes Festival prizewinner.

GANDAH, DJIBO. Diplomat. An educator by training, Gandah had been director of general affairs and judicial and cultural matters at the Ministry of Foreign Affairs (1962–64), deputy head of the Protocol Section (1964–65), director of the cabinet of the foreign minister (1965–66), and consul to Dahomey (1966–69). In 1970 he was promoted to ambassadorial rank, remaining in Dahomey until 1973. In that year he came home to a senior consultancy position in the Foreign Ministry, and later assumed administration of a state enterprise.

GANDE-BERI. The name by which the famine of 1914 is known among the Djerma. Equivalent to **Ka Kalaba** among the Hausa. *See also* DROUGHTS.

GANI, ISSAKA (1936–). Journalist and media specialist. Born in 1936 in Gaya, and educated locally, in Dosso, and in Niamey, Gani attended journalism school in Paris (1959–60) and upon his return to Niger was appointed director of programs at Radio Niger. In 1961 he was transferred to Zinder as director of that station, and in 1963 underwent specialized training in France. Upon his return the next year he became editor in chief of Radio Niger. He occupied a number of similar posts, all within the official communications media, including a period (1961–64) as director as ORTN—the Radio and Television Organization of Niger—before shifting in 1974 to become technical councillor at the Ministry of Information. He has since worked as an editor with one of Niamey's newspapers.

GANTE. Very big fish market on the Niger River.

GAO. Capital of the Songhay and Gao empires since 1010. Founded earlier, around 850, and at the outset also known as Kaw Kaw, Gao became the capital after the Islamization of the Songhay, replacing **Koukya** as capital. In the fourteenth century the scholar and adventurer Ibn Batuta visited Gao and described it as one of the largest and finest Sudanese towns. It was conquered by Moroccan troops in 1595, following which it went into a long decline. In it are found the tombs of the **Askias,** though in reality only one tomb remains. On the Niger River, it is the terminus of vessels from Mopti, and it is well connected by tracks and unpaved roads to both Niger and Algeria. At the time of the Songhay and Mali empires the town was also an important caravan entrepôt as the juncture of several important cross-Saharan routes. Currently the town of 25,000 is within the Republic of Mali.

GAO EMPIRE. *See* SONGHAY EMPIRE.

GAO N'GAZO. Temporary **Gobirawa** capital near Sabon Birni set up in 1823 and deserted in 1831, at the time of the anti-Fulani revolt.

GAOH, ABDOU (1922–). Former chef du cabinet of President Hamani Diori, key PPN official and secretary of the PPN politburo between 1956 and 1974. Born in Matankari in 1922 and of Maouri ethnic origin, the son of the chef de canton and traditional chief of Dogondoutchi, Gaoh acquired his education in Konni, Maradi, and Niamey and worked for three years (1940–43) as an assistant teacher in Dosso. Between 1943 and 1949 a commercial agent, he was dismissed for his activities on the part of the PPN. Between 1949 and 1953 he was the party's full-time secretary (and member of the executive committee), though in 1953 he had to resign the post in order to enter the civil service as an employee of the Treasury. With the rise to power of the PPN Gaoh was appointed Diori's chef de cabinet with a variety of responsibilities for PPN party activities, serving in this capacity until the 1974 coup d'état. A cofounder of the party in 1946, he served on its executive committee between 1949 and 1974. He was also secretary of the PPN Youth Wing (1955–56) and from 1956 to 1974 its president, as well as secretary of the Civil Servants Union. From 1964 to 1972 Gaoh was also president of the Niger Football Association. After the coup his personal property was confiscated, on the grounds of having been acquired through fraudulent means, and he was imprisoned. He was not released from prison until Kountché's death and the rise to power of General Saibou.

GAOH, AMADOU (1925–). Veteran Assembly deputy, unionist, and administrator. Born in 1925 in Matankari, and educated locally and at Dakar's Ecole William Ponty, Gaoh was involved in union activities at an early age and served as secretary general of the Civil Servants Union (until 1957) and leader of several other unions. An old PPN stalwart, Gaoh served on the latter's politburo until 1957 and on its steering committee through 1965. President of the party's Arewa branch, he was elected deputy to the Assembly in 1957, serving until the 1974 coup d'état, and holding a number of posts including that of financial officer (1958–74). He was also appointed to various administrative posts, such as director general of SONUCI (Société Nigérienne d'Urbanisme et de Construction Immobilière) and of SONARA, and between 1971 and 1974 was also commissioner of finance. A powerful personality in the outer periphery of Diori's clique in Niamey, Gaoh was purged from all positions of importance after the 1974 coup d'état, and he retired.

GAOH, BOUBACAR OUMAROU (1946–). Economist. Born in 1946 and educated in France where he secured a Ph.D. in finance, Gaoh was appointed on his return to Niger administrative director of programs and planning at the Ministry of Planning.

GAOH, DODY (1906–73). Former mayor of Niamey. Born in 1906 in Matankari to a chiefly family, and by profession an administrator, Gaoh served with the Ministry of Interior as subprefect of Illela, and between July 20, 1966, and August 12, 1968, as mayor of Niamey. Between 1967 and 1972 he also served as counselor to the Constitutional Chamber of the Supreme Court. He died on March 25, 1973.

GARAMANTIAN ROUTE. Caravan trail dating back to antiquity and linking Tripoli via Fezzan and Kaouar with the Bornu Empire. Control over the route constituted one of the major sources of wealth of ancient Carthage. Despite attempts to monopolize the route completely and to expand trade with the south, traffic was quite modest until the introduction of the camel by Rome in the first century A.D. *See also* CARAVAN ROUTES; FEZZAN–BORNU TRAIL.

GARBA, AHMED. Former secretary general of the Union Nationale des Travailleurs Nigériens, and head of the Service des Prestations Familiales de la Caisse Nationale de Securité. Following the 1974 coup d'état, Garba was promptly jailed on a host of charges and was not released until 1978.

GARBA, AMADOU. Former director general of the Union Nigérienne de Crédit et de Coopération.

GARBA, BELLO TIOUSSO. Political leader, head of a small, post-1991 political party—the Union pour la Démocratie et le Progrès (UDP-Amintchi)—aligned behind the anti-MNSD AFC alliance.

GARBA, DJIBO. Minister of secondary and higher education between April 1993 and the fall of the government in October 1994.

GARBA, ISSA (1898–1980). Former magistrate. Born in 1898 in Tondigamey and of Djerma ethnic origin, Garba was a veteran of the French colonial armies. He had a long administrative career that included serving as a court interpreter, a municipal councillor of Niamey, propaganda secretary of the PPN party, and after 1963 a member of the Conseil de Circonscription of Niamey. Between February 1967 and 1974 he served also as a judge in the Chambre de Contrôle de l'Instruction. Garba was one of the more influential PPN leaders in the Niamey region.

GARBA, OUMAROU (1931–). Former mayor of Niamey. Born in Dosso in 1931 and educated locally and in Paris (IIAP) with a certificate in law and economics, Garba served as principal comptroller of posts and communications for many years, and on the editorial board of *Le Niger* (until 1970). He was appointed director of the Caisse Nationale de Compensations, des Prestations Familiales et des Accidents de Travail (that is, the social security center) on January 1, 1965, and in 1971 became director of political affairs at the Ministry of Interior, a major promotion. In 1974 Garba was appointed mayor of Niamey, reverting to administrative duties in the Ministry of Interior a few years later. He is currently retired.

GARBA, OUMAROU YOUSSOUFOU (1940–). Former diplomat and current leader of the PPN political party in Niger. Born in Oungouar Rondji (Maradi) on March 15, 1940, and educated in Nigeria, England, and the U.S. (at American University in Washington, D.C.), Garba was with the Niger embassy to the U.S. as first secretary and head of protocol (June 1967 to January 1972), and as councillor (1972–74). Early in 1975 he was appointed ambassador to Nigeria and Cameroon, and served in a string of other postings until the mid-1980s when he returned to Niger. With the liberalizations of the 1990s Garba revived the PPN political party for the 1993 legislative elections, and also presented his candidacy for the presidential elections the same year. He garnered only a very small vote in each. In January 1995 Garba joined forces with another small splinter group to create a new party, the Front Démocratique Nigérien (FDN-Mountounchi), with Mohamad Mudur as secretary general and Garba as president.

GARBA, SAIDOU MAIGA. Key aide to **Mamadou Tandja,** especially during the latter's candidacy in the 1993 presidential elections, when he served as MNSD press attaché.

GARBA, SOUNAKOYE. Administrator. Formerly with the Ministry of Finance as deputy director of the budget and of the central accountancy services (since 1966), Garba joined the Ministry of Interior of 1970 and was appointed subprefect of the Tahoua arrondissement. In 1974 he was shifted back to the central administration in Niamey.

GARDE REPUBLICAINE. Former president Diori's personally loyal, elitist Tuareg Presidential Guard. The Garde Républicaine put up a fight before succumbing to the 1974 assault that toppled the Diori regime, and was subsequently totally restructured. It was placed under the command of Captain Moussa Hassane, one of President Kountché's cousins, and expanded, at one stage, to a force of 2,000. Trained by Moroccan officers who maintained high visibility in the Presidential Palace, the guard was one of the major props of both Kountché and Saibou, and played a major role in several military and civilian military skirmishes, including in the brutal suppression of the February 1990 student demonstrations and the Tuareg assaults in Aïr. Following a specific decision made in November 1991 by the

National Conference that ushered in civilian rule, the unit was dismantled on March 10, 1992, and its personnel dispersed among the country's other security forces.

GARI. "Village" in Hausa. The plural is *garuruwa*.

GAROUL. *See* DENDI.

GATE-GATE. One of the several names given by the local population to the rampaging Voulet-Chanoine column (*see* MISSION AFRIQUE CENTRALE). The term is Djerma; in other areas the local equivalent is *Sara-Sara*.

GATI, ALI (Marabout). Colonial-era marabout and leader of the Hamallist religious order that agitated for the emancipation of the **Bella** and other social groups oppressed (mostly by the Tuareg) in Niger. Arrested, imprisoned, and exiled for his various activities, Gati was amnestied in 1958, when he was finally allowed to return to Niger.

GAUTIER, EMILE-FELIX (1864–1940). French explorer and author. Established in Algeria where he was in charge of teaching African geography, Gautier explored parts of the Sahara Desert (as well as Madagascar), publishing accounts of his travels and discoveries in several books.

GAYA. Small town of 4,500 on the Benin-Niger border, demarcated by the Niger River, which is spanned by the Malanville Bridge. Also an arrondissement of 100,000 people. It is the main crossing point for much of Niger's imports and exports that use the OCDN railway and the port of Cotonou in Benin.

GAZERE, OUSMAN (Lieutenant Colonel). General Saibou's last minister of public health, Gazeré joined the cabinet in May 1989 and stayed in his ministry until September 1991 when the HCR government took over.

GAZOBI, ISSAKA (1943–). Physician and head of gynecological services at Niamey Hospital. Gazobi was educated at the University of Dakar Medical School and teaches at the University of Niamey.

GHADAMSI. Powerful merchants from Ghadames—an oasis south of Tripoli, in contemporary Libya. Called *Adamusawa* in Hausa, Ghadamsi had been established in small numbers in many centers in

Niger until the early years of the colonial area. Their economic power was far out of proportion to their actual numbers (for example, in 1899 there were only ten in Zinder and twelve in Djadjihouma); they were among the principal organizers and financial backers of trans-Saharan trade, many forming trading chains from the Mediterranean coast all the way to Kano. Their prime importance was in providing a bridge between the coastal communities, the economic condition of which they were familiar with, and the interior countries. With the decline of the caravan trade they either returned to Libya or settled permanently in some of the larger urban centers in the interior. In the case of the Niger communities, most relocated further south in northern Nigeria, especially Kano.

GIDA. The basic unit of the extended family, in Hausa. The supreme authority within it is called the *mai gida.*

GOBIR. Currently a district in the northern part of Sokoto state in Nigeria. For the history of the precolonial kingdom and people, *see* GOBIRAWA.

GOBIRAWA. Hausa ethnic group, founders of an important and powerful kingdom, Gobir, prior to its conquest early in the nineteenth century by the Fulani. Their origins are controversial, possibly traceable to Egypt—oral traditions refer to Istanbul—and they allegedly have a vague recollection of the ancient Israelites there. Possibly of mixed ethnic origin (with Toubou, or more likely some Semitic infusions), in the contemporary era they are not significantly different from other Hausa groups.

The Gobirawa first arrived in Bilma in the seventh century, led by Bana Tourmi, and then moved to Aïr where they settled, mixing with existing Hausa communities to form the Gobirawa people. In the twelfth century another clan arrived in Aïr, but Tuareg pressure from the north forced them to migrate south. Their capital for over two centuries was Birni-Lallé, which in Hausa means "citadel of well-being." From there they spread into the Konni and Maradi regions (in the seventeenth century), with their capital eventually shifting to Alkalawa, some 10 km northwest of Sabon Birni, both currently in Nigeria, and spreading their control over Sokoto, Kebi, Arewa, Ader, Dendi, and Konni, displacing in particular the Zamfara. Continually under pressure from the Tuareg, and fighting Katsina power in the eighteenth century, Gobir was crushed by Fulani armies led by Mohammed Bello. Alkalawa was placed under siege, pillaged, and its king killed (in 1804), with Gobir becoming a Fulani tributary state. In 1815 Alkalawa was abandoned in favor of Kadaye. A short-lived rebellion led to the latter's sacking and the founding of yet another capital at Dakourawa, 35 km southwest of Madaoua, which was also destroyed by the Fulani. One other attempt at independence also failed—and their new capital at Birni-N'Kounia was sacked in 1823—before hostilities died off for a decade. Based around Gao n'Gazo (near Sabon Birni) a new revolt flared in 1831, and Dakourawa was reestablished as the renascent Gobirawa capital, in alliance with Maradi. The revolt failed, and in 1835 the Gobirawa were again crushed—a major disaster—and many of the Gobirawa retreated to the Maradi area to regroup. Eventually Gobir's independence was reasserted at Tibiri. In 1860 a dissident Gobirawa faction seceded and, allied with the Sokoto Fulani, established Sabon Birni as a competing Gobirawa center which, developing into a major focal point of antiestablishment Gobirawa resistance, was eventually conquered by the legitimate forces of Gobir in Tibiri.

The current serkin Gobir, Muhammadu Bawa, in Nigeria, is a descendant of Serkin Gobir Babari, who led the Gobirawa forces in the eighteenth century in displacing the Zamfara. Enthroned in 1975 he resides in Sabon Birni. The former Gobir state lies partly in Niger and partly in Nigeria. The Gobirawa are to be found today in an arc from Maradi to Madaoua.

GOUNGUIA. *See* KOUKYA.

GOURE. Arrondissement of 102,000 people in the département of Zinder, with headquarters in the town of Gouré, which has an estimated population of 3,900, and is 170 km east of Zinder, on the main route of N'Guigmi. An important administrative and agricultural center, Gouré has lost most of its traditional village appearance.

GOURMANTCHE. Ethnic group much more numerous in neighboring states, found in Niger near the Burkina Faso border along the Niger River's W bend.

GOVERNMENT OF NIGER AT INDEPENDENCE, 1960:

Hamani Diori	President Council of Ministers
Saidou Djermakoy Issoufou	Minister of Justice
Diamballo Yansambou Maiga	Minister of Interior
Barcougne Courmo	Minister of Finance
Adamou Mayaki	Minister of Economy
Ibra Kabo	Minister of the Civil Service
Harou Kouka	Minister of Labor
Ikhia Zodi	Minister of Youth and Sports
Leopold Kaziendé	Minister of Public Works

Boubakar Ali Diallo	Minister of Public Health
Maidah Mamadou	Minister of Agriculture and Forestry
Yacouba Djibo	Minister of Stockbreeding
Mouddour Zakara	Secretary of State for Interior
Samna Maizoumbou	Secretary of State to the Presidency
Nicholas Leca	Director of the Presidential Cabinet

GOVERNMENT OF NIGER AS OF JULY 1995:

Mahamane Ousmane	Head of State
Hama Amadou	Prime Minister
Moussa Elhadj Ibrahim	Minister of Interior
Mamane Dobi (ret.)	Minister of Defense
Mohamed Bazoum	Minister of Foreign Affairs
Almoustapha Soumaila	Minister of Finance and Planning
Ibrahim Baidou	Minister of Justice
Alitor Mano	Minister of Agriculture
Issoufou Assoumane	Minister of Mines and Energy
Armstrong Karma	Minister of Public Health
Mouke Dji	Minister of Higher Education
Bouli Ali Diallo	Minister of National Education
Aissatou Dambo Dodo	Minister of Social Development and Women's Promotion

GOVERNORS, COLONIAL, OF NIGER:

COMMISSIONERS

1912–13	Lt. Col. Charles-Camille Thierry de Maugras
1914–16	Col. Paul-Celestin-Marie-Joseph Venel
1916–18	Col. Charles-Henri Mourin
1918–19	Col. Marie-Joseph-Félix Mechet
1919–20	Col. Claude-Paul-Emile Lefebvre
1920–21	Maj. Maurice-Gustave-Fernand Renauld
1921–22	Col. Lucien-Emile Ruef

LIEUTENANT GOVERNORS

1922–29	Jules Brévie
1930	Alphonse-Paul-Albert Choteau
1931	Louis-Placide Blacher
1932–33	Théophile-Antoine-Pascal Tellier
1933–34	Maurice-Léon Bourgine
1934–35	Leon-Charles-Adolphe Petre
1936–37	Joseph-Urbain Court

GOVERNORS

1937–38	Joseph-Urbain Court

1939–40	Jean-Alexandre-Leon Rapenne
1941–42	Maurice-Emile Falvy
1942–54	Jean-François Toby
1955–56	Jean-Paul Ramadier
1956–58	Paul-Camille Bordier
1958	Louis-Félix Rollet
1958	Don-Jean Colombani

HIGH COMMISSIONER

1959–60	Don-Jean Colombani

GREBOUN. *See* MONT GREBOUN.

GROS, AMADOU MOUSSA (Lieutenant Colonel) Secretary general of the Ministry of Defense. One of a clique of officers favored for political appointment by General Ali Saibou, and a friend of (then colonel) Mamadou Tandja, Gros joined Saibou's cabinet as a major in November 1987 when Saibou rose to power, and remained in it as minister of tourism until the new HCR civilian government was formed. With the dawn of the civilian era, he retired as lieutenant colonel, and in February 1995 he was appointed by the newly formed MNSD government to his current post.

GROUPEMENT MUTUALISTE. *See* CONSEIL NATIONAL DE DEVELOPPEMENT

GUBAWA. One of the two groups of the **Maouri,** the other being the **Arewa.** The adjectival form of Gubawa is *Gubanche*. The Gubawa, essentially hunters, were conquered by people arriving from Bornu.

GUELTA. Arab term designating a natural basin serving as a water reservoir. Equivalent to the *aguelman* of the Tuareg.

GUEZEBIDE. One of several names by which the **Toubou** are known in Kaouar.

GUINGAREY, BANAKOYE (1939–). Treasurer. Born in 1939 in Téra and educated at home and in Paris, Guingarey holds a diploma in administration from the Ecole Nationale d'Administration (Niamey) and from the Ecole Nationale de Trésor (Paris). For a long time the head of the financial office of the government's division for Territorial Collectives (1967–75), Guingarey was promoted to the post of treasurer general of the Caisse de Prêts aux Collectivités Territoriales as well as director general of that agency.

GULBI. The Hausa term for Niger's long, fossilized valleys and alluvial plains of 2 to 5 km in width. They are known in Fulani as **Dallol.**

GUM ARABIC. Crop of the acacia tree normally harvested by seminomadic clans during their transhumance patterns. Sudan has a quasimonopoly over world markets, exporting up to 80 percent of the tonnage. Since 1964 gum arabic has been a monopoly of COPRO-NIGER in Niger, which exported up to 1,000 tons of it per year in the 1970s. It is cultivated especially in the Gouré region of Niger, and is frequently smuggled into Nigeria, where it fetches a much higher price than that paid by COPRO-NIGER (in the 1970s, 65–75 CFA francs per kilogram). With the onset of the Sahel drought in the mid-1970s, which drained the region of its nomadic populations, a world shortage of the crop (used especially in paints), developed, boosting domestic prices to 200 CFA francs. Niger never attained the production levels of the 1960s, and indeed quantities harvested are very small.

-H-

HABIBOU, ALLELE EL HADJ. Former cabinet minister. Habibou was General Kountché's minister of justice between January 1983 and mid-1985, and rejoined the cabinet of General Saibou when he rose to power in November 1987, as minister of mines and energy. In 1989 he was shuffled to head the Foreign Ministry, remaining in office for a year.

HAJJ. The pilgrimage to Mecca, which is a duty required of all Muslims who have the means or opportunity to make the pilgrimage to the center of Islam. In 1970 official Saudi Arabian figures noted that the total number of pilgrims from Africa was 90,109, though the true figure is undoubtedly higher. Of this number, some 5,000 came from Niger. The figures for 1980 were of the same order, and those for 1990 slightly higher. Men who have concluded the hajj are entitled to add the prefix **Alhaji** or **El Hadj** to their names.

HALILOU, NOMA (1919–). Former mayor of Tahoua. Born in 1919 and a civil administrator by profession working for the army, Halilou's political career began with his election in December 1958 to the National Assembly. He sat in the Assembly for twelve years and occupied a variety of posts: chairman of the Tourism Committee, vice-president of the Assembly's Economic and Financial Affairs Committee, and Assembly delegate to the administration of the SMDR. In November 1967 he became mayor of Tahoua, serving in that post until April 1971. He has been in retirement since the mid-1980s.

HAMA. Members of a **Dumi,** or lineage group, among the Songhay.

HAMA, ABDOURAHMANE. Former foreign minister. Hama joined the cabinet in April 1993, remaining until the parliamentary crisis of October 1994.

HAMA, BOUBOU (1906–82). Until the 1974 coup d'état, president of the PPN and Niger's second most important leader; according to some he was the power behind the Hamani Diori regime. Born in 1906 in Foneko (Téra), the son of the village head and of Songhay ethnic origin, Hama was educated in Téra, in Dori, and Ouagadougou, Upper Volta (Burkina Faso) and continued his studies at the Ecole William Ponty in Dakar, Senegal (1926–29). He then taught for nearly twenty years in various localities in Niger (including Niamey and Tillabéry) and also in Burkina Faso. Hamani Diori, the future president, was one of his pupils.

A founder of the PPN party, and its president after 1956, Hama was elected in 1947 to the Territorial Council, concurrently being elected to the Grand Council of the AOF (in Dakar), in which he served until 1958. He was at the same time counselor to the French Union in Paris (to 1952) and in 1950 was appointed director of IFAN (serving until 1957). In 1956 Hama was elected municipal councillor of Niamey and served as deputy mayor of the city until 1959. With the PPN's ultimate rise to power, Hama became the president of the National Assembly (in 1958), retaining this position until the 1974 coup. Between 1959 and 1961 senator and vice-president of the French Community, Hama—greatly detested by segments of Niamey's urban population—was one of the first politicians of the ancien régime to be arrested after the coup. In more ways than one Boubou Hama was both the moving spirit and ideologue of the PPN and the backbone of the Diori regime. He was found guilty of embezzlement of 26 million CFA francs and of fiscal fraud of 12 million CFA francs. Following partial restitution of these sums he was granted clemency and not imprisoned, due to his advanced age and international prestige. Stripped of most of his property, and with no marketable skills, Hama was forced to adopt a very modest life-style, moving in to live with one of his children until his death in 1982.

As scholar and author, Hama published numerous books, monographs, and articles dealing with the oral traditions, history, and ethnography of Niger. In 1971 he was awarded the Grand Prix Littéraire de l'Afrique Noire for his autobiography, *Kotia Nima*. Niger's first indigenous teacher to complete his studies at William Ponty, Hama's huge literary output and personal library were renowned, and he assisted other budding scholars. He was president of the Association of Negro Writers, and on the boards of dozens of social, cultural, economic, and political state and private organizations, and president of such diverse bodies as the BDRN, UNCC, Crédit du Niger, COPRO-NIGER, and the BNCA.

HAMA, SAMBO. Former mayor of Niamey. Subprefect of Niamey until 1968, Hama became mayor of the capital on August 12, 1968, replacing Dody Gaoh. In 1971 he reverted to high-level administrative duties with the Ministry of Interior, and has been in retirement since the early 1980s.

HAMADAS. Rocky desert plateaus, a much more frequent feature of the Sahara Desert—especially within Niger—than the image of endless sand dunes (ergs) popularized in fiction.

HAMALLISM. A relatively xenophobic Muslim sect, named after its founder, Shaykh Hamahullah bin Muhammad bin Umar (1886–1943). Propagated in Mali, where it triggered disturbances starting in 1924, it spread to Niger in 1935. It gained further converts in west Niger during the Second World War among (especially) the rimaibe ex-Fulani slaves. Paradoxically, the order experienced a revival of sorts in Niger at a time when it had more or less disappeared elsewhere. Not fully a religious sect, but more of a protest movement by oppressed classes against the traditional order, the movement was led by Marabout **Ali Gati** and linked up with political elements in the post-1945 era. In favor of the emancipation of the **Bella,** youth, women, and other groups, and against compulsory labor for their traditional masters, various disturbances by Hamallists led to Gati's imprisonment and eventual banishment from Niger until 1958, when he was amnestied. The sect currently is still indirectly persecuted. Hamallism is in direct competition with the **Nyassism** order. Often called Reform Tidjaniya (*see* TIDJANIYA), Hamallism was introduced by a sharif from Touat at the turn of the century, though it was most strongly propagated in West Africa by his disciple (son of a Moorish father and a Fulani mother) from whom the movement acquired its name. Despite its xenophobic nature, to many Frenchmen Hamallism appeared no different from the Tidjaniya, and officials could see no fault with it except for its occasional anti-French forays. It was largely banned throughout the AOF (and in Niger) to satisfy Tidjani requests.

HAMANI, ABDOU (1942–). Director of the School of Letters at the University of Niamey. Hamani was born on December 21, 1942, and was trained in Paris in linguistics, concluding his studies in 1972.

HAMANI, DJIBO (1943–). Historian. Born in 1943 and having graduated from the universities of Grenoble (1971) and Aix (1975) with degrees in history, Hamani, who has written several books on Niger's history, is currently head of the history section of IRSH.

HAMAWIS. *See* HAMALLISM.

HAMIDOU, HASSANE DIALLO. Former interim foreign minister. Hamidou was appointed minister of foreign affairs by the HCR in November 1991 and remained until the regular civilian government took over in April 1993.

HAMIDOU, SIDIKOU. Head of the Geography Department at the University of Niamey, and author of several texts on Niger.

HARMATTAN. A dry, continental, sand-filled wind that blows in from the northeast during the dry season, especially in **Ader.**

HAROU, KOUKA. *See* KOUKA, HAROU.

HAROUNA, ADAMOU IDRISSA (Colonel). Former key officer in the military regime. Promoted to major with the coup of 1974, Harouna was a member of the CMS but was shunted to the periphery of power into prefectural duties during much of the Kountché era. Periodically rotated, he was, inter alia, prefect of Dosso (1979–81) and prefect of Niamey (1981–83). In 1983, after a disagreement with General Kountché he was arrested, and was released after the latter's death and the rise to power of General Saibou. He was then dispatched for one tour of diplomatic duty as ambassador to West Germany, and in 1988 was retired from the armed forces and put in charge of veterans' affairs.

HAROUNA, ALOU. Former cabinet minister. Head of a division of the civil service, Harouna was brought into the Kountché cabinet in September 1978 as minister of public works, labor, and posts, and was reassigned—exactly a year later—to head the Ministry of Justice. He remained in that post until June 1982, when he was dropped from the cabinet and nominated to head one of the state companies.

HASKE. *Haske* (weekly) and *Haske Magazine* (quarterly) are two independent publications. They were founded in Niamey in 1990 and are directed by Ibrahim Cheik Diop. The circulation of each is around 3,000.

HASSANE, AMADOU (1931–). Former vice-president of the National Assembly. Born on February 15, 1931, in Garendéyé (Dosso district) and educated in Niamey, Zinder, and Dosso, Hassane commenced his adult life as a nurse and founded the radiology station in Niamey Hospital, of which he later became head (1954–57). In 1957 he was elected PPN deputy from Dosso, and in December 1958 he was elected AOF grand councillor from Niger. Reelected to the National Assembly through 1974, he also represented Niger at the Organisation Commune des Régions Sahariennes (1959) and served as the Assembly's first vice-president after 1965. He also was (until the 1974 coup d'état) counselor to the Constitutional Chamber of the Supreme Court, vice-president of the Board of Directors of SOMAIR, secretary general of the PPN in the Dosso region, and president of the Board of Directors of the National Institute of Administration. After the 1974 coup he retained the last post.

HASSANE, MOUSSA (Major). Commander of the Garde Républicaine, restructured after the 1983 attempted putsch against General Kountché, whose cousin he is, until the Garde was dismantled in 1993.

HASSANE, SIDO (1932–80). Former secretary general of the UNTN. Born in Koygourou in 1932, the brother of **Amadou Hassane,** who became the vice-president of the National Assembly, Hassane attended schools at Dosso and Kolo and in 1948 commenced teaching on the primary level. He taught in Dogondoutchi, Abalak, and Kao (Tahoua region), Dosso and Bonkuku (Filingué), finally in 1958 becoming director of the Lycée National Issa Korombé in Niamey, remaining in that post until 1974. He was deeply involved in union activities after 1956, and was a member of the SNEN union of Niger schoolteachers. He was elected its deputy secretary general in 1961, after a 1960 union seminar in Tunis sponsored by the International Confederation of Free Trade Unions. In 1962 Hassane also became deputy secretary general of the UNTN and in 1969 the union's secretary general. In 1972 he became a member of the Conseil Economique et Social and traveled abroad widely. He was imprisoned after the 1974 coup and died in prison in Tillabéry.

HASSOUMI, MASSAOUDOU. Minister of commerce between April 1993 and October 1994, when the government fell.

HAUKA. A spirit cult that emerged in the mid-1920s similar in some respects to the **Bori** or **holey,** and which involved mimicry of French colonial authority and French mores. It first emerged in the winter of 1925 in the small village of Toudou Anza (in the Arewa region) under the animist priest Chibo (after whom the Chibo sect was to be called), in direct opposition to the serkin Arewa who had recently been improperly elevated to that post, and it carried strong anti-French overtones. The French administration intervened and punished those involved, but in May 1926 the antiestablishment phenomenon recurred south and east of the Dogondoutchi subdivision. It was again repressed. Chibo's success was so great, however, that by 1927 the cult—continually repressed—had spread throughout the **Kurfey** villages of the area, and the movement was spreading beyond. The death of the serkin Arewa (Gado Namalaya, in 1927) and the French administration's support of Chekou Seyni, one of his sons, as successor serkin (in opposition to Mainassara, a former French army NCO, and the Hauka choice) created new civil disturbances. Eventually, faced by strong French countermeasures, Hauka supporters melted into the bush and set up their own "new" villages and quasi-French imitation structures, complete with "police" and "army" equipped with wooden rifles. Officials who followed them into the bush were imprisoned. As this form of withdrawal from colonial rule spread into neighboring cantons (especially into Imanan) where **Bella** slaves of the Tuareg grasped at it in large numbers, and from them via the canton of Tondikandia into the Dosso region, the government increased its repressive policies to stamp out the revolt. Hauka dances were banned, Chibo was exiled for nine years, troops were sent out to bring back villagers who had fled from French authority, and all news about the spread of the cult was censored. Nonetheless, the practice continued, and as late as 1935 villagers in Lorma and in Chikal refused to obey the chef de canton's orders, demanding direct orders from the French. In Kobi antichiefly disturbances erupted in 1937, 1939, 1941, and 1947–48. What particularly alarmed the French was the Hauka possession dances, which allegedly made participants invulnerable, willing to brave both physical pain (flames, coals) and traditional sanctions by chiefs while mimicking French structures and hierarchies. The movement continued into the 1950s though it has assimilated various other tenets, becoming for all practical purposes a Bori variant.

HAUSA. A mostly Muslim people estimated at around 20 million in 1990, with figures cited in French sources consistently lower than those published in British ones. They are found mostly in northern Nigeria and southern Niger, with other smaller concentrations throughout West and Equatorial Africa. Though a Hausa "identity" does exist, there is a wide cultural heterogeneity among them. They speak the Hausa language, which belongs to the Chad group of the Hamito-Semitic language group and which is infused with Arabic words consequent to heavy Arab influence and their conversion to Islam. Many terms also come from the Kanuri language as a result of their former close contact with, and domination by, the Bornu Empire. Their language is the lingua franca of some 50 million people. In Niger the Hausa are found in the south-central regions in a broad arc from east of Dogondoutchi to east of Zinder. The 1988 census puts their numbers in Niger at around 3.8 million, or just about 53 percent of the total population.

Hausa history commences in the seventh century, when they started arriving in Aïr. Chased out during the twelfth century by the first Tuareg waves—essentially the **Isandalen**—and under pressure also from the Songhay in the west and Bornu in the east, the compact Hausa "wedge" was formed in between the former groups. Their name, *Hausa,* is actually a recent one. *Afuma* is the name by which they were called in ancient texts, and still are by many populations in Chad and Niger.

According to tradition, seven states were formed by the Hausa, who never knew political unity. Traditionally established in walled city-states, with a precise internal hierarchical organization, these were all headed by sons of the queen of Daura and an eastern hero. The states were Gobir, Daura, Kano, Katsina, Zazzau, and Rano (since disappeared). Gobir, at the height of its power straddled a large territory on both sides of the current Niger-Nigeria border (*see* GOBIR). The Fulani jihad at the beginning of the nineteenth century conquered most of the Hausa states and drove many groups into areas now in Niger, from which they tried to regain their homelands (from Maradi, Tsibiri, and Zango, for example). The area north of Katsina (now Fulani) became a major war zone for a whole century, as Fulani and Hausa armed might clashed. Following the Fulani conquests the major autonomous Hausa states, all in Niger, were Tessaoua, Maradi, Gobir, Konni, and Maouri. The Fulani states to their south were Sokoto, Gando, Katsina, Daura, and Kazaure.

HAUT CONSEIL DE LA REPUBLIQUE (HCR). Niger's provisional parliament formed after the National Conference in 1991, and in place after civilian elections were held in 1993. Its head was Professor André Salifou.

HAUTE COUR DE JUSTICE. Composed of Assembly deputies who elect their president, the Haute Cour de Justice, a section of the Cour Suprême, was empowered to impeach and try members of the government, including the president of the republic, for crimes while in office as well as for treason. The court was abolished after the 1974 coup d'état.

HEADS OF STATE. Since independence Niger has had four heads of state: Hamani Diori (1960–74); General Seynou Kountché (1974–87); General Ali Saibou (1987–93), and Mahamane Ousmane (1993–).

HILLANI. Name by which the Fulani are called by the Hausa in Niger.

HIMA, DJIBRILLA (1932–). Former commissioner general of youth and sports. Born on November 15, 1932, in Dosso and a teacher by profession, Hima was youth and sports commissioner (1961–63) and secretary general of the Niamey branch of the PPN between 1960 and 1974. In 1963 he was appointed director of youth and sports in the Ministry of Information and Youth, and held that post for eight years, until 1971. Concurrently, after August 29, 1966, he served as first deputy mayor of Niamey. In 1971 he was promoted within the ministry to the post of commissioner general of youth and sports, which he held until the 1974 coup. Since then Hima has been attached to the Ministry of Education.

HIMA, HAMANI (1905–). Born in 1905 in Niamey and trained as a veterinary nurse, Hima was elected deputy to the Territorial Assembly from Niamey in March 1957 and was subsequently reelected through 1974. In the assembly he was the vice-president of the Economic and Financial Affairs Committee and held several other committee assignments over the years. He was also a member of the Supreme Court's Constitutional Chamber between December 1958 and 1974, losing all positions with the 1974 coup d'état.

HIMOU, AMADOU MARANGA (1947–). Academic. Trained in physics and chemistry in Abidjan, Dakar, and Paris, Himou specializes in fluid mechanics and teaches at the School of Science at the University of Niamey.

HIRONDELLE. *See* OPERATION HIRONDELLE.

HOLEY. Spirits, in Songhay mythology. Similar to the *vodun* of the coastal Beninese, and the **Bori** of the Maouri. The holey are immortal and, though made like people, are invisible. The mother of the holey is Hara-ke, who is also the deity of water; there are over a hundred different spirits. The holey dance of possession is quite similar to the Bori rites and dances.

HOUDOU, ABDOULAYE (1940–). Radio broadcaster and poet. Born in 1940 in the Tillabéry region, Houdou was director of programming at Radio Niamey, the secretary of state of the Ministry of Information, and since August 1985 director of Niger radio and television services. He is the author of two volumes of poetry, one of which (thirty poems constituting *Sahéliennes*) received a prize for poetry.

-I-

IBBA, MOHAMED IBRAHIM. Minister of administrative reform from April 1993 until the government fell in October 1994.

IBOUNE, AMADOU. A civil administrator by profession, Iboune served with SONERAM (Société Nigérienne d'Exploitation des Ressources Animales) and with SOTRAMIL (Société de Transformation du Mil). He was also a technical councillor to the Ministry of Finance (1966–69) and deputy director of fiscal controls (1966–69). Between 1969 and 1973 director of the National Institute of Administration, Iboune was in April 1973 appointed director of the cabinet of the secretary of state to the presidency in charge of development. He lost his post after the coup d'état of 1974 and was shifted to administrative duties in the public sector. In 1976 he was appointed director of the Institut National de Gestion, serving until his retirement.

IBRA, KABO. *See* KABO, IBRA.

IBRAHIM, ARI TOUBOU. Former cabinet minister. Ibrahim joined Kountché's cabinet in February 1981 as minister of rural development, and was shifted to head the Ministry of State for Water and the Environment in September 1985, serving until Kountché's death in 1987.

IBRAHIM, MAHAMANE. Former interim secretary of state for the economy, between November 1991, when he was appointed in the HCR government, and March 1992 when he was shifted to be in charge of the budget. He left the cabinet after the civilian elections that produced a regular cabinet in April 1993.

IBRAHIM, MOUSSA ELHADJ. Minister of interior since March 1995 in the new MNSD government.

ID EL-FITR. Muslim festival of the breaking of the fast at the end of Ramadan, celebrated throughout Niger among the Muslim communities.

IDE, OUMAROU. *See* OUMAROU, IDE.

IFEROUANE. Major caravan stop 310 km north of Agadez in Aïr. Reached by a track after a spectacular but rugged nine- to ten-hour drive, the large oasis is at the foothills of the Tamgak Mountains (2,000 meters) and is surrounded by fine palm and date groves and vegetable gardens. Always competing with the much more prosperous and bigger Agadez for the trans-Saharan caravan trade terminus, by the nineteenth century Iférouane had essentially secured primacy, contributing to the further decline of its rival, so remarked upon by **Heinrich Barth** in 1850. Today still an important entrepôt for trade from the north, Iférouane is an important stop on the northern tourist circuit; many side trips from the village lead to stunningly beautiful sites, including to the peak of **El Mecki.** The oasis is a poste administratif in the arrondissement of Agadez, which numbers 130,000 people, of whom only 4,000 are sedentary, many of these in Iférouane itself. The oasis was especially hard hit by the drought in the 1970s and again in the 1980s, and lost much of its tourist traffic on which it had grown to depend with the onset of the Tuareg rebellion in Aïr in the 1990s.

IGDALEN. Tuareg class. Found especially in Mali, as well as in Agadez, the Igdalen form various maraboutic tribes in Niger. Very pious, religious, and honest, the Igdalen are not a political entity but are religious groups found attached to the other clans. The Igdalen—according to some traditions of Moroccan origin—were possibly the earliest Tuareg clan to enter Aïr, arriving before the eleventh century.

IKAZKAZAN. Tuareg group. The history and origins of the Ikazkazan are only vaguely known. They are found in two branches—as part of the Kel Tamat, mostly in Aïr, and the Kel Ulli, mostly in Damergou. According to some scholars they originated in Libya (in the Ghat district), though oral traditions point to the Ahaggar Mountains in Algeria. They are part of the larger **Kel Owey** confederation. The two segments of the Ikazkazan arrived in Niger at different times; the Kel Tamat in Aïr in the eighteenth century, the Kel Ulli in the nineteenth. As the junior clan in the Kel Owey confederation, the Ikazkazan have little voice in the selection of the **Anastafidet.**

IKELAN. Name of all black slaves formerly (or today, domestic serfs) of the Tuareg. Half of their agrarian produce goes to their masters. Exclusively cultivators and herders of the Tuareg livestock, the Ikelan do not nomadize like the Tuareg. The name is equivalent to **Bella** in Songhay and **Buzu** in Hausa.

IKOFAR. "Infidel" in Tamasheq.

ILELLAN. Tamasheq term (singular: *elelli*) signifying free men, as opposed to **ikelan** (singular: *akli*), or slaves. While there are distinct subcategories in the Tuareg social hierarchy, the most fundamental division is between the ilellan and the ikelan.

ILLABAKAN. Tuareg clan, part of the **Ouilliminden Kel Dinnik** confederation, numbering around 1,600 and nomadizing the Teguida area and in general the region between Tahoua and Agadez.

ILLELA. Small town of 10,000 some 90 km from Birni-N'Konni and 59 km from Tahoua, not to be confused with the village of the same name in Nigeria, also near Birni-N'Konni. Established by the Tuareg as the Ader capital of **Aggaba** after his conquest of the region and relocation from Birni-n-Ader around 1740. The title of serkin Illela was adopted by the Tuareg rulers as opposed to serkin Ader. Illela is currently an arrondissement in the département of Tahoua, with headquarters in the town itself. Illela has great tourist attractions in its well-preserved traditional Hausa architecture.

IMAJEGHEN. *See* IMAJEREN.

IMAJEREN. The highest Tuareg clan of nobility, corresponding to the Ahaggaren of the northern Tuareg. Literally "the Noble and the Free" (and in the singular, *imochar*), the Imajeren are the Tuareg warrior aristocracy with the **Imrad** (singular: *Amghid*) occupying the second rank in the traditional Tuareg hierarchy. Most of the Imajeren were killed in the various Franco-Tuareg clashes at the beginning of the twentieth century during when France established control over their areas.

IMGHAD. *See* IMRAD.

IMMOURAREN. Site of extremely rich uranium ore deposits (the richest by far in Africa). Some 70 km south of Arlit, the deposits are estimated (conservatively), at 70,000 tons of exploitable ore. Originally the site was to be developed by a consortium involving Niger's ONAREM, the French atomic energy commission, and CONOCO of the USA. Depressed global prices for uranium in the 1980s delayed implementation of the project, with CONOCO in particular reneging on its original participation agreement. With the continued uranium glut in global markets, prospects are dim that the deposits will be tapped in the near future. *See also* URANIUM.

IMOCHAR. *See* IMAJEREN.

IMOUZOURAG. Tuareg clan found mostly in Damergou, where they are considered to be the first of the Tuareg clans to have arrived there, in the sixteenth century. They eventually entered in competition with the Kel Owey (who arrived later, from Aïr) and their control over the **azalay** trade with Kaouar. The Imouzourag efforts to penetrate the azalay trade brought about intermittent clashes with the Kel Owey, which were not resolved until the entry of the French into the area. French military assistance to the Kel Owey (in exchange for camels for the impending invasion of Chad from Niger) brought about the complete eclipse of the Imouzourag. The French elevated to power an anastafidet from the Kel Owey who was made responsible for the peace and security over the entire region and the various clans residing there.

IMRAD. The second-ranking noble clan of free men and warriors in Tuareg traditional ranking, after the **Imajeren** aristocracy. The singular is *Amrid.* Formerly vassals, though in the distant past of noble freeman status, they were decimated in the Franco-Tuareg clashes at the beginning of the twentieth century.

IN-ABANGARIT. Traditional stop on the trail to Assamaka, an important Tuareg village 231 km north of Agadez. It is a center of the transhumance patterns of the Tamesna.

IN GALL. An oasis in southwestern Aïr at an altitude of 470 meters 118 km from Agadez and 760 km from Niamey. Also, an arrondissement in the département of Agadez with headquarters in the oasis itself. The village developed due to the presence of water in the area despite the very sparse vegetation surrounding it, and became for this reason an important secondary caravan stop on the east–west route. Local tradition relates to In Gall's being founded by troops left behind by Askia Mohamed of Songhay (*see* AGADEZ), and the local language is indeed Songhay. The population of In Gall, who had joined in the 1916 rebellion of **Kaocen,** was brutally repressed after the failure of the revolt. Hundreds of its notables were executed following the return of the French to Aïr. In 1969, when a detailed demographic study was conducted, the area had a largely nomadic population of 12,000, though this rose to more than 20,000 at the height of the Sahel **drought.** The original population included 3,596 Kel Ahaggar; 2,417 Fulani; 1,677 Kel Fadey; 1,600 Kunta, and 1,032 Igdalen. The village itself numbers 2,000 people but many work in the salt pits of **Teguidda n'Tesemt,** which is more or less a dependency of In Gall. (In 1970 all but 26 people of Teguidda's population were to be found in In Gall.) In Gall has important palm groves and date plantations, and the area is the favorite grazing grounds for clans on the annual **cure salée.** Outside the oasis, in the Agadez direction, are found deposits of fossilized wood, testimony to the heavily wooded nature of the region in a bygone era of plentiful water supplies and rainfall. When the Tuareg rebellion commenced in earnest in Aïr in the 1990s, In Gall was at least twice assaulted, leading to a further drift to more secure oases of its sparse resident population.

INADIN. Silversmith clan among the Tuareg. The Inadin are a nomadic group wandering from Tuareg encampment to encampment performing whatever chores have to be done. Respected for their craft though detested for their vagrant way of life, they also serve as fortune-tellers and healers. They are usually easily distinguished from the regular Tuareg clans by their shabby and simple dress, and their tents congregated at the outskirts of Tuareg encampments.

INCHA, EL MOCTAR. Traditional Tuareg governor of Agadez. He was arrested by the Niger army in October 1992 on suspicion of being sympathetic to the Tuareg rebellion.

INDEPENDANTS D'OUTRE-MER (IOM). Political grouping in the assembly of the French Union formed in 1948 by Leopold Sédar Senghor, future president of Senegal, with the purpose of uniting into a cohesive force the delegates from the colonies, then divided in allegiance among the various metropolitan political parties. In 1953 the IOM included fourteen African delegates loosely tied to the then French party of the moderate left, the MRP. Though attempts were made to transform the IOM into an interterritorial party with branches in each French colony along the lines of the RDA, the IOM never had any electoral support in the territories themselves and remained basically a caucusing group in the assembly. In Niger the UNIS party became an IOM affiliate under Ikhia Zodi and Francis Borrey's leadership after the bulk of its membership deserted the two leaders over this very issue.

INDIGENAT. Civil status established in 1924 and in existence until the reforms of 1946, restricting the civil rights of indigenous people who had not attained the status of **assimilé** or évolué. The restrictions included the obligation to perform corvée (including porterage), and legal jurisdiction under customary law and traditional authority with a French administrator presiding. The indigénat code was a major source of friction in much of Francophone Africa during the colonial era. *See also* ASSIMILATION POLICY.

INESLEMEN. Religious class among the Tuareg confederations, established after the penetration of Islam. Once a low, semivassal status (in the seventeenth century) the Ineslemen rapidly became a respected sacerdotal caste among the Ouilliminden confederation of clans, especially after the almost total decimation of the warrior and freeman clans in the Franco-Tuareg clashes at the beginning of the twentieth century. In Niger much of the population of Agadez claims Ineslemen origin and hence pays no taxes and performs no labor for the sultan of Agadez. Among the Ineslemen are found the extremely pious **Isherifen** who get special deference. The Ineslemen live on gratuities given them by the other castes and clans.

INNA. In the Gobir chiefdom in particular, but elsewhere as well (in the Hausa states), the inna is the second most important personality after the king or paramount chief. A woman of royal lineage, a Bori initiate, and with ultimate control over all the bori, she is chosen by the king to assist him in his duties. The exact title may vary from chiefdom to chiefdom and is synonymous with iya in Katsina, magaram in Zinder, and **magajiya** in Duara. So powerful was the magaram in Zinder that she was the only person given a state pension in 1906 by the French when they abolished the sultanate.

INNE, MARCEL. Minister of national education in General Saibou's government between May and December 1989.

INSA, ABDOU. Minister of commerce and industry in General Saibou's government between May and March 1990.

INSTITUT FRANCAIS D'AFRIQUE NOIRE (IFAN). Research and documentation center, part of a network of centers throughout Francophone Africa, set up in Niamey shortly after the end of the Second World War. After independence the agency's name was changed to **Centre National de Recherches en Sciences Humaines.**

INSTITUT NATIONAL DE GESTION (ING). Niamey-based National Institute of Administration. Founded in 1972 to train administrative cadres needed by Niger (and especially to replace middle-echelon foreign officials), the ING was for a long time headed by Amadou Hassane, under the directorship of Amadou Iboune.

INSTITUT NATIONAL DE LA RECHERCHE AGRONOMIQUE (INRA). Agronomy research organ set up by the post-1974 military regime (on January 7, 1975), which became operational in the 1990s.

INSTITUT NATIONAL DE RECHERCHE PEDAGOGIQUE (INDRAP). Advanced pedagogical institute based in Niamey.

INSTITUT PRACTIQUE DE DEVELOPPEMENT RURAL (IPDR). Vocational and technical training school in Niamey, recently expanded, and with a branch in Kolo, 25 km from the capital.

ISANDALEN (*or* Sandal). Part of the second wave of Tuareg clans to enter Niger's Aïr, in the eleventh century. Forced southward by the arrival of the Beni Hilal and other groups in Tripolitania and Fezzan, the Isandalen—originally from the Gulf of Sidra oasis of Aujila—founded under their chief (the *aghounbolou*) Aïr's oldest city, **Assodé.** Later, together with the **Itesen,** they provided the impetus for the creation of the **Sultanate of Agadez** in the fifteenth century. The Isandalen have long since disappeared, but some Itesen survive, mostly in the Madaoua area.

ISHERIFEN. Pious Tuareg clans that claim descent from the Prophet Muhammad. The name is practically synonymous with **Ineslemen**.

ISKOKI. Divinities such as **Bori.** Presiding over a person's destiny, iskoki can either help or hurt one's career and life, and hence must be appeased in various ways.

ISLAM. *See* ISLAMIC ORDERS; RELIGION.

ISLAMIC ORDERS. There are various Islamic orders in Niger, though as elsewhere in this region the **Tidjaniya** order is the most prevalent. For details, *see* HAMALLISM; KHALWATIYA; MIRGHANIYA; NYASSISM; QUADRIYA; RELIGION; SANUSIYA.

ISLAMIC UNIVERSITY OF SAY. Long-projected but only recently inaugurated Islamic university, financed by Arab petrodollars and aimed at modernizing the role of Say as a center of religious study (*see* SAY). The university project was finally approved in 1976—after deliberations as far back as 1969—with construction supposed to commence in 1978. The first funds were not released until 1982, however. Amounting to $18.5 million, they were scheduled for the building of the Arab language building and an administration and student hostel complex.

ISMAIL, OUMAR. Muslim religious leader and during the Kountché era president of the **Association Islamique du Niger.** Ismail is the son of a greatly venerated Muslim leader who taught at **Say.**

ISRAEL. Israel-Niger relations were quite cordial until 1969, with a multiplicity of mutual cooperation projects between the two countries. Relations began to cool—under Libyan pressure after the overthrow of King Idriss in Tripoli—and in 1973 diplomatic relations were severed and all formal contact terminated. In exchange Niger received Libyan pledges of grants and cooperation agreements. Informal relations with Israel continued, however, under both the Diori and the Kountché regimes, if only because Israel's specific developmental experience and competence in arid-zone agriculture and technology is second to none in the world and hence of direct and paramount importance to Niger. In the late-1970s Israel began to reassess the patterns of trade between Niger and Libya in particular, in light of growing shipments of enriched uranium to Libya and Iraq, both hard-line enemies of Israel with potential nuclear capabilities, albeit imported. In 1979 Niger was forced to admit—after embarrassing prevarications—that some 258 tons of uranium had been sold to Libya in 1978. The Libyan tonnage zoomed to 1,212 tons in the first half of 1981—

greatly disquieting Israel and making Libya Niger's primary client—before relations between Niger and Libya plummeted. Iraq also began to purchase enriched uranium for its nuclear reactor, which was later bombed by Israel. Since in all instances the sensitive details about Niger uranium sales to the Arab world were leaked out by Niger elements friendly to Israel, relations between Israel and Niger did not improve even when Libya-Niger relations soured. Full diplomatic relations were ultimately restored in the late 1980s.

ISSA, BOULAMA MAMADOU (1928–). Longtime Assembly deputy and diplomat. Born in 1928 in Ghettimari (Mainé) and educated as a teacher in Mali's Ecole Normale de Katibougou, Issa worked as a teacher and headmaster before joining the PPN party, where he rapidly rose to prominence. In 1956 he became the secretary general of its Zinder branch (serving in that capacity until 1958), and on December 14, 1958, he won an electoral contest and became deputy from Gouré. He remained in the Assembly until the 1974 coup d'état. He was also Niger's representative to the senate of the French Community (1959–61), and between 1964 and 1971 ambassador to Nigeria.

ISSA, IBRAHIM (1922–). Former cabinet minister. Born in 1922 in Zinder and of Hausa and chiefly origin, Issa completed his primary education in Zinder and worked for the next six years (1940–46) as a nurse. In 1946 he was one of the first to join the PPN party and consequently served as the party's publicity secretary (1947–50) and later (1950–58) secretary general of its Zinder branch. In 1959 he was elected to the National Assembly from Zinder, serving until 1965, and representing Niger at the senate of the French Community between 1959 and 1961. In 1965 he was brought into Diori's cabinet as minister of health, and in 1970 was shifted to head the Ministry of Posts and Telecommunications (as well as becoming a member of the Supreme Court), positions he held until the 1974 coup d'état. Issa has also served as a member of the executive boards or councils of COPRO-NIGER, OCDN, and the Caisse de Sécurité Sociale; as director general of Crédit du Niger; and as director of information of Niger. Following the 1974 coup Issa was imprisoned, to be released in April 1978.

ISSA, IBRAHIM (1929–86). Author and administrator. Born to a Fulani family in Niamey in 1929, Issa was trained as a teacher and studied under Hamani Diori. At independence he became Niger's first director of information, and later served as director of the Malbaza cement plant and regional director for Texaco. A published poet and author, Issa died in 1986 after a two-year confinement in a hospital in Niamey.

ISSA, MAZOU (Major). Chief of staff of the Niger armed forces. Issa was appointed directly by the National Conference in September 1991, after it dismissed from office the existing chief of staff (Colonel Toumba Boubacar) and his deputy over the February 1990 student brutalities and repression of Tuareg after the Tchin Tabaraden incident.

ISSA BERI. Name of the Niger River in Djerma.

ISSAKA, AMADOU (1924–). Serkin Kantché. Born in 1924 in Kantché, a Hausa and son of the chef de canton and serkin Kantché, Issaka had only primary education and at the age of twenty-two was elected to the regional council and as Conseil Général deputy from Zinder shortly later. He served in the latter body through 1952. He supported the MSA ticket in 1957 and was deputy to the National Assembly (from Magaria) between 1958 and 1965, though after 1958 he declared for the PPN. Between 1959 and 1961 he was also senator of the French Community. In 1965 he moved into Diori's cabinet as minister of labor and civil service and remained in that post until January 1970. For one year minister delegate to the presidency without any specific duties, he then became Diori's minister of economic affairs, commerce, and industry, holding that post until the 1974 coup d'état. Interned for over a year after the coup, he was finally granted clemency in mid-1975. An extremely powerful traditional chief, Issaka has been a member of various commissions, including the Chad Basin Commission. He has also been the general treasurer of the Association of Traditional Chiefs of Niger. Upon his release from detention he was fined 15 million CFA francs, of which he had been found guilty of fraudulent acquisition.

ISSAKA, MAIZOUMBOU (1929–). Traditional leader and longtime deputy to the National Assembly. Born in Tibiri to the traditional chiefly family, Issaka was to become chef de canton of Tibiri. Trained as a teacher, he was elected to the National Assembly in March 1957 from Dogondoutchi, and was reelected through the 1974 coup d'état. In the Assembly Issaka was a member of a powerful bloc of traditional chiefs who were the prime power source of the Diori regime.

ISSAKA, SOUNA. Briefly interim minister of justice appointed by the HCR. He served in the cabinet between November 1991 and March 1992.

ISSANDALAN. *See* ISANDALEN.

ISSOUFOU, MAHAMADOU (1932–). Former prime minister of Niger, leader of the **Parti Nigérienne pour la Démocratie et le**

Socialisme (PNDS-Tarayya), whose shift from supporting the AFC coalition to the MNSD allowed the latter to form the government of February 1995. A powerful Hausa leader, born in 1942 in the Tahoua region, Issoufou was educated as a mining engineer in France. When competitive politics were allowed in Niger, Issoufou forged a network of chiefs and influentials from his region supporting his PNDS party at the 1993 legislative elections, winning the third highest number of seats (thirteen) of the new National Assembly's eighty-three. He was also a presidential candidate who scored 15.92 percent of the vote in the first round, also in 1993. Barred from running in the second round (there were two other candidates with higher votes), Issoufou swung his electorate behind Mahamane Ousmane, helping ensure his victory on the second ballot, to beat the MNSD candidate, **Tandja.** The price for Issoufou's support was the prime ministership. An unruly cabinet shared by the six-party AFC alliance, and problems within the bicephalous executive, brought about Issoufou's resignation on September 28, 1994. His joining the opposition MNSD brought down the government and forced Ousmane to call for new legislative elections, which saw the MNSD coalition emerge victorious.

ITESEN. Tuareg clan once established in Aïr but practically extinct today except in the area of Madaoua, where they are found intermixed with the **Kel Gress.** The Itesen helped the **Isandalen** in setting up the **Sultanate of Agadez** and were one of the first Tuareg groups to arrive in Aïr.

IWILLIMINDEN. *See* OUILLIMINDEN.

IYA. *See* BORI; MAGAJIYA.

-J-

JAMA'AT IZALAT AL-BID'A WA IQAMAT AL-SUNNA. Religiously fundamentalist Muslim movement, spreading into Niger from Jos in Nigeria, and drawing many of the younger generation of Alhazai. It has been to a large extent behind the recent confrontations with animists in the country. *See also* RELIGION.

JEUNES PIONNIERS. Youth organizations aimed at raising civic consciousness and agrarian pioneering, established in the early 1960s as part of Israel's technical cooperation effort in Niger. Relations with Israel were ruptured on January 4, 1973 (they had been quite cordial though not extensive), as a result of Libya's drive against Israeli influence on the continent. At the time, all Israeli technical assistance was terminated, and remaining consultants with the Jeunes Pionniers were also withdrawn.

-K-

KA KALABA. Literally (in Hausa) "How [does one] hide [from the famine]?" Hausa name for the 1913–14 drought in Damagaram and Damergou that was the worst in Niger's history until the 1968–74 drought. During June and July 1914 alone, for example, Filingué lost 16 percent of its population to the famine sweeping the area, and a total of 80,000 died in Damagaram, while a mass exodus developed into north Nigeria, which was less affected by the ravages of the drought. *See also* DROUGHTS.

KABO, IBRA (1921–). Former cabinet minister and diplomat. Born in 1921 in Guidiguir (Gouré), and educated in Gouré, Zinder, and Niamey, and at Dakar's Ecole William Ponty (1938–41), Kabo obtained diplomas from the Posts and Telecommunications School of Dakar (1942, 1949) and also served for three years in the French army (1942–45). Appointed inspector of posts in Niger he joined the PPN in 1948, and from 1954 through 1959 was involved in union activities as secretary of the Telecommunications Union. He was briefly a member of the National Assembly (1958–59), following which he was integrated into Diori's cabinet as minister of the civil service (1959–64). In 1964 he was shifted to head the Ministry of Public Health but was dropped the following year on suspicion of basic disloyalty to the PPN (having previously been a leader of the opposition) as a consequence of a government purge that followed the **SAWABA** incidents of 1964–65. Appointed to diplomatic duties between 1966 and 1974, he served also as ambassador to France, Great Britain, Switzerland, Italy, and West Germany. After the 1974 coup d'état he was appointed head of the Personnel Service of the Ministry of Foreign Affairs, and retired in 1981.

KADAYE. Capital of the **Gobirawa** after the fall of their kingdom to the Fulani under Mohammed Bello and the sacking of their former capital of Alkalawa. Kadaye was founded in 1815 and was itself destroyed after a Gobirawa rebellion, and abandoned in favor of **Dakourawa.** *See also* GOBIR.

KADEY. In Fulani, "pagan," with the singular being *kado*. In the Tillabéry area most of the Songhay are known as Kadey.

KADI, OUMANI (1931–). Longtime Assembly deputy and traditional leader. Born in 1931 in Illela, where he is the traditional chief, Kadi was one of the chiefs who gave the MSA party (later the PRA) its early electoral edge. He was elected as MSA deputy from Birni-N'Konni in March 1957 and, after shifting to the PPN, continued being elected from his fiefdom until the 1974 coup d'état. In the Assembly he occupied various positions in the committees and was, among other things, secretary of the Assembly bureau between 1958 and 1965.

KADO. People of mixed Songhay-Gourmantché origins who are found in small numbers in the Téra area.

KAKA, NOMA (1920–). Former minister of defense. Born in Dogondoutchi in 1920 and of Maouri origins, Kaka was educated locally and at Dakar's Ecole William Ponty (1935–42), working for the next fifteen years as instructor and headmaster in various Niger schools and serving at the same time as secretary general of the Teachers Union. In 1958 he was elected deputy from Konni to the National Assembly and the next year was elected both senator to the French Union and grand councillor to Dakar's AOF (1959–61). In the National Assembly he was vice-president of the Social Affairs and Labor Committee and rapporteur of the Special Committee as well as Assembly administrator of the Caisse de Compensation des Prestations Familiales. In 1962 he was appointed by Diori president of the State Security Court, and in November 1965 he was brought into the cabinet as minister of national defense (and of information and youth), serving until 1971. In 1965 he was also integrated into the politburo of the PPN, where he served as the party's economics secretary until the 1974 coup d'état. In 1971 Kaka was shifted to head the Ministry of Rural Economy and, a year later, was given responsibility over the Ministry of Mines, Geology, and Water Resources. Kona (traditional chief) of Dogondoutchi since 1970, and hence one of the more powerful traditional leaders in the south, Kaka constituted part of the PPN inner elite until toppled from office in 1974. He was found guilty of embezzlement of 20 million CFA francs and fiscal fraud of 10 million CFA francs and had his private property confiscated pending payment to the Treasury of sums owed it.

KAKAKI. Long (two-and-a-half meter) trumpets used by the Damagaram mounted royal orchestra. Still used today, the *kakaki* are made of long, thin tubes of copper. They are found also in various other sultanates as far south as Benin. The king of Zinder (Damagaram) rarely ventured out without his orchestra, which also included great double bells and drums. Nowadays they are mostly used for ceremonial occasions.

KALALA. General Kanuri name for the salt pits of Kaouar, which they controlled. As in the case of **Bilma,** the Kanuri masters lived some distance away while the slave labor (later paid laborers) resided in the immediate proximity of the pits. Toubou and other raids eventually drove the Kanuri into the protective **ksars** of the villages.

KANDADJI DAM. Important dam on the Niger River between Ayorou and Tillabéry. A much debated project since the 1960s, its feasibility studies were finally concluded in 1980. The estimated cost of the project was then 185 billion CFA francs, a sum zooming up to 400 billion in 1988 due to inflation. Though there is some international backing for the dam, the cost (especially for transshipment of equipment and machinery from the coast), and the major vacillations in water levels of the Niger River (in late 1985 it was nearly dry at Niamey) have been stumbling blocks. Sited 65 km from the Mali border and 180 km from Niamey, the dam will allow the irrigation of 140,000 hectares of land and produce up to 900 gigawatts of electricity per year—which is of major importance in light of a 2,000 percent increase in electricity prices from Nigeria in 1996. The dam will also open up southwest Niger, assist internal fisheries projects, and make most of the Niger River navigable. Work on the dam is proceeding very slowly, however.

KANDINE, MALLAM ADAM. Minister of justice between April 1993 and the fall of the government in October 1994.

KANE, ABDOU. Director of the Caisse Nationale de Crédit Agricole.

KANE, AICHOUTOU. Secretary of state in charge of planning between April 1993 and the fall of the government in October 1994.

KANE, BOUKARI. Director general of the Société Nigérienne d'Electricité.

KANE, ILLA. Political leader and presidential candidate in the 1993 elections. A former secretary general of the Ministry of the Plan, with the onset of political liberalization Kané formed the PSDN party, later joining with **André Salifou** in the Union des Patriotes Démocratiques et Progrèssistes (UPDP-Shamuwa), and contested the 1993 parliamentary elections. The party won one seat. Kané also competed in the 1993 presidential elections, since Salifou, though better known, was barred from running (together with other former heads of state). Kané won 2.55 percent of the vote; though low, this placed him in fifth place after Niger's "big four" ethnic leaders (Tandja, Ousmane, Moumouni, and Issoufou).

KANE, MOUSSA SOULEYMANE. Secretary of state for transport and tourism between April 1993 and the fall of the government in April 1994.

KANE, OUMAROU (1942–). Secretary general of the Ministry of National Education. Born in April 23, 1942, in Madaoua and of Hausa ethnic origins, Kane was educated in Maradi, Tahoua, and Zinder, and in 1963 went to the U.S. to study psychology at Case Western Reserve University. In 1966 he returned to Zinder's Ecole Normale to teach child psychology and two years later went to Paris for further study at the Institute of Psychology at the Sorbonne, obtaining an M.A. and M.Ed. (1968–70). Upon his return to Niger, Kane taught for two years at Zinder's Ecole Normale but in 1972 was integrated into the Ministry of Education as director of secondary and technical instruction. Following the 1974 coup d'état he was promoted to the post of secretary general of the ministry.

KANEM-BORNU EMPIRE. One of the most powerful and longest lasting Sudanese states in Africa. Originally one of several small trading principalities in the ninth century in Kanem (Chad), in the twelfth century the kingdom began to expand and to control major east–west and north–south trade routes, prospering in the process. A major split among the federated clans in the middle of the thirteenth century resulted in the expulsion of the ruling Sefuwa dynasty to Bornu, west of Lake Chad. There it rapidly expanded and became one of the most powerful states in the entire region. The empire's capital was at Birni Ngazargama (founded in 1484) and later (in 1815) in Kukawa. Bornu conquered Kanem at the beginning of the sixteenth century and exacted tribute over a wide-ranging number of states including Aïr, Damagaram, Kano, Katsina, and Kaouar. In the seventeenth and eighteenth centuries the empire's control began to crumble in the peripheral areas, and in the nineteenth century the Fulani reassertion detached from it most of its Hausa dominions. The empire fell in 1893 to **Rabah,** though it was saved from occupation by the onset of the colonial era.

KANEMBU. Ethnic group located mostly in Kanem (Chad) and in smaller numbers in Nigeria and in Niger, where they are found in the vicinity of Lake Chad and in Kaouar.

KANTA. Chief, or king, of the **Kebi** ethnic group.

KANTOU. A salt cake of between 15 and 18 kilograms, produced in the salt pans of Kaouar.

KANURI. Usually called *Beri Beri* (their Hausa name), and lumped together with other small eastern groups (such as the **Manga**), the Kanuri are found in small numbers from Zinder to Mainé-Soroa and in the **Kaouar** oases. The dominant ethnic group of the **Kanem-Bornu Empire** and found in large numbers in the Borno province of Nigeria and in western Chad, the Kanuri spilled into Niger from their bases further south during their establishment of control over Kaouar. The 1988 census numbered the Kanuri at 320,000.

KAOCEN, AG MOHAMMED WAU TEGUIDDA (1880–1919). **Amenokal** of the **Ikazkazan** who led the major Tuareg insurrection in Aïr in 1916. Born around 1880 in Damergou to the Ghat clan of the Oraghen (and, according to some, the son of a Buzu), Kaocen witnessed several Tuareg defeats at the hands of the French (whose paramountcy he never accepted) and was converted to the militantly anti-Christian **Sanusiya** order in 1909). He became one of the order's most ardent supporters in the Niger region and helped in several anti-French assaults in Borkou-Ennedi-Tibesti in Chad in 1909, participating also in the bitter fighting for Ain Galakka. In 1910 he was given command of the defense of Ennedi by the Grand Sanusi. Defeated there, he was chased by French troops practically to Darfur (Sudan), and he slowly returned back first to Ounianga Kabir (Chad) and then to Fezzan (1913), where he made his plans for the assault against the French in Niger. In 1916 he mounted that assault with an attack and siege of Agadez that began on December 17. Accompanied by a thousand troops under **Kodogo,** one-third of whom possessed rapid firing guns and one cannon (leftovers from the fighting in Libya with the Italians), Kaocen maintained the siege of the French garrison until reinforcements from Zinder finally lifted it (*see* KAOCEN REVOLT). Slowly pushed into Tibesti and then Fezzan, he was captured by the Alifa of Zeila and hanged in Mourzouk on January 5, 1919.

KAOCEN REVOLT. Popular name for the rebellion of the Tuareg in northern Niger during the First World War. The holy war against the French, declared in Kufra (Fezzan) by the Grand Sanusi of the **Sanusiya** in October 1914 was ardently picked up by many, including Kaocen ag Mohammed, whose vision was to free Aïr from infidel rule (*see* KAOCEN). In close coalition with the sultan of Agadez (Tagama)—who had completely convinced the French commander of the loyalty of the Tuareg—Kaocen surprised the garrison on December 17, 1916, placing it under siege until March 3, 1917, when the siege was finally lifted by reinforcements from Zinder. During this period his troops controlled much of Aïr, defeating the occasional French columns sent out against them. When the French finally reentered Agadez and In Gall, they instituted severe, highly arbitrary, and savage reprisals. The marabouts—who in many instances had actually argued against the upheaval—were rounded up and most were massacred; up to 130 of them were killed by sword in the two centers.

KAOCENDO, NANAI (1918–). The daughter of the famous leader of the 1916 Tuareg revolt (*see* KAOCEN). Her mother was a Teda woman, Soukai, who bore Kaocen his daughter during his flight from the French after the collapse of the siege of Agadez. Raised as a Teda and residing in Agadez, Nanai Kaocendo faced official French discrimination even as she was not fully accepted by either Teda or Tuareg society. Since adulthood she has kept the memory of her father alive, glorifying his anti-French exploits through songs and fetes focusing on the rebellion.

KAOUAR. A series of ten oases in the desert running in a north-south direction for 150 km between Bilma and Séguédine, the biggest of which is **Bilma,** which has extensive date plantations, large salt pits, and used to be an important caravan stop on the main Fezzan–Bornu route. The sultan of Kaouar usually resides in Aney, a lesser center, and to this day is chosen from one of the two principal Toubou clans, the Kéfada and Kelimada. The Toubou sultanate continued even when power in the area passed into Tuareg hands. Each oasis was essentially a self-contained ministate. Originally most were Kanuri controlled and under the general suzerainty of the Kanem-Bornu Empire to the east until at least the eighteenth century. They eventually sought protection—in light of Bornu's declining strength and the oases' isolation and defenseless position—from the Toubou and later the Tuareg, who never settled in Kaouar though they became the masters of the area from Djado to Bilma and monopolized the salt-caravan trade (*see* AZALAY).

Known, inhabited, and visited by explorers since the end of the seventh century, Kaouar (and especially the Bilma area) has rock paintings and engravings indicating even earlier habitation. The original habitants were the legendary So, better known further east in Chad, followed by the Kanuri in the ninth century (who were their direct successors), then the Toubou, and finally the Tuareg, who made the entire region a tributary of Agadez around 1760. Notwithstanding Toubou and Tuareg protection, the area has numerous times been cruelly and bloodily pillaged by various assaulting forces, and its annual azalay required—right into the colonial era—extremely powerful military escorts to deter attacks. Occupied by France in 1606, Kaouar has been the center of strong Sanusiya proselytizing and influence coming from Fezzan, Tibesti, and other centers of that order. Even in the contemporary era, most of the established centers of that order in Niger are found in Kaouar, administratively a canton of some 3,000 people.

KAOUAR-TIBESTI. Early colonial cercle created by decree on December 7, 1915, and including Kaouar as well as the recently conquered Tibesti, which later (November 1, 1929) was attached to Chad.

KARIM, ALIO. Diplomat. During 1966–69 Karim served as first secretary at Niger's embassy to France. He returned to Niamey in 1970 to serve as director of the division of political and cultural affairs in the Foreign Ministry, returning to his old position in France in 1972. In 1975 he was appointed ambassador to Tunisia, and after six years in that post was reassigned to the ministry in Niamey.

KARIMOU, GOUKOYE (1933–). Former high-level administrator and prefect. Born in 1933 in Dagorou, and educated locally and in France (IHEOM), Karimou's first posting was as head of the Tanout circonscription (1961–62), following which he was named commander of the Magaria cercle (1962–65). On December 31, 1965, he was named commissioner general of development and simultaneously administrator of SOTRAMIL and president of the Niger River Commission. On October 19, 1968, Karimou was named prefect of Agadez, and in October 1972 he returned to Niamey as director of the National Lottery in the Ministry of Finance. Since then he has served a number of boards of parastatals, as well as on that of the BDRN.

KARMA, ARMSTRONG. Minister of public health in the MNSD-dominated government of February 1995.

KARMA REVOLT. Brief revolt in the Niger River valley, lasting from December 1905 to March 1906, headed by Oumarou Karma. The revolt came on the heels of the Kobakitanda rebellion of **Alfa Seydou** and had an anti-French and anti-European hue. Several French military columns converged on the region and firmly suppressed the rebellion.

KARUWAI. Traditional supporters and active members of the **Bori** spirit cult.

KATAMBA, GARBA (1938–). Former mayor of Niamey. Born in 1938 in Madaoua of Hausa ethnicity, Katamba was educated locally in Niamey and then was sent to Dakar's Ecole William Ponty (1956–59) and in 1960 was appointed to the Tahoua Teachers School.

The same year he joined the PPN party. In 1961–62 he studied in Abidjan (Côte d'Ivoire) at the Center for Higher Studies, taught science and mathematics at the Lycée National de Niamey, and again left for higher education in Caen, France, where he studied geology (1962–63). After obtaining a school inspector's certificate, he was appointed school inspector at Tahoua (1965) and Niamey (1966–68) before joining the ministry of education as director of the cabinet of the minister (1968–70). In 1970 he was dramatically promoted to the post of secretary of state for internal affairs, and in August 1972 assumed the post of minister of labor and civil service. Following the 1974 coup he was interned until August 1975 though no charges were levied against him. Indeed, fully rehabilitated, in 1979 he became mayor of Niamey, holding the post until 1984.

KATAMBA, ISSOUFOU. Secretary of state of the interior in charge of public security, between April 1993 and the fall of the government in October 1994.

KATKORE, AMADOU (1928–). Former senator to the French Community. A member of the nobility of Téra, where he was born in 1928, and educated as a teacher, Katkoré was elected to the National Assembly in December 1958 and shortly thereafter was sent to Paris to represent Niger in the senate of the French Community. Upon his return to Niamey in 1961 he continued as a member of the Assembly until the 1974 coup d'état. He also served for a year as director general of NIGELEC, Niger's electricity company, but lost the post after the coup. Katkoré has been in retirement since the early 1980s.

KATSINA. Town currently in Nigeria. Also a Hausa state originally stretching into what is today Niger, through Maradi, Tessaoua, and Kantché right up to Damergou, conquered by the Fulani in 1807. Part of the Hausa Katsinawa retreated to Damagaram to set up a "legitimate" successor Hausa Katsinawa state in **Maradi.** All these serkins have been titled serkin Katsinawa (and not Maradi), even though the original Katsina remained in Fulani hands and was never reconquered. Katsina was said to have been founded in the twelfth century by the son of a mythical white man called Kumayao.

KAURA. In the pre-Fulani Katsina, and in the legitimate Katsinawa successor state (as well as in some other states), the commander of the armies and especially of the cavalry. Nominally a slave, the kaura traditionally resided outside the capital city.

KAWAR. *See* KAOUAR.

KAZIENDE, LEOPOLD (1912–). Former minister of economic affairs. Born in 1912 in Kaya, Upper Volta (Burkina Faso) of Mossi (the dominant group) origins, Kaziendé (who is a Catholic) was educated at Kaya and Ouagadougou before proceeding to Dakar's Ecole William Ponty (1929–32). Graduating as a teacher, he spent the next twenty-six years teaching and as a headmaster, mostly in Niger (Konni, Filingué, Maradi, Dosso, and Niamey). In 1953 he obtained a diploma from France's Teachers Training School in Saint-Cloud. An early member of the interterritorial RDA political party, and Niger's branch—the PPN—Kaziendé came to know Hamani Diori as early as 1944 and was one of his early associates. With the rise of the Diori regime Kaziendé was appointed minister of public works (1958) and remained in that position (reappointed several times) until 1965. During this period he also served on several management boards, including as director general of Air Niger. One of the most experienced and competent people in Diori's cabinet, Kaziendé's ministry was expanded in 1965 to include mines, transportation, and urban affairs. In 1970 his abilities were given extra scope when he was appointed minister of economic affairs, commerce, industry, and mines—a veritable superministry—though the last three were dropped from his portfolio in 1971. Later the same year he was again shifted, this time to the sensitive Ministry of Defense, where he served until the 1974 coup d'état. He was imprisoned after the coup, and a commission of inquiry subsequently found him guilty of embezzlement of 38 million CFA francs and of fiscal fraud of 6.5 million, which he was ordered to pay back to the Treasury. He was released from prison in April 1978. Despite his age, in 1992 he was a cofounder of a resurrected PPN party headed by **Oumarou Youssoufou Garba.**

KEBI. Of unknown origins, Kebi was a state founded in 1513 when the local chief took the title of Kanta. In 1515 he accompanied Askia Mohamed of Songhay to Aïr, and since then Kebi had ascendance over Ader and the Tuareg clans living there. In the middle of the seventeenth century a Hausa usurper (Slimane) seized power and established a new dynasty, but in 1674 lost a major battle to the Tuareg, with Ader eventually passing over to the control of **Aggaba,** son of the sultan of Aïr. Kebi's capital was at Argoungou, an important site that effectively barred Sokoto's access, in the nineteenth century, to Dendi and the Djerma and Maouri regions.

KECHERDA. Major **Toubou** clan in Niger that, according to tradition, arrived from Kufra by way of Chad's Tibesti region. Pushed southwest, and raided heavily by the Ouled Sliman in the early nineteenth century, the Kecherda joined with the Tuareg of the Koutous to defeat their traditional enemies, in 1845, under the Kecherda leadership of Chief Barka Alafou. The Kecherda, like all the Toubou in Niger, are found primarily around Lake Chad, and in general in the eastern part of the country.

KEDEI. The uniquely constructed **Boudouma** papyrus pirogues on Lake Chad. They are called *tei tei* in Arabic, especially across the border in Chad.

KEITA. Town of around 6,500 people in the arrondissement of the same name (population 120,000) in the Tahoua département.

KEITA, ABDERAHMANE (1932–). Educator and administrator. Born in Birni-N'Konni on August 20, 1932, and educated in Niamey and at Dakar's Ecole William Ponty, Keita began his career as a teacher in Niamey and Zinder (1956–58). In 1958 he attended Dakar University and gained a diploma in literary studies. After a further year in Niger he went to the Ecole Normale Supérieure de Saint-Cloud in France and obtained a school inspector's diploma. Between 1961 and 1968 he headed Maradi's educational system, and between 1969 and 1970, Niamey's. In 1971 he was appointed director of primary instruction in the Ministry of Education, and between 1972 and 1974 he served as the cabinet director of the secretary of state for education, and of public works. After the 1974 coup d'état he was shifted to the Ministry of Education as head of a division, and recently retired.

KEITA, MICHEL (1949–). Sociologist. Born in 1949, and educated in sociology and ethnology, Keita has been head of sociology in IRSH, and a consultant to a variety of international bodies.

KEL. In **Tamasheq** meaning "people of." It is used as a prefix to a specific Tuareg clan (or clans) comprising a confederation.

KEL AHAGGAR. Confederation of Tuareg drum groups mostly in the Ahaggar Mountains of Algeria. One segment of the confederation—the Irregenaten and the Ibotenaten—nomadize periodically as far south as the Tamesna plains north of Agadez. Formerly known as the **Deremchaka,** the Kel Ahaggar were strongly, and with great casualties, repulsed in the nineteenth century when they tried to penetrate into Aïr and further south.

KEL AIR. Confederation of clans composed of the Kel Fadey (1,900), Kel Ferouane (6,600), Kel Tamat (5,200), and several other small groups. The Kel Aïr nomadize parts of Aïr.

KEL ATTARAM. Western branch of the **Ouilliminden.**

KEL AZANIERES. Part of the Kel Owey confederation, and one of the original seven clans of the confederation that arrived in Aïr in the fourteenth and fifteenth centuries, and that eventually dominated the region. *See also* KEL OWEY.

KEL DINNIK. The eastern branch of the **Ouilliminden.** Also referred to as the Ouilliminden Kel Dinnik.

KEL ES SUQ. A sacerdotal caste among the Tuareg. *See* INESLEMEN.

KEL FADEY. Confederation of Tuareg drum groups headed by an **amenokal** and an integral part of the larger Kel Aïr confederation. The Kel Fadey originated in the Ahaggar Mountains of Algeria, migrating south to Aïr and eventually settling and nomadizing in the general vicinity of In Gall. They have continually resisted, and rejected, the authority of the sultan of Agadez, and they also resisted the original French intrusions in the area. They number around 3,000.

KEL FEROUANE. Confederation of Tuareg drum groups arriving in Aïr from the Ahaggar Mountains in Algeria around the fourteenth century, eventually to settle and nomadize around Iférouane, north of Agadez, and as far south as Damergou. They number around 7,000.

KEL GRESS. One of the largest (70,000 people) Tuareg confederations of drum groups, and also the most southern extension of Tuareg influence, with several groups found in Nigeria. Arriving in Aïr between the twelfth and fourteenth centuries, they were in due course pushed further south by new Tuareg migrations. In the sixteenth century they acquired a monopoly of the **azalay** trade, providing Kaouar protection against other marauders, though they were to be displaced in this role by the Kel Owey. Around 1740 the continual clashes and battles with other Tuareg confederations forced the Kel Gress to migrate to the vicinity of Madaoua (north of Gobir). They resisted the entry of the French into Niger, and when harshly defeated, segments of the confederation fled as far afield as Sudan and Chad, though over the years most returned to Niger.

KEL OWEY. One of the largest and most powerful Tuareg confederations in Niger. The Kel Owey came to the Aïr and Agadez region from further north in several waves starting in the fifteenth century, and some were later to migrate further south. Their name (*Owey*) means "those of the beef" and refers to their prime activity of cattle herding, and their tribute (one head of cattle) to the sultan of Agadez to whom they owe allegiance. Upon their arrival in Aïr the confederation was formed of seven clans—Kel Tafidet, Kel Azanieres, Kel Amazefzel, Kel Tadek, Kel Aoualles, Kel Afess, and Kel Farras—and they came to dominate the Agadez area. Headed by an **anastafidet,** who is a nobleman and from the administrative point of view the most important Tuareg personage in Aïr, the Kel Owey have maintained control of Aïr since around 1740, pushing other clans either north or south. The Kel Owey also acquired control of the Kaouar azalay trade from other Tuareg groups, though in the nineteenth century this monopoly was challenged by the Imouzourag. The French, then assembling in Niger for the final push into Chad, intervened in the ongoing struggle between the two confederations and promised military help to whichever group could supply them with camels for the Chad expedition. The Kel Owey, because of their dominance of the caravan trade, were able to donate two hundred mounts and with French assistance entrenched their dominance in the area. The anastafidet of the Kel Owey is elected for three years at a time from the most important clans of the confederation—the Kel Tafidet and the Kel Azanieres. The Ikazkazan (Kel Tamat and Kel Ulli) are part of the Kel Owey confederation, though as the most junior members they have hardly any voice or prestige in communal decision making. There are currently around 7,000 members of the confederation who reside in the eastern, mountainous part of Aïr.

KEL TAFIDET. Part of the Kel Owey confederation of clans, and its most important component. One of the original seven clans to enter Aïr during the fourteenth and fifteenth centuries. *See* KEL OWEY.

KEL TAMASHEQ. "The Tamasheq People"—that is, the **Tuareg.**

KEL TAMAT. Tuareg drum group numbering 5,200 residing west of the **Kel Owey,** and acknowledging the sovereignty of their anastafidet. Their best-known subgroup, which played a dominant role in the **Kaocen revolt** of 1916, is the **Ikazkazan.**

KEL ULLI. *See* IKAZKAZAN.

KELETIGUI MARIKO, ABDOURAHMANE. A veterinary doctor by profession, Keletigui Mariko has been a top administrator in Niger since independence. He served as director of cooperation in the Ministry of Rural Economy (1962), head of the Development Service in the same ministry (1963–65) and simultaneously general director of the Société de Riz du Niger and administrator of SOTRAMIL. Since

1965 he has been the director of the trouble-ridden Union Nigérienne de Crédit et de Coopération (UNCC) and of the CNCA.

KHALWATIYA. Sufi order in Aïr, arriving there in the sixteenth century from Egypt and Turkey. Founded by Umar al-Khalwati (d. ca. 1397), the sect first took root in Azerbaijan, the Caucasus, and Turkey (ca. 1500) and then spread to set up lodges in Egypt. Its first influences in Aïr were probably felt around 1545. In some respects the Khalwatiya is the parent order of the **Tidjaniya.** It is most prevalent among segments of the Tuareg. *See also* RELIGIOUS ORDERS.

KOBAKITANDA. The site where two gardes cercles were assassinated in the beginning of what was to be a great anti-French Islamic uprising sparked by the blind marabout Seydou (or Saidou). The **djermakoy** of Dosso (Auta) was loyal to the French and helped avert a major disaster by contributing troops to the quelling of the popular revolt. Before it was crushed it had spread to Nigeria, to which Seydou had escaped. It was finally quelled on January 4, 1906.

KOBI. Important village in the canton of Tondikandia where the **Hauka** cult and anti-French movement took serious hold, leading to major disturbances in 1937, 1939, 1941, and 1947–48.

KODOGO, MOKHTAR (1880?–1920). **Kaocen**'s brother and principal lieutenant in the Aïr uprising and siege of Agadez (*see* KAOCEN REVOLT). After the failure of the revolt, Kodogo fled to Djado preaching revolt to the Toubou there. He mounted a Toubou uprising into Damergou which was repulsed into Tibesti (Chad), and was himself captured and killed near Zouar on May 11, 1920, on his way to Kufra.

KOIRAKINE. In Songhay meaning “the language of the country,” that is, the Songhay language.

KOLLO, KIMBA (Colonel). Former military commander of Agadez. Currently retired, Kollo was ordered placed under house arrest by the National Conference in 1991, to await trial for his role in executing the leader of the 1976 coup attempt, Major Sani Souna Sido.

KOMA BANGOU. One of the sites of gold deposits discovered in the mid-1980s. The gold field is 150 km northwest of Niamey, near Téra. Niger’s regime has been trying hard to spur the development and exploitation of the deposits in order to compensate for the decline of uranium exports. The discoveries, at Koma Bangou and in another dozen locations, yielding between 15 and 200 grams of gold per ton of rock, triggered an influx of illegal miners that the government is having difficulty in controlling. In May 1994 an agreement was signed with a Canadian company for feasibility studies, followed by the erection of a joint company with the Niger government to hold 33 percent of the equity.

KOMADUGU. River, flowing into Lake Chad, which for 150 km forms Niger's border with Nigeria. Along its valley—for which a development plan exists—is found a high density of population. The river was virtually dry for nearly a decade, starting to flow only in 1985. *See also* MANGA.

KOMBA, ADAMOU. Second vice-president of the HCR during 1991–92.

KOMMA, IBRAHIM. Interim secretary of state for interior, appointed by the HCR, between November 1991 and March 1992.

KONNI. Small Hausa state centered around **Birni-N'Konni** between Gobir, Ader, Sokoto, and Maouri. For some time tributary to Gobir, which conquered the region (1750), Konni submitted in the early nineteenth century to the Fulani under Othman Dan Fodio.

KORANIC SCHOOLS. Islamic primary schools found widely in small villages throughout Niger and neighboring countries. The highly informal and often extremely small schools offer a religious education (in some places teaching reading and writing of Arabic script) and a rudimentary amount of secular education. They are usually headed by a faki. These schools were prevalent long before the spread of Western education. In 1916, for example, there were 63 such schools in the Niamey cercle, with 232 students; the figures for the same year for other cercles were Zinder, 489 schools with 2,078 students; Tahoua, 344 schools with 1,547 students; N'Guigmi, 55 schools with 220 students; Gouré, 154 schools with 399 students; Agadez, 44 schools with 605 students; and Bilma, 8 schools with 135 students.

Parallel to these primary schools there are a growing number of *medersa* (secondary) schools in Niger. The first one, established in **Say** in 1957, provided the impetus and model for 35 additional ones by the time of Kountché's 1974 coup d'état, mostly in larger and urban centers (Agadez, Maradi, Tahoua, Zinder, for instance). Funding from Arab countries for the construction of mosques, of which there was an increase—Libya concentrated on such projects, fully funding, for example, the 1976–77 construction of Niamey's Grand Mosque with a capacity of 8,000—resulted in 8 more *medersa*s being set up by 1980, and an additional 12 by 1990. In 1978 there were 4,330 students enrolled in the *medersa*s, and by 1990 some 6,000. The teaching load is heavy (26 hours weekly), since the *medersa*s include normal educational subjects, intensive Koranic study, Islamic history, and some physical education. The language of instruction is French (11 hours) and Arabic (15 hours).

KORI. Hausa term synonymous to wadi, denoting a temporary watercourse in northern Niger.

KOROHOU, MAHAMANE (Lieutenant Colonel). Currently chief of staff of the Niger armed forces.

KOTONDI, AMADOU MAIDANDA (1940–). Former deputy director of the Sûreté Nationale. Born on October 28, 1940, and a graduate of the Ecole Nationale Supérieure de Police (Paris), Kotondi served first as police commissioner and head of personnel in the Sûreté Nationale (1965) before assuming the post of deputy director of the force in 1969. Following the 1974 coup d'état he was shifted to less sensitive duties in the Ministry of Interior.

KOUCHEWA. *See* TAOUA.

KOUILOU, MAHAMANE. Minister of public health in Niger's first post-1990 civilian government, serving between April 1993 and its collapse in October 1994.

KOUKA, HAROU (1922–). Physician and former cabinet minister. Born in 1922 in Zinder and of Mossi ethnic origin, Kouka was educated in Gouré, Zinder, and Niamey before going to Dakar's Ecole William Ponty (1940–43). He continued his studies at Dakar's School of Medicine (1943–47), joining the newborn PPN in 1947. He served as chief medical officer in Bilma (1948–50), Magaria (1950–54), Zinder (1954–55), Filingué (1955–56), and Tanout (1956–57). He was one of the early PPN leaders who joined with Condat to form the PINE party, which later merged with UNIS. Eventually Kouka made his peace with the establishment, and in 1958 he was elected to the National Assembly on the UCFA ticket (later, the PPN) and was reelected in 1965. In June 1959 he was also appointed minister of labor; in October of the same year his portfolio was enlarged to encompass social affairs, and in December 1960 he was shifted to head his original choice, the Ministry of Health. As one of Diori's close associates, Kouka was appointed in 1963 minister of education and held that post through 1972. His inflexibility vis-à-vis Niger's restless students, and his strong hand in the expulsion of over a hundred students in November 1970 (over grievances and strikes), brought upon him the wrath of the educational establishment and his removal from the ministry in which he had become largely ineffectual. He was shifted in 1972 to head the Ministry of Public Works, which post he held until the 1974 coup d'état. After the coup he was arrested together with most of Diori's cabinet and in 1975 was found guilty of embezzlement of 36 million CFA francs and fiscal fraud of 7 million CFA francs, which he was ordered to pay to the National Treasury. He was released from prison in April 1978. Not allowed to practice his long-neglected medical profession, Kouka currently lives a very modest life in Niamey.

KOUKYA. Also known as Gounguia, the ancient pre-Islamic capital of the Songhay on the Niger River, and currently in Mali. Its ruins have never been positively identified, though the town, founded in A.D. 690 is thought to be 140 km from Gao on the Niger River. Koukya was replaced by Gao as the capital of the **Songhay Empire** around the year 1010.

KOUNTCHE, SEYNI (General) (1931–87). President of Niger between 1974 and 1987. Born in 1931 in Fandou, Kountché obtained his primary education in Filingué and in 1944 went to the Kati (Mali) school for servicemen's children. In 1947 he attended secondary schools in Saint-Louis, Senegal, and in 1949 joined the French colonial army. Eight years later, in 1957, he was admitted as first sergeant to Frejus Officers' School and graduated as second lieutenant in 1959. Returning to Niger at independence, he served with the newly created Niger army in Zinder and in Agadez, and during 1965–66 he attended staff colleges in France, following which he was promoted to deputy chief of staff (1967) and major (1968). Despite reports of his political unreliability he was made chief of staff in 1973, and after the coup he staged in 1974 he became president of the Supreme Military Council and head of state of Niger. In 1979 Kountché was promoted to full colonel and in 1984 to major general.

The ascetic and severe-looking Kountché was an energetic officer who spent most of his army career in the field, not in the office. His manner was always abrupt, authoritarian, and abrasive, and he rarely stood on protocol. Simple and direct in tastes, he put in long (eighteen-hour) days and had similar expectations from subordinates. His manner, approach, and strict morals gained him many personal enemies, a fact that nurtured his innate suspicion of rivals. His ability to retain power within the officer corps rested on his de facto position at the head of the armed forces, a coterie of loyal supporters, a well-developed political-intelligence network, the elitist Presidential Guard—the last two headed by family members—and the strict punishment (death) he meted out to plotters. Notwithstanding this, his acute monopolization of power and unpopularity resulted in several mutinies and plots in which the prime conspirators were usually executed.

Though Kountché's 1974 coup may have been justified on the grounds of the corruption of the civilian regime—and military rule was for long regarded as untainted by corruption—by 1980 the picture was changed. All those close to his family had acquired immeasurable wealth. Kountché's brothers controlled many segments of Niger's trade. The president's (much detested) wife was raking in kickbacks from a variety of private enterprises, including a monopoly over the import of indigo cloth from Mali, which she shared with the wife of Mali's president. And one key aide, nicknamed "Bonkano," had amassed a huge fortune operating out of the head of state's office. After the eclipse of military rule, a commission of the National Conference investigating corrupt practices heard details of many of these occurrences (including from Bonkano, who gave evidence, having been granted immunity from prosecution), as well as of Kountché's routinely delving into the Treasury (and especially uranium receipts) for up to 10 billion CFA francs for unscheduled purposes by the presidency or the military forces.

KOUPE KOUPE BATTLE (1830). Major bloody clash between the Kel Owey and the Kel Gress in Damergou in which the expanding Kel Owey were harshly defeated. The outcome of the battle brought about the ascendance of the Kel Gress in the entire area, including Aïr and Agadez.

KOURFEY. *See* KURFEY.

KOUSSOU, IBRAHIM. General Saibou's last secretary of state for finance, serving between March 1990 and September 1991. Both prior to and after this stint in the cabinet, Koussou was the head of the Caisse de Stabilisation des Prix des Produits du Niger.

KOUTOUBI, SANI (Major). Former cabinet minister. Brought into Kountché's cabinet for the first time in January 1983 to serve as minister of information, Koutoubi was shifted in November 1983 to the Ministry of Mines and Industry, serving until Kountché's death in 1987.

KOUTOUKALE. Niamey quarter, currently populated by a large number of Kurtey.

KOY. "Chief" in Djerma, as in **djermakoy.**

KOYAM. Nearly extinct ethnic group. Arriving from Kanem (Chad) to the area west of Lake Chad, then a tributary of the Bornu Empire, the Koyam were decimated and pushed west by the Toubou. Their major center was the village of Belbelec. Remnants moved to Illela after the disaster.

KSAR. Fortresses of stone, banco, or natron, as the case may be, to which the population of the various Kaouar oases flee in time of attack. The first such walled encampments in Kaouar were built by the legendary So (who disappeared in the sixteenth century), and some of these ksars were later rebuilt by contemporary Kanuri residents of the oases.

KUMAYAO. Twelfth-century mythical white founder of **Katsina.** *See also* MARADI.

KUNTA. Saharan Arabic-speaking confederation of clans claiming descent from Sidi Muhamad al-Kunti, who lived in the fifteenth century. In Niger the Kunta were the traditional enemies of the Tuareg in the north, and the main propagators of the **Quadriya** Islamic order especially during the life of Sidi al-Mukhtar al-Kunti (1729–1811). Split up into various groups, including the Touajitom, Atourchan, Tagar, Echark, Almoussakare, and Ouldmelouk, the Kunta dominated—together with the **Ouilliminden**—the bend of the Niger River until the second half of the nineteenth century. Probably originating in Touat, they currently are to be found in Tahoua, In Gall, and Agadez.

KURFEY. Small, Hausa-speaking ethnic group that is also known as Soudié. The Kurfey (not to be confused with the Kurtey) migrated to villages north of Tahoua, pushing the resident Kallé further south. Many of their settlements are at the foot of major geological faults, which serve as protection against attacks by other groups.

KURTEY. Ethnic group usually attached to the Songhay-Djerma group of clans. They are the result of intermarriage of Fulani with Songhay and Djerma. As a Fulani clan (or former slaves) migrating consequent to an internal schism from Macina upstream on the Niger River, they came into Niger around 1750 under the leadership of Chief Maliki. Settling first at Gao, they later descended down the Niger River to settle on the riverain islands off Tillabéry and Niamey around 1820. Currently the area is populated by Kurtey and Wogo. Excellent pastoralists, they tended the cattle of the Songhay, assimilated the Sorko and Kado in the area, and adopted the local language and many of the local customs. They maintain several distinctly Fulani traits and customs and were in due course to fall out with the Songhay. Many Kurtey are currently to be found in Niamey, especially in the Koutoukalé quarter, and those outside that arrondissement are found mostly in the cantons of Dessa and Sonsoni, both in the Tillabéry area.

Prior to the onset of the colonial era the Kurtey were masters of the Niger River, and were greatly feared for their nighttime slave-raiding assaults up the river (in pirogues). These at times reached settlements as far away as 500 km and in general ranged from Say to Timbuktu, with those captured slaves not integrated into Kurtey households being sold at Say and Sansanné-Haoussa. Due to this preoccupation with slave raiding they were often regarded as nothing more than river pirates. Some Kurtey have migrated further downstream to near Zaria in Nigeria. There are around 35,000 of them in Niger. They cultivate river rice, millet, and tobacco and engage in fishing and cattle herding, a remnant of their Fulani origins. Like the **Wogo,** considerable numbers go south, to Ghana, to engage in seasonal labor; indeed, at any one time as much as 40 percent of the adult male population of Kurtey villages may be abroad.

KWARA-KOY. "Village chief" in Djerma.

-L-

LABO, ABDOU. Secretary general in charge of communications in Niger's first post-1990 civilian government, serving between April 1993 and its parliamentary ouster in October 1994.

LABO, KADO. MNSD militant who assumed the presidency of the party after General Saibou resigned from it on July 12, 1991, to remain above politics prior to the convening of the National Conference.

LAKE CHAD. Large, shallow, freshwater lake on which converge the international boundaries of Chad, Niger, Nigeria, and Cameroon. The lake's major source of water is the 1,200-kilometer Chari River, which is augmented in N'Djamena (Chad) by the Logone River, both entirely within Chad. The surface of the lake varies tremendously depending upon climatic conditions. In the past the lake encompassed as much as 25,000 sq km and as little as 3,500 sq km. During the Sahel drought of 1968–74, for example, the lake contracted to one-third of its normal size, and crossing from Niger to Chad was possible on foot. In 1985 it shrank to barely 3,500 sq km, and none of its surface water even fell within Niger's international boundaries.

In historic times Lake Chad was a vast inland sea stretching into Chad's Tibesti Mountains and was connected with the Nile River system via affluents. At the time the lake's surface covered some 300,000 to 400,000 sq km. Niger's portion of Lake Chad is 3,000 sq km of its northwest segment. The lake's altitude is 280 meters, and the average depth is from 1 to 4 meters, with annual variations of 1 to 3 meters.

LAOUALI, AMADOU. Minister of equipment and housing in Niger's first regular civilian cabinet, serving between April 1993 and its parliamentary ouster in October 1994.

LAYA, DIOULDE (1937–). Sociologist and director of the Centre National de Recherches en Sciences Humaines. Born in 1937 in Tamou (Say) and educated in Say, Kolo, and Bamako (Mali), Laya continued his higher studies in Dakar (1957–62 and 1967) in sociology. Between 1962 and 1970 secretary general of the Niger Commission of UNESCO (in the Ministry of Education in Niamey), he was appointed director of CNRSH in 1970. He has published a number of works on African oral traditions.

LAZARET. Tuareg drought-relief refugee camp near Niamey during the 1970s and again in the 1980s. Mostly settled by nomadic Tuareg from Mali who migrated into Niger in search of relief from the Sahel drought. The original camp was on the outskirts of Niamey, but when it became an eyesore with potential for the spread of epidemics, it was relocated to a site 40 km from the capital and dubbed Lazaret 2. This occurred in 1974. The camp is currently located some 11 km from Hamdallayé, the nearest village. Lazaret 1 was officially inaugurated by President Diori in early 1973, and by the time of its relocation in August 1974 it had a population of over 20,000. Its name, given it by Catholic missionaries, comes from *Lazarus*.

LETE ISLAND DISPUTE. *See* DAHOMEY-NIGER BOUNDARY DISPUTE.

LIBYA. Niger's northern neighbor, with whom relations have existed from antiquity. Their mutual boundaries have never been fully demarcated, and in 1970 there were several border skirmishes occasioned by rumors about the presence of oil in the area and by Niger's known uranium deposits. At the time several hundred nomads were expelled. When President Diori visited Libya in February 1971 he was informed that an administrative incident had been to blame, and some 3,000 million CFA francs in credits were offered to Niger. An agreement followed that established a variety of joint ventures, including a development bank and a joint chamber of commerce. An Islamic center for Niamey was later pledged when Niger broke relations with Israel after Libyan insistence. A mutual-defense treaty was signed between the two countries shortly before the 1974 coup d'état in Niamey. Relations between the two countries, however, have been deeply affected by the Qaddafi regime's insistence on the validity of the never-ratified **Mussolini-Laval boundary agreement,** according to which Libya's border was expanded some 200 miles further south into Aïr. This caused inevitable friction with Niger, as well as with other countries affected, such as Chad. The coup d'état of 1974 was to some extent the reaction of the Niger military to the overly close relations being established by Diori with Libya. After the coup all existing treaties with Libya, including a quasi-secret military one, were scrapped; some were later renegotiated.

Since 1974 Niger-Libya relations have been uneasy, and subject to vicissitudes. In the 1976 attempted coup of Major Bayeré, a "Libyan connection" was clearly visible (four tons of arms had been airlifted into Niamey, and Libya knew in advance of the imminent coup attempt), though diplomatic relations were not ruptured until 1981. This decision was made in the aftermath of Libya's increased military presence in neighboring Chad and the unilateral transformation of Libya's embassy in Niamey to a "People's Bureau." The impasse took a turn for the worse when Libya retaliated by calling upon Niger's Tuareg for support, reminding them that they were Libyan in origin and could be reunited (together with their counterparts in Mali and Algeria) within a "Sahel Republic." The irredentist call was viewed by Niamey as extreme provocation both in light of the sparsely patrolled northern regions of Niger (where the Tuareg nomadized) and the fact that the proposed Sahel Republic included Niger's major uranium and coal mines. Diplomatic relations were not fully reestablished until 1984 (after being briefly patched up in March 1982). In May 1985 a mostly Tuareg commando unit, trained in Libya, was intercepted prior to an assault on a Niger garrison town—part of an effort of **Abdoulaye Diori** to trigger an upheaval resulting in a comeback of his father, Hamani Diori. The incident, however, was not blamed on Libya, since the headquarters of Diori were in Algeria.

Libyan involvement with Tuareg irredentism in Niger did not end with this incident; in the 1990s Libya was a source of arms, refuge, and support for at least one of the liberation fronts that sprang up in Niger. On the other hand, for some time, and at least between 1979 and 1985—interrupted by the rupture in diplomatic relations—Niger has quasi-surreptitiously exported quantities of enriched uranium to Libya. Traveling overland by truck from Arlit, these shipments have been the subject of significant speculation.

On the cultural and economic fronts, relations between Niger and Libya have been freer of tension. Libya has cooperated in setting up, with Nigerien state participation, a number of joint companies, including a bank and, as Niger's economy nose-dived in the late 1980s, has pumped in new funds to keep it operational. In the mid-1970s Libya single-handedly picked up the tab for building Niamey's new Grand Mosque (inaugurated in 1977 by General Kountché, and accommodating 8,000 worshipers), when the previous structure was no longer adequate for the city's needs. In like manner, funds have been disbursed for a variety of mostly religious and cultural projects, in accord with long-standing Libyan priorities on foreign aid.

LISAWAN. Tuareg clan, named after an ancestor—Illiassou—currently settled in the Keita area of Niger. Their origin is not quite clear, though scholars think that they came south to Ader from **Azelik** in Aïr, then a rival of Agadez. They arrived in Ader with **Aggaba,** son of the sultan of Agadez, and conquered the region for Aïr, being placed in top administrative positions by Aggaba, who returned to Agadez. Nomadic stockbreeders, the Lisawan became sedentary only in the nineteenth century.

LISSOUANE. *See* LISAWAN.

LOGA. Arrondissement of 65,000 people in the département of Dosso, and a town of 4,000 which is the headquarters of the arrondissement.

LOI-CADRE. The "Enabling Act" passed by the French National Assembly in June 1956. The law expanded the legislative powers of the territorial assemblies in each of France's colonies at the expense of the two African federations, gave all overseas territories local autonomy, made suffrage universal, and established a single electoral college in each colony (*see* DOUBLE ELECTORAL COLLEGE).

LOUDOUDJI, BOUBAKAR. *See* DIOBO, ALFA MOHAMED.

LOULAMI. Capital of the **Dendi** branch of the Songhay Empire following its collapse to Moroccan power in the **Battle of Tondibi.** Long since disappeared, Loulami was probably in the vicinity of the contemporary Say.

LOUTOU, IBRAHIM (1934–). Former diplomat and secretary of state for information. Born in 1934 in Maradi and educated there and in Tahoua, Loutou was prepared for a teaching career and taught in Zinder and Gangara (1956–61) before being appointed cultural attaché in the

Niger embassy to France (1961–62). In 1962–63 he attended the University Institute for Higher International Studies in Geneva and on his return to Niamey was appointed director of the Foreign Ministry's Department of Political, Economic, and Cultural Affairs (1963–65). During 1965–66 he again served in Niger's embassy to France as first counselor, and between 1965 and 1967 he attended the Faculty of Law and Economics of the University of Paris. In 1966 he was appointed executive director of the African Groundnut Council based in Lagos and in 1971 became Niger's ambassador to Nigeria. In 1974 he was also accredited to Cameroon and Zaire. After the 1974 coup d'état Loutou was repatriated to Niamey and appointed technical councillor to the presidency, and in 1975 and 1976 he served as secretary of state for information and tourism. He was dismissed from his post and placed under house arrest early in January 1976 for issuing a "misleading and unauthorized" statement regarding Niger's recognition of the MPLA in Angola. In a sense reflecting the views of a faction in the military regime over which President Kountché did not have total control, Loutou was the victim of a difference of opinion on the Angola situation. He is currently in retirement.

LUGU. Azna village in the Dallol Maouri that is an important center for animist rituals.

LY, ABDOULAYE (1920–). High Ministry of Interior official. Born on June 13, 1920, in Fada N'Gourma, Upper Volta (Burkina Faso) and educated locally and abroad, Ly worked as an administrative official between 1941 and 1964. In September 1964 he was appointed cabinet director of the Ministry of Public Health. During 1967–68 he was also secretary of the Steering Committee of the PPN party, following which he was transferred to the newly created Arlit arrondissement. In 1974 he returned to Niamey to serve as head of the Personnel Bureau in the Ministry of Interior.

LY, SOULAYMANE (1919–). Former secretary general to the government. Born on October 23, 1919, in Fada N'Gourma, Upper Volta (Burkina Faso) and educated in Tenkodogo, Upper Volta, Niamey, and at the Teachers Training School of Katibougou (Mali), Ly—by profession a teacher and primary school inspector—was a schoolmaster in several Niger schools in Gouré, Zinder, Tahoua, and Manga between 1938 and 1942. After independence he became the cabinet director of the Ministry of Rural Economy and later of the Ministry of Defense before being appointed in 1965 deputy subprefect of Tillabéry, then subprefect of Illela (1966–67) and of Mirria (1967–68). In 1968 he returned to Niamey to become codirector of the Ecole Nationale d'Administration (1968–71), and in 1971 he became secretary general to the government. After the 1974 coup he went into retirement.

-M-

MADAOUA. Arrondissement of 118,418 people, of whom 45,100 are nomads, with headquarters in a town of the same name. The town itself, 510 km from Niamey, has a population of 5,000. It is an important regional center in Niger's cotton belt, with a big Sunday market.

MADI, MAYAKI (1906–). Assembly deputy. Born in 1906 in Filingué, and by profession a civil servant, Madi served in the Assembly from March 1957, when he was first elected, until the 1974 coup d'état. Now retired, he had been the chairman of the Assembly's important Finance and Economics Committee since 1960.

MADIBA. Diviners who, for a fee, can suggest propitious dates or days for travel or important business. The divination is usually based on analysis of signs on the sand.

MADOUDOU, FARMO. Former director of the National Tourist Office. An educator by training, Madoudou was chef de cabinet of the minister of economic affairs and planning (1960–61), head of the photo-cinematographic education division of the Ministry of Information and Press (July 1961 to April 1966) and on April 29, 1966, was appointed director of the Tourist Office. He held that post until 1972, when he was transferred to technical duties in the Ministry of Information.

MAGAGI, BOUREIMA (1942–). Journalist. Born on January 29, 1942, in Maradi and educated locally and abroad as a journalist, Magagi has been director of programs at the Ministry of Information since December 1971.

MAGAGIA. *See* MAGAJIYA.

MAGAJIYA (*also* Magagia). Queen of **Bori** and leader of the prostitutes. Though not initiated to Bori, the magajiya (also *Iya*) regulates all conflicts that arise between initiates. In the actual Bori ceremonies she is aided in her duties by the serkin Bori, who are usually men and collect taxes from each initiate, organize the ceremonies and Bori life in their communities, and in general serve as the regional administrators of the cult. The magajiya is a very powerful figure, chosen for her intelligence, leadership qualities, and strong personality, and because of her role in those regions where the ritual is widespread her political support is usually greatly sought after. In Niamey the magajiya played a major role during the Second World War and at the time of the 1958 referendum when she opted for the PPN party and delivered it a strong vote. Indeed, since then the chief magajiya (of Niamey), who presides over the other magajiyas of the various town quarters, has been a member of the PPN politburo. Moreover, it was the magajiyas of Niamey who created, in 1956, the **Association des Femmes** and in 1958 the Association de Jeunes Filles du Niger and the **Union des Femmes du Niger.** *Magajiya* is a Hausa term that is also used by the Songhay; other titles exist in non-Hausa areas.

MAGARAM. Synonymous with **inna.**

MAGARIA. Town of some 7,000 people 92 km west of Zinder and the acknowledged "peanut capital" of Niger. In the immediate pre-independence era a bastion of the **SAWABA** party, Magaria was founded by Massabaki, a prince of Daura Zongo (one of the original Hausa states) and eventually fell under the sway of Damagaram. Magaria is also the name of an arrondissement in the département of Zinder, with headquarters in the town of the same name. The area produces between 36 percent (in 1958) and 51 percent (1968) of Niger's peanut crop.

MAGORAWA. Ethnic group found in **Ader** originating from Bilma (in the eighth century) and first moving to Aïr, then to Arewa, and finally to Ader under Tuareg pressure in the seventeenth century. Their name comes from Magori, one of their chiefs. The Magorawa were the only group to resist successfully the Tuareg conquest of Ader (*see* AGGABA). Also called Magori at times, they are found in the east-central part of Ader, in Tamaské, Takwoshi, and in the Deulle regions.

MAGORI. *See* MAGORAWA.

MAHAMADOU, SEYDOU. Head of Personnel Division, Ministry of Foreign Affairs. Mahamadou has served as second secretary at Niger's embassy to the USA (1964–65), first secretary at Niger's embassy in France (1965–72), and since 1973 as head of the Personnel Division in the Foreign Ministry.

MAHAMANE, ABDOU GENTIL (1918–). Former mayor of Zinder and early politician. Born in 1918 in Magaria and by profession a postal official, Mahamane emerged early as an political figure. He was elected in 1946 to the Conseil Général and in 1959 served for two years as Niger's representative to the Counseil Economique et Social. In 1961 he moved into administrative duties with his appointment as head of the Tahoua district (1961–65) and administrator of SOTRAMIL. In 1966 he was elected mayor of Zinder as well as deputy to the National Assembly and served in the latter body as vice-president of the Committee on General Affairs. He is currently in retirement.

MAHAMANE, ANNOU. Former minister of planning, commerce, and transport. Educated in economics in Paris (and possessing a Ph.D. in that field), Mahamane joined the Kountché cabinet for the first time in 1976 as minister of planning. In February he was shifted to head the Ministry of Mines and Industry (a critical appointment as well) but was returned to his old post in July 1982. An extremely influential technocrat, Mahamane further consolidated his control over the Niger economy in January 1983 when he added to his duties the portfolios of commerce and transport. He left the cabinet in the 1985 cabinet shuffle.

MAHAMANE, KONDO (1938–). Diplomat. Born on July 19, 1938, in Birni-N'Konni, Mahamane was educated locally and worked between 1956 and 1967 with the Financial Service in the Ministry of Finance. On February 7, 1967, he was appointed chancellor at the Niger embassy to the U.S. in Washington, a post he held until 1977.

MAHAMANE, TAWAYE. Former serkin Madaoua between 1937 and 1955. A member of UNIS and of the Niger Territorial Assembly (1947–55), in 1955 Mahamane was deposed and imprisoned for several years.

MAHAMIDOU, ALIOU (1936–). Briefly prime minister of Niger, between March 1990 and September 1991, when the HCR government was set up after the National Conference. Prior to this appointment Mahamidou, a prominent industrialist, was chief executive of the Nigerien Cement Works.

MAIDJIRGUI. Small village near Zinder where Voulet and Chanoine, infamous French colonial officers (*see* MISSION AFRIQUE CENTRALE), were killed. Their tombs are found one hundred meters from the main road and village.

MAIDOKA, MOUSSA. Director of state lands. A high-level official in the Ministry of Finance, Maidoka was deputy director of fiscal controls (February 1966–June 1968), head of insurance and public establishments (June 1968–June 1970), deputy director of state lands (July 1970–April 1971), and has been director of state lands since April 1971.

MAIDOU, MAHAMADOU. Minister of commerce and industry in General Saibou's cabinet between November 1987 and May 1989.

MAIGA. A name found extensively among Songhay nobility, denoting descent from the former ruling **Askia** or **Sonni** families of the **Songhay Empire.** Sign of authentic Songhay nobility.

MAIGA, AMADOU FITI (1948–). Lawyer and former minister of interior. Born on May 23, 1948, in Dosso, and educated at the University of Toulouse and Paris, Maiga started his career as director of local government and was in 1982 integrated into General Kountché's cabinet as secretary of state for the interior. In 1984 he was promoted to minister delegate for the interior. Maiga was carried over into General Saibou's cabinet when he assumed power in November 1987 as minister of interior, and in May 1989 was shifted to head the Ministry of Administrative Reform. In December of that year he was reassigned as minister of state attached to the presidential office, and in March 1990 he left the government.

MAIGA, AMADOU SEYNI (Colonel). Former cabinet minister. Brought into Kountché's cabinet in June 1980 as minister of health and social affairs, Maiga retained his post until September 1981 when he was transferred to the civil service administration and appointed prefect of Zinder. He was promoted to major in 1981, and to colonel in 1987, at which time he became the deputy chief of staff of the Niger armed forces. Under mass pressure for his ouster due to his role in the army's brutal suppression of the student demonstrations in Niamey, he resigned in March 1990 from the MNSD party, in which he occupied the post of political secretary of the national executive bureau. Later he was dismissed from the armed forces.

MAIGA, BOUBOU IDRISSA (1932–). Civil and agricultural administrator. Born in Niamey on April 4, 1932, Maiga was educated in Tahoua and later in France where he studied agriculture and cooperatives. During his years in France he also developed an interest in poetry and in the arts, which he studied in Touraine. On his return to Niger, Maiga worked with rural-development mutual-assistance societies in the Niamey area, and on November 15, 1972, was appointed deputy prefect of Niamey. Following the 1974 coup he was reassigned to head a division in the administration of the Niamey district, continuing with a string of such appointments.

MAIGA, DIAMBALLA YANSAMBOU (1910–). Minister of interior between 1958 and 1974 and prior to the 1974 coup d'état the strongest of the triumvirate at the helm of Niger. Born in 1910 at Namarou (near Niamey) to a noble Songhay chef de canton, and tracing his lineage to the ruling family of the Songhay Empire, Maiga obtained only a rudimentary education, though through his flair for languages he has become extremely versatile linguistically. A simple clerk in the French colonial administration between 1929 and 1940, Maiga requested a posting in Aïr in 1940 (for health reasons); in five years he became thoroughly familiar with Arab and Tuareg life, customs, and languages. By 1949 he had become head of a section of the Treasury and a local leader of the PPN party, which he had helped found after attending the founding congress of the RDA in Bamako, Mali. Representing the powerful traditional chiefs of Niger, Maiga was after that date both the key member of the PPN and a basic fixture of Diori's cabinets. Elected to the National Assembly from Tillabéry in 1957, Maiga was appointed minister of interior in Diori's first government (1958) and remained in that post for the next sixteen years, setting an African record. At the time of the 1964 **SAWABA** uprising, Maiga was prominent in demanding the stiffest possible sentences against those involved and in his ruthless crushing of the assault on the regime. Between 1956 and 1974 the first vice-president of the PPN politburo, Maiga was part of the ruling triumvirate of Niger (with Hama and Diori) and according to some the real strongman. Accusations of corruption and fiscal mismanagement while in office did not tarnish his image until the 1974 coup d'état, when he was promptly imprisoned by the new military regime. An aggressive and intimidating as well as highly arrogant politician, his friends generally regard him as gentle and charming.

MAIGA, DINGARAYE. Cinematographer, best known for his 1979 production, *Nuages noirs*.

MAIGA, GAMATIE HAMIDOU (1913–). Veterinarian and former Foreign Ministry official. Born in 1913 in Say and educated abroad as a veterinary doctor, Maiga served as head veterinarian before being appointed ambassador to Nigeria in June 1961. He served there for a year and a half and was then transferred to head the Consular Affairs section and Secretariat at the Ministry of Foreign Affairs. In 1966 he became director of the cabinet of the Ministry of Rural Economy. He was shifted to other duties in 1971 and is currently retired.

MAIGA, HOUSSEINI (1949–). Hydrologist. Educated in hydrology at the universities of Nancy and Arizona, Maiga teaches at the University of Niamey and is attached to the Centre AGRHYMET.

MAIGA, YOUSSOUFFA AMADOU (Colonel). Former minister of national education, and currently commander of the national gendarmerie. A gendarmerie officer by training, Maiga joined Kountché's cabinet in February 1981 and is credited with soothing relations between the country's students and the regime as minister of education. In June 1982 he left the cabinet to become head of the gendarmerie, being progressively promoted from the rank of captain. Briefly presidential military adviser, appointed on October 26, 1994, by President Ousmane, in February 1995 he was appointed again commander of the national gendarmerie by Prime Minister Hama Amadou.

MAIGANA, MAI (1927–). Educator, former president of the Court of State Security and cabinet minister under both Hamani Diori and General Kountché. Born in 1927 in Kellé (Gouré) and of Beri Beri chiefly origins, Maigana was educated in Zinder and Niamey before attending Dakar's Ecole William Ponty (1945–48). He then taught in Niamey (1948–52) and served as school director in Madarounfa (Maradi) becoming also secretary general of the Niger Teachers Union. In 1955–56 he served as secretary for academic inspection in the Ministry of Education, following which he undertook higher studies in Paris (ENFOM), returning to Niamey to become cabinet director of the minister of interior (1958–59). During 1959–60 the administrative head of the Konni district, Maigana served in a similar capacity in Maradi (1960–63) and Zinder (1963–65), returning to Niamey in 1965 to an appointment as state inspector for African affairs attached to the presidency. He remained in the presidential office as secretary of state in charge of cooperation (1969–70), in charge of development and international cooperation (merely a change in the title of his office, 1970–72), and in 1972 he was made minister delegate to the presidency with general responsibilities. In December 1972 he was promoted to full ministerial rank as minister of human development and served in that capacity until the 1974 coup d'état. After 1968 he was on the Interministerial Committee on Uranium. In 1975 Maigana became the government's secretary general and in 1977 joined Kountché's cabinet as minister of economics, later also of trade and industry. One of the very few Diori appointees to be integrated into the Kountché regime, Maigana was dropped from the cabinet in February 1981 following his inability to resolve Niger's economic problems, and was appointed first to head a parastatal company and later as president of the State Security Court.

Because of his traditional status and importance, Maigana was utilized by General Saibou, after his rise to power, in a variety of advisory capacities, notably on the constitutional commission of 1988. He was again utilized during 1994–95, though now retired, by the civilian regime of President Mahamane Ousmane as chief negotiator with leaders of the Tuareg rebellion in Aïr.

MAI-GARI. Hausa for "chief," from *mai* of the **gari.**

MAIKASSOUA, ILLA. General Kountché's minister of higher education and research between July 1982 and November 1987. He was dropped from the cabinet with the rise to power of General Saibou.

MAIKOUREMA, ZEINAIBOU. Secretary of state in charge of agriculture in the post-Saibou civilian government, between April 1993 and its fall in October 1994.

MAINASSARA, BOUREIMA. During the Saibou era secretary general of the Union des Syndicats des Travailleurs du Niger, encompassing thirty-one constituent trade unions.

MAINASSARA, DAMBA (Colonel). Former chief of staff of the Niger army. Of Sudié ethnic origins, Mainassara was promoted through the ranks and at independence became Niger's first indigenous chief of staff (1960–63). He was then attached to the Ministry of Defense as military adviser and in 1968 was appointed director of the veterans office in the same ministry. He is currently in retirement.

MAINASSARA, MAIDADJI. Magistrate, president of the Niamey Court of Appeal, and between 1991 and 1993 president of the autonomous National Electoral Commission (CNE) that was charged with supervising the return to civilian rule and the series of elections attending it.

MAINE-SOROA. Arrondissement in the département of Diffa, which encompasses a population of 120,000 and includes a poste administratif at Goudoumaria. The village of Mainé-Soroa, which is the headquarters of the arrondissement, has a population of 3,000.

MAIZOUMBOU, SAMNA (1898–1967). Former minister of stockbreeding. Born in Tibiri in 1898 and during the colonial era serving as an interpreter, Maizoumbou, who was a local chief, served for two weeks (December 18, 1958, to January 3, 1959) as minister of stockbreeding before being shifted to the presidential office as secretary of state in charge of traditional customs. Found unsuitable for these sensitive political duties, Maizoumbou was returned to his chiefly duties on December 31, 1960.

MALAFIA, DJIBO (1928–). Forestry engineer. Born around 1928 in Karayé and educated locally and at the Ecole Fédérale de l'AOF (Abidjan) as a forestry engineer, Malafia served as director of forestry services between 1965 and 1973. In 1973 he was appointed administrator of a state enterprise and retired a few years later.

MALAM, BOUKAR ABA. Interim minister of agriculture appointed by the HCR government in November 1991 and serving in that capacity until April 1993 when an elected government emerged.

MALAM, TOULOU (1908–). Born in 1908 in Dori, and a well-known marabout and Koranic expert of Djerma ethnicity, Malam became a PPN militant in 1946 and the party's (largely inactive) second vice-president. Between 1968 and 1973 he was attached to the Ministry of Economic Affairs, also in a largely inactive capacity. Since 1973 he has been in retirement. A well-known religious fixture of the Diori regime and the PPN party, despite his low profile Malam was part of the innermost circle of Niger prior to the 1974 coup d'état.

MALAM AWAMI, MAMADOU. Magistrate and General Saibou's last president of the Supreme Court, appointed in December 1989.

MALAM YARO (1852?–1921). Important long-distance merchant. Born to a family that traced its origins from Egypt but was established in Damagaram for two generations, Malam Yaro—whose actual name was Moussa ben Abdoulahhi, and whose father was a religious scholar from the Kanuri town of Kulumfardo—grew up in Zinder and Agadez and established a vast commercial network stretching from Bornu to Tripoli on the coast. With strong family ties with the Tuareg (having married a woman of the Kel Tafidet drum group) that facilitated his trade, Malam Yaro became a prime supplier of goods to the French forces in Niger as well.

An important personality in the Damagaram court, and a trusted adviser to the sultan, Malam Yaro was very favorably regarded by the French until 1906. Indeed, they had earlier considered elevating him to the throne, an idea that he firmly turned down. (This was out of gratitude for his assistance to the ill-fated Mission du Haut-Soudan of Captain **Cazemajou.**) In 1906 he was accused, together with the sultan, of an anti-French conspiracy, and promptly exiled to Ivory Coast and Paris. The accusation was a false one and connected with internal court intrigues. Upon his return to Niger after three years exile, Malam Yaro's commercial empire was in shambles, and he died penniless in 1921.

MALBAZA CEMENT WORKS. Popular name for the SNC. Established in 1966 in Malbaza, 36 km east of Birni-N'Konni, to replace costly imports of cement from abroad, its product's price in 1969 was 13,000 CFA francs a ton, or twice the world market price of cement (though just about equal to the price of imported cement, given the high cost of transport from the coast). The factory has been working at two-thirds capacity and produces an average of 40,000 tons of cement a year.

MALKA, JEAN-GUY (1935–). Linguist. Born in 1935 and educated in linguistics and English in France, he commenced his career as a lecturer of English at the Ministry of National Education (1970–73), and was promoted in 1974 to head of linguistics in that ministry. In 1977 he joined IRSH as its head of linguistics.

MALLAM (1688?–1746). Only known name of the founder of Zinder and the Damagaram Sultanate at the end of the seventeenth century (*see* DAMAGARAM). Born around the end of the seventeenth century, Mallam studied under his father, a marabout named Maina Kadey, in the latter's center of Belbelec. He acquired local fame for his piety, miracles, and saintly demeanor and was made chief of the Gueza village in 1736. His lineage expanded the original dominions into the powerful Damagaram kingdom. Mallam's successor, his son, was Babami.

MAMADOU, AMADOU. General Saibou's first minister of agriculture, appointed in November 1987. In May 1989 Mamadou left the cabinet to become high commissioner for the Kandadji Dam project.

MAMADOU, MAIDAH (1924–). Former minister. Born in 1924 in Tessaoua and of Hausa noble origin, Mamadou is the son of a marabout and president of the Tessaoua indigenous tribunal. He was educated locally and in Maradi and Niamey before obtaining a teacher's certificate at the Katibougou (Mali) Teachers College (1941–45). He served with the French colonial army (1946–47) in Ivory Coast, and between 1947 and 1958 he worked as a teacher in a variety of schools in Niger. Elected in 1959 to the National Assembly from Tessaoua, he was immediately brought into Diori's cabinet as minister of agriculture, water resources, and forestry (1959–61) and in succession served as minister of education (1961–63), rural economy (1963–70), foreign affairs (1970–72), minister delegate to the presidency (1972), and minister of information (1972–74). His general decline in importance in the cabinet hierarchy after 1971 was a consequence of his general inactivity in office, though he was retained in the cabinet because of his gentle mannerisms, lack of ambition, and Hausa traditional credentials so needed in a government dominated by Djerma-Songhay interests. Following the 1974 coup-d'état Mamadou was arrested for fiscal fraud of 18 million CFA francs and embezzlement of 7 million CFA francs. He was under house arrest until 1976.

MAMADOU, MOUSSA (1939–). Rural development administrator. Born in 1939 in Gaya and educated in Gaya and Tahoua, Mamadou is a teacher by training. He taught in Logo (Dosso) and Say between 1958 and 1965, and in 1965 joined the Ministry of Rural Development, having taken a brief course (the same year) in Paris in development planning. In 1965–66 he served as deputy director of rural development, and between 1966 and 1972 he was head of the Human Development Section in that ministry. With the creation of a separate Ministry of Human Development in August 1972 he became the director of it and served in that capacity until the 1974 coup d'état. He has been active in party affairs, being a PPN member since 1958, secretary general of the Say branch (1962–65) and deputy secretary general of the PPN youth wing since 1969. Currently retired, he is the author of several works on development issues.

MAMANE, ABOU. Well-known Tuareg newspaper publisher. During the 1991 National Conference he served as head of the Crimes Commission investigating instances of abuse of power during earlier regimes. At the time of the October 1992 mass roundup in Aïr of Tuareg suspected of being sympathizers with the rebellion, Mamane fled via Burkina Faso to Paris.

MAMANI, ABDOULAYE (1932–). Journalist, author, and screenwriter. Born in 1932 and a journalist based in Zinder by profession, in 1972 Mamani published a collection of poems, and in 1980 a novel, both by Parisian presses. He has also written a number of theatrical dramas and other works.

MANGA. Region in Niger and name of ethnic group. The Manga are a Kanuri-speaking group of around 100,000 residing east of Zinder, north of Gouré between the Komadugu River and Mounio. Their origin is not known. Though regarding themselves as distinct from the Kanuri (whom they view as strangers), the Manga are quite probably of Kanuri extraction, and their territory was all along a province of the **Kanem-Bornu Empire,** and known as Mangari. The Manga never created any states in their territory, and in 1855, exploiting Bornu's decline and the Fulani pressures, Sultan Tanimoun of Damagaram annexed the entire area to his own kingdom. The area is astride the Niger-Chad border and is a series of plateaus without much vegetation. It is also inhabited by the Daza Toubou and the Hassaouna Arabs.

MANGA, BOULAMA (Major). Former minister in the Kountché regime. A little-known head of a gendarmerie unit prior to the 1974 coup d'état, Manga was one of the key officers in the clique that seized power. He was appointed minister of economic affairs, commerce, and industry in Kountché's first cabinet, and in December 1974 he was also appointed head of NITRA. Shifted to head the Ministry of Rural Development in February 1976, Manga was shortly thereafter (March 15, 1976) dropped from office and briefly imprisoned on suspicion of involvement in the attempted coup of that date. Cleared of these charges, he was reinstated in the cabinet as minister of youth, sport, and culture, serving until September 1979. By then differing with Kountché on a variety of policy issues, Manga was appointed, like many of the other officers Kountché sidelined, as prefect of one of Niger's regions. When he refused to leave Niamey on this assignment, he was arrested. He was not released until 1987 (after Kountché's death) by General Saibou, and he was then pensioned off.

MANO, ALITOR. Minister of agriculture in the MNSD-dominated government of February 1995.

MAOURI. Ethnic group found in the **Dallol Maouri** valley. Often called also **Azna** because of their animist beliefs, the Azna of Maouri are much more homogeneous than the Azna of Ader. There are various legends as to their origins. One refers to the derivation of this Hausa-speaking group from a temporary Bornuan dynasty in the valley following which the Arewa chiefdom was established as Kaosa (30 km southeast of Dogondoutchi) under nominal Gobirawa suzerainty. A highly localized ethnic group (with its core in the Dogondoutchi area), the Maouri can be differentiated into two groups: the Arewa and the Gubawa. The former have the strongest links with Bornu, arriving late and conquering the Gubawa and dividing power between the political head—the serkin Arewa, of their own group—and the saranuya head, the ritual queen of Lugu and of the Gubawa.

The term *Maouri* is mostly used by the Djerma and Fulani to refer to the Dogondoutchi region and population. The Fulani also use the term *Arewa* to refer to this population, though strictly speaking the term should be reserved for reference to the area and population around Matankari.

MARADI. Département encompassing 35,100 sq km and a population of 850,000 people with an average density of 21 per sq km. The département includes the arrondissements of Maradi, Dakoro, Mayaki, and the postes administratifs of Madarounfa, Gazaoua, Tibiri, and Tessaoua. The population is a composite of Hausa with smaller communities of Fulani, Buzu, and Tuareg. Centrally located, it is 670 km from Niamey, 250 km from Zinder, and 250 km from Kano in Nigeria, with which it is tightly connected for economic reasons. The

Maradi arrondissement within the département encompasses an area of 8,200 sq km and 330,000 people, giving it the highest density—33 per sq km—in all of Niger. The arrondissement is known as the peanut capital of Niger, producing fully 50 percent of Niger's peanut crop. The town of Maradi has a population of 75,000 making it Niger's third largest city, having ceded second rank to Zinder (85,000) around 1980. Much of the original town was badly damaged by the major floods that struck this region in 1945. The département was subject to much administrative reorganization during the colonial and postcolonial period and was finally reconstituted on October 17, 1963, after being temporarily disbanded on April 9, 1960. Previously suppressed as an individual region in 1926, it was reconstituted with three cantons in July 1944. The current arrondissement is divided into two—Maradi and Gobir. The former is the traditional fiefdom of the serkin Katsina and is divided into five local units, while the latter is under the authority of the serkin Gobir, who until recently was a member of the National Assembly.

The Maradi département is a large, sandy area that at all times has between 650 and 700 mm of rain and competes with Niamey as the economic capital of the country. It is the terminus of a paved road from Kano, where much of Niger's peanut crop is shipped. Much of Niger's imports also come via Maradi, being shipped from Lagos to Kano by rail and onward by truck. Maradi being the prime Hausa city of Niger, the Maradi Hausa are linked to their kinsmen across the international border, a fact that has at times disturbed both Niger's and Nigeria's leaders. Little is known of the history of the region prior to the arrival of the **Gobirawa** and, further south, the Katsinawa. The name of the region, and town, is also subject to some controversy, deriving from (*a*) a corruption of *Maryadi* (''the refuge''); (*b*) the name of a goddess to whom the valley belongs; or (*c*) the title of a Katsinawa official. A Katsina province that fell to Fulani rule (as did Katsina itself), the Maradi area became in the early nineteenth century the refuge of those Katsinawa expelled from their territory further south in the Fulani religious wars. In 1807 the Fulani under Umaru Dallaji overcame Katsina, defeating the Hausa ruler Magajin Halidou, who escaped to the northeast with some of his followers. After his suicide, **Dan Kassawa** was selected as the serkin Katsina. The Hausa refugees went to Damagaram, where they lived for two years before settling at Gafai on the border of Damagaram and the Maradi province, now under Fulani rule. They remained in Gafai for ten years, building up their strength and eventually occupying Maradi following a local revolt against the Fulani in the city. After installing themselves in Maradi, war became the prime rationale of the expatriate state, since all ardently believed—at least at the outset—that their stay would be only temporary until Katsina was regained. The history of Maradi in the nineteenth century is therefore the story of a never-ending tug-of-war between the Fulani of Katsina and the Katsinawa of Maradi. Maradi's allies in this struggle were the Gobirawa—also expelled by the Fulani—and, tacitly, Damagaram, which was not directly affected by the Fulani wars.

For some time the Gobirawa and Katsinawa lived together in Maradi, but eventually a joint effort was made and Tibiri was built for the Gobirawa in 1836 some 8 km northwest of Maradi. Under **Dan Baskore** a determined military assault of 10,000 warriors and a cavalry from Gobir, Maradi, Damagaram, and their Kel Owey allies reached to within 8 km of Katsina before being repulsed. By 1845 an uneasy stalemate had developed between Maradi and Katsina, with periodic mutual assaults across their respective frontier zones but without any major victories on the part of either of the two protagonists. Of the various rulers of Maradi, one of the most important was Dan Baskore, under whose leadership the kingdom prospered and became finally entrenched when a large wall was erected to protect the town. The most important officeholders in Maradi, after the king, were the kaura (commander in chief of the armies and especially of the cavalry, who was traditionally at least nominally a slave); the galadima (the most senior civil servant in the kingdom, a eunuch, and governor of territory south of Maradi town); and the yan daka (governor of areas southwest of the town). Together these officials constituted a check on the powers of the serkin. Though they could depose him, their interests usually coincided. The king lists of the Katsinawa successor state of Maradi are subject to various controversies as to the precise dates of the reigns of several rulers. The following is one chronology: Dan Kassawa, 1807–25; Rauda, 1825–35; Dan Mari, 1835–48; Binoni, 1848–53; Dan Mahedi, 1853–57; Dan Baura, 1857–58; Dan Baskore, 1858–79; Barmou, 1879–83; Mazawaje, 1883–85; Mallam, 1885–86; Mazallatchi, 1886–90; Dan Kaka, 1890–91; Dan Daddi, 1891; Mijinyawa, 1891–93; Kure, 1898; Mijinyawa, 1898; Kure, 1898–1904; Mahaman Burje, 1904; Kure, 1904–20; Ali Dan Kimalle, 1920–22; Dan Kolodo, 1922–44; Mahaman Dan Baskore, 1944–47; Mahaman Dan Zambadi Buzu, 1947–. To indicate the "temporary" nature of the Maradi state, all serkins have been titled serkin Katsina and not serkin Maradi, even though Katsina was never regained by the Hausa.

MARAFA, ABOUBACAR MAHAMADOU. One of the last prisoners of the Kountché era, released after the latter's death by General Saibou. Detained for his role in the 1983 attempted coup by "**Bonkano,**" and sentenced in 1988 to a ten-year term, Marafa was released on December 17, 1989.

MARANDET. Small Tuareg village approximately 90 km from Agadez, at the foot of cliffs where Fulani herdsmen traditionally graze their cattle. Archaeological evidence suggests a very early foundation for Marandet and for the arrival of civilization in the region. Some 40,000 Neolithic items, for example, have been recovered in the area. Oral tradition refers to the ouster of the Gobirawa from the area around A.D. 1200 by the first waves of the Tuareg.

MARCHE, LE. Independent Nigerien monthly publication, launched in 1989 by a former journalist at *Le Sahel,* **Abdoulaye Moussa Massalatchi.**

MARDI KIRI (1890?–1950). Head of the Nomadic Guard of Bilma, Marda Kiri was famous throughout the Niger Sahara area for his expert knowledge of the desert trails and all the routes connecting Kaouar with Aïr and Fezzan. He served for over twenty years as commander of the twenty-camel corps unit of Bilma.

MARIA THERESA DOLLAR. One of several currencies in Niger in the precolonial era and the first two decades of French rule in the country. Minted in Vienna and imported via the Maghrib, the Maria Theresa dollar was better accepted in Niger than the French franc right up to the 1920s. Indeed, the French themselves continued to import the coin (still minted though no longer legal tender in Europe) for some time in order to ensure receipt of services from the local population.

MARIAMA, MAILLELE. Educator and interim minister of national education. At the time director of the Kassoé High School in Niamey, Mariama was appointed in January 1991 to General Saibou's cabinet, leaving it when the HCR government was formed in September that year.

MASSALATCHI, ABDOULAYE MOUSSA. Editor of the monthly *Le Marché,* established in 1989. Massalatchi worked previously as a journalist with the main daily newspaper, *Le Sahel.*

MASSRAF FAYCAL AL ISLAMI. Saudi Islamic financial institution inaugurated in Niamey on May 4, 1983, and aimed at promoting nonusurious financial dealings between Saudi Arabia and Niger. It is an agency of the Dar Al Maal Al Islam, of which Prince Mohammed Al Faycal Al Saoud is the head.

MATAMAYE. Arrondissement of 92,000 people in the département of Zinder with headquarters in the village of the same name, which is 72 km from Magaria. Within the arrondissement is found the important village of Kantché.

MATANKARI. Important town in the arrondissement of Dogondoutchi in the Dosso département north of Dogondoutchi. Former capital of the Maouri of Arewa, Matankari has a population of 15,000 people and is named after the founder of the Maouri kingdom. In 1688 the town reputedly had a population of 20,000. The town and region later fell to the Bornu Empire. Prior to the French occupation, Matankari was the residence of the serkin Arewa. When the French set up their regional headquarters at Dogondoutchi, the serkin relocated his palace there. The region around Matankari is very scenic.

MAWRI. *See* MAOURI.

MAYAKI. Arrondissement of 125,000 people 45 km from Tessaoua with administrative headquarters in the town of the same name, which has a population of 2,200. Also title of chiefs among the Sudié and Maouri. It is of Tuareg origin.

MAYAKI, ADAMOU (1919–). Important political leader and former foreign minister. Born in 1919 in Filingué of Sudié chiefly origin (grandson of Fama, the first chief of the Sudié appointed by the French in Niger, and son of Gado Namalaye, the authoritarian serkin Filingué who died in 1935), Mayaki was educated locally and at Katibougou (Mali) Teachers College and eventually became a public works engineer. Active politically after 1946, Mayaki played a prominent early role in the BNA party and was one of Niger's early political leaders. In March 1952 he was elected to the Territorial Assembly on the UNIS ticket (later MSA) from Maradi and was reelected through 1958. In 1958 he was elected UCFA deputy to the National Assembly. Serving as grand counselor to the AOF in Dakar (1952–58) as well as Niger's counselor to the French Union (1953–58), Mayaki was appointed in May 1957 as minister of agriculture, in June 1958 became minister of interior, and in December of the same year minister of economics and planning. Two years later, in December 1960, Mayaki was shifted to head the ministry of industry and commerce (1960–62), following which he assumed the Foreign Ministry, serving through 1965. Leaving the cabinet in 1965 as part of a purge of all those not previously affiliated with the PPN and under suspicion of disloyalty to the regime after the **SAWABA** guerrilla assaults of 1964–65, Mayaki became ambassador to the USA, returning in 1970, at which time he was appointed prefect of Dosso (1970–73) as well as president of the SNTN. Following the 1974 coup d'état, Mayaki was appointed secretary general of the Ministry of Finance, a post he held for two years until his retirement.

MAYAKI, HAMIDOU. Managing director of the **Société Minière du Niger** and former head of the General Administration Bureau of the Ministry of Public Works (1972–78). Previously an agent of SAF and deputy director of the SMDN, Mayaki joined the Ministry of Public Works on March 23, 1961, and moving up the ranks became head of its Administration Division in September 1972.

MAYAKI, IBRAHIM. Current secretary general of the powerful USTN, Niger's trade union confederation.

MAYAKI, ISSOUFOU. Former minister of the civil service and labor. Of Tuareg origins, Mayaki joined Kountché's cabinet in September 1979 and retained the portfolio until mid-1985.

MAYAKI, MOUSSA (1925–). Educator. Born in Tounfalis-Filingué and educated at home and at Senegal's Ecole William Ponty, Mayaki served in succession as teacher, school principal, and primary school inspector. A member of the Syndicat des Enseignants du Niger, he joined the Ministry of National Education in 1958 as cabinet director of Maidah Mamadou. In 1967 he was appointed director of primary studies, reverting to instruction after the 1974 coup'état, and retiring in 1985.

MEANNA. Very important market town in northwest Niger founded by the French in 1920. It is on the Niger River.

MEDERSA. *See* KORANIC SCHOOLS.

MEHAOUA. Ruins, some 90 km from Agadez on the trail to Tabelot. The ruins are of an ancient village, very likely a contemporary of **Assodé.**

MEKROU. Elongated affluent of the Niger River flowing from the **Atakora** massif in Benin (maximum altitude, 640 meters), with a basin of 10,500 sq km. The **Parc National du W** covers the entire lower basin of the river within Niger.

MESSAN, LAMBERT (1940–). Diplomat. Born on September 20, 1940, and educated locally and in France, where he obtained an economics diploma, Messan was appointed third secretary at the Niger embassy to France in 1967, and was shifted to the U.N. mission in 1976. In the 1980s he was reassigned duties in the Foreign Ministry in Niamey.

MILLET. One of Niger's staple crops, a basic subsistence crop together with sorghum. Niger is Francophone Africa's biggest millet producer. Over 55 percent of Niger's surface is planted with the crop, the harvest of which is over a million tons, 85 percent of which is consumed locally. The rest of the harvest is sold in the cities, and between 8,000 and 10,000 tons is left for export, usually to Nigeria. The only processing center for millet is SOTRAMIL, which produces 1,000 to 1,500 tons of farina annually.

MINING. Until 1967 tin ore was the only mineral produced in Niger, extracted by the **Société Minière du Niger,** with an output of around 50 tons a year (*see* CASSITERITE). Since then uranium production has become Niger's prime export (*see* URANIUM). Iron ore was also discovered in the Say region, and there are huge coal reserves in Aïr. The iron deposits are not exploited, however, because of the large financial investments necessary. Gypsum is also produced in the important Maygia (Ader Doutchi) site, while limestone (with reserves of 30 million tons) is utilized by the Malbaza cement works. In 1985 significant gold deposits were discovered a few hundred kilometers from Niamey, and these are at the moment the subject of feasibility studies that could lead to joint Canadian-Nigerien exploitation.

MINISTERE DES AFFAIRES SAHARIENNES ET NOMADES. Cabinet ministry during the Diori era that was actually operative for only two months a year during the **cure salée** trek of herdsmen northward. The ministry was involved in coordinating technical services and socioeconomic activities in the In Gall–Agadez–Teguidda triangle where the bulk of the Tuareg influx occurs, during which the minister (usually an influential Tuareg amenokal), units of the gendarmerie, and the camel corps all relocate to Aïr in order to preserve peace among the volatile Tuareg clans.

MIRGHANIYA. Small religious order that arrived in Niger from Sudan, in the east. A small group of adherents are to be found in Niger in the Tahoua area. *See also* RELIGIOUS ORDERS.

MIRRIA (*also* Myrria). Large market town 20 km east of Zinder. In 1900 the market convened three times a week, greatly overshadowing Zinder's Thursday market. Formerly capital of one of the **Sossebaki** states of the area, Mirria's defeat at the hands of Damagaram cleared the way for the latter's rise to preeminence in the area in the nineteenth century. Currently Mirria is an arrondissement in the Zinder département and includes the poste administratif of Damagaram-Takaya, and has a population of 265,000. The town itself, southeast of Zinder, has a population of 8,000.

MISSION AFRIQUE CENTRALE. Ill-fated mission led by French officers Voulet and Chanoine and aimed, in part, at avenging the disastrous end of the former **Mission du Haut-Soudan** to Zinder in which Cazemajou was assassinated. Assembling in Sansanné-Haoussa on January 3, 1899, and numbering 1,700 (600 infantry, 800 porters, 200 women, and 100 children), the force descended down the Niger River. Due to crop failures in the area the mission was unable to buy any supplies and was forced to pillage areas which it crossed, leaving a swath of destruction still remembered in some villages to this day. In the process, the two commanding officers acquired ambitions to set themselves up as independent potentates. When news of the havoc caused by the mission reached French headquarters, Colonel Klobb and Lieutenant Meynier were sent after it to take command of the column. Leaving Say on June 12 via Dosso and Matankari, they intercepted the column at Dankori. Klobb was killed by the rebels, following which the other two officers were in turn killed by their troops. The column proceeded on its mission under Meynier to defeat the Damagaram forces in the Battle of Tirmini and to occupy Zinder, declaring a French protectorate over the kingdom.

MISSION BERLIET-TENERE. Mission of scientific exploration in 1960 sponsored by the French Berliet company into the Ténéré Desert. It reported a mass of newly discovered cave drawings and engravings and fossils of archaeological importance.

MISSION DU HAUT-SOUDAN. Led by Captain **Marius Gabriel Cazemajou** and aimed at exploring the little-known territories between the Niger River and Lake Chad, as well as reaching the slave raider **Rabah**—at the time a major force in the interior, having just defeated the vaunted **Kanem-Bornu Empire**—and inducing him to accept (with his territories) the "protection" of France. The mission arrived in Zinder, where it was regally entertained by Sultan Ahmadou of Damagaram. On its departure, however, a court faction murdered Cazemajou out of fear that his real intentions were to link up with Rabah against Damagaram. Cazemajou's murder brought about the dispatch of the **Mission Afrique Centrale** in retaliation, the occupation of Damagaram, and the killing of the sultan.

MOBEUR. Ethnic group estimated at 28,000 and found along the **Komadugu** River in east Niger. A mixture of Kanembu and the ancient So, the Mobeur are also found across the border in Nigeria. Originally settled at Ouri, the Mobeur were pushed out by Tuareg assaults in the mid–eighteenth century and in 1780 founded Bosso, fortifying the village. Continually under Tuareg pressure, the Mobeur acquired a very bad reputation from the first French explorers in the area who noted their aggression and suspicion.

MOCTAR, BIN SHARIF BASHIR (1892?–1972). Important Zinder economic figure. Born around 1892 in Zinder to a Kanuri woman and a **Ghadamsi** merchant, little is known about Moctar's early life. He obtained some education at a French school established in the town and attended Koranic schools. At the age of eighteen he moved to N'Guigmi and set up business as a merchant and importer. He rapidly prospered and became the prime supplier of the French garrison in N'Guigmi. He later established a network of agents stretching from Tripoli to Kano and branched off into various other commercial activities, such as importing goods directly from France and peanut brokering, operating gasoline stations, and retail trading. By 1940 he had a small fleet of trucks hauling peanuts to market, and by independence he was officially the seventh biggest exporter in Niger. He was a powerful economic figure with headquarters in Zinder. After Moctar's death his son inherited the business empire.

MODIBO. Fulani word for "teacher," equivalent of *mallam* in Hausa.

MODIELI, AMADOU. Trade unionist. Joining the cabinet of Kountché in February 1981 as secretary of state for education, Modieli was arrested in October 1983 in connection with the attempted putsch of that month.

MOHA, RABO (1916–). Traditional leader and longtime Assembly deputy. Born in 1916 and an important traditional chief, Moha was first elected territorial councillor in December 1946 on the UNIS ticket from Tahoua and was reelected (on the MSA slate) through 1957. In that year he again won reelection as PRA deputy but joined the PPN the next year and was reelected through 1974, when the coup d'état cut short his remarkable twenty-eight-year tenure as deputy. He served in the Assembly in several functions, most notably as vice-president of the Economics Committee.

MOHAMED, ABDOULAYE (1945–). Agricultural technician. Born on February 23, 1945, in Bonkoukou and educated locally and in Dakar, Senegal, as a public works engineer, Mohamed joined the Ministry of Agriculture as deputy head of agricultural services for Niamey (1966–67) at the age of twenty-one. He was then appointed head of Téra's agricultural services and codirector of N'Dounga's training center for young agrarian cadres (1967–68). In 1968 he was transferred to Gaya as head of agricultural services in that arrondissement, and he has occupied several similar appointments since, including in the ministry in Niamey.

MONT GREBOUN. Highest summit in Niger. Its precise height is subject to some controversy, with figures ranging from 1,944 to 2,310 meters.

MONZO. The representative of the sultan of Agadez at the Damagaram court, who dealt with all matters relating to the latter's sizeable and important Tuareg population. *See also* DAMAGARAM.

MOSSI, AMADOU (1920–). Former minister of public health. Born in Téra around 1920 Mossi was educated in Téra and Niamey and then attended Dakar's Ecole William Ponty (1942–45). He then worked in Conakry, Guinea, with the Financial Service Section in the colonial administration (1945–49), following which he completed his studies in Grenoble (1949–52) and in Paris (1952–59), obtaining an M.D. in tropical medicine. Between 1959 and 1962 a doctor in Niamey's hospital, he qualified as a surgeon between 1962 and 1965 at the Paris Medical Faculty and returned to Niamey Hospital in 1965 as chief surgeon. In 1970 he was brought into Diori's cabinet as secretary of state for public health and in 1972 attained full ministerial rank with the same portfolio, holding that post until the 1974 coup d'état. He was interned for one year after the coup for his activities while in office and was granted clemency in August 1975.

MOUDDOUR, AHMED (1941–76). Former director of the Union Nigérienne de Crédit et de Coopération. A Tuareg born in Bonkoukou (Filingué) on September 4, 1941, Mouddour was educated in Kao, Arzerori, Tahoua, and Niamey (1947–57) and continued his studies in Nogent-sur-Marne (France), where he obtained a diploma as public works engineer, and at the Paris Ecole Pratique des Hautes Etudes (1961–62), where he obtained a certificate in economics and social sciences. Mouddour returned to Niger to a posting as head of the agricultural region of Dosso (1962–65). In 1965 he became the head of agricultural services at Dosso, and in 1970 was appointed director of the UNCC. In 1972 he was also included in the Conseil Economique et Social of which he became vice-president. Between 1969 and 1974 he was also deputy secretary general of the Union Nationale des Travailleurs du Niger. After his purge, consequent to the 1974 coup d'état, he assisted the anti-Kountché plotters of 1976 by smuggling arms in trucks of COPRO-NIGER, of which he had been a director. For this he was arrested, sentenced to death, and executed on April 21, 1976.

MOUDDOUR, BADROUM. Secretary of state for interior in the interim HCR cabinet between March 1992 and April 1993.

MOUDDOUR, ZAKARA. *See* ZAKARA, MOUDDOUR.

MOUDI, ABDOU (Dr.). Minister of public health and social affairs between June 1983, when he joined the cabinet, and General Kountché's death in 1987.

MOUDI, MOHAMED. Secretary of state in charge of the budget in the first civilian government in the 1990s, between April 1993 and its parliamentary ouster in October 1994.

MOULOUL, AL HOUSSEINI. Former secretary of state for planning between July 1982, when he joined the Kountché cabinet, and 1985.

MOUMOUNI, ABDOU DIOFFO (1929–91). Physicist. Born on June 26, 1920, in Say and educated locally, in Dakar, and in Paris (where he studied science at the Sorbonne), Moumouni taught in Senegal, Guinea, and Niger, and traveled extensively. He conducted advanced research for two years at Moscow's Academy of Sciences, taught for some time at the University of Bamako (Mali), and published widely on both scientific and educational topics. In the mid-1980s he was named rector of the University of Niamey, serving also as director of the Niger Institute of Solar Energy. After his death in April 1991 the University of Niamey was renamed after him.

MOUMOUNI, AMADOU (1925–). Administrator. Born around 1925 in Harikanassou and an inspector of posts and telecommunications by profession, with a diploma from the Toulouse School for Telecommunications. Moumouni served as director of postal services between 1962 and 1968, and as deputy director of posts and telecommunications after July 1968.

MOUMOUNI, DIOFFO (1908–). Administrator. Born around 1908 in Kirtachi (Say) and a civil administrator by profession, Moumouni was elected to the National Assembly from Niamey in March 1957 and served in the Assembly continuously through 1974. He was third vice-president of the Assembly and administrator of Niamey's SMDR, the local electric company, and president of the Assembly's Committee on General Affairs.

MOUMOUNI, DJERMAKOY ADAMOU (Colonel). Influential Djerma leader, former key military officer, cabinet minister, ambassador to the United Nations, and with the onset of civilian rule head of the ANDP political party and president of the National Assembly. A descendant of the ruling family of the Dosso chiefdom favored by the French during the colonial era (*see* DJERMAKOY; DOSSO), Moumouni joined the Niger armed forces (following a family tradition) and moved up through the ranks. He was essentially apolitical until the 1974 coup d'état that brought Kountché to power. As one of the key Djerma officers in the army, with a personal fiefdom in Dosso to boot, he was then appointed to the senior post of minister of foreign affairs. Historic Djerma interclan competitions kept him from the summit of power, however (Kountché, and General Saibou later, come from an opposing clan), as did Kountché's jealous monopolization of real power and his policy of shunting aside potential competitors. In September 1979 he was shifted to the Ministry of Youth, Sport, and Culture, and was dropped from the cabinet in January 1983.

Keeping a low profile while standing above the interfactional fights within the military regime, Moumouni—a captain at the time of the coup—was promoted to major in July 1977, lieutenant colonel in 1982, and colonel in 1987. He headed a high-powered commission charged with the structural reorganization of Niger that led to the creation of the CND and later the MNSD. He was not appointed to head the former, as had been expected, but was sent instead to serve as prefect of Zinder. As Kountché's health took a turn for the worse in 1986, Moumouni was seen by some as a likely successor. Yet his somewhat overbearing personality, bon vivante penchants, and rival Dosso origins stood against him, and the Supreme Military Council chose instead Ali Saibou, of Kountché's clan and indeed from the same village. Moumouni was then (in 1988) dispatched far from the center of power as ambassador to the United Nations. He returned from New York early in 1991, and before the National Conference commenced he joined the MNSD, which he had helped create, as secretary for external affairs. Disillusioned about his prospects within the MNSD, controlled by elements beholden to the Old Guard (including former Colonel **Mamadou Tandja**), he then set up his own political party, the ANDP, and also presented his candidacy for the presidential elections.

Securing for both his party and his presidential candidacy a strong vote from his Dosso chiefdom, Moumouni and his party were part of the AFC anti-MNSD coalition, and he himself threw his electoral support in the second round of the presidential elections behind Mahamane Ousmane, who won against the MNSD candidate, Tandja. In exchange for his support he was appointed president of the National Assembly. Though the appointment was nullified by the Supreme Court of Niger on procedural grounds, he was later elected by the house and remained in that office until February 8, 1995, when the new MNSD-led government came to power.

MOUNKAILA, HAROUN. Former cabinet minister. Previously head of the Division of Studies and Research in the High Commission for Development (1970–76), Mounkaila was brought into the Kountché cabinet in September 1977 as minister of mines and hydrology. In June 1980 hydrology was removed from his ministry, and in February 1981 he was dropped from the cabinet altogether. He currently serves as head of a division in the Ministry of Rural Development.

MOUNKAILA, HASSANE (1937–). Born in 1937 in Garankiedey and a teacher of physical education by profession, Mounkaila taught at various schools in Niamey and Zinder (1957–63) and in 1963 was appointed head of the Physical Education and Sports Services in the Ministry of Youth and Sports.

MOUSSA, ABDOU MALAM. Former diplomat and cabinet minister. Moussa is the son of one of the principal marabouts who emerged after the Second World War (Malam Moussa) and brother of El Hadj Mustapha Moussa, first vice-president of the **Association Islamique du Niger.** In the early 1970s he served as secretary at Niger's embassy to Algeria, and later in a similar capacity at the embassy in Egypt. In September 1979 he returned to Niamey and was integrated into General Kountché's cabinet as secretary of state for interior, and was promoted to full ministerial rank in February 1981 when he was shifted to head the Ministry of Posts and Communications. In June 1982 he left the cabinet, on another series of low-level diplomatic assignments.

MOUSSA, ALI. Trade unionist and deputy secretary general of Niger's trade union confederation, the USTN.

MOUSSA, BAKO. *See* BAKO, MOUSSA.

MOUSSA, BOUBAKAR (1932–). Hamani Diori's half brother and former director of national security. Born on September 28, 1932, in Niamey, Moussa was educated in Filingué and obtained a teacher's certificate at Tahoua's Teachers Training School (1953). Between 1953 and 1958 he taught in Niamey, Magaria, and Karakara before going to Paris to obtain an IHEOM diploma (1958–61). He remained in Paris for a few months working at Niger's embassy as chancellor, and in October 1961 was appointed director of national security, serving in that post for the next eleven years (1961–72). In August 1972 he was appointed secretary of state for internal affairs, serving until the 1974 coup d'état. He was imprisoned after the coup on a host of charges, and was released in the 1990s.

MOUSSA, DOURAMANE. General Saibou's secretary of state for cooperatives, appointed in May 1989; his duties were redefined as agriculture in December 1989; and in March 1990 he was given duties relating to planning. Moussa was replaced in September 1991 by an appointee of the HCR government.

MOUSSA, EL HADJ MUSTAPHA. Religious leader and vice-president of the **Association Islamique du Niger,** Moussa comes from an illustrious maraboutic family (*see* MOUSSA, MALAM), and has a brother who became cabinet minister under General Kountché.

MOUSSA, MALAM. Major religious figure in Niger, viewed as the principal marabout in Aïr since the Second World War, Moussa is the father of **Abdou Malam Moussa** and **El Hadj Mustapha Moussa.**

MOUSSA, MOHAMED. Former interim minister of defense. A key Tuareg notable from the Agadez region and an active trade unionist, Moussa played a prominent role in the National Conference that took place in 1991, and was appointed minister of defense in Prime Minister Cheiffou's 1991 transitional government. In 1992 he was shifted to head the Ministry of Trade. Responsible for negotiations with rebel groups in Aïr, Moussa was arrested in Agadez in September 1992 during the army's sweep of suspected sympathizers with the Tuareg cause, and was not released until February 1993. He continued in the cabinet until April 1993, when a regular government emerged after parliamentary elections.

MOUSSA, OUMAROU. Civil administrator. Former administrator of SONICERAM and SOTRAMIL and director of the Banque de Développement de la République du Niger, Moussa was after 1969 director of Crédit du Niger, director of the CNCA, and director of the Société Nigérienne d'Urbanisme et de Construction Immobilière.

MOUSSA BEN ABDOULLAHI. *See* MALAM YARO.

MOUSSA BOUKAR, MAINA. General Saibou's minister of state firms and parastatals between November 1987 and May 1989.

MOUTARI, LAOUALI. Secretary general of the powerful USTN trade union confederacy.

MOUVEMENT DES FRONTS UNIFIES DE L'AZAWAD (MFUA). Militant coordinating organ of at least three liberation fronts operating in Azawak, and formerly joined in the **Mouvement Populaire pour la Libération de l'Azawad** (MPLA).

MOUVEMENT NATIONAL DE LA SOCIETE DE DEVELOPPEMENT (MNSD). Currently Niger's largest single party, and the one in control of the government. The MNSD had two distinct phases. First, as Niger's single political party, institutionalized as a party (from its previous status as a "movement") by General Saibou in 1988, and fielding a slate of candidates for that year's single-party elections, which resulted in the 1989 National Assembly. General Saibou was its president. Second, as a "normal" party, one among many, set up on March 12, 1991, with the onset of competitive politics. It then added the suffix "Nassara." Saibou, barred from seeking office by the 1991 National Conference, resigned from the MNSD on July 12, 1991, to remain above politics while he completed an interim role as head of state, and the party's leadership was assumed by **Hama Amadou** and **Mamadou Tandja.** The MNSD is currently largely a Songhay-Djerma party—but with the important exception of the Djerma of **Dosso,** solidly, as always, behind their leader, **Djermakoy Adamou Moumouni.** It is also the party of southwest Niger, and still largely the "ex-army party," in the sense that several key military officers (now resigned from the army, such as Tandja) play a dominant role in it.

When the new MNSD emerged to compete in the 1993 legislative and presidential elections (in the latter instance, behind Mamadou Tandja), all the other large organizations in the country (mostly Hausa, but also the Dosso Djerma) coalesced in an electoral alliance to prevent the comeback by the ballot box of the "Old Guard." The MNSD, benefiting from mass support in Songhay areas as a result of the previous military era's abundant dispensation of seed and drought relief, emerged as Niger's largest party in 1993, with twenty-nine of the eighty-three seats of the legislature. The party, however, could not find a single other large political partner with which to form a government, and the opposition (united as the AFC) formed Niger's first post–National Conference government. This collapsed in 1994 when Prime Minister Issoufou resigned and joined the opposition, and the subsequent elections produced the February 1995 MNSD government. In the 1993 presidential elections the MNSD candidate, former colonel Tandja, emerged the leader after the first round, but lost to current president **Mahamane Ousmane,** who benefited from the electoral support of all the other anti-MNSD candidates and parties.

MOUVEMENT NATIONAL DE LA SOCIETE DE DEVELOPPEMENT (MNSD-Nassara). *See* MOUVEMENT NATIONAL DE LA SOCIETE DE DEVELOPPEMENT (MNSD).

MOUVEMENT NIGERIEN DE COMITES REVOLUTIONNAIRES (MOUNCORE). Opposition group formed in March 1988 by the former MRLN, which, after General Saibou's accession to power, declared from Tripoli, Libya, an "all-out war" on the regime. A branch issued a similar manifesto in 1990 from Lagos, Nigeria, after brutal dispersal of the February 1990 student demonstrations.

MOUVEMENT POPULAIRE DE L'AZAWAD (MPA). Part of the larger **Mouvement Populaire pour la Libération de l'Azawad,** which seceded after the peace accords signed with the government in Mali in 1991.

MOUVEMENT POPULAIRE POUR LA LIBERATION DE L'AZAWAD (MPLA). Broad liberation front grouping Tuareg clans nomadizing parts of Azawak and portions of Mali. Headed by Secretary General Iyad ag Ghali, with headquarters in Mali, the movement signed peace accords with the government there in 1991, a fact that incensed most of the clans and resulted in the disintegration of the MPLA into its original components, which then began to operate as individual entities. The groups that emerged include the **Mouvement Populaire de l'Azawad,** the Front Populaire de Libération de l'Azawad (FPLA); the Armée Révolutionnaire de Libération de l'Azawad (ARLA); and the Front Islamique Arabe de l'Azawad (FIAA). These groups are distinguished in terms of clan membership, religion, degree of autonomy sought, and to a lesser extent territory claimed. They later combined to form the Mouvement des Fronts Unifiés de l'Azawad (MFUA).

MOUVEMENT REVOLUTIONNAIRE POUR LA LIBERATION NATIONALE (MRLN). Opposition group, aided by Libya in particular, set up probably in 1982, by elements hostile to General Kountché. Among them was the son of imprisoned former president Hamani Diori. The MRLN was responsible for several Tuareg armed sorties into Aïr, but was largely ineffective. In 1988 it merged with several other minuscule groups to form MOUNCORE.

MOUVEMENT SOCIALISTE AFRICAIN (MSA). Interterritorial party in French Africa to which **Djibo Bakary** affiliated his party (under the MSA title) prior to the adoption of the new party name—SAWABA. In the March 31, 1957, election Bakary's MSA took forty-one seats to the PPN's nineteen, but shortly after, in 1958, SAWABA's call for a "no" vote in the referendum regarding the future status of Niger brought about its eclipse as the PPN emerged with a smashing electoral victory.

MU KAARA SANI. Irregularly published information bulletin of Niamey's CNRS. Commenced in 1972, the originally mimeographed publication carried brief but informative articles of general interest on Niger.

MUDUR, MOHAMAD. Secretary general of the Front Démocratique Nigérien (FDN-Mountounchi), which emerged in January 1995 out of the merger of two small splinter groups, one of which was the Parti Progrèssiste Nigérien (PPN). The president of the FDN is **Oumarou Youssoufou Garba.**

MUSEE NATIONAL DU NIGER. Opened in December 1959, the museum is modest in size but includes an impressive collection of local art, including of the Tuareg, Djerma, Hausa, and Fulani, as well as their jewelry. One hall includes the famous tabol of Amenokal Fihroun, a war trophy. Set up by IFAN in a large park within which are constructed huts typical of Niger's main ethnic groups, the museum attracted a great deal of local and international attention when it was opened, and was visited by 25,000 people in its first forty-five days. Sited between the town itself and the Niger River, the museum grounds also include botanical exhibits and a thirty-foot fossil tree. There are also local craftsmen who sell their wares on the grounds.

MUSSOLINI-LAVAL BOUNDARY AGREEMENT. The unratified Franco-Italian boundary treaty that extended southern Libya (then an Italian possession) some 200 miles further south into Niger, Chad, and a corner of Sudan. Since independence, Libya has regarded the unsigned agreement as binding, and with the rise to power of the Qaddafi regime, troops have been sent to occupy the strip of land unilaterally. Some 7,500 sq m of Niger territory are affected, souring Libyan-Niger relations. In the case of Chad (where fully 50,000 sq m were occupied), a charge of aggression was lodged with the U.N. Security Council late in 1977. *See also* LIBYA.

MUSTAPHA, ALASSANE. One of Niger's principal cinematographers. Attached to Niamey's CNRSH, Mustapha has filmed a number of acclaimed short films, including *Aouré, La Bague du Roi Koda, La Mort de Gandji,* and *Bon Voyage Sim.*

MUSTAPHA, MAITOURNAN. Early political militant of a family of Kanuri notables, Mustapha served as UNIS delegate to the Territorial Assembly between 1947 and 1958.

-N-

NABA, ALBORA (1935–). Former deputy director general of Crédit du Niger. Born in Goudel (near Niamey) in 1935, Naba was educated in Niamey, joined the civil service in Filingué, and between 1958 and 1961 was attached to the Ministry of Justice. He then attended the Center for Administrative Training (Niamey) and in 1962 became bureau chief in the Ministry of Finance. In June 1964 he was promoted to cabinet chief of the minister and in 1965 became the cabinet director of the minister. Between 1969 and 1971 he attended the International Institute of Administration in Paris, and upon his return was appointed secretary general of the Conseil Economique et Social. In October 1973 he was appointed deputy director general of Crédit du Niger, and shortly thereafter also of the Caisse de Prêts aux Collectivités Territoriales. Reassigned to head SONUCI (Société Nigérienne d'Urbanisme et de Construction Immobilière), Naba was dismissed from his post in 1985 on charges of embezzlement after a 318-million-CFA-franc shortfall was discovered in Crédit du Niger's accounts. All his property was subsequently confiscated. In 1989 he was partly recompensed after General Saibou came to power.

NACHTIGAL, GUSTAV (1834–85). German explorer. Better known for his exploits elsewhere, and for his role in expanding the German colonial empire in Togo and Cameroon, Nachtigal's mission to the court of Bornu (1869–74) brought him also into areas currently within Niger. Everywhere he visited he kept meticulous notes, historical records, and king lists that were, and still are, invaluable.

NADJIR, HADJI. Minister of justice between October 1984 and November 1987. Prior to that Nadjir briefly served as minister of labor and the civil service.

NAGOGO, AGADA. *See* AGADA, NAGOGO.

NATIONAL CONFERENCE. *See* CONFERENCE NATIONALE.

NATIONAL INSTITUTE OF ADMINISTRATION. *See* INSTITUT NATIONAL DE GESTION.

NATRON. Low-grade carbonate of soda (table salt) found in pans in several locations in Niger in the oases of **Kaouar,** and especially in

Bilma. Used throughout the area for human and animal consumption, natron is one of those commodities still carried by caravans across the desert expanses. In the past the average biannual salt caravan (**azalay**) would stretch single-file for 25 km, include up to 10,000 camels, and be headed by a representative of the **amenokal** of Aïr. The azalays continued, to some extent, despite the competitiveness of trucked natron in Agadez, until the Tuareg rebellion of the 1990s. In the past Niger's natron satisfied local needs, and surplus was exported to neighboring ones. In 1960 the exchange rate was 3 kg of millet for 1 kg of natron. Salt has been a popular exchange medium in the past, and served as a quasi-currency.

NAYAYA, AMADOU OUSMANE (1935–). Labor inspector. Born in 1935 in Tessaoua and originally a nurse, Nayaya went to France to study labor administration at the IHEOM. Active from youth in the RDA interterritorial party and serving as secretary general of one of the PPN branches (1957–60) and as deputy secretary general of its Youth Division (1960–62), Nayaya joined the Ministry of Labor in 1962 as chef de cabinet of the minister, transferring to the same position in the Ministry of Education in 1963. In 1967 he returned to his old occupation as labor inspector in Maradi.

NEINO, RABO. Civil administrator. Neino served as deputy subprefect of Maradi (1970), prefect of Maradi and of Tillabéry (1966–68), and since 1970 as head of the Personnel Division in the Ministry of Civil Service and Labor.

NENI. Small island facing Niamey on the Niger River.

N'GUIGMI. Arrondissement on the border of Chad, including part of **Lake Chad,** with a seminomadic population of 40,000. The town of N'Guigmi, which is an important border-control post and garrison base, is very isolated at the end of a poor track from Zinder. It has a population of 7,000 and is the capital of the arrondissement. Another sand track skirts the northern edge of Lake Chad ending at Rig Rig in Chad and is a favorite route for cattle smugglers from that country. Once a fishing village on Lake Chad with few water problems, the periodic contractions of the lake in the past two decades have made the town virtually a desert oasis. The arrondissement (then a cercle) was administered for security purposes by the French military right through January 1, 1947. In the late 1970s commercially exploitable oil reserves were discovered in the region.

NIAMEY. Modern capital of Niger and nerve center of the country, though sharing economic pride of place with Maradi and Zinder.

Niamey became capital of Niger in 1926 (making it one of the youngest of the capitals in Africa), having been at the outset an insignificant minor fishing village not once mentioned in any of the accounts of exploration in the nineteenth century. Five years after being designated capital it had a population of 1,731; just prior to independence (1959) it still numbered only 31,000 people. Rapid growth since independence raised Niamey's population to 90,000 in 1971; 155,000 in 1977; 343,000 in 1983; and an estimated 600,000 in 1995. Demographic projections from the 1988 census estimate Niamey's urban population may reach 2.1 million in the year 2010.

Stretching along 7 km of the Niger River, and since 1970 connected with its southern bank by the Kennedy Bridge, the town is a sprawling and very disorganized urban center. It is in the middle of largely Djerma country; the origin of the town's name is subject to controversy: one tradition refers to it as the name of a tree (though long since disappeared, its site is still venerated) by which the first settlers once rested (*Niami*); another tradition refers to its origins from *Oua Niammane* (later *Namma* or *Niame*) stemming from the first Djerma inhabitants of the area led by the founder of the village, chief Kouri Mali. Later a Wazi named Balo set up a settlement nearby, forming the foundation of the Kalley quarter of the town. Other small groups arrived, spreading the confines of the budding village. Several other legends exist as to the origin of its name and the original village.

The town's **zongo,** which has a relatively low population density, is geographically in the center of the town, stretching between Niamey-Plateau and Niamey-Haut to the back of the mayoralty building and Avenue Salama, north of the Gaouey district. Forty percent of the zongo is occupied by Hausa. At the two extremities of Niamey lie Yantala and Gamkallé, formerly outlying Djerma villages that are now suburbs and contain important military camps. The cattle market is in the northern suburbs, beyond the Kalley-Nord quarter. The town had no traditional chief until 1931 when Djibo Salifou was made Amirou Niamey in gratitude for his services to the French in the colony. The city is organized into a "European" quarter (in the west) and an "African" one (in the east) separated by a park, which has since become the **Musée National.** The town has expanded not to the west, as anticipated, but inward from its two extremities (east and west), filling in all the open spaces in and between the two zones. The highest population density occurs in the Gaouey quarter and Kalley-Ouest; the lowest in Kalley-Nord. The town has a picturesque Place du Grand Marché that was totally renovated (with cement foundations) in 1962 (though it was ravaged by fire in the 1980s).

There are small Yoruba and Beninese-Togolese communities that have a quasi monopoly over several aspects of retail trade and imports into Niger. Apart from other small non-Niger minorities, the town's population is roughly 50 percent Djerma, 12 percent Hausa, and the rest a variety of local and foreign minorities the largest (10 percent) being Beninese-Togolese. Niamey is connected by a scenic road along the Niger River with Mali, passing by **Ayorou,** and is also connected via Fada N'Gourma with Burkina Faso. This unpaved, 297-km track is totally impassable during the rainy season. The main road runs from Niamey to Maradi and hence to Zinder, or north to Agadez.

In 1992 the Niamey département encompassed a territory of 90,417 sq km and a population of 995,000, most of whom are Djerma and Songhay, with smaller concentrations of Fulani and Hausa. The département was divided into the arrondissements of Niamey, Filingué, Ouallam, Say, Téra, and Tillabéry, with postes administratifs of Abala, Ayorou, Banibangou, Bankilaré, and Gothéye. In 1992 the headquarters of the Niamey département was shifted to Tillabéry.

NIANDOU, HAROUNA. Director of information between March 1982 and 1987.

NIANDOU, IDE. Interim secretary of finance and planning between March 1992 and the formation of an elected government in April 1993.

NIANDOU, ZADA (1924–). Former civil administrator. Born in 1924 in Dosso and educated locally and abroad, Niandou served as the chef de cabinet of the minister of stockbreeding and animal husbandry (1959) before being appointed deputy head of the administration of the Madaoua cercle. In January 1961 he became head of the Agadez arrondissement; between October 1962 and March 1963 he was subprefect of the Tanout arrondissement; between March 1963 and July 1964 he was subprefect of Tillabéry, and in May 1966 of Filingué. For the next four years he served as prefect of Zinder, and in March 1970 he was shifted to head the Maradi prefecture. Shortly after the 1974 coup d'état, he was appointed director of the Social Security Fund of Niger.

NIGELEC. Niger's electricity company, scheduled for privatization in 1996. The company has had difficulties keeping up with demand for electricity, consumption having quadrupled between 1970 and 1987, and it has increased more since. Domestic generation of electricity is nearly all thermal, and only covers half of the demand, with the major consumers being the uranium companies. The remainder of Niger's need is met from Nigerian sources that have been notoriously unreliable. There is an ongoing program of expanding domestic electricity development, based, in part on the coal supplies in Aïr.

NIGER, LE. Until its 1974 dissolution, the weekly newssheet of the PPN party. Founded in 1961 and with a circulation of 1,500, *Le Niger* was edited and distributed by the Niger Information Service.

NIGER AUTO PNEUS. Large private enterprise involved in the import and marketing of tires. Headquartered in Niamey with a branch in Maradi, the company has a large share of the market.

NIGER EN MARCHE. Annual government publication issued each Independence Day.

NIGER RIVER. Africa's third longest river, and the world's ninth longest, the Niger rises 250 km from the sea in the Futa Djallon highlands of Guinea (height: 800 meters) and spirals in a huge 2,600-mile arc through Mali (where it forms a large inland delta), Niger, Burkina Faso, Benin, and Nigeria before emptying into the Atlantic Ocean. The river's drainage basin is 1,484,800 sq. km. The river flows for some 550 km through the Niger Republic, and a small portion of it forms the border between Niger and Benin. One of the river's half-submerged islands, Lété, was the source of the 1964 border dispute between Niger and Benin. The river offers Niger limited navigation possibilities for only 200 km (essentially between Gaya/Malanville and Niamey), a stretch navigable by shallow vessels, except in times of drought. It receives, in Niger, no affluents on its left side between Tossayé and Malanville, though there are large vestiges of former hydrographic features—the fossilized valleys of Tilemsi, Azawak, and Dallol Bosso. On its right bank it receives (in Burkina Faso) the Goroubi, Diamangou, and Tapoa affluents. Above the W National Park the river is joined, from the Benin side, by the Mekrou, Alibori, and Sota rivers. The series of Sahel droughts since the mid-1970s has depressed water levels throughout the river's course. In 1985 the Niger River was nearly dry at Niamey, and at its lowest level since 1922. The projected **Kandadji Dam**—between Ayorou and Tillabéry—is supposed to make the river (in normal years) fully navigable throughout its entire course.

NIGER TRANSIT (NITRA). State agency created by the Ministry of Economic Affairs in December 1974, with the SNTN possessing 48 percent of the shares. Capitalized with 5 million CFA francs and with administrative headquarters in Niamey, NITRA is the state's customs agent, manages Nigerien port facilities in Lomé, Togo, and handles warehousing and freighting of goods to and from landlocked Niger.

NIGERIA INTERNATIONAL BANK OF NIAMEY. A fusion of Nigerian banking interests (NIBOIC, 60 percent, and Citibank 40 percent), the bank achieved a turnaround in 1991 after bad losses in 1990. Its director general was Adnan A. Mohamed. In 1992 it acquired the assets and liabilities of the bankrupt Bank of Commerce and Credit and was renamed Nigerian Trust Bank.

NIGERIA-NIGER JOINT COMMISSION FOR COOPERATION. Joint-development commission of the two bordering states, involved in projects of mutual interest. The exploitation of the Say iron deposits, the Kamadugu-Yobé River Basin development project, and several other activities have fallen under the purview of the commission. Its headquarters are in Niamey, and its meetings are attended by the respective ministers of development and cooperation.

NIGERIA TRUST BANK. *See* NIGERIA INTERNATIONAL BANK OF NIAMEY.

"NIGERIENNE, LA" National anthem of Niger, adopted on July 12, 1961.

NIGNON, JACQUES (1909–). Former general manager of COPRO-NIGER. Born in 1909 in Kanembatacké (Mayaki district) and educated in Porto Novo (Benin) and Zinder (1919–24), Nignon worked for thirty-two years in the Niger Finances Department, rising to head of department. During this period he was also very active in, and an officer of, several trade unions and served as treasurer of Niamey's Cultural Center. Elected in 1959 to the National Assembly as deputy from Tessaoua (through 1965), Nignon served as president of the Assembly's Economics Committee and as president of Niger's Chamber of Commerce. Between 1964 and 1977 he also was general manager of COPRO-NIGER, president of the Société des Produits Chimiques du Niger (SPCN) and on several other industrial boards.

N'KONNI. *See* BIRNI-N'KONNI.

NOMA, SAFIETOU. Secretary general of the **Union des Femmes du Niger.**

NOUHOU, AMADOU. Former minister of commerce and transport, serving between November 1983 and 1987. Previously Nouhou had been the director general of the Banque de Développement de la République du Niger.

NOUHOU, ASKIA. Son of Daoud, and grandson of Askia Mohamed I. Founder of the Kingdom of **Dendi** and first in the short lineage of the

Askias of the southern branch of the **Songhay Empire** following the fall of Gao and the Battle of Tondibi. Ruling for seven years, during which all his efforts were channeled into the struggle to regain the lost heartland of the empire, Nouhou has not been given sufficient credit or attention by many historians. He assumed leadership over Songhay after the Moroccan conquest and the deposal of his brother, and hid in the Niger bend (the W) until troops sent to capture or kill him retreated, following which he organized his own forces to harass the enemy now entrenched in Gao.

NOUHOU, MAIGA (Major). Director of the Veterans' Association at the Ministry of Defense between July 1968 and Kountché's coup of 1974. He was then reassigned to other duties in the armed forces.

NYASSISM. Islamic fraternity found in the Niger River valley settlements (*see* RELIGION). Cofounded by Abdoulaye and his son, Ibrahim Nyass (who was born in Kaolack, Senegal), and becoming less orthodox over time, it spread especially among the Senegalese communities along the coast of West Africa. In 1982 it was estimated that Nyassism had over two million converts in Africa, right through to Khartoum (Sudan), and that the sect was still growing, slowly but steadily, due to its rather unique mix of fundamentalism and social responsibility. It arrived in Niger via northern Nigeria, where it had sunk roots earlier. The order's most important leader in Niger is the marabout **Sheik El-Hadj Aboubakar** of Kiota (near Dosso, in the Niamey arrondissement), who is married to one of Nyass's daughters. Nyass himself visited Niger in 1953, giving the sect a needed boost. In Niger adherents are found today especially in villages in the areas of Maradi and Dogondoutchi, with Hausa in particular, and to a lesser extent Djerma, attracted by its doctrine. The order is in direct competition with **Hamallism** in espousing the emancipation of the oppressed classes. It is discriminated against by the orthodox Muslim establishment, including in the **Association Islamique du Niger,** though the Nyassite sect on its part does not seek involvement, and indeed eschews much contact, with any power hierarchies, today as during colonial days. The order has developed a strong sense of social responsibility, but equally strongly rejects modernization, and espouses the Arabization of all aspects of culture and society.

-O-

OFFICE DE RADIODIFFUSION-TELEVISION DU NIGER (ORTN). Niger's state broadcasting authority, under Director General Mahamane Adamou, which carries programs in French, Hausa, Djerma,

Tamasheq, Kanuri, Fulfulde, English, and Arabic. In 1992 Niger had 500,000 radios and 37,000 T.V. sets in use. Four television transmitting stations are operational—at Arlit, Agadez, Bilma, and Diffa. *See also* RADIO NIGER; TELEVISION; VOIX DU SAHEL.

OFFICE DES EAUX DU SOUS-SOL (OFEDES). State agency under Adou Adam, charged with exploiting and maintaining subterranean water resources in Niger, as well as digging new wells and boreholes. The country's needs are roughly 10,000 wells, while OFEDES maintains only 3,000 and is digging only 50 new wells per year. Most of Niger's boreholes are 20 to 30 meters deep, though some are as deep as 100 meters.

OFFICE DES PRODUITS VIVRERS DU NIGER (OPVN). State organ created in August 1970 to handle the marketing and price stabilization of some 85 percent of Niger's agricultural produce, including millet and sorghum. The company had immense difficulties through the mid-1970s in building up its stock of commodities for stabilization purposes. As part of the reorganization of the public sector, some of the activities of OPVN were privatized in 1985. It is headed by Adamou Souna.

OFFICE DU LAIT DU NIGER (OLANI). State company set up in 1971 to spur the centralized development of milk products in Niger, and to market them more effectively. The company falls under the Ministry of Rural Development. This is one state organ the government has specifically stated it will not privatize. It is headed by Abdou Kabo.

OFFICE NATIONAL DE L'ENERGIE SOLAIRE (ONERSOL). State agency with headquarters in Niamey. Created on May 15, 1975, with U.N., ECA, and Libyan fiscal support (subsequent to a March 1972 agreement), ONERSOL carries out basic research on the utilization of solar energy, installs solar energy units in public buildings, and converts solar energy into electricity to drive well pumps and irrigation systems in the countryside. It operates seven solar furnaces, all subsidized by France, and has long been headed by **Albert Wright.**

OFFICE NATIONAL DE RECHERCHES, D'EXPLOITATION ET DE COMMERCIALISATION DE L'URANIUM DU NIGER. State organ charged with the licensing, research, and marketing of Niger's uranium resources. The office was set up by the military regime on December 19, 1974, as a central clearinghouse holding a share in all uranium companies in the country. In September 1975 it increased the government's share in SOMAIR from 16.75 percent to 33 percent. The office was also known as URANIGER, and was replaced in 1976 by the **Office National des Recherches et Exploitation Minière** (ONAREM).

OFFICE NATIONAL DES AMENAGEMENTS HYDRO-AGRICOLES (ONAHA). State agency set up on December 28, 1978, charged with the systematic extension of irrigated lands tapping the Niger River waters. Founded with French funds, ONAHA has opened several tracts of land for intensive cultivation. Its activities are to be privatized.

OFFICE NATIONAL DES PRODUITS PHARMACEUTIQUES ET CHIMIQUES (ONPPC). State company set up in 1972 with 440 million CFA francs capital, to produce a limited number of drugs under foreign license. These include aspirin and the antimalarial chloroquine. Its capitalization has since increased to 770 million CFA francs. It is headed by Dr. Maidana Saidou Djermakoye.

OFFICE NATIONAL DES RECHERCHES ET EXPLOITATION MINIERE (ONAREM). Public industrial and commercial company created on August 26, 1976, and charged with promoting the research, development, and exploitation (as well as sale) of all mineral resources in the Republic of Niger, and to participate in all joint companies set up. ONAREM holds 33 percent of the shares of SOMAIR, and holds similar equity in the other mining companies. In the mid-1980s gold was discovered in a dozen sites two hundred miles from Niamey, and ONAREM initialed an agreement with a Canadian company for the joint exploitation of the ore on the same terms, following more detailed feasibility studies in the mid-1990s. ONAREM is headed by Ousmane Gaouri. *See also* OFFICE NATIONAL DE RECHERCHES, D'EXPLOITATION ET DE COMMERCIALISATION DE L'URANIUM.

OIL. Oil exploration, interrupted in 1965, was resumed in the early 1970s with the Niger government's encouragement and consequent to various promising signs of possible deposits in Aïr as well as in neighboring countries. Among the major concessions granted are (1) 245,000 sq km north of Lake Chad, given to Texaco (across the border in Chad, several wells came on-line in the early 1970s), which committed itself to spend 910 million CFA francs in explorations over five years; (2) Continental Oil Company, which obtained a concession over 290,000 sq km in southern Niger, pledging investments amounting to 1,650 million CFA francs over five years; and (3) Bishop Oil and Refining Company, which holds a potentially valuable Djado concession of 110,000 sq km and 85,000 sq km in the Agadez area, with the commitment to invest 550 million CFA francs in explorations. By the late 1970s sufficient actual deposits had been discovered (especially in the distant Tin Touma sands in the N'Guigmi arrondissement) to ensure Niger self-sufficiency in oil, if and when the resources are exploited.

OPERATION CHEVAL NOIR. Secret French contingency plan, allegedly devised by de Gaulle himself, to protect Hamani Diori, his family, and key aides with French troops stationed in Niger, and to spirit them away to Camp Leclerc in case of a coup d'état in Niamey. The plan was not put into motion when the actual coup erupted in 1974, allegedly since there was "no one" in Paris at the time (Easter) to authorize its execution, and the French garrison of Niamey was likewise preoccupied with a hunt over the holiday.

OPERATION HIRONDELLE ("Operation Swallow"). The evacuation of Niger's peanut crop via the OCBN railroad to the Atlantic port of Cotonou in Benin and thence to Europe. Introduced in 1953 as the practical alternative to exporting via Nigerian ports, Opération Hirondelle is a very slow, cumbersome, and inefficient arrangement due to the major problems of evacuating the big-volume crop in just a few weeks onto a rail-and-truck network that is both outdated and in a state of disrepair. It is advantageous to Benin, however, for its Cotonou–Parakou railway would otherwise be grossly underutilized in the southbound direction. The projected expansion of the railway to Niger—discussed "seriously" for six decades—could alleviate some of these problems.

ORGANISATION COMMUNE AFRICAINE, MALGACHE ET MAURITIENNE (OCAMM). A grouping (originally) of most of Francophone Africa, later joined also by Mauritius, for the purpose of economic, social, and cultural cooperation. Indirect successor of the Brazzaville group, the UAM, and the OACME, OCAMM's most successful venture in many respects was the creation of Air Afrique—the multinational airline of French Africa—as well as several joint technical colleges and a common telecommunications system. Since 1970 OCAMM has suffered some attrition (as has Air Afrique) as member states have pulled out of the organization or its joint ventures.

ORGANISATION COMMUNE BENIN-NIGER DES CHEMINS DE FER ET DES TRANSPORTS (OCBN). Joint Benin-Niger organization (known as OCDN when Benin was known as Dahomey), founded in 1959 with a Beninese majority control (63 percent) of the shares. The OCBN's main activities are running the railroad from Cotonou to Parakou (entirely in Benin), the Parkou–Niamey transshipment by trucks of goods destined for Niger, the joint management of the Cotonou wharf, and coordination of **Opération Hirondelle.** The Cotonou–Parakou line is 438 km long, and the remaining 880-km section to the border and Dosso has been projected for decades. The high building costs and low traffic (except when Niger's crops have to be evacuated) have stalled execution of the project, despite the fact that feasibility and fund-raising efforts have been mounted periodically.

ORGANISATION COMMUNE DAHOMEY-NIGER DES CHEMINS DE FER ET DES TRANSPORTS (OCDN). *See* ORGANISATION COMMUNE BENIN-NIGER DES CHEMINS DE FER ET DES TRANSPORTS (OCBN).

ORGANISATION COMMUNE DES REGIONS SAHARIENNES (OCRS). Regional organization created on January 10, 1957, with the purpose of the socioeconomic development of the Sahara area, the coordination of programs of research, and interstate communications in the region. The agency had a High Commission with thirty-two members, sixteen of whom represented the countries concerned (two from each) and sixteen representing the ethnic groups living in the regions. The OCRS's last program in Niger was in 1962—shortly thereafter the organization collapsed as each country opted to push for the separate development of its Saharan regions. Much of central and northern Niger fell under the purview of the OCRS. Total investments in Niger under the OCRS amounted to 2,199 million CFA francs between 1959 and 1962.

ORGANISATION DE LA RESISTANCE ARMEE (ORA). Successor, in 1995, to the **Coordination de la Résistance Armée,** which signed the April 1995 peace agreement with the Niger government, formally ending the Tuareg rebellion. The organization was somewhat looser than the CRA, and was headed by Ghissa Ag Boula, who was also head of the CRA and leader of one of the main Tuareg liberation movements in Niger. *See also* TUAREG REBELLION.

OUALLAM. Town of 5,000 people in the arrondissement of the same name (population 150,000) in the Niamey département.

OUBANDAKAWI, MALLAM (Major). Former commander of the gendarmerie. A hard-liner, Oubandakawi presided over the 1989 State Security Court's trial of the plotters of the 1983 attempted coup, meting out harsh sentences. He was removed from the gendarmerie in 1989.

OUHOUMOUDOU, MAHAMADOU. Interim minister of mines and energy in the HCR government between March 1992 and the rise of a new government in April 1993.

OUILLIMINDEN. Major Tuareg confederation found in Mali and in Niger, numbering 240,000, of whom 130,000 are slaves or former slaves. The confederation is composed of two major branches: the western branch called Ouilliminden Kel Attaram, and the eastern branch called Ouilliminden Kel Dinnik, the latter of which nomadizes areas in Niger. It is headed by **amenokal** traditionally chosen by the Kel Nan clan, which is also the repository of the confederation's **ettebel.** The French suppressed the confederation's amenokal after several upheavals in Niger, and replaced his authority by that of eight regional and clan chiefs. The Ouilliminden Kel Dinnik emerged as a confederation at the beginning of the eighteenth century, after a split that formed the two branches in 1650, in the Menaka region of Mali, and by 1840 reached the Koria region, superimposing themselves on all groups encountered. They were unable to penetrate further due to Djerma and Kurtey resistance, which blocked their path of advance. They clashed with the **Kel Ahaggar** in a series of bloody battles in the Tahoua area that greatly diminished the latter's strength vis-à-vis the Kel Gress in the region, and they fought many other battles with Tuareg clans that had preceded them into Niger.

During the colonial era the French had to suppress a major rebellion by **Fihroun,** the amenokal of the Ouilliminden, who later were, in part, supporters of the **Kaocen revolt** in Aïr. It was subsequent to this that the cohesiveness of the Ouilliminden was shattered by the French decision to separate the tribe artificially by the establishment of eight centers of authority. The Ouilliminden Kel Dinnik currently nomadize the Azawak area and especially the Tchin Tabaraden arrondissement in the Tahoua département. They raise camels, sheep, and other livestock, and with the arrival of the rainy season they commence their drive north in the In Gall area for the **cure salée.** Each of the confederation's eight groups has a very specific transhumance route. They have the same castes as all other Tuareg groups in the area.

The Ouilliminden Kel Dinnik had thirteen amenokals between 1655 and 1917, when they were forcibly split up. Subject to the normal date variations in various lists established, the amenokals were: Khadakhada, 1655–80; Mohammed agh Abuyakhya, 1680–1700; Atifrij, 1700–1750; Kharoza agh Atifrij, 1750–70; Muda agh Kharoza, 1770–1804; Khettutu agh Muda, 1804–7; Aljilani agh Ibrahim, 1807–16; Aghaba agh Khettutu, 1816–19; Budal Bala agh Khatami, 1819–40; Mussa agh Budal Bada, 1840–72; Mahamat agh Elkhumati, 1875–1905; Ismail agh Lasu, 1905–8; and Alkhurer agh Arragabi, 1908–17.

OUILLIMINDEN KEL DINNIK. The Ouilliminden Kel Dinnik number around 98,000, making them Niger's largest Tuareg subgroup, nomadizing in particular the Tchin Tabaraden arrondissement. *See also* OUILLIMINDEN.

OULED SLIMAN. Arab tribe, prevalent in much larger numbers in neighboring Chad and Nigeria, that arrived in Niger's Kaouar and Chad's Kanem from Fezzan in Libya. There were essentially two different waves: one peaceful, the second a rampaging invasion that swept destruction through Kanem and caused unsettled conditions in Kaouar. The Ouled Sliman entered these areas in the latter part of the nineteenth century and the early twentieth century. In 1923 another branch came to Niger's Tintouma area from Chad's Kanem.

OUMAROU, ABDOU. Educator. Born in Niamey and educated for a teaching career, Oumarou taught at Maradi before being appointed director of popular education (in the Ministry of Youth) in Niamey. He served in that capacity between 1961 and 1967, and under a slightly different title between 1967 and his retirement from the civil service in 1980.

OUMAROU, ABOU (Colonel). Former chief of staff of the Niger armed forces. In 1991 he was stripped of his command and ordered imprisoned for the brutal repression of Tuareg dissidents in Aïr. Mutinous troops released him from prison at Kolo in February 1992, claiming he had been made a scapegoat for the Tchin Tabaraden massacres.

OUMAROU, ADAMOU (1929–). Public prosecutor of Niamey and former diplomat. Born on January 27, 1929, in Nogharé and educated locally and at the Islamic University of Boutilimi (Mauritania), Oumarou was director of Islamic studies in Niger and councillor of the Niamey arrondissement before his appointment in 1966 as chargé d'affaires at the Niger embassy to Saudia Arabia, Sudan, Libya, and Algeria, with residence in Khartoum, Sudan. He held this post for eight years, until the 1974 coup d'état, following which he was repatriated and appointed public prosecutor of Niamey.

OUMAROU, AMADOU (Lieutenant) (1943–). Key conspirator in the famous 1983 attempted coup against Kountché. Better known in Niamey as "Bonkano," a nickname, Oumarou was President Kountché's personal aide and confidant. Virtually illiterate, he used his control of the portals of the presidential office to dispense patronage, in the process enriching himself tremendously. His interests included construction, commerce, trucking, and banking. A devout Muslim, known in expatriate circles as "Niger's Ayatollah," he built himself a personal mosque at the cost of 100 million CFA francs, and donated various sums for charitable purposes. In 1983 Oumarou utilized his status in the presidential office to lure and arrest a number of key military officers (including Saibou, the future president, after Kountché's death) as a prelude to a takeover. When the conspiracy failed, due to the alertness of one of the commanders, Oumarou slipped into exile to Europe (*see also* COUP OF OCTOBER 5, 1983). In 1991, during the proceedings of the National Conference in Niamey, Oumarou was given personal immunity and returned to testify before a committee investigating the fiscal improprieties of the Kountché era, throwing further light on the latter's ad hoc utilization of public funds and on the corruption of his inner circle of confidants, including his own wife.

OUMAROU, IDE (1937–). Former secretary general of the Organization of African Unity (OAU) and former foreign minister of Niger. Born in Niamey, and a graduate of Ecole William Ponty and IHEOM in Paris, Oumarou was trained as a journalist. He commenced his career as an editor in the Ministry of Information, and at the age of twenty-four was appointed editor of *Le Niger* (1961–63). In 1963 he became director general of information, serving until October 1972, when he became director of posts and telecommunications. Shortly after Kountché's 1974 coup he joined his presidential staff as chef du cabinet, becoming Kountché's closest aide for the next five years. In 1980 he was promoted by Kountché to head Niger's delegation to the U.N., and in that capacity he presided between May 1980 and January 1981 over the Security Council. On November 14, 1983, Oumarou was recalled to Niamey to become foreign minister, serving until July 1985 when the OAU elected him its secretary general. He ran for another term of office in July 1988 but was defeated by Tanzania's Salim Salim, returning to Niamey to serve as General Saibou's minister of state and special adviser. Oumarou is an author as well. His first book, *Gros Plan,* won the coveted Grand Prix Littéraire of French Africa in 1978.

OUMAROU, MAMANE (1946–). Diplomat and former prime minister. A Kanuri from eastern Niger, Oumarou served as ambassador to Canada, mayor of Maradi, and minister of youth, sports, and culture under Kountché. Briefly prime minister of Niger, in November 1983 Oumarou was appointed head of the **Conseil National de Développement,** serving until 1988 in what was at the time envisaged as the second most important post in Niger. After Kountché's death, his successor, General Saibou, reappointed Oumarou prime minister of Niger in May 1989. The position was eliminated in December 1989.

OUMAROU, OUSMANE. Minister of interior in Niger's first post-1990 civilian cabinet, serving between April 1993 and the government's fall in October 1994.

OUMAROU, SANDA (1904–84). Former sultan of Zinder. Born in 1904 and the son of Ahmadou Dan Bassa and grandson of Tanimoun, Oumarou came to the throne in 1950.

OUSMANE, BEN MAMADOU (1934–). Former mayor of Niamey and a civil administrator. Born in N'Guigmi on June 2, 1934, and educated locally and in Paris (IHEOM, IDEP), Ousmane was appointed deputy head of the Niamey cercle on his return to Niger in 1961, following which he was shifted to head the administrative staff of the Niamey commune (1961–64), and in July 1964 he was appointed administrative director of the General Commissioner's Office for Development (1964–67), and head of the Research and Studies Unit within it. In September 1967 he was made deputy prefect of Niamey and in August 1968 subprefect of Konni. He stayed in the latter post through 1972, at which time he became secretary general of Niger's Chamber of Commerce and mayor of Niamey (through 1975). He has also served on a number of boards of commercial enterprises, including the SNC and SONICERAN.

OUSMANE, BOUKAR. Former secretary of state in General's Saibou cabinet. Appointed in charge of the Interior Ministry when Saibou rose to power in November 1987, he was shifted to Animal Resources in May 1989, and left the cabinet in December 1989.

OUSMANE, BOUREIMA (1948–). Academic. Head of geologic services in the School of Sciences at the University of Niamey. Ousmane earned a doctorate in hydrology in 1978.

OUSMANE, ISSAKA (Major). General Saibou's last minister of public works and housing, appointed in May 1989 and staying in office until the HCR-appointed cabinet took over in September 1991.

OUSMANE, MAHAMANE (1950–). President of Niger. Prior to the convening of the National Conference in 1991, a relatively unknown Hausa statistician and economist from Zinder, Ousmane founded the CDS party in 1991 as a powerful Hausa political machine. Strongly supported financially by his hometown's rich traders, he then linked his party with most of the other parties that emerged within an AFC alliance to block the return to power of the "new" MNSD party of the Old Guard. With the support of the Hausa in the east, he ran in the

1993 presidential elections and emerged in second place (with 26.59 percent of the vote, behind the 34.22 percent of **Mamadou Tandja** of the MNSD), and was one of the two candidates entitled to compete in the runoff round. Prior to the second ballot, he obtained the electoral support of just about all former presidential candidates, and defeated Mamadou Tandja in the second ballot to emerge as Niger's president. His term of office, renewable by election once, expires in 1998.

Neither charismatic, flexible, nor particularly political astute, his attempts to run Niger without due attention to some of his allies in parliament led to a break with the AFC prime minister, which brought the civilian government down. Rather than compromising, and thus probably gluing the governing coalition together (as counseled by France), he sought a new verdict at the polls, and in the ensuing parliamentary elections an MNSD alliance secured a majority of the seats, forcing Ousmane to appoint Tandja as prime minister. (Ousmane and Tandja have been on very bad terms all along.) In the new government that subsequently emerged in February 1995, there was not a single AFC member or anyone politically friendly to Ousmane.

OUSMANE, SEMBENE. One of Niger's greatest cinematographers, directing, inter alia, *Samory* in 1985.

OUSSENI, HAMADOU (1937–). Physician and president of the Council of Health of Niger. Born in 1937, and with a medical degree from the University of Dakar (1975), Ousseni is with the School of Sciences at the University of Niamey and head physician at Niamey Hospital.

OUSSENI, INOUSSA. One of Niger's best-known cinematographers and managing director of the Inter-African Cinematography Distribution Center (CIDC) and the Inter-African Center for the Production of Films (CIPROFILM).

OUSSENI, MAMANE (Captain). Former minister of national education between July 1982 and October 1983, when he was arrested in connection with the "**Bonkano**" anti-Kountché attempted putsch of that month. He was kept in prison for five years before a trial in 1988 (after Kountché's death), in which he received a sentence of eight years for his part in the coup bid. Shortly thereafter he was amnestied by General Saibou.

-P-

PARASTATAL SECTOR. Prior to the 1970s, Niger had a limited number of public companies. The uranium boom in the 1970s triggered the establishment of a large number of state enterprises in various sectors of the economy, with the figure reaching fifty-four in 1981, and sixty-six in 1984. Shortly thereafter, and escalating as the decade progressed, declining global market prices for uranium and losses piled up by the state sector sharply contracted government revenues, leading to a series of closures and privatizations.

In 1986 as many as twenty of Niger's parastatal companies were slated to be closed in the first round of a rationalization program that was supposed eventually to contract the public sector to only twenty-five enterprises. The commitment was confirmed by General Saibou, who signed a series of agreements with the IMF (the first one in 1983, three others in 1986) and subsequently cut borrowing, restricted credit, froze wages, and pledged to downsize the civil service. Subsequently a Structural Adjustment Plan called for major employment cuts in a parastatal sector then employing more people than the civil service itself (29,000 *vis* 24,000), in a country with only 14,000 workers employed in the private sector. The SAP was not implemented, however, nor was the line held on other matters, despite the fact that Niger desperately needed the loans that would then have ensued, and the disengagement of the state from the economy (and especially companies losing money) has been a slow process. Vociferous resistance from unionists (who have paralyzed the economy by general strikes, including a five-day one in 1990 on this very issue), students (directly affected by freezes in hiring by the civil service and the state sector, which their degrees "entitle" them to, and also twice striking on this issue), and youth (competing for the manual jobs), have made implementation of an austerity regimen impossible and privatization much slower than envisaged. This has been compounded by the facts that (*a*) many foreigners left the country with the onset of its economic decline; (*b*) other entrepreneurs have avoided investments in such countries as Niger, where climatic vagaries can wipe out even the best-run enterprise, or have been deterred by the growing political restlessness in the country; and (*c*) several of the former state enterprises (for instance, SONICERAM) required infusions of new capital and renovations (to make them at least minimally attractive to private capitalists) that the government could not afford.

By the mid-1980s eight state enterprises had been privatized, eight (through a reduction in the government's equity) were under private management, five had been liquidated, and three had had their activities merged within a ministry. Among the first affected were the UNCC and OPVN, which were drastically restructured and partially privatized. In the late 1980s several banks and financial institutions collapsed, and a few more parastatals were restructured, but during the turbulent transitional years (1990–93) there was little further progress on the issue. In October 1994 the (now civilian) government again opened the issue, stating that an additional fifteen of the country's state enterprises would soon be privatized, starting with Niger's electricity company (NIGELEC), main transport company (SNTN), and the SNC cement works, and that the country's main hotels would be handed over to private managerial consortia. Among the former state companies now private are SONICERAM, SONERAM, SONITAN, SOTRAMIL, SNP, SOPAC, CMAN, NITRA, SICONIGER, SNT, SONIFAC, SEPANI, SNCF, VETOPHARM.

PARC NATIONAL DU W. Wildlife refuge and nature preserve shared by Niger (300,000 hectares), Burkina Faso (330,000), and Benin (500 hectares) in the double bend of the Niger River area as it flows through the last outcroppings of the **Atakora** Mountains. The park gets its name from the W shape of the double bend of the Niger. The Niger portion of the park, the most accessible and developed (*see* CAMPEMENT DE LA TAPOA) is 165 km south of Niamey. The best time for visits is between November and February. It is reached (1) via a road from Niamey that passes through Diapaga; (2) by boat from Niamey to Boumba and to hence the next 15 km by road to Tapoa; or (3) by DC3 air service during the tourist season. The park has some lovely, though modest, gorges, swamps, and rocky outcroppings, and varied wildlife that includes elephants, lions, buffalo, gazelle, and monkeys.

PARTI INDEPENDANT DU NIGER-EST (PINE). *See* UNION DES NIGERIENS DE L'EST (UNE).

PARTI NIGERIEN POUR LA DEMOCRATIE ET LE SOCIALISME (PNDS-Tarayya). Post–National Conference political party, headed by **Mahamadou Issoufou** and gaining in the 1993 elections the third largest number of seats. Though largely a Hausa party, the PNDS—whose cadres previously were members of various clandestine radical groups—is the most nonethnic, and ideologically strident, of Niger's parties. Issoufou served as President Ousmane's first Premier. In a dramatic split between the two leaders in September 1994, however, Issoufou resigned and joined the MNSD opposition; this led to the fall of the government and new elections in 1995. In the subsequent rearray of power, the PNDS became part of the MNSD-led coalition that constituted the new government of February 1995. *See also* POLITICAL PARTIES.

PARTI POUR L'UNITE NATIONALE ET LA DEMOCRATIE (PUND-Salama). Small Tuareg post-1991 political party, part of the AFC, headed by **Akoli Dawel.** *See also* POLITICAL PARTIES.

PARTI PROGRESSISTE NIGERIEN (PPN). Niger's ruling party between 1958 and 1974. Formed in 1946 by a group of intellectuals, trainees, and évolués of the Ecole Primaire Supérieure de Niamey (some sixty-five of whom had gone on to study at the Ecole William Ponty) as the Niger branch of the interterritorial **Rassemblement Démocratique Africain.** The PPN was very briefly a mass party (1948–49) before succumbing to oligarchic tendencies. Between 1946 and 1951 very anti-French, the PPN eventually mellowed. In 1946 a group in the PPN bolted the party as a number of Djerma chiefs, including the **djermakoy of Dosso** together with Dr. **Francis Borrey**—a Frenchman—and some low-status évolués deserted the PPN with administrative support. In June 1948 they set up the UNIS party. Earlier, in the 1946 elections for the French National Assembly, Hamani Diori had been elected. When the PPN selected **Djibo Bakary** as its second candidate for the National Assembly (a second seat was allotted to Niger), another segment bolted the party following the lead of **Harou Kouka** and **Georges Condat,** who eventually set up PINE. Some of this group later merged with UNIS.

In 1951 the PPN split in two with the disassociation of the RDA from the French Communist party with which it had been allied. The leftist branch of the PPN, following Djibo Bakary, constituted itself as the Union Démocratique Nigérienne, which was later to become the MSA and still later SAWABA. The other segment retained the PPN label. In the 1952 elections the PPN was shut out from the local Territorial Assembly, and the party had already been unsuccessful in the 1951 French National Assembly elections when it failed to elect its candidates who lost to UNIS's Condat and **Ikhia Zodi.** In the 1956 French National Assembly elections, the PPN again lost to a UPN-BNA alliance, and specifically to the Condat-Seydou ticket, by garnering only 83,000 votes to the former's 127,000. Again in 1957 the PPN lost the local elections to the MSA led by Bakary, but rallied back in the form of a broad alliance campaigning for a "yes" vote in the 1958 referendum. It won the referendum against SAWABA by 358,000 votes to 98,000 votes and shortly thereafter won the territorial elections as well, gaining 49 of the 60 seats at stake. In 1959 SAWABA was banned, and Niger became a one-party state under PPN rule.

Though a new name was supposed to be adopted to denote the coalition that had joined the PPN to defeat SAWABA, the PPN convinced the other groups to merge with it. All cabinets since have been more or less balanced ethnically, but in the politburo of the party power has been held very tightly—since 1956—by a clique of Djerma, Songhay, and Maouri, with no members whatsoever from the country's large Fulani and Hausa communities. Indeed, the PPN was always in reality the party of west Niger and of the Djerma and Songhay, and came to power when Bakary's control over the east, and the Hausa, slipped.

The party was an elitist grouping of power wielders and had a virtually septuagenarian leadership. Its core triumvirate was Hamani Diori, Boubou Hama, and Diamballa Maiga. Its politburo was unchanged between 1956 and 1974 (*see below*), and its lists for the National Assembly were for all practical purposes compilations of the more powerful traditional leaders of the country not integrated into the cabinet and the administration. Officially boasting 300,000 members in 1968 (*vis* 5,000 in 1946), the PPN had not even specified its purpose, functions, or goals by that date. It has held no congresses since independence, and as the party ossified, it was criticized for tolerating, if not encouraging, corruption in high places. Not until 1968 was a PPN policy "Guideline" issued, and not until 1974 was the party's first congress in fifteen years scheduled to meet. (It never did, for the coup of that year preceded the scheduled congress.) After the 1974 coup d'état, the party was dissolved and numerous cabinet ministers and other PPN officials were arrested on charges of corruption, embezzlement, and/or fraud.

PPN POLITBURO, 1956–74

President	Boubou Hama	Songhay
1st Vice-Pres.	Diamballa Maiga	Songhay
2nd Vice-Pres.	Toulou Malam	Djerma
Sec. Gen.	Hamani Diori	Djerma
Dep. Sec.	Mahamane Dan Dobi	Maouri
Political Sec.	Barcougne Courmo*	Djerma
Economics Sec.	Noma Kaka	Maouri
Social Sec.	Réné Delanne*	(Mestiso)
Treasurer	Barkiré Halidou	Djerma
Propaganda Sec.	Himadou Alou Badarou	Songhay
Propaganda Sec.	Issa Garba	Djerma
Secretary	Abdou Gaoh	Maori

*The only members ever dismissed from the politburo in the period 1956–71. They were dismissed in 1971.

Paradoxically, the old party name was resurrected with the onset of civilian rule in the 1990s, and a "new" PPN party emerged, headed by **Oumarou Youssoufou Garba** and **Leopold Kaziendé,** competed in the 1993 legislative elections, and supported Garba's presidential bid the same year. The party won only 2 of the national assembly's 83 seats, and seeking a greater political impact, in January 1995 merged with another small party to form the Front Démocratique Nigérien (FDN), headed by Oumarou Youssoufou Garba and Mohamad Mudur. It is part of the AFC coalition. Its prize candidate, Diori's son Abdullahi, failed, however, to secure his election to the legislature.

PARTI REPUBLICAIN POUR LES LIBERTES ET LE PROGRES DU NIGER (PRLPN-Nakowa). Small post-1991 political party, part of the AFC alliance though without National Assembly representation. The party is headed by Alka Almou. *See also* POLITICAL PARTIES.

PARTI SOCIAL-DEMOCRATE NIGERIEN (PSDN–Alheri). Small post-1991 political party, headed by El Hadj Kazelma Oumar Taya and part of the AFC alliance though without representation in the National Assembly. *See also* POLITICAL PARTIES.

PEANUTS. Peanuts were first introduced in Niger in 1930, and Niger rapidly attained the rank of second largest producer of peanuts in the Franc Zone. In 1945 Niger exported 10,566 tons; by 1952, 39,855 tons; and at independence, 76,720 tons. The highest production ever occurred in 1966–67, when 191, 303 tons were exported. With the onset of the Sahel drought, production and exports plummeted to an insignificant 3,758 tons in 1975, and have only slowly rebounded since. Peanuts are grown primarily in two départements, which together account for 90 percent of the crop. These are, in order of importance, Maradi and Zinder, with Magaria the acknowledged peanut capital of the country. Producer prices have in general been low, ranging between 24,000 CFA francs (1970) per metric ton and 17,500 CFA francs (1968). Worldwide shortages and the Sahel drought pushed prices up in the mid-1970s to the vicinity of 28,000 CFA francs.

A monopoly over the commercialization of peanuts was deemed necessary in Niger, and SONORA was given this task in 1963, with three shelling factories in Tchadaoua (capacity of 45,000 tons), Dosso (30,000 tons), and Malbaza (15,000). Deliveries to the two oil mills (since the 1960 closure of SIAM) have varied between 20,000 tons in 1964 and 30,000 tons in 1969. The oil mills are SICONIGER and SHN. In 1970 SICONIGER produced 20,656 tons, and SHN 9,982 tons. Since then three new oil mills have been constructed in Niger, one each by SICONIGER, SHN, and SEPANI. Since 1965 the UNCC's role in the marketing of the crop has diminished, purchasing in the 1970s some 30–35 percent of the crop, the rest being bought by the private sector (since 1970, largely local). In 1986 the UNCC was dismantled, making peanut marketing more or less a private activity.

Peanut exports are transported largely via Apapa in Nigeria (75 percent of the crop goes this way), which is some 1,400 km from Zinder. The rest goes through Cotonou (1,060 km from Niamey) via **Opération Hirondelle.** Transportation costs are very high—between 13,000 and 15,000 CFA francs per ton—and are rising. The three Niger parastatal organs most involved with peanut farmers (until the privatizations of 1986) were UNCC, which provided assistance and materials and purchased part of the crop; CNCA, which extended credit to the various cooperatives that grew the crop; and SONORA, which undertook the sale of the harvest after its collection and centralization.

Postindependence figures for peanut production are provided below. The low figures for 1975–77 reflect the fact that much of the harvests was destroyed by insects. The 1977–78 harvest was similarly hard hit by pests. Figures cited are tons:

1960–61	76,720
1961–62	66,671
1962–63	91,843
1963–64	114,180
1964–65	106,201
1965–66	156,081
1966–67	191,303
1967–68	182,701
1968–69	163,732
1969–70	164,824
1970–71	130,134
1971–72	144,658
1972–73	109,588
1973–74	25,563
1974–75	90,220
1975–76	3,758
1976–77	7,148
1977–78	14,209

PERSPECTIVES DECENNALES, 1965–74. *See* PLANS.

PEUL. *See* FULANI.

PLANS. First Three-Year Plan (1961–64): Submitted on June 15, 1961, as an intermediate research plan to permit the enactment of a comprehensive economic plan in 1964. Anticipated expenditures in 1961–64 were 30,100 million CFA francs, of which 63 percent was to come from public sources, 37 percent from private ones. Only 84 percent of the anticipated expenditures were actually available, in practically equal percentages insofar as the state/private sectors were concerned.

Intermediate Plan of Development (1964–65): Enacted on February 7, 1964, to complete the goals of the First Three-Year Plan (1961–64) that were not completed at the time. The projects included research on a textile plant and a tannery at Maradi, with anticipated expenditures of 9,380 million CFA francs.

First Four-Year Plan (1965–68): Part of a larger 1965–74 Ten-Year Plan (called Perspectives Décennales, 1965–74), anticipated financing during 1965–68 was 43.2 billion CFA francs allocated among social infrastructure (25.6 percent), administrative infrastructure (2.3 percent), economic infrastructure (21.9 percent), productive sector (45.4 percent), and research (4.8 percent). Adopted on September 19, 1964, the largest sum was allocated for hydrogeological services and studies. The expenditures amounted to a 71 percent increase over the previous plan. The plan was subsequently revised downward to a grand total of 30 billion CFA francs (a 31 percent cut). The exact sums actually obtained from private sources have never been published, but public expenditures were barely 12.7 billion CFA francs, or 38 percent of targeted sums. Only 70 percent of the revised goals of the plan were actually achieved.

Second Four-Year Plan (1968–72): Envisaged 37.1 billion CFA francs of public expenditures and 10.7 billion CFA francs of private funds, with the overall foreign financing needed standing at 89 percent. Due to the Sahel drought, the plan remained largely on paper and most of its goals were not fulfilled.

Third Four-Year Plan (1971–72): Part of a new master plan for the ten-year period 1973–82. Few of its goals or targeted sums were attained due to the continuation of the Sahel drought.

Three-Year Plan (1976–78): Adopted on April 30, 1976, by the new military regime to free Niger from "outside geographical factors," "install a dynamic developing society," and "lead to economic independence." The plan included an administrative reorganization of state agencies, especially limiting SONORA's activities to the marketing of peanuts and derivatives (oil), while COPRO-NIGER was given a total monopoly over the imports of consumer goods and their sale through retail outlets throughout Niger. The government also undertook all outstanding shares in Crédit du Niger. Total investment envisaged during the life of the plan was 1,024 million CFA francs in industry (eleven projects) out of a grand total of 135,281 million CFA francs. The plan was described as an intermediate one with the primary aims being (1) feeding the population and attaining self-sufficiency, especially in cereals; it stressed accelerated growth in food crops and the opening up of virgin lands along the fertile Niger River valley at the expense of cash crops, such as cotton and peanuts; (2) compensating as fast as possible for the decimation of the Niger livestock herds by the Sahel drought and bringing them up to 1972 levels; and (3) research on the Kandadji Dam leading (once constructed) to a major growth in electricity production and also of solar power. Some 21 percent of the sums budgeted in the plan were to be obtained from Niger's FNI. The plan had a reasonable chance of attaining most of its goals, especially at the outset, despite shortfalls in financing, but like other plans met only a minority of its goals.

POISSON, JEAN (1929–). Diplomat. Born in Filingué on March 15, 1929, and educated locally and in France (ENFOM), Poisson was Niger's delegate to the U.N.'s fifteenth and sixteenth sessions before joining the Ministry of Industry and Commerce in 1962 as director of economic affairs. In June 1969 he was dispatched to Brussels to serve as ambassador to the Benelux countries and the EEC. He remained in that post until 1974, when he was returned to Niamey to a senior post in the Foreign Ministry. In March 1977 he was reassigned to diplomatic duties abroad, serving inter alia as Niger's representative to the U.N. He has been in retirement since the mid-1980s.

POLICE ECONOMIQUE. Post-1976 police force charged with investigating economic and customs crimes and offenses (including hoarding and smuggling) as well as fiscal irregularities. It was under the control of General Kountché and was active during the Sahel drought and its aftermath. The force was dismantled in 1978.

POLITICAL PARTIES. The evolution of political parties in Niger has been somewhat less convoluted than in neighboring states. For clarity's sake this entry will be divided into the country's three periods of political activity.

Pre-Independence Through the Diori Presidency

The first political movement to be set up in Niger was the **Parti Progrèssiste Nigérien,** which was an affiliate of the interterritorial **Rassemblement Démocratique Africain.** All the other parties in Niger in essence seceded from the PPN or its offshoots. Locked out of power until 1958–59 (first by UNIS and then by the MSA-SAWABA), the PPN won the 1958 referendum on the continued status of Francophone Africa and the subsequent territorial elections, banned the SAWABA party, and established a one-party system that lasted until it was ousted from power in 1974. Niger's most important parties during the multiparty era of 1946–59 follow.

Parti Progrèssiste Nigérien (PPN): the de facto party of the Songhay-Djerma-Maouri alliance of the country's west. Founded in 1946 by a group of évolués, many of whom had attended the elitist Ecole William Ponty in Dakar, Senegal, and including such future political leaders as Boubou Hama, Hamani Diori, and Djibo Bakary, the very first schism in the PPN was over its continued affiliation with the interterritorial RDA, then affiliated in France with the French Communist party. The faction that opposed continued affiliation with the RDA opted out of the PPN in 1948 and formed the Union Nigérienne des Indépendants et Sympathisants (UNIS). From 1946 to 1951 very militantly anti-French (which is why the French administration actively supported the UNIS party), the PPN had mellowed by the mid-1950s. The party lost yet another faction, which organized around Georges Condat and Harou Kouka, who after an attempt to set up their own party, merged with UNIS. The most serious split in the PPN, however, occurred in 1951–54, following the RDA's disassociation from the French Communist party. The PPN went along with this policy, though a significant leftist faction opted to follow **Djibo Bakary,** who set up the Union Démocratique Nigérienne (UDN), which eventually became the MSA and SAWABA (*see below*). The PPN lost the 1957 elections to the latter party, gaining only nineteen seats to SAWABA's forty-one, but scored a dramatic upset both in the 1958 referendum and in the subsequent territorial elections. In this they were helped in part by the French administration's change of heart regarding Djibo Bakary, and his progressive alienation of the Hausa-Fulani chiefs in east Niger, on whom his power really rested. Shortly thereafter the PPN legislated itself the only legitimate party in Niger. *See also* PARTI PROGRESSISTE NIGERIEN.

Union Progrèssiste Nigérienne (UPN). Splinter group formed around Georges Condat that left the PPN to form the UNIS party and then, in March 1953, left that party in an effort to realign with the PPN. This effort aborted, the UPN rejoined the UNIS party, which by this time had changed its name to Bloc Nigérien d'Action.

Union Nigérienne des Indépendants et Sympathisants (UNIS). Founded in 1948 by former members of the PPN and other previously unaffiliated elements. At its core was a powerful group of Djerma chiefs including the **djermakoy of Dosso.** The origin of the UNIS party is traceable to the schism earlier, in 1946, over the PPN's continued affiliation with the interterritorial RDA party (*see above*). Its main non-Djerma chiefly leaders included Georges Condat and Ikhia Zodi. It suffered major secessions in 1953–55 when the former opted out of UNIS over their demand that links be reestablished with the PPN in an effort to unite the Niger nationalist movement. Establishing the UPN party, Condat's efforts were rebuffed by the PPN and he returned to the UNIS fold. By that time the party had practically collapsed over the question of affiliation with the new interterritorial movement, the Convention Africaine (a successor to the French National Assembly caucusing group, Indépendants d'Outre-Mer, in which the future president of Senegal, Leopold Sédar Senghor, was most active). The bulk of UNIS—including Condat's defunct UPN—formed the Bloc Nigérien d'Action (*see below*) leaving a few leaders totally isolated within the shell of UNIS. These leaders, including Dr. Francis Borrey and Ikhia Zodi, trailed very badly in the 1957 elections, and the party disappeared shortly thereafter, being transformed into the Convention Africaine–affiliated Forces Démocratiques Nigériennes (*see below*).

Bloc Nigérien d'Action (BNA). Successor to the UNIS party (*see above*) after the major schism that split it apart over affiliation with the interterritorial Convention Africaine, successor to the IOM. The BNA was constituted of the rump of the UNIS party that opposed affiliation with the latter, leaving their former leaders Ikhia Zodi and Francis Borrey with the empty shell of UNIS. The BNA was also rejoined by a faction that had left UNIS previously, the UPN. In the 1955 elections the party's Condat-Seydou (the latter being the djermakoy of Dosso) ticket obtained 127,000 votes to the PPN's 83,000. In November the BNA merged with Djibo Bakary's Union Démocratique Nigérienne (*see below*) to form the Mouvement Socialiste Africain that was later renamed SAWABA (''freedom" in Hausa). The main leaders of the BNA were Djermakoy Issoufou Seydou and Amadou Mayaki.

Forces Démocratiques Nigériennes (FDN). Successor party of UNIS after the split that brought about the formation of the BNA. The FDN was affiliated with the interterritorial Convention Africaine and was very short-lived since it had hardly any followers. *See also* UNIS, *above*.

Parti Indépendant du Niger-Est (PINE), or Union des Nigériens de l'Est (UNE). Largely stillborn party formed of a faction that opted out of the PPN in 1946 over the latter's affiliation with the interterritorial RDA. The faction merged with UNIS in 1948. It had a small following in the Hausa east.

Mouvement Socialiste Africain (MSA). Name of an interterritorial movement with which Djibo Bakary's UDN became affiliated. Though Bakary's party also campaigned under the MSA label, his party is discussed under SAWABA, *below*. For the interterritorial movement, *see below*.

SAWABA. The rallying call (*sawaba* means "freedom" in Hausa) of the MSA branch in Niger that became the party of the Hausa east even though led by non-Hausa from the west (such as Bakary himself). SAWABA originated from the previous Union Democratique Nigérienne (*see above*), which had also benefited from support from the French colonial administration. After its loss in the 1958 referendum (in which SAWABA called for a "no" vote leading to immediate independence) and the subsequent elections in which the party lost its status as governing party of Niger, the party was banned by the resurgent PPN and some of its leadership placed in prison. With most of its leadership eventually either in exile (in Guinea, Ghana, and Algeria) or in prison, Bakary attempted a comeback through violent means (1963–65), which included a grenade attack on Hamani Diori, an attempted assault on Niger border posts, and efforts to foment upheaval. The lack of success of these tactics, and indeed the negative reaction in Niger to the loss of innocent lives, brought about the relapse into inactivity of SAWABA. After the 1974 coup d'état Bakary finally returned home from exile. In 1975–76 he was accused of contravening his pledge to refrain from politics during the duration of the military regime.

Union Démocratique Nigérienne (UDN). SAWABA's predecessor. Formed in 1954 by PPN dissidents objecting to the parent interterritorial (RDA) party's disaffiliation from the French Communist party, the UDN was led by former coleader of the PPN, Djibo Bakary, and was quite popular and powerful in the Hausa east, though it counted very few Hausa among its leaders. Aided, for a time, by the French colonial administration (according to some scholars, it was a "creation" of the French leftist administration), and by traditional chiefs, especially Hausa and Fulani, the UDN absorbed the BNA party in 1956 and joined the radical interterritorial party—the MSA—campaigning under this name until the new party name of SAWABA was adopted (*see above*). The UDN, and SAWABA successor, controlled Niger's political life, being in a majority in the Territorial Assembly and with Bakary as head of the local executive, until the party lost control in 1958 with its dual defeat in that year's referendum and territorial elections.

Union des Nigériens de l'Est (UNE): *see* Parti Indépendant du Niger-Est (PINE) *above*.

Union pour la Communauté Franco-Africaine (UCFA). Temporary loose electoral alliance led by the PPN party in its ultimate electoral fight with SAWABA in 1958, which was to result in the latter's collapse and the rise of the PPN to the status of governing party. The UCFA obtained fifty-four of the sixty seats in the National Assembly, and SAWABA only four. Following the elections a new political party was supposed to be established, but the PPN leadership convinced its allies in the UCFA to merge with the PPN and keep its name.

Interterritorial parties: There were several interterritorial movements with which Niger's parties affiliated themselves. These have all been noted previously, including their alliances. In summary they were (1) Rassemblement Démocratique Africain (the Niger affiliate from its inception was the Parti Progrèssiste Nigérien). (2) Indépendants d'Outre-Mer (more of a caucusing group of Francophone African deputies in the French National Assembly; its prime supporters in Niger were Ikhia Zodi and Francis Borrey of UNIS; the IOM was later to create the Convention Africaine). (3) Convention Africaine (in many ways successor to the IOM, its Niger affiliate was the practically stillborn Forces Démocratiques Nigériennes after the bulk of UNIS deserted Ikhia Zodi and Francis Borrey over the issue of affiliating the party with the C.A.). (4) Mouvement Socialiste Africain (the Niger affiliate had for some time the same name; later it became the SAWABA party). (5) Parti de Regroupement Africain (in many ways the outgrowth of the Mouvement Socialiste Africain interterritorial party, the Niger affiliate was the SAWABA party).

The Military Era of Generals Kountché and Saibou

The only legal party during the prolonged military era (1974–91) was the MNSD (*see below*), which first emerged in protoform under General Kountché as a mobilization tool—a "movement"—and was not institutionalized as a political party by General Saibou until 1988–89, and under which Niger's single-party elections of 1989 were held. At the time General Saibou was its president, and all those who aspired to power or influence were at least nominal members. The party was largely under military control and reflected the continued political stranglehold by the Songhay and Djerma, unbroken since the rise of the Diori regime and the PPN. Over 70 percent of the members of government that ensued from the subsequent single-party elections were from those ethnicities. For the "transformed" MNSD following the return to civilian politics, *see below*.

At the same time there were a number of illegal political parties abroad, aiming largely at the "liberation" of Niger from military rule. Most were inactive or content with issuing manifestos. Among these was the Front Populaire de Libération du Niger (FPLN), which was the organ used by Diori's son in an attempt to realize his father's comeback in the early 1980s. The party was headquartered in Libya and had in it several members who had plotted against Kountché, such as Khamed Moussa and Liman Chaafi, its president. Other such movements include the Mouvement Révolutionnaire pour la Libération Nationale (MRLN); Parti Islamique Intégriste (PII); Front Dém-ocratie Uni (FDU); Parti Socialiste Révolutionnaire (PSR); Mouvement Nigérien des Comités Révolutionnaires (MOUNCORE).

The National Conference and the New Civilian Era, 1991–

A large number of political parties emerged after the liberalizations in Niger in 1991 and the convening of the National Conference. According to one count there were as many as forty, and some new groups are being formed continually, though most are mergers of splinter groups of personal power vehicles. Niger's rather simple ethnic array (compared to other more heterogeneous countries) brought about considerable consolidation of the picture by the time the first parliamentary and presidential elections were held, and this was further aided by the drive to capture power that resulted in the formation of two coalitions of parties. One, the (originally) nine-party coalition AFC (*see below*)—though only six gained seats in the National Assembly—represented forces aiming to prevent at all costs the electoral return to power of the Djerma-Songhay Old Guard under a restructured MNSD party. The tactic worked, and the AFC formed Niger's first post-1991 regular government. The other alliance was the MNSD itself, backed by some splinter groups, but after the second parliamentary elections (1995) joined by another partner, formerly in the AFC, which allowed the new MNSD alliance to form the government in power as of July 1995.

At the same time the onset of the Tuareg rebellion resulted in the formation of a number of fluid fronts or movements of liberation, which are also noted below.

The following array of power existed in September 1994, prior to the collapse of the ruling coalition; subsequent changes in party affiliations to the two coalitions are noted, but they entailed primarily the shift of the PNDS from the AFC coalition to the MNSD.

Alliance des Forces du Changement (AFC)

Originally a nine-party alliance (of which only six won seats in the Assembly), and after the 1994 parliamentary crisis a five-party alliance, aimed at preventing the considerably more united Songhay-Djerma (minus the always maverick Dosso branch) from winning control of the legislature and the presidency. The alliance captured fifty of the eighty-three Assembly seats in the 1993 elections, and its support for Mahamane Ousmane gave him the presidency over **Mamadou Tandja,** the MNSD front-runner after the first ballot. The AFC's senior partner (with twenty-two seats) is the CSD of President Mahamane Ousmane, but each party is of great value, since without internal cohesion, the MNSD (which is more homogeneous) could come to power. This indeed happened with the fall of the AFC government in 1994. An MNSD goverment subsequently was formed in February 1995, after an electoral rearray of power that gave the former opposition forty-three of the seats in the National Assembly in the January 1995 elections. The AFC group (except for the PNDS turncoat and another political splinter group) is currently the opposition in Niger.

Alliance Nigérienne pour la Démocratie et le Progrès (ANDP–Zaman Lahiya): This is the powerful political machine of **Djermakoy Adamou Moumouni** with the Tuareg Brigi Raffini as vice-president. The ANDP coalesces the Djerma of Dosso, Moumouni's ethnic fief. Though a Djerma party, the ANDP—which is very cohesive behind their djermakoy—is in the AFC due to (*a*) historic intra-Djerma rifts between Dosso and the Djerma-Songhay of the west (grouped largely behind the MNSD, and the power in both the civilian regime of Hamani Diori and that of generals Kountché and Saibou); and (*b*) personality cleavages from the days of military rule, when the djermakoy was sidelined by both generals Kountché and Saibou, who are from the western branch. The ANDP obtained eleven seats in the 1993 legislative elections, making it the country's fourth largest, two seats behind the PNDS. (These two seats later gave Moumouni the presidency of the National Assembly rather than the prime ministership.) Moumouni's presidential bid likewise resulted in his coming in fourth on the first ballot. Urging his supporters to throw their second-ballet vote behind Mahamane Ousmane, Moumouni was personally rewarded with the presidency of the National Assembly. After the parliamentary crisis of 1994 and the new elections of January 1995 the ANDP and the AFC emerged in the opposition vis-à-vis a new MNSD government.

Convention Démocratique et Sociale (CDS-Rahama): This is the party of President Mahamane Ousmane, which secured twenty-two seats in the 1993 legislative elections, making it the second largest in Niger, after the MNSD (which got twenty-nine). The CDS also delivered to Ousmane the second largest number of votes in the first ballot of his 1993 presidential bid, and following the coalescence behind him of virtually all the other non-MNSD parties, he beat Tandja, the MNSD candidate. The CDS is largely a Hausa party, and more specifically a party of **Damagaram** or Zinder, heavily supported by the rich Hausa traders of that region, and sustained by the general dissatisfaction of the Hausa at their being shunted from the center of power since independence despite being the largest ethnic group in the country. The CDS was the senior partner in the AFC government until the parliamentary crisis of 1994 that led to new elections in January 1995. At these the former opposition (MNSD), the PNDS (which had precipitated the crisis), and another small party gained forty-three of the assembly's eighty-three seats, forming the government, with the CDS transformed into part of the opposition.

Parti Nigérien pour la Démocratie et le Socialisme (PNDS-Tarayya): The party of Mahamadou Issoufou, with coleader Mohamed Bazoum, that managed to edge out the ANDP in the 1993 legislative elections, gaining thirteen seats (to eleven of the ANDP) of the eighty-three seats at stake. Issoufou (who had to withdraw from the second round of his presidential bid after coming in third, behind Tandja and Ousmane), threw his support to **Mahamane Ousmane,** who eventually was elected president of Niger. In exchange Issoufou was appointed prime minister, heading the AFC coalition. A falling out with President Ousmane late in 1994 created a parliamentary crisis when Issoufou resigned and joined the opposition (then the MNSD), bringing down the government. In the subsequent elections of January 1995, which Ousmane unwisely called for, the former opposition plus PNDS edged out the AFC (gaining forty-three seats to the AFC's forty) and formed the new government. Issoufou became president of the National Assembly. The PNDS should thus now be considered part of the governing MNSD alliance.

Parti Progrèssiste Nigérien (PPN-RDA): This was a resurrection of the governing party in Niger between 1960 and 1974. Led by Oumarou Youssoufou Garba and **Leopold Kaziendé,** it won two seats in the 1993 legislative elections (and Garba just less than 2 percent in the same year's presidential elections). In the January 1995 elections the PPN gained only one seat and joined the MNSD. It also merged with another splinter group to form the Front Démocratique Nigérien (FDN-Mountounchi), with Garba as president and Mohamad Mudur as secretary general.

Union pour la Démocratie et le Progrès Social (UDPS-Amana): Tuareg party, securing one seat in the elections. Headed by Mohamed Abdoulahi.

Parti Social-Démocrate Nigérien (PSDN-Alheri): Small splinter party headed by Kazelma Oumar Taya, winning one seat.

The MNSD Coalition

This coalition is dominated by the heavyweight MNSD; even after it was joined by the PNDS in 1994, the MNSD is still the main partner of this alliance.

Mouvement National de la Société de Développement (MNSD-Nassara): This is the resurrected MNSD from military days, transforming itself (from the governing single party) into a "normal" party on March 12, 1991, and with General Saibou resigning as its president in July of the same year in order to remain above politics. Despite its association with the military junta and military era, the MNSD was, and remains, very powerful among the Songhay and Djerma of the west. The party had two years to organize itself (1991–93) prior to elections, and draws strong support in the countryside from farmers and chiefs who remember and appreciate General Saibou's distribution of seed and drought relief during the 1980s. The leadership of the party is under Hama Amadou, who is its secretary general, and it is supportive of the presidential aspiration of former colonel Mamadou Tandja, the strongman of the party. In the 1993 legislative elections the MNSD received twenty-nine of the eighty-three seats, becoming the largest party in Niger. It could not, however, find a single other major political party to join it to form the government, which went to the AFC alliance. In like manner, its strong support for Tandja made him the front-runner in the first ballot of the presidential elections. On the second ballot, all the other candidates threw their electoral support behind Ousmane as the AFC candidate, and he won the election. In the 1995 parliamentary elections the fact that Mahamadou Issoufou and his PNDS had joined the MNSD alliance gained it forty-three of the eighty-three seats and allowed the MNSD to form the February 1995 government of Niger.

Union Démocratique des Forces Progrèssistes (UDFP-SAWABA):

This is a resurrection of a segment of Djibo Bakary's pre-independence political vehicle, headed by Bakary, claiming to represent the "authentic" old SAWABA. It has two seats.

Union des Patriotes Démocrates et Progrèssistes (UPDP-Shamuwa): Headed by André Salifou and Illa Kané, winning two seats.

Other Parties and Newer Formations

These are not represented in the National Assembly, though they are supportive of one or another of the political alliances.

Parti pour l'Unité Nationale et la Démocratie (PUND-Salama): Tuareg party under **Akoli Dawel** and **Khamed Abdoulaye,** former rebel leaders, standing officially for a federal structure for Niger, but part of the AFC.

Front Démocratique Nigérien (FDN-Mountounchi): Formed in January 1995 when the PPN merged with another splinter group, the joint party now headed by Oumarou Youssoufou Garba as president and Mohamad Mudur as secretary general.

Front Nigérien National (FNN): Fulani political party, set up in February 1993 by Fulani elements feeling marginalized and taken for granted by the other political formations. The FNN is under the secretary generalship of Salifou Sadikou.

Parti Républicain pour les Libertés et le Progrès au Niger (PRLN-Nakowa): Headed by Alka Amou, and part of the AFC, though the party gained no seats.

Parti Nigérien pour l'Autogéstion (PNA): New party, formed in February 1995 as the first secession from President Ousmane's CDS party, which lost control over the government after the previous month's elections. The PNA is headed by Jacoub Tamagui Sanoussi.

Parti Sociale-Démocrate Nigérien (PSDN-Alheri): Headed by Kazelma Oumar Taya. Part of the AFC.

Union pour la Démocratie et le Progrès (UDP-Aminchi): Headed by Bello Tiousso Garba. Part of the AFC.

Union pour la Démocratie et le Progrès (UPDP-Amana).

Union Nigérienne Démocratique (UND-SAWABA): This is a wing of the old SAWABA, headed by Pascal Mamadou.

The Liberation Movements

A dozen liberation movements have emerged in Niger. Four of these were, until 1995, coordinated in Paris by the Coordination de la Résistance Armée (CRA), and four formed the Mouvement des Fronts Unifiés de l'Azawad (MFUA). They are separated along clan lines (and in one instance—the FIAA—ethnic lines), and have different aims and visions for the Tuareg north (autonomy, federalism, independence) and various religious goals.

The Mouvement des Fronts Unifiés de l'Azawad (MFUA) was set up in 1991 after a splintering into its constituent parts of the previous

Mouvement Populaire pour la Libération de l'Azawad (MPLA), headed by Iyad ag Ghali and headquartered in Mali. (The latter mobilized a segment of the Tuareg there.) After the MPLA initialed peace accords with the Mali government, the following groups opted out and later set up the MFUA): Mouvement Populaire de l'Azawad (MPA); Front Populaire de Libération de l'Azawad (FPLA); Armée Révolutionnaire de Libération de l'Azawad (ARLA); Front Islamique Arabe de l'Azawad (FIAA).

The Coordination de la Résistance Armée (CRA) was formed in 1993 and is headed by **Mano Dayak,** who is head of the ARLN, and **Ghissa Ag Boula** to group the following liberation fronts (the first [the FLAA] was the first to organize in Niger and is the only one to claim a sphere of operations in both Aïr and Azawak): Front de Libération de l'Aïr et de l'Azawad (FLAA); Front de Libération Temust (FLT); Armée Révolutionnaire de Libération du Nord Niger (ARLN); Front Patriotique de Libération du Sahara (FPLS). The CRA gave way in 1995 to the Organisation de la Résistance Armée (ORA), a somewhat looser organization that initialed the final peace accord in mid-April 1995 formally ending the Tuareg rebellion.

Finally, one other alleged liberation movement can be noted: the Front pour le Démocratique Renouveau (FDR), formed in 1993 but primarily active since 1995, and distinct from all the others in that it operates in the southeast (near Lake Chad) rather than in the north, and is a Toubou–Kanuri–Shoa Arab movement. For additional details on most of these fronts and movements, see the individual entries in this Dictionary.

POSTE ADMINISTRATIF. Basic administrative unit inherited from the colonial era, of which there were thirteen in 1960, and by 1975, thirty-one. Administrative authority in the poste administratif is lodged in the sous-préfet of the arrondissement, which delegates authority over the post to the local traditional leader. *See also* ADMINISTRATIVE ORGANIZATION.

PRESIDENTS OF NIGER (1960–95). Niger has had four heads of state to date: Hamani Diori, 1960–74; General Seyni Kountché, 1974–87; General Ali Saibou, 1987–93; Mahamane Ousmane, 1993–.

PROGRAMME DE DEVELOPPEMENT REGIONAL DE L'ADM. Regional development program of the Ader-Doutchi-Maggia area in the region of Tahoua–Keita–Madaoua–Birni-N'Konni. FAC funds totaling 2.4 billion CFA francs were granted to the project between 1960 and 1972; until 1966 for preliminary studies, and since for soil conservation, dams, and water dikes. The area has a very high population density (50–65 people per sq km) and has traditionally suffered from soil erosion and the negative effects of droughts. Though the original project was very ambitiously conceived (20 billion CFA francs were called for in the period 1965–84), much less capital was available, and many of the scheduled expenditures had to be cancelled.

PROGRAMME TRIENNAL, 1976–78. *See* PLANS.

-Q-

QUADRIYA. Historically the most important Muslim religious order in much of Niger, especially in Damagaram, and including Fulani, Hausa, and Tuareg adherents. The order was founded by Abdel Kadir al-Jilani (1077–1166) in Baghdad and spread to Morocco around 1450. The oldest branch established in sub-Saharan Africa was set up in Kano, Nigeria, in the seventeenth century, probably after lodges were founded in Aïr. The order was strong in Zinder, Tahoua, and Agadez but rapidly lost ground in the 1920s to the **Tidjaniya** order. Its current strongholds are Zinder and Agadez, and it is especially prevalent among the Tuareg (who also flocked to the **Khalwatiya**) and the Arab **Kunta** clans.

-R-

RABAH ZUBEIR (*also* Rabih Fadl Allah) (1845?–1900). Sudanese slave raider and builder of a vast personal empire stretching from Sudan through parts of Chad into northern Cameroon. Rabah commenced his swath of military conquest, destruction, and slave raids from the east, from Darfur (now in Sudan), and by 1893 his troops had defeated the once mighty Bornu Empire and pillaged its capital, Kukawa. Though he never entered areas currently within Niger, both his presence at the periphery of Damagaram and his ambitions for a further westward expansion influenced Zinder's court, especially at the time of the arrival of the French mission of Captain **Cazemajou.** Cazemajou's murder in Zinder was in part out of fear in one segment of the court that his true mission was to link up French ambitions with Rabah's aspirations in the area. Niger was the staging ground for one of the three military columns mounted by the French aimed at his destruction. It was within Niger that one of the columns recruited porters, auxiliaries, and camels for its drive toward Chad and the 1900 Battle of Kousseri, which brought about the destruction of Rabahist power and the death of Rabah himself.

RABO, MAI ADA MAMADOU. Secretary of state in charge of national education in the first post-military era civilian government of Niger, between April 1993 and its collapse in October 1994.

RABOIU, DAOUDA. Interim secretary of state in charge of Defense, with specific responsibilities to negotiate with the Tuareg rebel leaders. Formerly prefect of Maradi, he was secretary of state (and later minister of interior) between March 1992 and the creation in April 1993 of a regular elected government.

RADIO NIGER. Set up on March 3, 1962, and broadcasting in French, English, Arabic, and five local languages, Radio Niger's name was changed in 1974 to **Voix du Sahel.**

RAFFI. Hausa name for the **Dallol Maouri,** which is also known as Fadama.

RAFFINI, BRIGI. Tuareg leader. Raffini served as General Saibou's secretary of state for agriculture between November 1987 and May 1989, and then in 1990 was named president of the Conseil National de Développement. With the onset of civilian politics, he quit his alliance with the MNSD and joined **Djermakoy Adamou Moumouni's** ANDP as vice-president of the party. He was arrested by the army in October 1992 in their sweep of Aïr for suspected Tuareg sympathizers.

RASSEMBLEMENT DEMOCRATIQUE AFRICAIN (RDA). Francophone Africa's first and most influential political movement, with branches in most of France's African territories. Founded in 1946 at a congress in Bamako (Mali) which various Francophone leaders attended (including an important delegation from Niger) and headed by Côte d'Ivoire's Houphouët-Boigny, the RDA was initially very militant and allied, at the French National Assembly in Paris, with the French Communist party. The RDA's territorial affiliate in Niger was the Parti Progressiste Nigérien (PPN). *See also* POLITICAL PARTIES.

RASSEMBLEMENT DEMOCRATIQUE DE FEMMES DU NIGER (RDFN). Civic organization for women founded in Niamey in March 1992. Its secretary general is Bayard Mariama Gamatie.

REBELLIONS. Since the French occupation of the territory that was to become the colony of Niger, there have been a number of rebellions in various parts of the country. Among these are the following:

(1) *The 1906 disturbances in the Djerma areas.* Not a generalized rebellion but a series of reactions against colonial authority organized under the guise of a holy war. Most of the important Djerma chiefs remained loyal to the French. The revolt began in December 1905 un-

der Seydou, the blind marabout of Kobakitanda (65 km south of Dosso). His village was razed on January 4, 1906, but the revolt was picked up elsewhere. Seydou eventually made his way to Nigeria where he was captured and executed (March 1906), for the revolt had also spread into neighboring territories and appeared dangerous in light of its "anti-infidel" hue. In Niger it was picked up by the chief of the Karma, Oumarou, who carried the revolt into the area between Goudel and Sansanné-Haoussa. Pacification continued through April 1906.

(2) *The alleged Zinder plot of 1906 by the sultan of Damagaram,* which led to the dissolution of the Sultanate. The plot was a fictitious one, concocted by a courtier who later was elevated to the post vacated by the banished sultan. In light of their natural suspicions, and the general unease in the area (*see above*), the French gave undue credence to the alleged conspiracy.

(3) *The several revolts in the Tuareg north.* A holy war had been declared by the **Sanusiya** order, which had been expanding from Kufra into Kanem and B.E.T. in Chad, clashing with the northward expansion of the French. This resulted in numerous skirmishes between French troops and Sanusiya believers. The Niger upheaval was picked up, in particular, by **Kaocen Ag Mohammed** and, earlier, by **Fihroun.** Other factors adding fuel to the revolts were the general independent spirit of the Tuareg (who did not submit easily to domination), loss of Tuareg camel wealth in the various French levies—or unpaid "purchases"—for the earlier conquest of Chad, the French abolition of slavery and the slave trade, and the severe 1911–14 drought that hit Damergou and Aïr especially hard. The most serious of the Tuareg revolts was the second one—of Kaocen—who arrived secretly at Agadez in December 1914 with a large force of troops armed with modern rifles and a cannon. After a siege of three months, and control of Aïr for that period, the siege was lifted by reinforcements from Zinder. The rebels held out for another two years in various parts of the Aïr wilderness but were finally driven east in 1918 with major losses. The French undertook a series of severe reprisals, which saw massive and indiscriminate executions of marabouts and other leaders in Agadez and In Gall. The second major revolt of the Tuareg occurred under the leadership of Fihroun, the amenokal of the Ikazkazan, starting in 1911. Considered alternately as pro- and anti-French, Fihroun was arrested and exiled in Mali, but escaped in February 1916, raised his armies, and initiated a march on Filingué. He was defeated at the gates of that center.

(4) *The Dori rebellion in December 1915.* This was a rebellion of the Tuareg of the Dori region influenced by the Sanusiya leaders in the area, and especially the important marabout Mohammed Ahmet, at a

time when the French were preoccupied with putting down a rebellion in Mossi areas in Upper Volta. The revolt also spread to neighboring Songhay areas in Niger (especially in the Téra area), though it did not become widespread and was put down in June of the same year. For the contemporary revolt in Aïr, *see* TUAREG REBELLION.

REFERENDUM OF DECEMBER 26, 1992. A referendum on the constitution for the post-military era. Some 3.9 million voters were entitled to vote, 2.7 million registered to vote, and 2.2 million actually voted. Of those who voted, 1,945,653 (89.79 percent) approved of the constitution, while 221, 267 rejected it. For details of the proposals, *see* CONSTITUTIONS.

REFORME ADMINISTRATIVE, 1964. Administrative reform of July 17, 1964, effective October 1, 1965, which divided Niger into seven départements, 32 arrondissements, and approximately 150 communes. The administrative reform was directed toward both rationally setting up the country's administrative framework and decentralizing as much as possible decision making to allow better development prospects and greater mass participation. Toward this end a **Conseil d'Arrondissement** was set up in each of these local units. They were, until 1972, consultative, and since then executive. *See also* ADMINISTRATIVE ORGANIZATION.

RELIGION. The bulk of Niger's population is Muslim (90 percent), with the rest being animist (8 percent) and Christian (2 percent), though the animist population is undoubtedly underrepresented and has been estimated as high as 14.5 percent, and the Muslim as low as 85 percent. Most of the animists are **Maouri** and **Manga,** with some Boudouma and Songhay. The majority denomination among the Christians is Catholicism, with twelve mission centers (and a diocese founded in 1961), twenty-five priests, and thirteen thousand converts. The Catholic mission in Niger was originally set up by Bishop Steinmetz of Dahomey in January 1931. In the 1940s other missionaries (not affiliated with the latter's Missions Africaines de Lyon) started their work in the Zinder area. The Protestant sects in Niger have thirteen mission centers, a personnel of ninety, and some three thousand converts in the entire country. Several of the missions came to Niger via northern Nigeria, as, for example, two American societies—Sudan Interior Mission and the Africa Christian Mission—established in Zinder, Dogondoutchi, Madaoua, and Galmi. Among the Muslim majority, the Tidjaniya order is the dominant one after wresting primacy from the Quadriya during the first decades of the twentieth century. Other orders, badly trailing these two, are Hamallism and Sanusiya, though **Nyassism** has in recent decades been making some steady inroads, and the Wahhabite sect is also now present.

The Songhay-Djerma areas of west Niger have been mostly affected by the Islam of the western Sahel and its maraboutic fraternities. In **Say** especially, but also along the Niger River valley, strong fraternities of the Hamallist-Nyassite order sprang up. In east Niger Islam came mostly via Bornu (which dominated the area until roughly 1736), and Islam has retained its original eastern flavor and peculiarities. In the north the Sanusiya influence has been felt strongly, especially by the Tuareg and the Toubou of Aïr and Kaouar, respectively, who played a prominent role in the various anti-French upheavals in the first two decades of the twentieth century. (Most of Niger's Toubou are Muslim in name only, and their Islam has numerous pre-Islamic practices.)

Pilgrimage figures for Niger show the paradox of one of Africa's most Muslim countries having the distinction of one of Africa's lowest pilgrimage-to-Mecca figures (only forty-eight in 1956). Among Niger's Fulani are found many Bororo quasi animists. Niger's Hausa, and some of the Fulani in the south, maintain close links with their kinsmen across the border and especially with the marabouts of Kano and Zaria, something that at various times caused apprehension in French and British colonial circles. For more details on the various orders, *see* HAMALLISM; NYASSISM; QUADRIYA; RELIGIOUS ORDERS; TIDJANIYA.

Over the past two decades, and especially in the early 1990s, part of the Muslim community in Niger became more assertive and militant, affected by similar developments in north Nigeria and the spread of more militant fundamentalism from there. A hard-line movement, originating in Jos, Nigeria, was behind a number of violent clashes with animists, whose alleged irreverent or immoral behavior has been blamed for ecological shortfalls, and a greater proselytizing effort has been mounted. (The movement is called *Jama'at izalat al-bid'a was igamat al-Sunna,* meaning "Movement for suppressing innovations and restoring Sunna-Izal.") More recently, a progressive family bill being considered by Niger's National Assembly in 1994 was strongly opposed by six Muslim associations. *See also* ASSOCIATION ISLAMIQUE DU NIGER; KORANIC SCHOOLS.

RELIGIOUS ORDERS (Muslim). There are numerous Muslim religious orders in Niger, though the dominant one by far is the **Tidjaniya,** which attained primacy over the **Quadriya** in the first decades of the twentieth century. Established by Umar al-Tidjani in Fès, Morocco, at the turn of the century, and encouraged by the French in their colonies, Tidjaniya is an orthodox sect. The Quadriya has been established in Niger since the eighteenth century, when it was the local majority order. Founded in Baghdad early in the twelfth century, it arrived in Niger in the seventeenth century. Because of its connection with the Middle East, and the "influences" it could bring in from the outside world, the "local" Tidjaniya was strongly supported by the French during the colonial era. Apart from these two major groups, Niger has been influenced by several other Islamic orders, but to a lesser extent or on a regional basis only.

Hamallism struck roots mostly among the oppressed slaves or former slaves (especially Fulani)—*ramaibe*—during the Second World War. **Khalwatiya** became one of two dominant orders among the Tuareg (the other being Sanusiya) arriving in Niger from Egypt in the mid–sixteenth century but not spreading much beyond the Tuareg of Aïr. The Sanusiya established itself in Aïr around 1870 and spread via the caravan trade to Kaouar, In Gall, and Iférouane; one of its important centers became Djididouna, though contemporarily Kaouar, and Bilma specifically, are probably its main centers. It adopted a virulent anti-French, anti-infidel line in the first decade of the twentieth century and declared, from Kufra, Libya, a jihad against the French that was headed by the Tuareg and Toubou in Niger, and by other groups in France's other Saharan colonies. For this reason the French did their utmost to stamp out the order wherever they could.

Other minor orders to be found in Niger include Chadelia, Nyassism, and Taibia. A 1920 census of the marabouts in Niger found that there were 771 belonging to the Quadriya, 332 to the Tidjaniya, 21 to the Sanusiya, 3 to the Chadelia, and 1 to the Taibia. The Zinder cercle at the time counted 169 Tidjaniya, 91 Quadriya, 4 Sanusiya, 3 Chadelia, and 1 Taibia marabout. In the Tahoua cercle the figures were 420 Quadriya and 8 Tidjaniya. Since this census the Quadriya membership has drastically shrunk and the Tidjaniya expanded, though the other sects have remained stable. No reliable figures such as these of 1920 are currently available, however.

REPATRIATIONS. Large numbers of Nigeriens, resident in other African states (but mostly in West Africa), have been forcibly repatriated over the years for a variety of reasons. The two best-known instances were the 200,000 Nigeriens expelled from Ghana in 1970 for reasons of economic nationalism in Ghana. Their reintegration into the Niger economy caused the government a great deal of fiscal stress. Earlier, in 1964, an undetermined though smaller number of Nigeriens were expelled from Dahomey as a retaliation against Niger's earlier expulsion of its large Dahomean expatriate community arising from the unconnected Lété Island boundary dispute between the two countries. And in 1982 the massive expulsions of foreigners from Nigeria caused major dislocations and fiscal hardships to Niger, which was faced with an influx of over 100,000 of its nationals.

RIOU, YVES. Civil administrator. Riou served in a variety of capacities in the colonial administration of Niger between 1936 and independence, and was retained as inspector of administrative affairs of the new republic until 1965. Being of French nationality, at that date he became consul of France in Zinder (1965–69) and later consul general of France in Niamey (1969–73).

RIZ DU NIGER (RINI). A largely (98.5 percent) state company set up in 1968 with 250 million CFA francs in capital to process rice planted by farm cooperatives. It commenced with the capacity of producing 10,000 tons of rice annually, a sum since doubled, though rice production plummeted in the 1980s. The company has three plants, in Tillabéry, Kirkissoyé, and Kollo. Consistently operating below capacity (and never producing over 17,250 tons), the company has long been scheduled for restructuring or privatization.

ROSI. Archaeologically important site 15 km southwest of Birni N'-Gaouré, of a village from the fifteenth century. Pottery and bracelets from various ages have been dug up.

ROUCH, JEAN PIERRE (1917–). French anthropologist, filmmaker, and one of the foremost scholars of Niger. Born on May 31, 1917, and trained originally as a civil engineer. Rouch worked in Niger (1941–42), served with the Free French Forces (1942–45), and following anthropological studies commenced his career as intructor, scholar, and cinematographer. He made the first descent of the Niger River by canoe in 1946–47. He has taught at the Musée de l'Homme, has directed a large number of films (several of which have won prizes), and set up (in 1962) the Niamey branch of IFAN.

ROUMJI. A small village in southern Damagaram, famous as the site where the French finally caught up with Sultan Ahmadou on September 16, 1899, and killed him, avenging the murder of Captain Cazemajou in Zinder.

ROUTE DE L'UNITE. Name of the paved Gouré–N'Guigmi road that connects east and west Niger. The first part of the road was completed in 1972–73.

ROUTE DE L'URANIUM. Name of the main route through which Niger's uranium exports travel. The road commenses at **Arlit**—with feeder roads from the other mines in the vicinity—and runs through Agadez to Tahoua where it connects with the main southern east-west artery. The 650-km road was paved between 1976 and 1980. It was completed at a cost of over 200 billion CFA francs, most of which was covered by the mining companies, which need it most (with little other north-south traffic) and which also committed themselves to the road's upkeep for the next twenty years.

-S-

SABIRI. The most ancient population of **Dosso.** Under their *sandi* (chief) the Sabiri had a privileged status in Dosso until Auta became **djermakoy** of Dosso.

SABO, BOUKARY (1924–). Former foreign minister of Niger. Born in 1924 in Dan-Amario (Maradi district), and of Hausa nobility, being the son of Sabo Bawa, serkin Mayaki (1932–50). He was educated locally and at the Frederic Assomption Teachers Training College at Katibougou (Mali) in 1945–49, where he remained as an instructor (1950–59). Sabo returned to Niger in 1959 and, due to his traditional credentials, was elected deputy to the National Assembly from the Tessaoua district. He served in the Assembly until 1965 and was the rapporteur of its Social Affairs and Labor Committee. In 1965 he was brought into Diori's cabinet as minister of youth, information, and sports and in 1970 was shifted to head the Ministry of Civil Service and Labor. In 1972 he was promoted to the key post of foreign minister, which he held until the 1974 coup.

SABO, NASSIROU. General Saibou's last minister of communications, serving between March 1990 and September 1991 when the HCR government took over.

SABON BIRNI. Founded in 1860 by a dissident **Gobirawa** faction aided by the Sokoto Fulani (with whom the legitimate Gobirawa regime had been fighting for some fifty years), who rejected the authority of Tibiri. Becoming an important center of Gobirawa dissidence Sabon Birni was ultimately conquered by the legitimate Gobirawa forces. The town is very remotely located in northern Nigeria. It is the headquarters of the serkin Gobir, Muhamadu Bawa, who ascended the throne in 1975.

SADIO, DJOULDE. Minister of agriculture between April 1993 and the collapse of the government in October 1994.

SAHARAN ROCK DRAWINGS. *See* ARCHAEOLOGY.

SAHEL. Arid transitional zone between the desert north and the subtropical south. Running across much of Central and West Africa, the zone encompasses most of central and northern Niger. Though the Sahel usually has regular rainfall, any disruption of the climate (as during the recent series of prolonged droughts) can transform the affected areas into desert. The term *Sahel* is Arabic for "fringe" or "border." *See also* DROUGHTS.

SAHEL-HEBDO. Niger's principal weekly newspaper, formerly named ***Le Temps du Niger.*** Edited and distributed by the Ministry of Information its circulation has inched up over the years to 4,000. The ministry also publishes a daily—*Le Sahel*— with a similar circulation. The editor of both is Sahidou Alou. Following civilianization, press freedoms were extended and a number of other newspapers emerged.

SAIBOU, ALI (General) (1940–). President of Niger between 1987 and 1993, and former chief of staff of the Niger armed forces. Born in Dingajibanda (in the arrondissement of Ouallam), Seyni Kountché's home village, and a Djerma like Kountché, Saibou has often been referred to as the latter's cousin (which he is not) because of Kountché's propensity to place family members in key military posts. Saibou decided at an early age on a military career, and enrolled in the Saint-Louis (Senegal) preparatory school in 1954. He then joined the First Senegalese Tiralleurs Regiment. He saw military action in 1960 in Cameroon (where he was wounded), while with the Fifth RIOM regiment. He was transferred to the Nigerien army in August 1961 with the rank of sergeant. After attending officers' school he was placed in command of units at N'Guigmi (1969) and Agadez (1973), attaining the rank of captain. He was in that city when Kountché mounted his coup d'état against President Hamani Diori, and his prompt overnight drive with his troops to Niamey in support of Kountché brought about his promotion to major and elevation to the cabinet as minister of rural economy and the environment. On November 20, 1974, he was also named chief of staff of the armed forces.

By nature not politically minded—and Kountché's complete opposite, a gregarious, easygoing bon vivant—Saibou was dropped from the cabinet in June 1975, when Kountché, ever suspicious of all those surrounding him, suggested that Saibou relinquish command of the armed forces to assume a largely ceremonial post. Saibou's response (that since this would indicate Kountché's lack of trust in him, he would prefer to be dismissed altogether and return to his home village) sealed a bond between the two officers, and Saibou was retained at the head of the army until Kountché's death, despite the latter's disposing of virtually all military officers in the original clique that seized power. He proved his loyalty to the head of state on a number of occasions, including during Kountché's last, seriously ailing years, when France tried unsuccessfully to nudge Saibou to assume power.

On Kountché's death in a Paris hospital on November 10, 1987, Saibou engineered his own nomination by a clique in the CMS (the supreme military command) to succeed Kountché, averting a possible bid by another group in support of Djermakoy Adamou Moumouni. He then proceeded to send overseas on diplomatic assignments all potential military rivals from the Old Guard, while increasing the size of his cabinet and the numbers of military officers in it. Aware that some form of mass political participation was overdue in Niger, he transformed the MNSD into Niger's sole political party with himself at its head. Following the adoption of a new constitution, and Niger's first National Assembly since 1964, Saibou was elected president of Niger in the single-party elections that followed.

Saibou failed, however, to grasp that the days of symbolic participation were numbered. The years after 1989 were hectic, with mounting social unrest due to Niger's deteriorating economy, increased international pressures for structural adjustment programs in exchange for debt rescheduling (which Saibou reluctantly agreed to), and domestic union and student strikes against the austerity regimen and later for true democratization. In the first part of 1990 occurred two events that ultimately doomed the regime: a student strike (over bread-and-butter issues), which was brutally suppressed by the armed forces, and a few months later a Tuareg armed assault (not the first) on Tchin Tabaraden, which was followed by mass, indiscriminate repression and hundreds of deaths. Both led inexorably to (*a*) the dismantling of military rule via the National Conference route, a process Saibou could not avert due to the bankruptcy of the regime, and (*b*) a full-fledged Tuareg rebellion in the north (but progressively closer to Niamey), which for similar reasons the Niger armed forces could not stem.

At the 1991 National Conference Saibou was retained (despite some opposition) as titular head of state until the 1993 presidential elections. He remained virtually invisible in this role, and presided over an orderly transfer of power, which in the case of Niger was not only from military to civilian rule, but also one which saw Djerma-Songhay domination of power (1960–93) terminated and the rise in importance of the Hausa east. After the presidential elections that saw his replacement by the civilian Mahamane Ousmane, Saibou retired to his home village.

SAIDOU, AMADOU. General Saibou's secretary general of the government in charge of relations with the National Assembly, a post necessitated when a new (single-party) Assembly was created in 1989.

Saidou served in that capacity until the rise of the HCR government, between December 1989 and September 1991.

SAIDOU, SOULEYMANE. Political newcomer and interim HCR minister of public health between November 1991 and April 1993 when Niger's new civilian government took office.

SALA, MOUSSA (Lieutenant Colonel). Former commander of Niger's armored unit and minister of public health. Since 1966 head of Niger's small armored unit, Moussa joined the military cabinet after the 1974 coup d'état as minister of public health and social affairs. In mid-1975 he was shifted to head the Ministry of Transport and Public Works but was returned to his old ministry (stripped of social affairs) in 1976, when he was also promoted to major. Appointed minister of education in September 1978, Sala was held personally responsible for the eruption of student unrest in the country in 1980 and was dropped from the cabinet in February 1981. Sala was rehabilitated after General Saibou's rise to power, and in 1989 was named MNSD deputy from Dosso to the National Assembly. He served in that capacity until the Assembly was dissolved by the National Conference of 1991.

SALAOU, BARMOU. Organizing secretary of the **Société de Développement du Niger** during the reign of generals Kountché and Saibou, and currently performing a similar task in the MNSD.

SALEY, ABDOU EL NADJ. A civil administrator by profession who served for several years as subprefect in some of the nomadic arrondissements, Saley became in November 1977 Niger's first resident ambassador to Senegal. In 1980 he was shifted to another diplomatic posting, and in 1987 integrated into the Ministry in Niamey.

SALIAH, ASSANE (1930–). Civil administrator. Born in Filingué and educated locally and at the Katibougou Teachers College in Mali, Saliah taught in a number of schools before joining the Niger administration as prefect of Dosso in April 1966. He was moved to head the Diffa prefectural system in 1970, and in 1973 was again shifted to become prefect of Zinder. Since the 1974 coup he has been appointed to several administrative postings throughout the country, usually subservient to military prefects.

SALIFOU, ADAMOU. Interim secretary of state in charge of tourism and trade, serving in the HCR government between November 1991 and April 1993, when it stepped down. In March 1992 his portfolio was defined that of commerce.

SALIFOU, ANDRE (1942–). Historian, author, former president of the HCR, and political leader. Born in 1942 in Zinder and educated locally, in France (at Toulouse University) and at the Abidjan (Ivory Coast) Ecole Nationale d'Art Dramatique, Salifou possesses a Ph.D. in history. He has written several plays, one of which—*Tanimoune*—was first performed in Algiers in 1969 and gained him much acclaim. He also founded and directed many amateur theatrical groups. Between 1967 and 1973 teaching at the Ecole Normale in Zinder, he was its director between 1969 and 1970. In 1973 he went to Dakar to serve with UNESCO's office there until 1978, and then became director of social and cultural affairs of OCAM. In 1979 he returned to Niamey to become the director of the School of Education at the local university, in due course emerging as its dean. He participated in focusing pressure on the military regime of General Saibou, and when the National Conference was convened in 1991 was elected president of the HCR, the interim (until elections produced a regular) legislature of Niger. Barred, together with other former heads of state and government leaders from running in the forthcoming presidential elections, Salifou joined forces with **Illa Kané** to form a party, the Union des Patriotes Démocratiques et Progrèssistes (UPDP-Shamuwa). The party won only one seat in the National Assembly, and Kané's parliamentary bid secured him roughly 2.5 percent of the vote. Disenchanted with the outcome of civilian rule, by 1993–94 Salifou was active in antiestablishment campaigns against it, and he was twice briefly arrested. The UPDP has been aligned in the National Assembly with the MNSD.

SALIFOU, BAZEYE. Attorney general of Niger, appointed on January 7, 1988, by General Saibou. She was replaced after the National Conference by El Hadj Mati Ousmane.

SALIFOU, ILLA (1932–). Former ambassador to the U.S. and the U.N. Born on February 17, 1932, in Madaoua and educated locally and abroad, including at the Graduate Institute for International Studies in Geneva, Salifou joined the Foreign Ministry in 1961 after serving for one year as director of administration and legislation in the Ministry of Justice (1960–61). One of Niger's delegation to the U.N. General Assembly (1961–66) and counselor at the Niger embassy to the U.S. (1960–66), he was brought back to Niamey and appointed (in 1968) cabinet director of the minister of foreign affairs. In 1970 he became technical councillor and director of consular and administrative affairs in the ministry (1970–71). Throughout 1967–71 he also was Niger's delegate to the OAU and attended the 1968, 1969, and 1971 U.N. General Assembly sessions. Following the 1974 coup d'état Salifou was named Niger's ambassador to the United States and representative to the United Nations, serving until 1976. In that year he was appointed ambassador to the Soviet Union. In 1979 Salifou was repatriated to Niamey to become secretary general of the Foreign Ministry. His tenure was brief; in 1980 he left for Paris to become personnel director of the Francophone organization, the Agence de Cooperation Culturelle et Technique des Pays Francophones (ACCTF).

SALISSOU, MADOUGOU. Minister of the civil service and labor between April 1993 and the fall of the government in October 1994.

SALT MINES. *See* NATRON.

SAMA, OUMAROU IBRAHIM (1943–). Economist. Born in Say on February 27, 1943, and educated at home and in France, Sama served as head of the Economic Relations Service in the Ministry of Economic Affairs between 1970 and the coup of 1974. Since the coup he has been shifted to head a division in the Ministry of Planning.

SAMARIA. Traditional organizations resurrected by Kountché's military regime and given a modern developmental function. Meaning "youth" in Hausa (the singular being *samari*), the samaria were groups of youth (organized by age) coordinated at the village level under a serkin samaria to perform whatever tasks they were delegated by the village chief or the serkin samaria. Largely stagnating in the 1960s, the groups were resurrected after the 1974 coup d'état by Kountché, who called upon them to assume a major effort in several developmental tasks, such as brick making and the construction of schools and classrooms. In 1981–82 the samaria—by now officially set up in every one of Niger's nine thousand villages—were given a key role in the newly enunciated **Société de Développement,** though their economic role has always been modest, and as a tool for popular mobilization even less.

SAMBO, HAMA. Former mayor of Niamey. A civil administrator by profession, Sambo was a former sous-préfet of the Niamey arrondissement and PPN propaganda secretary when elected to the Niamey mayoralty on August 12, 1968. He served as mayor until the coup of 1974. Imprisoned for a while, he has been in retirement since his release.

SAMBO, MAHAMANE MARIAMA. Secretary of state in charge of women's issues and the protection of children between April 1993 and the fall of the government in October 1994.

SANA, IBRAHIM EL HADJ (1916–). Powerful former member of the inner core of the PPN party. Born in 1916 in Tanda and a petty administrative functionary until his election to the National Assembly in 1957 from Dosso. He remained in the Assembly until its dissolution in 1974 serving on a host of committees, including as president of the Economic Affairs Committee and rapporteur of the Finance Committee.

SANDA, OUMAROU. *See* OUMAROU, SANDA.

SANDAL *See* ISANDALEN; ITESEN

SANDI. Head of the non-Djerma indigenous population, which in the Dosso chiefdom is roughly equal to the **djermakoy** whom he actually formally enthrones after selection from the Auta family. The Sandi is always consulted by the djermakoy on important matters.

SANI, KOUTOUMI. Administrator. Formerly director of the Office National des Recherches Minières (UNAREM), Sani was named in 1976 Director of URANIGER.

SANOUSSI, JACOUB TAMAGUI. Leader of a splinter political group that in February 1995 deserted President Ousmane's own CDS party to form the Parti Nigérien pour l'Autogéstion (PNA).

SANSANNE-HAOUSSA. A **Kado-Kurtey** village on the Niger River some 45 km south of Tillabéry and Zinder where Djerma country merges with Kurtey country. In 1990 a small village with a population of 2,000 and a popular Friday market, Sansanné-Haoussa was in the nineteenth century the principal slave market of the entire area (drawing slaves from the Kurtey islands in the Niger River) and a major jumping-off point for French expeditions to the east. Indeed, for all practical purposes Sansanné-Haoussa was the biggest "urban" center in the entire area. Today it is in the Tillabéry arrondissement of the Niamey départment.

SANUSIYA. A Sunni (orthodox) sufi (mystic) order stressing return to the basic precepts of Islam, avoidance of contaminating influences from the infidel world, and direct interpretation of Islam. The order struck roots in Libya in the nineteenth century and had a deep impact further south toward the latter part of that century. Founded by the Algerian scholar al-Sayyid Muhamad bin Ali al-Sanusi al-Khattabi (called in Libya either the Grand Sanusi or al-Sanusi al-Kabir), Sanusiya was established in Libya after his return from Mecca where he had organized his first lodge. Moving his headquarters to the interior Jaghbub (160 miles from the coast) where an Islamic university was also founded (the second after Cairo's Al-Azhar), al-Sanusi won the allegiance of various tribes in the interior of Libya, and others involved in long-distance trading. In light of this success, the order developed a more African-oriented proselytizing ambition, and the center of the order was shifted to Kufra in 1895, and then into Chad's B.E.T., from which its influence radiated into Aïr and Kaouar (in Niger) and Kanem and Ouadai (in Chad). Much of the conversion of these areas to the Sanusiya occurred after al-Sanusi's death, and was carried out by his two lieutenants, Sidi Muhammad al-Barrani and Muhammad al-Suni. The Sanusiya's expansion southward coincided with France's, and the two forces clashed bitterly from the turn of the century into the 1920s. In Niger the Sanusiya established itself first in Aïr in 1870 (especially in Agadez, In Gall, Iférouane, and a few other minor centers). Emissaries were sent as far afield as Zinder, both to gain converts and open lodges and to mobilize the population against the French. The order did not strike deep roots among the Tuareg and the Toubou. It currently has a number of lodges, especially in Kaouar.

SARANUYA. The **Gubawa** head of Lugu, a major **Azna** center in the Dallol Maouri. *See also* MAOURI.

SARARI-N-MESALLAJE. The great mosque of Agadez. Its spiky minaret dominates the entire countryside. First built in the sixteenth century, it was thoroughly rebuilt in 1847.

SARA-SARA. One of the several indigenous names for the rampaging Voulet-Chanoine column in Niger. In Djerma the local equivalent is Gate-Gate. *See* MISSION AFRIQUE CENTRALE.

SARGAJI REVOLT (1899–1900). Localized anti-French revolt lasting from August 1899 to December 1900 and affecting the region north of Dosso (and flaring up again in 1905), ethnically a mixed area of Gubey, Tuareg, Maouri, and Djerma. Among the complex reasons for the revolt was the attachment of the traditionally "independent" villages of Sargaji and Loga to the authority of the djermakoy of Dosso, a prime ally of France. The refusal of the two villages to submit to Dosso's authority led to hostilities that spread throughout the area. Two campaigns (in August 1899 and February 1900) led to French defeats and only in November 1900 did a strong column armed with rapid-firing weapons succeed in razing the villages and setting the prime conspirators to flight.

SARKI (*also* Sarkin, Serki, Serkin). "Chief." The term is used for the chief of a village or region, or the official head of any ritual or ceremony, for instance, serkin Bori.

SASSALE. Kurtey slaves, originating in the Sassalé village near Dessa, who developed a reputation as griots specializing in obscene songs and dances.

SAWABA. In Hausa, "independence" or "freedom"—the rallying call of Djibo Bakary's **Mouvement Socialiste Africain** and later the official name of that party. Successor name of Djibo Bakary's Union Démocratique Nigérienne (*see* POLITICAL PARTIES). Founded in 1957. The party lost the 1958 referendum (in which it called for a "no" vote) by 358,000 (for the PPN) and 98,000 for SAWABA, and shortly thereafter lost the territorial elections, thus losing political primacy in Niger. With the rise of the PPN the SAWABA party was banned (in 1959) and several years later attempted a comeback through violent means (*see* UNION DEMOCRATIQUE NIGERIENNE), among which were the October 1964 attacks on several border and customs posts and the April 1965 grenade attack on President Diori, the reaction to which was so harsh, as well as negative, that SAWABA for all practical purposes stopped its quest for power. In 1964, moreover, it was estimated that it had only about 300 to 400 militants and fewer guerrillas trained (in particular) in Nkrumah's Ghana. The party had at various times been labeled Communist, which is erroneous, though certainly it was radical. After the 1974 coup d'état SAWABA leaders, including Djibo Bakary, were invited to return to Niger on the condition that they refrain from politics for the duration of the military regime. The party name, as a suffix, was resurrected by Djibo Bakary with the onset of competitive elections in the early 1990s, but not only has it not garnered more than a small number of votes, it has also split into two, with Bakary heading one of its components.

SAY. Historically important Fulani and Muslim stronghold. Founded in the early part of the nineteenth century by **Alfa Mohamed Diobo,** who came to the area from Djenné (Mali) in 1810 via Gao, and was in full control of the area around Say by 1854. At the time of **Heinrich Barth's** visit Say was a thriving Fulani political and religious center of renown numbering some 8,000 people. The town was occupied by France on May 9, 1897, and administered from Dahomey until 1907. Located about 55 km from Niamey near the **Parc National du W,** the village today has barely 3,000 people, is of little importance, and bears no resemblance to the ancient center of Islamic learning and piety. In recognition of its former role, however, in 1974 the Islamic

Conference in Lahore designated Say as the site for the new **Islamic University,** to be built (the first in West Africa) with Arab oil money. After much delay the new university finally opened its doors in October 1986, with Dr. Abdullah Ben-Abdul-Muhsin El-Turki as its rector. Say is connected to the capital by an all-weather road, and has a colorful Friday market to which many tourists flock. Nearby are found iron deposits with a 50 percent iron content. At its heyday the town of Say was widely known from Gao to Gaya as a center for Islamic learning and piety. It is reputed to have had at one time 30,000 inhabitants, and to have launched its own trans-Saharan caravans. Currently Say is an arrondissement of 75,000 in the Niamey département.

SAY, BANIA MAHAMADOU (1935–). Administrator, youth leader, and poet. Born in 1935 in Tillakalna and educated as an administrative accountant, Say served as a teacher before being selected to become director of the national budget. Currently he is with the International Labor Office's Niamey bureau and a director of the **samaria** movement. In 1980 a book of his poems was published in Niger.

SAY–BARROUA LINE. A straight line between Say and Barroua (on Lake Chad) that delineated, in the Anglo-French Treaty of 1890, the French (northern) and British (southern) spheres of influence in the area. France's haste in ratifying the border was indicative of a gross overestimation of the extent of British control and influence south of the line, costing France the highly populated areas of northern Nigeria. The Say–Barroua Line was later somewhat revised in favor of France. *See also* ANGLO-FRENCH TREATIES, 1890–1906.

SEGUEDINE. Rich oasis in Kaouar, 90 km south of Djado, 190 km from Bilma. Despite a strong **ksar** and a population of over 1,000, Séguédine fell in the mid–eighteenth century to a joint force of Toubou and Tuareg, and many of its inhabitants fled to neighboring oases in Kaouar. Séguédine was again raided and razed in February 1918 by Kaocen's brother (*see* KAOCEN REBELLION). Like most oases in the area Séguédine possesses salt pans and some palm groves.

SEKOU, HAMIDOU. Former minister of national education. Appointed by General Saibou in May 1989, it was under his tenure that the brutal suppression of student demonstrations took place in February 1990, and he was dropped from the cabinet the next month.

SENOUSI. *See* SANUSIYA.

SENOUSSI, JACKOU. Former deputy president of the National Assembly during Niger's first post-1991 civilian government, and former chairman of the CSD party. Senoussi resigned from the CSD in mid-1994 over the AFC coalition's decision not to debate a USTN demand for higher wages.

SERKI. *See* SARKI.

SERKIN AZNA. Chief of the animists, and especially of the **Bori** cult in the Birni-N'Konni region.

SEYDOU, ABDOUL RAHAMANE (Major). General Saibou's minister of youth, brought in as a newcomer to the cabinet in November 1987, dropped in a reshuffle in May 1989, and brought in again in the same post after the February 1990 student demonstrations and their brutal dispersal. He served until September 1991, when the HCR government was formed.

SEYDOU, ALFA (1865?–1906). Frequently referred to as the "Blind Marabout" who set southern Niger ablaze with anti-French rebellions in 1905–6. Triggering the revolt of several ethnic groups primarily in the area of the **dallols** and especially in the Niamey-Gaya and Dallol Maouri, the center of the upheaval was at Kobakitanda and Sambera Kuré. Coming from a noble family and of the chiefly lineage of Kobakitanda, Seydou was blind but exerted tremendous charismatic pull. Though the rebellion reflected deep social grievances at the inequities of colonial rule, it was equally Seydou's personal vendetta against the infidel French. Declaring a holy war against all Europeans, Seydou witnessed his ideas spreading like wildfire and farmers refusing to pay taxes or to obey colonial officials. The revolt even had repercussions in neighboring Nigeria. In December 1905 violence broke out and Djermakoy Auta of Dosso, a staunch ally of the French, was ordered to bring about order in the region. Seydou managed to escape into Nigeria, fanning the revolt there, too, before his arrest and execution.

SEYDOU, AMADOU (1928–). Scholar and diplomat. Born in 1928 and educated locally, at Dakar's Institut des Hautes Etudes, at Cairo's Al-Azhar University, and at the University of Paris (studying philosophy, psychology, and Arab languages and literature), Seydou started his career as a teacher and later founded the National School of Medersa in 1960. He was then appointed chargé d'affaires at the Niger embassy in Paris and in 1961 was appointed ambassador. He served in that post for five years and concurrently during 1964–66 as ambassador to

Great Britain. In October 1967 he was appointed director of the Department of Culture of UNESCO in Paris. Shortly after the 1974 coup in Niamey he was again named ambassador to France, and in 1982 became secretary general of the Ministry of Finance. In 1988 he retired.

SEYDOU, AMADOU (Colonel) (1943–). Former military commander of the Niamey Battalion. One of the conspirators in the October 1983 anti-Kountché putsch, Seydou was arrested and, after a trial that did not take place until 1988 (after Kountché's death), was sentenced to twenty years in prison. He was nevertheless released on December 17, 1989, as General Saibou prepared to assume office as a politically elected president. At the time he was dubbed Niger's "last political prisoner." He was later appointed inspector general of Niger's armed forces, and was pensioned off in 1993.

SEYDOU, DJERMAKOY (1889–1938). **Djermakoy** of **Dosso** and father of **Djermakoy Issoufou Seydou.** A staunch ally of France, as was his father before him, he assisted in the colonization of Niger and supported the French cause with his own cavalry. Seydou assumed the throne in 1912. During the First World War he volunteered for the French army and was at the bloody siege of Verdun. He was decorated twice, and demobilized with the rank of lieutenant.

SEYDOU, DJERMAKOY ISSOUFOU (1920–). **Djermakoy** of **Dosso,** former cabinet minister, key early political leader, and United Nations administrator. The son of the famous **Djermakoy Seydou,** who assisted in the French conquest and colonization of Niger, Seydou was born on July 10, 1920, and was educated in Dosso, Algeria, and the Lycée Faidherbe in Saint-Louis, Senegal (through 1942). Seydou—the traditional leader of the Djerma of Dosso, and at the time the most prestigious Djerma chief, évolué, and ally of the French administration—volunteered in the Free French forces for the duration of the Second World War (as had his illustrious father, who served in Verdun in the First World War). After the war Seydou continued his studies in mathematics and commenced his political career by participating in the foundation of the PPN party in Niger. A former president of the party though opposed to its link to the interterritorial RDA, Seydou bolted the PPN to form the UNIS party. In 1947 he was elected on that ticket as deputy to the French Union (serving through 1957) and between 1952 and 1957 also served as grand councillor to the AOF Council in Dakar, and in 1958 as senator of the French Community. During these years he was also UNIS's key leader, and president of its successor, the BNA party. He was also a cofounder and briefly president of the MSA party that later became **SAWABA,** though he left the party to join with the PPN president of the UCFA electoral alliance that swept the polls in 1958. Seydou was vice president and minister of justice between December 1958 and October 1959 and was retained in Diori's cabinet after 1960 as minister attached to the presidency. In March 1961, partly due to personality difficulties with Diori, he left Niamey to become Niger's ambassador to the U.S. and representative to the United Nations. In 1962 he returned to Niamey to rejoin the cabinet as minister of international cooperation, and between 1963 and 1965 he served as Diori's minister of justice. In 1965 he returned to New York as Niger's representative to the U.N. and in 1967 was appointed U.N. deputy secretary general in charge of nonautonomous territories. In 1972 he assumed the post of deputy secretary general in charge of African questions, and between 1973 and his retirement he was deputy secretary general and commissioner for U.N. technical assistance.

SEYNI, ABDOULKARIMOU. Secretary of state in charge of cooperation between April 1993 and the fall of the government in October 1994.

SEYNI, AMADOU (Colonel). Prefect of Maradi. Seyni, who is of a chiefly family, attended military staff colleges in France and was President Hamani Diori's aide-de-camp prior to the 1974 coup d'état. A key officer of the supreme military command (CMS), and a good friend of General Kountché, Seyni was nevertheless shunted aside to prefectural duties, first in charge of the important Maradi prefecture, and later in charge of Zinder in a similar capacity. In 1990 he was brought in a little closer to the center of power by an appointment to the political bureau of the General Saibou's newly institutionalized political party, the MNSD.

SI. *See* SONNI.

SIDI, MUHAMMAD (Captain). Ringleader of the March 1976 uprising against the Kountché regime (*see* COUP OF MARCH 15, 1976), who was wounded in the fighting. Sidi, a Tuareg, was condemned to death in his subsequent trial and was executed on April 21, 1976. Prior to the 1974 coup d'état that led to the rise of Kountché, he had been chef de cabinet of the minister of defense.

SIDI AL-MUKHTAR IBN AHMED IBN BAKR AL-KUNTI. *See* AL-MUKHTAR AL-KUNTI.

SIDI MUHAMAD BIN SIDI UMAR BIN SIDI MUKHTAR AL-WAFI. *See* BAY AL-KUNTI, SHAYKH.

SIDIBE, ABOUBAKAR (1933–). Former diplomat. Born on March 13, 1933, in Madaoua and educated locally and abroad (obtaining a degree from IHEOM), Sidibé served as first secretary at Niger's embassy in France (1961–64), minister plenipotentiary (also to France, 1964–66), ambassador to West Germany (1966–67), and ambassador to France and Great Britain. Between 1969 and his retirement he served as Niger's representative to UNESCO.

SIDIKOU, AROUNA HAMIDOU (1946–). Geographer. Born on March 4, 1946, and educated in Zinder and the University of Abidjan, Sidikou then proceeded to obtain a doctorate in geography from the University of Rouen. He taught at several lycées in Niamey in the 1970s before joining the University of Niamey. The author of numerous studies, in 1985 he was named director of IRSH.

SIDIKOU, GARBA (1932–). Administrator and former minister of higher education. Born in 1932 in Birni N'Gaouré, Sidikou was educated in Niamey and taught primary schools between 1951 and 1959. For the next two years he was responsible for educational radio programs and in 1961 obtained specialized radio training in France. He then worked for nine years (1961–70) as deputy director of Radio Niger and in 1968–69 was the elected vice-president of URTNA (the union of African radio and television stations). In 1969 he was elected its president for two years. In 1970 Sidikou was appointed head of the press section in the Department of Information, and in 1972 became director general of information. Following the 1974 coup d'état Sidikou took over the direction of Radio Niger and a few months later (December 1974) was named secretary of state in charge of youth and sports. In February 1976 he was given full ministerial rank as minister of youth, sports, and culture. Later the same year, after the purge of Ibrahim Loutou, Sidikou was appointed in his stead as secretary of state for information. In 1979 he became minister of youth and sport, and in July 1982 Sidikou was shifted to head the Ministry of Information. He lost this position in January 1983 and was reassigned to technical duties in the Ministry of Interior, as well as being deputy president of the National Development Council (CND). In 1983 he was also elected mayor of Niamey, serving for four years.

SIDIKOU, MAHAMANE. Journalist and former cabinet director of Prime Minister Mamane Oumarou. Sidikou was deeply implicated in the attempted putsch of October 1983, and for some time there was suspicion of Oumarou's own involvement in light of the close links between the two men. Arrested after the putsch, he was released on Kountché's death by his successor, General Saibou, early in 1989.

SIDIKOU, OUMAROU (1938–). Former treasurer general of Niger. Born in 1938 in N'Dounga and educated locally and abroad, Sidikou was director of fiscal contributions in the Ministry of Finance, government representative on the board of SONERAN, and president of NITEX until August 1973. On that date he assumed the post of treasurer general of Niger. He retained his position after the coup of 1974, but was soon appointed director of administrative affairs of the BCEAO branch in Niamey.

SIDIKOU, SALIFOU. Secretary general of the Front Nigérien National (FNN), one of Niger's newer parties, set up in 1993 by Fulani elements feeling left out of the political distribution of power in Niger.

SIDO, CHEIK AMADOU. Religious leader. Head of the fundamentalist Muslim Izala sect in Niamey, Sido was behind the proselytizing campaign against the capital's animists in April 1994 that led to interethnic fighting and violent clashes with the police.

SIDO, SANI SOUNA (Major) (1933–77). Former minister in the Kountché military regime. The chef de cabinet of Diori's military cabinet prior to the coup d'état of 1974, Sido was not brought into the conspiracy because of his proximity to Diori. After the coup, however, in part because of his popularity among the troops, he was brought into the CSM and appointed its vice-president and also minister of interior, mines, and geology. He rapidly developed into a strong competitor to Kountché, and friction multiplied between the two officers though they appeared on the surface to be on good terms. By the end of 1974 Sido was stripped of his other military duties and demoted from the Ministry of Interior to directorship of the Conseil National de Développement. Of Djerma origins, but Hausa-speaking and Hausa-oriented, he was accused on August 2, 1975, of plotting Kountché's demise and seeking a reassertion of the Hausa east, and was imprisoned. He died in Agadez in June 1977, allegedly of epilepsy, but in reality was murdered by then-prefect of Agadez, Lieutenant Colonel Bagna Beidou. Verfication of this took place at the time of the 1991 National Conference, and a number of officers, including Beidou, were imprisoned for his murder.

SOCIETE AFRICAINE DES PILES ELECTRIQUES (SAPELAC). Mixed-economy enterprise producing batteries of various kinds. Capitalized at 10 million CFA francs, and set up in 1978, SAPELAC's recent turnover has been in the vicinity of 500 million CFA francs per year.

SOCIETE DE DEVELOPPEMENT DU NIGER (SDN). Part of General Kountché's conception of Niger's road to development. Rejecting the lessons of both East and West, Kountché set up a committee by decree on October 29, 1979, to establish a Society of Development in Niger, replete with the requisite organizational structures aimed at transforming the typical Nigerien mentality while utilizing indigenous forms of cooperative action. The two pillars of the new society were to be the **samaria** youth groups and the cooperative movement. Both were supposed to elect delegates by "consensus" to serve at higher levels of the organizational pyramid, which commenced at the village level (with 9,000 village or nomadic district agencies allegedly created by 1984), through the cantonal, regional, to the national Council of Development.

Though the experiment was hailed as a somewhat unique innovation aimed at decentralized, nonpolitical decision making and mobilizing the masses to developmental tasks, like many other "animating" structures and hierarchies tried elsewhere the SDN was more a success on paper. Though some development work was carried out, especially by the samaria, in the early years (mostly building rural schools and leveling dirt roads), apathy and lethargy set in in the 1980s. Moreover, the collapse of uranium producer prices in 1982 placed in jeopardy all development planning in Niger, adding constraints on the anticipated new structures of society. In the late 1980s the stress shifted to developing a political-participation mechanism, and the SDN was absorbed within the MSDN.

SOCIETE DE PRODUITS CHIMIQUES DU NIGER (SPCN). Mixed-economy company set up in Niamey in 1980 though in existence since 1965 under a different share distribution. Capitalized at 225 million CFA francs with the original participation of the Blohorn Group, the company produces an array of soaps, cosmetics, powders, and detergents. Its productive capacity is over 4,500 tons of soap a year.

SOCIETE DE TRANSFORMATION DU MIL (SOTRAMIL). Originally a state enterprise set up in 1967 with 100 million CFA francs in capital for the processing of millet and preparation of biscuits, flour, pasta, and other items in its Zinder plant. Its capital was later increased to 566 million CFA francs (1975). SOTRAMIL has the capacity of producing 7,000 tons of farina, 600 tons of biscuits, and some 2,000 tons of other items, negating the need for imports from abroad. The company is now privatized, and is working at 30 percent of capacity.

SOCIETE DES BRASSERIES DU NIGER. *See* BRASSERIES DU NIGER.

SOCIETE DES GAZ INDUSTRIELS DU NIGER (SOGANI). Subsidiary of Air Liquide, SOGANI was set up in 1971 in Niamey with a productive capacity of 200,000 cubic meters of oxygen and 50,000 of acetylene, the production of which has in reality been quite low.

SOCIETE DES HUILERIES DU NIGER (SHN). Oil mills at Matamayé, processing locally produced peanuts. Set up in 1954 with an original capitalization of 25 million CFA francs (since increased to 110 million), the SHN employs sixty-seven workers. The company experienced severe problems of supply in 1968–69 and had to close down for over a year. With a maximum capacity of 8,000 tons the company produced only 4,200 tons of oil in 1971. Though its capacity was expanded to 30,000 tons in the 1970s, the plant was completely inactive in 1979–80 due to the devastation of Niger's peanut crop by the Sahel drought.

SOCIETE DES MINES DU DJADO (SMD). Uranium company formed on May 14, 1974, after a 1973 protocol of agreement. Jointly owned by the Niger government (25 percent), the German Urangesellschaft (25 percent), the French Atomic Energy Commission (25 percent), and a Japanese company (25 percent), the company prospected for uranium in the vicinity of Djado.

SOCIETE DES SALINES DE TIDEKELT (SST). Formed in 1988, this mixed-economy company plans to produce modern table salt from the deposits near the ancient copper and salt works at Teguidda-n'Tesemt in Aïr.

SOCIETE D'EXPLOITATION DES PRODUITS D'ARACHIDE DU NIGER (SEPANI). Peanut-processing oil mill founded in Magaria in March 1971. The factory has the capacity of processing 56,000 tons of peanuts and producing 19,000 tons of oil and 21,000 tons of cakes. Capitalized at 450 million CFA francs, until recently it was a joint company, with the German Hobum Afrika holding 66.6 percent of the shares and the Niger government the rest. At peak activity (for instance, in 1975) the company employs some 165 workers and produces 14,000 tons of oil and 17,635 tons of cakes. The mill was adversely affected by the successive Sahel droughts that devastated the peanut crops, and was closed for much of 1979–80, and later in the mid-1980s. The government of Niger is liquidating its stake in the company.

SOCIETE DU DEVELOPPEMENT. *See* CONSEIL NATIONAL DE DEVELOPPEMENT.

SOCIETE INDUSTRIELLE ET ALIMENTAIRE DE MAGARIA (SIAM). Former oil mill at Magaria with a capacity of 7,000 tons of oil, which produced in 1961—its last year of operations—1,400 tons of oil.

SOCIETE INDUSTRIELLE ET COMMERCIALE DU NIGER (SICONIGER). Established in 1942 and by 1971 Niger's thirteenth largest enterprise, SICONIGER is a mixed-economy company in which the government originally held 33 percent of the shares and the German Eechman Group 54.2 percent. Capitalized at 980 million CFA francs, SICONIGER owned an oil mill at Maradi (constructed in 1942 with the capacity to process 25,000 tons of peanuts), which was replaced in 1974 with a new plant with a capacity of 50,000 tons. At full production it employs over 120 workers including a few Europeans. In 1975 SICONIGER produced 22,000 tons of oil, with a turnover of 2,000 million CFA francs. Immediately after that came the Sahel droughts, with the supply of peanuts dropping badly, and the mill produced negligible amounts of oil: 1,508 tons in 1980, and 1,800 tons in 1981. A second drought in the mid-1980s led to the plant's shutdown in 1986, and in 1987 it was open for only six months. Though since then production has picked up, it has never regained anything like the levels of the early 1970s; the government, to avert the company's liquidation, assumed a majority stake (90 percent) in SICONIGER, while trying to find new investors to take over the company.

SOCIETE MINIERE D'AIR (SOMAIR). Uranium-processing company, the first to be established in Niger. Established on July 7, 1967, after an accord granting it a concession over 360 sq km in the **Arlit** area, SOMAIR is capitalized with 60 million French francs, with 45 percent of the shares originally held by the French Atomic Energy Commission, 40 percent by two private French companies (Compagnie de Mokta–EI Hadid and Compagnie Française des Minerais d'Uranium), and 15 percent by the Niger government, which retained the right to increase its share to 20 percent. Niger's share—through ONAREM, which holds the equity—has since increased to 36.6 percent.

Preliminary exploration for uranium commenced ten years earlier and involved a thousand depth soundings and an outlay of 55 million French francs. SOMAIR's prime site is Arlit, which has known reserves of 20,000 tons of concentrated ore, making it a much more abundant site than Gabon's and probably at par with the rich Colorado (U.S.) mines. SOMAIR is also undertaking mining at **SMTT**'s Tassa N'Taghalgué concession, which was leased to SOMAIR in 1986. The company's initial capacity was 750 tons of processed uranium concentrate per year, but by 1975 Niger had jumped to become the world's fifth largest exporter of **uranium,** and the government increased its shares in the company to 33.3 percent following prorated adjustments on the part of the other partners. The capacity of the plant was also increased to 1,800 tons, produced after the processing of 350,000 tons of rock. The ore is evacuated by truck to Parakou (Benin) and on to the port of Cotonou for export abroad. The company built Arlit as its uranium city and, until the slowdown in the mid-1980s, employed 1,260 workers (mostly Tuareg) and some 170 Europeans. The global uranium glut that developed in the 1980s contracted operations, production, profitability, and earnings. Niger's share of the global output of uranium zoomed to second—despite a halving in production—though uranium royalties as percentage of the budget declined to between 5 and 13 percent. With the recession in the industry, a lot of European personnel pulled out, a process that escalated with the onset of the Tuareg rebellion in the 1990s. The World Bank in particular has been critical of the cost structure of Niger's uranium mines, which are not economical except for the direct subsidy by France, which continues to buy uranium at prices well above the global market.

SOCIETE MINIERE DE TASSA N'TAGHALGUE (SMTT). Mixed-economy uranium ore mining company, constituted on September 24, 1979, to exploit the Arni concession (at Tassa N'Taghalgué), which is 4 km southwest of **Arlit.** Capitalized at 7 billion CFA francs, half of the capital from ONAREM and the rest from French public and private interests. At one time there was a Kuwaiti consortium involved as well. Peak capacity was supposed to be 1,500 tons of processed ore a year, but the global uranium glut that developed in the 1980s halved production. Before the recession in uranium mining the company employed some 1,200 workers, and had on the drawing boards a plan to produce some 7,000 tons of sulfuric acid per year by the late 1980s. The latter project was shelved due to cash-flow problems since 1983, and SMTT itself has been semidormant in light of the serious global glut in uranium ore. In 1986 SMTT leased its prime concession of Taza to SOMAIR, which began mining operations there, and a year later the Tassa N'Taghalgué concession was likewise leased, with SOMAIR beginning mining it in 1987. *See also* URANIUM.

SOCIETE MINIERE DU DAHOMEY-NIGER (SMDN). *See* SOCIETE MINIERE DU NIGER.

SOCIETE MINIERE DU NIGER (SMDN). **Cassiterite**-mining company founded in 1941 to explore the Aïr massif. It discovered cassiterite at several locations, the most prominent of which was **El Mecki.** At the time the company was operated under a slightly different name—Société Minière du Dahomey-Niger (SMDN). Two centers for extraction of the ore were eventually formed—the El Mecki site, from which 60 percent of the ore comes, and Tarrouadji to its south. The company had to stop most of its activities in 1955 due to difficulties encountered (shortage of water, problems of evacuating the ore to the coast, and its high cost). In 1964 the Niger government took over the El Mecki site on its own account, and assumed 75 percent of the shares of the company, which slightly changed its name (though not its acronym) to its current one. The remaining shares are owned by the French Banque de l'Indochine. Output in the 1950s and 1960s was around 70 tons per year; in the 1970s, 125 tons; in 1974–75 production reached 140 tons, but progressively declined to 38 tons in 1990 as ore has been stockpiled pending improved prices. Capitalized at 30 million CFA francs, when working at full capacity SMDN employs 526 workers, and until SOMAIR's creation in 1967 was Niger's only mining company. The ore produced used to be transported by truck to the Makeri Smelting Company in Jos, Nigeria, which purchased the entire output of SMDN. In recent years the mine's entire output has been purchased by the Netherlands.

SOCIETE MUTUELLE DE DEVELOPPEMENT RURAL (SMDR). Successor to the Société de Prévoyance (of the 1930s and 1940s) and of the pre-1958 Société Mutuelle de Production Rurale (SMPR), the SMDR is a state-controlled development agency. One of its main functions is to operate peanut markets in various locations deemed "unprofitable" for private collectors of the crop. In its first full year of operations the SMDR had a net profit of 620,000 CFA francs. A significant degree of anti-SMDR sentiment developed, however, among private and French expatriate interests, who feared that the organization would undermine and undercut their operations. Operating funds were derived from a subscription added to the head tax. Major abuses of fiscal responsibility finally brought the SMDR's dissolution in 1962 and its replacement by the mixed-economy COPRO-NIGER and the UNCC, both of which have, however, faced a host of problems of a similar nature.

SOCIETE MUTUELLE DE PRODUCTION RURALE (SMPR). *See* SOCIETE MUTUELLE DE DEVELOPPEMENT RURAL.

SOCIETE NATIONALE DE COMMERCE ET DE PRODUCTION DU NIGER (COPRO-NIGER). Better known as COPRO-NIGER, the company was originally capitalized with 150 million CFA francs, but after major deficits this was raised to 600 million CFA francs. The shares are owned by the state (33 percent), the BDRN (18.2 percent), the UNCC (15 percent), and twenty-eight individual shareholders. Created as a state trading organization in April 1962, COPRO-NIGER has, throughout the country, twenty-eight agencies and sixty sales outlets employing more than two hundred workers. It holds a monopoly over certain imports, the full list of which has varied, and is assigned a monopoly over the purchase of certain locally produced crops. Thus, in 1969 COPRO-NIGER was given the monopoly over the import of concentrated milk, green tea, sugar, salt, cigarettes, textiles, and sacks. Earlier, in 1964, it lost its monopoly over the purchase of Niger's peanut crop, and in 1968 over meat and several other commodities. COPRO-NIGER has been plagued by a host of deficit-producing problems stemming in part from Niger's poor transportation system, the immense distances involved, and a poor commercial network in the country outside the urban centers. Its primary purpose—for which the monopolies are granted—is to ensure stability of food prices, and to ensure a system of retail and wholesale outlets throughout the country. Most of these are in rural areas where cooperatives do not operate. In 1985 COPRO-NIGER had some of its monopolies lifted in order to spur greater competition in the country.

SOCIETE NATIONALE DES GRANDS TRAVAUX DU NIGER (SNGTN). Mixed-economy company with a majority state equity (81 percent), set up in 1963 to engage in construction work. Capitalized at 529 million CFA francs and employing 2,300 workers, in 1980 the company's turnover was 6,500 million CFA francs.

SOCIETE NATIONALE DES TRANSPORTS NIGERIENS (SNTN). Originally a mixed-economy company with a capitalization of 1,000 million CFA francs, owned by the Niger government (53 percent) and the Compagnie Trans-Africaine (47 percent). The SNTN is the country's most important national road hauler and enjoys a monopoly over certain routes. It connects Niamey with Parakou (Benin) weekly (a thirty-six-hour trip), Ouagadougou (Burkina Faso, forty-eight hours), and Zinder (daily). It was originally created when Transafricaine-Niger (formed in August 1961) was transformed from a private company to a mixed-economy company with the entry of the government into the transportation arena (November 1964). The company owns 500 trucks and 400 other vehicles, and employs 1,800. SNTN hauls the produce of all state and parastatal organs, military supplies, the mails, and uranium ore concentrate, and ensures regular connections among Niamey, Zinder, and N'Guigmi, as well as Agadez in the far north. Its turnover in 1980 amounted to 11,000 million CFA francs. In October 1994 the government announced that the SNTN would be privatized.

SOCIETE NIGERIENNE D'ARLIMENTATION (SONIA). State enterprise set up in Niamey on September 1, 1982, with 10 million CFA francs in capitalization, to produce foodstuffs. The company was from inception unprofitable, and in any case only biscuits were produced with regularity. The cause of the company's poor finances was the fact that it purchased raw materials from one of the partners at prices 25 percent above their real cost. The practice was stopped in 1986, and another 245 million CFA francs were pumped into the company, but the deficits continued. Private partners could not be found, and SONIA was closed down.

SOCIETE NIGERIENNE DE BANQUE (SONIBANQUE). Private bank set up in Niamey on September 7, 1990, to take over the deposits of the BDRN, which was in liquidation and possessed 70 billion CFA francs in unrecovered debts. It was capitalized at 2 billion CFA francs, and the Tunisian banking company STB contributed 25 percent, private local and foreign investors hold 25 percent of equity, with smaller shares held by a variety of other groups, including 5 percent by public Niger funds. The general director is a Tunisian.

SOCIETE NIGERIENNE DE CERAMIQUE (SONICERAM). Originally a state enterprise producing bricks and tiles for the building industry in Niger, and especially Niamey. Set up in 1966 with an investment of 69 million CFA francs, in 1982 the company moved to another site and two years later faced liquidation. The government has pumped new funds into it in order to make it more attractive for privatization. Its problems stemmed from general inefficiency, the poor competence of its workers, and the high costs of its energy needs.

SOCIETE NIGERIENNE DE CIMENTERIE (SNC). For a long time Niger's second largest company (after SOMAIR), established in 1963 with an original capitalization of 650 million CFA francs, since augmented to 900 million. The mixed-economy enterprise operates in semiperpetual deficit, its prime purpose being to ensure stable supplies of locally produced cement. Its product is much more costly than comparable cement in Europe or elsewhere in Africa, but the heavy transportation costs of foreign cement to Niger make it nearly coequal in price with that produced locally. Currently the state controls 74.5 percent of the share capital, up from the original 32 percent. With headquarters in Malbaza, in the late 1970s the SNC's productive capacity was raised to 50,000 tons from its original 40,000 tons, and again to 100,000 in 1982. In 1985 Niger's cement needs were so large that a second cement factory was envisaged (with a capacity of 300,000 tons, since scaled down by 50 percent), but final negotiations with

Japanese investors had to be postponed in light of Niger's problems with the World Bank, which had been insisting on a SAP program with major cost restructuring of the uranium and parastatal industries. In October 1994 the government announced the SNC would be privatized or closed down.

SOCIETE NIGERIENNE DE COLLECTE DES CUIRS ET PEAUX (SNCF). Originally a largely (93 percent) state-owned enterprise, SNCF was set up in 1973 with eighty-five employees and capitalized at 180 million CFA francs. It was privatized in 1986.

SOCIETE NIGERIENNE DE COMMERCIALISATION DE L'ARACHIDE (SONARA). Mixed-economy company established in May 1962 as the sole exporter of peanuts from Niger, charged also with centralization of all peanut purchases in the country in order to reduce costs and speed the process of Nigerienization in this domain. The state controls 60 percent of the share capital. All intermediate purchasers of peanuts are required by law to sell their stocks to SONARA. In 1970 SONARA was one of Niger's largest enterprises, being capitalized at 1,400 million CFA francs. It has peanut-cracking plants at Dosso and Tchadoua (a third one in Malbaza had to be closed down), with a capacity of 70,000 tons. The company employs four hundred seasonal workers, and in 1980 had a turnover of 5,000 million CFA francs.

SOCIETE NIGERIENNE DE CREDIT AUTOMOBILE (SONICA). Private company, capitalized at 41,125 million CFA francs, offering financing of the purchase of vehicles.

SOCIETE NIGERIENNE DE FABRICATIONS METALLIQUES (SONIFAME). Former public metal and woodwork factory in Niamey set up in 1965 and greatly expanded in the 1970s. Employing 350 workers the company produced an array of furniture in both wood and metal. After a number of heavy deficits the company was closed down in mid-1983.

SOCIETE NIGERIENNE DE PRODUITS PETROLIERS (SONIDEP). State agency capitalized at 500 million CFA francs, created on January 20, 1977, to ensure the regularity of import and distribution of Niger's petroleum supply.

SOCIETE NIGERIENNE DE TANNERIE (SONITAN). Former Maradi mixed-economy tannery enterprise, set up in 1969 with 27 million CFA francs in capitalization. Operating with a deficit, it was rescued in 1980 when new funds were pumped into it, and in 1987 the company was finally fully privatized when it was sold to nine private entrepreneurs in Maradi.

SOCIETE NIGERIENNE DE TELEVISION (STN). State television organ set up in October 1981 under the overall supervision of the ORTN. Apart from programing, the STN is involved in providing repairs on electronic equipment and magnetoscopes.

SOCIETE NIGERIENNE D'ELECTRICITE (NIGELEC). Set up in 1968 as a mixed-economy enterprise (though with a 94.6 percent state ownership), the company is Niger's second largest employer, having experienced a quintupling of demand for electricity in the last fifteen years. Capitalized at 2,300 million CFA francs, later increased to 3,400 million, NIGELEC is currently further expanding. It operates nineteen thermal centers, including two in the capital. Some 45 million kh are imported, mostly from Nigeria, and sales are at the level of 130 million kh per year. In 1993 the government announced that NIGELEC would be privatized, though the process is not yet complete.

SOCIETE NIGERIENNE DES PRIMEURS (SONIPRIM). Mixed-economy company with headquarters in Niamey involved in the marketing of a number of fruits and vegetables.

SOCIETE NIGERIENNE DES TEXTILES (NITEX). *See* SOCIETE NOUVELLE NIGERIENNE DES TEXTILES.

SOCIETE NIGERIENNE DES TRANSPORTS AERIENS (SONITA). Air transport company set up in 1989 with headquarters in Niamey, and restructured on September 22, 1991. Capitalized at 50 million CFA francs, 51 percent of equity is owned by private local interests, 30 percent by local enterprises, and 19 percent by a Cypriote combine. The company serves mostly the interior of the country but also flies to neighboring countries. It possesses one Fokker 27 chartered from Libya and is about to purchase a Boeing 737. Its routes are Niamey–Ouagadougou–Abidjan–Cotonou–Lomé–Gao; Niamey–Agadez–Arlit; Niamey–Zinder–Maradi; and Niamey–Agadez–Sebha–Tripoli. Its director general is Abdoulaye Maiga Goudoubaba.

SOCIETE NIGERIENNE DES TRANSPORTS FLUVIAUX ET MARITIMES (SNTFM). State company capitalized at 64.6 million CFA francs and based in Niamey, involved in all aspects of Niger's river and sea transport needs.

SOCIETE NIGERIENNE D'EXPLOITATION DES RESSOURCES ANIMALES (SONERAN). Founded in 1968 with 270.4 million CFA francs of capital, SONERAN produces fresh and processed meat both for local consumption and for export to (in particular) Côte d'Ivoire. In 1967 it was given the management of the Ranch d'Ekrafane, north of Filingué, and in 1980 acquired another one near Say. The company has the capacity of processing 10,000 head of cattle and producing 450 tons of meat.

SOCIETE NIGERIENNE D'HOTELLERIE (SNH). State organ set up in Niamey in 1977 with the express purpose of managing the country's state hotels: the Grand Hôtel and the Hôtel Le Sahel in Niamey and the Hôtel de l'Aïr in Agadez. The agency is in the process of dissolution as management of hotels is transferred to private enterprise.

SOCIETE NIGERIENNE DU CHARBON D'ANOU ARAREN (SONICHAR). Mixed-economy enterprise set up on May 5, 1975, with a capital of 760 million CFA francs—later more than doubled, making it Niger's largest enterprise—to exploit the six million tons of coal deposits discovered in Anou Araren, some 1,000 km northeast of Niamey and 40 km northwest of Arlit. Production commenced at the opencut mine in 1981, and output is around 150,000 tons a year. The coal extracted is used to produce electricity on-site for the various uranium mines in the immediate vicinity. The state's share has gone up since SONICHAR was inaugurated and currently stands at 62.4 percent; minority shareholders include the Islamic Development Bank (15.8 percent) and COMINAK, SOMAIR, and SMTT. One of the largest coal-producing companies in Africa, SONICHAR employs over 400 workers. Running costs have been higher than anticipated, and the electricity produced is also very expensive, considerably diluting earlier expectations that SONICHAR could help spur the transformation of Niger's north. The quadrupling of Niger's demand for electricity between 1970 and 1985, and more since, however, has brought about expansion in SONICHAR's operations. The company started off in 1981 with a capacity of 16 MW of electricity, increased it in 1982 to 37.7 MW, and is currently undertaking further capacity expansions.

SOCIETE NIGERIENNE POUR LE DEVELOPPEMENT DU TOURISME ET L'HOTELLERIE (NIGERTOUR). State organization distinct from the Office du Tourisme du Niger, engaged in building and planning the tourist infrastructure of Niger.

SOCIETE NIGERO-ARABE-LIBYENNE (SONAL). Niger-Libya developmental organ, set up to develop specific sectors of the Niger economy. Projects for which funds have been allocated involve agricultural development along the Niger River and in the Lake Chad basin.

SOCIETE NOUVELLE NIGERIENNE DES TEXTILES (SONITEXTIL). Joint company founded in 1968 as the Société Nigérienne des Textiles (NITEX) with the participation of the Agache Willot combine (70 percent) and the Niger government (15 percent). In 1978, when faced by major financial problems, the Niger government assumed 49 percent of the shares of NITEX, and the company was renamed SONITEXTIL. Capitalized at 725 million CFA francs (later increased to 1,000 million) and employing 830 workers (up from the original complement of 609), NITEX was Niger's third largest company. Production in 1975 was 6 million meters of textiles, and by that date plant expansion had raised the number of workers to 950. The plant is involved in all aspects of textile and fiber production and printing using local cotton and has an annual capacity of 7.5 million meters of yarn and printed cloth. The highly automated factory covers 15,000 square meters in the industrial zone of Niamey and satisfies 80 percent of Niger's textile needs.

SOMAIR. *See* SOCIETE MINIERE D'AIR.

SONAIKINE. Indigenous name for the **Songhay** language, also called, more popularly, *koirakine* ("language of the country"). The language, which has no vernacular literature, has three principal, mutually intelligible, dialects. It is, however, totally unrelated to any of the existing categories of African language groups or families. It exhibits some Arab, Berber, and Hausa influences. Songhay is also used as a "secret" language by the northern Gourma in some of their rites.

SONGHAY (*or* Songhai). Broad constellation of ethnic clans including the Songhay, **Djerma,** and **Dendi** found from Djenneé (in Mali) along the Niger River valley to Gaya (including in Burkina Faso in the Dori and Yatenga districts), and in some other locations, such as in northern Benin. The Djerma component of the Songhay are also known as Zerma or Zaberma. The Dendi are principally found on the Niger-Benin border (and in a few areas of northern Benin) and are essentially those Songhay elements which resisted the Moroccan conquest of the heartland of Songhay and of **Gao** (*see* BATTLE OF TONDIBI). The Djerma, east of the Niger River between Niamey and the Hausa "bloc" are a Songhay branch that fled from the Mali Empire before the rise of the Songhay Empire. Other groups frequently lumped together with the Songhay are the **Kurtey,** who are ex-Fulani, strongly intermarried with Sorko, and found on the islands of the Niger between Niamey and

Tillabéry and between Niamey and Say, as well as in Nigeria near Zaria; the **Wogo**—who are found intermingled with the Kurtey—and the Tyenga of Dendi. Songhay islands also can be found in Mopti, Djenné, Bamako (Mali), and in Kumasi (Ghana). The Niger Songhay were estimated in 1951 at 113,000, with a further 228,000 Djerma, 16,500 Kurtey, and 26,000 Wogo, Dendi, and Tyenga. Their numbers were estimated in 1972 at around 305,000, and in 1990 at 500,000. Together with the more numerous Djerma, they constitute around 30 percent of Niger's population. Some 6,000 of the pure Gao-originating Songhay are also found in Agadez, presumably having arrived there during the conquest of Aïr by Gao in the sixteenth century. The Songhay are mostly agriculturalists (some clans engaged also in fishing activities), growing millet and letting the Fulani tend their small livestock herds. Farming, a male occupation, is not regarded as demeaning. The origin of the Songhay is quite controversial and can be traced at least to the foundation of Koukya around A.D. 700 and the arrival of the Lemta Christian Berbers from Libya and the establishment of the Za dynasty. Fifteen of the latter rulers assumed the throne before the Songhay became Islamized, transferring their capital to Gao. The son of the twentieth Za of Gao revolted against the Mali Empire then holding Gao under a tributary relationship, and took office under the title of Sonni, or Si. The Gao lineage, however, remained undisturbed. The eighteenth Sonni, Sonni Ali, took power in 1464 and was the true founder of the Songhay Empire, expanding its dominions in all directions including into contemporary Niger. In 1493 an internal revolt brought to power one of Sonni Ali's prime lieutenants, who set up the Askia dynasty that expanded the empire's dominions into Aïr. In 1591 the empire collapsed to musket-bearing Moroccan troops, though the southern part—Dendi—remained independent under a legitimate lineage. Eventually, however, Dendi disintegrated into a series of small kingdoms, such as Téra. *See also* SONGHAY EMPIRE.

SONGHAY EMPIRE. One of the largest of the Sudanese empires centered around **Gao** (currently in Mali) during the fourteenth through sixteenth centuries, and at its height stretching from Aïr, Kano to Djenné (Mali). Its origin was a small chiefdom in eastern Mali that slowly expanded to found Koukya with its Za (or Dya) dynasty under Dya Aliaman. The latter dynasty was to rule for some 600 years. In 1009 Dya Kosoy—the twenty-fourth king—converted to Islam, though the complete Islamization of the Songhay was to take several more centuries. The new capital of the state was also shifted to Gao (also known as Kaw Kaw) the next year. The kingdom became a vassal of the Mali Empire, throwing off tributary status under a Dya who took office under the title of Sonni (or Si). There were nineteen Sonni kings between 1335 and 1493, the most famous of whom was Sonni Ali Ber (1464–92), who was the true founder of the Songhay Empire. In 1493 the dynasty fell in an internal upheaval to one of Sonni Ali's lieutenants, who established the Askia dynasty. The empire reached the heights of its territorial expansion under Askia Daoud (1549–82) before collapsing in 1591 to a musket-bearing semimercenary Moroccan invasion across the Sahara Desert. A segment of the southern part of the empire remained free of Moroccan control and with a legitimate lineage (*see* DENDI), though it eventually disintegrated into a number of small kingdoms. *See also* SONGHAY.

SONGHAY EMPIRE, RULERS OF: ?–1464, Sulayman Dandi; 1464–92, Sonni Ali; 1492–93, Sonni Barru; 1493–1528, Muhammad Ture; 1528–31, Farimundyo Musa; 1531–37, Muhammad Bunkan; 1537–39, Ismail; 1539–49, Ishaq I; 1549–82, Daoud; 1582–86, Muhammad II; 1586–88, Muhammad Bani; 1588–91, Ishaq II.

SONNI. Title of the rulers of the **Songhay Empire** at Gao, assumed by the son of the twentieth Za (or Dya) of the **Songhay.** There were nineteen Sonni kings between 1335 and 1493, when the Askia dynasty replaced it.

SONNI ALI (Ali Ber). Eighteenth **Sonni** of the **Songhay** at Gao, and the true founder of the Songhay Empire. Assuming power in 1464, he greatly expanded Songhay's territory, including into areas currently in Niger. It was under Sonni Ali that Timbuktu was captured in 1468, followed by Djenné (1473) and Mopti (1477). Sonni Ali died in battle in 1492. His successor, Sonni Barru, was toppled in 1493 by one of Ali's lieutenants, who set up the Askia dynasty.

SONRAY. *See* SONGHAY.

SONYANKE. A hereditary and closed high caste of **zima.**

SORBO-HAOUSSA. Early temporary capital of the Territoire Militaire du Zinder before Niamey was designated capital. The village is found between Sansanné-Haoussa and Karma.

SORKAWA. *See* SORKO.

SORKO. One of the over twenty-four major **Songhay** clans, found mostly in Mali along the Niger River. Divided into two branches—the Faran and the Fono—the Sorko are master fishers, and dominate all riverain commercial activity between Djenné and Gao (both in Mali).

They were prominent in the foundation of the Songhay Empire. Their number in Niger is relatively small. Descendants from a priestly clan, the Sorko have been an important component of the Songhay in Mali, and played a major role in Sonni Ali's conquests and expansion of the **Songhay Empire.** In Niger they are mostly found in the immediate vicinity of Niamey.

SOSSEBAKI. A Bornuan lineage that ruled a series of small states in the area between Zinder and Kano. Sossebaki was the surname given to Mohammed Ouba n'Saraki, one of the successors of Mohammed Nafarko, meaning "mouth-sucker." The latter, a son of the sultan of Bornu, had been sent to pursue escaping slaves in the tenth or the twelfth century, and was made chief of the population among which he found himself. The small chiefdoms that were eventually established were initially tributaries of Kano, and then of Bornu. One of the better-known ministates was centered around Mirria. Most of them were eventually conquered by Zinder in the establishment of the Damagaram kingdom in the seventeenth and eighteenth centuries.

SOUDIE. Also known as **Kurfey,** the Soudié are an ethnic group of mixed Hausa animist ancestry, originally residing in Gobir and forming a small confederation of clans. Chased from Tahoua by the Ouilliminden, 1820–50, and settling in the Dosso region, the Soudié adopted the Djerma language and customs, except for those Kurfey who remained Hausa-speaking and are still referred to as Kurfey rather than Soudié.

SOUMAILA, ALMOUSTAPHA. Niger's long-serving minister of planning, and current minister of finance and planning. Soumaila first joined the cabinet when appointed in September 1984 to General Kountché's government, and was retained in that capacity by General Saibou right until the HCR government took over in September 1991. Of Tuareg origins, Soumaila had earlier served under General Kountché as secretary of state for commerce and transportation between January 1983 and September 1984. Soumaila was reappointed to the new MNSD government in February 1995 as minister of finance and planning.

SOUMANA, IDRISSA (1941–). Niger's head of Agronomical Services, born on July 17, 1941; he has a doctorate in biology.

SOUMANA, ISSAKA MAIGA (1932–). Civil administrator. Born in 1932 in Tillabéry and educated locally and abroad, Soumana is a primary school teacher by profession. He entered politics while teaching and became PPN secretary general of a district in Dargol (1956–64) and was later appointed arrondissement councillor (1962). In December 1965 he dropped his teaching career to join the Ministry of Economic Affairs, Commerce, and Industry as chef de cabinet of the minister, assuming in December 1970 the same position in the Ministry of Justice. Since 1974 he has been involved in teaching.

SOUNA, ADAMOU (1937–). Former cabinet minister. Born in Niamey in 1937 and educated locally, in Dakar, Paris, Toulouse, and Nogent-sur-Marne, Souna obtained degrees in agricultural engineering. Upon his return to Niger in June 1964 he was appointed deputy director of agriculture in charge of hydro-agricultural development. In September 1964 he was made acting director of the division and in July 1965 director of agricultural services. He served in that post until August 1972 when he was appointed secretary of state for rural development, and just prior to the 1974 coup d'état he was made secretary of state attached to the presidency (October 1973–April 1974), in charge of all mixed-economy companies and public enterprises. Interned for over a year after the coup, Souna was granted clemency in August 1975, and assumed technical duties in the Ministry of Agriculture. After Kountché's death he was brought back into General Saibou's cabinet in May 1989 as minister of mines, shifting in March 1990 to head the Ministry of Agriculture. He stayed in the cabinet until the HCR government took over in September 1991.

STATE ENTERPRISES. *See* PARASTATAL SECTOR.

STUDENTS. Students have been a thorn in the flesh of all governments of Niger, but especially with the wave of fiscal austerity that afflicted the country in the late 1980s. The Hamani Diori regime had for a long time been opposed by the country's modern youth, and government-youth confrontations were numerous, especially in the 1970s. Of the various eruptions that occurred one in particular was the 1969 disorder in Zinder and Niamey, which was repeated on January 19, 1970, when students in the three secondary schools of Zinder went on strike. When the minister of education declared the strike illegal—it was over higher stipends, shorter terms, and diplomatic recognition of the USSR and China—and closed the schools in town, Niamey's students went on a sympathy strike. The situation was further inflamed by an open letter to the strikers by the unpopular Boubou Hama, who addressed the students paternally as "my children" and reminded them of the privileged status they occupied in the country. The strike eventually collapsed after three weeks.

In November 1970 Nigerien students joined in a strike at the University of Abidjan where they were pursuing higher studies. The Ivory

Coast government promptly expelled them (as well as nationals from other countries). Even as Niger initiated its own national university, its expelled students were transported directly to military camps where many were roughed up, sparking secondary school strikes in sympathy. The armed forces were called out a month later to restore order. Student unrest continued into 1971 and erupted again in 1972 over the visit to Niger of French president Pompidou. On February 12, the Niger embassy in Paris was taken over by Nigerien students in France opposing the Diori regime, though their invasion was brief. Since in this instance, as in others, French technical assistants and teachers in Niger had given the students moral support (and according Diori and Hama, active support), relations with France deteriorated during the year. Schools were closed for some time due to the strike in Niamey in sympathy with the Paris demonstrators, but they were reopened on February 21, and in May 1972 a commission was set up to initiate educational reforms. The gesture did not succeed in soothing student grievances, and again the Paris embassy was seized on November 9, 1973, in sympathy with continued student unrest in Niger (which had been going on for some six months) and a strike that had paralyzed Niger's schools since October of the previous year. The Niamey strike was a long one, and lasting from October 22, 1972, until February 1973. Student ringleaders were arrested, and in a closed trial in Tillabéry many, together with a handful of teachers allegedly inciting the students, were given stiff prison sentences.

It was not surprising, therefore, that when the 1974 coup d'état erupted, the country's students were solidly behind it. Yet, within six months disenchantment set in with the nonideological tenor of the new military regime. Kountché had notoriously poor relations with young people; and in both 1975 and 1976 strikes and calls for major reforms (many of these of an academic nature) were directed at him. Intermittent confrontations continued until the 1980s. Strikes occurred in 1979, 1982, and again in the mid-1980s, necessitating the closure of the educational establishment for varying periods of time.

By the late 1980s, however, the frequency of confrontations began to escalate, caused primarily by the harsh austerity regimen that began to affect all aspects of the Nigerien social fabric. The parastatal sector was in shambles and piling up deficits, the size of the civil service had grown unchecked and was also a major expenditure, all at a time when uranium revenues—which once had fueled the transformation of the country from a peanut-producing Sahelian backwater—were declining. Decisions to trim the civil service and stem the automatic recruitment of college graduates into it, as well as projected closures of a large number of parastatals—demanded by international donor agencies as a precondition for bailing out the parlous economy—were violently resisted by youth, often joined by the USTN in sympathy strikes.

On February 9, 1990, a huge boycott of classes commenced, developing into a demonstration in downtown Niamey (over various academic cuts and a government decision to restrict civil service employment), which was prevented by military troops from crossing a bridge. When the procession would not stop the troops fired at the students, killing around twenty. Though the Saibou regime tried to contain the damage by selective reshuffling of the cabinet and military high command, outrage at the incident merged with budding sentiment to call for an end to military rule. Neighboring Benin had just had its National Conference. The massacre of innocent people after the Tuareg attack on Tchin Tabaraden resulted in the convening of the National Conference of 1991, which led to civilianization.

Neither the interim HCR government (1991–93) nor civilianization since 1993 has brought respite from ongoing student unrest and government-student confrontations. Indeed, on May 18, 1993, students expressed their disgust with the new government (triggered by shortages of school supplies) by going on a rampage that saw the setting on fire of the headquarters of four political parties (PNDS, RDA, PSDN, and CDS). The financial straits of Niger, despite debt forgiveness by various governments and world agencies, still require fiscal austerity. At the same time the recession and the departure of a large number of expatriates and foreign companies and the jobs they created have made even more acute the desperate search for a salaried position in a country where all along the public payroll had been the major employer. Periodic strikes and demonstrations have erupted in every year since over late payment of student grants, just as the civil service (and the armed forces) have rebelled over similar delays in backpay.

SUBDIVISIONS. Predecessors of the contemporary arrondissements. The subdivisions were local administrative units into which the colonial cercles were divided. In 1922 there were nine cercles and twenty-seven subdivisions; after independence, on January 1, 1962, the country was divided into thirty-one circonscriptions replacing the former cercles, and following the Réforme Administrative of 1964 these were regrouped into seven départements and (originally) thirty-two arrondissements, with many of the latter being direct successors of the previous subdivisions. *See also* ADMINISTRATIVE ORGANIZATION.

SUSSAY. Annual tribute offered to the amenokals by tributory clans. Usually paid in kind—grain, animals, butter—it is not to be confused with another such tribute, the **tamessedek.**

SYNDICAT DES COMMERCANTS, IMPORTATEURS ET EXPORTATEURS DU NIGER (SCIMPEXNI). Niamey-based organization of traders involved in the import/export trade.

SYNDICAT DES PETITS ET MOYENS COMMERCANTS DU NIGER (SPMC). Niamey-based organization grouping together the country's commercial interests. The organization is presided over by El Hadj Yacouba Djibo.

SYNDICAT DES TRAVAILLEURS DES MINES DU NIGER (SYNTRAMIN). Trade union of the mining sector. The union is rather conservative since conditions of work tend to be far superior in the mining sector compared to other areas.

SYNDICAT NATIONAL DES PETITES ET MOYENNES ENTREPRISES ET INDUSTRIES NIGERIENNES (SYNAPEMEIN). Organization grouping together all the local industrialists and entrepreneurs of the private sector of Niger. Its headquarters is in Niamey.

SYNDICAT NATIONAL DES TRANSPORTEURS ET COMMERCANTS (SYNTRACOM). National organization of all long-distance truckers and major commercial interests.

SYNDICAT PATRONAL DES ENTREPRISES ET INDUSTRIES DU NIGER (SPEIN). Niamey-based employers union.

-T-

TABELOT. Small Tuareg village of 1,400 around 150 km from Agadez. Growing a variety of crops in watered gardens, Tabelot has received help from the World Church Service, and raises three cereal crops per year. The village is the principal springboard for the difficult trek to the spectacular Baguézane massif.

TABLA. Small Djerma village on the right bank of the Dallol Boboy, the ancient riverbed of Azawak. Tabla is 105 km from Niamey on the road to Filingué.

TADELIZA. Capital of the nascent Agadez sultanate prior to the designation of Agadez as its permanent capital in 1434. Despite the shift of the center of political authority to Agadez, Tadeliza remained the principal center of Aïr for a century. It was conquered around 1500 by the Songhay Empire, and later razed. The city's precise location was subject to much speculation. There is a small village, and a wadi with the same name, but that was not the location of the ancient center, which was finally traced in 1973 by Lhote to the area on the right bank of the Irazer-n-Agadez, near the small village of Irezen Melouldnin, 20 km from Agadez, the inhabitants of which had not forgotten the nature of the ruins nearby. *See also* AGADEZ, SULTANATE OF.

TAGHLALT. Smallest unit of salt produced for the local salt trade in Teguidda-n' Tesemt. The least fragile and most extensively traded, in the 1970s the salt cake sold for 15 CFA francs a pair in Teguidda and 20 francs further south in In Gall.

TAGLEM. Hausa name for the huge annual or biannual salt caravans between **Kaouar** and Agadez. The more familiar name for these is the Tuareg **azalay.**

TAGUELMOUST. The traditional veil or headdress of the Tuareg. An elaborately arranged length of light cotton up to six and a half meters long (over twenty feet), the taguelmoust differs slightly from clan to clan. Women are barefaced, contrary to orthodox Muslim tradition observed among other groups in the Sahara.

TAHI, MOUSTAPHA. (1937–). Former ambassador to Côte d'Ivoire. Born in 1937 in Agadez, and educated for a teaching career in Tahoua, Tahi served as a teacher in Bilma, In Gall, and Agadez (1955–61), obtaining further training as an educator in France in 1961. Upon his return to Niamey he was attached to the Ministry of Defense, Youth, and Sports (1963–64) and in 1964 joined the administration as assistant to the prefect of Filingué. He then continued in similar posts, including as subprefect of Madoua (1966–67), Tchin Tabaraden (1967–68), Tahoua (1968–70), Mainé-Soroa (1970–71), and again of Tchin Tabaraden (1972–73). In August 1973 he was appointed prefect of Diffa. Following the coup d'état of 1974 Tahi was appointed prefect of Maradi and in July 1976 was named ambassador to Côte d'Ivoire. Since 1980 Tahi has been back in Niamey with the Ministry of Foreign Affairs.

TAHIROU, AMADOU. Minister of defense between April 1993 and the fall of the government in October 1994.

TAHIROU, DJIBO (Major) Deputy chief of staff of the Niger armed forces, appointed in September 1991 by the National Conference after the dismissal of the army's two most senior officers for their role in the brutal repression of Niamey's 1990 student demonstrations.

TAHOUA. A département and arrondissement in Niger, as well as an important Hausa market town and trade crossroad roughly equidistant (at 440 km) from Niamey and Agadez. The town is Niger's fourth largest, with 48,000 people. The arrondissement encompasses 170,000 people, while the département covers 150,260 sq km and has a population of 1,000,000 and a density of 6.6 per sq km. The population of the département is a mixture of Aderawa, Buzu, Fulani, Tuareg, Gobirawa, and Maouri. The town of Tahoua was originally formed of three **Azna** villages that were eventually absorbed into the municipality. The département includes the arrondissements of Tahoua, Birni-N'Konni, Bouza, Illela, Keita, Madaoua, and Tchin Tabaraden, and the postes administratifs of Tillia, Abalak, Dogueraoua and Bogaraoua. Though a typical Hausa town, and important communications and trade artery, Tahoua has little of interest for the tourist.

TAIBIA. Minor religious order in Niger. *See* RELIGIOUS ORDERS.

TAKEL NAKEL. Tamasheq for "building the country," a Tuareg irredentist, pronationalist movement that sprang into the limelight in the 1990s as Tuareg gripes against Niamey escalated with the 1990 Tchin Tabaraden incident.

TAKOUKOU. Small village on the Agadez–Zinder road, some 260 km from the former and 215 km from the latter. It marks the beginning of the zone of regular cultivation of millet.

TAKURABOW. Female protecting divinity, or **iskoki,** of the **Gobir** chiefdom that is also venerated, under a different name, in Katsina and in several non-Gobirawa areas.

TALAK. A steppelike desert called **Tamesna** by the Ouilliminden Tuareg and located between the Aïr massif and Adrar des Ifora.

TALBA, MOUSSA. Former prefect of Tahoua (1962–64), Maradi (1964–66), and Niamey (1966–68). Between 1968 and 1974 Talba served as a member of the Constitutional Chamber of the Supreme Court.

TAMASHEQ (*also* Tamarshek). The Tuareg language. The written script, Tifinagh, is linguistically limited. There are essentially four Tamasheq dialects, which are related to ancient Libyan.

TAMASKE. Town of 10,000 in the Keita arrondissement of the Tahoua département. Tamaské is 20 km west of the village of Keita.

TAMBARI. Royal drums, part of the symbols of chiefdom in Tuareg clans. They are of pre-Islamic Tuareg origin, though they are also found among several non-Tuareg ethnic groups.

TAMESNA. The Ouilliminden name for Talak, the steppelike dessert between Aïr and Adrar des Ifora.

TAMESSEDEK. Precolonial annual tribute to the amenokal by tributary clans. The tribute has a religious origin, with specific rules governing its size. It is not to be confused with the **sussay**.

TAMGAK. One of several peaks of Aïr in the 1,400- to 1,800-meter range.

TANAMARI, BATTLE OF. Damagaram site where French troops, allied with the **Kel Owey,** defeated and put to flight the **Imouzourag** overlords of the region. France had promised to aid militarily whichever of the two groups could supply it mounts (essentially camels) for the forthcoming French advance into Chad and the impending major confrontation with **Rabah.** The Kel Owey were the only ones who could fill France's needs (eventually contributing over two hundred camels) since they dominated the **azalay** trade.

TANDJA, MAMADOU (Colonel) (1938–). Former minister of interior, strong presidential candidate in the 1993 civilian elections, and current strongman of the MNSD political party, which constitutes the government of February 1995. Born in 1938 in Diffa near Lake Chad of mixed Fulani-Sarakollé origins, Tandja opted early for a military career and was educated in colonial military schools in Senegal and Mali. He was integrated into General Kountché's cabinet in September 1979 as minister of interior, and was promoted to major in 1980. He retained his ministerial post until September 1981, when he was shifted, like so many of the officers surrounding Kountché, into the prefectural system, to serve as prefect of Tahoua, and was later posted as ambassador to Nigeria. He was brought back by General Saibou in March 1990 after the previous month's military repression of the student demonstrations in Niamey, to serve as a "strong" minister of interior. Paradoxically he was to witness the National Conference and civilianization, remaining until the HCR government took over in September 1991. Tandja presented his candidacy in the 1993 presidential elections and scored heavily on a "law and order" campaign in Songhay-Djerma areas, ending up as the front-runner (with 34.22 percent of the vote) in the first ballot. In the runoff second round, he lost to **Mahamane Ousmane** when nearly all the other candidates rallied behind Ousmane to prevent a member of the former governing military elite from capturing the presidency. A tall (6′3″), imposing person, he resigned from the armed forces and helped build the MNSD into a genuine political machine, especially in the Songhay-Djerma areas of southwest Niger. The party was able to capture twenty-nine of the seats in the subsequent parliamentary elections, forming the opposition, and in the 1995 elections that followed the fall of the AFC coalition the preceding September, the MNSD emerged in control of the government with forty-three of the eighty-three seats.

TANIMOUN DAN SULEYMAN (1811–84). Sultan of **Damagaram**, 1841–43 and 1851–84, and one of that kingdom's most illustrious kings. Known also as Baki Jataw or Tanimoun Dari, Tanimoun was a son of Suleyman, and his rule over Damagaram alternated with that of his brother Ibrahim. He was appointed sultan by the king of Bornu, at the time Damagaram's nominal suzerain, but was expelled from the throne by his brother Ibrahim. He regained the throne in 1851 after returning to the good graces of the court of Bornu, where he resided for part of the intervening years. A strong sovereign and leader, Tanimoun centralized Damagaram's government and administration, encouraged Tuareg settlement in the outskirts of Zinder (thus gaining their military allegiance in his expansionist policies), and greatly built up Damagaram's army, of which he is regarded as the true founder. In 1871 the kingdom possessed six thousand rifles and forty cannon, and could draw many thousands of foot soldiers. Despite seven rejections by Bornu of Zinder's request to fortify the city, Tanimoun ordered the walls built, and the remnants remain to this day. At their construction they were reputed to be nine to ten meters high and twelve to fourteen meters thick at the base, with seven city gates and a total circumference of four and a half kilometers. Tanimoun's tomb is found on the old sultanate's palace grounds in Zinder.

TANIMOUNE, ARY (1930–). Former diplomat. Born in 1930 in Gouré and educated locally and in Paris (IHEOM) Tanimoune was elected to the National Assembly in 1958, and reelected through 1970, serving as that body's first vice-president. Appointed ambassador to Ghana in 1961, he returned to Niger in 1966 to become prefect of Dosso and director general of the Societé Nigérienne de Cimenterie (SNC). In August 1971 he again assumed diplomatic duties as ambassador to Canada, and later to the U.S. and the U.N. In 1973 he returned to Niamey and was appointed to a senior post in the Ministry of Interior.

TANKOANO, AMADOU (1953–). Academic. Born on February 7, 1953, and educated at the University of Nice in public law and international economic law, on his return to Niamey Tankoano rapidly rose through the ranks at the local university, being appointed the first dean of the School of Economics and Law, which he had helped found, in 1985. He has also been counselor to the Supreme Court since 1987.

TANOUT. Arrondissement in the département of Zinder, with a population of 135,000 and headquarters in the important village of the same name, 160 km from Zinder.

TAOUA. Daughter of the leader of the second wave of Gobirawa to move into Aïr in the twelfth century. Remnants of her tomb, at Kouchewa, are still visible, and are venerated by the animist population of the area.

TAPOA. Niger River affluent in the immediate vicinity of the **Parc National de W.** With a basin of 5,500 sq km and a length of 260 km the Tapoa forms a twenty-meter waterfall near the park, joining the Niger via a narrow and sinuous gorge obstructed by large boulders. The region has phosphate deposits. In 1981 an agreement was reached with Nigeria for their joint exploitation, but little has come of it. *See also* CAMPEMENT DE LA TAPOA.

TARGUI. The singular for a Tuareg male.

TASAR. Ruler of the Tessaoua dependency of Maradi until its break from Maradi (*see* TESSAOUA). The name comes from the founder of the dynasty, Tasar Ibrahim, who was succeeded by twenty-four chiefs, until the onset of the colonial era.

TASSA N'TAGHALGUE. Site of major uranium ore concentrations, part of the SMTT concession (*see* SOCIETE MINIERE DE TASSA N'TAGHALGUE). In 1987 the concession and especially the Tassa N'Taghalgué site, was leased to SOMAIR, which began exploiting it.

TASSAWA. *See* TESSAOUA.

TASSILI. Tuareg name for the **Hamadas**—the rocky desert plateaus of Niger.

TAYA, EL HADJ KAZELMA OUMAR. Head of the **Parti Sociale-Démocratique Nigérien** (PSDN). Taya's party performance in the 1993 and 1995 legislative elections, and his presidential bid in 1993, secured only small support, in the latter contest only 1.68 percent of the vote.

TAZA. *See* TASSA N'TAGHALGUE.

TCHELLE, LEON. A physician and epidemiologist, Dr. Tchéllé has been deputy director of public health in the Ministry of Health since 1966, and deputy director of epidemics in the same ministry.

TCHERNAKA, YACOUBA. Secretary general of the Ministry of Planning since 1978.

TCHIN TABARADEN. Arrondissement in the Tahoua département that is the prime area of nomadization of the **Ouilliminden Kel Dinnik.** Formerly known as Tahoua-Nomade, it encompasses the postes administratifs of Abalak and Tillia and has a population of 95,000. During the height of the Sahel drought (1973–74) a refugee camp in the arrondissement had a population of 18,000, mostly Tuareg. The arrondissement has its administrative headquarters in the important village of the same name—75 km north of Tahoua—which has an abundance of water from wells and boreholes. The Niger armed forces armory at Tchin Tabaraden has been the focus of several Tuareg armed assaults, including one in the early 1980s organized by Hamani Diori's son. More recently Tchin Tabaraden was attacked in 1990, in the aftermath of which the Niger armed forces undertook mass reprisals on the civilian population of the area, brutalizing and humiliating it. The exact scope of the massacre is unknown, figures ranging from 63 (according to the government) through 600 to 700 (estimated by humanitarian organizations), to 1,500 (according to the Tuareg). The incident marked the onset of the **Tuareg rebellion** in Niger, which ended in May 1995. In 1991 both Niger's minister delegate for defense, Bagno Beida, and the-then military prefect of Agadez, Kimba Kollo, were arrested for their role in the repressions; a shake-up in the high command of the Niger armed forces also took place at the insistence of the National Conference.

TEDA. A branch of the **Toubou** found mostly in northern Chad, and in much smaller numbers in eastern Niger. They call themselves *Tedagada* ("those who speak Tedaga"). Both Toubou branches speak similar dialects, which are related to the Kanuri language. In Niger the Teda are to be found in Kaouar and especially in the Djado area the between Agadem and Soutellan, and are often called by other ethnic groups *Braouia*. The Teda are Muslim, with most of the clans in Niger belonging to the Sanusiya order. Both in Niger and in neighboring Chad the Teda spearheaded the anti-French, anti-infidel drives from the onset of the colonial era into the 1920s. In Chad, the Teda have been in rebellion against the regimes of Ndjamena since 1966. Certain clans have been pushed into Niger by this rebellion, and the Niger government has been extremely apprehensive about the possibility of the rebellions spreading into its territory. This did not occur, despite several incidents in the late 1960s, but after Hissene Habre's ouster in Chad in 1990 elements of his army fled to Niger, sold their arms to the rebelling Tuareg, and in 1993 joined in a rebellion in Niger's desolate southeastern region.

TEFLIS. Site, 8 km south of Tagabel, of a mosque, the oldest structure in Aïr, dating from A.D. 750.

TEGAMA AGH BAKHARI, ABDERAHMAN (1880?–1920). Sultan of Agadez at the time of the **Kaocen revolt.** Born in Dogarawa around 1880 Tegama was an energetic leader in very trying times for his people (and much maligned by the French as ineffective). He sided with the budding rebellion in Aïr aimed at freeing it from colonial and infidel rule. After the rebellion collapsed and the siege of Agadez was lifted, Tegama escaped to Kaouar (Bilma) but was betrayed to the French by the local Toubou in May 1919. He was brought to Zinder and imprisoned. The French were afraid to put him on trial, and Tegama was murdered in his cell on April 29, 1920. His death was for years passed off as suicide.

TEGUIDDA-N-TAGAIT. Small Tuareg village 85 km from Agadez with important vegetable and fruit gardens and palm groves. The village is archaeologically of great interest, being the center of a vast Neolithic site, possibly the most important in all the Sahara. Some 250 prehistoric engravings have been discovered to date. Teguidda-n-Tagait was also a base for the Songhay sovereign Askia Mohammed during his assault on the Sultanate of Agadez, 1500–1515.

TEGUIDDA-N' TESEMT. Tuareg oasis in Aïr, and famous former caravan stop on the western route to Gao. Twenty kilometers northeast is the ancient site of Azelik, which in the fifteenth century competed for primacy with Agadez. Teguidda—193 km from Agadez—developed due to the presence of salt pans east of the village, and became a desolate, sedentary outpost in the midst of a nomadic region. Because of its location and the presence of water close to the surface, Teguidda was in the past an important caravan stop on the trails connecting Aïr with Gao. Currently, many of Teguidda's prime mercantile and social families reside permanently in **In Gall,** coming to Teguidda only on a seasonal basis. Indeed, during the winter the village is practically deserted; in a 1970 demographic study, only twenty-six people were found residing in the village. Because of Teguidda's historical and mythical association with **Azelik,** Teguidda is ceded ritual political primacy over In Gall, though the latter possesses religious and judicial supremacy. Both are the personal fiefdoms of the sultan of Agadez.

TELEVISION (educational). An experimental program for which Niger became widely known, financed by Niger and by outside donors, and affecting twenty-two schools northwest of Niamey along the Niger River. First launched in 1964 it involved only eight hundred children. Lessons were prepared in Niamey and reached students in twenty weekly transmissions of fifteen minutes each, followed by the distribution of papers in school. Extremely costly, the program was terminated in 1969, though originally it had been hoped that it could be extended to encompass a large number of Niger's school-age population. *See also* EDUCATION.

TEMPS DU NIGER, LE. Daily mimeographed newspaper published since 1960 by the Niger Information Service in Niamey, with a circulation of 1,300. Following the coup, on April 29, 1974, the paper's name was changed to *Le Sahel*. See also *SAHEL-HEBDO*.

TENDE. Spirit cult practiced by some Tuareg in Aïr, similar to the **Bori** cult further south.

TENEKERT. Tamasheq for the **cure salée** trek.

TENERE. Area of shifting dunes stretching over some 400,000 sq km between Aïr and Kaouar. In prehistoric, wetter days fully vegetated and settled (by inhabitants who left numerous cave engravings), the Ténéré is now totally uninhabited. In the western part some stunning sand-dune formations dominate the landscape, while in the north the desert is essentially a monotonous sand plain. The term *Ténéré* is actually the Tamasheq word for "desert"; the equivalent Arab word is *Sahara*. *See also* ARBRE DU TENERE.

TERA. Town of 9,600 some 180 km from Niamey. Also an arrondissement encompassing 216,000 people in the département of Niamey. During the precolonial era the town was totally destroyed a number of times, including by the Tuareg in 1885. In the seventeenth century Téra was a small Songhay state centered around the village. *See also* DENDI.

TERRITOIRE MILITAIRE AUTONOME DE ZINDER. Original name (July 23, 1900) of what was to become first (June 22, 1910) the **Territoire Militaire du Niger** and later (1922) the **Colonie du Niger.**

The Territoire Militaire Autonome de Zinder was part of the large **Colonie du Haut-Sénégal-Niger,** which stretched into the French Sudan (Mali).

TERRITOIRE MILITAIRE DU NIGER. Designation (June 22, 1910) of the territory that was to become in July 1922 the Colonie du Niger (*see* ADMINISTRATIVE ORGANIZATION). The Territoire was detached from the **Colonie du Haut-Sénégal-Niger,** which it had been a part of from 1900 to 1910, but included the cercle of Gao (currently in Mali). Later, on June 21, 1911, the Gao cercle was returned to French Sudan (Mali), and the territory was directly attached to the AOF. The Territoire Militaire du Niger was the direct successor of the Territoire Militaire Autonome de Zinder.

TESSAOUA. Important historic town of 10,000 people 137 km from Maradi and 117 km from Zinder. Also, an arrondissement of 300,000 people in the Maradi département. Historically a vassal of Hausa Katsina (before the Fulani conquest), Tessaoua continued its allegiance to Maradi after the Katsinawa relocated to that town (*see* MARADI). Far to the east of the continuing Hausa-Fulani tug-of-war, Tessaoua (which in 1851 had a population of 15,000) was ruled by the **tasar** and was quite independent in most matters. This de facto independence eventually led to a split from the nominal suzerainty of Maradi.

TIARI, MAMADOU (1895–1974). For a long time, chief of the Bilma canton. Of the ruling Kanuri lineage, Tiari was instrumental in promoting the commercial importance of Bilma in the **azalay** trade, despite the insecurity of the desert trails.

TIBESTI. Large western sous-préfecture in neighboring Chad's (B.E.T.) département, with headquarters in Bardai. A desert mountain massif encompassing 150,000 sq km, Tibesti was in prehistoric times much wetter, and lushly vegetated, supporting a large population. The region was conquered by French troops coming in three columns, one from Niger. It was originally part of the French colony of Niger, and hence within the AOF federation. In 1930 it was removed from Niger and attached to Chad, becoming part of the second French colonial federation, the AEF.

TIBIRI. Ultimate independent capital of the **Gobirawa** following their long series of clashes with, and rebellions against, the Fulani. Currently the political center of Niger's Gobirawa, with a population of 10,000 and a very important weekly market. The **Inna** of Tibiri, the main mosque, and the royal palace are prominent sites in the town. Located

8 km from Maradi, Tibiri was built in 1836 by a joint Katsinawa-Gobirawa effort after the two groups lived peacefully together in Maradi for several years. The two groups also cooperated in the struggle to regain their territories to the south from which they had been expelled by the Fulani. In 1860 a dissident Gobirawa group seceded from Tibiri and set up its own center of antiestablishment dissidence (with Fulani help) at Sabon Birni, which was some time later conquered by the legitimate forces of Gobirawa. *See also* GOBIR.

TIDJANIYA. Dominant religious order in Niger that since the 1920s nearly completely replaced the Quadriya, previously dominant in the area. The order is popular in particular among the Beri Beri (though Bilma itself is Senousi), the Djerma, and the Songhay. Its most important strongholds are Tahoua, Niamey, Gouré, and N'Guigmi. Founded by Si Ahmed al-Tidjani (a Moor from Trarza) in the late eighteenth century, the order spread widely in subsequent centuries. The Tidjaniya in Niger opposed the French intrusion, but an understanding was reached and the order became the one "favored" by the French administration. Later, **Hamallism** arose as a reaction to this alliance. *See also* RELIGIOUS ORDERS.

TIENGA. *See* TYENGA.

TILLABERY. Historically an important Djerma village of 4,000 people, and arrondissement encompassing a population of 160,000. Midway on the scenic road connecting Niamey (140 km south) with Ayorou. Tillabéry is the center of a grain-growing region and currently also produces rice and cane sugar. It has big market days on Thursday and Sunday. The arrondissement includes the towns of Ayorou and Sansanné-Haousa, and is in the département of Niamey. In 1992 Tillabéry was designated the headquarters of the département of Niamey.

TIMIA. Stunningly beautiful palm grove amid impressive mountain wilderness in the Agalak Mountains. Reached from the Telouess palm groves (and oasis) by a rough 256-kilometer track, Timia is often visited by the hardy tourist exploring the Aïr massif. The village has a fort built by the French in 1951, and its cascades and **guelta** are unrivaled in Niger. The area is currently unsafe due to the Tuareg rebellion.

TIMIDRIA. New association of the "black" Tuareg, or Bella (domestic slaves), that emerged in December 1991 as part of the politicization of the entire north with the eruption of Tuareg irredentism. The word means "fraternity." The association aims at peaceful cohabitation of pastoralists and farmers.

TIN CHAMAN. *See* TADELIZA.

TIN TOUMA. Desert area in the N'Guigmi arrondissement, site of important recent oil discoveries that, if developed fully, could give Niger energy self-sufficiency. *See also* OIL.

TIOUSSO, ABDOU. Interim minister of justice between March 1992 and April 1993, when a regular government was formed.

TIRMINI, BATTLE OF (July 30, 1899). The village of Tirmini, 10 km west of Zinder, was where a French-commanded force of Senegalese soldiers defeated **Damagaram's** armies prior to the occupation of Zinder. The action was in retaliation for the earlier murder of Captain **Cazemajou** while at the court of Damagaram. Following the battle Zinder was deserted, and the French occupied the town without a fight.

TONDI, MOUSSA (Colonel). Former quartermaster general of the Niger army and minister of finance. Quartermaster general between November 1968 and 1974, Tondi was appointed minister of finance after the 1974 coup d'état, remaining in that post until late 1983. He was promoted to lieutenant colonel in 1975 and chaired the commission of inquiry into the abuses of the preceding Diori regime. An unassuming officer, he tended to remain above some of the infighting of the officer corps following Kountché's assumption of power. In 1979 Tondi was promoted to full colonel. He left the cabinet in November 1983 due to illness, and retired.

TONDIBI, BATTLE OF (April 12, 1591). Tondibi was the site of the major clash between Moroccan (and some Spanish mercenary) troops and the armies of the Songhay Empire. The Moroccan trans-Saharan assault was mounted in November 1590 and succeeded by virtue of surprise and the muskets carried by a sizable contingent of the 4,000-man force. By contrast the 40,000 troops sent to oppose them did not have a single musket among them, and had not been exposed to rifle power in the past. The battle changed the course of history in the region, leading to the collapse of the **Songhay Empire.** Eventually the northern area conquered by the Moroccans fell to the Tuareg (Ouilliminden), and Gao specifically in 1770.

TONDIBIA. Important military camp 12 km from Niamey. It was to Tondibia that the Diori regime brought political prisoners for initial confinement and before dispersal to other garrisons, and it was from Tondibia that the 1876 attempted coup d'état of Moussa Bayeré was mounted.

TOUBOU. Collective name for several branches of an ethnic group found in the southern Sahara, and specifically in northern Chad and Niger and in southern Libya. Their name comes from the **Kanuri** for "inhabitants of Tu," the local name for the Tibesti Mountains to the east of Kaouar. The two major Toubou branches are the **Teda**—found in large numbers in Chad and in smaller concentrations in Djado, Bilma, Agadez, and in general in Kaouar in Niger—and the Daza, who are found in much larger numbers in Chad and Libya but in very small numbers around Lake Chad in Niger and in general in the N'Guigmi area. Estimates of the total population of the Toubou vary greatly, but it is thought that their maximum numbers do not exceed 250,000, most found in Chad (some 50 percent) and Libya (30 percent).

The ethnic origin of the Toubou is still clouded with mystery, especially since their dark complexion and their language are quite different from the Berbers from whom it is assumed they originated and with whom they share unique and strikingly similar ABO blood-group patterns. According to one reconstruction of their origin, the Toubou are descendants of white nomads from the Nile Valley who arrived between the seventh and ninth centuries in the region of B.E.T. (Chad)–Kaouar, where they helped found the Kanem kingdom and then, in the early thirteenth century were pushed out of the region northward. In subsequent centuries, by now ethnically intermixed with other groups, they arrived in the areas they formerly occupied in search of new pastures. Early in the nineteenth century this new migration gained momentum under Ottoman pressure from Libya. At the onset of the colonial era the Toubou, fierce **Senoussi** adherents and highly independent, resisted for nearly two decades the entry of the French into their regions. Muslim, nomadic, and aggressive, the Toubou have traditionally exacted a levy (10 percent) on all caravans (that they did not plunder) passing through their strongholds, or from sedentary settlements (for instance, Kaouar), exacting a tribute from the populations there. In 1966 in neighboring Chad, the Toubou took up arms against the N'Djamena government, eventually emerging victorious against the southern government then in power.

Niger's Toubou, mostly in the vicinity of N'Guigmi and Kaouar, control the salt pans of the area and have a political entity called the Sultanate of Kaouar. Their supremacy of the region was shattered, however, by the Tuareg in the nineteenth century, though they were allowed to retain their intermediary role between the Kanuri population of the oases and the Tuareg overlords. They arrived in Niger from Kufra (Libya) via Tibesti (Chad) and first settled in the Komadugu River area before being pushed further north by the existing, and more powerful, Mobeur. Among the most important Toubou clans, which are all quasi-autonomous, are the **Kecherda,** Azza, Dogordo, Gadana, and Ouandalla. Since the onset of the Tuareg rebellion in Niger in 1990, the Toubou have been restless. Augmented by those remnants of Hissene Habre's armies which fled N'Djamena after losing out to a rival, in 1993 the Toubou set up a new "liberation front" for their region in southeastern Niger.

TOUDOU, OUSMANE (1923–) Former political leader. Born in Guécheme (in the Dogondoutchi area) in 1923, and a stockbreeding assistant originally, Toudou was an important PPN leader in his region. He secured election to the National Assembly in 1965, remaining in it through 1974, and serving as the vice-president of its Social Affairs Committee. He also served as a member of the Diori regime's Cour de Sûreté de l'Etat. After the 1974 coup Toudou was appointed to an administrative posting in the Ministry of Social Affairs, and retired in the early 1980s.

TOUDOU ANZA. Small village in the Arewa region where in 1925 the Hauka rites first commenced. *See also* HAUKA.

TOUNKARA, YAHAYA. Former cabinet minister and National Assembly deputy. Tounkara was Niger's director of stockbreeding when he was first brought into the government, in December 1977, to serve as General Kountché's minister for water resources and the environment. He served until November 1985 when he returned to his old post. With the rise to power of General Saibou in 1987 he was again integrated into the cabinet as minister of higher education, and was later shifted to head the Ministry of Planning. He was dropped in 1989 and nominated to the MNSD list for the forthcoming elections to the new National Assembly. He served as a deputy until 1991 when the HCR government took over, and returned to technical duties in the Ministry of Agriculture.

TOURAWA. Title of the war chief of the sultan of Agadez, corresponding to the Hausa kaoura. The second most important personality after the sultan, the tourawa has traditional command over all the Arabs residing in Aïr and also leads the annual or biannual Bilma caravan. *See also* AGADEZ, SULTANATE OF.

TOURISM. Despite some impressive tourist attractions (along the Niger River, the W National Park, the Tuareg encampments, and of course the stunningly beautiful Aïr massif), tourism has been slow to develop in Niger. This has been in part a result of the relatively undeveloped tourist infrastructure and in part because exploration of Aïr has been largely for the venturesome and hardy. Only 18,000 tourists visited Niger in 1977, of whom 55 percent came from Europe, just over a third from France. In that year the entire country had only sixteen hotels (seven in Niamey, the others rather minuscule), with fewer than seven hundred beds in all. Since the advent of the military regime, a serious program of developing the country's tourism was embarked upon. Also, the paving of the Uranium Road made distant Agadez and Aïr a long day's drive from Niamey rather than a rugged expedition in its own right. Hotel construction and renovation increased room and bed capacity. A new hotel—the Gaweye—on the Kennedy Bridge in Niamey by itself (with its 250 rooms) increased capacity by 30 percent, while a Sheraton (or Novotel) in Agadez—still in planning stages—aimed to raise capacity in that center by a hundred percent. A decade later, in 1987, over 43,000 tourists visited Niger (a 25 percent increase), giving the country's hotels a 2 billion CFA franc turnover. The country's image was damaged, however, by the revelation that despite a ban on hunting of wildlife in Niger since 1964, members of the Saudi royal family had visited Niger on several occasions for hunting purposes.

In 1990 the Tuareg rebellion in Aïr put an end to rosy hopes of the tourist industry's further coming of age. At the same time the government's acute budgetary straits forced it to pass the running of most of the larger state-run hospitals to private management teams. In that year Niger had nearly a thousand rooms, Agadez's airport was upgraded to an international airport to accept charter flights from Europe, and the tourist possibilities in the Tahoua and Zinder regions were being developed. All these options have been put on hold as tourist figures plummeted.

TRANSAFRICAINE. Long-distance transport and trucking concern that had, during the colonial era, a monopoly over trucking in Chad, Niger, Upper Volta, and several other territories. In most of these areas it was either nationalized or, more commonly, was forcibly transformed into a joint mixed-economy company with government participation. *See also* COMPAGNIE TRANSAFRICAINE.

TRANS-NIGER AVIATION. Aviation company set up in 1989 in Niamey to assist in domestic and regional services. Its shares are held by private Nigerien interests with a 38 percent stake each by SNTN and a French combine.

TRANSONORA. The trucking branch of **SONORA,** which evacuates Niger's peanut crop. The company has about twenty trucks of ten- to twenty-five-ton capacity.

TRANSPORTATION. *See* COMMUNICATIONS.

TROUPE, LA. Name of the armed forces regiment charged with the security of Aïr. It is that unit which mounted a much-criticized wave of two hundred arrests of Tuareg influentials in Agadez in October 1992, further exacerbating the Tuareg unrest.

TUAREG. Largely nomadic ethnic group found in a large area between 14° and 30° north and 5° west and 10° east, centered around the Ahaggar Mountains (Algeria) and including concentrations in Niger, Algeria, Mali, and Libya. In Niger their number is 720,000, according to the most recent census (1988), or 10.4 percent of the population. (During the Sahel droughts of the 1970s over 100,000 are estimated to have migrated to Niger, temporarily, from Mali.) Estimates of their total number in Africa vary widely, from a million upward. Most of these are not, however, the "white" (or true) Tuareg free nobles, but their black **Iklan** or **Bella** slaves or serfs. The nobles claim common Berber descent, are habitually veiled with the **tagelmoust,** and though some are quasi-sedentary (especially in Niger), all regard nomadization in the Sahara or Sahel with their camels as the Tuareg way of life and a sign of nobility and freedom.

Arriving in several waves from the north under pressure from the North African Beni Hillal and Beni Soleim, the Tuareg entry into Niger (via Aïr) pushed existing Hausa communities there (such as the Gobirawa) southward. The original seven clans to arrive in Aïr were united in a federation as the **Itesen.** The Tuareg never call themselves Tuareg—this being an Arab appellation—but rather refer to themselves by their clan's or their confederation's name. Each clan (*taousit*) is composed of various families under the leadership of one of several chiefs, the *amrar*. Several large clans, or tribes, form a Tuareg *Kel,* or "People of . . . " (*For details on the various Tuareg clans, see the entries under* KEL.) Several Kels may combine to appoint a joint supreme chief, or **amenokal,** though this term may also signify any chief on the clan level. Tuareg hierarchy recognizes several distinct castes. The most noble and pure are the **Imajeren,** which literally means "The Proud and Free," followed by the **Imrad,** also freemen but subordinate to the former. The Ineslemen are a religious, nonfighting, sacerdotal caste that has gained status (from virtual servility in the past) as a result of the utter decimation of the warrior freemen castes in the various Franco-Tuareg battles and skirmishes in the late nineteenth and early twentieth centuries. At the bottom of the caste system come the Ikelan (in Tuareg) or Bella (in Songhay) or Buzu (Hausa) slaves, currently in peonage. The last do not nomadize with their masters but remain to tend palm groves or vegetable gardens. There are also several specialized occupational castes, including the **Inadin** artisan and silversmith caste, which is considered separate and outside regular Tuareg society, being freemen, but detested for their vagrant way of life.

The Tuareg language is **Tamasheq,** which comes in four closely related dialects; its written script, Tifinar, is related to the ancient Libyan language. Some scholars trace the origins of the Tuareg to the Mycenaeans, to the ancient Egyptians, or to groups from the Aegean Sea region, though the ancient Garamantians (of Libya) are probably their immediate ancestors. With the Arab conquests of the Maghrib the Tuareg migrations south commenced (in the seventh century), though one branch did join in the Arab conquest of Spain.

Following the arrival in Aïr of the first Itesen wave, other clans drifted in over the centuries. The Kel Gress, for example, arrived in the thirteenth and fourteenth centuries; the Kel Owey in the fourteenth and fifteenth centuries. These constant and aggressive migrations from the north exerted powerful pressures on preexisting settled groups in Aïr, forcing some of the clans to migrate further south, into Ader, Damergou, and even Damagaram. Certain of these clans eventually became sedentary; most remained nomadic or seminomadic, and their patterns of transhumance have at times covered large areas. The Illabakan, for example, nomadize a region of 12,000 sq km, roughly 150 km from east to west and 80 km from north to south, from Abalak to Teguidda. Others migrate from Damergou to the In Gall region on the **cure salée** trek.

Politically the Tuareg have never constituted one entity. They formed a number of sultanates, however, such as that in Agadez (*see* AGADEZ, SULTANATE OF) in the fifthteenth century. Elsewhere, smaller entities were established after the conquest of territory and sedentary populations, as in the Ader and Tahoua. Outside Niger, the Tuareg finally conquered Gao (in 1770) after constant pressure, as well as Timbuktu (both currently in Mali). Converted to Islam, and later to the **Sanusiya** religious order, though retaining many pre-Islamic customs, the Tuareg spearheaded the resistance to the imposition of French (regarded as infidel) rule over their areas. Their independent spirit and religious fanaticism continued into the first decades of the twentieth century, which saw a number of rebellions, including in Niger (*see* REBELLIONS). Even with the approach of independence in West Africa, several top Tuareg chiefs in Niger and Mali attempted to form a federation to keep themselves outside the political control of the still-despised and inferior "black south." In Mali the Tuareg have been intermittently severely repressed, and incidents of rebellion and unrest have been frequent. Indeed, to some extent the current rebellion in Niger had its origins in events in Mali in the late 1980s.

In Niger the sultan was deposed in favor of his son, and exiled to Birni-N'Konni, while the anastafidet was likewise deposed and exiled to Tillabéry, being replaced by his brother. In Niger, however, and unlike in Mali, this incident did not lead to further agitation on the part of the Tuareg. During the Hamani Diori regime (1960–74), the Tuareg were treated with special consideration, and one of their amenokals served in the cabinet (as often as not resident in Agadez) as minister of Saharan affairs. Free salt, tea, and sugar were distributed to the migrating clans during the cure salée at In Gall, and Aïr was administered with a gentle hand—part of a general awareness of Tuareg sensitivities and their potential volatility.

Following the 1974 coup d'état the Kountché regime "regularized" the treatment of the Tuareg. Though a number of Tuareg joined his cabinet in key posts (including one, Algabid, as prime minister), many Tuareg chiefs tended to look back with nostalgia to the Diori days when Aïr was, in many ways, free from southern interference. In 1980 Libya tried to foment the growth of subnationalism among Niger's Tuareg following the break in diplomatic relations with Niamey. (*See* LIBYA.) A number of Tuareg civil servants were enticed by Libyan blandishments and left for Tripoli, and on at least three occasions Diori's self-exiled son, with Libyan support, led groups of Tuareg in assaults against Nigerien military installations in Aïr (including Tchin Tabaraden, a favorite target) in an effort to attain a comeback for his father. After one armed incident in 1985 Kountché expelled from Niger tens of thousands of "non-Nigerien" Tuareg (difficult to distinguish in light of their nomadic nature), which indirectly set the stage for the Tuareg rebellion of 1990.

Increased Tuareg grievances against Niamey began with the greater intrusion of the central government in Aïr in the 1970s as uranium and other mining enterprises were set up. Much of the work force in these mines was Tuareg; yet, though employment provided a source of income unavailable anywhere else, their cultural alienation and marginalization from cherished values (such as the *tagelmoust* that they had to remove to work in the pits), produced a love/hate relationship. The fact that "black southerners" or "infidel French" were their immediate masters rankled; the influx of brazen tourists wandering "without respect" in their domain further attested to the suppression of the "noble and free" way of life. This growing alienation from Niamey may not have been anything more than a symptom of the pain of transition to modernity; but in the 1980s, however, a bout of repression in neighboring Mali (to which some clans migrate on their transhumance patterns), and General Kountché's expulsion of tens of thousands from Niger after an armed incident, solidified a renascent desire to attain their former autonomy. This was expressed in a variety of ways, including the emergence of liberation movements (at the outset in Mali) and the beginning of talk of a Tuareg "Sahara Republic." When in mid-1990 an isolated Tuareg assault on Tchin Tabaraden resulted in a rampage of the Niger army, severe beatings, humiliations, and massacres, the Tuareg rebellion in Niger finally crystallized. *For details on the latter, see* TUAREG REBELLION.

TUAREG, POPULATION DISTRIBUTION IN NIGER OF. Recent figures on the precise population distribution of the largely nomadic Tuareg are not available, since at the time of the most recent census (1988) a large number of Tuareg who had fled the drought of the mid-1980s had not yet returned to Niger. The only reliable figures are from 1962, and these are badly dated since at that time Niger's population stood at 2.6 million people, as compared to the 7.6 million of 1992. Only in one département, however, that of Agadez, have the Tuareg ever formed a majority (75 percent) of the population. Within the subdivision of Tchin Tabaraden (in the département of Tahoua) most of the population (90.5 percent) has also been Tuareg, with significant numbers (25 percent) in Madoua also, though overall their percentage of the population of Tahoua amounts to only 18.4. Elsewhere Tuareg are found in concentrated numbers only in the Filingué subdivision of the département of Niamey (35 percent, though overall they are only 5.1 percent of the population) and in the subdivision of Tanout in the département of Zinder (19.3 percent; overall, 3.8 percent).

TUAREG REBELLION (1990). In retrospect the 1990 Tuareg rebellion in Niger, still simmering though formally ended, started with the severe military repression and massacres that followed a mid-1990 Tuareg armed assault on the Niger army outpost at **Tchin Tabaraden,** a popular target for such isolated Tuareg attacks. The assault, to capture arms, took place against a general background of (*a*) the return to Niger of tens of thousands of "non-Nigerien" Tuareg from Mali, having been expelled by General Kountché in 1985 after an armed incident, abetted by Libya and aimed at bringing back to power Hamani Diori; (*b*) their grievances against Niamey's not fulfilling pledges made by General Saibou (who rescinded the expulsion order) to assist in their resettlement (funds were stolen by local officials); and (*c*) a general escalation of the Tuareg crisis in neighboring Mali, where Bamako's relations with the Tuareg had historically been bad.

Early talk of the carving out of an all-Tuareg Saharan Republic encompassing Mali's, Niger's, Libya's, and Algeria's desert wilderness, was not a cause espoused by many, though it captured global headlines. Within Niger prior to the 1990 assault, there had been growing discontent in Tuareg circles with their cultural marginalization and the sidelining of their interests by Niamey. Sporadic incidents, and a certain spillover of the Mali rebellion notwithstanding, an actual crisis had not developed until the 1990 incident. (*For the general background and Niamey-Tuareg relations, see* TUAREG.)

The repression, massacres, and similar heavy-handed attempts by the Niger army to stamp out Tuareg irredentism after the 1990 Tchin Tabaraden assault ignited a full-scale rebellion. Intermittent armed groups, at times outgunning the Niger forces (with weapons secured either from neighboring countries or from Toubou remnants of Hissene Habre's armies in Kaouar), made all of Aïr insecure, including the uranium mining town of Arlit, but also regions further south (in Tahoua), only 320 kilometers from Niamey. Around a dozen liberation fronts formed, linked in 1991 and 1993 in two coordinating organs, one of which—the CRA—with a leader in Paris, **Mano Dayak,** has been the most active, with press conferences and appeals to the United Nations. Mano Dayak also wrote a book on Tuareg grievances against Niamey, triggering a book in response by **André Salifou.**

By 1995 there were a dozen liberation movements in Niger. Four of these are coordinated in Paris, and allegedly in the field, by the Coordination de la Résistance Armée, and four have formed the Mouvement des Fronts Unifiés de l'Azawad. They are separated along clan lines (and in one instance—the FIAA—along ethnic lines), have different aims and visions for the Tuareg north (cultural and administrative autonomy, federalism, independence), and varying religious (Muslim) goals.

The Mouvement des Fronts Unifiés de l'Azawad (MFUA) was set up in 1991 after the splintering into its constituent parts of the previous Mouvement Populaire pour la Libération de l'Azawad (MPLA), headed by Iyad ag Ghali and headquartered in Mali, which mobilized a segment of the Tuareg there. After the MPLA initialed peace accords with the Mali government, the following groups opted out and later set up the MFUA: Mouvement Populaire de l'Azawad (MPA), Front Populaire de Libération de l'Azawad (FPLA); Armée Révolutionnaire de Libération de l'Azawad (ARLA); Front Islamique Arabe de l'Azawad (FIAA).

The Coordination de la Résistance Armée (CRA) was formed in 1993 and was headed by Mano Dayak, head of the ARLN, to group four liberation fronts. (The CRA gave way in 1995 to the looser Organisation de la Résistance Armée [ORA], which recently initialed a peace agreement with Niamey.) The FLAA was first to organize in Niger, the only one to claim spheres of operation in both Aïr and Azawak, and the largest (possibly mobilizing over a thousand men), though figures about each armed group are highly speculative. The four fronts are Front de Libération de l'Aïr et de l'Azawad (FLAA); Front de Libération Temust (FLT); Armée Révolutionnaire de Libération du Nord Niger (ARLN); Front Patriotique de Libération du Sahara (FPLS). *For more details on most of the above, see their individual entries.*

In light of the vastness of the desert regions that the Tuareg know well from their transhumance patterns, and the smallness and severely underfunded nature of the Nigerien army charged with securing law and order, Tuareg forces roamed virtually at will, with the government's forces taking up static strategic positions or mounting punitive forays against any Tuareg they encountered. The number of armed clashes has been estimated at no more than around thirty. Casualties on both sides (other than in the massacres—those casualties numbering in the hundreds) have been relatively minor, since Tuareg assaults are hit-and-run operations mounted by at most two hundred warriors. Indeed, the total armed Tuareg "might" that kept the Niger army at bay has been estimated at fewer than two thousand. By 1995 the Tuareg held some sixty hostages (mostly from the army or gendarmerie or civil servants, some subsequently released) and had caused several tourist deaths. (In one incident, a Tuareg attack left a number of tourists unharmed, but jittery Nigerien reinforcements opened fire on the tourists, mistaking them for Tuareg.)

The National Conference that took place in Niamey in 1991 recognized the Tuareg grievances, dismissed some senior military officers for their role in the Aïr atrocities, and tried to initiate a dialogue with the Tuareg, considered for several years as "bandits" or rogue elements seeking revenge. Reflecting the historically decentralized nature of the fiercely independent Tuareg confederations, there was no single set of Tuareg leaders to negotiate with, nor was the CRA empowered to negotiate for the individual groups in the field. Each front was composed of members of one confederation; they had different demands for peace, articulated by spokesmen with little influence over the actual fighting forces.

The common demands, however, were (*a*) the evacuation of all Nigerien armed forces from Aïr; (*b*) a federal system, with the north (Aïr and Azawak) one component with total cultural, religious, administrative, and military autonomy; (*c*) an infusion of funds for the benefit of the hitherto ignored north; and (*d*) integration of Tuareg into the army—all conditions that Niger was unwilling originally to consider. The extremist position—independence for a Sahara confederation of Tuareg clans—was voiced, but seemingly only nostalgically, and mostly by Tuareg normally in Mali.

Sporadic negotiations between Niamey and rebel leaders and sympathizers in Agadez resulted in several truces as early as 1992, but they led nowhere. It was essentially only in mid-1994, with Niger totally drained by the war effort, that negotiations in Ouagadougou (Burkina Faso) brokered by the latter and by France, resulted in a more serious truce, confirmed in mid-April 1995 as a cease-fire. Under it Niger agreed to virtually all the Tuareg demands, including setting up ethnically homogeneous administrative regions with their own regional assemblies, governors, and cultural autonomy.

TYENGA. Oldest inhabitants of the lower Niger River valley, and especially of **Dendi.** The Tyenga language—which is nearly extinct—is also spoken by a few clans in Nigeria, though most members adopted Songhay and later Hausa. The Tyenga were pushed into the Dendi from Sokoto, which they had been chased out of by the Hausa. There are only about six thousand of them in Niger, though many more live in northern Nigeria. The Djerma of Dendi consider them Hausa today, in light of their assimilation of the latter's customs and language. In Nigeria they are called Tyengawa.

-U-

UNION DEMOCRATIQUE DES FORCES PROGRESSISTES (UDFP-SAWABA). Small, post-1991 political party, claiming to represent the "original" veteran political leader **Djibo Bakary.** The SAWABA "constituency," and label, is claimed by two groups in the post-1991 period. Bakary's party is aligned behind the MNSD, in power since February 1995, while another "SAWABA" faction, the Union Démocratique de Forces Révolutionnaires (UDFR-SAWABA) is part of the AFC alliance, which until 1994 was part of the governing coalition in Niger. *See also* POLITICAL PARTIES.

UNION DEMOCRATIQUE DES FORCES REVOLUTIONNAIRES (UDFR-SAWABA). Small, post-1991 political party, claiming to represent the **SAWABA** party of the 1950s, and part of the anti-MNSD AFC alliance, which until 1994 formed the government of Niger. The party won two seats in the National Assembly. The other faction of SAWABA, the Union Démocratique de Forces Progrèssistes (UDFP-SAWABA), headed by the original SAWABA leader of the 1950s, **Djibo Bakary,** is part of the MNSD coalition. *See also* POLITICAL PARTIES.

UNION DEMOCRATIQUE NIGERIENNE (UDN). Founded in 1954 by PPN dissidents led by **Djibo Bakary** following the 1951 dissociation of the RDA (with which the PPN was affiliated) from the French Communist party. Despite strong administrative opposition the UDN obtained a respectable showing in the 1956 elections, polling 74,000 votes. It then merged with the Bloc Nigérien d'Action (BNA)—successor to the Union Nigérienne des Indépendants et Sympathisants—to form the local branch of the new interterritorial Mouvement Socialiste Africain, which in 1958 became SAWABA. *See also* POLITICAL PARTIES.

UNION DES FEMMES DU NIGER (UFN). Women's organization of Niger, though in large respect operative mostly in Niamey. Successor to efforts to organize women that commenced with the 1956 Association des Femmes, formed by the four principal **magajiyas** of Niamey, and the 1958 Association de Jeunes Filles du Niger. The honorary president of the UFN was **Alissa Diori,** wife of President Diori. Its stated purpose was to promote, educate, and mobilize women. Following the 1974 coup the organization's name was changed to **Association des Femmes du Niger.**

UNION DES FORCES POUR LA DEMOCRATIE ET LE PROGRES (UFDP). Political party formed late in 1991 and holding its first congress in February 1992 to elect Djibo Bakary as their president. Neither he in the presidential elections nor the party at the parliamentary elections, both in 1993, gained more than a minute percentage of the votes. The party split into two. *See also* POLITICAL PARTIES.

UNION DES NIGERIENS DE L'EST (UNE). Loose faction in the PPN in 1946—also known as the Parti Indépendant du Niger-Est (PINE)—led by Georges Condat and Harou Kouka. It seceded from the PPN in 1946 after the party's selection of Djibo Bakary as its second candidate for the forthcoming elections. The UNE was largely a stillborn party, and it merged with UNIS in 1948. *See also* POLITICAL PARTIES.

UNION DES PATRIOTES DEMOCRATIQUES ET PROGRESSISTES (UPDP-Shamuwa). Small, post-1991 political party, headed by **André Salifou** and **Illa Kané,** with one seat in the National Assembly, aligned with the MNSD party currently in office.

UNION DES SCOLAIRES NIGERIENS (USN). Organization of students, increasingly combative vis-à-vis the government since the late 1970s. The union was not recognized by the government until 1982, and its officers were harassed during the Kountché and Saibou eras. In May 1983 the USN supported the UENUN demonstrations, and its leaders were arrested. The USN's main planks at the time were democratization of society and radicalization of social policies. Since the dawn of the new civilian era, the USN has been at the forefront of the intermittent student demonstrations in Niger's cities, calling for greater, and more timely, allocations of student grants.

UNION DES SYNDICATS DES TRAVAILLUERS DU NIGER (USTN). Successor, after the 1974 coup d'état, of the UNTN trade union federation. The USTN encompassed thirty-one individual unions, and was for a long time headed by Secretary General

Boureima Mainassara. In the 1990s the USTN was a major force—via actual strikes and even threats of strikes—in the drive toward democratization and civilianization of Niger. Restless for some time, their strike of June 10–11, 1990, in particular forced General Saibou to agree to multipartyism on June 16, and in May 1991 their threat of a strike prevented him from packing the scheduled National Conference with loyalist "delegates" from the country's parastatal agencies. Though USTN supported Saibou (with the threat of a general strike) in his February 1992 confrontation with mutinous troops (unpaid for two months), the next month they supported a strike by teachers on the same matter, and resisted the imposition of a national solidarity tax or any other tax to bolster the finances of the armed forces fighting the Tuareg rebellion in Aïr. It was also the USTN's ability to paralyze all activity in the capital city that prevented both President Saibou and successor civilian governments from executing civil service cuts, budgetary reductions, privatization, or the closure of state enterprises, and implementing the Structural Adjustment Plan that Saibou had been forced by the IMF to accept as early as 1988. In 1994 the USTN mounted a very protracted and economically debilitating strike over their demand for a pay hike for the civil service of (originally) 30 to 50 percent, and they remain a major force to be reckoned with today. The secretary general is Ibrahim Mayaki, with Ali Moussa as his deputy. In 1993 four unions broke from the USTN to form the Confédération des Syndicats Libres des Travailleurs du Niger (CSLTN); USTN retained the loyalty of thirty-one affiliates and 200,000 members. *See also* UNIONS.

UNION NATIONALE DES TRAVAILLEURS DU NIGER (UNTN). Niger's first single trade union federation. Founded in 1960 with three sections for labor (in Maradi, Zinder, and Niamey), the UNTN had thirty-one individual union affiliates and was itself internationally linked with the African Trade Union Confederation. Its secretary general was **René Delanne.** The UNTN was dissolved after the 1974 coup d'état and replaced by the USTN.

UNION NIGERIENNE DE CREDIT ET DE COOPERATION (UNCC). Founded on September 20, 1962, and capitalized at 245 million CFA francs, the UNCC was charged with helping form cooperatives and assisting them with credit, technical assistance, and commercializing their agricultural crops. Originally granted a partial monopoly over several peanut markets previously under the jurisdiction of the SMDR, in 1967 the UNCC's role was increased to include 50 percent of the peanut crop of Niger. Private entrepreneurs, however, continued to dominate major markets (such as Magaria proper). Other crops the UNCC has handled (in 1970, for example) included Niger's entire rice crop, and 85 percent of Niger's small cotton harvest. The record of the UNCC has been very checkered. It faced numerous fiscal problems in its earlier years as farmers refused to, or could not, repay their debts, and eventually the company left the credit field altogether. New funding was necessary on several occasions due to the inefficient and bloated central personnel and fiscal abuses. Near bankruptcy in 1965, when several scandals rocked it, its budget was cut and credit operations transferred to the CNCA. Yet again in 1968–69 the UNCC capital was depleted and fresh scandals abounded. By the 1980s the fiscally hard-pressed government could no longer continue to absorb the massive deficits of the state sector. In 1985 the UNCC was privatized.

UNION NIGERIENNE DES INDEPENDANTS ET SYMPATHISANTS (UNIS). Political party founded on June 4, 1948. In essence a regional (especially in the beginning), traditionalist, and anti-RDA party, its origins can be traced to splits within the PPN over its continued links with the RDA, itself affiliated internationally with the French Communist party. Very strongly supported by the French administration in Niger—and in particular by then-governor Jean Toby—UNIS was born out of a cleavage of the PPN, and though formed only twenty-three days before the French National Assembly elections, Condat (its leader) easily defeated Djibo Bakary of the PPN, and in 1951 again Condat and Ikhia Zodi won elections against Hamani Diori. Moreover, in the 1952 Territorial Assembly elections, UNIS gained thirty-four of the thirty-five seats of the second electoral college (*see* DOUBLE ELECTORIAL COLLEGE). In 1953 UNIS lost a splinter group under Condat, which formed the UPN party in favor of a reconciliation with the PPN now that the RDA had cut its links with the French Communist party. In 1955 the UNIS party for all practical purposes folded, as most of its membership followed Seydou and Mayaki in forming the BNA party, leaving the shell, and name, of the party to Francis Borrey and Ikhia Zodi, who had pushed for the party's affiliation with the IOM and interterritorial C.A. UNIS fared very poorly in the subsequent elections and obtained only 24,000 votes. On February 24, 1957, the party became the Niger section of the Convention Africaine under the name of Forces Démocratiques Nigériennes.

UNION POUR LA COMMUNAUTE FRANCO-AFRICAINE (UCFA). Temporary, PPN-led electoral list that won fifty-four of the sixty seats of the National Assembly in the December 14, 1958, elections, unseating the ruling party, SAWABA. The alliance was supposed to bring about the formation of a new party, but the PPN convinced its partners to merge with the PPN and retain its name. *See also* PARTI PROGRESSISTE NIGERIEN.

UNION POUR LA DEMOCRATIE ET LE PROGRES (UDP-Amintchi). Small, post-1991 political party, aligned behind the AFC anti-MNSD alliance, headed by Bello Tiousso Garba. The party did not win any seats in the 1993 parliamentary elections.

UNION POUR LA DEMOCRATIE ET LE PROGRES SOCIAL (UDPS-Amana). Small, post-1991 political party, aligned behind the AFC anti-MNSD alliance, headed by Mohamed Abdoullahi.

UNION PROGRESSISTE NIGERIENNE (UPN). Political party set up on March 24, 1953, by Georges Condat and his supporters formerly within the UNIS party, eager for a reconciliation with the PPN, from which they had originally seceded. The attempts to link up with the PPN ultimately failed, and the UPN returned to the fold—renamed the Bloc Nigérien d'Action. *See also* POLITICAL PARTIES.

UNIONS. Thirty-five worker unions with some 35,000 members are grouped within the USTN, of which Ibrahim Mayaki is the secretary general. On the owners' side Niger has three unions: SCIMPEXNI (Syndicats des Commerçants, Importateurs et Exporteurs du Niger), SPEIN (Syndicat Patronal des Entreprises et Industries du Niger), and S.T. (Syndicat des Transporteurs), the last affiliated with the UNTN. In 1993 four affiliates broke off from UNTN to form an "independent" confederation, the Conféderation des Syndicats Libres des Travailleurs du Niger (CSLTN).

UNITY ROAD. *See* ROUTE DE L'UNITE.

UNIVERSITE DE NIAMEY. Niger's main university. An outgrowth of the Centre d'Enseignement Supérieur set up in 1974. The university has schools of science, education and letters, medicine, and agronomy, and enrolls around 6,000 students. In 1994 it was renamed after one of its rectors, though the new name has not yet been adopted widely.

UNIVERSITE ISLAMIQUE DU NIGER. *See* ISLAMIC UNIVERSITY OF SAY.

URANEX. Organization set up on October 1969 to market uranium ore produced by the Franc Zone countries, especially Niger, Gabon, Central African Republic, and France. *See also* URANIUM.

URANIGER. Popular name for the **Office National de Recherches, d'Exploitation et de Commercialisation de l'Uranium du Niger.**

URANIUM. For about a decade uranium was Niger's prime export, foreign-currency earner, and major source of income. In the 1990s Niger became the world's second largest uranium producer, up from her fifth rank in the late 1970s. This was attained, however, with around half the uranium produced in the 1970s, due to a major global uranium glut and France's disinclination to continue her direct subsidies to Niger's uranium sector by means of grossly inflated prices for all the uranium Niger was capable of producing.

Niger's ore is found in several locations in Aïr, which, it is estimated, contain over 10 percent of the world's known reserves. In the 1980s other sources of uranium were detected, including outside Aïr (especially in Kaouar), reinforcing indications that its spread in Niger is much more extensive than originally thought. Exploitation at most sites other than the original ones have been indefinitely shelved, however.

Uranium was first discovered, quite accidentally, in 1958 by the French Atomic Energy Commission in the Arlit area of Aïr, and by 1966 detailed searches and evaluations confirmed its presence in commercially exploitable quantities, leading to the creation of Niger's first uranium company, SOMAIR. Subsequent discoveries, and the grant of further concessions, saw the creation of several other companies, including the Société de Mines de Diado, COMINAK, and the **Société Minière de Tassa N'Taghalgué.**

While originally the government assumed a small share in these various enterprises, with the rise of the Kountché military regime in 1974 a more aggressive policy raised the government share and more revenues began to flow into the state treasury. These uranium royalties were used for budget-balancing purposes, and fueled a massive bout of infrastructure work, development projects, and the creation of a plethora of parastatal enterprises, all of which stabilized military rule in Niger.

In December 1974 ONAREM was formed to centralize and administer the government's uranium holdings and to watch over the government's interests. Moreover, alleging friction with France—which controls much of their market—the Francophone uranium-producing countries set up a joint-marketing organization whose task was to ensure high prices for the mineral (*see* URANEX). Uranium exports from Niger slowly increased after the first shipment of 400 tons in 1971. By 1974, SOMAIR (then the sole fully operative mining company) was exporting 1,400 tons of processed/enriched mineral ore valued at 15,000 million CFA francs. (A huge amount of rock has to be crushed and processed to yield each kilogram of uranium.) With the entry of new uranium companies, tonnage increased to over 4,500, and (highly optimistic) estimations projected a possible annual production of 10,000 tons by the year 1990.

The uranium boom collapsed, however, in 1980. Lower global demand, coupled with excess production by other countries, first seriously depressed prices and later severely eroded global demand. Niger's uranium production began to decline in the 1980s, since excess ore could not be sold economically at the depressed prices—30,000 CFA francs a kilogram in 1980; 17,000 in 1992. Production declined from a peak of 4,400 tons in 1980, first to around 3,500 tons, and then more sharply to 2,000 tons, before rebounding somewhat. Recent production has not exceeded, however, the 3,000 tons of 1987. The role of uranium royalties in the Niger budget likewise declined sharply, to between 8 and 12 percent of state revenues, the lower percentage being the most recent. By contrast, uranium exports constituted 80 percent of Niger's foreign earnings in the late 1970s, when they made up fully 50 percent of the state's budget.

A significant percentage of Niger's uranium exports were from the outset purchased by France at well above world market prices. Though this indirect subsidy to the Nigerien economy was somewhat curtailed in the 1980s as France began to "normalize" its relations with Francophone Africa, France continued into the 1990s to purchase (unneeded) Nigerien uranium at higher than global market prices. By 1994 the price paid by France for Niger's uranium was reduced to 15,450 CFA francs per kilogram, compared to the 20,400 CFA francs of 1990, but at the time the spot market price for uranium was as little as 9,000 CFA francs. These revenue declines have further undermined Niger's uranium sector, which has all along been hard-pressed by abnormally high production costs. The World Bank has criticized Niger's uranium cost structure, insisting upon a major restructuring as a prime condition for a structural adjustment loan, since on the face of it Niger's uranium had been grossly uncompetitive even in the boom years. Even with a cost restructuring (which Niger is resisting), and a currently projected uranium shortage by the turn of the century, Niger's mines would remain uncompetitive.

Declining uranium-generated revenues raised Niger's need to intensify peanut production and exports, as in previous decades when it was a prime foreign-exchange earner. Equally important, lowered royalties and budgetary infusions inexorably spelled the end of Niger's developmental boom and the onset of civil-military strife over bread-and-butter issues, something greatly intensified by the uncontrolled expansion of parastatals and the civil service in the 1970s and 1980s.

With the meltdown in Niger's uranium prospects, international consortia that were in the process of developing mining operations abruptly pulled out completely. Prospecting (for both uranium and many other ores, though not gold) dried up. Foreigners in the uranium mines, and entrepreneurs attracted into the service sector of a booming economy, left Niger. Indeed, what has been referred to as the French "disinvestment" from Francophone Africa of the mid-1980s affected Niger the most. In 1990 it was estimated that fully 80 percent of Niger's resident foreigners had already left the country, a figure no doubt since augmented by the effects of the Tuareg rebellion in Aïr (in close proximity to the uranium mines), the urban unrest in Niamey since 1990, and the country's continued pauperized state.

URANIUM ROAD. *See* ROUTE DE L'URANIUM.

URBAN CENTERS. In 1988 Niger's latest census estimated the country's population at some 7 million people, with the following ranking of its major urban centers (the figures are not overly reliable, however, since even the same government department—Statistics—disseminates different figures for the country's towns):

(1)	Niamey	400,000
(2)	Zinder	90,000
(3)	Maradi	70,000
(4)	Tahoua	46,000
(5)	Agadez	30,000
(6)	Arlit	20,000

UTHMAN DAN FODIO. *See* DAN FODIO, OTHMAN.

-V-

VOIX DE L'ISLAM. Libyan-financed Arab-language Niamey radio transmission system, initiated as a consequence of one of the accords signed by President Hamani Diori shortly before the 1974 coup that overthrew him. The project was scrapped by the subsequent Kountché administration.

VOIX DU SAHEL. Niger's radio station, founded in 1958 and previously known as Radio Niger. It was renamed on April 29, 1974, following the Kountché coup d'état. The station broadcast in the 1970s in French, Hausa, Djerma, Tamasheq, Kanuri, Fulfulde, English, and Arabic, and expanded in the 1980s with broadcasts also in Kanuri, Gourmantché, and Toubou. It is directed by Omar Tiello.

VOULET. *See* MISSION AFRIQUE CENTRALE.

-W-

W. *See* PARC NATIONAL DU W.

WAHAD, AICHATOU BEN. Former secretary of state for small and medium enterprises between April 1993 and the fall of the government in October 1994.

WODAABE. Meaning "the rejected," this is the name by which the Bororo Fulani of Niger are also known. *See also* BORORO; FULANI

WOGO. Small ethnic group found in Mali, Nigeria, and Niger. In Niger they are often found intermingled with the **Kurtey** on the Niger River islands off Tillabéry and Niamey. Arriving from the vicinity of Lake Debo to Bourra (Ansongo)—in Mali—and of Sarakolé-**Sorko** ethnic mixture, a Wogo branch came down the Niger River, reaching its present locations in Niger and Nigeria starting round 1810. Islamized, the Wogo fought numerous battles with the Kurtey, whom they found settled on the islands before them. Courageous and very industrious, the contemporary Wogo are excellent agriculturalists, and many become seasonal farm workers in Ghana. They are ethnically homogenous, and the three Wogo segments (in Mali, Niger, and Nigeria—the latter migrating from Bourra to Zaria around 1890) are strongly linked. Their numbers in Niger are hard to determine but estimates revolve around 26,000. They speak the Songhay language.

WRIGHT, ALBERT. Former interim minister of education, appointed by the HCR in November 1991 and serving until April 1993, when a new government was formed. In 1992 he was appointed government spokesman, and in January 1993 he was given ministerial duties relating to quelling the Tuareg rebellion.

WRIGHT, ANDRE JOSEPH (1937–). Diplomat and former ambassador to the U.N. and the U.S. Born in Niamey on December 1, 1937, Wright has a law degree from the University of Montpellier (1959) and a diploma from the IHEOM (1961) where he studied diplomacy. In 1962 he joined Niger's Foreign Ministry and became a member of Niger's delegation to the U.N. General Assembly (1964–67). Between 1967 and 1972 he was seconded to the OAU, where he served as acting executive secretary of the OAU Office at the U.N., and in 1968 he became head of the Political Affairs Section of the OAU in Addis Ababa. He returned to Niger in 1973 and was appointed technical advisor in the Foreign Ministry and in 1974 director of the Department of International Organizations and Economic Affairs in that ministry.

In August 1974 he resumed diplomatic duties as ambassador to the Ivory Coast, Guinea, and Sierra Leone, and in July 1976 he was appointed ambassador to the U.S. and representative to the U.N. In April 1978 he was also accredited ambassador to South Korea. He later became head of a division in the Ministry of Foreign Affairs.

WRIGHT, EMMANUEL (1910–). Former educator. Born on November 2, 1910, in Fotoba (in Guinea, and the origin of the Nigerien Wright family), he became a naturalized Nigerien in 1962. Wright was an educator who worked for many years in Niger (1932–57), mostly in the Niamey area, serving also as inspector of primary education. During 1957–65 he was primary school inspector for the Niamey district, and in 1966 he was appointed director of primary education in the Ministry of Education. Wright is currently retired.

WRIGHT, FRANCOIS (Lieutenant Colonel). Commander of the Nigerien air force.

WRIGHT, JOHN (1934–). Physician. Born in Niamey on May 14, 1934, and holding an M.D. from the University of Montpellier (1962), with a diploma in tropical medicine (Montpellier, 1958) and physiology (Lyons University, 1962), Dr. Wright has been attached to Niamey Hospital since 1963, serving also as director of the National School for Nursing.

-Y-

YACOUBA, HENRI DUPUIS (General) (1924–). Former inspector general of the Niger armed forces, and at the time the most senior officer in the armed forces. Of Djerma commoner origins, Yacouba was born on March 10, 1924, in Timbuktu (Mali), and was trained from an early age for a military career by his father, a soldier in the French colonial armies. Just prior to independence he was promoted to officer rank, and returned to Niamey as one of the few indigenous officers of the newly created Niger army. Yacouba then served as head of personnel services in the Niger Ministry of Defense (December 1961–August 1966) while simultaneously chef de cabinet of the minister of defense (December 1962–August 1966). He was then appointed director of national defense in the ministry of the same name and in July 1973 also assumed the post of inspector general of the armed forces. After the 1974 coup d'état, in which Yacouba was involved in a nonactive way, he was promoted; by August 1976 he had attained the highest rank in the armed forces. Immediately after the coup he was brought into the military cabinet as minister of education, youth, and sports. In a 1975 shuffle he dropped the portfolios of youth and sports, and in another shuffle the same year he was named minister of posts and telecommunications. The following year Yacouba was implicated in the March 15, 1976, attempted coup, having recently been dismissed from the cabinet. At the time his "driving ambition" was cited as the reason both for his purge from the cabinet and for his involvement in the anti-Kountché conspiracy. He was reintegrated into the government in a minor, mostly honorific, post consequent to a reassessment of his minor role in the 1976 plot, and he served in that capacity between 1976 and 1985, when he was retired from the armed forces. After Kountché's death in 1987, Yacouba—though in retirement since 1985—was reappointed by General Saibou to his honorific post, as token compensation for his being shunted aside by Kountché.

YACOUBA, IDE. Former prefect. By training a stockbreeding assistant, Yacouba joined the administrative arm of the Ministry of Interior and in June 1966 was appointed prefect of Diffa. He was then shifted in 1969 to fill a similar function in Maradi, and in 1971 he became prefect of Agadez. After the 1974 coup d'état Yacouba was reassigned as consultant in the Ministry of Interior.

YACOUBA, ISSA KONE. Former director of labor and social security. Born in 1925 in Zinder and by training a labor inspector, Yacouba was in charge of labor inspection and the execution and enforcement of social laws in east Niger for two years (1962–63) before assuming in December 1964 the post of director of labor and social security in the Ministry of Civil Service and Labor. Prominent also in trade union activities, Yacouba retired in 1985.

YACOUBA, MOUMOUNI. Former minister of public works and town planning between July 1982 and November 1985.

YAKIN AGGABA. "The War of Aggaba," as referred to in Ader, in popular remembrance of the conquest of the region in the eighteenth century by **Aggaba,** son of the sultan of Aïr. *See also* ADER.

YAKUDIMA. In the precolonial Damagaram hierarchy, a son or brother of the sultan, and heir apparent, who resided as governor of the village of Damagaram ta-Kaya.

YAM BORI. "The Children of **Bori,**" that is, Bori initiates.

YANSAMBOU, AMADOU (1924–). Former prefect of Niamey. Born around 1924 in Saga, in the Niamey district, and obtaining his education locally, Yansambou worked with the local public works department (1943–45) followed by service with the local administration (1945–52). In 1953 he was shifted to the district administration of Agadez (1953–58). Since 1946 a PPN militant, and first secretary of the PPN Youth Wing, with the rise of the PPN to power Yansambou's career took an upward turn. After the creation of the first Diori cabinet Yansambou was appointed deputy prefect of Agadez (1959–60), sous-préfet of Ouallam (1960–61), prefect of Dosso (1961), and of Agadez. In August 1968 he returned to Niamey to become prefect of the Niamey département. After the 1974 coup d'état he was reassigned to administrative duties in the Ministry of Interior, and retired in 1984.

YANTALA. Niamey quarter, originally a small suburban village, at the northwestern extremity of the city, and site of a military camp. The quarter is practically all Djerma (87 percent). The Presidential Palace is also located in this general vicinity.

YATTARA, HAMA BEIDARI (1920–). Former minister. Born in Agadez on August 2, 1920, and a stockbreeding assistant by training, Yattara joined the Ministry of Agriculture in 1958 and a year later was selected to be the minister's chef du cabinet. He later performed similar duties for the minister of rural economy while serving also as deputy prefect of Tessaoua. In 1962 he was dispatched to Nigeria to serve as consul, and remained there for five years. Since 1968 an administrator in the Ministry of Rural Economy and Saharan Affairs, Yattara has also served as deputy prefect of N'Guigmi (1970–71). After the 1974 coup d'état he was shifted to the administration of Agadez, where he served until his retirement.

YAYE, BONZOUGOU (1948–). Chemical engineer. Born in 1948, and having received a doctorate in chemistry from the University of Paris in 1979, Yaye is head of the chemistry section of the School of Sciences at the University of Niamey.

YENENDI. Important **holey** rite, usually performed in May or June (at the end of the hot season) and aimed at invoking the rains. It is especially celebrated in the Niamey region.

YORUBA. Large ethnic group found mostly in west Nigeria and east Benin, along the coast or immediate hinterland, and in smaller concentrations as traders in many other countries. Though the Yoruba number only 2 percent of Niamey's population (their numbers outside Niamey are minimal), they are the most dynamic ethnic group in the city, especially after the 1964 expulsion of the **Dahomeans** also resident in Niamey. Their arrival—mostly from Nigeria—was spontaneous, and was not encouraged by the local French administration, as was the arrival of the Dahomeans or the Togolese. Very industrious and agile merchants, most repatriate their capital back to Nigeria. They have not entered areas of commerce where there is indigenous commercial competition. Normally cultivators and artisans at home, they never engage in these activities abroad. They specialize in the sale of basic necessities that are produced in north Nigeria and small manufactured goods from Hong Kong. The community's total ethnic solidarity and developed social life allow newcomers to set up business with little personal capital and to benefit from advice and support of old-timers in the community. Most of Niamey's Yoruba community arrived there in one wave around 1950–55. They speak Yoruba and some Hausa and English, but little French. *See also* AJO OMO SAHKI KPARAPO.

YOUNOUS, SULTAN OF AIR (1405?–1424). Legendary first sultan of Aïr. According to tradition Younous was the son of the sultan of the Ottoman Empire and a slave concubine, sent to rule Aïr in response to a Tuareg deputation to the court (*see* AGADEZ, SULTANATE OF). In reality he probably came from the Fès region. The tradition of the sultans of Agadez being of low birth stems from the slave origins of Younous. Seminomadic in this era, the capital of the sultanate was not fixed in Agadez until around 1440. In 1424 Younous was deposed from the throne by his nephew, Agh Hassan.

-Z-

ZA. *See* DYA.

ZABERMA. Another name for the **Djerma.** *See also* SONGHAY.

ZAGHAWA. Group of seminomadic Arab clans found in a broad arc across Chad and reaching into parts of western Sudan and eastern Niger. Formerly much more widespread, including in Niger, their numbers are now, in that country, very small. In the Middle Ages the Zaghawa—thought to be of nomadic Berber origin and currently speaking a language similar to the **Teda**—controlled much of the trans-Saharan trade and helped in the founding of the Kanem and Gobir kingdoms.

ZAKARA, MOUDDOUR (1916–77). Former **amenokal** of the **Ouilliminden** and important former minister of finance and of Saharan and nomadic affairs, and after 1959 in effect minister resident in Agadez. Born in 1916 in Diguina (Filingué) and eventually (after 1952) the Tuareg chef de canton of Imanan (composed of largely sedentary Tuareg) and amenokal of the Ouilliminden Kel Dinnik (one of the largest Tuareg confederations), Zakara was educated in Niamey and worked as a simple clerk in the colonial treasury (1932–38). He was transferred to Tahoua in 1938, and between 1940 and 1947 he served as Tamasheq interpreter in the Nomad Affairs Division of the colonial government's Tahoua headquarters. Between 1947 and 1957 special agent and representative of the government (after his appointment as chef de canton), Zakara was elected to the Territorial Assembly in 1957 as MSA deputy and in 1959 as UCFA deputy, serving in that body as its vice-president. In 1958 he was brought into the cabinet as secretary of state for interior affairs, a key post, and served in this capacity until 1962. Zakara's responsibilities were enlarged in 1965 to include posts and telecommunications. In 1970 his duties were again redefined as minister of finance, Saharan, and nomadic affairs, and he held these portfolios until the 1974 coup d'état. Descendant of the conqueror and warrior Ahrli, and the amenokal of the Ouilliminden (and hence one of the most important traditional leaders of Niger's Tuareg), Zakara's power in Niger could not be exaggerated, though he chose not to flaunt it. The treasurer of and main figure in the Association of Customary Chiefs in Niger, he participated in various traditional ceremonies, leading the traditional **cure salée** departure of the Ouilliminden livestock in August. In Niamey, too, he was a striking figure, appearing always in his flowing Tuareg robes. After the 1974 coup d'état Zakara was imprisoned for embezzlement of 55 million CFA francs and fiscal fraud of 19 million CFA francs—the second worst offender of the Diori associates. He was serving a jail sentence for those offenses when he fell ill and died in the hospital in May 1977.

ZAMFARA. Principality and ethnic group displaced by the **Gobirawa** upon the latter's own displacement from Aïr with the arrival of new Tuareg waves in the mid-eighteenth century.

ZAWAYA. Religious centers or chapter houses established by the **Sanusiya** brotherhood. The zawayas were centers where proselytizing as well as religious education was carried out. Most of the Sanusiya lodges in the region were in Tibesti, in Chad, though there were several in Kaouar and Damergou.

ZEM. Metalworker caste among the Songhay who, as among numerous other ethnic groups, are credited with supernatural powers and are hence envied while being feared and despised. They are endogamous.

ZENGOU. Zinder's **zongo,** currently an integral quarter of the town. Originally a Tuareg caravan stop and resting area outside Zinder's walls (*see* DAMAGARAM), it is today the town's center and principal commercial quarter with a huge Thursday market. Between the *zengou* and *birni* (the walled inner section of town) there is a residential area and a military camp.

ZERMA. *See* DJERMA.

ZIMA. Priestly caste of the traditional Songhay spirit rites. One is not born into the caste, however, but initiated into it. A zima is a medium who is capable of receiving the **holey** spirits in himself and of serving as a bridge between the human and spirit worlds. Forbidden to intercede with the major spirits, the zima are the priests most in contact with the average person. A "superior" high caste, hereditary, closed, and very secretive zima group, the **sonyanké** are the nobility of the zima, and deal directly with the major deities of the Songhay spirit world.

ZIN. *See* DJINN.

ZINDER. Niger's second largest (formerly third) city and historic capital of the Damagaram Sultanate; also département with a population of just under a million people and encompassing a territory of 152,863 sq km with the dominant ethnic group being Hausa, Fulani, Beri Beri, Manga, Buzu, Tuareg, and Toubou. The département includes the arrondissements of Gouré, Magaria, Matamayé, Mirria, and Tanout, and the poste administratif of Damagaram-Takaya. As Niger's prime, indeed only, major city in the immediate precolonial era, the town served for a while as the capital of the colony (1911–26).

Despite the relocation of the capital to Niamey—908 km to the west—Zinder remains the second of three focal points of Niger (Niamey of the Djerma, Zinder of the Hausa, and Agadez of the Tuareg), squarely in the center of Niger's peanut-growing region (centered actually around nearby Maradi) and with the country's second largest cattle market after **Barmou.** During the precolonial era an important terminus of the trans-Saharan caravan trials, Zinder rose to prominence slowly as a result of the expansion of the Damagaram Sultanate (*see* DAMAGARAM). It greatly benefited in the nineteenth century from the shift in caravan trade away from Katsina to Kano consequent to the Fulani conquests of Othman Dan Fodio. It also possessed a developed "double" slave market to which many suppliers flocked (the kingdom's two biggest slave markets were both in Zinder—at **Zengou** and Birni), shipping northward once a year (to Fezzan via Aïr) more than 3,000 slaves, and receiving guns from the coast. With the repression in the first decade of French rule, coupled with the collapse of the caravan trade (which had already begun to bypass Zinder in the latter decades of the nineteenth century), the town's importance declined, though it was to see a commercial revival starting in the 1950s.

Zinder is located 908 km from Niamey, 488 km from Agadez, and 604 km from N'Guigmi. The oldest part of the town is the *birni,* the old walled city, which is still surrounded by remnants of **Tanimoun's** massive ramparts, a tourist site. One kilometer from it (the separating area is filled in by the "modern" urban sprawl of residential areas and a military camp) is **Zengou,** which was once a Tuareg caravan stop and residence. Today it is Zinder's liveliest commercial center. Dominating the town is Fort **Cazemajou,** since independence renamed Camp Tanimoun. The town numbered only 9,200 people in 1951, but the population climbed to over 33,000 by 1971, overtook Maradi as the second largest city in Niger around 1980, and currently stands at around 90,000. For a long time Zinder—and not Niamey—was the principal headquarters of the various European trading houses purchasing Niger's commercial crops (cotton, peanuts), though today most have relocated their headquarters to Niamey while retaining branches in Zinder. Within the *birni* the tombs of three former sultans can be found—Tanimoun, Hanatari, and Moustapha. The city has a big Thursday market and is a major artisan center.

ZODI, IKHIA. Educator, early political leader, and former cabinet minister. Of Tuareg origins and one time director of IFAN (Niamey), Zodi was an early party militant in the PPN. In 1946–47 he joined in the groundswell of opposition in the party that gave rise to the UNIS faction and later political party. One of its prime leaders despite his youth, his attempt in 1955 to force the party to affiliate internationally with the IOM split the party apart and resulted in the desertion of most of its leaders and membership. Some time later the party changed its name (to FDN) and affiliated with IOM's successor, the Convention Africaine (*see* POLITICAL PARTIES). Earlier, Zodi had secured his election to the French National Assembly (beating Diori in 1951) and in 1952 was elected Territorial Assembly deputy from Filingué, and between 1952 and 1957 he sat on the Grand Council of the AOF. In December 1958, he made his peace with PPN and was integrated into Diori's cabinet as minister of education, youth, and sports. In December 1960 he was appointed minister of state in charge of national defense. It was in that role that he was implicated in the 1963–64 anti-Diori attempted coup (*see* DIALLO, HASSAN A.), purged, sentenced to death, and with the sentence commuted, imprisoned in a military camp in the south. He was not released from prison until February

1971. For all practical purposes, Zodi's driving ambition brought his early promising career to a standstill. He has played no significant role in Niger since.

ZONGO. Throughout most of West Africa, and parts of Equatorial Africa, the "temporary" residence of strangers. The zongo is often outside the village or town proper. (Often with rapid urbanization the zongo finds itself swallowed up, becoming the center of the town.) In general, however, it is a separate and distinct quarter altogether, which in larger zongos is divided internally along ethnic lines. The term means "thorn enclosure" implying temporary living quarters, as opposed to habitation within the **birni,** or fortified city. Of Niger's various zongos, that of Zinder is by far the most important (*see* ZENGOU). In Niamey a zongo quarter has existed since 1936 (though a serkin zongo has existed since 1906). It sprang up next to the town's then only market (today's Petit Marché).

ZOUME, BOUBE (1951–). Poet. One of Niger's new generation of poets, Zoumé was born in Caya on December 30, 1951, to a Sorko fishing family. He was educated in Niamey and obtained a diploma from the National School of Administration. While pursuing a minor administrative career, Zoumé wrote several collections of poetry that were published in Paris.

Bibliography

As is true for much of Francophone Africa, most of the literature on Niger is in French. The bibliography that follows, though comprehensive, stresses in particular the social sciences. Though a considerable amount of research has accumulated on Niger, the quantity camouflages the existence of serious gaps in several fields and the contemporary nature of much of it. Not a single book on Niger was published between 1927 and 1952, for example, and for the last phase of the colonial period (1945–60) the material available is hardly satisfactory. It is for this reason that the series of monographs entitled *Etudes Nigériennes* (jointly published in Niamey and Paris), though they tend to stress history and ethnology, are invaluable, since they fill some of these gaps. The bibliographic notes that follow aim at providing a brief guide to some of the more significant literature in several of the categories into which the bibliography is divided.

In the "Archaeology and Prehistory" section, the published works of Paul Huard, Henri Hugot, and Henri Lhote are both voluminous and seminal. Hugot has also reported on the 1960 Berliet-Ténéré scientific expedition, and Lhote on the discovery of the site of the ancient Tadeliza (see his article in *Notes Africaines* [1973] under this heading). Also worth noting is the research by Mauny and De Zeltner.

On the early explorations of Niger, many articles have been written by military officers and administrators who participated in the territory's conquest and early administration. Though not including much material specific to Niger, the massive volumes by Heinrich Barth—*Travels and Discoveries in North and Central Africa*—are strongly recommended, as well as those by Gustav Nachtigal, *Sahara and Sudan*.

Many excellent works exist in the fields of anthropology and ethnology, and much additional research accumulates yearly in these fields. Of particular note is the fact that by now a number of outstanding works exist in English (especially those by Stoller). In general, however, some of Niger's ethnic groups, notably the Tuareg, continue to receive an inordinate amount of attention, while others still tend to be less studied.

The two studies by Briggs (in English) are seminal on the populations of the Sahara (including the Toubou), as are the works by Capot-Rey and Chapelle on the same groupings. Ligers has published extensively on the Sorko; Jean Rouch on the Songhay; and of great importance are the studies of Marguerite Dupire on Niger's Fulani (including her solid *Peuls Nomads*). This last is directly comparable with Stenning's book in English on the Wodaabe Fulani.

On Niger's Hausa (who constitute over one-half of the population), Guy Nicholas's many works are all-encompassing and can be supplemented by Claude Reynaut's, especially his microstudy, *Structure Normatives et Relations Electives: Etude d'une communauté villageoise Hausa*. For the country's Maouri, the work of Marc Henri Piault is unrivaled, while Colette Piault's study of the life of traditional Maouri women spans several disciplines in its breadth. For both the Kurtey and Wogo, the studies of Olivier de Sardan constitute the best introduction. Cline's English-language monograph on the Teda branch of the Toubou is also valuable.

When one approaches the study of the Tuareg, who have been particularly fascinating to French scholarship, one is faced with a truly voluminous body of research that is regularly being augmented. In view of the modest numbers of the Tuareg, this is even more impressive. Numerous excellent studies abound, and any selection here would perforce be highly idiosyncratic. Of particular note, however, would be the works of Edmond Bernus. His *Les Illabakan,* for example, is a solid microstudy, and his monumental *Touaregs Nigériens* (1981) is the definitive work on this ethnic group. Also noteworthy are his *Quelques aspects de l'évolution des Touareg de l'Ouest de la République du Niger,* and his joint work with Suzanne Bernus on the salt pan oases of In Gall and Teguida (*Du Sel et des Dates*), which is fascinating. Chapelle's many briefer reports, including one on the Tuareg, are also useful though not easily accessible, as they must be examined in the CHEAM archives in Paris. The Danish scholar Nicolaisen has also published some noteworthy work in English on the Tuareg, including his articles in *Folk* (Copenhagen) and his large *Ecology and Culture of the Pastoral Tuareg*. Francis Nicholas is yet another prolific scholar of world renown who has contributed much outstanding material on the Tuareg. For one earlier study, still of great use today, see Urvoy's seminal "Histoire des Ouilliminden de l'Est." More recently, Hélène Claudot-Hawad has contributed some important work on the Tuareg.

In the "Sociology and Demography" section of this Bibliography, Suzanne Bernus's study of Niamey is sadly outdated by the major expansion of the capital since 1960, but is nevertheless practically the only study of its kind and is a solid piece of research. Nicole Echard, whose work spans several subfields, has also written much of interest on the sociology of the Ader region.

There are numerous good works in the "History" section. Any discussion of this subfield needs to note the many contributions by Boubou Hama, the prolific former president of Niger's National Assembly, who was not just one of the trio ruling Niger for two decades, but an avid scholar and writer as well. His books, by now mostly out of print at *Présence Africaine* in Paris, tend to be long, rambling, and disjointed, but they contain invaluable material especially on oral history and tradition. They range from studies of the Fulani to the Hausa, Songhay, Djerma, and Tuareg. The two American books by Stephen Baier and Roberta Dunbar on the Sultanate of Damagaram (and especially its political economy) are extremely useful, and not only because they are in English. Sir Herbert Palmer's, A. Adu Boahan's, and E. William Bovill's works on trans-Saharan trade patterns and the Sahara-Sudan in previous centuries should need no introduction to Africanists. Though their major focus is on the trade itself, and regions outside contemporary Niger, since one terminal of the caravan trade was in Niger, their books are vital to any understanding of the outside factors affecting Niger. In this connection one could also refer to the excellent 1986 study by Paul Lovejoy on salt production and salt trade in the Sahara.

David's study of Maradi is one of the best concise histories of this city-state. Finn Fugelstad's articles fill several important gaps as well, and his *History of Niger, 1850–1960,* though much too concise to reveal the richness of the primary data available, remains a good synthesis in the English language of Niger's recent history. (See also his contributions under "Politics.") In like manner, Rash (a former Israeli ambassador to Niger) has written a good monograph on France's role in the Damergou interclan Tuareg rivalry at the turn of the century. André Salifou's *Le Damagaram ou Sultanat de Zinder au XIXe siècle* is possibly the best single-volume study of this kingdom. Salifou has written another invaluable study on the Aïr rebellion during the First World War—*Kaoussan ou la révolte senoussite*—which surprisingly is one of very few recent reanalyses of the siege of Agadez. He has written on other historical themes, such as the Fihroun rebellion and Malan Yaro, one of the key leaders of Damagaram at the time of the French conquest. And, in 1992, as both historian and a politician, he wrote a book on the Tuareg as a rebuttal to their grievances, as documented by one of the leaders of the Tuareg rebellion of the 1990s, Mano Dayak. Gregoire's work on the Hausa merchants of Maradi is one of the first such studies in general, and it is all the more valuable in that it was translated into English in 1992. Finally, Séré de Rivières's *Histoire du Niger,* though weak on the more contemporary era, is the best single-volume introduction to Niger in general, containing chapters on the geography, ethnology, and history of the country. One could also note here Urvoy's 1934 article on the historically important Agadez Chronicles.

Much more has been written in English on Niger politics than on other subjects, this having always been a major weakness of French scholarship, anxious not to offend former colonies and their leaders. Still, there is little work, in any language, on the immediate pre-independence era (1945–60), and precious little on the Diori era. By and large, for those interested in post-independence Niger, the best combination of materials would be the books by Séré de Rivières and Fugelstad (noted previously under "History"), the chapters on Niger in *Année Politique Africaine, Année Africaine,* and *Africa Contemporary Record* (the last sadly now no longer being issued), supplemented by American scholarship (the book by Charlick, the chapter by Decalo), and by reports on ongoing developments in the two series of *Africa Research Bulletin, Africa Confidential,* and *West Africa.* As usual, one should refer to *Politique Africaine,* which intermittently comes out with a special volume on an individual country, as it did with no. 38 on Niger.

In the field of economics, a basic research tool supplying much needed raw statistical data that cannot easily be obtained elsewhere is the Central Bank's (BCEAO) quarterly "Indicateurs Economique Nigériens" and other occasional monographs on Niger. Belloncle's writings are invaluable for any discussion of the Niger cooperative movement and the UNCC. The International Monetary Fund has a very dated though solid chapter on Niger in its *Surveys of African Economics.* With the onset of the continentwide economic stagnation and debt crisis in the 1980s, however, there has been a massive spurt of books and articles on economic issues, as attested in the items listed in this section, many of which are in English.

On the Sahel droughts that have intermittenly ravaged Niger, Jean Copans's *Sécheresses et famines du Sahel* has a number of valuable contributions by various scholars (including Raynaut's chapter on the Maradi region, mentioned above), which can be contrasted with Michael Glantz's *Politics of Natural Disaster: The Case of the Sahel Drought.* The political effect of the drought in Niger (leading indirectly to the 1974 coup d'état) is treated in Victor du Bois's *Fieldstaff Reports.* The United Nations Special Sahelian Office has also published several studies in recent years, as have a large number of scholars.

In the section on education, much attention has been focused on Niger's unique (for Africa) experiment with educational television and with radio clubs. A sprinkling of new contributions have appeared more recently as well. The "Science" section is only a sampling of a much more voluminous selection of work available and is dominated by studies on the important 1960 Berliet-Ténéré expedition. Chudeau's works are also noteworthy, as are those by Urvoy—though these are from several decades ago and deal with areas somewhat to the west of the Niger Republic.

Among the studies on African religions and cosmologies, one can note the many studies on the Bori cult and the Azna Hausa, especially by Besmer, Broustra-Monfouga, and Jacqueline Nicholas, including the last's *'Juments' des Dieux: Rites de possession et condition féminine en pays hausa* and *Ambivalence et culte de possession. Contribution à l'étude du Bori Hausa.* One should also note Stoller's research, in English, which is seminal and has already been cited under "Anthropology."

Niger's literary output is well represented by Dandobi's *Kabrin Kaba* and the various books by Boubou Hama and by the latter in cooperation with Andrée Clair. André Salifou's much-acclaimed play, *Tanimoune,* is no doubt familiar to many, and new books and plays are published intermittently.

The section on linguistics lists many of the standard works on Niger's languages and dialects. The section on the arts includes the comprehensive article by Dieterlen and Ligers on Tuareg jewelry and one by Dupuis and Echard on Ader's pottery. Another noteworthy work is the study by Ligers, *La Sculpture Nigérienne.*

The prospective tourist has by now a more than adequate selection of material from which to chose in English. Among the French titles, Bourget's *Fascinant Niger* is particularly good.

Among the best continuing sources for the further study of Niger are *Africa Research Bulletin, Année Politique Africaine,* and the occasional articles on Niger that appear in *Politique Africaine, West Africa,* and *Africa Confidential.*

The books and articles in this bibliography have been organized under the following subject headings:

General Works

Afrique Occidentale Française. 2 vols. Paris: Encyclopédie Coloniale et Maritime, 1949.

Blanguernon, Claude. *Le Hoggar*. Paris: Arthaud, 1955.

Bourges, Hervé, and Claude Wauthier. *Les 50 Afriques*. Paris: Le Seuil, 1979.

Brass, William. "The Demography of the French-Speaking Territories." In A. J. Coale (ed.), *The Demography of Tropical Africa*. Princeton, N.J.: Princeton University Press, 1968, pp. 342–439.

Brunschwig, Henri. *Le Partage de l'Afrique Noire*. Paris: Flammarion, 1971.

Chailley, Marcel. *Les Grandes Missions Françaises en Afrique Occidentale*. Dakar: IFAN, 1953.

———. *Historie de l'Afrique Occidentale Française*. Paris: Berger-Levrault, 1968.

Corbett, Edward M. *The French Presence in Black Africa*. Washington, D.C.: Black Orpheus Press, 1972.

Cornevin, Robert. *Historie de l'Afrique*. 2 vols. Paris: Payot, 1967.

———. *Histoire des Peuples de l'Afrique Noire*. Paris: Berger-Levrault, 1960.

Delavignette, Robert. *Afrique Occidentale Française*. Paris: Editions Géographiques, Maritimes et Coloniales, 1931.

Deloncle, Pierre. *L'Afrique Occidentale Française: Découverte, Pacification, Mise en Valeur*. Paris: Editions Ernest Leroux, 1934.

Deschamps, H. *Histoire Générale de l'Afrique Noire*. 2 vols. Paris: Presses Universitaires de France, 1970–71.

Dossiers Niger. Paris: Recontres Africaines, 1988.

Englebert, Victor. *The Goats of Agadez*. New York: Harcourt Brace Jovanovich, 1973.

Fage, J. D. *An Introduction to the History of West Africa*. Cambridge: Cambridge University Press, 1959.

Finley, Diana. *The Niger*. London: Macdonald Education, 1975.

Food and Agricultural Organization. *FAO Africa Survey*. Rome, 1961.

France. Ministère de la Coopération. *Etude Monographique de trente et un pays Africains*. 4 vols. Paris, 1965.

Gann, L. H., and P. Duignan (eds.). *Colonialism in Africa, 1870–1960*. 4 vols. London: Cambridge University Press, 1969+.
Gardi, René. *Sahara*. Bern: Kümmerly et Frey, 1969.
Gautier, E. F. *L'Afrique Noire Occidentale*. Paris: Larose, 1935.
———. *Le Sahara*. Paris: Payot, 1948.
Gouzy, René. *Du Leman au Niger par le Sahara*. Geneva: A. Jullien, 1935.
Green, Scott, et al. *The New Urbanization*. New York: St. Martin's Press, 1967.
Hallett, Robin. *Africa to 1875; A Modern History*. Ann Arbor: University of Michigan Press, 1970.
Hance, William A. *Geography of Modern Africa*. New York: Columbia University Press, 1967.
Hänny, E. R. *Vom Sudan zum Mittelmeer*. Saint Gall: Verlag Zollikofer & Co., 1944.
Hanotlaux, G., and A. Martineau. *Histoire des Colonies Françaises*. 6 vols. Paris: Plon, 1932.
Jenness, Aylette. *Along the Niger River: An African Way of Life*. New York: Crowell, 1974.
Kimble, George H. T. *Tropical Africa*. 2 vols. New York: Twentieth Century Fund, 1960.
Kitchen, Helen. *A Handbook of African Affairs*. London: Pall Mall, 1964.
Klotchkoff, Jean-Claude. *Le Niger aujourd'hui*. Paris: Editions Jeune Afrique, 1982.
Lusignan, G. de. *French-Speaking Africa Since Independence*. London: Pall Mall, 1969.
MacArthur, Wilson. *The Desert Watches*. Indianopolis, Ind.: Bobbs-Merrill, 1954.
Martel, André. "Pour une Histoire de Sahara Français." *Revue Française d'Histoire d'Outre-Mer* 55, no. 200 (1968):335–51.
Martin, Gaston. *Histoire de l'Esclavage dans les colonies françaises*. Paris: Presses Universitaires de France, 1948.
Meillassoux, Claude. *L'Esclavage en Afrique précoloniale*. Paris: Maspero, 1975.
Moberg, G. *Rädslansland 16,000 kilometer genom Sahara och Sudan*. Stockholm: A. Bonnier, 1927.
Morgan, Ted. *The Strong Brown God: The Story of the Niger River*. Boston: Houghton Mifflin, 1976.
Morgenthau, Ruth Schachter. *Political Parties in French-Speaking West Africa*. Oxford: Oxford University Press, 1964.
Mourgues, Gaston. *Le Moyen Niger et sa Boucle*. Paris: Comité de l'Afrique Française, 1933.
"Niger." Special section in *Jeune Afrique*, no. 953 (Apr. 12, 1979).

"Niger." Special issue of *Europe Outre-Mer* 59, no. 624 (1982).
Olkes, Cheryl. "Information-Seeking with Mass Media in the Republic of Niger." Ph.D. diss., University of Texas, 1978.
Richard-Molard, J. *Afrique Occidentale Française*. Paris: Berger-Levrault, 1949.
Roucek, J. S. "The Niger and Its People." *New Africa* 7, no. 8/9 (1965):9–10, 23.
Sarraut, A. *Le Mise en valeur des colonies françaises*. Paris: Payot, 1953.
Spitz, G. *L'Ouest Africain Français*. Paris: Editions Géographiques, Maritimes et Coloniales, 1947.
Stride, G. T., and Caroline Ifeka. *Peoples and Empires of West Africa*. New York: Africana, 1971.
Suret-Canale, J. *L'Afrique Noire Occidentale et Centrale*. 2 vols. Paris: Editions Sociales, 1972.
Tenaille, Frank. *Les 56 Afriques*. 2 vols. Paris: Maspero, 1979.
Thompson, Virginia. *West Africa's Council of the Entente*. Ithaca, N.Y.: Cornell University Press, 1972.
———, and Richard Adloff. *French West Africa*. Stanford, Calif.: Stanford University Press, 1957.

Archaeology and Prehistory

Alionen, H. *Préhistoire de l'Afrique*. Paris: N. Boubée & Cie., 1955.
Ba, Amadou Hampaté, and G. Dièterlen. "Les fresques d'époque bovidienne du Tassili, N'Agger et les traditions des Peul; hypothèses d'interprétation." *Journal de la Société des Africanistes* 36, no. 1 (1966): 141–157.
Beltrami, Vanni. "Repertorio dei monumenti cosiddetti 'pre-Islamici' presenti nel territorio dell'Air ed aree limitrofe." *Africa* (Rome) 34, no. 4 (1979):417–23.
———. "Repertori delle stazioni paleolitiche e neolitiche dell'Air e delle regioni circostanti." *Africa* (Rome) 35, no. 3/4 (1980):489–504.
———. *Repertorio preistorico-archeologico del territorio dell'Air ed aree limitrofe*. Rome: Istituto Italo-Africano, 1987.
Bernus, S., and P. L. Gouletquer. "Approche archéologique de la Région d'Azalik et de Tegidda n Tesemt." Paris: CNRS, 1974.
———. "Die Salinen von Tegidda n Tesemt." *Ethnographisch-archäologische Zeitschrift,* no. 16 (1976):209–36.
———. "Du Cuivre au Sel, recherches ethnoarchéologiques sur la région d'Azelik." *Journal des Africanistes* 46, no. 1/2 (1976):7–68.
Binet, C. "Notes sur les ruines de Garoumélé (Niger)." *Notes Africaines,* no. 53 (Jan. 1952):1–2.
Bouesnard, L., and R. Mauny. "Gravures rupestres et sites néolithiques des abords est de l'Aïr." *Bulletin d'IFAN* (ser. B) 24, no. 1/2 (Jan.–Apr. 1962):1–11.

Brouin, G. "Du nouveau au sujet de Takedda." *Notes Africaines,* no. 47 (1950):90–91.

———. "Un îlot de vieille civilisation africaine: le pays de Ouacha (Niger Française)." *Bulletin du Comité d'Etudes Historiques et Scientifiques de l'AOF* 21, no. 4 (Oct.–Dec. 1938):469–79.

———. *Le pays de Ouacha (Niger Française).* Paris: Larose, 1938.

Camps, Gabriel. "Le chars sahariens: Images d'une société aristocratique." *Antiquités Africaines* (Paris) 25 (1989):11–40.

———. "Ten Years of Archaeological Research in the Sahara, 1965–1975." *West African Journal of Archaeology* 7 (1977):1–15.

Castro, R. "Examen de creusets de Marandet (Niger)." *Bulletin d'IFAN* (ser. B) 36, no. 4 (Oct. 1974):667–75.

Chamla, M. C. *Les Populations anciennes du Sahara et des régions limitrophes. Etudes des restes osseux humaine néolithiques et protohistoriques.* Paris: Arts et Métiers Graphiques, 1968.

Chantret, F., R. de Bayle des Hermens, and H. Merle. "Deux nouveaux gisements néolithiques de la région d'Agadès: Ibadanan et Ntarhalgé." *Notes Africaines,* no. 132 (Oct. 1971):85–93.

———. "Le Gisement préhistorique de Madaouéla, République du Niger." *Bulletin de la Société Préhistorique Française* 65 (1968): 623–28.

Chudeau, René. "Les monuments lithiques du Sahara." *Anthropologie* 30, (1920):111–14.

Clark, J. Desmond. "An Archeological Survey of Northern Aïr and Ténéré." *Geographical Journal* 137, no. 4 (1971):455–57.

———. "Human Populations and Cultural Adaptation in the Sahara and Nile During Prehistoric Times." In Martin A. J. Williams (ed.), *The Sahara and the Nile Quaternary Environments and Prehistoric Occupation in Northern Africa.* Rotterdam: Balkema, 1980, pp. 527–82.

Close, Angela A. "Current Research and Recent Radiocarbon Dates from Northern Africa." *Journal of African History* 29, no. 2 (1988): 143–76.

Courtin, J. "Le Ténéréen du Borkou, Nord Tchad." In *La Préhistoire, problèmes et tendances.* Paris: CNRS, 1968, pp. 133–38.

De Beauchêne, Guy. "Niger 1963: Recherches archéologiques." *Objets et Mondes* 6, no. 1 (1966):69–80.

———. "Nomades d'il y a 5000 ans." *Niger* (Niamey), no. 1 (Oct. 1967):47–50.

———. "Prehistory and Archeology in Niger, Togo, Upper Volta, Dahomey and Ivory Coast." *West African Archeological Newsletter* (Nov. 5, 1966):6–8.

———. "Recherches archéologiques au Niger en 1966." *Actes du Premier Colloque Internationale d'Archéologie Africaine (Fort-Lamy)* (1969):50–61.

Desplagnes, L. "Une mission archéologique dans la vallée du Niger." *Géographie* 13 (1906):81–90.

De Zeltner, Franz. "Des Dessins sur les rochers à Aïr qui appartient au territoire des Touareg." *Anthropologie* 23 (1912):101–4; 24 (1913): 171–84.

———. "Les gravures rupestres de l'Aïr." *Anthropologie* (1916): 171–84.

———. "Objets en pierre polié de l'Aïr." *Anthropologie* (1910):21–27.

———. "Objets en pierre polié de l'Aïr." *Bulletin et Mémoire de la Société d'Anthropologie de Paris* (1912):394–97.

Echellier, J. C., and S. P. Roset. "La céramique des gisements de Taqalaqal et de l'Adrar Bousio." *Cahiers des Sciences Humaines* 22, no. 2 (1986):151–58.

Fagan, B. M. "Radiocarbon Dates from Sub-Saharan Africa." *Journal of African History* 8 (1967).

Faure, Hugues. "Disque néolithique trouvé dans la région du Nord-Est de l'Adrar Bous (Niger)." *Notes Africaines* (Oct. 1960):110–11.

———. "Sur quelques dépôts du Quaternaire du Ténéré." *Comptes Rendu de l'Académie des Sciences* 249, no. 25 (1959):2807–9.

———, et al. "Formations lacustres du Quaternaire supérieur du Niger oriental." *Bulletin du Bureau de Recherches Geologiques,* no. 2 1963.

Feger. "Note sur les pyramides de pierre de la région de Konni (Niger)." *Notes Africaines* no. 29 (Jan. 1946):5.

Franz, H. "On the Stratigraphy and Evolution of Climate in the Chad Basin During the Quaternary." In *Background to Evolution in Africa.* Chicago: University of Chicago Press, 1967, pp. 273–83.

Gallay, Alain. "Peintures rupestres récentes du bassin du Niger." *Journal de la Société des Africanistes* 34, no. 1 (1964):123–39.

Gardi, René, and Jolantha Neukom-Tscudi. *Peintures rupestres du Sahara.* Lausanne: Payot, 1962.

Gironcourt, Georges de. "Les inscriptions lithiques du Niger et de l'Adrar." In *Bulletin de la Section Géographique du Ministère d'Information Publique.* Paris, 1914.

Grebenart, D. "Néolithique final et âge des métaux au Niger, près d'Agadez." *Anthropologie* 89, no. 3 (1985):337–50.

———. "Note sur deux gravures rupestres de l'Aïr, Niger." *Notes Africaines,* no. 157 (Jan. 1978):1–2.

———. *La région d'In Gall–Tegidda n'Tesemt. Niger: Programme archéologique d'urgence. 1977– 1981.* Niamey: IRSH, 1985.

Greiget, J. "Description des formations retracées et tertiares du bassin des Iullemeden." Paris: BRGM, 1966.

Huard, Paul. "Contribution à l'étude des spirales au Sahara central et nigéro-tchadien." *Bulletin de la Société Préhistorique Française* 63, no. 2 (1966):433–64.

———. "Gravures rupestres des confins nigéro-tchadiens." *Bulletin d'IFAN* 15, no. 4 (1953):1569–81.

———. "Nouvelles gravures rupestres du Djado, de l'Afafi et du Tibesti." *Bulletin d'IFAN* (ser. B) 19, no. 1/2 (1957):184–223.

———, G. Breaud, and J. M. Massip, "Répertoire des sites paléolithiques du Sahara central, tchadien et oriental." *Bulletin d'IFAN* (ser. B) 31, no. 3 (1969):853–74.

———, and G. Feval. "Figurations rupestres des confins Algéro-Nigéro-Tchadiens." *Travaux de l'Institut de Recherches Sahariennes* 23, (1964):61–94.

———, and L. Leonardi. "Nouvelles gravures rupestres des chasseurs du Fezzan méridional, du Djado et du Tibesti." *Rivista di Scienze Prehistoriche* 21, no. 1 (1966):135–56.

———, and J. M. Massip. "Monuments du Sahara nigéro-tchadien." *Bulletin d'IFAN* (ser. B) 29, no. 1/2 (1967):1–27.

———. "Nouveaux centres de peintures rupestres au Sahara nigéro-tchadien." *Bulletin d'IFAN* (ser. B) 28, no. 1/2 (Jan.–Apr. 1966): 44–81.

———, and B. Rosso. "Grands outils de pierre polié du Sahara nigéro-tchadien." *Bulletin de la Société Préhistorique Française* 65, no. 2 (Feb. 1968):629–41.

———, and Mark Milburn. "Nouvelles stations rupestres de confins nigéro-algériens." *Bulletin d'IFAN* 40, no. 1 (1978):1–14.

Hugot, Henri J. "Au sujet de l'Atérien du Ténéré." *Bulletin de la Société Préhistorique Française* 60 (1963):149–51.

———. *Mission Berliet Ténéré-Tchad.* Paris: Arts et Métiers Graphiques, 1962.

———. "Les missions Berliet au Sahara (1960)." *Libyca* 8 (1960): 323–35.

———. "Une nouvelle date pour le néolithique saharien: celle du Ténéréen." *Libyca* 8 (1960):259–60.

———. "Premier aperçu sur la préhistoire du Ténéré du Tafassasset." *Documents Scientifiques du Mission Berliet.* Paris: Arts et Métiers Graphiques, 1962, pp. 149–78.

———. *Le Sahara avant le désert.* Toulouse: Editions des Hesperides, 1974.

———, and R. Mauny. "Prises de dates résultant des travaux de la mission Berliet-Ténéré." *Bulletin de la Société Préhistorique Française* 65, no. 5/6 (1960):270–72.

Joleaud, L. "Vertèbres subfossils de l'Azaoua." *Comptes Rendu de l'Académie des Sciences* (1934):599–601.

Joubert, C., and R. Vaufrey. "Le néolithique du Ténéré." *Anthropologie* 50 (1941–46):325–30.

Kelessi, Mahamadou. *Etat actuel des recherches sur le néolithique dans l'Aïr et ses régions adjacentes*. Niamey: Université de Niamey, 1987.

Kelley, Harper. "Harpons, objets en os, travailles et silex taillés de Taferjit et Tamaya Mellet (Sahara nigérien)." *Journal de la Société des Africanistes* (1934):135–43.

Killick, D., et al. "Reassessment of the Evidence for Early Metallurgy in Niger, West Africa." *Journal of Archeological Science* 15, no. 4 (1988):367–94.

Laforgue, P. "Quelques objets néolithiques du Niger." *Bulletin du Comité d'Etudes Historiques et Scientifiques de l'AOF* 21 (1938): 147–48.

Lapparent, A. F. de. "Reconnaissance des gisements à dinosauriens du Tamesna." *Travaux de L'Institut de Recherches Sahariennes* 10 (1953).

———. "Les dinosaures du Sahara central." *Travaux de l'Institut de Recherches Sahariennes* 19, no. 1/2 (1960):7–24.

Law, R. C. C. "Garamantes and Trans-Saharan Enterprise in Classical Times." *Journal of African History* 8, no. 2 (1967);181–200.

Lebeuf, Jean Paul. *Carte Archéologique des abords du lac Tchad*. Paris: CNRS, 1969.

Le Coeur, Charles. "Une chambre des hôtes de la ville morte de Djado." *Notes Africaines,* no. 43 (Oct. 1943):9–10.

Lhote, Henri. "Découverte de chars de guerre en Aïr." *Notes Africaines,* no. 127 (July 1970):83–85.

———. "Découverte des ruines de Tadeliza, ancienne résidence des sultans de l'Aïr." *Notes Africaines,* no. 137 (Jan. 1973):9–15.

———. *L'Epopée du Ténéré*. Paris: Gallimard, 1961.

———. *Les Gravures de Nord-Ouest de l'Aïr*. Paris: Arts et Métiers Graphiques, 1972.

———. "Gravures, peintures et inscriptions repéres du Kaouar, de l'Aïr et de l'Adrar des Iforas." *Bulletin d'IFAN* 14, no. 4 (Oct. 1952): 1268–1340.

———. "La Mission Berliet-Ténéré." *Europe France Outre-Mer,* no. 363 (Feb. 1960) 20–23.

———. "Note complémentaire au sujet du puits à balancier en Aïr." *Encyclopédie Berbère* (Aix en Provence), 1972.

———. "Nouvelle contribution à l'étude des gravures et peintures rupestres au Sahara central: La station du Tit (Ahaggar)." *Journal de la Société des Africanistes* 29, no. 2 (1959):147–92.

———. "Nouvelle contribution à l'histoire des sultans de l'Aïr." *Notes Africaines,* no. 148 (Oct. 1975):102–9.

———. "Les peintures pariétales d'époque bovidienne du Tassili: éléments sur la magie et la religion." *Journal de la Société des Africanistes* 36, no. 1 (1966):7–27.

———. "Pierres dressées à Tadeliza, en Aïr, et monuments lithiques de la même région." *Notes Africaines,* no. 138 (Apr. 1973):29–35.

———. "Problèmes touaregs." *Encyclopédie Mensuelle d'Outre-Mer,* no. 44 (Apr. 1954):109–13.

———. "Quelques coutumes en usage chez les Kel Oui." In *Contribution à l'étude de l'Aïr*. Paris: Larose, 1950, pp. 504–7.

———. "Recherches sur Takedda, ville décrite par le voyageur Ibn Battouta et situé en Aïr." *Bulletin d'IFAN* (ser. B) 34, no. 3 (1972): 430–70.

———. "Route antique du Sahara Centrale." *Encyclopédie Mensuelle d'Outre-Mer* 1, no. 15 (1951):300–305.

———. "Saharan Rock Art." *Natural History* 69, no. 6 (June–July 1960):28–43.

———. "Les salines du Sahara: La saline de Taguidda-n-tisemt." *Terre et la Vie* 3, no. 12 (Dec. 1933).

———. "Les sandales." In *Contribution à l'étude de l'Aïr*. Paris: Larose, 1950, pp. 512–33.

———. "Au sujet du Port du voile chez les Touareg et les Tedah." *Notes Africaines,* no. 52 (Oct. 1951):108–11.

———. "La technique de la poterie à Agadez." In *Contribution à l'étude de l'Aïr*. Paris: Larose, 1950, pp. 507–12.

———, and Paul Huard. "Gravures rupestres de l'Aïr." *Bulletin d'IFAN* (ser. B) 27, no. 3/4 (July–Oct. 1965):445–78.

———, et al. *Les gravures du pourtour occidental et du centre de l'Aïr*. Paris: Editions Recherche sur les Civilisations, 1987.

Maley, J., et al. "Nouveaux gisements préhistoriques au Niger oriental." *Bulletin ASEOUA,* no. 31/32 (1971):9–18.

Mascarelli, M., and R. Mauny. "Découverte d'un biface de longeur exceptionelle au Kaouar." *Notes Africaines,* no. 70 (Apr. 1956):38–39.

Mauny, R. "Contribution à la préhistoire de l'Aïr." In *Contribution à l'étude de l'Aïr*. Paris: Larose, 1950, pp. 537–40.

———. "Découverte d'un atelier de fonte du cuire à Marandet (Niger)." *Notes Africaines,* no. 58 (Apr. 1953):33–35.

———. "Etat actuel de nos connaissances sur la préhistoire de la colonie du Niger." *Bulletin d'IFAN* 11, no. 1/2 (Jan.–Mar. 1949):141–58.

———. "Objets subactuels en fer trouvés en pays Teda et à l'est de l'Aïr." *Notes Africaines,* no. 97 (Jan. 1963):24–25.

———, and Maurice Colombel. "Découverte de nouveaux sites rupestres au Kawar (Niger)." *Notes Africaines,* no. 113 (Jan. 1967): 15–16.

Milburn, Mark. "Aïr Occidental: essai de chronologie relative de quelques monuments lithiques." *Almogaren* (Hallein) 7 (1976):147–54.

———. "On Pre- and Protohistory of Ténéré Tafassasset." *Leba* (Lisbon) 6 (1987):37–60.

Monod, Théodore. *Contributions à l'étude du Sahara occidental. Gravures, peintures et inscriptions rupestres*. Paris: Larose, 1938.

Morris, R. W. B., and Mark Milburn. "Some Cup-and-Ring Marks of Western Aïr." *Almogaren* (Hallein) 7 (1976):143–45.

Mourgues, Gaston. "Gravures rupestres chez les Touaregs nigériens." *Afrique Française* 44, no. 8 (Aug. 1934):145–48.

Nicolas, Francis. "Inscriptions et gravures rupestres." In *Contribution à l'étude de l'Aïr*. Paris: Larose, 1950, pp. 541–51.

Niger '86: Viaggio nella preistorica. Milan: Centro Studi Archeologica Africana, 1987.

Pedrals, Denis Pierre de. *Archéologie de l'Afrique Noire: Nubie, Ethiopie, Niger sahélien, L'Aïr tchadien. Niger inférieur* . . . Paris: Payot, 1950.

Poncet, Yveline. *La Région d'In Gall. Tegidda n Tesemt*. Niamey: IRSH, 1983.

Posnansky, Marrick, and Roderick McIntosh. "New Radiocarbon Dates for Northern and Western Africa." *Journal of African History* 17, no. 2 (1976):161–96.

Prevost, Marius, and Lucien Mayet. "L'Oasis du Kaouar et la préhistoire du Sahara oriental." *Nature,* no. 2658 (Mar. 15, 1925):161–68.

Quéchon, G. "Groupements de lances néolithiques de la région de Termit." *Cahiers des Sciences Humaines* 22, no. 2 (1986):203–16.

———, and J. P. Roset. "Prospection archéologique du massif de Termit (Niger)." *Cahiers d'ORSTOM* 11, no. 1 (1974):85–104.

Regelsperger, G. "Du Niger au Tchad. La Mission Tilho." *Mois Colonial et Maritime* 1 (1909):97–109.

La Région d'In Gall Tegidda n Tesemt: Programme archéologique d'urgence, 1977–1981. Niamey: IRSH, 1985.

Reygasse, M. "Le Ténéréen: Observations sur un faciès nouveau du Néolithique des confins algéro-soudanais." In *Congrès Préhistorique de France. XIe session, Periqueux 1934*. Paris: SPF, 1935, pp. 577–84.

Rodd, F. R. "Some Rock-Drawings from Aïr in the Southern Sahara." *Journal of the Royal Anthropological Institute* 68, (1938):99–111.

Roset, Jean-Pierre. "Art rupestre en Aïr." *Archaélogia* (Paris), no. 39 (Mar.–Apr. 1971):24–31.

———. "Deux Modes d'inhumation néolithique au Niger." *Cahiers d'ORSTOM* 14, no. 3 (1977):325–30.

———. "Une meul néolithique ornée du Ténéré." *Archaélogia,* no. 58 (1973):66–68.

———. "Un gisement néolithique ancien près de Faci (Erg du Ténéré)." *Cahiers d'ORSTOM* 11, no. 1 (1974):105–10.

Rouch, Jean. "Gravures rupestres de Kourki (Niger)." *Bulletin d'IFAN* (1949):34–53.

Roy, A. "Vestiges de Takedda, ancienne capitale des Igdalens, centre minier et caravanier d l'Aïr au XIVe siècle." *Notes Africaines,* no. 29 (Jan. 1946):5–6.

Ruhlmann, Armand. "Le Ténéréen." *Bulletin de la Société de Préhistoire du Maroc* (1936):3–15.

Rumeur. "Le témoin d'une civilisation disparue dans le Cercle de Tahoua." *Bulletin du Comité des Etudes Historiques et Scientifiques de l'AOF* 16, no. 2 (Apr.–June 1933):299–318.

Schobel, Jürgen. *Ammoniten der Familie Vascoceratidae aus dem Unteren des Damergou-Gebietes. République du Niger*. Uppsala: Palaeontological Institution of the University of Uppsala, 1975.

Smith, Andrew B. "The Neolithic Tradition in the Sahara." In Martin A. J. Williams and Hugues Faure (eds.), *The Sahara and the Nile: Quaternary Environment and Prehistoric Occupation in Northern Africa*. Rotterdam: Balkema, 1980, pp. 451–65.

Spruyette, J. "Les chars et les chevaux de Tamajert." *Bulletin de la Société Royale Belge d'Anthropologie* 76, (1965):73–78.

Tillet, Thierry. *Le Paléolithique du bassin tchadien septentrional*. Paris: CNRS, 1983.

Toucet, P. "La Préhistoire au Niger." *Communauté France-Eurafrique*, no. 126 (Nov. 1961):31–36.

Vedy, Jean. "Contribution à l'inventaire de la station rupestre de Dao Timni-Woro-Yat (Niger)." *Bulletin d'IFAN* (ser. B) 24, no. 3/4 (Jul.–Oct. 1962):325–82.

———. "La station rupestre de Ziri-Betidai (Niger)." *Bulletin d'IFAN* (ser. B) 23, no. 3/4 (July–Oct. 1961):456–75.

Early Explorations

Alexander, Boyd. "From the Niger by Lake Chad to the Nile." *Annual Report of the Smithsonian Institution* (1909): 335–400.

———. "From the Niger by Lake Chad to the Nile." *Geographical Journal* 30 (1907):119–52.

Alexander, J. *Whom the Gods Love: Boyd Alexander's Expedition from the Niger to the Nile, 1904–7, and His Last Journey, 1908–10*. London: Heinemann, 1977.

Arnaud, E., and M. Cortier. *Nos Confins sahariens. Etude d'Organisations militaire*. Paris: Larose, 1908.

Auguste, T. "Le Pays de Zaberma." *Afrique Française* (1901):25–32.

Auzou, Emile. "La Boucle du Niger." *Revue des Deux Mondes* 147 (1898):163–88.

Ayasse. "Première reconnaissance: N'guimi, Agadem, Bilma." *Revue des Troupes Coloniales* 1, (1907):552–82.

Baillaud, E. "Les territoires français du Niger: Leur valeur économique." Géographie (1900):9–24.

Barbier, J. V. *A travers le Sahara. Les Missions du Colonel Flatters*. Paris: Librairie de la Société Bibliographique, 1884.

Barth, Heinrich. *Travels and Discoveries in North and Central Africa.* 3 vols. Reprint. London: Frank Cass, 1965.

Baudry L. "Le Niger économique." *Géographie Commerciale* (1897): 337–46.

Bernus, S. *Henri Barth chez les Touaregs de l'Aïr.* Niamey: Etudes Nigériennes, 1972.

Bindloss, Harold. *In the Niger Country.* 1898. Reprint. London: Frank Cass, 1968.

Binger, Louis-Gustave. *Du Niger au Golfe de Guinée par le pays de Kong et le Mossi.* Paris: Musée de l'Homme, 1982.

Bovill, E. W. (ed.). *Mission to the Niger.* 4 vols. Reprint. Cambridge: Cambridge University Press, 1966.

Bouchez. *Guide de l'Officier méhariste au territoire militaire du Niger.* Paris: Larose, 1910.

Brosselard, G. *Voyage de la mission Flatters au Pays des Touareg Azdjers.* Paris: Jouvet, 1911.

Buchanan, Angus. *Exploration of Aïr: Out of the World North of Nigeria.* New York: Dutton, 1922.

———. *Sahara.* London: John Murray, 1926.

Buret, A. *Le Territoire Française Niger-Tchad.* Brussels: Imprimerie Nouvelle, 1905.

Burthe d'Annelet. *A Travers l'Afrique Française. Du Cameroun à Alger par . . . le Zinder, l'Aïr, le Niger, le Ahagar . . .* 2 vols. Paris: Roger, 1932.

———. *A Travers l'Afrique Française. Du Sénégal . . .* 2 vols. Paris: Didot, 1939.

Chudeau, René. "L'Aïr et la région de Zinder." *Géographie* 15, no. 6 (May 15, 1907):321–36.

———. "D'Alger à Tombouctou par l'Ahaggar, l'Aïr et le Tchad." *Géographie* 15, no. 5 (1907):261–70.

———. "Le cercle de Bilma." *Géographie* 21, no. 4 (Apr. 1910): 264–66.

———. "De Zinder au Tchad." *Comptes Rendus de l'Académie de Sciences* 143 (1906):193–95.

———. "Notes sur l'ethnographie de la région du Moyen-Niger." *Anthropologie* (1910):661–66.

———. *Sahara Soudanais, Mission au Sahara.* 2 vols. Paris, 1909.

Cortier, Maurice. *Mission Cortier 1908, 1909, 1910.* Paris: Larose, 1914.

———. "Le pays des Touaregs Ioulliminden." *Géographie* 21 (1910): 221–36.

———. "Teguidda-n-tesemt." *Géographie* (Sept. 5, 1905):159–64.

De Bary, Erwin. *Le Dernier Rapport d'un Européen sur Ghat et les Touareg de l'Aïr.* Paris: Librairie Fischbacher, 1898.

Delevoye, M. *En Afrique Centrale, Niger-Bénoué-Tichad.* Paris: Le Soudier, 1906.

Denham, Dixon, and H. Clapperton. *Narrative of Travels and Discoveries in Northern and Central Africa in the Years 1822, 1823, and 1824.* London: John Murray, 1826.

Desplagnes, Louis. "Notes sur l'origine des populations nigériennes." *Anthropologie* 17 (1906):525–46.

———. *Le Plateau central nigérien.* Paris: Larose, 1907.

"Die Wasserverbindung zwischen Niger und Tschadsee." *Globus,* no. 87 (1905):168–73, 186–90.

Foureau, F. *D'Alger au Congo par le Tchad.* Paris: Masson, 1902.

———. "De l'Algérie au Congo Français par l'Aïr et le Tchad." *Géographie* 2 (1900):936–61.

———. *Documents scientifiques de la Mission Saharienne (Mission Foureau-Lamy) 1898–1900.* 3 vols. Paris: Masson, 1905.

François, G. "La Mission Desplagnes dans le Plateaux central Nigérien." *Bulletin du Comité d'Afrique Française* (Apr. 1907):159–63.

———. "La Mission Tilho. La frontière entre le Niger et le Tchad." *Afrique Française,* no. 2 (1909):56–62.

Gadel, A. "Notes sur l'Aïr." *Bulletin de la Société de Geographie de l'AOF,* no. 1 (Mar. 31, 1907):28–52.

———. "Notes sur Bilma et les oasis environnants." *Revue Coloniale* 7, no. 51 (1907):361–86.

———. "Les oasis de la région de Bilma." *Bulletin de la Société de Géographie de l'AOF* 2, no. 30 (1907):85–114.

Gaden, Henri. "Notice sur la résidence de Zinder." *Revue des Troupes Coloniales* 2 (1903):608–56, 740–94.

Gallieni, Joseph Simon. *Explorations du Haut-Niger.* Paris, 1883.

Gautier, E. F., and R. Chudeau. *Missions au Sahara.* Paris: Armand Colin, 1909.

Goldstein, Ferdinand. "Die Saharastädte Ghat und Agades." *Globus* 92 (1907):171–75, 186–88.

Hall, D. N., et al. "The British Expedition to the Aïr Mountains." *Geographical Journal* 137, no. 4 (Dec. 1971):445–67.

Hallett, Robin (ed.) *The Niger Journal of Richard and John Lander.* New York: Praeger, 1965.

Hourst, Emile Auguste Leon. *French Enterprise in Africa: The Personal Narrative of Lieutenant Hourst of His Exploration of the Niger.* London: Chapman and Hall, 1898.

Ibn-Batouta. *Voyages d'Ibn-Batouta.* 5 vols. Paris: Imprimerie Nationale 1914–26.

Jacobs, A. *Les voyages d'exploration en Afrique du Docteur Barth en 1849. Le désert, le Tchad, le Niger.* Paris, 1860.

Kerillis, Henri de. *De l'Algérie au Dahomey en Automobile*. Paris: Plon, 1925.

King, W. J. Harding. *A Search for the Masked Twareks*. London: Smith, Elder, 1903.

Laird, M. G., and R. K. Oldfield. *Narrative of an Expedition into the Interior of Africa by the River Niger*. London: Bentley, 1920.

Lander, R., and J. Lander. *Journey of an Expedition to Explore the Course and Termination of the Niger*. London: Murray, 1833.

———. *The Niger Journal of the Landers*. Reprint. London: Routledge and Kegan Paul, 1965.

Lanoye, F. de. *Le Niger et les explorations de l'Afrique centrale depuis Mungo-Park jusqu'au Docteur Barth*. Paris: Hachette, 1860.

Lenfant, Eugène Armand. "De l'Atlantique au Tchad par la voie Niger-Bénoué-Toubouri-Logone." *Afrique Française*, no. 6 (1904):186–99.

———. "Exploration hydrographique du Niger." *Comité des Travaux Historiques et Scientifiques. Bulletin de Géographie Historique et Descriptive* (1903):25–133.

———. *Le Niger, voie ouverte à notre empire africain*. Paris: Hachette, 1903.

Mattei, A. *Bas Niger, Bénoué, Dahomey*. Grenoble: Vallier, 1890.

Meniaud, Jacques. Les Pionniers du Soudan avant, avec et après Archinard, 1879–94. 2 vols. Paris: Société des Publications Modernes, 1931.

Mohamed ben Otsmane el-Hachaichi. *Voyage au Pays des Senoussia à travers la Tripolitaine et les pays Toureg*. Paris: Challamel, 1903.

Monteil. *De Saint-Louis à Tripoli par le Lac Tchad*. Paris: Alcan, 1894.

Moullet. "Le Ténéré, Kaouar, Tibesti. Du Tibesti au Hoggar." *Revue des Troupes Coloniales* 28 (1934):105–25, 269–90.

———, and d'Alberny. "A travers le désert du Tibesti au Hoggar par le Tassili." *Revue des Troupes Coloniales* 1 (1938):229–45.

Muteau. *Le Niger et la Guinée*. Dijon, 1882.

Nachtigal, Gustav. *Sahara and Sudan*. Trans. by A.G.B. and H.J. Fisher. 4 vols. London: Hurst, 1971+.

Paulhiac, H. "Maures et Touareg." *Revue de Géographie* 55 (1905): 74–79, 99–103.

"Le pays de Zaberma." *Bulletin du Comité de l'Afrique Française* 11 (1901):25–32.

Regelsperger, G. "Du Niger au Tchad. La Mission Tilho. *Mois Colonial et Maritime* 1 (1909):97–109.

Richardson, James. *Narrative of a Mission to Central Africa Performed in the Years 1850–51*. 2 vols. London: Chapman and Hall, 1853.

Richardson, Robert. *A Story of the Niger*. London: Nelson and Sons, 1888.

Rodd, Francis J. Rennell. "A Journey in Aïr." *Geographical Journal* 62 (1923):81–102.

———. "Une mission anglaise en Aïr." *Bulletin du Comité d'Etudes Historiques et Scientifiques de l'AOF* 11, no. 4 (1928):695–707.

———. "A Second Journey Among the Southern Tuareg. *Geographical Journal* 73 (1929):1–19, 147–58.

Salaman. "Notice sur le Moyen Niger." *Revue Economique Française* 27 (1905):471–90.

Smith, Andrew Brown. "Adrar Bous and Karkarichinkat: Examples of Post-Paleolithic Human Adaptation in the Saharan and Sahel Zones of West Africa." Ph.D. diss., University of California/Berkeley, 1974.

Toutée, Georges Joseph. *Dahomé, Niger, Touareg*. Paris: Armand Colin, 1905.

———. *Du Dahomé au Sahara*. Paris: Armand Colin, 1907.

Von Bary, Erma. *Le Dernier Rapport de Von Bary sur les Touaregs de l'Aïr, Journal de Voyage 1876–77*. Paris: Fischbacher, 1898.

Anthropology and Ethnology

Aboubakar, I. "Le problème de l'acces aux opérations concrètes en un milieu africain." *Archives de Psychologie* 54, no. 210 (1986):159–75.

Arnould, Eric J. "Anthropology and West African Development: A Political Economic Critique and Auto-Critique." *Human Organization* 48, no. 2 (1989):135–48.

Audette, Raymond. "Stockage traditionnel de céréales vivrieres en milieu paysan au Niger." M.S. thesis, University of Laval, 1983.

Baroin, Catherine. *Les marques de bétail chez les Daza et les Azza du Niger*. Paris: Etudes Nigériennes, no. 29, 1972.

———. "Techniques d'adoption en milieu animal." *Homme et l'Animale* (1975):493–95.

Bellot, Jean Marc. "Les femmes dans les sociétés pastorales du Gorouol. *Cahiers d'Outre-Mer* 33, no. 130 (Apr.–June 1980):145–65.

Bernus, S., et al. *Le Fils et le Neveu*. Cambridge: Cambridge University Press, 1988.

Bovin, Mette. "Ethnic Performances in Rural Niger: An Aspect of Ethnic Boundary Maintenance." *Folk* (Copenhagen) 16/17 (1974): 459–74.

Brémaud, O., and J. Pagot. "Grazing Lands, Nomadism and Transhumance in the Sahel." In *The Problems of the Arid Zone*. Paris: UNESCO, 1962.

Briggs, L. D. *The Living Races of the Sahara Desert*. Cambridge, Mass.: Peabody Musuem, 1958.

———. *Tribes of the Sahara*. Cambridge, Mass.: Harvard University Press, 1960.

Calame-Griaule, G. "Notes sur l'habitation du plateau central nigérien." *Bulletin d'IFAN* 17 (1995):477–98.

Capot-Rey, R. *L'Afrique blanche française. Le Sahara française*. 2 vols. Paris: Presses Universitaires de France, 1953.

———. "Le nomadisme pastoral dans le Sahara français." *Travaux de l'Institut de Recherches Sahariennes* 1 (1942):63–86.

———. "The Present State of Nomadism in the Sahara." In *Problems of the Arid Zone*. Paris: UNESCO, 1962.

Chapelle, Jean. "Les nomades du Sahara méridional." *Tropiques* (Mar. 1949).

———. *Nomades Noirs du Sahara*. Paris: Plon, 1958.

Chudeau, R. "Peuples du Sahara central et occidental." *Anthropologie* 24 (1913):185–96.

Cohen, Ronald. "The Structure of Kanuri Society." Ph.D. diss., University of Wisconsin, 1960.

Coutouly, F. de. "Les populations de cercle de Diori." *Bulletin du Comité Scientifique et Historique de l'AOF* (1923):269–301, 471–96, 638–71.

"Coutoumiers Azna." In *Coutoumiers juridiques de l'AOF*. Paris: Larose, 1939, 3:303–16.

David, Phillippe. *La geste du grand K'Aura Assao*. Paris: Etudes Nigériennes, no. 17, 1964.

Desplagnes, L. "Notes sur l'origines des populations nigériennes." *Anthropologie* 17 (1906):525–46.

Dieterlen, G., and Y. Cissé. *Les fondements de la société d'initiation du Komo*. Paris: Mouton, 1972.

Donaint, P. *Les Cadres Géographiques à travers les langues du Niger*, Contribution à la pédagogie de l'étude du milieu. Paris: Etudes Nigeriennes, no. 37, 1975.

Drouin, J. "The Bestiary of Rupestrian and Literary Origin in the Sahara and Sahel: An Essay in the Investigation of Correlations." In H. Morphy (ed.), *Animals in Art*. London: Unwin Hyman, 1989.

Dupire, Marguerite. "Situation de la femme dans une société pastorale." In D. Paulme (ed.), *Femmes d'Afrique Noire*. Paris: Mouton, 1960, pp. 51–92.

Echard, Nicole. "Histoire et phénomènes religieux chez les Asna de l'Ader." In *Systèmes de Pensée en Afrique Noire*. Paris, 1975, pp. 53–77.

Ethnologie Régionale i Afrique-océanie. Paris: Gallimard, 1972.

Fuchs, Peter. *Das Brot der Wüste: Sozio-Ökonomie der Sahara Kanuri von Fachi*. Wiesbaden: Steiner, 1983.

Gallais, Jean. *Hommes du Sahel*. Paris: Flammarion, 1984.

Gaudio, Attilio. *Les Civilisations du Sahara*. Marabout Université, 1972.

Gerster, G. "River of Sorrow, River of Hope." *National Geographic* (Aug. 1975):152–89.

Grall. "Le Secteur nord du Cercle du Gouré." *Bulletin d'IFAN* 7, no. 1/4 (1945):1–46.

Griaule, Marcel. "L'Arche du Monde chez les populations nigériennes." *Journal de la Société des Africanistes* 18, no. 1 (1948):117–26.

Guermond, Yves. "Paysans du Niger sahélien." *Cahiers de Sociologie Economique* (Le Havre) (May 1966):1889–2170.

Halam, W. K. R. "The Chad Basin." *Nigeria Magazine* (Lagos), no. 91 (Dec. 1966):255–64.

Helfritz, Hans. *Schwarze Ritter Zwischen Niger und Tschad. Ein Reisebericht von Westafrika*. Berlin: Safari-Verlag, 1958.

Horowitz, Michael M. "Ecology and Ethnicity in Niger." *Africa* 44, no. 4 (1974):371–82.

———. "Ethnic Boundary Maintenance Among Pastoralists and Farmers in the Western Sahara (Niger)." *Journal of Asian and African Affairs* 7, no. 1/2 (Jan.–Apr. 1972):16–114.

———. *The Manga of Niger*. New Haven, Conn.: Human Relations Area Files, 1972.

———, et al. *Niger: A Social and Institutional Profile*. Binghamton, N.Y.: Institute for Development Anthropology, 1985.

Jaffre, Joël, and J. Dorou. *La Caravane du Sel*. Paris: Denoel, 1978.

Karl, Emmanuel. *Traditions Orales au Dahomey-Niger*. Niamey: Centre Regional de Documentation pour la Tradition Orale, 1974.

Kimba, Idrissa. *Guerres et Sociétés*. Niamey: IRSH, 1981.

Konrad, W. Zad. *Geheimnis zwischen Niger und Nil. Ein ethnographischer Beitrag zur Kenntnis der Tschadsee-Insularen*. Hildesheim: Gebr. Gerstenberg, 1955.

Latour, E. "Maîtres de la terre, maîtres de guerre." *Cahiers d'Etudes Africaines* 24, no. 3 (1984):273–97.

Le Coeur, Charles. "Initiation à hygiene et à la morale de l'alimentation chez les Djerma et les Peuls de Niamey." *Bulletin d'IFAN* no. 8 (1946):164–80.

———. "Méthodes et conclusions d'une enquête humaine au Sahara nigéro-tchadien." In *1ère Conférence Internationale des Africanistes de l'Ouest, Comptes Rendus*. Paris: Maisonneuve, 1951, 2:374–81.

———, and M. Le Coeur. "Tombes antéislamiques du Djado." *Notes Africaines,* no. 21 (1944):1–2.

Le Coeur, M. "Mission au Niger; juillet-décembre 1969." *Journal de la Société des Africanistes* 40, no. 2 (1970):160–68.

———, and Catherine Baroin. "Rites de la naissance et de l'imposition du nom chez les Azza du Manga (République du Niger)." *Africa* 44, no. 4 (Oct. 1974):361–70.

Leroi-Gourhan, André, and Jean Poirier. *Ethnologie de l'Union Française (Territoires Extérieures), 1, Afrique*. Paris: Presses Universitaires de France, 1953.

Lhote, Henri. *Aux Prises avec le Sahara*. Paris: Les Oeuvres Françaises, 1936.

Ligers, Z. *Atlas d'Ethnographie Nigérienne*. 2 vols. Paris: 1974.

Lobsiger-Dellenbach, Marguerite. "Contribution à l'étude anthropologique de l'Afrique Occidentale Française (Colonie du Niger); Haoussas, Bellahs, Djermas, Peuls, Touaregs, Maures." *Extraits des Archives Suisses d'Anthropologie Générale* (Geneva) 16, no. 1 (1951).

Malfettes, Raymond. "Le canton de Dessa." *Archives des Etudes Nigériennes,* no. 1 (1964).

Mathis, Constant. *L'Oeuvre des Pastoriens en Afrique Noire. Afrique Occidentale Française*. Paris: Presses Universitaires de France, 1946.

Monod, T. (ed.). *Méharées Explorations au vrai Sahara*. Paris: Larose, 1937.

———. (ed.). *Pastoralism in Tropical Africa*. London: Cass, 1975.

Morel, Alain. "Villages et oasis des Monts Bazzans (Massif de l'Aïr–Niger)." *Revue de Géographie Alpine* 1 (1973):247–66.

Muller, Jean-Claude. *Du bon usage du sexe et du mariage. Structures matrimoniales du haut plateau nigérien*. Paris: Harmattan, 1992.

Nicholas, Guy. "Aspects de la vie économique dans un canton du Niger: Kantché." *Cahiers de l'SEA,* no. 5 (1962).

———. *L'Evolution du Canton de Kantché. Etude ethnologique d'une société de l'Est du Niger*. Thesis, Bordeaux University, 1957.

Oxby, Clare. *Les Pasteurs nomades face au développement*. London: International African Institute, 1975.

Perron, M. "Le Pays Dendi." *Bulletin du Comité Historique et Scientifique de l'AOF* (1924):51–83.

Piault, Marc H. *Populations de l'Arewa. Introduction à une étude régionale*. Paris: Etudes Nigériennes, no. 13, 1964.

Poncet, Yveline. *Cartes ethno-démographiques du Niger*. Paris: Etudes Nigériennes, no. 32, 1973.

Raulin, Henri. "Cadastre et terroirs au Niger." *Etudes Rurales,* no. 9 (Apr.–June 1963):58–77.

———. "Société san classes d'âge au Niger." In D. Paulme (ed.), *Classes et associations d'âge en Afrique de l'Ouest*. Paris: Plon, 1971, pp. 320–39.

———. "Techniques agraires et instruments oratoires au sud du Sahara." *Cahiers d'ORSTOM* 20, no. 3/4 (1984):339–58.

Raynaut, C. "La circulation marchande des céréales." *Cahiers du Centre d'Etudes et Recherches Ethnologique* (Bordeaux), no. 2 (1973): 1–48.

———. "Outils agricoles de la région de Maradi, Niger." *Cahiers d'ORSTOM* 20, no. 3/4 (1984):505–36.

Riou, A. "Le Niger géographique et ethnologique." *AOF Magazine* (Dakar), no. 6 (May 1954).

Robin, Jean. "Description de la province de Dosso." *Bulletin d'IFAN* 9, nos. 1–4 (1947):56–98.

———. "Note sur les premières populations de la région de Dosso (Niger)." *Bulletin d'IFAN* 1, no. 2/3 (Apr.–July 1939):401–4.

Robinson, Pearl T. "African Traditional Rulers and the Modern State: The Linkage Role of Chiefs in the Republic of Niger." Thesis, Columbia University, 1975.

Rochette, R., A. Guillon, and J. Hernandez. "Dogondoutchi, petit centre urbain du Niger." *Revue de Géographie Africaine* 56, (1968):349–58.

Rosman, Abraham. "Social Structure and Acculturation Among the Kanuri of Northern Nigeria." Ph.D. diss., Yale University, 1962.

Roucek, J. S. "The Niger and Its Peoples." Special issue of *New Africa,* nos. 7–10 (Aug.–Sept. 1965).

Rouch, Jean. "Les pêcheurs du Niger: Techniques de pêche, organisation économique." *Comptes Rendus de l'Institut Français d'Anthropologie* 5 (Jan.–Dec. 1951):17–20.

———. "Toponymie légendaire du 'W' du Niger." *Notes Africaines,* no. 46 (Apr. 1950):50–52.

———, O. H. Mokhtar, and A. Leriche. "Batons à inscriptions magiques du Niger." *Notes Africaines,* no. 70 (Apr. 1956):40–41.

Sidikou, Arouna Hamdou. "Les Gaouankey de Karoubedji (République du Niger)." *Bulletin des Instituts de Recherche de l'Université d'Abidjan,* no. 1 (1961):14–21.

———. *Sedentarité et mobilité entre Niger et Zgaret.* Niamey: Etudes Nigériennes, 1974.

Sigwarth, G. "La Vie économique dans l'oasis de Djanet." *Travaux de l'Institut des Recherches Sahariennes* 4 (1947):175–80.

Spittler, Gerd. "Wüste, Wildnis and Zivilisation—die Sicht der Kel Ewey." *Paideuma* (Frankfurt) 35 (1989):273–87.

Stoller, Paul. *The Taste of Ethnographic Things.* Philadelphia: University of Pennsylvania Press, 1989.

Sundstrom, Lars. *Ecology and Symbiosis: Niger Waterfolk.* Uppsala: Studia Ethnografica Upsaliensa, 1972.

Terrier, Auguste. "L'Oasis de Bilma et les oasis environnants." *Bulletin du Comité de l'Afrique Française* (1907):287–89.

"Trois grandes chefferies au Niger." *Bulletin d'Information et de Renseignements* (Dakar), no. 207 (Dec. 5, 1938):510–11.

Urvoy, Yves. *Histoire des Populations du Soudan Central (Colonie du Niger).* Paris: Larose, 1936.

———. *Petit Atlas ethno-démographique du Soudan entre Sénégal et Tchad*. Paris: Larose, 1942.

Valaskakis, Kimon. *Relations Nord-Sud en Afrique de l'Ouest*. Montreal: University of Montreal CRDE, 1988.

Van Hoey, Leo Frans. "Emergent Urbanization: Implications of the Theory of Social Scale Verified in Niger, West Africa." Ph.D. diss., Northwestern University, 1966.

Vital, Laurent. *Rituels de possession dans le Sahel*. Paris: Harmattan, 1992.

Bozo/Sorko

Dièterlen, Germaine. "Note sur le génie des eaux chez les Bozo." *Journal de la Société des Africanistes* 12 (1942):149–55.

———, and Z. Ligers. "Un objet rituel bozo: le maniyalo." *Journal de la Société des Africanistes* 28, no. 1/2 (1958):33–42.

———. "Les *tengere*: Instruments de musique bozo." *Objets et Mondes* 7, no. 3 (1967):185–216.

Francis-Boeuf, Jean. "Etude sur les Bozos du Niger occidental." *Outre-Mer* 3 (1931):391–405.

Griaule, Marcel, and Germaine Dieterlen. "L'Agriculture rituelle des Bozo." *Journal de la Société des Africanistes* 19, no. 2 (1949): 209–22.

Ligers, Z. "La chasse à l'éléphant chez les Boso." *Journal de la Société des Africanistes* 30, no. 1 (1960):95–99.

———. *Les Sorko (Bozo), maîtres du Niger—Etude ethnographique*. 3 vols. Paris: Cinq Continents, 1964–67.

Rouch, Jean. "Banghawi—Chasse à l'hippopotame au harpon par les pêcheurs sorko du Moyen-Niger." *Bulletin d'IFAN* (1948): 361–77.

———. "Les Sorkawa, pêcheurs itinérants du Moyan-Niger." *Afrika* 20, no. 1 (Jan. 1950):5–25. Translated to English in *Farm and Forest* 10 (1950):36–53.

Ydewalle, Serge d'. "Avec les pêcheurs Sorko du Niger." *Jeune Afrique*, no. 897 (Mar. 1978):71–73.

Djerma/Songhay

Ardant du Picq, Charles Pierre. *Une population Africaine: Les Dyerma*. Paris: Larose, 1933.

———. "Une population Africaine: Les Dyerma." *Bulletin du Comité d'Etudes Historiques et Scientifiques de l'AOF* 14, no. 4 (Oct.–Dec. 1931).

Bisilliat, J. "Maladies de village et maladies de brousse en pays songhay." *Cahiers d'ORSTOM* 18, no. 4 (1981/82):475–86.

———, and D. Laya. "Représentations et connaissances du corps chez les Songhay-Zarma: Analyse d'une suite d'entretiens avec un guérisseur." In *La Notion de personne en Afrique*. Paris: CNRS, 1973, pp. 331–58.

———, E. Pierre, and C. Pidoux. "La notion de Lakkai dans la culture Djerma Songhai." *Psychopathologie Africaine* 3, no. 2 (1967):207–63.

Clauzel, J. "Des noms songhay dans l'Ahaggar." *Journal of African Languages* 1, no. 1 (1962):43–44.

Davis, Richard Eugene. "Response Innovation in a Zarma Village: Contemporary Tradition in Niger, West Africa." Ph.D. diss., University of Connecticut, 1991.

Diarra, A. "La notion de personne chez les Zarma." In *La Notion de personne en Afrique Noire*. Paris: CNRS, 1973, pp. 359–72.

Diarra, Fatoumata-Agnes. *Femmes Africaines en devenir: Les femmes Zarma du Niger*. Paris: Editions Anthropos, 1971.

———. "Les relations entre les hommes et les femmes et les migrations des Zarma." In Samir Amin (ed.), *Modern Migrations in Western Africa*. London: Oxford University Press, 1974, pp. 226–38.

"Documents jerma: les coutumes." Cahier 53, ____. Niger et Pays Voisin series, Fonds Vieillard, IFAN Library, Dakar.

Ducroz, Jean-Marie, and Marie-Claire Charles. *L'Homme Songhay tel qu'il se dit chez les Kaado du Niger*. Paris: Harmattan, 1982.

Dupois-Yakouba, A. *Les Gow, ou chasseurs du Niger. Légendes songai de la région de Tombouctou*. Paris: Leroux, 1911.

Dutel, Réné. "Apparition d'une nouvelle amulette chez les Sonrai et Zarma du moyen Niger." *Notes Africaines,* no. 25 (Jan. 1945):1–2.

Gado, Boubé. *Le Zarmatarey. Contribution à l'histoire des populations entre Niger et Dallol Mawri*. Niamey: IRSH, 1980. Also diss., University of Paris, 1979.

Hale, T. A. "Kings, Scribes and Bards: A Look at Signs of Survival for Keepers of Oral Tradition Among the Songhay-Speaking Peoples of Niger." In S. Biernaczky (ed.), *Folklore in Africa Today*. Budapest: Lorand Eotros University, 1984. Also in *Artes Populares* 1 (1983): 207–20.

Houis, M. "Notes sur les Songhay." *Bulletin d'IFAN* 20, no. 1/2 (1958): 225–40.

Kaba, Lansine. "Le pouvoir politique, l'essor économique et l'inégalité sociale au Songhay 1464–1591." *Bulletin d'IFAN* 45, no. 1/2 (1983).

Karimou, M. "Role du 'griot' dans la société sonrai-djerma (Niger)." *Annales de l'Université d'Abidjan* 1, no. 1 (1972):97–102.

LaCroix, P. F. "L'ensemble songhay-jerma. Problèmes et thèmes de travail." *Annales de l'Université d'Abidjan* 1 (1971):87–99.

Lateef, N. V. "A Techno-Environmental Analysis of Zarma Cultural Organization." *Bulletin d'IFAN* 37, no. 2 (Apr. 1975):388–411.

———, and N. L. Lateef. "Zarma Ideology." *Bulletin d'IFAN* 38, no. 2 (Apr. 1976):377–89.

Mounkaila, Fatimata. *Le mythe et l'histoire dans la geste de Zabarkane.* Niamey: CELTHO, 1989.

Olivier de Sardan, Jean-Pierre. "Un barde, des scribes, et la geste du Songhay." *Cahiers d'Etudes Africanes* 30, no. 2 (1990):205–10.

———. *Concepts et conceptions songhay-zarma.* Paris: Nubia, 1982.

———. "Contradictions sociales et impact colonial." Ph.D. diss., University of Paris, 1982.

———. "Esclavage d'échange et captivité familiale chez les Songhay-Zerma." *Journal de la Société des Africanistes* 43, no. 1 (1973): 151–67.

———. "Personnalité et structures sociales (à propos des Songhay)." In *La Notion de personne en Afrique.* Paris: CNRS, 1973, pp. 421–45.

———. *Les sociétés songhay-zerma (Niger-Mali).* Paris: Karthala, 1984.

Palmeri, Paolo. "Traditional Lifeways and Modernization in a Niger Village." In Bernardo Berdichewski (ed.), *Anthropology and Social Change in Rural Areas.* Paris: Mouton, 1979, pp. 49–65.

Prost, André. "Notes sur les Songhay." *Bulletin d'IFAN* 16, no. 1/2 (1954):167–213.

———. "Statut de la femme Songhay." *Bulletin d'IFAN* 32, no. 2 (Apr. 1970):486–517.

———. "La vannerie chez les Songhay." *Notes Africaines,* no. 60 (Oct. 1953):115–16.

Rouch, Jean. "Le calendrier mythique chez les Songhay-Zarma (Niger)." *Systèmes de Pensée en Afrique Noire* (1975):52–62.

———. "Contribution à l'histoire des Songhay." *Mémoires d'IFAN,* no. 29 (1953).

———. "Rites de pluie chez les Songhay." *Bulletin d'IFAN* 15, no. 4 (Oct. 1953):1655–89.

———. "Sacrifice et transfer des âmes chez les Songhay du Niger." *Systèmes de Pensée en Afrique Noire* (1976):55–66.

———. *Les Songhay.* Paris: Presses Universitaires de France, 1954.

Sarr, M. "Les Songhay." Special Issue of *Etudes Maliennes* (Bamako), no. 4 (Jan. 1973).

Stoller, Paul. "The Dynamics of Bankedano: Communications and Political Legitimacy Among the Songhay." Ph.D. diss., University of Texas/Austin, 1978.

———. *Fusion of the Worlds: The Ethnography of Possession Among the Songhay of Niger*. Chicago: University of Chicago Press, 1989.

———. "The Negotiation of Songhay Space: Phenomenology in the Heart of Darkness." *American Ethnologist* 7, no. 3 (1980):419–31.

———. "Ritual and Personal Insults in Sonrai Sonni." *Anthropology* 2, no. 1 (1977):31–37.

———. "Signs in the Social Order: Riding a Songhay Bush Taxi." *American Anthropologist* 9, no. 4 (Nov. 1982):750–62.

———. *The Cinematic Griot: The Ethnography of Jean Rouch*. Chicago: University of Chicago Press, 1992.

———. "Social Interaction and the Management of Songhay Socio-Political Change." *Africa* (London) 51, no. 3 (1981):765–80.

———. "Son of Rouch: Portrait of a Young Ethnographer by the Songhay." *Anthropological Quarterly* 60, no. 3 (1987):114–23.

Streicher, Allan Joseph. "On Being Zarma: Scarcity and Stress in the Nigerien Sahel." Ph.D. diss., Northwestern University, 1980.

Surugué, B. *Contribution à l'étude de la musique sacrée Zarma-Songhay*. Paris: Etudes Nigériennes, no. 30, 1972.

Terrier, Auguste. "Le pays de Zaberma." *Afrique Française* 11 (1901): 25–32.

Fulani

Ba, Amadou Hampaté, and Germaine Dièterlen. *Koumen: Texte initiatique des pasteurs Peul*. Paris: Ecole Pratique des Hautes Etudes, 1974.

Baba, Diallo. *La Tradition Historique Peule*. Niamey: Centre d'Etudes Linguistique et Historique par Tradition Orale, 1977.

Beauvilain, Alain. *Les Peuls du Dallol Bosso*. Niamey: Institut de Recherches en Sciences Humaines, 1977.

Beckwith, Carol. "Niger's Wodaabe: People of the Taboo." *National Geographic* (Oct. 1983):482–509.

———. *Nomads of Niger*. New York: H. N. Abrams, 1993.

Bonfiglioli, Angelo Maliki. *Dud'al Histoire de famille et histoire de troupeau chez un groupe de Wodaabe du Niger*. Cambridge: Cambridge University Press, 1988.

———. "Evolution de la propriété animale chez le WoDaaBe du Niger." *Journal des Africanistes* 55, no. 1/2 (1985):29–37.

"Les Bororo." *Niger* (Niamey), no. 1 (Oct. 1967):25–42.

Botting, Douglas. *The Knights of Bornu*. London: Hodder and Stoughton, 1961.

Bovin, Mette. "Nomads of the Drought: Fulbe and Wodaabe Nomads Between Power and Marginalization in the Sahel of Burkina Faso and the Niger Republic." In Mette Bovin and Leif Manger (eds.), *Adap-*

tive Strategies in African Arid Lands. Uppsala: Scandinavian Institute of African Studies, 1990, pp. 29–57.

Brackenberry, E. A. "Notes on the 'Bororo Fulbe' or 'Nomad Cattle Fulani.'" *Journal of the African Society* 23, no. 91/92 (1924).

Brandt, H. *Nomads du Soleil*. Lausanne: Clairefontaine, 1956.

Dièterlen, Germaine. "Initiation Among the Pastoral Peul Tribes." In M. Fortes and G. Dièterlen, *African Systems of Thought*. London: Oxford University Press, 1965.

Dupire, Marguerite. "Contribution à l'étude des marques de propriété du bétail chez les pasteurs Peuls." *Journal de la Société des Africanistes* 24, no. 2 (1955):123–44.

———. *Les facteurs humaines de l'économie pastorale*. Paris: Etudes Nigériennes, no. 6, 1972.

———. *Organisation sociale des Peul. Etude d'Ethnographie comparée*. Paris: Plon, 1970.

———. *Peuls Nomades. Etude descriptive des Wodaabe du Sahel Nigérien*. Paris: Institut d'Ethnologie, 1962.

———. "Pharmacopée peule du Niger et du Cameroun." *Bulletin d'IFAN* 19, no. 3/4 (July–Oct. 1957):382–417.

———. *La Place du commerce et des marchés dans l'économie des Bororo (Fulbe) nomades du Niger*. Paris: Etudes Nigériennes, no. 3, 1961. Also, in English, in Paul Bohanan and George Dalton (eds.), *Markets in Africa*. Evanston, Ill.: Northwestern University Press, 1961, pp. 335–64.

———. "The Position of Women in a Pastoral Society: The Fulani WoDaaBi." In Denise Paulme (ed.), *Women in Tropical Africa*. Berkeley: University of California Press, 1963.

———. "Trade and Markets in the Economy of the Nomadic Fulani of Niger." In Paul Bohanan and George Dalton (eds.), *Markets in Africa*, Evanston, Ill.: Northwestern University Press, 1962, pp. 335–64.

———, and Michel De Lavergne de Tressan. "Devinettes peules et Bororo." *Africa* 25, no. 4 (Oct. 1955):375–92.

Gallais, Jean. "Les Peuls en question." *Revue de Psychologie des Peuples* (Le Havre), no. 3 (1969):231–51.

Hama Beidi, Boubakar. *Les Peuls du Ballol Dosso: Coutumes et mode de vie*. Saint-Maur, Fr.: Sépia, 1993.

Hopen, C. E. *The Pastoral Fulbe Family in Gwandu*. London: Oxford University Press, 1958.

Johnson, H. A. S. *The Fulani Empire of Sokoto*. London: Oxford University Press, 1967.

Kaartinen, Timo. "The Wodaabe Flight: Inversions of Hierarchy in a West African Pastoral Community." *Soumen Anthropologi* 14, no. 4 (1989):3–10.

Kintz, D. "Les Peuls du Maradi." Diss., University of Bordeaux, 1977.

Layya, Juuldé. *La Tradition Peule des Animaux d'Attache*. Paris: Anthropos, 1973.

———. *La Voie Peule*. Paris: Nubia, 1984.

Legal, V. "Acculturation spontanée at acculturation forcée chez les Wodaabe nomades du Niger." M.A. thesis, University of Paris, 1971.

Luhi, Charles. "Les Bororo et leurs légendes." *France Eurafrique,* no. 218 (July, 1970):28–31.

Mohamadou, Eldridge. "Les peuls du Niger oriental: groupes ethniques et dialectes." *Camelang* (Yaoundé), no. 2 (1969):57–93.

Mornet, P., and Kassoum Kone. "Le Zebu peulh bororo." *Bulletin des Services Zootechniques et des Epizooties de l'AOF* (Dakar) 4, no. 3/4 (Sept.–Dec. 1946).

Nicolaisen, Johannes. "The Pastoral Kreda and the African Cattle Complex." *Folk* (Copenhagen), no. 19/20 (1977/78):251–307.

Paden, John. *Religion and Political Culture in Kano*. Berkeley: University of California Press, 1973.

Riesman, Paul. *Freedom in Fulani Social Life*. Chicago: University of Chicago Press, 1979.

Riou, A. "Les Populations du Niger." *AFO Magazine* (May 1954):____.

Seydou, Christiane. *Bibliographie Générale du Monde Peul*. Niamey: IRSH, 1977.

———. "Eléments d'analyse de la notion de temps dans la langue des Peuls du Niger." In P. E. Lacroix (ed.), *L'Expression du Temps dans quelques langues de l'Ouest africain*. Paris: SELAF, 1972, pp. 71–85.

Soehring, A. "Nomadenland im Aufbruch. Bericht über die Cure Salee 1965 in der Republik Niger." *International Afrika Forum* 2, no. 2 (Apr. 1966):178–81.

Stenning, Derrick J. "Cattle Values and Islamic Values in a Pastoral Republic." In I. M. Lewis, *Islam in Tropical Africa*. London: Oxford University Press, 1966.

———. "Household Viability Among the Pastoral Fulani." In James L. Gibbs, *Peoples of Africa*. New York: Holt, Rinehart and Winston, 1965.

———. *Savannah Nomads: A Study of the Wodaabe Pastoral Fulani*. London: Oxford University Press, 1959.

———. "Transhumance, Migrating Drift, Migration: Patterns of Pastoral Fulani Nomadism." In Simon Ottenberg and Phoebe Ottenberg (eds.), *Cultures and Societies of Africa*. New York: Random House, 1960. Also in *Journal of the Royal Anthropological Institute* 87 (1957):57–73.

Tauxier, L. *Moeurs et Histoire des Peuls*. Paris: Payot, 1937.

Thom, Derrick J. "The Morphology of Maradi." *Africa Urban Notes* 8, no. 1 (1972).

———. "The Niger-Nigeria Borderlands: A Politico-Geographical Analysis of Boundary Influence upon the Hausa." Ph.D. diss., Michigan State University, 1971.

———. *The Niger-Nigeria Boundary*. Papers in International Studies, Africa series, no. 23. Athens: Ohio University Press, 1975.

Tremearne, A. J. *The Niger and the Western Sudan*. London: Hodder and Stoughton, 1910.

Van Offelen, Marion, and Carol Beek. *Nomades du Niger*. Paris: Editions Chene, 1983.

———. *Nomads of Niger*. New York: Abrams, 1983; London: Collins, 1984.

Wilson, Wendy. "Resource Management in a Stratified Fulani Community." Ph.D. diss., Howard University, 1984.

Zaborowski, S. "Les Habés et les Peuhls du Niger oriental." *Revue Anthropologique* 22, (1912):242–47.

Maouri

Karimou, Mahamane. *Les Mawri Zarmaphone*. Niamey: IRSH, 1977.

Latour Dejean, Elaine de. "Shadows Nourished by the Sun: Rural Social Differentiation Among the Mawri of Niger." In *Peasants in Africa*. Beverly Hills, Calif.:Sage, 1980, pp. 104–41.

Leroy, P. "Une population nigérienne. Les Maouri." CHEAM, no. 1486 (1949).

Monteil, V. "Note sur la toponomie, l'Astronomie et l'orientation chez les Maures." *Hesperis* 26, (1949):189–220.

Piault, Colette. *Contribution à l'étude de la vie quotidienne de la femme Mawri*. Paris: Etudes Nigériennes, no. 10, 1965.

Piault, Marc Henri. *Histoire Mauri—Introduction à l'étude des processus constitutifs d'un état*. Paris: CNRS, 1970.

———. "Les Mawri de la République du Niger." *Bulletin du cercle des Jeunes Anthroplogues* (1966).

———. "Les Mawri de la République du Niger." *Cahiers d'Etudes Africanes* 7, no. 28 (1967):673–78.

———. "La personne du pouvoir ou la souveraintè du souverain en pays mawri (Hausa du Niger)." In *La Notion de personne en Afrique Noire*. Paris: CNRS, 1973, pp. 459–65.

Rochette, R. "Au Niger Tibiri, village Maouri." *Revue Géographie Alpine*, no. 1 (1965):101–30.

———, J. D. Gronoff, F. Masseport, and A. Valancot. *Doumega, Dioundiou, Kawara, Debe. Villages des Dallols Maouri et Fogha*. Paris: Etudes Nigériennes, no. 19, 1967.

Soudié/Kurtey/Wogo

Da Silva, M. "Enquête sur les moeurs et coutumes soudiées avant l'occupation française." *Bulletin d'Enseignement AOF* 23 (Jan.–Mar. 1934).

Echard, Nicole. "Histoire du Peuplement: Les traditions orales d'un village sudyé, Shat (Filingué, République du Niger)." *Journal de la Société des Africanistes* 39, no. 1 (1969):57–78.

Kaziendé, Leopold. "Origine des Sudiés." *Education Africaine* 29, no. 104 (1940):32–44.

Olivier de Sardan, Jean-Pierre. "Marriage Among the Wogo." In D. Seddon (ed.), *Relations of Production: Marxist Approaches to Economic Anthropology*. London: Frank Cass, 1978, pp. 357–87.

———. *Systèmes des relations économiques et sociales chez les Wogo (Niger)*. Paris: Institut d'Ethnologie, Musée de l'Homme, 1969.

Rousselot, R. *Les Wogo du Niger*. Paris: Etudes Nigériennes, no. 20, 1965.

———. *Les voleurs d'hommes. Notes sur l'histoire des Kurtey*. Paris: Etudes Nigériennes, no. 25, 1969.

Hausa

Barkow, J. H. "Strategies for Self-Esteem and Prestige in Maradi, Niger Republic." In T. R. Williams (ed.), *Psychological Anthropology*. The Hague: Mouton, 1975, pp. 373–88.

Bartel, Noirot. "Une province hausa du Niger: le Tessaoua—essai dur les coutumes." *Renseignements Coloniaux* (Feb. 1937): 20–24; (May 1937):41–45.

Bonté, Pierre, and N. Echard. "Histoire et histoires. Conception du passé chez les Hausa et les Twareg Kel Gress de l'Ader." *Cahiers d'Etudes Africanes* 61/62 (1976):237–96.

Charlick, R. B. "Power and Participation in the Modernization of Rural Hausa Communities (Niger)." Ph.D. diss., University of California/Los Angeles, 1974.

"Coutumes haoussa et peul." In *Coutumiers juridiques de l'Afrique Occidentale française*. 3 vols. Paris: Larose, 1933, vol. 2:261–301.

Echard, Nicole. *Bori, aspects d'un culte de possession hausa dans l'Ader et le Kurfey*. Paris: EHESS, 1989.

———. "L'Habitat traditionnel dans l'Ader (pays hausa, République du Niger)." *Homme* 7, no. 3 (July–Sept. 1967):48–77.

———. "Note sur les forgerons de l'Ader (pays haoussa, République du Niger)." *Journal de la Société des Africanistes* 35, no. 2 (1965): 353–72.

———. "La pratique religieuse des femmes dans une société d'hommes. Les Hausa du Niger." *Revue Française de Sociologie* 19, no. 4 (Oct.–Dec. 1978):551–62.

"La famille haoussa." *Niger* (Niamey), no. 8 (Nov. 1969):18–27.

Faulkingham, Ralph H. "Political Support in a Hausa Village." Ph.D. diss., Indiana University 1970.

Fusier. "Une population Haoussa. Les Gobiraoua." CHEAM, no. 1299 (1948).

Keith, Nancy Jean. "Feeding, Weaning and Illness in Young Hausa Children." Ph.D. diss., Michigan State University, 1991.

Levy-Luxereau, A. *Etude Ethno-zoologique du pays hausa en République du Niger*. Paris: Musée d'Histoire Naturelle, 1972.

Mainet, G. "La vie des Haoussa de la région de Maradi." Mémoire de D.E.S. de Géographie, Bordeaux University, 1964.

Nicolas, Guy. "Les Catégories d'ethnie et de fraction au sein du système social Hausa." *Cahier d'Etudes Africaines,* no. 59 (1975):359–441.

———. *Cosmologie Hausa.* Paris: CNRS, 1965.

———. "Developpement rural et comportement économique traditionnel au sein d'une société africaine." *Genève Afrique,* no. 2 (1969): 359–441.

———. *Dynamisme sociale et appréhension du monde au sein d'une société Hausa.* Paris: Musée de l'Homme, 1969.

———. "Essai sur les structures fondamentales de l'espace dans la cosmologie Hausa." *Journal des Africanistes,* 36, no. 1 (1966):65–107.

———. "Etude de marchés en pays Haoussa (République du Niger)." *Documents Ethnographiques* (Bordeaux) (Feb. 1964).

———. "Fondements magico-religieux du pouvoir politique au sein de la principauté Hausa du Gobir." *Journal de la Société des Africanistes* 39, no. 2 (1969):199–231.

———. "Une forme attenuée du 'potlach' en pays hausa (République du Niger): Le dubu." *Economies et Sociétés* (Paris), no. 2 (Feb. 1967): 151–214.

———. *Notes ethnographiques sur le terroir, l'agriculture et l'élevage dans la vallée de Maradi.* Paris: Etudes Nigériennes, no. 8, 1963.

———. "Particularismes régionaux au sein de la culture Haoussa: Aspects Nigériens," *Bulletin des Etudes Africaines* 1, no. 1 (1981): 111–31.

———. "La pratique traditionnelle du crédit au sein d'une société subsaharienne, vallée de Maradi, Niger." *Cultures et Développement* 6, no. 4 (1974):737–73.

———. "Processus de résistance au 'développement' au sein d'une société africaine." *Civilisations* 21, no. 1 (1971):45–66.

———. "Processus oblatifs à l'occasion de intronisation des chefs traditionnels en pays hausa (République du Niger)." *Tiers Monde* 9, no. 33 (Jan.–Mar. 1968):43–93.

———. "Les relations sociales dans la société haoussa." *Synthèses Nigériennes, no. 1 (Feb. 1968):17–27.*

———. Structures fondamentales de l'espace dans le cosmologie d'une société hausa." *Journal de la Société des Africanistes* 36, no. 1 (1966):65–108.

———. "Un système numerique symbolique." *Cahiers d'Etudes Africaines* 8, no. 4 [no. 32] (1968):566–616.

———. "Un village Haoussa de la République du Niger: Tassao Haoussa." *Cahiers d'Outre-Mer* 13 (1960).

———, Hubert Doumesche, and Maman dan Mouche. *Etude sociéconomique de deux villages hausa: Enquête en vue d'un aménage-*

ment hydro-agricole, vallée de Maradi. Paris: Etudes Nigériennes, no. 22, 1968.

———, and Guy Mainet. *La Vallée du Gulbi de Maradi.* Paris: Etudes Nigériennes, no. 16, 1964.

———. "The 'Other' Hausas." *West Africa,* no. 3130 (July 4, 1977): 1348–49.

Persyn, René. *Les Talakas.* Paris: La Pensée Universelle, 1978.

Pilaszewicz, S. "The Craft of the Hausa Oral Praise-Poets." In S. Biernaczky (ed.), *Folklore in Africa,* Budapest: Lorand Eotros University, African Research Project, 1984, pp. 269–76.

Pucheu, Jacques. "Techniques traditionelles des maîtres fondeurs haoussa de l'Ader." *Bulletin des Etudes Africaines* 3, no. 5 (1983):139–51.

Raynaut, Claude. "Organisation spatiale et organisation sociale d'un village Hausa du Niger." *Cahiers d'Outre-Mer,* no. 94 (Apr.–June 1971):123–57.

———. *Structures Normatives et Relations Electives: Etude d'une communauté villageoise haoussa.* Paris: Mouton, 1972.

———. "Transformation d'un système de production et inégalité économique: Le cas d'un village hausa (Niger)." *Canadian Journal of African Studies* 10, no. 2 (1976).

Renault, Philippe. "Echelle de corde de fabrication haoussa." *Notes Africaines,* no. 55 (July 1952):83–84.

Roger, Robert. "Le nationalism Haoussa." CHEAM, no. 3543, (1961).

Rousselot, R. "Notes sur la faune ornithologique des cercles Maradi et de Tanout." *Bulletin d'IFAN* (1947):99–137.

Salamone, F. A. *The Hausa People.* 2 vols. New Haven: HRAF, 1983.

Saunders, Margaret Overholt. "Marriage and Divorce in a Muslim Hausa Town: Mirria, Niger." Ph.D. diss., Indiana University, 1978.

Smith, Mary F. *Baba of Karo: A Woman of the Muslim Hausa.* New Haven: Yale University, 1981.

Smith, Michael. "The Hausa Markets in Peasant Economy." In Paul Bohanan and George Dalton (eds.), *Markets in Africa.* Evanston, Ill.: Northwestern University Press, 1962.

———. "The Hausa of Northern Nigeria." In James Gibbs, Jr., *Peoples of Africa.* New York: Holt, Rinehart and Winston, 1965.

———. "The Jihad of Shehu Dan Fidio." In I. M. Lewis (ed.), *Islam in Tropical Africa.* London: Oxford University Press, 1966.

Spittler, G. "Herrschaft über Bauern: Staatliche Herrschaft und islamischurbane Kultur in Gobir." Paper, Frankfurt University, 1978.

Sutter, John William. "Peasants, Merchant Capital and Rural Differentiation: A Nigerian Hausa Case Study." Ph.D. diss., Cornell University, 1982.

Thom, Derrick. "The City of Maradi: French Influence upon a Hausa Urban Center." *Journal of Geography* 70 (1971):472–82.

———. "The Niger-Nigeria Borderlands: A Politico-Geographical Analysis of Boundary Influence upon the Hausa." Ph.D. diss., Michigan State University, 1970.

Toubou

Baroin, Catherine. *Anarchie et Cohésion sociale chez les Toubou: Les Daza Késerda (Niger)*. Paris: Editions de la Maison des Sciences de l'Homme, 1985.

———. "Dominant-dominé: Complémentarité des roles et des attitudes entre les pasteurs deda-daza du Niger et leurs forgerons." In Yves Monino (ed.), *Forge et Forgerons*. Paris: ORSTOM, 1991, pp. 329–81.

———. "Effets de la colonisation sur la société traditionnelle Daza." *Journal des Africanistes* 47, no. 2 (1977):123–31.

———. "Esclaves chez les Daza du Niger." In *Itinéraires en pays peul et ailleurs*. Paris: Société des Africanistes, 1981, pp. 321–41.

———. *Les Marques des Bétail chez les Daza et Azza du Niger*. Niamey: Etudes Nigériennes, 1972.

———. "The Position of Tubu Women in Pastoral Production: Daza Kesherda, Niger." *Ethnos* 52, no. 1/2 (1987):137–55.

———. "Techniques d'adoption en milieu animal. Les Daza du Niger." In *L'homme et l'Animal*. Paris: Institut Inter-Ethnoscience, 1975.

Chapelle, J. "Etude sur les Toubous, nègres sahariens." CHEAM, no. 804 (1946).

———. "Les Toubous." CHEAM, no. 1039 (1947).

Cline, Walter. *The Teda of Tibesti, Borku and Kawar in the Eastern Sahara*. Menasha, Wis.:George Banta, 1950.

Gamory-Dubourdeat, P. M. "Notes sur les coutumes des Toubous du Nord." *Bulletin du Comité d'Etudes Historiques et Scientifiques de l'AOF* (1926):131–52.

Heseltine, Nigel. "The Toubbou and Gorane." *South African Archaeological Bulletin* 14, no. 1 (1953):21–27.

Le Rouvreur, Albert. "Agadem et Djado: Deux aspects du Teda." CHEAM, no. 1142 (1948).

Tuareg

Aghali Zakara, Mohamed. *Psycholingustique touaregue*. Paris: INALCO, 1992.

———, and Jeannine Drouin. *Traditions touaregues nigériennes*. Paris: Harmattan, 1979.

Altanine ag Arias. *Iwillimiden*. Niamey: CNRSH, 1970.

———. *Traditions Historiques des Touaregs de l'Imannan*. Niamey: CELTHO, 1977.

———, and E. Bernus. "La Jardin de la sécheresse, l'histoire d'Amumen ag Amastan." *Journal des Africanistes* 47, no. 1 (1977):83–94.

Arkell, A. J. "Forms of the Talhakim and the Tanaghibit as Adopted from the Tuareg by the Various West African Tribes." *Journal of the Royal Anthropological Institute* 65 (July–Dec. 1935):307–9.

———. "Some Tuareg Ornaments and Their Connection with India." *Journal of the Royal Anthropological Institute* 65 (July–Dec. 1935): 297–306.

Aymand, A. *Les Touaregs*. Paris: Hachette, 1911.

———. "Les Touregs du Sud." *Le Tour de Monde* (1908):109–58.

Barth, Heinrich. "Die Imoscharch oder Tuareg, Volk und Land." *Petermanns Mittelungen* 3 (1857):239–60.

Bernus, Edmond. "Afarag." *Encyclopédie Berbère* (Aix-en-Provence) 12 (1974).

———. *Atlas des structures agraires au Sud du Sahara: Les Illabakan*. Paris: ORSTOM, 1974.

———. "Azakka." *Encyclopédie Berbère* (Aix-en-Provence) 12 (1974).

———. "Azawagh." *Encyclopédie Berbère* (Aix-en-Provence) 16 (1978).

———. "Le berger touareg sahélien." In *L'Elevage en Méditerranée Occidentale*. Paris: CNRS, 1984, pp. 269–79.

———. "Les composantes géographiques et sociales des types d'élevage en milieu touareg." *Notes et Documents Voltaiques* (Ouagadougou) 6, no. 3 (Apr.–June 1973):12–22.

———. "Cueillette et exploitation des ressources spontanées du Sahel Nigérien par les Kel Tamasheq." *Cahiers d'ORSTOM* 4, no. 1 (1967): 31–52.

———. "Espace géographique et champs sociaux chez les Touareg Illabakan." *Etudes Rurales,* nos. 37–39 (Jan.–Sept. 1970):46–64.

———. "L'évolution des relations de dépendance depuis la période précoloniale jusqu'à nos jours chez les Iullemmeden Kel Dinnik." *Revue de l'Occident Musulman et da le Méditerranée* 21 (1976):85–99.

———. "L'Evolution récente des relations entre éleveurs et agriculteurs en Afrique tropicale: L'exemple du Sahel nigérien." *Cahiers d'ORSTOM* 11, no. 2 (1947):137–43.

———. "Géographie humaine de la zone Sahélienne." In *Le Sahel*. Paris: UNESCO, 1974, pp. 67–73.

———. "Histoire parallèles et croisées: Nobles et religieux chez les Touaregs Kel-Denneg. *Homme* 30, no. 115 (Sept. 1990).

———. *Les Illabakan (Niger): Une Tribu Touaregue Sahélienne et son Aire de Nomadisation*. Paris: ORSTOM, 1974.

———. "Incongruités et mauvaises paroles touaregues." *Journal de la Société des Africanistes* 42, no. 1 (1972):89–94.

———. "Maladies humaines et animales chez les Touaregs Sahéliens." *Journal de la Société des Africanistes* 39, no. 1 (1969):111–38.

———. "Médications Touaregs Sahéliens." *Encyclopédie Berbère* (Aix-en-Provence) 13 (1973).

———. "Les palmeraies de l'Aïr." *Revue de l'Occident Musulman* 11, no. 1 (1972):37–50.

———. "Possibilités et limites de la politique hydraulique pastorale dans le Sahel nigérien. *Cahiers d'ORSTOM* 11, no. 2 (1974):119–26.

———. "La Problème du berger chez les Touaregs Nigériens." Paper presented at the Colloque sur l'Elevage, N'Djamena, Chad, 1969.

———. *Quelques aspects de l'évolution des Touareg de l'Ouest de la République du Niger*. Paris: Etudes Nigériennes, no. 9, 1963.

———. "Techniques agricoles de l'Aïr." *Encyclopédie Berbère* (Aix-en-Provence), vol. 3 (1971).

———. "Les Touareg du Sahel nigérien." *Cahiers d'Outre-Mer* 19, no. 73 (Jan.–Mar. 1966):5–34.

———. "Les Touaregs," *Ethnies,* no. 6/7 (1987):7–13.

———. *Touaregs, chronique de l'Azawak*. Paris: Plume, 1991.

———. *Touaregs Nigériens, Unité Culturelle et diversité régionale d'une peuple pasteur*. Paris: ORSTOM, 1981.

———, and A. A. Arias. "Récits historiques de l'Azawagh. Traditions des Iullemmeden Kel Dinnik." *Bulletin d'IFAN* 32, no. 2 (Apr. 1970):434–85.

———. and Suzanne Bernus. *Du sel et des dates. Introduction à l'étude de la communauté d'In Gall et de Tegidda-n-Tesent*. Paris: Etudes Nigeriénnes, no. 31, 1972.

———. "L'évolution de la condition servile chez les Touaregs sahéliens." In C. Meillassoux (ed.), *L'Esclavage en Afrique Précoloniale*. Paris: Maspero, 1975, pp. 27–47.

———. "Les Kel Illagatan: Une pratique carnavalesque dans le mariage touareg." In *Itineraires en pays peul et alleurs*. Paris: Société des Africanistes, 1981, pp. 345–53.

———, and Ekhya Agg-Albostan. "L'amour en verte: poème touareg." *Journal des Africanistes* 57, no. 1/2 (1987):109–16.

Bernus, Suzanne. "Hypothèses sur le processus de constitution d'une *tawshet*: L'exemple *desimeghad* Illabakan." In V. Hull and M. Simpson (eds.), *Breastfeeding, Child Health and Child Spacing*. London: Croom Helm, 1985.

———. "Recherches en pays Touareg." *Mu Kaara Sani* (Niamey), no. 1 (n.d.):14–19.

———. "Stratégie matrimoniale et conservation du pouvoir dans l'Aïr et chez les Iullemmeden." *Revue de l'Occident Musulman et de la Méditerrannée* 21 (1976):101–4.

———, et al. "Die Salinen von Tegidda-n-tesemt." *Ethnographie-Archäologische Zeitschrift* (Berlin) 17, no. 2 (1976):209–36.

Bisson, J. "Eleveurs caravaniers et vieux sédentaires de l'Aïr." *Travaux de l'Institut de Recherches Sahariennes* 23 (1964):95–110.

Bleeker, Sonia. *The Tuareg, Nomads and Warriors of the Sahara.* New York: Morrow, 1964.

Bonté, Pierre. "Production et échanges chez les Touareg Kel Gress du Niger." Thesis, University of Paris, 1970.

———. "Structures et classes sociales chez les Kel Gress." *Revue de l'Occident Musulman et de la Méditerranée,* no. 21 (1976):141–62.

———, and N. Echard. "Histoire et Histoires. Conception du passé chez les Hausa et les Twareg Kel Gress de l'Ader." *Cahiers d'Etudes Africaines,* no. 61/62 (1976):237–96.

Bordeau, B. "Attisi ag Amellal." *Encyclopédie Berbère* (Aix-en-Provence) 21 (1978).

Bourgeot, André. "Affranchi (chez les Touaregs)." *Encyclopédie Berbère* (Aix-en-Provence) 21 (1978).

———. "Le désert quadrillé: Des Touaregs au Niger." *Politique Africaine,* no. 38 (1990):68–75.

———. "Identité touaregue: L'aristocratie à la révolution." *Etudes Rurales,* no. 120 (1990).

———. "Idéologies et appelations ethniques, l'exemple Twareg." *Cahiers d'Etudes Africaines* 12, no. 48 (1967):533–54.

———. "Le Lion et la gazelle: Etats et Touaregs." *Politique Africaine,* no. 34 (1989):19–29.

———. "Structure de classe, pouvoir politique et organisation de l'espace en pays touareg." In *Pastoral Production and Society.* Proceedings of the International Meeting on Nomadic Pastoralism, Paris, 1976. London: Cambridge University Press, 1979.

Brock, Lina Lee. "The Tamejirt: Kinship and Social History in a Tuareg Community." Ph.D. diss., Columbia University, 1984.

Cabannes, R., et al. "Etude hémotypologique des populations du massifs du Hoggar et du plateau de l'Aïr." *Bulletin et Mémoire de la Société d'Anthropologie de Paris* 4 (1969):143–46.

Cadenat, P. "Notes d'ethnographie touaregue." *Libyca* 12 (1964): 315–24.

Campbell, Dugald. *On the Trail of the Veiled Tuareg.* London: Seeley, Service and Co., 1928.

Casajus, Dominique. "Autour du rituel de la nomination chez les Touaregs Kel Ferwan." *Journal of the Anthropological Society of Oxford* 13, no. 1 (1982):57–67.

———. "Islam et noblesse chez les Touaregs." *Homme,* no. 115 (1990):7–30.

———. "Jeux touaregs de la région d'Agadez." *Journal des Africanistes* 58, no. 1 (1988):23–50.

———. "Le mariage préférentiel chez les Touaregs du nord du Niger." *Journal de la Société des Africanistes* 52, no. 1/2 (1983):95–117.

———. "Parole retenue et parole dangereuse chez les Touaregs Kel Ferwan." *Journal des Africanistes* 57, no. 1/2 (1987):97–107.

———. *La tente dans la solitude: La société et les morts chez les Touaregs Kel Ferwan*. London: Cambridge University Press, 1987.

———. "The Wedding Ritual Among the Kel Ferwan Tuaregs." *Journal of the Anthropological Society of Oxford* 14, no. 2 (1983): 227–37.

———. "Why Do the Tuareg Veil Their Faces?" In R. H. Barnes et al. (eds.), *Contexts and Levels: Anthropological Essays on Hierarchy*. Oxford: JASO, 1985.

Chaker, Salem (ed.). *Etudes Touaregues: Bilan des recherches en sciences sociales: Institutions—chercheurs—bibliographie*. Aix-en-Provence: Edisud, 1988.

Chapelle, J. "Les Nomades du Sahara méridional—Les Touareg." *Tropiques,* no. 38 (1950):25–38.

———. "Les Touareg." CHEAM, no. 1031 (1946).

———. "Les Touareg de l'Aïr." *Cahiers Charles de Foucault,* 3rd series (1949):20–95.

Chaventre, André. "Etude généalogique d'une tribu saharo-sahélienne, les Kel Kummer, et leur apparentés." Thesis, University of Paris, 1972.

———. *Evolution anthropo-biologique d'une population touaregue: Les Kel Kummer et leurs apparentés*. Paris: Presses Universitaires de France, 1983.

Claudot-Hawad, Hélène. "Des Etats-nations contre un peuple: Le cas des Touaregs." *Revue de l'Occident Musulman et de la Méditerranée* (Aix-en-Provence) 44 (1987):48–63.

———. "Femmes touaregues et pouvoir politique." *Peuples Méditerranéens* (Paris) 48/49 (1989):69–79.

———. "Les Touaregs ou la résistance d'une culture nomade." *Revue de l'Occident Musulman et de la Méditerranée* 51 (1989):63–73.

———. *Les Touareges: Portrait en fragments*. Aix-en-Provence: Edisud, 1993.

Clauzel, J. "L'Evolution contemporaine de l'économie et de la société chez les Touareg." *Actualitiés d'Outre-Mer,* no. 24 (July 1963):5–23.

———. "Les hiérarchies sociales en pays tuareg." *Travaux de l'Institut de Recherches Sahariennes* 21, no. 1 (1962):120–75.

———. "La situation en pays Touareg." *Afrique et l'Asie,* no. 58 (1962):23–40.

Coulomb, J. *Zone de Modernisation Pastorale du Niger*. Paris: IEMVT-SEDES, 1971.

Couret, B. "L'Avenir des Touaregs." *Connaissance du Monde,* no. 122 (Feb. 1969):61–72.

De Zeltner, Franz. "Etudes anthropologiques sur les Touaregs du Sud." *Anthropologie* 25 (1914):459–76.

———. "Les Touareg du Sud." *Journal of the Royal Anthropological Institute* 44 (1914):351–75.

"Dix Etudes sur l'Organisation sociale des Touaregs." Special issue of *Revue de l'Occident Musulman et de la Méditerrannée,* no. 21 (1976).

Dresch, J. "Notes de géographie humaine sur l'Aïr." *Annales de Géographie,* no. 367 (May–June 1959):257–62.

Drouin, J. "De quelques conception esthétiques de la parole dans la société touaregue." *Journal des Africanistes* 57, no. 1/2 (1987):77–96.

Dudot, Bernard. "Les *cigittawan* ou poteaux de mariage d'Agadès." *Notes Africaines,* no. 123 (July 1969):89–90.

———. "Notes sur la fabrication des anneaux de bras en pierre portés par les Touareg de l'Aïr." *Notes Africaines,* no. 122 (Apr. 1969): 58–61.

Duveyrier, Henri. *Les Touaregs du Nord.* Paris: Challamel, 1864.

———. "Notes sur les Touaregs et leurs pays." *Bulletin de la Société de Géographie* 5 (1863):102–25.

Englebert, Victor. *The World of Three Young Nomads.* New York: Harcourt, Brace, Jovanovich, 1971.

Feral, Gabriel. "Note sur le régime successoral en coutume tamacheq." *Notes Africaines,* no. 65 (Jan. 1955):21–22.

Gabus, Jean. "La colonisation chez les Touareg de la boucle du Niger." *Acta Tropica* 2, no. 4 (1945):353–73.

———. "Les Tuaregs." *Ville de Neuchâtel Bibliothèques et Musées* (Neuchâtel, Switz.) (1971):85–156.

Garba, Amadou. "Chez les Touareg on prend le voile quand on est devenu un homme." *France-Eurafrique,* no. 196 (June 1968):39–40.

Gast, M. "Notes d'ethnographie touaregue." *Libyca* 12 (1964):325–34.

Gaubert. "Les Kels Owey, groupement Touareg de l'Aïr." CHEAM, no. 1315 (1948).

Goetz, F. *Méharistes et Touaregs.* Paris: La Pensée Universelle, 1991.

Guillaume, Henri. *Les nomades interrompus: Introduction à l'étude du canton twareg de l'Imanan.* Paris: Etudes Nigeriénnes, no. 35, 1974.

Hama, Boubou. *Recherche sur l'histoire des Touaregs Sahariens et Soudanais.* Paris: Présence Africaine, 1967.

Huguet, J. "Sur les Touareg. *Bulletin et Mémoires de la Société Anthropologique* 5, no. 3 (1902):614–39.

Ichefegh, Attoujani. "Problèmes économiques, sociaux et politiques du développement chez les Touaregs Iwellemmendan de la République du Niger." Ottawa: Ottawa University Institute of International Cooperation, [1974?]

Jean, Camille-Charles. *Les Touareg du sud-est; Leur role dans la politique saharienne.* Paris: Larose, 1909.

Joubert. "Les coutumes et le droit chez les Kel Tadélé. *Bulletin d'IFAN* 1, no. 1 (Jan. 1939):245–81.

Keenan, Jeremy. "Some Theoretical Considerations on the 'Temazlayt' Relationship." *Revue de l'Occident Musulman.* no. 21 (1976):33–46.

———. *The Tuareg: People of Ahaggar*. London: Allen Lane, 1978.

Krebser, Markus, and Frederika de Cesco. *Touareg: Nomades du Sahara*. Paris: Hachette, 1971.

Laurent, C. "L'Aïr et ses gens." CHEAM, no. 1879 (1966).

Leblanc, Lancelot. "Les Touareg." *Revue Anthropologique* (Jan.–Mar. 1929).

Lefevre, Witier, and J. Ruffie. "Note sur l'hétérogénéité biologique des Touaregs." *Revue de l'Occident Musulman,* no. 11 (1972):99–105.

Leupen, A. H. A. *Bibliographie des populations Touaregues*. Leiden (Neth.): Afrika-Studiecentrum, 1978.

Lhote, Henri. "Un bijou anthropomorphe chez les Touareg de l'Aïr." *Notes Africaines,* no. 44 (Oct. 1949):114–16.

———. *La Chasse chez les Touaregs*. Paris: Editions Amiot-Dumont, 1951.

———. *Comment Campent les Touaregs*. Paris: J. Susse, 1947.

———. "Contribution à l'anthropologie somatique des Touaregs." *Revue Anthropologique* 48 (1938):284–306.

———. "Contribution à l'étude des Touaregs soudanais." *Bulletin d'IFAN* 17 (1955):234–70.

———. "Contribution à l'histoire des Touareg soudanais." *Bulletin d'IFAN* 17, no. 3/4 (July–Oct. 1955):334–70, 391–407.

———. "Le cycle caravanier des Touaregs de l'Ahaggar et la saline d'Amadror. Leurs rapports avec les centre commerciaux du Soudan." *Bulletin d'IFAN* 21, no. 4 (Oct. 1969):104–27.

———. *Dans les campements Touaregs*. Paris: Amiot-Dumont, 1952.

———. "Note complémentaire: Au sujet du puits à balancier en Aïr." *Encyclopédie Berbère* (Aix-en-Provence) (1972).

———. "Note sur l'origine des lames d'epée des Touaregs." *Notes Africaines,* no. 61 (1954):9–15.

———. "Quelques coutumes en usage chez les Kel Oui." In *Contribution à l'étude de l'Aïr*. Paris: Larose, 1950, pp. 504–7.

———. "Les Sandales." *Contribution à l'étude de l'Aïr*. Paris: Larose, 1950, pp. 512–33.

———. *Les Touaregs du Hoggar*. Paris: Payot, 1955.

———. "'Varia' sur la sandale et la marche chez les Touaregs." *Bulletin d'IFAN* 14, no. 2 (1952):596–622.

———. *Vers d'Autres Tassilis*. Paris: Arthaud, 1976.

Maillocheau, J. "Les touaregs de la subdivision de Tanout." CHEAM, no. 2618 (1956).

Mariko, Keletigui. *Les Touaregs Ouelleminden*. Paris: Karthala, 1984.

Mounier, A. "Le travail des peaux chez les Touareg Haggar." *Travaux de l'Institut de Recherches Sahariennes* (1942):133–75.

Murphy, R. F. "Social Distance and the Veil." *American Anthropologist,* no. 66 (1964):1270–74.

———. "Tuareg Kinship." *American Anthropologist,* no. 69 (1967): 163–70.

Museur, M. "De Tradition à Modernité: analyse des structures socio-économiques 'en devenir' des classes sociales de la communauté targuia du Hoggar." 2 vols. Thesis, Monpellier, 1975.

———, and R. Pirson. "Une Problématique de passage chez les populations du Hoggar-Tassili: Du nomadisme à la sedentarité." *Civilisations* 26, no. 1/2 (1974):64–82.

Nicolaisen, Johannes. "Ecological and Historical Factors: A Case Study from the Ahaggar Tuareg." *Folk* (Copenhagen) 6, no. 1 (1964): 75–81.

———. *Ecology and Culture of the Pastoral Tuareg*. Copenhagen: National Museum of Copenhagen, 1963.

———. "Political Systems of Pastoral Tuareg in Aïr and Ahaggar." *Folk* (Copenhagen) 1 (1959):67–131.

———. "Some Aspects of the Problem of Nomadic Cattle Breeding Among the Tuareg of the Central Sahara." *Geografisk Tidsskrift* (Copenhagen) 53 (1954):67–105.

———. "The Structural Study of Kinship Behavior with Particular Reference to Tuareg Concepts." *Folk* (Copenhagen) no. 13 (1971): 167–94.

———. *Structures politiques et sociales des Touareg de l'Aïr et de l'Ahaggar*. Paris: Etudes Nigeriénnes, no. 7, 1963.

Nicolas, Francis. "Aperçu sur les populations berbères du groupe Touareg aux points de vue historique, social, politique." CHEAM, no. 753 (1945).

———. "Aspects politiques de l'administration chez les Touaregs du Niger." CHEAM, no. 505 (1941).

———. "Contributions à l'étude des Twareg de l'Aïr." In *Contribution à l'étude de l'Aïr*. Paris: Larose, 1950, pp. 459–503.

———. *Coutumes et traditions chez les Twareg: Matriarcat et patriarcat*. Paris: Institut des Belles Lettres Arabes, 1946.

———. "Les industries de protection chez les Twareg de l'Azawagh." *Héspèris* 25, no. 1 (1938):43–84.

———. "Notes sur la société et l'état chez les Twaregs du Dinnik (Iullemenden de l'Est)." *Bulletin d'IFAN* 1, no. 2/3 (Apr.–July 1939): 579–86.

———. "Pièces du folklore des Twaregs Ioullemmenden." *Anima,* no. 29 (Jan.–Feb. 1942):3–12.

———. "Les populations Touareg du Niger et leur participation à l'économie moderne." CHEAM, no. 495 (1941).

———. "Superstition et magie chez les Ioullemmenden de l'est (Colonie du Niger)." *Anima,* no. 33 (July–Sept. 1943):106–7.

———. *Tamesna: Les Ioullemenden de l'Est*. Paris: Imprimerie Nationale, 1950.

———. "Textes ethnographiques de la 'tamajeq' des Iullemmeden de l'est." *Anthropos* 46, no. 5/6 (Sept.–Dec. 1951):754–800; 48, no. 3/4 (1953):458–84; 50, nos. 4–6 (1955):655–58; 51, no. 1/2 (1956): 129–56; 52, no. 1/2 (1957):49–64; 52, no. 3/4 (1957):564–80.

———. "La transhumance chez les Iullemmeden de l'Est." *Travaux de l'Institut de Recherches Sahariennes* 4 (1947):111–24.

Nicolas, Guy. "Un village bouzou du Niger: Etude d'un terroir." *Cahiers d'Outre-Mer* 15, no. 58 (Apr.–June 1962):138–65.

Norris, H. T. *The Tuaregs: Their Islamic Legacy and Its Diffusion in the Sahel*. London: Aris and Phillips, 1975.

Oxby, C. "The 'Living Milk' Runs Dry: The Decline of a Form of Joint Ownership and Matrilineal Inheritance Among the Twareg, Niger." In P. T. W. Baxter (ed.), Property, Poverty, and People: Changing Rights in Poverty and Problems of Pastoral Development. Manchester: Department of Social Anthropology and the International Development Centre, 1989.

———. "Women Unveiled: Class and Gender Among Kel Ferwan Twareg (Niger)." *Ethnos* 52, no. 1/2 (1987):119–36.

Palmer, H. R. "The Tuareg Veil." *Geographical Journal* 68 (Nov. 1926):412–18.

Papy, Louis. "Le Déclin des Hoggaras au Sahara." *Cahiers d'Outre-Mer* 12, no. 48 (Oct.–Dec. 1959):401–6.

Ramir, Sylvie. *Les pistes de l'oubli: Touaregs au Niger*. Paris: Editions du Felin, 1991.

Rasmussen, Susan J. "Accounting for Belief: Causation, Misfortune, and Evil in Tuareg Systems of Thought." *Man* 24, no. 1 (1989):124–44.

———. "Gender and Curing in Ritual and Symbol: Women, Spirit Possession and Aging Among the Kel Ewey Tuareg." Ph.D. diss. Indiana University, 1986.

———. "Interpreting Androgynous Woman: Female Aging and Personhood Among the Kel Ewey Tuareg." *Ethnology* (Jan. 1987):17–30.

———. "Modes of Persuasion: Gossip, Song and Divination in Tuareg Conflict Resolution." *Anthropological Quarterly* 64, no. 1 (Jan. 1991):30–46.

———. *Spirit Possession and Personhood Among the Kel Ewey Tuareg*. Cambridge: Cambridge University Press, 1995.

Reeb. "L'avenir économique du pays touareg." CHEAM, no. 1284 (1948).

———. "Les Iklan ou les Touaregs Noirs." CHEAM, no. 1226 (1947).

———. "Les Noirs au sein de la société touaregue." CHEAM, no. 1291 (1948).

Renaud, J. "Etude sur l'évolution des Kel Gress vers la sédentarisation." *Bulletin du Comité des Etudes Historiques et Scientifiques de l'AOF* 2 (1922):252–62.

Richer, A. *Les Touareg du Niger: Les Ouilliminden.* Paris: Larose, 1924.

Rodd, Francis Rennel. "The Origin of the Tuareg." *Geographical Journal* 67 (1926): pp. 27–52.

———. *People of the Veil.* London: Macmillan, 1926.

———. "A Second Journey Among the Southern Tuareg." *Geographical Journal* 73 (1929):1–19, 147–58.

Saenz, Candelaris. "They Have Eaten Our Grandfather: The Special Status of Aïr Twareg Smiths (Niger)." Ph.D. diss., Columbia University, 1991.

Si Gunga Mayga. "Les Touaregs en pays Songhay." Cahier 18, texte 1, Niger et Pays Voisin series, Fonds Vieillard, IFAN Library, Dakar.

Slavin, K., and J. Slavin. *The Tuareg.* London: Gentry Books, 1973.

Soehring, Anneliese. "Nomadenland im Aufbruch: Berichte über die 'cure salée' 1965 in der Republik Niger." *Internationales Afrikaforum* (Apr. 1966).

Spittler, Gerd. *Les Touaregs face aux sécheresses et aux famines: Les Kel Ewey de l'Aïr (Niger) 1900–1985.* Paris: Karthala, 1993.

"Les Touareg de l'Azawack." *Niger* (Niamey), no. 4 (July 1968):22–49.

Traditions Historiques de Touaregs de l'Imannan. Niamey: CELTHO, 1977.

Urvoy, Yves. "Histoire des Ouilliminden de l'Est." *Bulletin du Comité d'Etudes Historiques et Scientifiques de l'AOF* 16, no. 1 (Jan.–Mar. 1933):66–97.

Vallet, M. "Les Touaregs aujourd'hui." CHEAM, no. 4113 (1966).

Wellard, J. "The Tuaregs." *Geographical Magazine* 37 (Sept. 1964): 386–96.

Worley, Barbara. "Property and Gender Relations Among Twareg Nomads." *Nomadic Peoples* 23 (1987):31–35.

———. "Women's War Drum, Women's Wealth: The Social Contribution of Female Autonomy and Social Prestige Among Kel Faday Twareg Pastoral Nomads (Niger)." Ph.D. diss., Columbia University, 1991.

Zakara, Mohamed Aghali, and Jeannine Drouin. *Traditions touareg nigeriénnes.* Paris: L'Harmattan, 1979.

Sociology and Demography

Arnaud, M., and B. Spire. *Urbanisme et habitat—République du Niger.* Paris, 1960.

Arnould, Eric J., and Helen K. Henderson. "Women in Niger." In *Women in Development.* Tucson: University of Arizona, International Agricultural Programs Working Paper no. 1, 1982.

Bandiane, Ali. "L'Enfant dans la société nigérienne." *Revue Juridique et Politique,* no. 2 (Apr.–June 1977):371–79.

Barkow, Jerome H. "Strategies for Self-Esteem and Prestige in Maradi." In T. R. Williams (ed.), *Psychological Anthropology.* Paris: Mouton, 1975, pp. 373–88.

Barou, Jacques. "L'Emigration dans un village du Niger." *Cahiers d'Etudes Africaines* 6, no. 63/64 (1976):627–32.

Bataillou, C. "Modernisation du nomadisme pastoral." In *Nomadisme et Nomades au Sahara.* Paris: UNESCO, 1963, pp. 165–77.

Belloncle, Guy. *Femmes et Développement en Afrique Sahélienne.* Paris: Nouvelles Editions Africaines, 1980.

Berdichewsky, Bernardo (ed.). *Anthropology and Social Change in Rural Areas.* The Hague: Mouton, 1979.

Bernus, Suzanne. *Niamey, Population et habitat.* Paris: Etudes Nigeriénnes, no. 11, 1962.

———. *Particularismes ethniques en milieu urbain; L'exemple de Niamey.* Paris: Institut d'Ethnologie, Musée de l'Homme, 1969.

———. "Recherches sur les centres urbains d'Agadez et d'In Gall." *Revue de l'Occident Musulman* 11, no. 1 (1972):51–56.

———. "Besoins et participants des femmes rurales au Niger." *Carnets de l'Enfance* (Paris) 41 (Jan.–Mar. 1978):74–92.

Borrey, F. "La formation sanitaire nomade du Niger." *Marchés Coloniaux,* no. 237 (1950):1185–88.

Castinel, J. "Le mariage et la mort dans la région du Yanga." *Bulletin d'IFAN,* no. 7 (1945):148–55.

Ciucci, L., and D. Maffioli. "L'impact de l'urbanisation sur les modèles de consommation alimentaire de base au Niger." *Africa* (Rome) 43 no. 2 (1988):292–97.

Clair, Andrée. "Au Niger, les Touareg à l'ombre des transistors." *Afrique* (Oct. 1962):30–33.

Clerson, Gérard. "Habitat à Niamey." M.A. thesis, Université de Sherbrooke, 1972.

Dandobi, Mahamane. "Les institutions martimoniales basées sur la tradition et la coutume ne sont pas restées immeubles." *Niger* (Niamey), no. 12 (Mar. 6, 1967):3; no. 13 (Mar. 13, 1967):5, 8.

———. "Le mariage au Niger." *Revue Juridique et Politique,* no. 1 (Jan.–Mar. 1967):105–17.

Dankoussou, Issaka, et al. "Niger." In John C. Caldwell et al. (eds.), *Population Growth and Socio-Economic Change in West Africa.* New York: Columbia University Press, 1975, pp. 679–700.

Davis, Richard Eugene. "Responses to Innovation in a Zarma Village: Contemporary Tradition in Niger." Ph.D. diss., University of Connecticut, 1991.

Decoudras, P. M. "Condition Sahélienne et pauvreté rurale: Les sauniers des Dallols du Niger." In A. Singaravelou (ed.), *Pauvreté et développement dans les pays tropicaux.* Bordeaux: Centre de Recherches sur les Espaces Tropicaux, 1989, pp. 55–72.

Demain, H. M., and J. Lugassy. "L'Artisanat rural en Haute-Volta et au Niger." *Bulletin Chambre du Commerce du Niger* (Niamey) (1965).

Desiré-Vuillemin, G. "Les capitales de l'Ouest Africain." 2 vols. Paris: Service d'Etudes et de Recherches Pedagogiques pour les pays en Voie de développement, 1963.

Diado, Amadou. "Le coût du mariage est trop élevé. *Niger* (Niamey), no. 7 (Feb. 26, 1968):1–2; no. 8 (Mar. 4, 1968):2, 7.

Diop, M. "Etude sur le salariat: Haute-Sénégal, Niger, Soudan, Mali, 1884–1963." *Etudes Maliennes* (Bamako), no. 14 (1975).

Dresch, J. "Notes de géographie humaine sur l'Aïr." *Annales de Géographie,* no. 367 (May–June 1959):259–62.

Du Boucher. "Aspects du nomadisme au Niger." CHEAM, no. 1009 (1945).

Dudot, Bernard. "Traditions sur les origines de la ville de Niamey." *Notes Africaines,* no. 117 (Jan. 1968):19–20.

Echard, Nicole. *Etude socio-économique dans les vallées de l'Ader Doutchi Majya.* Paris: Etudes Nigériennes, no. 15, 1964.

———. "Espace politique Nigérien." In A. Diagne, *Pouvoir Politique en Afrique Noire.* Paris: Mouton, 1967.

Faulkingham, R. H. "Fertility in Tudu: Analysis of Constraints on Fertility in a Village in Niger." In J. C. Caldwell (ed.), *The Persistence of High Fertility.* Canberra: Australian National University, 1977.

———, and P. F. Thorbahn. "Population Dynamics and Drought in a Village in Niger." *Population Studies* (London) 23, no. 3 (Nov. 1975):463–77.

France. Ministère de la Coopération. Institut National de la Statistique et des Etudes Economique. *Les Budgets familiaux africains, Niamey,* by D. Michaud. Paris, 1964.

———. *Etude Démographique du Niger.* Paris, 1963.

———. *Mission Démographique du Niger—Enquête par sondage (1959–62).* 2 vols. Paris, 1963.

Galaty, John G, and Philip C. Salzman. *Change and Development in Nomadic and Pastoral Societies.* Leiden: Brill, 1981.

Gervais, Raymond, "Les conséquences démographiques de la sécheresse au Sahel: Le cas du Niger, 1969–1974." M.Sc. thesis, Université de Sherbrooke, 1982.

Hama, Boubou. *Le Double d'hier rencontre demain.* Paris: UGE, 1973.

———. *L'Exode rural: Un problème de fond.* Niamey: Editions de la Croix Rouge Nigérienne, 1968.

———. "Textes et Documents sur la ville de Niamey." Niamey: IFAN, 1955.

Hoogvelt, Ankie. "Indigenization and Technological Dependency." *Development and Change* 11, no. 2 (1980):257–72.

Horowitz, M. M. "Ethnic Boundary Maintenance Among the Pastoralists and Farmers in the Western Sudan (Niger)." *Journal of Asian and African Studies* 12 (1972):106–14.

King, M. H.W. "Rural–Urban Migration in Niger." Thesis, University of Michigan, 1977.

Laval, Gilbert. "Enquête sur le 'tabliers' de Niamey." *Cahiers d'Etudes Africaines* 21, no. 81–83 (1981):211–20.

Le Coeur, Charles, and Marguerite Le Coeur. "Initiation à l'hygiène et à la morale de l'alimentation chez les Djerma et les Peuls du Niamey." *Bulletin d'IFAN* 8 (1946):164–80.

Le Thin, Kim Dung. "Etude de la fécondité au Niger à partir d'une sondage, 1970–1971." M.Sc. thesis, University of Niamey, 1976.

Louis-Joseph, Raymond. "Note sur l'habitat traditionnel—Schéma d'études des possibilités d'amélioration." Niamey: Crédit du Niger, 1964.

Martini, P. "Amélioration des conditions de vie des nomades dans L'Eghazer." Rome: FAO, 1974.

Maygueskia. "Niamey, ville indigène." *Bulletin d'Information et de Renseignements* (Dakar), no. 204 (Oct. 24, 1938):436–37.

"Médicins nomades pour Nomades malades." *Niger* (Niamey), no. 1 (Oct. 1967):60–69.

Monnier, A. "Les organisations villageoises de jeunes: Samari." Niamey: CNRSH, 1967.

———. "Les Vallées d'Ibohamane et de Tégèf." Niamey: CNRSH, 1967.

Morichau-Beauchant, A. "Santé et Développement en milieu rural: L' expérience au Niger du département de Maradi." *Revue Tiers Monde,* no. 53 (Jan.–Mar. 1973):173–76.

Mortimer, M. J. "The Changing Resources of Sedentary Communities in Aïr, Southern Sudan." *Geographical Review* (Jan. 1972):71–91.

Moulton, Jeanne Marie. *Animation Rurale: Education for Rural Development.* Amherst, Mass.: Center for International Education, 1977.

Museur, M. "Quelques aspects récents de l'économie sociale du Hoggar." *Revue de l'Institut de Sociologie* 2 (1974):299–315.

"Niamey: Capital of the French Niger Colony." *Geographical Journal* 76 (1930):364.

"Niamey, perle du Niger." *Europe France Outre-Mer,* no. 503 (Dec. 1971):8–10.

Niger. Ministère de l'Economie et de Finances. *Recensement général de la population 1988.* Niamey, 1992.

———. Ministère du Plan. Direction de la Statistique et de l'Information. *Estimations de quelques parametres démographiques de la population du Niger de 1977 à l'an 2000.* Niamey, 1985.

———. *Recensement général de la population 1977.* Niamey, 1987.

Niger. Service de la Statistique. "La population dans la République du Niger," by H. Wiesler. 2 pams. Niamey, 1973.

Painter, Thomas Michael. "Making Migrants: Zarma Peasants in Niger,

1900–1920." In Dennis D. Cordell and Joel W. Gregory (eds.), *African Population and Capitalism: Historical Perspectives*. Boulder, Colo.: Westview Press, 1987, pp. 122–33.

———. "Peasant Migration and Rural Transformation in Niger." Ph.D. diss., State University of New York/Binghamton, 1986.

Palmeri, Paolo. "Traditional Lifeways and Modernization: Social Transformation in a Niger Village." In Bernardo Berdichewsky (ed.), *Anthropology and Social Change in Rural Areas*. The Hague: Mouton, 1979.

Piault, M. "Cycles de marché et 'espaces' socio-politiques (au Niger)." In C. Meillassoux (ed.), *The Development of Indigenous Trade and Markets in West Africa*. London, 1971, pp. 285–302.

Poitou, Daniele. "Approche sociologique de la jeunesse délinquante au Niger." *Afrique et l'Asie Moderne*, no. 120 (1979):43–61.

———. "Délinquance juvenile et urbanisation au Niger et au Nigeria." *Cahiers d'Etudes Africaines* 21, nos. 81–83, (1981):111–27.

———. *La Délinquance juvenile au Niger*. Niamey: INRSH, 1978.

———. "Un exemple d'urbanisation sauvage: Le quartier Talladje à Niamey, Niger." In N. Haumont and A. Maric (eds.), *Actes du colloque international: Stratégie urbaine dans les pays en voie de développement*. Paris: Harmattan, 1987.

Pool, D. I. "Enquête sur la fécondité et la famille en Niger." Niamey: Collection Méthodologiques, no. 1, CNRSH, n.d.

———, and Victor Piche. "Enquête sur la fécondité au Niger Central." Niamey: Collection Méthodologiques, no. 2, CNRSH, n.d.

Pool, Janet E. "A Cross-Comparative Study of Aspects of Conjugal Behavior Among Women of Three West African Countries." *Canadian Journal of African Studies* 6, no. 2 (1972):233–60.

Raulin, H. "Société sans classes d'âge au Niger." In D. Paulme (ed.), *Classes d'âge et Associations d'âge en Afrique de l'Ouest*. Paris: Plon, 1971, pp. 320–40.

Ravignan, François de. "L'Afrique des paysans." *Economie et Humanisme* (Paris), no. 248 (July–Aug. 1979):5–15.

Raynaut, Claude. "Circulation monétaire et évolution des structures socio-économiques chez les Haoussas du Niger." *Africa* 47 (1977).

———. "Disparités et homogénéité à Maradi, Niger, et la santé comme révélateur d'une réalité urbaine." In A. Singaravelou (ed.), *Pauvreté et développement dans les pays tropicaux*. Bordeaux: Centre de Recherches sur les Espaces Tropicaux, 1989, pp. 525–40.

———. "Les privilege urbain: Conditions de vie et santé au Niger." *Politique Africaine*, no. 28 (1987):42–52.

———. "Transformation d'un système de production et inégalité économique: Le cas d'un village haoussa." *Canadian Journal of African Affairs* 10, no. 2 (1976):279–306.

Rovagny, Albert. "Villes d'Afrique: Niamey." *Afrique Française* 40, no. 6 (June 1930):329–37.

Saunders, M. O. "Marriage and Divorce in a Muslim Hausa Town: Mirria, Niger." Ph.D. diss., University of Indiana, 1978.

Sauvy, Jean. "Un marché africain urbain: Niamey." *Notes Africaines,* no. 38 (Apr. 1948):1–5.

Sekou, Touré, and A. Prokhoroff. *Etude Démographique du Niger.* Paris: INSEE, 1963.

Séré de Rivières, Edmond. "La Chefferie au Niger." *Penant* 77, no. 718 (Oct.–Dec. 1967):463–88.

Shapiro, Barry Ira. "New Technology Adoption in Two Agricultural Systems of the Niamey Region of Niger." Ph.D. diss., Purdue University, 1990.

Sidikou, Arouna Hamidou. "Niamey." *Cahiers d'Outre-Mer,* no. 111 (July–Sept. 1975):201–17.

———. *Sédentarité et mobilité entre Niger et Zgaret.* Paris: Etudes Nigériennes, no. 34, 1974.

———. "Sédentarité et mobilité entre le Niger et Zgaret." Ph.D. diss., University of Rouen, 1973.

Silla, O. "Villes historiques de l'Afrique Saharo-Soudanaise." *Revue Française d'Etudes Politiques Africaines,* no. 29 (May 1968):25–37.

"Social Security Fund in the Republic of Niger." *International Labor Review* (Feb. 1966):177–78.

Spittler, G. "Urban Exodus: Urban-Rural and Rural-Urban Migration in Gobir." *Sociologica Ruralis* 17 (1977):223–35.

Thom, Derrick J. "The City of Maradi: French Influence upon a Hausa Urban Center." *Journal of Geography* (Nov. 1971):472–82.

———. "The Morphology of Maradi, Niger." *African Urban Notes,* no. 7 (Winter 1972).

Thomson, J. T. "Ecological Deterioration: Local Level Rule-Making and Enforcement Problems in Niger." In M. H. Glantz (ed.), *Desertification: Environmental Degradation in and Around Arid Lands.* Boulder, Colo.: Westview Press, 1977.

Van Hoey, Leo Fralls. "The Coercive Process of Urbanization: The Case of Niger." In S. Green et al., *The New Urbanization.* New York, 1968.

———. "Emergent Urbanization: Implications on the Theory of Social Scale Verified in Niamey, West Africa." Ph.D. diss., Northwestern University, 1966.

Wiesler, Hans. "Estimation de la mortalité au moyen de la théorie sur la population stable: Un cas typique, la République du Niger." *Schweizerische Zeitschrift für Volkswirtschaft und Statistik* (Basel) (Apr. 1975):229–43.

Willaert, Y. "L'emploi dans les pays du Sahel: Situation et perspectives de l'emploi au Niger." Addis Ababa: International Labor Organization, 1977.

History

Abdelkader, A. "Histoire de l'Aïr du Moyen Age à nos jours." *Niger* (Niamey), no. 19 (Mar. 1973):10–13.

Aboubacar, Adamou. "Agadez et sa région. Contribution à l'étude du Sahel et du Sahara nigérien." Thesis, University of Niamey, 1968. Also Niamey: Etudes Nigériennes, no. 44, 1979.

Adamu, Mahdi. *The Hausa Factor in West African History*. London: Oxford University Press, 1978.

———. "The Role of the Fulani and Twareg Pastoralists in the Central Sudan, 1405–1903." In Mahdi Adamu and A. H. M. Kirk-Green (eds.), *Pastoralists of the African Savanna*. Manchester: Manchester University Press, 1986, pp. 55–61.

Afrique Occidentale Française. Gouvernement Général. *Le Niger*. Paris: Société d'Editions Géographiques, Maritimes et Coloniales, 1931.

Ag Arias, Alatnine, and Edmond Bernus. "La jardin de la sécheresse. L'histoire d'Amamen ag Amastan." *Journal des Africanistes* 47, no. 1 (1977):83–93.

"Aïr et Kaouar." Special issue of *Niger* (Niamey), no. 19 (Mar. 1973).

Alkali, M. Nur. "The Political System and Administrative Structure of Kanem Bornu Under the Saifawa." In J. F. Ade Ajayi and Bashir Ikara (eds.), *Evolution of Political Culture in Nigeria*. Ibadan: Ibadan University Press, 1985, pp. 33–49.

Alibert, Louis. *Méhariste 1917–1918*. Paris: Delmas, 1936.

Amed Toihir, S., and J. Mahi Matike. "Famine du 1931 au Niger." In C. Barnes et al. (eds.), *Wood, Energy and Households*. Uppsala: Scandinavian Institute of African Studies, 1984, pp. 51–58.

Arnett, E. J. *The Rise of the Sokoto Fulani*. Kano, Nigeria, 1929.

Ba, A. K. *Sonni Ali Ber*. Niamey: INRSH, 1977.

Baa, M. *La geste de Fanta Maa, archétype du chasseur dans la culture des Bozo*. Niamey: CELTHO, 1987.

Baba Kake, Ibrahima. *Djouder, la fin de l'Empire Songhay*. Dakar: Nouvelles Editions Africaines, 1975.

Baier, Stephen. "African Merchants in the Colonial Period: A History of Commerce in Damagaram (Central Niger) 1880–1960." Ph.D. diss., University of Wisconsin, 1974.

———. *An Economic History of Central Niger*. London: Oxford University Press, 1981.

———. "The Transsaharan Trade and the Sahel: Damergou, 1870–1930." *Journal of African History* 18, no. 1 (1977):37–60.

———, and D. J. King. "Drought and the Development of Sahelian Economies: A Case Study of Hausa-Tuareg Interdependence." *LTC Newsletter,* no. 45 (1974):11–22.

———, and Paul Lovejoy. "The Tuareg of the Central Sahara: Gradations of Servility at the Desert Edge." In Suzanne Meiers and Igor

Kopytoff (eds.), *Slavery in Africa*. Madison: University of Wisconsin Press, 1977, pp. 391–411.

Ballif. "Les Française en Aïr pendant la guerre." *Bulletin du Comité d'Etudes Historiques et Scientifiques de l'AOF* (1924).

Baquet. *La Pénétration saharienne: Resumé historique*. Paris: Charles Lavauzelle, 1908.

Baroin, Catherine. "Effets de la colonisation sur la société traditionnelle Daza." *Journal de la Société des Africanistes* 47, no. 2 (1977):123–32.

Beauvilain, Alain. *Les Peuls du Dallol Bosso*. Niamey: CNRSH, 1977.

Beltrami, Vanni. "Arte parietale dello Djado e delle regioni prossime al margine occidentale del Tibesti." *Africa* (Rome) 44, no. 3 (1989): 445–72.

Benoit, J. "La guerre au désert. Le sénoussisme et l'attaque du Sahara et du Soudan." *Revue des Sciences Politiques* 49 (Apr.–June 1926): 224–45.

Beraud-Villars, J. *L'Empire de Gao*. Paris: Plon, 1942.

Bernus, Edmond. "Récits Historiques de l'Azawagh." *Bulletin d'IFAN* 32, no. 2 (1970):431–85.

———. *Touaregs: Chroniques de l'Azawak*. Paris: Plume, 1991.

———, et al. *Nomades et commandants: L'administration et sociétés nomades dans l'ancienne AOF*. Paris: Karthala, 1993.

Bernus, Suzanne (ed.), *Henri Barth chez les Touaregs de l'Aïr*. Paris: Etudes Nigériennes, no. 28, 1972.

———. "Recherches sur les centres d'Agadez et d'In Gall." *Revue de l'Occident Musulman et du Monde la Méditerranéen,* 11 (1972): 51–56.

Berthelot, A. *L'Afrique saharienne et soudanaise. Ce qu'en ont connu l'anciens*. Paris: Les Arts et les Livres, 1927.

Bétrix, Jean. *La pénétration Touareg*. Paris: Charles Lavauzelle, 1911.

Biobaku, Saburi, and Muhammad Al-Hajj. "The Sudanese Mahdiyya and the Niger-Chad region." In I. M. Lewis (ed.), *Islam in Tropical Africa*. London: Hutchinson, 1966, pp. 226–39.

Bisilliat, Jeanne, and Dioulde Laya. *Les Zamou*. Niamey: CNRS, 1972.

Boahen, A. Adu. *Britain, the Sahara and the Western Sudan, 1788–1861*. London: Oxford University Press, 1964.

———. "The Caravan Trade in the Nineteenth Century. *Journal of African History* 3, no. 2 (1962):349–59.

———. "The Caravan Trade in the Nineteenth Century." In P. J. M. Smith (ed.), *Nineteenth Century Africa*. London: Oxford University Press, 1968, pp. 90–98.

Boisselot, R. "Une subdivision nomade au Niger: Le cercle de Tanout." *Afrique Française* 44, no. 4 (Apr. 1934):81–85.

Bonardi, Pierre. *La République du Niger*. Paris: APD, 1960.

Bonfiglio, Angelo Maliki. *Dudal: Histoire de famille et histoire de troupeau chez un groupe de Wodaabe du Niger*. New York: Cambridge University Press, 1989.

———. *Introduction à l'histoire des WoDaaBe du Niger*. Niamey: Ministère du Développement Rurale, 1982.

Bouchet, Alain Paul. "Perspectives thérapeutiques et sociales des phénomènes de transe de pays songhay." Diss., University of Paris, 1988.

Boulnois, Jean, and Boubou Hama. *L'Empire de Gao: Histoire, coutumes et magie des Sonrai*. Paris: Maisonneuve, 1954.

Bourgeot, André. "Les échanges transsahariens, la senussiya et les révoltes twareg de 1916–17." *Cahiers d'Etudes Africains* 18, no. 1/2 (1978):159–86.

———. "Le Lion et la gazelle: Etats et Touarges." *Politique Africaines*, no. 34 (June 1989):19–29.

———. "Rapports esclavagistes et conditions d'affranchissements chez les Imuhagh." In Claude Meillassoux (ed.), *L'Esclavage en Afrique précoloniale*. Paris: Maspero, 1975.

Bovill, E. William. *Caravans of the Old Sahara*. London: Oxford University Press, 1933.

———. *The Golden Trade of the Moors*. London: Oxford University Press, 1958.

———. "The Niger and the Songhai Empire." *Journal of the Africa Society* 25, no. 98 (Jan. 1926):138–46.

———. *The Niger Explored*. London: Oxford University Press, 1968.

Briggs, L. C. "European Blades in Tuareg Swords and Daggers." *Journal of the Arms and Armour Society* 5, no. 2 (1965).

Britsch, J. "Le Sahara et ses pionniers." *Eurafrique* (Algiers), no. 26 (Apr. 1961):15–20.

Brock, Lina Lee. "The Tamejirs: Kinship and Social History in a Tuareg Community." Ph.D. dissertation, Columbia University, 1984.

Brulard, M. "Aperçu sur le commerce caravanier Tripolitaine–Ghat–Niger vers la fin du XIXe siècle." *Bulletin de Liaison Saharienne* 9, no. 31 (1958):202–15.

Buret, Joseph. *Le Territoire Française Niger-Tchad*. Brussels: Société d'Etudes Coloniales de Belgique, 1905.

Casajus, Dominique. "Deux touaregs de la région d'Agadez." *Journal des Africanistes* 58, no. 1 (1988):23–50.

Chailley, Marcel. "La Mission du Haut-Soudan et le drame de Zinder." *Bulletin d'IFAN* 16, no. 3/4 (July–Oct. 1954):243–54; 17, no. 1/2 (Jan.–Apr. 1954):1–58.

Chanoine, Charles P. J. "Mission Voulet-Chanoine." *Bulletin de la Société de Géographie* 20, no. 7 (1899):220–35.

Chapelle, Jean. *Souvenirs du Sahel: Zinder, lac Tchad, Komadougou*. Paris: Harmattan, 1987.

Chatelain. "L'Exode des Djerma de l'Andiarou vers le Dallol Bosso, le Djigui et la Fakara." *Bulletin du Comité d'Etudes Historiques et Scientifiques de l'AOF* no. 2 (Apr.–June 1921):273–79.

———. "Traditions relatives à l'éstablissement de Bornuans dans le Dallol Maouri et le pays Djerma." *Annuaire et Mémoire du Comité d'Etudes Historiques et Scientifiques de l'AOF* (1918):358–61.

Clair, Andrée. *Le Niger, pays à découvrir*. Paris: Hachette, 1965.

Clarke, Thurston. *The Last Caravan*. New York: Putnam, 1978.

Claudot-Hawad, H., et al. *La politique dans l'histoire Touaregue*. Aix-en-Provence: Cahiers de l'IREMAM, 1993.

Clauzel, J. "L'administration française et les sociétés nomades dans l'ancienne Afrique Occidentale Française." *Politique Africaine*, no. 46 (1992):99–116.

Collion, Marie-Hélène Josephine. "Colonial Rule and Changing Peasant Economy in Damagherim, Niger Republic." Ph.D. diss., Cornell University, 1982.

"Le commerce tripolitain dans la région du Lac Tchad et le Sokoto." *Renseignements Coloniaux* (Aug. 1898):208–11.

"La convention franco-anglaise du Niger: Le 14 juin 1898." *Afrique Française*, no. 7 (1898):209–18.

Cressier, Patrice. "La grande mosquée d'Assodé." *Journal des Africanistes* 59, no. 1/2 (1989):133–62.

Cross, Nigel, and Rhiannon Barker (eds.). *At the Desert's Edge: Oral Histories from the Sahel*. London: Panos, 1991.

———. *Mémoires du désert: Des Sahéliens se souviennent*. Paris: Harmattan, 1994.

Daniel, F. "Shehu Dan Fodio." *Journal of the African Society* 25 (1926).

Dankoussou, Issaka. *Histoire du Dawra*. Niamey: Centre Régional de Recherche de la Documentation pour la Tradition Orale, 1979.

———. *Katsina: Traditions historiques des Katsinaawaa après le Jihad*. 1974. Reprinted. Niamey: CNRSH, 1988.

David, P. *Maradi, l'ancien état et l'ancienne ville*. Paris: Etudes Nigeriénnes, no. 18, 1964.

———. "Maradi précoloniale: L'état et la ville." *Bulletin d'IFAN* 31, no. 3 (July 1969):638–88.

———. "Portraits de transition: Niger, 1961–1963." *Le Mois en Afrique* 21, no. 239/40 (1985):157–66.

"De Zinder au Tchad." *Afrique Française*, no. 1 (1905).

Delafosse, Maurice. *Haut-Sénégal-Niger*. 3 vols. Paris: Larose, 1912.

Delavignette, Robert. "Souvenirs du Niger." *Revue Française d'Histoire d'Outre-Mer* 54, no. 1947 (1967):13–21.

Derriennic, Hervé. *Famines et Dominations en Afrique Noire*. Paris: Harmattan, 1977.

Dionmansu, Sy. *La Pénétration Européenne au Niger*. Niamey: Imprimerie de Souza, 1972.

Djibo, Hamani. *Contribution à l'étude de l'histoire des états hausa: L'Ader précolonial*. Paris: Etudes Nigériennes, no. 38, 1975.

———. "Histoire d'une région du Niger: L'Ader du XVIe siècle au XIXe siècle." *Mu Kaara Sani* (Niamey), no. 1 (1967):10–13.

"Documents Djerma." Cahiers 36, Niger et Pays Voisins series, Fonds Vieillard, IFAN Library, Dakar.

Donaint, Pierre, and François Langrenon. *Le Niger*. Paris: Presses Universitaires de France, 1972.

Doombos, Martin R. "The Shehu and the Mullah: The Jehads of Usuman Dan Fodio." *Génève Afrique* 14, no. 2 (1975):7–31.

Duboc, A. A. L. *L'Epopée Coloniale en Afrique Occidentale Française*. Paris: Editions Egar Malfère, 1938.

Dubois, Felix. *Notre Beau Niger: Quinze Années de Colonisation Française*. Paris: E. Flammarion, 1911.

Dufour, J. L. *La révolte de l'Aïr (1916–1917)*. Paris: Centre d'Etudes sur l'Histoire du Sahara, 1987.

Duhard, Jean-Pierre. "La résistance des Tuaregs de l'Aïr." *Saharien,* no. 109 (1989):8–13.

Dunbar, Roberta Ann. "Damagaram (Zinder, Niger) 1812–1906: The History of a Central Sudanic Kingdom." Ph.D. diss., University of California, 1971.

———. "Recherches historiques au Damagaram." *Mu Kaara Sani* (Niamey), no. 2 (n.d.):15–19.

Echard, Nicole. *L'Expérience du passée: Histoire de la Société paysanne hausa de l'Ader*. Paris: Etudes Nigériennes, no. 36, 1975.

———. "Histoire du peuplement et histoire des techniques: L'exemple de la metallurgie hausa du fer au Niger." *Journal des Africanistes* 56, no. 1 (1986):21–34.

———. "Notes sur les forgerons de l'Ader. *Journal des Africanistes* 35, no. 1 (1965):352–72.

———. "Répertoire historique des communautés rurales de la Province de Tawa." Paris, 1972.

Edwards, F. A. "The French on the Niger." *Fortnightly Review* 63 (1898):576–91.

Egg, J., F. Lerin, and M. Venin. "Analyse descriptive de la famine des années 1931 au Niger et implications méthodologiques." Paris: INRA, 1975.

Ekechi, F. "Relations Between the Royal Niger Company and the French Missions on the Niger, 1885–1900." *Umoja* (New York) 2, no. 2 (July 1975):13–28.

Elliot, G. S. McD. "The Anglo-French Niger-Chad Boundary Commission." *Geographical Journal* 24 (1904):505–24.

Escher, Jean. "Evolution avec l'occupation française du groupement Hausa formant le sultanat de Zinder." CHEAM, no. 812 (1946).

Estienne, G. "Les voies de communication entre l'Afrique du Nord et l'Afrique Centrale." *Renseignements Coloniaux d'Afrique Française* (Oct. 1929):550–60.

Etievant. "Le commerce tripolitain dans le centre africain." *Afrique Française* 9 (Sept. 1910):277–82.

Ferry, R. "Les voies de pénétration et de communication en Afrique Occidentale Française." *Annales des Sciences Politiques* 22 (1907): 338–58, 503–23, 739–57.

Fievet, Maurice. "Salt Caravan . . . Expedition with One of the Touareg Trains Which Bring Desert Salt to Nigeria." *Nigeria,* no. 41 (1953):4–21.

Fonferrier. "Etudes historiques sur les mouvements caravaniers dans le cercle d'Agadez." *Bulletin du Comité d'Etudes Historiques et Scientifiques de l'AOF* 17 (1923):202–15.

Foulkes. "The New Anglo-French Frontier Between the Niger and Lake Chad." *Scottish Geographical Magazine* 22 (1906):565–75.

Foussagrives, J. B. "Française, anglais et allemands dans l'arrière-pays du Dahomey." *Bulletin du Comité Afrique Française* 2 (1895).

France. Ministère de la France d'Outre-Mer. "Le Niger." Paris, 1950.

———. "Ministère des Affaires Etrangères. *Niger et Tchad.* Paris: Cussac, 1918.

Fugelstad, Finn. "A propos de travaux récents sur la mission Voulet-Chanoine." *Revue Française d'Histoire d'Outre-Mer* 67, no. 246/47 (1980):73–87.

———. "Archival Research in Niger: Some Practical Hints." *African Research and Documentation,* no. 16/17 (1978):26–27.

———. "Le grande famine de 1931." *Revue Française d'Histoire d'Outre-Mer* 61, no. 222 (1974):18–33.

———. "Les Hauka: Une interprétation historique." *Cahiers d'Etudes Africaines,* no. 58 (1976):217–38.

———. *A History of the Niger, 1850–1960.* Cambridge: Cambridge University Press, 1983.

———. "Les révoltes des Touareg du Niger (1916–17)." *Cahiers d'Etudes Africaines* 13, no. 1, (1973):82–120.

———. "Niger in the Colonial Period." Ph.D. diss., University of Birmingham, 1976.

———. "Reconsideration of Hausa History Before the Jihad." *Journal of African History* 19, no. 3 (1978):319–39.

———. "Révolte dans le désert. Les mouvements de révolte chez les nomades du Sahara Nigérien (1915– 31). Diss., University of Aix-en-Provence, 1971.

———. "The Expedition that Lost Its Head." Paper. University of Birmingham, 1975.

Gadel. "Notes sur les sections méharistes de la région Zinder-Tchad." *Revue des Troupes Coloniales* 2 (1907):288–303, 427–45.

Gado, Boube. *Le Zarmatarey: Contribution à l'histoire des populations d'entre Niger et Dallol Mawri.* Niamey: IRSH, 1980.

Gaffiot. "L'Aïr en feu (1916–17)." *Revue Militaire de l'AOF* 11, no. 42 (July 15, 1939):19–52.

Gamory-Dubourdeau, P. M. "Etude sur la création de cantons de sédentarisations dans le cercle de Zinder et particulièrement dans la subdivision centrale." *Bulletin du Comité d'Etudes Historiques et Scientifiques de l'AOF* 7, no. 2 (Apr.–June 1924):239–58.

Gautier, E. F. "Anciennes voies de commerce transsaharien." *Geografiska Annaler* (1935):550–62.

Gersi, Douchan. *La Dernière Grande Aventure des Touareg*. Paris: Robert Laffont, 1972.

Ghubayd agg Alawjali. *Attarikh en Kel Denneg*. Copenhagen: Akademisk Forlag, 1975.

Gouraud, Henri J. *Zinder-Tchad: Souvenirs d'un Africain*. Paris: Plon, 1944.

Grandin. "Notes sur l'industrie et le commerce du sel au Kaouar et au Agram." *Bulletin d'IFAN* 13, no. 2 (Apr. 1951):488–533.

Great Britain. Foreign Office. Historical Section. *Upper Senegal and Niger*. London, 1920.

Gregoire, Emmanuel. *The Alhazi of Maradi: Traditional Hausa Merchants in a Changing Sahelian City*. Boulder, Colo.: L. Rienner, 1992.

Guilleux, C. *Journal de route d'un caporal de tirailleurs de la mission saharienne (Mission Foureau-Lamy), 1898–1900: Sahara, Aïr, Soudan, Lac Tchad, Chari, Congo*. Belfort: Schmit, 1904.

Guitard, Françoise. "Les conditions de l'évolution du commerce: Agadez." Ph.D. diss., University of Paris, 1988.

Hama, Boubou. *Contribution à la connaissance de l'Histoire des Peuls*. Paris: Présence Africaine, 1968.

———. "Documents nigériens: Tome 1. L'Aïr." Niamey: mimeo, 1963.

———. *L'Empire Songhay: Ses ethnies ses légendes et ses personnages historiques*. Paris: P. J. Oswald, 1974.

———. *Histoire des Songhay*. Paris: Présence Africaine, 1968.

———. *Histoire du Gobir et de Sokoto*. Paris: Présence Africaine, 1967.

———. *L'Histoire d'un peuple: Les Zarma*. 3 vols. Niamey: mimeo, 1964.

———. *Histoire Traditionelle d'un peuple: Les Zarma-Songhay*. Paris: Présence Africaine, 1967.

———. *Histoire Traditionelle d'un village Songhay Foneko*. Paris: Présence Africaine, 1970.

———. *Le Niger. Unité et Patrie. Ses Bases historiques à travers l'unité de l'histoire humaine de notre pays*. 2 vols. Paris and Niamey: mimeo, 1962.

———. *Recherche sur l'histoire des Touaregs sahariens et soudanais*. Paris: Présence Africaine, 1967.

———, and A. Boulnois. *L'Empire du Gao, Histoire, coutumes, et agie des Songhay*. Paris: Maisonneuve, 1954.

Hamani, D. M. *Au carrefour de Soudan et de la berbèrie: Le sultanat Tourag de l'Ayar*. Niamey: IRSH, 1989.

Hirshfield, Claire. "British Policy on the Middle Niger, 1890–1898." In N. N. Barker and M. L. Brown (eds.), *Diplomacy in an Age of Nationalism*. New York: Columbia University Press, 1968.

Humwick, J. O. "Religion and State in the Songay Empire." In I. M. Lewis (ed.), *Islam in Tropical Africa*. London: Oxford University Press, 1966.

———. "Songhay Bornu and Hausaland in the Sixteenth Century." In J. F. A. Ajayi and M. Crowder (eds.), *History of West Africa,* vol. 1. New York: Columbia University Press, 1971.

Issa, Ibrahim. *Nous de la coloniale*. Paris: La Pensée Universelle, 1982.

Janvier, J. "Autour des missions Voulet-Chanoine en Afrique Occidentale." *Présence Africaine* 22 (Oct.–Nov. 1958):86–100.

Joalland, P. "De Zinder au Tchad et la conquête du Kanem." *Géographie* 3 (1901):369–80.

———. *Le Drame de Dankori, Mission Voulet-Chanoine, Mission Joalland-Meynier*. Paris: Argo, 1930.

———. "Du Niger au Tchad." *Bulletin de la Société Normande de Géographie* 24 (1902):65–84.

Johnson, Marion. "Calico Caravans: The Tripoli–Kano Trade After 1880." *Journal of African History* 17, no. 1 (1976):95–117.

Kaba, Lansine. "Les chroniquers musulmans et Sonni Ali: Ou un aperçu de l'Islam et de la politique au Songhay au XVe siècle." *Bulletin d'IFAN* 4, no. 1 (Jan. 1978):49–65.

———. "The Pen, the Sword, and the Crown: Islam and the Revolution in Songhay Reconsidered." *Journal of African History* 25 (1984):241–56.

Kaké, Ibrahima Baba. *Djouder, la fin de l'Empire Songhay*. Dakar: Nouvelles Editions Africaines, 1975.

———. and Gilbert Comte. *Askia Mohamed, l'apogée de l'Empire Songhay*. Paris: Editions ABC, 1976.

Karimou, M. *Tradition Orale et Histoire: Les Mawri zarmaphones des origines à 1898*. Niamey: IRSH, 1976.

Kaziendé, Leopold. "L'Odysée du vieux Daidié." *Education Africaine* 28, no. 102/3 (1939):57–72.

Khorat, Pierre. "La défense d'Agadez." *Correspondant* (Paris), no. 289 (1922):41–62.

Kimba, Idrissa. "Niger." In *L'Afrique occidentale au temps de française*. Paris: Editions la Découverte, 1992, pp. 221–50.

———. *Guerres et Sociétés: Les populations du Niger au XIXe siècle et leurs réactions face à la colonisation*. Niamey: IRSH, 1981.

———. "La formation de la colonie du Niger (1880–1922)." Diss., University of Paris, 1988.

Klobb. *A la Recherche de Voulet*. Paris: Argo, 1931.

Konaré, A. B. *Sonni Ali Ber*. Niamey: IRSH, 1976.

Lambert, R. "Les Salines de Teguidda-n-Tesoum." *Bulletin du Comité d'Etudes Historiques et Scientifiques de l'AOF* 18, no. 2/3 (1934): 366–71.

Lange, Dierk. "Notes sur le Kwar au Moyen-Age." *Mu Kaara Sani* (Niamey) 3, no. 1 (1984):12–18.

———. "Trois hauts dignitaires bornuans de XVIe siècle." *Journal of African History* 29, no. 2 (1988):177–89.

Latour, Elaine de. "La paix destructrice." In Jean Bazin and Emmanuel Terray (eds.), *Guerres de lignages et guerres d'etats en Afrique*. Paris: Editions des Archives Contemporaines, 1982, pp. 237–65.

Laval, Gilbert. "Enquête sur les 'tabliers' de Niamey: Dépérissement et reconquête d'un ville." *Cahiers d'Etudes Africaines* 21, no. 81 (1981): 211–20.

Laya, Diouldé. "La brousse est morte." In Mahdi Adamu and A. H. M. Kirk-Greene (eds.), *Pastoralists of the African Savanna*. Manchester: Manchester University Press, 1986.

———. "Migrations et intégration politique dans la Gourma oriental au XIXe siècle." *Journal des Africanistes* 61, no. 2 (1991):65–90.

Le Coeur, Marguerite. *Les oasis du Kawar*. Niamey: IRSH, 1985.

Le Sourd, Michel. "Tarikh el Kawas." *Bulletin d'IFAN* 8 (1946):1–54.

Lombard, J., and R. Mauny. "Azelick et la question de Takedda." *Notes Africaines,* no. 64 (1954):99–101.

Lovejoy, Paul E. *Salt of the Desert Sun: A History of Salt Production and Trade in Central Sudan*. Cambridge: Cambridge University Press, 1986.

Low, A. "The Border States: A Political History of Three Northwest Nigerian Emirates." Ph.D. diss., University of California/Los Angeles, 1967.

McDougell, Ann E. "Camel Caravans of the Saharan Salt Trade." In C. Coquery-Vidrovitch and Paul Lovejoy (eds.), *The Workers of African Trade*. Beverly Hills, Calif.: Sage, 1985, pp. 99–122.

———. "Salts of the Western Sahara: Myths, Mysteries and Historical Significances." *International Journal of African Historical Studies* 23, no. 2 (1990):231–58.

Mangeot, P. "Le siège d'Agadès raconte par un prisonnier de Kaossen." *Renseignements Coloniaux,* no. 8 (1930):479–84.

Martin, B. G. "Kanem, Bornu and the Fazzan: Notes on the Political

History of a Trade Route." *Journal of African History* 10, no. 1 (1969): 15–27.

Marty, A. "Histoire de l'Azawagh nigérien." Thesis, University of Paris, 1975.

Mathieu, M. "La Mission Afrique Centrale." Thesis, University of Toulouse, 1975.

Meyerowitz, E. L. R. "The Origins of the 'Sudanic' Civilizations." *Anthropos* 67, no. 1/2 (1972):161–75.

Meynier, O. "La guerre sainte des Senoussya dans l'Afrique Français (1915–18)." *Revue Africaine* 83, no. 2 (1939):227–75.

———. *Mission Joalland-Meynier*. Paris: Editions de l'Empire Française, 1947.

Miles, William F. S. *Hausaland Divided: Colonialism and Independence in Nigeria and Niger*. Ithaca, N.Y.: Cornell University Press, 1994.

———. "Partitioned Royality: The Evolution of Hausa Chiefs in Nigeria and Niger." *Journal of Modern African Studies* 25, no. 2 (1987): 233–58.

Monteil, Charles. *Les empires du Mali*. Paris: Maisonneuve et Larose, 1968.

Monteil, P. L. *De Saint-Louis à Tripoli par le Lac Tchad . . . 1890–1892*. Paris: Felix Alcan, 1894/95.

Morel, H. M. "Essai sur l'epée des Touaregs de l'Ahaggar." *Trauvaux de l'Institut de Recherches Sahariennes* (1943).

———. "Note sur les takoubas historiques." *Travaux de l'Institut de Recherches Sahariennes* (1948).

Morou, Alassane. "Etude de l'équilibre vivrier et de sa problématique au Niger." M.Sc. thesis, Laval University, 1981.

Museur, Michel. "Un exemple specifique d'économie caravaniere: l'échange sel-mil." *Journal des Africanistes* 47, no. 2 (1977):49–80.

Nachtigal, Gustav. *Sahara and Sudan,* trans. from German by Allan G. B. and Humphrey J. Fischer. 4 vols. London: C. Hurst, 1980.

Niandou, Harouna. "Les salines de Bilma." *Niger* (Niamey), no. 19 (Mar. 1973):38–39.

Le Niger au quotidien: Recueil d'histoires vécues au temps de la présence coloniale. Maisons-Laffite: Imprimerie Finet, 1992.

Obichere, Boniface. *West African States and European Expansion: The Dahomey-Niger Hinterland, 1885–1898*. New Haven: Yale University Press, 1971.

Olivier, E. "La délimitation de la frontière Niger-Tchad." *Revue de Géographie* 55 (1905):52–56.

Olivier de Sardan, Jean-Pierre. "Le cheval et l'arc." In Jean Bazin and Emmanuel Terray (eds.), *Guerres de lignages et guerres d'états en Afrique*. Paris: Editions des Archives Contemporaines, 1982, pp. 191–231.

———. *Quand nos pères était captifs . . . récits paysans du Niger*. Paris: Nubia, 1976.

O'Mara, Kathleen Khadija. "A Political Economy of Ahir (Niger)." Ph.D. diss., Columbia University, 1986.

Owen, Richard. *Saga of the Niger*. London: Robert Hale, 1961.

Painter, Thomas M. "From Warriors to Migrants: Critical Perspectives on Early Migrations Among the Zarma of Niger." *Africa* 58, no. 1 (1988):87–100.

———. "Making Migrants: Zarma Peasants in Niger, 1900–1920." In Denis D. Cordell and J. W. Gregory (eds.), *African Population and Capitalism: Historical Perspectives*. Boulder, Colo.: Westview Press, 1987, pp. 122–33.

Palmer, Sir Herbert Richmond. *Bornu, Sahara and Sudan*. London: Murray, 1936.

———. "The Central Sahara and the Sudan in the Twelfth Century A.D." *Journal of the African Society* 28, no. 112 (July 1929): 268–378.

———. "Notes on Some Asben Records." *Journal of the African Society* 9, no. 36 (July 1910):388–400.

———. "The Tuareg of the Sahara." *Journal of the African Society* 31 (1931):153–73, 293–308.

Perie, Jean. "Notes historiques sur la région de Maradi." *Bulletin d'IFAN* 1, no. 2/3 (Apr.–June 1939):377–400.

———, and Michel Sellier. "Histoire des populations du cercle de Dosso (Niger)." *Bulletin d'IFAN* 12, no. 4 (Oct. 1950):1015–74.

Perron, Michel. "Le pays Dendi." *Bulletin du Comité d'Etudes Historiques et Scientifique de l'AOF* (1924):51–83.

Piault, Marc H. "Le héros et son destin." *Cahiers d'Etudes Africaines* 22, no. 87/88 (1982):403–40.

Pineau, Guy. "La Guerre du Kaossen 1916–19." *Afrique Littéraire et Artistique* 10, (1970):50–55.

Porch, Douglas. *The Conquest of the Sahara*. Oxford: Oxford University Press, 1986.

Porter, Andrew. "The Hausa Association: Sir George Goldie, the Biship of Dover and the Niger in the 1890s." *Journal of Imperial and Commonwealth History* 7, no. 2 (Jan. 1979):150–79.

Pourage, Gérard, and Jean Vanaye. *Le passé du Niger de l'antiquité à la pénétration coloniale*. 2 vols. Paris: mimeographed, 1973.

Rash, Yehoshua. *Des Colonisateurs sans enthousiasme*. Paris: Paul Geuthner, 1973.

———. "Des colonisateurs sans enthousiasme: Les premières années françaises au Damergou." *Revue Française d'Histoire d'Outre-Mer* 59, no. 214 (1972):5–69; no. 215 (1972):240–308.

———. "Un établissement colonial sans histoire. Les premières années française au Niger 1897–1906." Diss., Univeristy of Paris, 1972.

Raynaut, Claude. "Circulation monétaire et évolution des structures socio-économiques chez les haoussas du Niger." *Africa* 47, no. 2 (1977):160–71.

Regelsperger, G. "Mission pour la délimitation de la frontière Niger-Tchad." *Quinzaine Coloniale* (1908):63, 349–50; (1909):61, 614–15; (1910):215–17, 518–19, 659–61; (1911):638–39.

Regnier, J. "Les salines de l'Amadror et le trafic caravanier." *Bulletin de Liaisons Sahariennes* 12, no. 43 (1961):234–61.

Relations interethniques et culture matérielle dans le bassin du Lac Tchad. Paris: ORSTOM, 1990.

Riou, L. "L'Azalay d'automne 1928." *Afrique Française* (May 1929).

Riou, Yves. *La Révolte de Kaocen et le siège d'Agadès 1916–17*. Niamey, 1968.

Rivet. *Notice sur le Territoire Militaire du Niger et le Bataillon de Tirailleurs de Zinder*. Paris: Lavauzelle, 1912.

Rolland, J. F. *Le Grand Capitain: Un Aventurier inconnu de l'époque coloniale*. Paris: Grasset, 1976.

Rothiot, Jean-Paul. *L'ascension d'un chef africain au début de la colonisation: Aouta le conquérant (Dosso-Niger)*. Paris: Harmattan, 1988.

———. *Le Niger: Textes et documents d'histoire du 16e siècle au 20e siècle*. Niamey: INDRAP, 1979.

Rottier, A. "Le Sahara oriental. Kaouar, Djado, Tibesti." *Renseignements Coloniaux,* no. 1 (1924):1–24; no. 2 (1924):78–88; no. 3 (1924):101–8.

Salifou, André. "Colonisation et sociétés indigènes au Niger de la fin du XIX siècle au début de la deuxième guerre mondiale." Thesis, University of Toulouse, 1977.

———. "La Conjuration manquée du sultan de Zinder, 1906." *Afrika Zamani,* no. 3 (1974):69–103.

———. *Crise Alimentaire au Niger: Les Leçons du Passé*. Dakar: Institut Africain de Développement Economique et de Plantification, 1974.

———. *Le Damagarem ou Sultanat de Zinder au XIXe siècle*. Paris: CNRSH, Etudes Nigériennes, no. 27, 1971.

———. "The Famine of 1931 in Niger." *African Environment* 1, no. 2 (1975):22–48.

———. "Les Française, Fihroun et les Kounta 1902–1916." *Journal de la Société des Africanistes* 43, no. 2 (1973):175–95.

———. *Histoire du Niger*. Paris: Nathan, 1989.

———. "Kaocen et le siège d'Agadez 1916–17." *Journal de la Société des Africanistes* 42, no. 2 (1972):193–95.

———. *Kaoussan ou la révolte senoussite*. Paris: Etudes Nigériennes, no. 28, 1973.

———. "Malan Yaroh, un grand négociant du Soudan central à la fin du XIXe siècle." *Journal de la Société des Africanistes* 42, no. 1 (1972): 7–27.

———. "Quand l'histoire se répéte: La famine de 1931 au Niger." *Environnement Africain* 1, no. 2 (1975):25–52.

Salmon, Pierre. "Les Touaregs de l'Ahaggar et du Tassili-n-Ajjer." *Revue des Etudes* (Brussels) (1971–72):48–65.

Sauvaget, J. "Les épitaphes royales de Gao." *Bulletin d'IFAN* 12, no. 2 (Apr. 1950):418–40.

———. "Notes préliminaires sur les épitaphes de Gao." *Revue des Etudes Islamiques* 1 (1948):1–12.

Séré de Rivières, Edmond. *Histoire du Niger*. Paris: Berger-Levrault, 1966.

———. *Le Niger*. Paris: Editions Maritimes et Coloniales, 1952.

Smith, Michael G. "A Hausa Kingdom: Maradi Under Dan Baskore, 1854–1875." In D. Forde (ed.), *West African Kingdoms in the Nineteenth Century*. London: Oxford University Press, 1967, pp. 93–122.

———. "The Hausa of Northern Nigeria." In James Gibbs, Jr. (ed.), *The Peoples of Africa*. New York: Holt, Rinehart and Winston, 1965.

———. "The Jihad of Shehu Dan Fodio." In I. M. Lewis (ed.), *Islam in Tropical Africa*. London: Oxford University Press, 1966.

Spittler, Gerd. "Durren im Air: eine historische analyse." *Die Erde* 116, no. 2/3 (1985):177–84.

———. "Etude sur le mouvement caravanier entre l'Aïr, Bilma et Kano." *Mu Kaara Sani* 3, no. 1 (1984):1–11.

———. *Herrschaft über Bauern, die Ausbreitung staatlicher Herrschaft und einer islamisch-urbanen Kultur in Gobir*. Bonn: Campus Verlag, 1978.

———. "Traders in Rural Hausaland." *Bulletin d'IFAN* 35, no. 2 (1977):362–85.

Staudinger, Paul. *In the Heart of the Hausa States*. 2 vols. Athens: Ohio University Center for International Studies, 1990.

Stewart, Bonnie Ann. "An Operational Assessment of the National Organization of Commerce and Production in Niger." *Agricultural Administration* (May 1981):209–19.

———. "Peanut Marketing in Niger." *Journal of African Studies* 7, no. 2 (Summer 1980):123–28.

Stoller, Paul Allen. "The Dynamics of Bankwano: Communication and Political Legitimacy Among the Songhai." Ph.D. diss., University of Texas/Austin, 1978.

———. *Embodying Colonial Memories: Spirit Possession, Power and the Hauka in West Africa*. New York: Routledge, 1995.

———. "Horrific Comedy: Cultural Resistance Among the Hauka Movement in Niger." *Ethos* 12, no. 2 (1984):165–86.

———. "Son of Rouch: Portrait of a Young Ethnographer by the Songhay." *Anthropological Quarterly* (July 1987):114–36.

Streicker, Allen Joseph. "On Being Zarma: Scarcity and Stress in the Nigerien Sahel." Ph.D. diss., Northwestern University, 1980.

"Terre d'Afrique: Le Niger." *Nations Nouvelles,* no. 5 (Sept. 1965): 31–37.

Terrier, Auguste. "La délimitation de Zinder." *Questions Diplomatiques et Coloniales* 14 (1902):481–91.

Toihir, Amed, and Jacques Mahi. "*Matiko*: Famine de 1931 au Niger." In C. Coquery-Vidrovitch (ed.), *Histoire Démographique*. Paris: Harmattan, 1985, pp. 51–58.

Tymowski, Michal. "Le Niger: Voie de communication de grands états du Soudan occidental." *Africana Bulletin* (Warsaw) 6 (1967):73–95.

Urvoy, Yves. "Chroniques d'Agadez." *Journal de la Société des Africanistes* 4, no. 2 (1934):145–77.

———. *Histoire des Populations du Soudan Central*. Paris: Larose, 1938.

Vallet, M. *Les Touaregs aujour'hui*. CHEAM, no. 4113 (1966).

Van der Laan, H. Laurens. "Marketing West Africa's Crops: Modern Boards and Colonial Trading Companies." *Journal of Modern African Studies* 25, no. 1 (1987):1–24.

Venel. "Le Territoire militaire du Niger au commencement de 1909." *Revue des Troupes Coloniales* (1909):307–23.

Verdot, Marguerite. "A propos de la révolte du sultan de Zinder in 1906." *Notes Africaines,* no. 30 (Apr. 1946):3.

Vignes, K. "Etudes sur la rivalité d'influence entre les puissances européene en Afrique équatoriale et occidentale dupuis l'acte général de Berlin jusqu'au seuil du XIXe siècle." *Revue Française d'Histoire d'Outre-Mer* 48, no. 1 (1961):5–96.

Vikor, Knut S. "The Desert-Side Salt Trade of Kawar." *African Economic History* 11 (1982):115–44.

———. "The Early History of the Kawar Oasis: A Southern Border of the Maghrib or a Northern Border of the Sudan." *Maghreb Review* 12, no. 3/4 (1972):78–83.

———. "An Episode of Saharan Rivalry: The French Occupation of Kawar, 1906." *International Journal of African Historical Studies* 18, no. 4 (1985):699–715.

———. *The Oasis of Salt: The History of Kawar, a Saharan Centre of Salt Production*. Bergen: Universitetet i Bergen, 1979.

Wallerstein, Immanuel. "How Seven States Were Born in Former West Africa." *Africa Report* 6, no. 3 (Mar. 1961):3, 4, 7, 12.

Wedderburn, Agnes. "The Koyam." In Mahdi Adamu and A. H. M. Kirk-Greene (eds.), *Pastoralists of the African Savanna*. Manchester: Manchester University Press, 1986.

Zakari, Maikoréma. *Contribution à l'histoire des populations du sud-est nigérien (Le cas de Mangari, XVIe–XIXe siècles)*. Niamey: IRSH, 1985.

———. *Tradition orales du Mangari*. 2 vols. Niamey: CNRS, 1986.

Politics, Administration, and Foreign Relations

Abba, Souleymane. "La chefferie traditionelle en question." *Politique Africaine,* no. 38 (1990):51–60.

Agoro, I. O. "The Establishment of the Chad Basin Commission." *International and Comparative Law Quarterly* 15, no. 2 (Apr. 1966):542–50.

Ahmad, Syed Salahuddin. "Niger-Nigeria Relations, 1960–75." *Kano Studies* 2, no. 1 (1980):59–72.

Alexandre, Pierre. "The Land-Locked Countries of the AOF: Mali, Upper Volta and Niger." In Zdenek Cervenka (ed.), *Landlocked Countries of Africa*. Uppsala: Scandinavian Institute of African Studies, 1973, pp. 137–45.

Allakayé, Joseph Seydou. "La Société de Développement." *Europe Outre-Mer,* no. 624 (Jan. 1982):11–14.

Amuwo, K. "Military-Inspired Anti-Bureaucratic Corruption Campaigns: An Appraisal of Niger's Experience." *Journal of Modern African Studies* 24, no. 2 (1986):285–301.

L'Année Politique Africaine. Dakar: Société Africaine d'Edition, 1980.

Asiwaju, A. J, and B. M. Barkindo (eds.). *The Nigerian-Niger Transborder Cooperation*. Lagos: Malthouse Press, 1993.

Bandiare, Ali. "L'enfant dans la société nigérienne." *Revue Juridique et Politique,* no. 2 (Apr.–June 1977):371–79.

Baulin, Jacques. *Conseiller du président Diori*. Paris: Eurafor-Press, 1986.

Belima, E. "Fondements naturels, politiques et moraux des travaux nigériens." *Outre-Mer* 6 (1934):177–87.

Belloncle, Guy, et al. *Alphabétisation et géstion des groupements villageois en Afrique Sahélienne*. Paris: Karthala, 1982.

Bellot, Jean-Marc. "La Politique Africaine de la Libye: Le Cas du Niger." *Revue Française d'Etudes Politiques Africaines* (Aug.–Sept. 1980):20–36.

Berthier, Thierry. "Le Régime politique de la République du Niger." 2 vols. Thesis, University of Roanne, 1973?

Beuchelt, Eno. *Niger*. Bonn: Kurt Schroder, 1968.

Biarnes, P. "Niger: Les raisons de la Chute." *Revue Française d'Etudes Politiques Africaines,* no. 101 (May 1974):25–28.

Bois de Goudusson, Jean du. "La réorganisation de la chefferie traditionnelle au Niger." In *Année Africaine 1983*. Paris: Pedone, 1985, pp. 108–11.

Borella, F. *L'évolution politique et juridique de l'Union Française depuis 1946*. Paris: R. Pichon & Durand-Auzias, 1958.

Bourgeot, André. "Mouvement de libération nationale et réalité du Sahara." *Pensée,* no. 229 (1982):91–97.

———. "Révoltes et rébellions en pays touareg." *Afrique Contemporaine,* no. 170 (1990):3–18.

Brownlie, Ian. *African Boundaries: A Legal and Diplomatic Encyclopedia*. Berkeley: University of California Press, 1979.

Carter, Gwendolyn M. (ed.). *National Unity and Regionalism in Eight African States*. Ithaca, N.Y.: Cornell University Press, 1966.

Casajus, Dominique. "Les amis française de la 'cause touarege.'" *Cahiers d'Etudes Africaines* 35, no. 137 (1995):237–50.

Chaffard, Georges. *Les Carnets secrets de la décolonisation*. Paris: Calmann-Levy, 1967.

———. "Les carnets secrets de la décolonisation: La subversion au Niger en 1965." *France Eurafrique,* no. 190 (Dec. 1967):35–37.

Charlick, Robert B. "Power and Participation in the Modernization of Rural Hausa Communities." Ph.D. diss., University of California/Los Angeles, 1974.

———. *Niger: Personal Rule and Survival in the Sahel*. Boulder, Colo.: Westview Press, 1991.

Clair, André. *Le Niger Indépendant*. Paris: ATEOS, 1966.

Clary, Jean. *Législation et techniques financiares au Niger*. Paris: CHEAM, 1966.

Claudot-Hawad, Hélène. "La coutume absente ou les métamorphoses contemporaines du politique chez les Touaregs." *Cahiers de l'IREMAM,* no. 4 (1993):67–85.

———. "Histoire d'un enjeux politique: La vision évolutionnaire des événements touaregs 1990–1992." *Politique Africaine* (June 1993): 32–40.

———. *Les Touaregs: Portrait en fragments*. Aix-en-Provence: Edisud, 1993.

Colin, Roland. "Dynamiques populistes en cristallisations institutionelles 1960–1990." *Politique Africaine,* no. 38 (1990):30–39.

Comité d'Etudes Historiques et Scientifiques de l'Afrique Occidentale Française. *Coutumiers Juridiques de l'Afrique Occidentale Française,* vol 3. *Mauritanie, Niger, Côte d'Ivoire, Dahomey, Guinée Française*. Paris: Larose, 1939.

Comte, Gilbert. "Le Dahomey au sein de l'Entente. La réconciliation avec le Niger." *Europe France Outre-Mer* 42, no. 426/27 (July–Aug. 1965):22–24.

———. "Niger: De l'uranium et des jardins." *France Eurafrique,* no. 193 (Mar. 1968):19–22.

———. "Le Niger: Un pays qui à vocation de charnière." *Europe France Outre-Mer,* no. 430 (Nov. 1965):10–12.

———. "Un pays raisonnable: Le Niger." *Europe France Outre-Mer,* no. 373 (Dec. 1960):35–37.

———. "Les principaux dirigeants nigériens." *Europe France Outre-Mer,* no. 430 (Nov. 1965):16–20.

———. "Treize années d'histoire Nigérienne." *Revue Française d'Etudes Politiques Africaines,* no. 72 (Dec. 1971):28–40.

Conac, Gérard. *Le Cours Suprêmes en Afrique*. Paris: Economica, 1988.

———. *Les institutions administratives des états francophones d'Afrique Noire*. Paris: Economica, 1979.

Constitution du 24 Septembre 1989. Niamey: Secrétariat Général du Gouvernement, 1989.

Coordinative Observers to the 1993 Elections in Niger. Washington, D.C.: National Democratic Institute for International Affairs, 1993.

"Coup d'état au Niger." *Afrique Contemporaine,* no. 73 (May–June 1974):14–15.

Dagui, N'Gabo. "Le nouveau code de la nationalité Nigérienne." *Penant* 98, no. 797 (June–Oct. 1988):262–92.

Dahomey. Service d'Information. *The Truth About the Dispute Between Dahomey and Niger*. Porto Novo, 1963.

Dandobi, Mahamane. "L'Organisation judiciaire du Niger en matière penale." *Revue Juridique et Politique,* no. 4 (Oct.– Dec. 1969): 819–22.

David, Phillipe. "Portrait de transition: Le Niger 1961–1963." *Le Mois en Afrique,* no. 239/40 (1985–86):157–66.

Dayak, Mano. *Touareg, la tragédie*. Paris: Jean-Claude Lattès, 1992.

Decalo, Samuel. "Modernizing Tradional Society under the Ascetic General," in his Coups and Army Rule. New Haven: Yale University Press, 1990, pp. 241–84.

Decoudras, Pierre-Marie. "L'Aide internationale." *Politique Africaine,* no. 38 (1990):87–96.

———. "Niger: démocratisation réussie, avenir en suspension." In *L'Afrique politique 1994*. Paris: Karthala, 1994, pp. 134–58.

Deniau, Jean François. "L'Aide française aux pays du Sahel." *Coopération Technique,* no. 73 (Mar. 1974):6–9.

Diori, Hamani. *Parole à la nation*. Niamey, 1963.

Discours et messages: Ali Saibou. Niamey: Agence Nigérienne de Presse, 1988.

"Djibo Bakaré parle." *Politique Africaine,* no. 38 (1990):97–110.

Djirmey, Aboubacar, et al. "Lutte d'identité culturelle au Niger." *Politique Africaine* (Mar. 1992):142–48.

Dugue, Gil. "L'Affaire Nigérienne." In *Vers les Etats-Unis d'Afrique*. Paris: Editions Lettres Africains, 1960, pp. 151–62.

Etats et sociétés nomades. Special issue of *Politique Africaine,* no. 34 (June 1989).

Faujas, Alain. "La Politique Etrangère du Niger." *Revue Française d'Etudes Politiques Africaines,* no. 72 (Dec. 1971):41–57.

Flottes, Pierre. *Institutions et Structures de l'Etat*. Niamey: Ecole Nationale d'Administration, 1971.

France. La Documentation Française. "L'Organisation judiciare en AOF, au Togo et au Cameroun." *Notes et Etudes Documentaires,* no. 1947 (1954).

———. "La République du Niger." *Notes et Etudes Documentaires,* no. 2638 (1960).

———. "La République du Niger." *Notes et Etudes Documentaires* no. 3994/95 (1973).

Fugelstad, Finn. "Djibo Bakary, the French and the Referendum of 1958 in Niger." *Journal of African History* 14, no. 2 (1973):313–30.

———. "UNIS and BNA: The Role of 'Traditionalist' Parties in Niger, 1948–60." *Journal of African History* 16, no. 1 (1975):113–35.

Gabas, Jean-Jacques. *Aides extérieures dans les pays membres du CILSS: Investissement en panne*. Paris: OCDE, 1987.

Gandin-Blanc, Nicole, and Robert Buijtenhuijs. *Tensions politiques et ethniques au Sahel*. Leiden: Afrika-Studiecentrum, 1977.

Golan, Tamar. "The Conseil de l'Entente." Ph.D. diss., Columbia University, 1980.

Gonidec, P. F. *Constitutions des Etats de la Communauté*. Paris: Sirey, 1959.

Graybeal, N. Lynn, and Louis A. Picard. "Internal Capacity and Overload in Guinea and Niger." *Journal of Modern African Studies* 29, no. 2 (1991):275–300.

Gregoire, E. "Une système de production agro-pastorale en crise." In Emile Le Bris et al. (eds.), *Enjeux Fonciers en Afrique Noire*. Paris: Karthala, 1982.

Grove, A. T. *The Niger and Its Neighbors*. Rotterdam: A. A. Balkema, 1985.

Guillemin, Jacques. "Chefferie Traditionnelle et administration publique au Niger." *Revue Française d'Etudes Politiques Africaines,* no. 213/14 (Oct.–Nov. 1983):115–24.

———. "Note sur l'évolution de l'organisation administrative territoriale de la République du Niger." *Revue Française d'Etudes Politiques Africaines,* no. 201/2 (Oct.–Nov. 1982):97–103.

Haaringen, P. "Cheminements migratoires maliens, voltaiques et nigériens en Côte d'Ivoire." *Cahiers d'ORSTOM,* no. 2/3 (1973): 195–201.

Habsburg, Erzherzogin Adelheid von. "Niger oder wie man mit Stäatskrisen fertig wird." *Afrika Forum,* no. 2 (Feb. 1965):24–29.

Hama, Boubou. "Das Geschichtsbewusstsein Afrikas." *Afrika Forum* (July–Aug. 1966):341–45.

———. *Les Grands Problèmes de l'Afrique des Indépendances*. Paris: Jean Oswald, 1974.

———. *Histoire Traditionnelle des Peuls du Dallol Bosso*. Niamey: INSH, 1969.

———. *Hon si suba ben*. Paris: Jean Oswald, 1973.

———. *Kotia-Nima*. 2 vols. Paris: Présence Africaine, 1969.

———. *Les Problèmes brûlents de l'Afrique*. 3 vols. Paris: Jean Oswald, 1973.

———. *Le retard de l'Afrique*. Paris: Présence Africaine, 1972.

———, and Andrée Clair. *L'Aventure d'Albarka*. Paris: Julliard, 1972.

"Hamani Diori." *Afrique Contemporaine* (Nov.–Dec. 1970):30.

"Hamani Diori, Staatsprasident der Republik Niger." *Afrika Forum* (Sept.–Oct. 1969):578–81.

Hargreaves, J. O. *West Africa: The Former French States*. Englewood Cliffs, N.J.: Prentice Hall, 1967.

"Has Niger a Future?" *Africa Report* (June 1962):7–8.

Hentgen, E. F. *L'Organisation régionale et locale de la République du Niger*. Niamey: Ecole Nationale d'Administration, 1974.

Hetzel, W. "Problems of the Inland Situation of the Republic of Niger." *Erdkunde* (Mar. 1970):1–14.

Higgot, Richard A. "Colonial Origins and Environmental Influences on the Foreign Relations of a West African Land-locked State: The Case of Niger." Ph.D. diss., University of Birmingham, 1979.

———. "Niger." In T. Shaw and O. Aluko, *The Political Economy of African Foreign Policy*. London: Gower, 1984, pp. 165–89.

———. "Politics in Niger, 1945–71." M.A. thesis, Birmingham University, 1974.

———. "Structural Dependence and Decolonization in a West African Land-locked State: The Case of Niger." *Review of African Political Economy,* no. 17 (July–Aug. 1980):43–58.

———, and Finn Fugelstad. "The 1974 Coup d'Etat in Niger: Towards an Explanation." *Journal of Modern African Studies* 13, no. 3 (Sept. 1975):383–98.

Hinkmann, Ulrich. *Niger*. Munich: R. Oldenbourg Verlag, 1968.

Houlet, G. "Niger aux multiples visages." *Connaissance du Monde,* no. 29 (Apr. 1961).

"Interview de Lieutenant-Colonel Seyni Kountché." *Europe Outre-Mer,* no. 554 (Mar. 1976):10–13.

Janke, B. "Regenfeldbau und Bewässerungsfeldbau im Niger und ihre Bedeutung besonders in Dürrezeiten." *Afrika-Spectrum,* 9, no. 3 (1974):268–77.

Jouvé, Edmond. "Du Niger de Diori Hamani au gouvernement des militaires." *Revue Française d'Etudes Politiques Africaines,* no. 149 (May 1978):19–44.

———. "Niger 1977–78." *Revue Française d'Etudes Politiques Africaines,* no. 149 (1978):19–44.

Keita, Mariama. "L'Action emancipatrice en faveur des femmes. *Europe Outre-Mer,* no. 624 (Jan. 1982):15–16.

Khalil Diallo, Ibrahima. "L'Introduction de l'Article 141 de l'ancien code de procédure civile française en droit positif nigérien." *Penant,* no. 793 (Jan.–Apr. 1987):37–48.

Kiba, Simon. "Problèmes Nigériens." *Afrique* (Jan. 1962):9–15.

Kotoudi, Idimama. *Transition à la Nigérienne*. Niamey: Nouvelle Imprimerie du Niger, 1993.

Kountché, Seyni. *Discours et Messages, 1974–5*. Niamey: Secrétariat d'Etat à la Présidence Chargé d'Information et Tourisme, 1975.

———. *Discours et Messages, 1975–6*. Niamey: Secrétariat d'Etat à la Présidence Chargé de l'Information, 1976.

Laine, Bernard. "Régime Militaire et Société de dévoloppement au Niger 1974–83." *Afrique Contemporaine* (Jan.–Mar. 1983):38–44.

Lame, G. "Evolution du régime foncier dans une société d'éleveurs nomades." In Emile Le Bris et al. (eds.), *Enjeux Fonciers en Afrique Noire*. Paris: Karthala, 1982, pp. 195–201.

Latour, Eliane de. *Les temps du pouvoir*. Paris: Ecole des Hautes Etudes en Sciences Sociales, 1992.

Lavroff, D. C., and G. Peiser. *Les Constitutions Africaines*. Paris: Pedone, 1963.

LeVine, Victor T. *Political Leadership in Africa: Post-Independence Generational Conflict in Upper Volta, Senegal, Niger, Dahomey and the Central African Republic*. Stanford: Hoover Institution, 1967.

McEwen, A. C. "The Establishment of the Niger/Nigeria Boundary, 1889–1989." *Geographic Journal* 157, no. 1 (Mar. 1991):62–70.

Maidoka, Aboubacar. "La constitution nigérienne du 24 Septembre 1989." *Revue Juridique et Politique,* no. 2 (May–Sept. 1991):112–32.

Mangin, G. "Le Code pénal du Niger." *Penant,* no. 691 (Apr.–May 1962):289–96; no. 692 (June–Aug. 1962):458–67.

Manouan, A. "L'Evolution du Conseil de l'Entente." *Penant,* no. 746 (Oct.–Dec. 1974):447–97; no. 747 (Jan.–Mar. 1975):19–92; no. 748 (Apr.–June 1975):211–36.

Martens, George R. *Trade Unionism and Politics in Niger*. Lomé, Togo: Regional Economic and Research Center, 1986.

Martin, François. *Le Niger du Président Diori 1960–1974*. Paris: Harmattan, 1991.

Materi, Yem Gouri. "La responsabilité civile de l'état." *Revue Juridique et Politique* 41, no. 3 (1987):199–214.

Mayaki, Adamou. *Les partis politiques nigériens de 1946 à 1958*. Niamey: Imprimerie Nationale de Niger, 1991.

"Message à la nation de Lt. Colonel Seyni Kountché." *Bulletin d'IFAN* (May 1979): pp. 19431–33.

Meyer, Reinhold. "Legitimität und Souveränität des nigerischen Staates." *Afrika-Spectrum* 22, no. 2 (1989):193–207.

———. *Die Franzosische Politik der Cooperation Culturelle et tech-*

nique und die Nationale Entscheidung: Funktionale in Niger. Hamburg: Buske, 1973.

Milcent, Ernest. "L'Evolution de M. Djibo Bakary." *Chronique Sociale de France,* no. 4 (July 1956):366–67.

Miles, William F. S. "Partitioned Royalty: The Evolution of Hausa Chiefs in Nigeria and Niger. *Journal of Modern African Studies* 25, no. 2 (June 1987):233–58.

———. "Self-Identity, Ethnic Affinity and National Consciousness: An Example from Rural Hausaland." *Ethnic and Rural Studies* 9, no. 4 (1986):427–44.

———. "Traditional Rulers and Development Administration." *Studies in Comparative International Development* 28, no. 3 (Fall 1993): 31–50.

———, and David A. Rochefort. "Nationalism Versus Ethnic Identity in Subsaharan Africa." *American Political Science Review* (June 1991):393–403.

Mounkaila, S. "Informatics in the Niger." *Cahiers Africaines d'Administration Publiques* (Tangiers) (Dec. 1977):31–33.

Mouralis, Jean-Louis. "La Cour d'Etat, jurisdiction suprême de la République du Niger." In Gérard Conac, *Les Cours Suprêmes en Afrique*. Paris: Economica, 1988, pp. 290–306.

"Le Nation tout entière fête aujourd'hui le 26ème aniversaire du PPN-RDA." *Niger* (Niamey), no. 18 (May 1972):1–16.

Newbury, C. W. "The Formation of the Government-General of French West Africa." *Journal of African History* 1, no. 1 (1961):11–128.

Niandou Soulaye, Abdoulaye. "L'Armée et le pouvoir." *Politique Africaine,* no. 38 (1990):40–50.

———. "Le Niger après Seyni Kountché." In *Année Africaine 1989*. Paris: Pedone, 1990, pp. 243–79.

———. "Tractes et démocratisation au Niger." In *Année Africaine 1990–91*. Bordeaux: CEAN, 1991, pp. 431–43.

Niger. *Répertoire général des textes*. Niamey, [1974?].

———. Centre d'Information du Niger. *Le Niger en marche 1960–1970*. Paris, 1970.

———. Direction de l'Information et de la Presse. *Le Niger en marche*. Paris, 1962.

———. Secrétariat d'Etat à l'Information. "Discours et messages du Lieutenant-Colonel Seyni Kountché." Niamey, 1976.

"Niger." In Colin Legum and John Drysdale (eds.), *Africa Contempory Record*. Annual. London and Exeter: Africa Research; London: Rex Collings; New York: Africana Publishing Co., 1968–89.

"Niger." In Donald G. Morrison et al., *Black Africa: A Comparative Handbook*. New York: Free Press, 1972.

"Niger." *Europe France Outre-Mer,* no. 430 (Nov. 1965).

"Niger." *Europe France Outre-Mer,* no. 503 (Dec. 1971).
"Niger." *Année Africaine.* Annual. Paris: Pedone, 1964.
"Niger." *Le Courrier/ACP-CEE* (Brussels), no. 54 (Mar.–Apr. 1979): 7–28.
"Niger After Kountché." *Africa Confidential* (Feb. 18, 1987).
"Niger Builds." *Africa Report* (Dec. 1970):11–12.
"Niger Chroniques d'un Etat." *Politique Africaine,* special issue, no. 38 (1988).
"Niger Coup." *Africa Confidential* (Apr. 19, 1974):8.
"Niger Diversifies." *Africa Report* (June 1971):8–9
"Niger: Der Französiche Botschafter verlässt Niamey." *Internationales Afrika Forum* (Mar. 8, 1972):162–68.
"Niger: The French Disconnection." *Africa Confidential* (Sept. 8, 1972): 3–5.
"Niger Government." *Africa Confidential* (May 17, 1974).
"Niger: Kountché's Anxiety." *Africa Confidential* (Mar. 25, 1981):4–5.
"Niger—Putsch Manquée." *Afrique Contemporaine* (Jan.–Mar. 1984):37–38.
"Niger: Un Président à écouté de son peuple." *Europe Outre-Mer,* special issue on Niger, no. 624 (Jan. 1982).
"Niger: Rebels, Official and Unofficial." *Africa Confidential* (Nov. 6, 1992):4–5.
"Niger: Rester vigilant face au danger libyen." *France Outre-Mer* (Feb. 1981):31–33.
"Niger: Saibou's Hand." *Africa Confidential* (Mar. 3, 1989):3–4
"Niger: Soutien populaire au Coup d'état militaire." *Revue Française d'Etudes Politiques Africaines,* no. 101 (May 1974):20–24.
"Niger: Stabilité politique, amélioration économique." *Europe France Outre-Mer,* special issue on Niger, no. 430 (Nov. 1965).
"Niger Unrest." *Africa Confidential* (Feb. 8, 1974).
"Niger—Uranium Politics." *Africa Confidential* 21, no. 17 (Aug. 13, 1980):6–8.
Noblet, R. *Le Niger,* Paris: Armand Colin, 1978.
Nomads of the Sahel. London: Minority Rights Group, 1979, 1989.
Novicki, Margaret. "Interview: Ide Oumarou." *Africa Report* (July–Aug. 1986):9–13.
Nubukpo, K. C. "Les conseils nationaux de chargeurs des pays en voie de développement: L'exemple du Niger." *Revue Juridique et Politique* 41, no. 3 (1987):168–84.
Ofoegbu, Mazi Ray. "Nigeria and Its Neighbors." *Journal of West African Studies* 12, (1975):3–24.
"Opération 'Urgence Niger 1984.'" *Afrique Contemporaine* (Jan.–Mar. 1985):33–42.
Oumarou, Amadou. "Interférences de la loi, la coutume et la 'charia' is-

lamique devant les juridictions nigériens." *Penant* (Apr.–June 1979): 129–33.

———. "La Loi sur la liberté de la presse au Niger." *Penant,* no. 769 (July–Sept. 1980):254–61.

Ousman, Amadou. *Chroniques judiciaires.* Niamey: Imprimerie Nationale du Niger, 1987.

"Pages nouvelles du Niger." *Afrique* (Dec 1961):28–31.

"Un Pays qui émerge; Le Niger." *Europe Outre-Mer,* special issue, no. 570 (July 1977):2–52.

"Perspectives de Yaoundé II." *Niger* (Niamey), no. 9 (Jan. 1970):20–28.

Pietrantoni. "La subdivision de Madoua." CHEAM, no. 4402 (1949).

Pons, R. "Le problème touareg: Hier, aujourd'hui et demain." *Marchés Tropicaux et Méditerranéens* (May 7, 1993):1185–91.

"Les postes et télécommunications au Niger." *UAMPT,* no. 2 (Mar. 1965):6–9.

"Les premières assises de la francophonie à Niamey." *Afrique Contemporaine,* no. 42 (Mar.–Apr. 1969):20–21.

"Le Président Ali Saibou et la jeunesse." *Bingo,* no. 433 (Feb. 1989): 8–11.

"Les problèmes du Niger." *Marchés Tropicaux et Méditerranéens,* no. 28 (Feb. 1969):309–12.

"Le putsch de Niamey ne résoudre pas les problèmes dramatiques du Niger." *Marchés Tropicaux et Méditerranéens,* no. 1484 (Apr. 1974): 1049–50.

Rashidi, Lucienne el. *Cours de Fonction Publique.* Niamey: Ecole Nationale d'Administration, 1973.

Raynal, Jean-Jacques. "De la démocratisation à la démocratie? La constitution nigérienne du 24 septembre 1989." *Afrique Contemporaine,* no. 155 (1990):68–79.

———. *Les institutions politiques du Niger.* Saint-Maur, Fr.: Sepia, 1993

Raynal, Maryse. "La diversité dans l'unité: Le système juridictionnel Nigérien." *Penant,* no. 805 (Jan.– May 1991):61–110.

Raynaut, Claude, and Souleymane Abba. "Trente ans d'indépendance: Repères et tendances." *Politique Africaine,* no. 38 (1990):3–29.

"Recensement des repatriés du Niger." *Bulletin de Statistiques* (Porto Novo), no. 4 (Apr. 1965):8–12.

"Réforme constitutionnelle au Niger." *Revue Juridique et Politique,* no. 2 (Apr.–June 1966):363.

"La République après ses 18 ans." Special Issue of *Sahel-Hebdo* (Dec. 18, 1976).

"République du Niger." *Europe France Outre-Mer,* annual (1960–87).

Retaille, D. "La mise en place d'une région en Afrique sahélienne autour du Koutous, Niger oriental." In R. A. Prete and A. H. Ion (eds.),

Armies of Occupation. Waterloo, Belg.: Wilfrid Laurien University Press, 1984, pp. 181–203.

"La Révolution Africaine en marche." Paris: Maspero, 1972, pp. 18–29.

Revue Encyclopédique de l'Afrique. *République du Niger*. Abidjan, 1968.

Riedel, Jürgen. *Sozio-kulturelle Herausforderungen für die Entwicklungspolitik: die Republik Niger*. Munich: Weltforum Verlag, 1990.

Rifrac, S. "Développement et reconquête de la souveraineté." *Cahiers du Communisme* 69, no. 12 (Dec. 1993):76–84.

Robinson, Pearl Theodora. "African Traditional Rulers and the Modern State: The Linkage Role of Chiefs in the Republic of Niger." Ph.D. diss., Columbia University, 1975.

———. "Traditional Clientage and Political Change in a Hausa Community." In Pearl T. Robinson and E. Skinner (eds.), *Transformation and Resiliency in Africa*. Washington, D.C.: Howard University Press, 1983, pp. 105–28.

Sabourin, Louis. "Problems and Prospects of the Seven Landlocked Countries of French-Speaking Africa." In Z. Cervenka (ed.), *Landlocked Countries of Africa*. Uppsala: Scandinavian Institute of African Studies, 1973, pp. 146–60.

Salifou, André. La question touaregue au Niger. Paris: Karthala, 1992.

"Les 'Samara' au service du pays." *Europe Outre-Mer,* no. 554 (Mar. 1976):19–20.

Sao, Marankan. "Les dispositions transitoires du Code de la nationalité nigérienne." *Revue Juridique et Politique,* no. 4 (Oct.–Dec. 1971): 545–46.

Scofield, John. "Freedom Speaks French in Ouagadougou." *National Geographic* (Aug. 1966):153–203.

Sidikou, Abdou. "Dure ce que l'on pense, faire ce que l'on dit." *Niger* (Niamey), no. 5 (Jan. 1969):22–31.

"Social Security Fund in the Republic of Niger." *International Labour Review* (Feb. 1966):177–78.

Spittler, Gerd. "Administration in a Peasant State." *Sociologia Ruralis* (Essen) 23, no. 2 (1983):130–44.

———. "Peasants and State in Niger." *Peasant Studies* (Winter 1979): 30–47.

Stewart, Bonnie Ann. "Government Intervention and the Commercialization of Subsistence Food Crops in Niger." *Journal of African Studies* 14, no. 4 (1987/88):199–206.

Stoller, Paul Allen. "The Dynamics of Bankwano." Ph.D. diss., University of Texas/Austin, 1978.

"Le Syndicats en Afrique Noire." *Revue d'Etudes Politiques et Economiques Africaines,* no. 172/73 (Apr.–May 1980):22–45.

Thollard, G. "Le problème de l'enclavement du Niger." Mémoire, University of Bordeaux, 1983.

Thompson, Virginia, and Richard Adloff. "Niger." In *French West Africa*. London: Allen and Unwin, 1958, pp. 155–61.

———. "Niger." In Gwendolen Carter (ed.), *National Unity and Regionalism in Eight African States*. Ithaca, N.Y.: Cornell University Press, 1966, pp. 151–230.

———. *West Africa's Council of the Entente*. Ithaca, N.Y.: Cornell University Press, 1972.

Thomson, James Trevor. "Law, Legal Process and Development at the Local Level in Hausa-Speaking Niger: A Trouble Case Analysis of Rural Institutional Inertia." Ph.D. dissertation, Indiana University, 1976.

———. "Le processus jurdique, les droits fonciers et l'aménagement de l'environnement dans un canton du Niger." In Emile Le Bris et al. (eds.), *Enjeux Fonciers en Afrique Noire*. Paris: Karthala, 1982.

Tixier, Gilbert. "Les états du Conseil de l'Entente." *Penant,* no. 686 (Apr.–May 1961).

Touval, Saadia. "Disengagement I: Dahomey and Niger." In *The Boundary Politics of Independent Africa*. Cambridge: Harvard University Press, 1972, pp. 198–203.

Triaud, J. L. "L'Islam et l'Etat en République du Niger." In Olivier Carré, *Islam et Etat dans le monde aujourd'hui*. Paris: Presses Universitaires de France, 1982.

Vallet, M. "Nomades blancs et gouvernements noirs." CHEAM, no. 141 (1966).

Van Rensburg, A. P. J. "Seyni Kountché, Niger—Discipline and Authority Are Fundamental Necessities." In *Contemporary Leaders of Africa*. Cape Town: Haum, 1975, pp. 272–78.

Verdier, R. "Problèmes fonciers nigériens." *Penant* 74, no. 703/4 (Oct.–Dec. 1964):587–93.

Vieillard, Gilbert. "Coutumiers du cercle de Zinder, 1932." In *Coutumier Juridique de l'Afrique Occidentale Française,* vol. 3. Paris: Larose, 1939.

"Voyage du Président Pompidou en Afrique: Niger." *Afrique Contemporaine,* no. 59 (Jan.–Feb. 1972):pp. 16–17.

Wall, Roger. "Niger: Politics and Poverty in the Sahel." *Africa Report* (May–June 1983):59–65.

Weerd, Guido de. "La comptabilité du receveur d'arrondissement au municipal." Niamey: Ecole Nationale d'Administration, 1972.

Weiss, Danielle. "Interview du Colonel Seyni Kountché." *Europe Outre-Mer,* no. 597 (Oct. 1979):9–14.

———. "Interview du Colonel Seyni Kountché." *Europe Outre-Mer,* no. 624 (Jan. 1982):1–5.

———. "Seyni Kountché, un soldat pragmatique." *Europe Outre-Mer,* no. 554 (Mar. 1976):pp. 14–15.

Economic and Development Issues

Abdoulaye, Diallo. "Rechercher, conçevoir, coordonner, contrôler . . ." *Niger* (Niamey), no. 5 (Jan. 1969):32–39.

Adesina, Akinwumi Ayodeji. "Farmer Behavior and New Agricultural Technologies in the Rain-Fed Agriculture of Southern Niger." Ph.D. diss., Purdue University, 1988.

———, and B. W. Brorsen. "A Risk Responsive Acreage Resonse Function for Millet in Niger." *Agricultural Economics* 1, no. 3 (1987): 229–39.

———, et al. "Ex-ante Risk Programming Appraisal of New Agricultural Technology in Southern Niger." *Agricultural Systems* 27, no. 1 (1988):23–34.

Afrique, Industrie, Infrastructure, special issue on Niger, no. 154 (Jan. 1978):pp. 42–81.

Afrique Occidentale Française. *Compte Definitif des Recettes et des Dépenses de la colonie du Niger*. Dakar, 1922+.

———. *Etude Economique du trafic et de l'équilibre budgétaire du chemin du fer de Cotonou au Niger et au-delà*. Marseilles: Sémaphore, 1928.

———. *Les sels alimentaires: Sels du Manga (Niger),* by L. Soula. Dakar, 1950.

Agence Nigérienne de Publicité. *Annuaire Economique du Niger 1973–4*. Niamey, [1973?]

Agnew, Clive. "Spatial Aspects of Drought in the Sahel." *Journal of Arid Environments* (London) 18, no. 3 (1990):279–93.

Ajustement structurel, ajustement informel: Le cas du Niger. Paris: Harmattan, 1991.

Albenque, A. *Le Département d'Agadez 1974–5*. Niamey: Ministère de la Plan, 1975.

Alibert, Jacques. *Le Guide Bancaire du Niger*. Paris: EDITM, 1988.

Amadou, Ousmane. "Les transports en République du Niger." *Industries et Travaux d'Outre-Mer,* no. 179 (Apr. 1970):269–74.

Aménagement hydro-agricole de Karma. Rome: Ifagraria, 1964.

Aménagement hydro-agricole de la cuvette de Koutoukalé. Rome: Ifagraria, 1964.

"Aménagements hydro-agricoles de 6,000 hectares." *Europe Outre-Mer,* no. 624 (Jan. 1982):37–39.

Amin, Samir. *L'Afrique de l'Ouest Bloquée: L'Economie politique de la Colonisation, 1880–1970*. Paris: Editions de Minuit, 1971.

Anderson, Peggy. "The African Farmer II. New System in Niger." *Africa Report* 13, no. 7 (Nov. 1968):12–17.

Annuaire Economique du Niger. Niamey: ANIP, 1974.

"Aperçu global de la compagne agricole 1975–6 du Niger." *Bulletin de l'Afrique Noire,* no. 915 (June 1977):17866–69.

"Aperçus sur l'économie du Niger." *Notes d'Information BCEAO,* no. 143 (Aug.–Sept. 1967).

Arditi, Claude. *La commercialisation des céréales dans trois pays du Sahel.* Paris: Ministère de la Coopération, 1980.

Arnould, Eric J. "Anthropology and West African Development: A Political Economic Critique and Auto-Critique." *Human Organization* 48, no. 2 (1989):135–48.

———. "Changing the Terms of Development: Collaborative Research in Cultural Ecology in the Sahel." *Human Organization* 49, no. 4 (1990):339–54.

———. "Evaluating Regional Economic Development: The Results of a Marketing System Analysis in Zinder Province." *Journal of Developing Areas* 19, no. 2 (Jan. 1985):209–44.

———. "Marketing and Social Reproduction in Zinder, Niger." In R. McNettling and Eric Arnould (eds.), *Households: Comparative and Historical Studies of the Domestic Group.* Los Angeles: University of California Press, 1984, pp. 130–62.

———. "Merchant Capital, Simple Social Reproduction, and Underdevelopment: Peasant Traders in Zinder, Niger Republic." *Canadian Journal of African Studies* 20, no. 3 (1986):323–56.

———. "Petty Craft Production and the Underdevelopment Process in Zinder, Niger." *Dialectical Anthropology* 6 (1981):61–70.

———. "Process and Social Formation: Petty Commodity Producers in Zinder, Niger." *Canadian Journal of African Studies* 18, no. 3 (1984): 501–22.

———. "Regional Market System Development and Changes in Relations of Production in Three Communities in Zinder Province, Niger." Ph.D. diss., University of Arizona, 1982.

———. "Social Reproduction in Zinder Province, Niger Republic." In Robert McNettling, R. R. Wilk, and Eric J. Arnould (eds.), *Households: Comparative and Historical Studies of the Domestic Group.* Los Angeles: University of California Press, 1984.

Audette, Raymond. "Stockage traditionnel de céréales vivrières en milieu paysan au Niger." M.Sc. thesis, Laval University, 1983.

"L'autosuffisance alimentaire, priorité des priorités." *Europe Outre-Mer,* no. 624 (Jan. 1982):26–28.

Azam, Jean-Paul. *Le Niger: La pauvreté en période d'adjustement.* Paris: Harmattan, 1993.

Ba, B. "The Problem of Transferring Technology to the Least Industrialized Countries (the Case of Niger)." *Labour and Society* (Geneva) 1, no. 3/4 (July–Oct. 1976):121–26.

Badinand, B. "La situation économique du Niger." *Agronomie Tropicale,* no. 10 (Oct. 1967):1037–40.

Badoin, Robert. "Structures rurales et développement économique au Niger." *Droit Social* (Paris) (Dec. 1962):599–601.

Baier, Stephen. "The Development of Agricultural Credit in French-Speaking Africa, with Special Reference to Niger." M.A. thesis, University of Wisconsin, 1969.

———. "Economic History and Development: The Sahelian Economics of Niger." *African Economic History* (Spring 1976):1–16.

———. *An Economic History of Central Niger*. Oxford: Clarendon Press, 1980.

———. "Long Term Structural Change in the Economy of Central Niger." In B. K. Swartz and R. E. Dumett (eds.), *West African Cultural Dynamics*. The Hague: Mouton, 1980, pp. 587–602.

Baillaud, Emile. "La mise en valeur des territoires du Niger française." *Annales des Sciences Politiques* 14 (1899):744–65.

———. "Les territoires française du Niger: Leur valeur économique.' *Terre-Air-Mer* 2 (1900):9–24.

Bako Dankassoua. "Le Développement de l'Industrie nigérienne." *Niger* (Niamey), no. 7 (Feb. 16, 1970):8; no. 11 (Feb. 23, 1970):3–4; no. 12 (Mar. 2, 1970):2, 4; no. 13 (Mar. 9, 1970): 2–3.

"La balance commerciale: Un important déficit." *Europe France Outre-Mer,* no. 503 (Dec. 1971):29–30.

"La Balance de la culture cotonnière." *Europe Outre-Mer,* no. 624 (Jan. 1982):29–30.

"Balance des paiements extérieurs du Niger: Années 1970 et 1971." *Notes d'Information BCEAO,* no. 222 (Nov. 1974); "Année 1969," no. 195 (May 1972); "Année 1968," no. 176 (Aug.–Sept. 1970).

"Balance des paiements extérieurs du Niger; Année 1974." *Notes d'Information BCEAO,* no. 246 (Jan. 1977); "Année 1973," no. 241 (July 1976); "Année 1972," no. 230 (July 1975).

Banque Africaine de Développement. *Etude des possibilités de coopération économique entre le Ghana, la Côte d'Ivoire, la Haute-Volta, le Niger, le Dahomey et le Togo*. 3 vols. Paris: SEDES, 1970.

Banque Central des Etats de l'Afrique de l'Ouest. "Balance de Paiements extérieurs," no. 223 (1974); no. 234 (1975); no. 246 (1977); no. 256 (1977); no. 278 (Dec. 1979); no. 324 (Feb. 1984).

———. "Les Budgets généraux des Etats de l'Union Monétaire Ouest Africaine." No. 317 (June 1983).

———. "Commerce extérieur 1972–6." No. 269 (1979).

———. "Le Commerce extérieur du Niger en 1981." No. 322 (Dec. 1983).

———. "Le Commerce extérieur de la République du Niger." *Notes d'Information,* no. 76 (Nov. 1961).

———. "La commercialisation des arachides en Niger en 1962–3." *Notes d'Information,* no. 102 (Jan. 1964).

———. "Conjoncture économique fin 1983." No. 324 (Feb. 1984).

———. "Installation du Directeur National de la BCEAO pour le Niger." No. 325 (Mar. 1984).

———. "Niger: Chronologie Economique et Politique." No. 259 (Mar. 1978); no. 263 (July 1978); no. 267 (Dec. 1978); no. 271 (Apr. 1979); no. 275 (Aug.–Sept. 1979); no. 279 (Jan. 1980); no. 283 (May 1980); no. 287 (Oct. 1980); no. 291 (Feb. 1981); no. 295 (June 1981); no. 299 (Nov. 1981); no. 303 (Mar. 1982); no. 307 (July 1982); no. 311 (Dec. 1982); no. 315 (Mar. 1982); no. 319 (Aug.–Sept. 1983); no. 323 (Jan. 1984); no. 327 (May 1984); no. 331 (Sept. 1984); no. 339 (June 1985); no. 343 (Nov. 1985); and quarterly since.

———. "Notes d'Information." No. 279 (Jan. 1980); no. 283 (May 1980); no. 287 (Oct. 1980); no. 291 (June, 1981); no. 299 (Nov. 1981).

———. "Niger: Statistiques Economique et Monétaires." No. 259 (Mar. 1978); no. 263 (July 1978); no. 267 (Dec. 1978); no. 271 (Apr. 1979); no. 275 (Aug.–Sept. 1979); no. 279 (Jan. 1980); no. 283 (May 1980); no. 287 (Oct. 1980); no. 291 (Feb. 1981); no. 295 (June 1981); no. 299 (Nov. 1981); no. 303 (Mar. 1982); no. 307 (July 1982); no. 311 (Dec. 1982); no. 315 (Mar. 1982); no. 319 (Aug.–Sept. 1983); no. 323 (Jan. 1984); no. 327 (May 1984); no. 331 (Oct. 1984); no. 335 (Feb. 1985); no. 339 (June 1985); no. 343 (Nov. 1985); and quarterly since.

Banque de Développement de la République du Niger. "Rapport d'Activité." Niamey, 1962+.

Barclay, A. H. et al. "L'Impact des organisations bénévoles et privées sur le développement: Kenya et Niger." In *La rôle des organisations non-gouvernementales dans la coopération pour le développement.* Paris: OCDE, 1983.

Bortolani, Sergio. *The Banking System of Niger.* Milan: CRPL, 1971.

Battles, Ralph U. "Study of Agricultural Credit and Cooperatives in Niger." USAID/esd-2219. Washington, D.C.: Agency for International Development, 1974.

Baumhauer, Roland, and Horst Hagedorn. "Probleme der Grundwassererschliessung im Kawar." *Die Erde* (Berlin) 120, no. 1 (1989):11–20.

Beaussou, Jean-Jacques. "Le Niger Central." Thesis, University of Paris, 1980.

———. "Genèse d'une classe marchande au Niger." In *Entreprises et Entrepreneurs en Afrique.* Paris: Harmattan, 1988, pp. 205–20.

Beauvilain, Alain. "Eleveurs et élevage le long du fleuve Niger dans le département de Dosso." *Cahiers d'Outre-Mer* 32, no. 125 (Jan.–Mar. 1979):66–102.

———. *Les peuls du Dallol Bosso.* Niamey: IRSH, 1977.

Beck, Alois J. *Theorie und Praxis der 'Animation Rurale' im Frankophonen Afrika: Landliche Entwicklung Im Departement Zinder. Republik Niger*. Bochum, Ger.: Studienverlag Brockmeyer, 1981.

Belgium. Administration Générale de la Coopération au Développement. "Les Belges aux Niger: Coopération entre la Belgique et le Niger pour des projets de développement." Brussels, 1976.

Belgium. Service Information et Relations Publiques. "Les Belges au Niger." Brussels, 1976.

Belloncle, Guy. "Une expérience d'animation coopérative au Niger." *Archives Internationales de Sociologie de la Coopération et du Développement,* no. 21 (Jan.–June 1967):47–73.

———. *Coopératives et développement en Afrique noire sahélienne.* Sherbrooke, Can.: Centre d'Etudes en Economie Coopérative, 1978.

———. "Une éxperience d'animation coopérative au Niger." In H. Desroche and P. Rambaud (eds.), *Villages en Développement.* Paris: Mouton, 1971, pp. 201–27.

———. "Formation des hommes et développement au Niger. Introduction à la problématique nigérienne." *Développement et Civilisations,* no. 49/50 (Sept.–Dec. 1972):27–37.

———, and D. Gentil. "Pédagogie de l'implantation du mouvement coopératif au Niger." *Archives Internationales de Sociologie de la Coopération et de Développement,* no. 23 (Jan.–June 1968):50–71.

Bellot, Jean-Marc. *Commerce, Commerçants de bétail et migration régionale; L'exemple de l'Ouest du Niger*. Bordeaux: Institut d'Etudes Politiques, 1982.

———. "Exportations du bétail et politique nationale: L'exemple des exportations de l'Ouest du Niger." Revue Française d'Etudes Politiques Africaines, no.207/8 (Apr.–May 1978):77–105.

Belotteau, Jacques. "Le problème du déficit vivrièr au Sahel." *Afrique Contemporaine* (Oct.–Dec. 195):47–62.

Bernus, Edmond. "Azakha, mesure de capacité en Aïr." *Encyclopédie Berbère* (Aix-en-Provence) (1975).

———. "Le composants géographiques et sociales des types d'élevage en milieu touareg." In Theodore Monod (ed.), *Pastoralism in Tropical Africa.* London: Oxford University Press, 1975.

———. "Le contrôle du milieu naturel et du troupeau par les éleveurs touaregs sahéliens." In *Pastoral Production and Society: Proceedings of the International Meeting on Nomadic Pastoralism, Paris, Dec. 1976.* Cambridge: Cambridge University Press, 1979, pp. 67–74.

———. "Cueillette et exploitations des ressources spontanées du Sahel nigérien par les Kel Tomasheq." *Cahiers d'ORSTOM,* no. 1 (1967): 31–52.

———. "Dates, Dromedaries, and Drought: Diversification in Tuareg Pastoral Systems." In John G. Galaty and Douglas L. Johnson (eds.),

The World of Pastoralism: Herding Systems in Comparative Perspective. New York: Guilford Press, 1990.

———. "Graines sauvages." *Encyclopédie Berbère* (Aix-en-Provence) (1971).

———. "Jeu et élevage; Vocabulaire de l'élevage." *Jounal d'Agronomie Tropicale* 22, nos. 4–6 (1975):167–76.

Bairnes, Pierre. *L'Economie Africaine*. Dakar: Société Africain d'Edition, 1970+.

———. "Bilan de l'activité de la Caisse Centrale de Coopération Economique en Afrique Noire en 1978." *Bulletin de l'Afrique Noire,* no. 1011 (July 1979):19612–13.

———. "Bilan d'exécution du programme triennal 1976–8." *Bulletin de Afrique Noire,* no. 964 (June 1978):18816–18.

Billaz, R., and Y. Diawara. *Enquêtes en milieu rural sahélien*. Paris: Presses Universitaires de France, 1981.

Bisson, J. "Eleveurs caravaniers et vieux sédentaires de l'Aïr sud-oriental." *Travaux de l'Institut de Recherches Sahariennes* 23 (1964): 97–112.

Blum, W. E. *Rapport préliminaire. Ecologie, sols. Lutte contre l'érosion, mesure forestières et agricoles*. Niamey, 1975.

Bonté, Pierre. *L'Elevage et le commerce du bétail dans l'Ader Doutchi-Majya*. Paris: Etudes Nigériennes, no. 23, 1967.

Bortolani, Sergio. *The Banking System of Niger*. Milan: Finafrica, 1984.

Bovin, Mette. "Nomads of the Drought: Fulbe and Wadabee Nomads Between Power and Marginalization in the Sahel, Burkina Faso and Niger Republic." In Mette Bovin and Leif Manger (eds.), *Adaptive Strategies in African Arid Lands*. Uppsala: Scandinavian Institute of Afican Studies, 1990, pp. 29–58.

Breman, Henk, and Nico de Ridder. *Manuel sur les pâturages des pays sahéliens*. Paris: Karthala, 1991.

British Overseas Trade Board. *Ivory Coast, Niger and Upper Volta*. London, 1977.

Brosch, J. "Canada et Niger: De la francophonie à la coopération." *France Eurafrique,* no. 210 (Oct. 1969):28–30.

Brousse, Philippe. "Maîtriser le Développement." *Jeune Afrique,* no. 953 (Apr. 12, 1979):45–49.

Carle, P. "Une expérience d'assistance technique: La création de la Société Nigérienne de Commercialisation de l'Arachide (SONORA)." Coopération et Développement (Oct.–Dec. 1964):14–20.

Carre, M. "L'Electricité." *Industries et Travaux d'Outre-Mer,* no. 122 (Jan. 1964):66–69.

Catherinet, M. D., S. Dumont, and A. A. Mayaki. "Le Mil et le Sorgho dans l'agriculture du Niger." *Agronomie Tropicale* 18, no. 1 (1963): 108–25.

Catrisse, Benoit. "Le Textile." *Afrique Industrie,* no. 178 (Feb. 1979): 34–91.

Chambre de Commerce d'Alger. *Missions Economiques dans le Hoggar et au Niger*. Algiers: Imprimerie Africa, 1932.

Chantereau, J., and C. Etasse. "Création de populations naines de mil pennisetum au Niger." *Agronomie Tropicale,* no. 3 (July–Sept. 1976): 254–64.

Charbonnier, François. "Niger: Expansion économique lente mais continue." *France Eurafrique,* no. 169 (Jan. 1966):20–21.

Charlick, Robert B. "Induced Participation in Nigerien Modernization: The Case of Matamaye County." *Rural Africana,* no. 18 (Fall 1972): 5–29.

———. "Participatory Development and Rural Modernization in Hausa Niger." *African Review* (Dar es Salaam) 2, no. 4 (1972):499–524.

Charoy, J. "Les cultures irriguées au Niger." *Agronomie Tropicale,* no. 9 (Sept. 1971):979–1002.

———. "Dynamique de l'eau dans un type de sole du Goulbi de Maradi au Niger. Application à l'irrigation du blé et d'une culture de saison des pluies de coton avec complément d'irrigation." *Agronomie Tropicale,* no. 10 (Oct. 1974):983–94.

Chauleur, Pierre. "Les problèmes du Niger." *Marchés Tropicaux et Méditerranéens,* no. 1369 (Feb. 4, 1972):309–12.

Cheramy, Pierre. "Les Canadiens ont des projets ambitieux pour le développement du Niger." *France Eurafrique,* no. 222 (Dec. 1970): 29–31.

Chevalier, A. "Les productions végétales du Sahara et de ses confins Nord et Sud, passé, présent, avenir." *Revue de Botanie Appliqué et Agronomie Tropicale* 12 (Sept.–Oct. 1931).

Chevalier, Jerome. *Programmation régionale au Niger*. Paris: IRFED, 1969.

Chevillard, Nicole. "Afrique: Six pays en quête de partenaires." *Moniteur Africain du Commerce International,* no. 228 (Feb. 7, 1977): 18–26.

———. "Niger: Terre pauvre vengée par son sous-sol." *Moniteur du Commerce International,* no. 373 (Nov. 1979):13–16.

Chirot, David. "Urban and Rural Economies in the Western Sudan: Birni N'Konni and Its Hinterland." *Cahiers d'Etudes Africaines* 8, no. 32 (1968):547–65.

Cloud, Kathleen. "Sex Roles in Food Production and Distribution Systems in the Sahel." In Lucy E. Creevy (ed.), *Women Farmers in Africa: Rural Development in Mali and the Sahel*. Syracuse, N.Y.: Syracuse University Press, 1986, pp. 19–49.

Collins, John Davison. "The Clandestine Movement of Groundnuts Across the Niger-Nigeria Boundary." *Canadian Journal of African Studies* 10, no. 2 (1976).

———. "Government and Groundnut Marketing in Rural Hausa Niger: The 1930s to the 1970s in Magaria." Ph.D. diss., Johns Hopkins University, 1974.

Collion, Marie Helene. "Colonial Rule and Changing Peasant Economy in Damagherim, Niger Republic." Ph.D. diss., Cornell University, 1982.

Colombe, J. *Textes généraux sur la plantification nigérienne.* Niamey: Ecole National d'Administration, [1972?].

"Le commerce extérieur réel de la République du Niger." *Notes d'Information BCEAO,* no. 76 (Nov. 1961).

"La commercialisation des arachides au Niger." *Notes d'Information BCEAO,* no. 102 (Jan. 1964); no. 137 (Feb. 1967).

Commission des Communautés Européennes. *Les conditions d'installation d'entreprises industrielles dans les états africaines: Niger,* vol. 6. Brussels, 1974.

Commission Economique pour l'Afrique. *Monographie de la République du Niger,* Niamey, 1964.

Compagnie Française pour le Développement des Fibres Textiles. *Rapport d'activité de la CFDT en République du Niger: Campagne 1967–68.* Niamey, 1968.

Condat, G. "Présentation du Niger." *Revue de la Société Etudes et Expansion* (Liège), no. 207 (Sept.–Oct. 1963):523–28.

"Conditions et perspectives de l'agriculture au Niger." *Nations Nouvelles,* no. 14 (Dec. 1967):21–26.

"Conférence sur l'harmonisation des programmes de développement industriel à Niger." *Niger* (Niamey), no. 28 (July 9, 1962).

"Les Coopératives." *Niger* (Niamey), no. 5 (Jan. 1969):50–60.

Copans, Jean. "The 'New' International Division of Labour and the Sahel of the 1970s." In R. E. Boyd (ed.), *International Labour and the Third World.* Aldershot, Eng.: Avebury, 1987, pp. 179–99.

"Le Coton." *Afrique Agriculture,* no. 48 (Aug. 1979):22–43.

"Le Coton." *Afrique Agriculture,* no. 57 (May 1980):28–36.

"Le Coton en Afrique de l'Ouest et du Centre." *Afrique Agriculture,* no. 36 (Aug. 1978):24–47.

"Le Coton—Moteur du développement rural." *Africa,* no. 89 (Mar. 1977):53–90.

Coulomb, J. *Zone de Modernisation pastorale du Niger: Économie du tropeau.* Paris: IEMVT, 1971.

Courmo, Barcougne. "Les finances publiques de la République du Niger depuis son indépendence." *Notes d'Information BCEAO,* no. 134 (Nov. 1966).

———. "La loi de Finances du Niger pour l'année budgetaire 1970." *Notes d'Information BCEAO,* no. 168 (Dec. 1969).

———. "La Place capitale de l'arachide." *Europe France Outre-Mer,* no. 430 (Nov. 1965):25–27.

———. "La politique du Gouvernement en matière de sociétés d'économie mixte." *Niger* (Niamey) (May 27, 1969):2–3, 6.

———. "Promotion humaine et croissance économique au Niger." *Revue de la Société d'Etudes et d'Expansion* (Liège), no. 213 (Nov.–Dec. 1964):757–60.

Coyaud, Y., and J. M. Lienart. "La recherche rizicole au Niger." *Agronomie Tropicale,* no. 1 (Jan. 1966):56–64.

Cuevas, Carlos. "Niger." In Mario Masini (ed.), *Rural Finance Profiles in African Countries.* Milan: Finafrica, 1985, 1:119–84.

Curry, John James. "Development and Dissertation: Field Research Opportunities on a Pastoral Development Project in Niger." In E. C. Green (ed.), *Practicing Development Anthropology.* Boulder, Colo.: Westview Press, 1986.

———. "Local Production, Regional Commerce, and Social Differentiation in a Hausa Village in Niger." Ph.D. diss., University of Massachusetts, 1984.

Cys, Monique. "Niger: De l'élevage au pool de la viande." *Entente Africaine,* no. 3 (Jan. 1970):64–71.

"Dahomey, Niger, Togo: Le décollage économique est commencé." *Moniteur du Commerce International,* no. 1083 (Aug. 26, 1971): 3387–3401.

Damiba, Pierre-Claver, and Paul Schrumpf. *Quel avenir pour le Sahel?* Lausanne: Editions Pierre-Marcel Favre, 1981.

Dan Moussa, L. "L'Information en tant que stimulant du développement rural au Niger." Diss., University of Paris, 1974.

Decupper, J., and Kelefa Decupper. "Les problèmes économiques du Niger." *Africa* (Dakar) 9, no. 48 (1969):31–35.

Delpy, Jacques. "Le Développement économique de la République du Niger." Thesis, University of Paris, 1960.

Delwaulle, S. C. "Le Bois de feu à Niamey. *Bois et Forêts des Tropiques,* no. 152 (Nov.–Dec. 1973):55–60.

Derriennic, Hervé. *Famines et Dominations en Afrique Noire: Paysans et Eleveurs du Sahel sous le Joug.* Paris: Harmattan, 1977.

Desroche, Henri, and Placide Rambaud. *Villages en Développement.* Paris: Mouton, 1972.

"La Deuxième tranche de la centre thermique de la SONICHAR." *Europe Outre-Mer,* no. 624 (Jan. 1982):46–49.

Diallo, Hamidou. "SONORA: Un déficit de plus de deux milliards." *Sahel-Hebdo* (Niamey), no. 71 (Oct. 6, 1975):6–9.

Diallo, S., and Philippe Brousse. "Le Niger hier negligé, demain courtisé." *Jeune Afrique,* no. 935 (Apr. 1979):31–66.

Diarra, S. "Les problèmes de contact entre les pasteurs peul et les agriculteurs dans le Niger central." In Theodore Monod (ed.), *Pastoralism in Tropical Africa.* London: Oxford University Press, 1975, pp. 284–97.

Diawara, I. "Les transports au Niger." *Niger* (Niamey), no. 17 (May 1972):7–13.

Doizelet, A. "Travaux d'irrigation du Niger." *Revue de Génie Militaire* (Nancy) 71 (1972):439–76, 554–86.

Dorosh, Paul Anthony, and B. Essema Nssah. *External Shocks, Policy Reform, and Income Distribution in Niger*. Ithaca, N.Y.: Cornell University Food and Nutrition Policy Program, 1993.

Le Dossier Sahel. Paris: Ediafric, 1978.

Doutresscule, Georges Alexis-Helie. "L'Elevage au Niger." Thesis, Mortain University, 1924.

Dupire, Marguerite. "Exploitation du sol, communautés résidentielles et organisation lignagère des pasteurs woDaaBe (Niger)." In Theodore Monod (ed.), *Pastoralism in Tropical Africa*. London: Oxford University Press, 1975, pp. 322–37.

———. *Les Facteurs humaines de l'économie*. Niamey, INSH, 1972.

Durand, C. L., et al. *Les Produits Vivrièrs au Niger*. Paris: SEDESS, 1963.

Dynamique de l'emploi dans un système sahélien, le Niger. Addis Ababa: Bureau International du Travail, 1980.

Eberhart, Frederick B. "Equitable Distribution in Small-Scale Agricultural Projects in the Niger Republic: Trade-Offs in Reaching the Poor." M.A. thesis, University of Indiana, 1985.

"Les échanges commerciaux entre les pays de l'Union Monétaire Ouest Africaine 1969–78." *Banque Centrale des Etats de l'Afrique de l'Ouest,* no. 292 (Mar. 1981).

Economic Commission for Africa. *Le développement industriel du Niger*. Mimeo. Addis Ababa, 1965.

———. *Monographie de la République du Niger*. Niamey, 1964.

L'Economie Africaine. Annual. Dakar: Société Africaine d'Edition, 1972 + .

L'Economie des Pays d'Afrique Noire de la Zone Franc. Paris: Ediafric, 1972.

Eddy, Edward D. "Labor and Land Use on Mixed Farms in the Pastoral Zone of Niger." Ann Arbor, Mich.: Center for Research on Economic Development, 1979.

———. "Prospects for the Development of Cattle Production on Mixed Farms in the Pastoral Zone of Niger." Ann Arbor, Mich.: Center for Research on Economic Development, 1980.

Ediafric. *Les Plans de Développement des Pays d'Afrique Noire*. Paris, 1972.

Elbow, Kent M. "Popular Participation in the Management of Natural Resources: Lessons from Baban Rafi, Niger." Ph.D. diss., University of Wisconsin, 1992.

"L'Electricité en Afrique." *Industries et Travaux d'Outre-Mer,* no. 168 (Nov. 1967):961–1058.

"L'Electricité: Niger." *Industries et Travaux d'Outre-Mer* (Jan. 1964): 66–69.

Eliott Berg Associates. *Joint Program Assessment of Grain Marketing in Niger*. 2 vols. Niamey: USAID, 1983.

———. *Cereal Policy Reform in the Sahel*. 7 vols. Paris: Club du Sahel, 1986.

Englebert, V. "I Joined a Sahara Salt Caravan." *National Geographic* (Nov. 1965):694–711.

Erceville, d'. "L'Elevage des animaux de boucherie au Niger." CHEAM, no. 1525 (1950).

"Etudes du barrage de Kandadjisé." *Europe Outre-Mer,* no. 624 (Jan. 1982):35–36.

Everts, Arjaan. "Development Planning in Niger." *Research in Economic Anthropology* 3 (1980):254–64.

"Evolution économique et financière de la République du Niger." In *BCEAO*. Annual. Paris, 1970+.

"L'évolution récente de l'économie nigérienne." *Notes d'Information BCEAO,* no. 128 (Apr. 1966); no. 130 (June 1966).

"Un Expérience d'assistance technique: La création de la Société Nigérienne de Commercialisation de l'Arachide (SONORA)." *Coopération et Développement* (Oct.–Dec. 1964):14–20.

Favard, L. *Sahara et Soudan. Essai sur la mise en valeur du Sahara et sur les communictions du Centre Africain avec l'Europe*. Paris: Imprimerie F. Levé, 1905.

"Le fichier industriel." *Europe Outre-Mer,* no. 554 (Mar. 1976):42–47.

Fond Européen de Développement. *Niger 1960–1975*. Brussels, 1975.

"Le Fonds national d'investissement." *Bulletin de l'Afrique Noire,* no. 999 (Apr. 1979):19401–2.

Food and Agricultural Oganization. *Rapport au Gouvernement du Niger. Le Commerce du poisson dans la vallée du Niger,* by J. M. Remo. 1970.

———. *Rapport au Gouvernement du Niger. Le Développement et la rationalisation de la pêche sur le fleuve Niger,* by N. B. Dobrovici. 1971.

"Forest Land Use: Guessolbodi, Niger." In Paul Kerkhof, *Agroforestry in Africa*. London: Panos Publications, 1990.

France. La Documentation Française. "La législation du travail dans les états africains et malgache d'expression française." *Notes et Etudes Documentaires,* no. 3018 (Sept. 13, 1963).

———. Institut National de la Statisique et des Etudes Economiques. *Commerce Extérieur des Etats d'Afrique et de Madagascar 1949 à 1960. Rétrospectif*. Paris, 1962.

———. *Compendium des Statistiques du commerce extérieur des pays de la Zone Franc*. Paris, 1938–46.

———. *Resumé des Statistiques d'Outre-Mer. Bulletin Accéléré.* Monthly (Oct. 1958–64).

———. Ministère de la Coopération. *Le Développement régional et sa problématique étudiés à Travers l'expérience de Tahoua,* by J. M. Funel. 1976.

———. *Industrialisation des pays d'Afriques sub-saharienne: Le cas du Niger,* by C. Brochet and J. Pierre. 1986.

———. *Niger: Données statistiques sur les activités économiques, culturelles et sociales.* Paris, 1975.

———. *Les produits vivrièrs au Niger.* Paris, 1963.

———. *Situation éonomique des Etats africains et de l'Océan indien.* Paris, 1979.

———. *Niger. Analyse et conjoncture 1978.* Paris, 1978.

———. *Le Coût des transports routiers au Niger.* Paris, 1964.

———. Secrétariat d'Etat aux Affaires Etrangères. *Enquête agricole au Niger.* Paris: INSEE, 1970.

———. *Le marché du riz au Niger,* by G. Gassend. Paris, 1969.

———. *Méthodologie de la planification: L'expérience nigérienne de planification permanente,* by J. Nemo and J. Bethany. Paris, 1974.

———. *Niger 1968–69—Dossier d'information économique.* Paris, 1970.

———. Service de Coopération. *Enquête agricole au Niger.* Paris, 1970.

———. Secrétariat du Comité monétaire de la Zone Franc. *La Zone Franc en 1978.* Paris, 1979.

Franke, Richard W., and Barbara H. Chasin. "Peanuts, Peasants, Profits and Pastoralists: The Social and Economic Background to Ecological Deterioration in Niger." *Peasant Studies* 8, no. 3 (1979):1–30.

Frelastre, Georges. "La Nouvelle stratégie rurale du Niger." *Revue Française d'Etudes Politiques Africaines,* no. 211/12 (Aug.–Sept. 1983):69–106.

———. "Le séminaire de Zinder et la nouvelle stratégie de la République du Niger." *Revue Française d'Etudes Politiques Africaines,* no. 211/12 (1983):69–80, 97–106.

———. "Le Troupeau nigérien en peril." *Revue Française d'Etudes Politiques Africaines,* no. 247/48 (Aug.–Sept. 1986):97–105.

Fuchs, P. "Sozio-Ökonomische Aspekte der Dürrekatastrophe für die Sahara-Bevölkerung von Niger." *Afrika Spectrum* 9, no. 3 (1974): 308–16.

Furon, R. "A Propos du cuivre de la région d'Azelick (Niger)." *Notes Africaines,* no. 48 (1950):127.

Gado, Kaka. "Production Schedule of Sorghum in Niger: A Times Series Study." M.A. thesis, Virginia State University, 1984.

Garba, Amadou. "Contributions de l'irrigation à l'amélioration de l'agriculture dans les pays du Sahel: Le cas du Niger." M.A. thesis, University of Sherbrooke, 1982.

Gaudio, Attilio. "Un rêve millénaire devient realité: La route transsaharienne." *France Eurafrique,* no. 218 (July 1970):11–15.

Gavin, Sarah. "Land Tenure and Fertility Management in Niger." Ph.D. diss., Stanford University, 1993.

Genné, Marcelle. *Autosuffisance alimentaire ou famine en l'an 2000.* Paris: Economica, 1991.

Gentil, Dominique. *Les Coopératives Nigériennes: Traditions Villageoises et Modernisation Coopérative*. Paris: Harmattan, 1971.

———. "Méthodologie de l'implantation du nouveau système coopératif coopératif au Niger." *Développement et Civilisations,* no. 52/53 (Apr.–Sept. 1973):51–64.

Giesecke, J., and A. B. Simon. "Rénovation de la route Parakou-Malanville." *Routes,* no. 509 (May 1975):53–60.

Giffard, Pierre-Louis. "Les gommiers, essences de reboisement pour les régions sahéliennes." *Bois et Forêts Tropiques,* no. 161 (May–June 1975):3–21.

Giri, Jacques. *Le Sahel au XXIe siècle: Une essai de réflexion prospective sur les sociétés sahéliennes*. Paris: Karthala, 1989.

Gregoire, Emmanuel. "L'Artisanat dans la Ville de Maradi, République du Niger." Maradi: Service du Plan, 1979.

———. "L'Etat doit-il abandonner le commerce des vivres aux marchands?" *Politique Africaine* 37 (1990):63–70.

———. "Le fait économique haoussa." *Politique Africaine* 38 (1990): 61–67.

———. "Les perspectives d'accumulation dans le petite industrie de transformation: L'exemple de la menuiserie metallique à Maradi." *Cahiers d'Etudes Africaines* 21, no. 81 (1981):221– 35.

Grelon, Bruno. "Pour un politique novatrice en matière d'élevage." *Europe Outre-Mer,* no. 624 (Jan. 1982):31–34.

"Les greniers de réserve dans le territoire du Niger—Note faite d'après plusiers rapports." *Agronomie Tropicale,* no. 56 (1949):321–22.

Guide de l'entreprise et de l'investisseur au Niger. Le Vésinet, Fr.: EDITM, 1983.

Guilbert-Nignon, Louise. "Les ouvriers mineurs du Niger." Ph.D. diss., University of Paris, 1989.

Guillaumont, Patrick, and Sylvaine Guillamont. *L'Ajustement structurel, ajustement informel: Le cas du Niger*. Paris: Harmattan, 1989.

Hall, William E., and Grover E. Murray. *The Niger Cereals Projects: An Experience with Technical Assistance*. Lubbock, Tex.: International Center for Arid and Semi-Arid Land Studies, 1983.

Hamildil, A., and O. Hamil. "Aligning Practice with Theory in Niger." In *Strengthening Environmental Cooperation with Developing Countries*. Paris: OECD, 1989.

Heermans, John G. "The Guesselbodi Experiment: Bushland Management in Niger." *Rural Africana,* no. 23/24 (1985/86):67–77.

Hetzel, W. "Problems of the Inland Situation of the Republic of Niger." *Erdkunde,* no. 24 (1970):1–14.

Horowitz, Michael. "Herdsmen and Husbandmen in Niger: Values and Strategies." In Theodore Monod (ed.), *Pastoralism in Tropical Africa.* London: Oxford University Press, 1975.

Houdet, J. "Le projet d'extension du réseau de l'OCDN de Parakou à Dosso." *Industries et Travaux d'Outre-Mer,* no. 163 (June 1967): 525–28.

Hugon, Pierre. "Les programmes d'ajustement structurel du Niger et l'impact de l'économie nigérienne." *Afrique Contemporaine,* no. 155 (1990).

L'Huilerie au Niger. Paris: Compagnie Générale d'Etudes et Recherches pour l'Afrique, 1964.

"Les hydrocarbures dans l'économie africaine." *Europe France Outre-Mer,* no. 413 (June 1964):14–59.

Ichard, A. "La coopérative des éleveurs de Toukounans (Cercle de Filingué-Niger)." *Notes Documentaires du Secrétariat Social d'Outre-Mer,* no. 32 (1959):1–7.

"Inauguration de l'agence de la BCEAO." *Note d'Information,* no. 295 (June 1981).

"L'Inauguration de l'ensemble minier de la SOMAIR—14 Décembre 1971." *Industries et Travaux d'Outre-Mer,* no. 218 (Jan. 1972):47–51.

"Indicateurs Economiques Nigériens." *BCEAO Notes d'Information.* Quarterly. 1960+.

"Industrial Development in the Niger." In *Industrial Development in Africa.* New York: United Nations, 1967, pp. 281–87.

"L'Industrialisation du Niger de 1960 à 1970." *Afrique, Industrie, Informations,* no. 4 (Nov. 16, 1970):55–58.

"L'Industrie du ciment en Afrique Noire." *Bulletin de l'Afrique Noire,* no. 968 (July 1978):18888–94.

International Labour Office. *Rapport au gouvernement de la République du Niger sur la création de coopératives rurales et la formation de leurs dirigeants.* Geneva, 1964.

———. *Rapport au gouvernement de la République du Niger sur l'organisation de coopératives de construction et de transports.* Geneva, 1964.

"Les interventions du FAC de 1973 à 1976." *Marchés Tropicaux,* no. 1637 (Mar. 1977):691–93.

"Les investissements du F.A.C. et du F.E.D." *Europe France Outre-Mer,* no. 430 (Nov. 1965):38–40.

Jabara, Cathy L. *Structural Adjustment and Stabilization in Niger.* Ithaca, N.Y.: Cornell University Food and Nutrition Policy Program, 1991.

Jacquemin, André. *La Fiscalité des Collectivités Territoriales du Niger.* Niamey: Ecole Nationale d'Administration, 1974.

Jobs and Skills Programme for Africa. Addis Ababa: International Labour Office, 1982.

Jouan, B., and M. Delassus. "Principales maladies des mils et sorghum observées au Niger." *Agronomie Tropicale,* no. 8 (Aug. 1971): 830–60.

Judet, P., and R. Tiberghien. *L'Industrialisation de l'economie nigérienne: Diagnostic, éléments pour une problématique, premières pistes pour des stratégies*. Niamey: Ministère du Plan, 1986.

Julienne, Roland. "Les plans de développement des états de l'Afrique francophone." *Industries et Travaux d'Outre-Mer,* no. 195 (Feb. 1970):85–91.

———. "Les plans de développement des états de l'Afrique francophone en 1975." *Industries et Travaux d'Outre-Mer,* no. 266 (Jan. 1976):11–18.

Justice, C. O., and P. H. Y. Hiernaux. "Monitoring the Grasslands of the Sahel." *International Journal of Remote Sensing* 7, no. 11 (1986): 1475–97.

Karimou, Goukoye. "L'Animation des collectivités au développement." *Europe France Outre-Mer,* no. 430 (Nov. 1965):41–43.

Kassapu, Samuel. *Les dépenses de recherche agricole dans 34 pays d'Afrique tropicale*. Paris: Centre du Développement de l'OCDE, 1976.

Kaziendé, Leopold. "L'Activité minière au Niger en 1961 et le programme pour 1962." *Industries et Travaux d'Outre-Mer,* no. 106 (Sept. 1962):691–99.

Keita, T. "Problématique le l'integration des femmes aux coopératives agricoles du Niger." In *Women in Rural Development in Africa.* Dakar: AAWord, 1986.

Klein, R. "Flächennutzung im westlichen Sahel der Republik Niger und Abundanzdynamik des Goldsperlings." *Die Erde* 120, no. 3 (1989): 203–12.

Kondo, M., et al. "Effect of Phosphorous on Azolla and Its Utilization in Rice Culture in Niger." *Plant and Soil* 120, no. 2 (1989):165–70.

Lachenman, Gudrun. "Ecology and Social Structure in the Sahel." *Economics* (Tübingen), no. 32 (1985):84–106.

Ladjimi, Mohamed Habib. "Niger: L'espoir." *Jeune Afrique,* no. 904 (May 1978):30–35.

Lapott, Jacek. "*Kadei* des papyrus des Tschad-Sees." *Jahrbuch des Museums für Volkerkunde zu Leipzig* 37 (1987):221–40.

Latremolière, F. "La Crise financière du Niger." *Marchés Tropicaux,* no. 1943 (Feb. 1983):253–55.

Laucoin, Guy. "L'animation des aménagements hydro-agricoles: Vers l'autogestion des aménagements au Niger." *Développement et Civilisations,* no. 44 (June 1971):54–62.

———. "La gestion des aménagements hydro-agricoles au Niger." *Développement et Civilisations,* no. 51 (Jan.–Mar. 1973):21–31.

Laya, Diouldé. "Interviews with Farmers and Livestock Owners About the Famine." *African Environment* 1, no. 2 (1975):49–70.

———. *Recherche et Développement. Le projet de mise en valeur des cuvettes de Kutukale et Karma en pays Songhay*. Paris: Etudes Nigériennes, no. 24, 1969.

Lefebre, F. "Précis de la fiscalité nigérienne à l'usage des entreprises." *Droit et Fiscalité d'Outre-Mer,* no. 9 (May 1, 1972).

Le Houerou, Henri Noel. *The Grazing Land Ecosystems of the African Sahel*. Berlin: Springer, 1989.

Le Nay, Jean, and Jean Mathis. "The Impact of the Drought on the National Accounts for Livestock in the Sahelian Countries." *Review of Income and Wealth* (New Haven, Conn.) 35, no. 2 (1989): 209–24.

Leroy, M. "Securité alimentaire au Niger." CHEAM, no. 1622 (1949).

Lhote, H. "La mission Berliet-Ténéré ouvre la route directe Alger–Tchad." *Europe France Outre-Mer,* no. 363 (Feb. 1960):20–23.

Lolito, Gaston. *Sahel: Crise, survie, développement.* Nice: Comité Française pour l'UNICEF, 1987.

Louis-Joseph, J. "Note sur l'habitation traditionnel." Niamey: Crédit du Niger, 1964.

Lovejoy, Paul E. "The Borno Salt Industry." *International Journal of the African Historical Society* 11, no. 4 (1978):629– 68.

Luc, Jean-Claude. "L'Economie du Niger depuis indépendance." *Revue Française d'Etudes Politiques Africaines,* no. 72 (Dec. 1971):61–84.

McCorkle, C. M., et al. *A Case Study of Farmer Innovations and Communication in Niger*. Washington, D.C.:Academy for Educational Development, 1988.

McIntire, J., and C. L. Delgado. "Statistical Significance of Indicators of Efficiency: Examples from West African Agriculture." *American Journal of Agricultural Economics,* 67, no. 4 (1985):733–38.

McIntire, J, and L. K. Fussell. "On-Farm Experiments with Millet in Niger." *Experimental Agriculture* 25, no. 2 (1989):217–33.

Maiga, Issaka Doulaye. "Difficultés et limites de l'animation rurale: Le cas du Niger, 1964–1974." In A. C. Mondjanagni (ed.), *La participation populaire au développement en Afrique Noire*. Paris: Karthala, 1984, pp. 155–70.

Maina, Sanda. "On Food Security in Niger Republic." M.S. thesis, Michigan State University, 1982.

Mainet, Guy. "L'Elevage dans la région de Maradi, République du Niger." *Cahiers d'Outre-Mer,* no. 69 (Jan.–Mar. 1965):32–72.

———, and G. Nicolas. *La Vallée de Gulbi de Maradi. Enquête socio-économique*. Paris: Etudes Nigériennes, no. 16, 1965.

"Majjia Valley Windbreak project, Niger." In Paul Kerkhof, *Agroforestry in Africa*. London: Panos Publications, 1989, pp. 113–23.

Malou, Ada R, and Sharon E. Nicholson. "A Study of Rainfall and Vegetation Dynamics in the African Sahel." *Journal of Arid Environments* 19, no. 1 (1990):1–24.

Mamoudou, A. "Food in the Sahel: Helping the People Grow Their Own." *World Health Forum* 7, no. 4 (1986):410–11.

Mamoudou, Maidah. "L'Elevage une richesse potentielle considérable." *Europe France Outre-Mer* no. 430 (Nov. 1965):30–32.

"Le marché hôtellier à Niamey." *Informations Economiques* (Niamey), no. 2 (June 1971):3–9.

"Le marché Nigérien." *Marchés Tropicaux et Méditerranéens,* no. 1301 (Oct. 17, 1970):2961–3330.

Martinet, D., et al. *Le commerce des engrais au Niger: L'impacte de la politique nigeriene*. Muscle Shoals, Ala.: International Fertilizer Development Center, 1994.

Marty, J. P., J. Greigert, and B. Peyre de Fabrègues. "Mise en valeur du complexe pastorale situé au nord de l'axe Filingué–Tahoua au Niger." Paris, 1966.

"Matières premières: Le poids de l'Afrique." *Europe Outre-Mer,* no. 531 (Apr. 1974):9–56.

Mayaki, Amadou. "Les problèmes économiques de la République du Niger." *Notes d'Information BCEAO,* no. 59 (June 1960).

Merlin, P., E. Kleinmann, and J. M. Payen. "Problèmes de transport au Niger et au Dahomey." Paris, 1963.

Meunier, Michel. "Le rôle de l'armature urbaine dans le processus de formation de l'éspace: Le cas du Niger." M.A. thesis, University of Montreal, 1975.

Meyer, R. "Die "animation rurale" in Niger: Möglichkeiten und Verwirklichungschancen in einer peripheren Gesellschaftsformation." *Afrika Spectrum* 11, no. 2 (1976):145–55.

Michaud, D. "Les Budgets familiaux Africains à Niamey." Paris: Ministère de la Coopération, 1964.

"Les Mines." *Afrique Industrie,* no. 189 (July 1979):35–57.

"Mise en oeuvre des budgets économiques au Niger." *Economie et Pension,* no. 75 (1983).

"Mise en place de la Commission de Contrôle et d'Enquête." *Marchés Tropicaux et Méditerranéens,* no. 1486 (May 3, 1974):1197–98.

Mix, Ulrike. *Les jardins de la sécheresse: Tamazalak versant ouest de l'Aïr*. Geneva: Institut Universitaire d'Etudes du Développement, 1988.

"Modalités du Budget du Niger pour 1980." *Bulletin de l'Afrique Noire,* no. 1038 (Feb. 1980):20045–47.

Montagne, Pierre. "Contributions of Indigenous Siviculture to Forestry Development in Rural Areas: Examples from Niger and Mali." *Rural Africana,* no. 23/24 (1985–86):61–65.

Morel, A. "Faire renaître le Sahel? Experiences de développement agricole dans le Massif de l'Aïr." *Cultures et Développement* 8, no. 2 (1976):266–86.

Morou, Alassane. "Etude de l'équilibre vivrier et de sa problématique au Niger: Une perspective à long terme." M.Sc. thesis, Laval University, 1981.

Moulton, J. "Development Through Training: *Animation Rurale* in Niger and Senegal." In J. C. Bock and G. J. Papgiannis (eds.), *Nonformal Education and National Development*. New York: Praeger, 1983, pp. 25–41.

Moumouni, Abdou. "Une richesse méconnue . . . L'énergie solaire." *Niger* (Niamey), no. 17 (May 1972):15–20.

Mourgues, G. "La mise en valeur de la vallée du Niger." *Géographie* 63 (1935):77–101.

Müller, J. O. *Problèmes d'élevage contractuel des bovine par les pasteurs Foulbé (Peulh) en Afrique Occidentale*. Munich: IFO Institut, 1967.

Munier, P. *Prospection phénicole en territoire de la République du Niger*. Paris: Institut des Fruits et Agrumes Coloniaux, 1963.

———. *Le palmier-dattier*. Paris: Maisonneuve et Larose, 1973.

Murgue, Bernard. "Les échanges commerciaux." *Europe Outre-Mer,* no. 554 (Mar. 1976):48–50.

Nabukpo, C. "Le concept de banque et d'établissement financier dans les pays de l'OMOA: Le cas du Niger." *Revue Juridique et Politique* 41, no. 4 (1987):328–44.

Najada, Ibrahim. "La pêche au Niger." *Afrique Agriculture,* no. 49 (Sept. 1979).

Newby, J. E., and J. F. Grettenberger. "The Human Dimension in Natural Resource Conservation: A Sahelian Example from Niger." *Environmental Conservation* 13, no. 3 (1986):249–56.

Nicolas, Guy. "Circulations des biens et échanges monétaires au nord du Niger." *Cahiers de l'Institut des Sciences Economiques Appliqués* (Sept. 1962):49–62.

———. "Circulations des richesses et participation sociale dans une société hausa du Niger." Diss., University of Bordeaux, 1965.

———, et al. *Etude Socio-Economique de Deux Villages Hausa*. Paris: CNRS, 1968.

Niger. *Code des Douanes*. Niamey, 1965.

———. *Legislation et réglementation de travail*. Boulogne: Editions Delroisse, 1968; Niamey, 1981.

———. *Le programme triennal 1976–78*. Niamey, 1976.

———. *Table ronde sur le secteur privé*. Niamey, 1988.

———. Chambre de Commerce. *Règlement des prix au Niger*. Niamey, 1971, 1985.

———. "Comité permanent inter-Etat de lutte contre la sécheresse. *Etude sur l'amélioration des cultures irriquées dans les pays du Sahel.* Niamey, 1987.
———. Commissariat Général au Dévelopement. *Annuaire Statistique 1967.* Niamey, 1967.
———. *Annuaire Statistique.* Irregular. Niamey, 1960+.
———. *Documents des 'perspectives décennales' du Niger: 1964–1975.* 2 vols. Niamey, n.d.
———. "L'Elaboration et l'exécution du Plan au Niger. La planification permanente." *Notes d'Information BCEAO,* no. 177 (Oct. 1970).
———. *Plan de Développement Economique et Sociale, 1961–63.* 2 vols. Niamey, 1961.
———. *Programmation quadriennale, 1971–1974, investissements public.* Niamey, 1970.
———. *Rapport partiel d'exécution du Plan, 1965–1968.* Niamey, 1969.
———. Direction de l'Elevage et des Industries Animales. "Les produits de l'élevage et de la pêche au Niger." *Notes d'Information BCEAO,* no. 82 (May 1962).
———. Ministère du Plan. *Plan quinquennal de développement économique et social, 1979–1983.* Niamey, 1980.
———. *Plan de développement économique et social du Niger, 1987–1991.* Niamey, 1987.
———. *Programme de développement de la recherche agronomique au Niger.* 2 vols. Niamey, 1989.
———. Ministère de la Santé Publique. *Perspectives décennales (1965–1974) de développement des Services de Santé.* Niamey, 1964.
———and Ministère de l'Economie Rurale. "Rapport Annuel." Niamey, 1969+.
———. Ministère des Travaux Publiques. "Direction des Mines et de la Géologie: Rapport Annuel." Niamey, 1972+.
———. Présidence de la République. *Plan Quadriennal (1965–1968).* 2 vols. Niamey, 1965.
———. "Renseignements économiques sur la République du Niger." Niamey, 1964 [by Robert L. Clifford].
———. Union Nigérienne de Crédit et de Coopération. *L'Experience Nigérienne dans le Domaine Coopératif.* Niamey, 1967.
"Niger." *Afrique Industrie, Infrastructure,* no. 154 (Jan. 1978):42–61.
"Niger." In *L'Agriculture Africaine.* Paris: Ediafric, 1970, 1975.
"Niger." In *L'Economie Africaine.* Annual. Dakar: Société Africaine d'Edition, 1972+.
"Niger." In *L'Industrie Africaine.* Paris: Ediafric, 1975.

"Niger." In *Surveys of African Economies,* vol. 3. Washington, D.C.: International Monetary Fund, 1970.

"Niger." In *L'Usine Africaine*. Paris: Ediafric, 1972, pp. 291–310.

"Niger." In *La Zone franc et l'Afrique*. Paris: Ediafric, 1977.

"Le Niger." *Afrique Industrie,* no. 173 (Nov. 1978):162–69.

"Niger 1980." *Marchés Tropicaux,* no. 1751 (June 1979): 1383–1462.

"Niger 1966." In *Momento de l'Industrie Africaine*. Paris: Ediafric, 1966, pp. 319–40.

"Niger." In Willard Johnson and Vivian R. Johnson, *West African Governments and Volunteer Development Organizations*. Lanham, Md.: University Press of America, 1990, pp. 25–40.

Niger: Atlas Jeune Afrique. Paris: Jeune Afrique, 1979.

"Le Niger dans l'attente d'un bon hivernage." *Courier ACP-CEE* (Brussels), no. 92 (July–Aug. 1985):12–27.

"Niger: Mise en service d'un complexe thermique en Anou-Araren." *Afrique Contemporaine* (July–Aug. 1981):21–23.

"Niger: Une Mutation rapide." Special issue of *Europe Outre-Mer,* no. 597 (Oct. 1979).

"Niger: Un nouveau code des investissements." *Industries et Travaux d'Outre-Mer,* no. 180 (Nov. 1968):1015–16.

"Niger on the Hoof." *Africa Report* (June 1970):6–7.

Le Niger: La pauvreté en periode d'ajustement. Paris: Harmattan, 1993.

"Le Niger: Le Plan quinquennal 1979–83." *Afrique Industrie,* no. 211 (July 1980):52–89.

"Niger—Programme intérimaire consolidation 1984–5." *Afrique Industrie,* no. 311 (Dec. 15, 1984):47–55.

"Niger: Le programme triennal de développement 1976–78." *Industries et Travaux d'Outre-Mer,* no. 272 (July 1976):508–12.

Niverd, C. *Etude des problèmes d'exploitation et de commercialisation du bétail au Niger*. Niamey, 1964.

Nnadozie, E., and M. Dwight. "The Political Economy of Islamic Penetration and Development in Niger." *Scandinavian Journal of Development Alternatives* 9, no. 2/3 (June–Sept. 1990):205–20.

———. "Les conseils nationaux de chargeurs des pays en voie de développement: l'exemple du Niger." *Revue Juridique et Politique* 41, no. 3 (July–Sept. 1987):168–84

O'Mara, Kathleen Khadija. "A Political Economy of Ahir: Historical Transformations in a Pastoral Economy." Ph.D. diss., Columbia University, 1986.

Oudin, Patrick. *Les jardins du Bas-Téloua—République du Niger*. Grenoble, 1974.

Ouendaba, Botorou. "Diversity, Combining Ability and Heteroric Patterns Among African Pearl Millet Landraces (Niger)." Ph.D. diss, Purdue University, 1991.

Over, Mead. "The Effect of Scale on Cost Projections for a Primary Health System in a Developing Country." *Social Sciences and Medicine* 22, no. 3 (1986):351–60.

Painter, Thomas Michael. "Bringing Land Back In: Changing Strategies to Improve Agricultural Production in the West African Sahel." In P. D. Little et al. (eds.), *Lands at Risk in the Third World*. Boulder, Colo.:Westview Press, 1987, pp. 144–63.

———. "In Search of the Peasant Connection: Spontaneous Cooperatives, Introduced Cooperatives and Agricultural Development in Southwestern Niger." In Michael M. Horowitz and Thomas M. Painter (eds.), *Anthropology and Rural Development in West Africa*. Boulder, Colo.: Westview Press, 1986, pp. 195–220.

———. "Peasant Migrations and Rural Transformations in Niger." Ph.D. diss., State University of New York/Binghamton, 1986.

Pallier, Ginette. *Les Problèmes de Développement dans les Pays Intérieures de l'Afrique Occidentale*. Isle, Fr.: G. Paller, 1984.

"Panorama de l'industrie minière du continent africain en 1966." *Annales des Mines* (Sept. 1967):613–35.

"Participation populaire au développement: Quelques réflexions à partir d'exemples du projet réalisés au Cap Vert, au Niger, en Gambie et au Tchad." *IFDA Dossiers* (Nyon, Switz.), no. 62 (1987):3–15.

Pauvreté et développement dans les pays tropicaux. Bordeaux: Institut de Géographie, 1989.

"Le pays sachemine vers l'autosuffisance alimentaire." *Europe Outre-Mer,* no. 597 (Oct. 1979):23–26.

Pehaut, Yves. "L'Arachide au Niger." *Etudes d'Economie Africaine,* (Paris), no. 1 (1970):11–103.

Perrier, G. K. *Limiting Livestock Pressure on Public Rangeland in Niger*. London: Overseas Development Institute, 1986.

Petit, Henri. "L'Elevage et la production de la viande en République du Niger." CHEAM, no. 4384 (1971).

"Le Plan quadriennal de développement 1965–68 et les perspectives décennales." *Europe France Outre-Mer,* no. 430 (Nov. 1965):21–24.

"Le Plan quadriennal du Niger (1971–74) réserve la priorité à l'infrastructure de communication." *Industries et Travaux d'Outre-Mer* no. 208 (Mar. 1971):185–90.

"Le Plan quinquennal 1979–83." *Europe Outre-Mer,* no. 597 (Oct. 1979):19–21.

Planification du Développement aux Niveaux Régional et Local: La Participation des Cadres et la Population à la Planification Locale. Niamey: Ecole Nationale d'Administration, 1973.

Planhol, X. de, and P. Rognon. *Les Zones Tropicales arides et subtropicales*. Paris: A. Colm, 1970.

"La production d'arachides au Niger." *Notes d'Information BCEAO,* no. 159 (Feb. 1969).

Le programme de développement de la recherche agronomique au Niger. 2 vols. The Hague: Service Internationale pour la Recherche Agricole Nationale, 1989.

"Le programme triennal 1976–80 du Niger." *Marchés Tropicaux et Méditerranéens,* no. 1609 (Sept. 10, 1976):2324–29.

"Le projet de chemin de fer Parakou–Niamey." *Europe Outre-Mer,* no. 597 (Oct. 1979):51–52.

"Le projet prioritaire: Le barrage de Kandadji." *Europe Outre-Mer,* no. 597 (Oct. 1979):49–50.

"Le projet de prolongement du chemin du fer de Parakou à Dosso." *Europe France Outre-Mer,* no. 453 (Oct. 1967):38–39.

Raulin, Henri. "Communautés d'entraide et développement agricole au Niger. L'Exemple de la Majya." *Etudes Rurales,* no. 33 (Jan.–Mar. 1969):52–56.

———. "Développement agricole au Niger et au Maroc. Etude ethnologique du changement technique dans les sociétés rurales." *Economie Rurale,* no. 88 (Apr.–June 1971):103–10.

———. *Enquête socio-économique rurale 1961–3.* Niamey: Etudes Nigériennes, no. 4, 1963.

———. "Organized Cooperation and Spontaneous Cooperation in Africa." In J. Nash et al. (eds.), *Popular Participation in Social Change.* The Hague: Mouton, 1976, pp. 35–43.

———. *Techniques et bases socio-économiques des sociétés rurales nigériennes.* Paris: Etudes Nigériennes, no. 12, 1963.

———. "Travail et régimes fonciers au Niger." *Cahiers de l'ISEA,* no. 166 (Oct. 1965):119–39.

Raynaut, Claude. "Aspects socio-économiques de la préparation et de la circulation de la nourriture dans un village hausa." *Cahiers d'Etudes Africaines* 17, no. 4 (1977): 596–97.

———. "Aspects of the Problem of Land Concentration in Niger." In R. E. Downs and S. P. Reyna (eds.), *Land and Society in Contemporary Africa.* Hanover, N.H.: University Press of New England, 1988, pp. 221–42.

———. "Le cas de la région de Maradi (Niger)." In J. Copans (ed.), *Sécheresses et Famines du Sahel.* Paris, 1975, 2:5–43.

———. *Le Développement rural: De la région au village: Analyser et comprendre la diversité.* Bordeaux: Groupe de Recherches Interdisciplinaires pour le Développement, 1988.

———. "L'Opération de développement et les logiques du changement: La nécessité d'un cas nigérien." *Genève-Afrique* 27, no. 2 (1989): 7–38.

———. "Outils agricoles de la région de Maradi, Niger." In J. J. Swift (ed.), *Pastoral Development in Central Niger*. Niamey: Ministry of Rural Development, 1984.

———. "La privilège urbaine: Conditions de vie et santé au Niger." *Politique Africaine,* no. 28 (1987):42–52.

———. *Quelques données de horticulture dans la vallée de Maradi.* Paris: Etudes Nigériennes, no. 26, 1969.

———. *Recherches multidisciplinaires dans le région de Maradi: Rapport de synthèse*. Bordeaux: University of Bordeaux, 1980.

———. "Transformation du système de production et inégalité économique: Le cas d'un village haoussa (Niger)." *Canadian Journal of African Studies* 10, no. 2 (1976):279–306.

République du Niger: Evaluation de la situation agricole et alimentaire. Rome: FAO, 1988.

Retaille, Denis. "Interventions externes et réponses des pasteurs: L'exemple de la zone des forages Nord-Gouré: Niger Oriental." *Cahiers d'Outre-Mer,* no. 150 (Apr.–June 1985):103–20.

Rippstein, G., and B. Peyre de Fabrègues. *Modernisation de la zone pastorale du Niger*. Paris: Maison-Alfort, 1972.

"Le riz du Niger." *Sahel-Hebdo,* no. 14 (Jan. 12, 1976):17–19.

"La riziculture en Afrique de l'Ouest." *Bulletin de l'Afrique Noire,* no. 997 (Mar. 1979):19367–71.

Roberts, Pepe. "Rural Development and the Rural Economy in Niger." In J. Heyer, P. Roberts, and G. Williams (eds.), *Rural Development in Africa*. New York: St. Martin's Press, 1981. pp. 193–221.

Robinet, A. H. "La chèvre de Maradi et le problème de l'exportation des peaux au Niger." *Bulletin de la Chambre de Commerce du Niger,* no. 120 (Oct. 29, 1962):2–12; no. 121 (Nov. 5, 1962):1–10. Also in *La Nouvelle Revue Française d'Outre-Mer,* no. 47 (1955):221–26.

———. "La chèvre de Maradi et l'élevage caprin au Niger." *Courrier de l'Association,* no. 12 (Mar.–Apr. 1972):32–37.

———. "La chèvre rousse de Maradi: Son exploitation et sa place dans l'économie et l'élevage de la République du Niger." *Revue d'Elevage et du Médicine Vétérinaire de Pays Tropicaux,* no. 20 (1967):129–86.

Rodary, Pierre. "L'Organisation Commune du Dahomey-Niger (OCDN)." *Bulletin de la Chambre du Commerce du Niger,* no. 144 (Apr. 15, 1963):1–9.

———. "L'Organisation Commune Dahomey-Niger des chemins de fer et des transports." *Industries et Travaux d'Outre-Mer,* no. 116 (July 1963):634–38.

Roesch, M. *Des exploitants agricole face au commerce privé et à un projet de développement rural: Le cas de la région de Maradi au Niger*. Nogent-sur-Marne, Fr.: Institut de Recherches Agronomiques Tropicales, 1986.

Rouch, Jean. *Rapport sur les migrations nigériennes vers la Basse Côte d'Ivoire*. Niamey: IFAN, 1957.

"La Route Trans-saharienne." *Industries et Travaux d'Outre-Mer,* no. 195 (Feb. 1970):120–21.

Sabatier, J. L., and A. Paquier. "Irrigation et développement: Le cas du Dallol Bosso, Niger." *Cahiers de la Recherche-Développement,* no. 18 (1988):23–37.

"Le Sahel et ses problèmes: L'apport de la recherche." *Afrique Contemporaine* (Jan.–Mar. 1984):11–17.

Le Sahel face aux future: Dépendance croissante ou transformation structurelle. Paris: OCDE, 1988.

Saint André, Christian. "La Compagnie de culture cotonnière du Niger 1919–1927: Intérêts nationaux ou intérêts privés?" Diss., University Paul Valéry, 1978.

Sanders, John H. "Agricultural Research and New Technology Introduction in Burkina Faso and Niger." *Agricultural Systems* 29, no. 2 (Feb. 1989):139–54.

Sauer, P. "Poultry Production in the Republic of Niger: Assistance to Middle-Sized Versus Small Farmers." *Quarterly Journal of International Agriculture* 26, no. 1 (1987):86–97.

Schaefer, Kurt Carpenter. "A Portfolio Model of Mixed Farming in Less Developed Countries, with an Application to Project Evaluation in Southeastern Niger." Ph.D. diss., University of Michigan, 1984.

Schneider, James B. "Development as Dialogue: The UNCC story." *Community Development Journal* 4, no. 3 (July 1969):151–58.

Scott, Sarah. "Le méthodes de tissage employés à Niamey et au Niger." *Mu Kara Sani*. 4, no. 1/2 (1985):38–71.

Sere, J. M. "Dépenses récurrentes, déficit en ressources et développement financier: Quelques observations autour du cas nigérien." *Etudes Internationales* 16, no. 1 (1985):87–101.

Sholton, Erwin J., and Edward A. Sholton. *Niger's Industrial Potential*. Washington, D.C.: Continental Allied Co., 1965.

Situation de l'élevage en République du Niger. Paris: SEDES, 1970.

"Situation et perspectives de l'énergie électrique au Niger en 1977." *Bulletin de l'Afrique Noire,* no. 995 (Mar. 1979):19329–30.

Sizaret, A. "Le déficit fruitier du Niger." *Fruits* (June 1972):485–88.

Smith, Michael G. "The Hausa Markets in Peasant Economy." In Paul Bohannan and George Dalton (eds.), *Markets in Africa*. Evanston, Ill.: Northwestern University Press, 1962.

Société d'Etudes et de Réalisations Economiques et Sociales dans l'Agriculture. "Niger." *Eléments de Documentations sur l'Afrique Occidentale*. (Dakar), no. 8 (1959).

Sociétés et fournisseurs d'Afrique Noire. Paris: Documentation Africaine, 1979, pp. 383–402.

Somerville, Carolyn M. *Drought and Aid in the Sahel: A Decade of Development Cooperation.* Boulder, Colo.: Westview Press, 1986.

"Le SONORA dans l'économie du Niger." *Marchés Tropicaux et Méditerranéens,* no. 1092 (Oct. 15, 1966):2614–15.

Sordet, Monique. "Une Terre ingrate, un exemple d'équilibre ethnique." *Europe France Outre-Mer,* no. 503 (Dec. 1971):5–7.

Spittler, G. "Niger als exportabhängiger Bauernstaat." *Afrika Spectrum* 11, no. 2 (1976):127–44.

———. "Traders in Rural Hausaland." *Bulletin d'IFAN* 39, no. 2 (1977):362–85.

Starr, Martha. "Risk, Environmental Variability and Drought-Induced Poverty: The Pastoral Economy of Central Niger." *Africa* (London) 57, no. 1 (1987):29–56.

"Les statistiques du bétail, des produits et sous-produits animaux." *Revue Trimestrielle d'Information Technique et Economique,* no. 14 (Oct.–Dec. 1975):10–19.

Stecker, Allen Joseph. "On Being Zarma." Ph.D. diss., Northwestern University, 1980.

Stemplat, Axel V. *The Impact of Food Aid and Food Security Programmes on the Development in Recipient Countries.* Saarbrücken, Ger.: Verlag Breitenbach, 1981.

Stewart, Bonnie Ann. "Cooperative and Agricultural Development: A Case Study of the Credit and Cooperative Union of the Republic of Niger." *Journal of African Studies* 11, no. 2 (Summer 1984):66–73.

———. "Government Intervention and the Commercialization of Subsistence Food Crops in Niger." *Journal of African Studies* 14, no. 4 (1987–88):199–206.

———. "The Impact of Marketing Organizations Serving the Agricultural Sector in Zinder, Niger." Ph.D. diss., University of Arizona, 1978.

———. "The Organization for the Collection of Hides and Skins in the Province of Zinder." *Journal of African Studies* 13, no. 1 (1986): 25–30.

———. "Technology and Development: The Case of a Millet Factory in Niger." *Journal of African Studies* 9, no. 2 (1982):83–88.

Sutter, John W. "Commercial Strategies and Monetary Pressures: Wodaabe Nomads." *Nomadic Peoples* (Montreal), no. 11 (Oct. 1982): 26–60.

———. "Commercial Strategies, Drought and Monetary Pressures: Wodaabe Nomads of the Tanout Arrondissement, Niger." In C. Salzman and J. G. Galaty (eds.), *Nomads in a Changing World.* Naples: Istituo Universario Orientale, 1990, pp. 339–82.

———. "Peasants, Merchant Capital and Rural Differentiation: A Nigerien Hausa Case Study." Ph.D. diss., Cornell University, 1982.

Swift, Jeremy, and Angelo Maliki. "Cooperative Associations for Nomadic Herders in Niger." *Yearbook of Agricultural Cooperatives* (1985):119–39.

Sy, Papa Ibrahima. "Sous-développment et politique de développement en Afrique Sahélienne." *Présence Africaine,* no. 143 (1987):101–12.

"Tableau de l'assistance extérieure au Niger à 1978." *Bulletin de l'Afrique Noire,* no. 1025 (Nov. 1979):19843–44.

"Tableau de l'industrie du Niger." *Bulletin de l'Afrique Noire,* no. 1018 (Oct. 1979):19720–22.

"Tableau des industries manufacturières." *Europe Outre-Mer,* no. 597 (Oct. 1979):39–42.

"Tableau des industries textiles en Afrique Noire." *Bulletin de l'Afrique Noire,* no. 987 (Jan. 1979):19195–210.

"Tableau de la production cotonnière de l'Afrique Noire." *Bulletin de l'Afrique Noire,* no. 949 (Mar. 1978):18535–45.

"Tableau de la production cotonnière de l'Afrique Noire." *Bulletin de l'Afrique Noire,* no. 996 (Mar. 1979):19343–53.

Taton, Robert. "Un début d'industrialisation." *Europe France Outre-Mer,* no. 503 (Dec. 1971):25–27.

———. "Un pays qui attire les investisseurs." *Europe Outre-Mer,* no. 597 (Oct. 1979):15–19.

———. "Le programme triennal (1976–78)." *Europe Outre-Mer* (Mar. 1976):24–28.

Thebaud, Brigitte. *Elevage et développement au Niger: Quel avenir pour les éleveurs du Sahel?* Geneva: ILO, 1988.

Thollard, G. "Le problème d'enclavement du Niger." M.A. thesis, University of Bordeaux, 1983.

Thomas-Peterhans, Randall. "The Stratification of Livestock and the Production and Marketing of Livestock in Southeastern Niger." Ph.D. diss., University of Michigan, 1983.

Thomson, James T., et al. *Options pour promouvoir le contrôle et la gestion par les usagers des ressources naturelles renouvelables au Sahel.* Burlington, Vt.: Associates in Rural Development, 1989.

Tinguiri, Kiari Liman. "Crise économique et ajustement structurel 1982–86." Politique Africaine 38 (1990):78–86.

———. "Stabilization Without Structural Adjustment: The Case of Niger." In G. A. Cornia et al. *Africa's Recovery in the 1990s.* New York: St. Martin's Press, 1992, pp. 72–92.

Toh, K. "Niger's External Debt: Legacy of Uranium-Led Strategy." *Eastern Africa Economic Review* 3, no. 1 (1987):27–41.

Torres, Paul. *Le processus budgétaire dans les collectivités au Niger.* Niamey: Ecole Nationale d'Administration, 1973.

"Transactions, objets de commerce, monnaies des contrées d'entre le Niger et la Côte d'Or." *Economie Ouest Africaine, BCEAO,* no. 179 (Dec. 1970).

"Les travaux de l'Office de l'Energie Solaire." *Europe Outre-Mer,* no. 554 (Mar. 1976):55–56.

United Nations. Economic Commission for Africa. *L'Entretien des routes au Niger,* by M. Bako. Addis Ababa, 1974.

———. *Foreign Trade Statistics of Africa.* Series A: *Direction of Trade;* Series B: *Trade by Commodity.* New York, 1960/62+.

United States. Department of Commerce. Bureau of International Programs. World Trade Information Service. "Basic Data on the Economy of Niger." Washington, D.C., 1962.

———. Peace Corps. *Conservation and Forestry Manual, Niger.* Washington, D.C., 1971.

"Une usine à élever le niveau de vie." *Niger* (Niamey), no. 2 (Jan. 1968): 22–31.

Valaskakis, Kimon. *Relations Nord-Sud en Afrique de l'Ouest: Le cas Niger-Nigeria.* Montreal: Centre de Recherche en Développement Economique, 1974.

Vanbercie, R. "Le Tabac en République du Niger. Possibilité d'un production de tabacs légers." *Agronomie Tropicale,* no. 11 (Nov. 1963): 1095–1104.

Vereinsbank Hamburg. Länderberichte. "République du Niger." Hamburg, 1966.

Viguier, Serge. *Crédit et coopération à Tilibiri.* Paris: Ecole Pratique des Hautes Etudes, 1969.

Vourc'h, Anne, and Maina Boukar Moussa. *L'expérience de l'allégement de la dette du Niger.* Paris: OCDE, 1992.

Weerd, Guido de. *Manuel d'exécution du budget et de comptabilité des collectivités territoriales.* Niamey: Ecole National d'Administration, 1972.

Weicker, Martin. "Vie statt Hirse oder Vie gene Hirse: Probleme der Ressourcennutzung und der Nahrungsmittelversorgung bei den Iforas-Tuarge." *Die Erde* 199, no. 4 (1988):243–51.

Weiss, Roland. *Wandel des agrarsystem und ernahrungssichesung im Niger.* Hamburg: Institut für Afrika-Kunde, 1990.

Werquin, J. "Le Niger province uranifière d'avenir." *Industries et Travaux d'Outre-Mer,* no. 294 (May 1978):419–21.

White, Cynthia. "Changing Animal Ownership and Access to Land Among the Wodaabe of Central Niger." In P. T. W. Baxter and Richard Hogg (eds.), *Property, Poverty and People: Changing Rights in Property.* Manchester: University of Manchester International Development Center, 1990, pp. 240–54.

———. "Food Shortages and Seasonality in WoDaaBe Communities." *IDS Bulletin* 17, no. 3 (1986):19–26.

———. *Herd Reconstitution: The Role of Credit Among the Wodaabe Herders in Central Niger.* London: Overseas Development Institute, 1984.

Whitehead, E. E. *Arid Lands, Today and Tomorrow.* Boulder, Colo.: Westview Press, 1988.

Wilde, J. C. de. *Expérience de développement agricole en Afrique Tropicale*. 3 vols. Paris: Maisonneuve et Larose, 1968.

Wilson, Wendy. "Resource Management in a Stratified Community." Ph.D. diss., Howard University, 1984.

Wright, J. A. "Banker in the Desert." *Canadian Banker* 70 (Winter 1963):38–50.

Wrigley, C. "Speculations on the Economic Prehistory of Africa." *Journal of African History* 1, no. 2 (1960):189–203.

The Sahel Drought

Aboubacar, Adamou. "Agadez et sa region: Contribution à l'étude du Sahel et du Sahara." Thesis, University of Niamey, 1968.

Ag Arias, Alatnine, and Edmond Bernus. "Le jardin de la sécheresse. Histoire d'Amumen Amastan." *Journal des Africanistes* 47, no. 1 (1977): 83–93.

Angstreich, Michael. "Are Trees Effective Against Desertification? Experience from Niger and Mali." In P. T. W. Baxter (ed.), *When the Grass Is Gone: Development Intervention in African Arid Lands*. Upp-sala: Scandinavian Institute of African Studies, 1991, pp. 141–51.

Arrighi de Casanova, J. "Demain, le Sahel." *Revue Juridique et Politique* 30, no. 4 (Dec. 1976):429–34.

Berg, Eliott. *The Recent Revolution of the Sahel*. Ann Arbor, Mich.: University of Michigan Center for Research on Economic Development, 1975.

Bernus, Edmond. "Drought in Niger Republic." *Savanna* (Zaria) 2, no. 2 (1973):129–32.

———. "Etude de cas sur la désertification: Région d'Eqhazer et Azaouak, Niger." In *Conférence de Nations Unies sur la Désertification*. Paris, 1977.

———. "Les éleveurs face à la sécheresse." In D. Dalby et al. (eds.), *Drought in Africa*. London: International African Institute, 1977, pp. 140–47.

———. "Exploitation de l'éspace désertification en zone sahélienne." *Travaux de l'Institut Géographique de Reims,* nos. 30–40 (1979): 49–54.

———. "Famines et sécheresses chez les Touaregs sahéliens." *Africa* 50 (1980):1–7.

———. "Possibilités et limites de la politique d'hydraulique pastorale dans le Sahel Nigérien." *Cahiers d'ORSTOM 11,* no. 2 (1974):119–26.

———. "Les tactiques des éleveurs face à la sécheresse: Le cas du sud-ouest de l'Aïr." In *Strategies pastorales et agricoles des sahéliens*. Bordeaux: CNRS, 1977, pp. 201–17.

———, and G. Savonnet. "Les problèmes de la sécheresse dans l'Afrqiue de l'Ouest." *Présence Africaine,* no. 88 (1973):113–38.

———, et al. "Evolution et formes modernes d'élevage dans les zones arides et tropicales." *Cahiers d'ORSTOM* 11, no. 2 (1974):115–18.

Beudot, Françoise. *Elements de bibliographie sur la sécheresse au Sahel*. Paris: OCDE, 1981.

Beauvilain, Alain. "Les peul du Dallol Bosso et la sécheresse 1969–1973." In J. Gallais (ed.), *Stratégies pastorale et agricoles des Sahéliens durant la sécheresse 1969–1974*. Talance, Fr.: CEGET, 1977.

Bonfils, Michel. "L'UNICEF et le Sahel pendant et après la sécheresse." *Revue Juridique et Politique* 30, no. 4 (Dec. 1976):403–11.

Bonté, P. *Sécheresse et Imperialisme en Afrique*. Paris: Notes et Etudes, 1975.

Bunting, Edward. "Africa Wakes Up to the True Extent of Its Ecological Disaster." In Colin Legum (ed.), *Africa Contemporary Record, 1985–86*. New York: Africana, 1987, A149–57.

———. "Africa's Great Drought." In Colin Legum (ed.), *Africa Contemporary Record, 1983–84*. New York: Africana, 1985, A110–23.

———. "The Sahel: The Anguish of Uncertainity." In Colin Legum (ed.), *Africa Contemporary Record, 1985–86*. New York: Africana, 1987, A141–48.

———. "The Sahel: The Hunger Is Here to Stay."In Colin Legum (ed.), *Africa Contemporary Record, 1984–85*. New York: Africana, 1985, A95–101.

———. "The Sahel: Struggle for Food and Self-Sufficiency." In Colin Legum (ed.), *Africa Contemporary Record, 1981–82*. New York: Africana, 1982, A147–51.

———. "The Worst Climatic Disaster in Modern Times." In Colin Legum (ed.), *Africa Contemporary Record, 1984–85*. New York: Africana, 1985, A102–11.

Caldwell, John C. *The Sahelian Drought and Its Demographic Implications*. Washington, D.C.: American Council on Education, 1975.

Campbell, David John. "Strategies for Coping with Drought in the Sahel: Recent Population Movements in Maradi." Ph.D. Thesis, Clark University, 1977.

Centre de Développement de l'OCDE. *Sécheresse au Sahel. Selection d'articles de périodiques à partir de Décembre 1972*. Paris, 1974.

Chambard, Paul. "Le déficit alimentaire: Un million de personnes menacées de famine." *Europe Outre-Mer*, no. 554 (Mar. 1976):29–31.

Chauleur, Pierre. "Les plans mis au point par les Etats du Sahel pour lutter contre la sécheresse." *Revue Juridique et Politique*, no. 4 (Oct.–Dec. 1976):412–20.

Clarke, Thurston. *The Last Caravan*. New York: G. P. Putnam's Sons, 1978.

Cloudsley-Thompson, J. L. (ed.). *Sahara*. Oxford: Pergamon Press, 1984.

Copans, Jean (ed.). *Sécheresses et famines du Sahel*. 2 vols. Paris: Maspero, 1975.

Crouzet, A. "La sécheresse en zone sahélienne." *Notes et Etudes Documentaires de BCEAO,* no. 4216/17 (Sept. 23, 1975).

Dalby, David, and R. J. Harrison Church (eds.). *Drought in Africa*. London: London School of Oriental and African Studies, 1973.

Delwaulle, J. C. "Désertification de l'Afrique au Sud du Sahara." *Bois et Forêts des Tropiques,* no. 149 (May–June 1973):3–20.

Derrick, Jonathan. "The Great West African Drought, 1972–74." *African Affairs* 76, no. 305 (Oct. 1977):537–86.

Derriennic, Hervé. *Famines et dominations en Afrique noire: Paysans et éleveurs du Sahel sous le joug*. Paris: Harmattan, 1977.

"Desertification in the Eghazer and Azawak Region." In J. A. Mabbutt and C. Floret (eds.), *Case Studies on Desertification*. Paris: UNESCO, 1980, pp. 115–46.

"The Drought—Easing the Transport Bottleneck." *Africa Report* (Sept.–Oct. 1974):13–16.

Drouhin, M. "La sécheresse, drame de l'Afrique sahélienne." *Industries et Travaux d'Outre-Mer,* no. 236 (July 1973):576–82.

Du Bois, Victor D. "The Drought in Niger." *Fieldstaff Reports* (Africa series) 15, nos. 4–7 (1974).

———. "A Note on the Sahel." *Fieldstaff Reports* (Africa series) 16, no. 4 (1975).

Durand, Jacques-Henri. "A propos de la sécheresse et de ses conséquences au Sahel." *Cahiers d'Outre-Mer,* no. 120 (Oct.–Dec. 1977): 383–403.

"Les effets de la sécheresse sur l'élevage nigérien." *Revue Trimestrielle de la Communauté Economique du Bétail et de la Viande,* no. 4 (Apr.–June 1973):31–39.

"Elevage: Reconstituer le chaptel." *Europe Outre-Mer,* no. 554 (Mar. 1976):33–34.

Englebert, Victor. "Drought Threatens the Tuareg World." *National Geographic* (Apr. 1974):544–71.

Environmental Change in the West African Sahel. Washington, D.C.: AID, 1983.

Fabrègues, B. Peyre de. "Aspects pastoraux de développement de l'élevage en zone sahélienne dans le contexte de la période de sécheresse: Le cas du Niger." In *Le Développement rural: Comprendre pour agir*. Paris: ORSTOM, 1987.

Faulkingham, Ralph Harold, and Peter Thorbahn. "Population Dynamics and Drought: A Village in Niger." *Population Studies* 24, no. 3 (1975).

France. La Documentation Française. Notes et Etudes Documentaires. "La Sécheresse en zone sahélienne." No. 4216–17, Sept. 1975

Gallais, J. "Stratégies pastorales et agricoles des sahéliens durant la sécheresse 1969–74." *Travaux et Documents de Géographie Tropicale,* no. 30 (1977).

Glantz, Michael H. (ed.). *Desertification: Environmental Degradation in and Around Arid Lands*. Boulder, Colo.: Westview Press, 1977.

——— (ed.). *The Politics of Natural Disaster: The Case of the Sahel Drought*. New York: Praeger, 1976.

——— (ed.). *Drought and Hunger in Africa: Denying Famine a Future in Africa*. Cambridge: Cambridge University Press, 1987.

Haig, E. F. G. "Famine in the Sahel." *Nigerian Field* 40, no. 1 (1975): 23–40.

Haquin, René. *Sahel: La vague jaune ou le Sahara sans rivage*. Brussels: Rossel Editions, 1973.

Harrigan, Peter. "Drought Brings Niger to Its Knees." *African Development* (June 1974):17–22.

Johnson, D. L. "The Human Dimension of Desertification." *Economic Geography* 53 (Oct. 1977):417–31.

Joyce, Stephen J., and F. Beudot. *Eléments de Bibliographie sur la Sécheresse au Sahel*. Paris: OCDE, 1977.

Klein, Roland. "Flächennutzung im westlichen Sahel der Republik Niger und Abundanzdynamik des Goldsperlings." *Die Erde* (Berlin) 120, no. 3 (1989):203–12.

Le Gal, P. Y. "L'Agriculture sahélo-soudanaise face à la sécheresse: L'exemple de la région de Maradi, Niger." *Cahiers de la Recherche-Développement,* no. 16 (1987):42–50.

Marie, J. "Stratégie traditionnelle d'adaptation à la sécheresse chez les éleveurs sahéliens." In J. Gallais (ed.), *Strategies Pastorales et agricoles de sahéliens durant la sécheresse 1969–74,* 1977.

Marnham, Patrick. *Nomads of the Sahel*. London: Minority Rights Group, 1979.

Martini, P. *Amélioration des conditions de vie des nomades dans l'Eghazer (Agadez)*. Rome: FAO, 1974.

Matheson, Alastair. "The African Environment: A Continent Under Threat." In Colin Legum (ed.), *Africa Contemporary Record, 1987–88*. New York: Africana, 1989, A46–51.

———. "The Year of the Locust." In Colin Legum (ed.), *Africa Contemporary Record, 1986–87*. New York: Africana, 1988, A141–48.

Monimart, Marie. *Femmes du Sahel: La désertification au quotidien*. Paris: Karthala, 1989.

Morel, Alain. "Faire renaître le Sahel? Expériences de développement agricole dans le massif de l'Aïr Niger." *Cultures et Développement* 8, no. 2 (1976):266–86.

Morris, Roger, and Hal Sheets. *Disaster in the Desert: Failures of International Relief in the West African Drought.* Washington, D.C.: Carnegie Endowment for International Peace, 1974.

Pauvreté et développement dans les pays tropicaux: Hommage à Guy Lasserre. Paris: Institut de Géographie, 1989.

Perrier, G. K. "Limiting Livestock Pressure on Public Rangeland in Niger." London: Overseas Development Institute, 1986.

Poncet, Yveline. *La sécheresse en Afrique Sahélienne: Une étude micro-régionale en République du Niger.* Paris: OCDE, 1974.

———. *Variations climatiques et incidences sur les mouvements migratoires des nomades et des troupeaux au Niger.* Niamey: UNESCO Conference Proceedings, 1974.

Qui se nourrit de la famine en Afrique? Paris: Maspero, 1974.

Reining, Priscilla. *Challenging Desertification in West Africa: Insights from "Landsat" into Carrying Capacity, Cultivation and Settlement Sites in Upper Volta and Niger.* Athens: Ohio University Center for International Studies, 1980.

Rosenthal, Jerry E. "Drought—the Creeping Catastrophe." *Africa Report* (July–Aug. 1973):7–13.

"Sahel." Special issue of *Revue Juridique et Politique* (1976).

Sahel Dürre. Hamburg: Afrika-Spectrum, 1974.

Scott, Earl (ed.). *Life Before the Drought.* Boston: Allen and Unwin, 1984.

"La sécheresse, ennemi numéro I du développement." *Europe France Outre-Mer,* no. 503 (Dec. 1971):18–20.

Starr, M. A. "Risk, Environmental Variability and Drought-Induced Impoverishment: The Pastoral Economy of Central Niger." *Africa* 57, no. 1 (1987):29–50.

Stuckmann, G. "Probleme der Wassernutzung im Sahel der Republik Niger." *Afrika Spectrum* 9, no. 3 (1974):260–67.

Suret-Canale, J. "Sécheresse et famine dans le Sahel." *Culture et Développement* 8, no. 2 (1976):327–34.

Swinton, S. M. "Drought-Survival Tactics of Subsistence Farmers in Niger." *Human Ecology* 16, no. 2 (1988):123–44.

Thomson, James T. "Deforestation and Desertification in Twentieth Century Arid Sahelian Africa." In J. F. Richards and R. P. Tucker, *World Deforestation in the Twentieth Century.* Durham, N.C.: Duke University Press, 1988, pp. 70–90.

———. "Ecological Deterioration: Local-Level Rule-Making and Enforcement Problems in Niger." In M. H. Glantz (ed.), *Desertification: Environmental Degradation in and Around Arid Lands.* Boulder, Colo.: Westview Press, 1977.

United Nations. Special Sahelian Office. *Towards a Strategy for Development in the Sahelian and Sudano-Sahelian Zones.* New York, 1973 [by Michel C. Baumer].

———. *Response of Pastoral Nomads to Drought in the Absence of Outside Intervention.* New York, 1973 [by D. L. Johnson].

———. "Sahel Recovery and Rehabilitation Program." Washington, 1973.

Uranium

"Activité minière dans la République du Niger en 1964." *Chronique des Mines et de la Recherche Minière,* no. 345 (Aug. 1965):259–62.

Adamou, Aboubakar. "Les ressources minières dans l'économie du Niger." *Etudes Scientifiques* (Dec. 1981):35–40.

"Arlit, c'est le Niger de demain." *Entente Africaine,* no. 1 (July 15, 1969):38–39.

Arlit et les retombées économiques de l'uranium sur le Niger. Paris, 1974.

Baudet, J., and C. Brizard. "Le gisement d'uranium Arlette." *Revue de l'Industrie Minérale-Mines* 53 (May 1971):1–12.

Beulaygue, M. "Le Mine d'uranium d'Arlit, République du Niger." *Annales des Mines* (Mar. 1972):29–40.

"Bilan de l'activité minière au Niger en 1978." *Bulletin de l'Afrique Noire,* no. 1022 (Oct. 1979):19783–85.

Chambard, Paul, and Genévième Sigisbert. "L'Aide Publique bilaterale à l'Afrique Noire Francophone." *Europe Outre-Mer,* no. 564 (Jan. 1977):13–54.

Charbonneau, René. "L'Uranium africain." *Afrique Contemporaine,* no. 76 (Nov.–Dec. 1974):7–11.

Charbonnier, François. "L'Uranium, nouvelle ressource africaine." *France Eurafrique,* no. 22 (July 1971):26–29.

Cys, Monique. "Niger: Du côté d'Arlit." *Entente Africaine,* no. 3 (Jan. 1970):34–37.

Diallo, Siradiou. "Uranium ne fait pas le Printemps." *Jeune Afrique,* no. 953 (Apr. 12, 1979):37–42.

"L'exploitation de l'uranium du Niger." *Industries et Travaux d'Outre-Mer,* no. 188 (July 1969):579–81.

Garba, Amadou. "Sous les sables nigériens un trésor était caché: l'uranium." *France Eurafrique,* no. 191 (Jan. 1968):35–36.

Gerard, M. "Arlit et les retombées économiques de l'uranium sur le Niger." Thesis, University of Aix-Marseilles, 1974.

"Une grande 'province uranifère': L'Ouest de l'Aïr." *Europe France Outre-Mer,* no. 503 (Dec. 1971):21–23.

Hoban, Carol. "Reajustement des politques économique et financière au fonction de l'évolution des cours mondiaux de l'uranium." *Bulletin du Fond Mondiale* (Washington) 11, no. 5 (Mar. 1982):66–69.

Lawless, R. I. "Uranium Mining at Arlit in the Republic of Niger." *Geography,* no. 59 (Jan. 1974):45–48.

"Les mines en général . . . et l'uranium en particulier." *Niger* (Niamey), no. 10 (May 1970):63–73.
Moyal, M. "Uranium Find in Niger." *Nuclear Engineering,* no. 13 (Apr. 1968):333–34.
"Niger—l'exploitation des mines d'uranium." *Afrique Contemporaine,* no. 33 (Sept.–Oct. 1967):14–15.
"Niger—l'exploitation de l'uranium un tournant pour l'économie nigérienne." *Moniteur Officiel du Commerce International,* no. 741 (Mar. 27, 1968):1298–1302.
"Niger Hopes for Uranium." *West Africa* (July 9, 1979): 1210–12.
"Niger Uranium." *Africa Confidential* (Oct. 24, 1975):8.
Pallier, Ginette. "L'Uranium au Niger." *Cahiers d'Outre-Mer,* no. 146 (1977):175–90.
Poitou, Daniele. "Arlit, ville pionnière de l'industrialistion nigérienne." *Afrique et l'Asie,* no. 133 (1982):29–47.
"La route d'Uranium." *Europe Outre-Mer,* no. 597 (Oct. 1979):43–48.
Sigisbert, Genéviève. "Le Grand atout économique: l'Uranium." *Europe Outre-Mer,* no. 554 (Mar. 1976):35–41.
———. "Uranium: Espoir d'une amélioration progressive des marchés internationaux." *Europe Outre-Mer,* no. 624 (Jan. 1982):41–45.
———. "L'Uranium en flèche." *Europe Outre-Mer,* no. 597 (Oct. 1979):27–31.
"Situation et perspectives de l'industrie minière du Niger." *Bulletin de l'Afrique Noire,* no. 959 (Mar. 1978):18726–29.
"L'Uranium africaine." *Europe Outre-Mer,* no. 528 (Jan. 1974):17–21.
"L'Uranium au Niger." *Cahiers d'Outre-Mer,* no. 146 (Apr.–June 1984): 135–58.
"L'Uranium d'Arlit." *Europe France Outre-Mer,* no. 452 (Sept. 1967): 38–40.
"L'Uranium du Niger." *Echos du CEA,* no. 4 (July–Aug. 1967):8–9.
"L'Uranium du Niger." *Uniafrique,* no. 54 (Mar. 1969):1–5.
"L'Uranium Nigérien." *Industries et Travaux d'Outre-Mer,* no. 197 (Apr. 1970):262–66.
Verhack, Caroline. "Le Niger malade d'uranium." *Afrique Industrie,* no. 276 (May 1983):46–65.
Wright, Albert. "Les Activités de l'Office de l'Energie Solaire." *Revue Trimestrielle d'Information Technique* (Ouagadougou), no. 20/21 (Apr.–Sept. 1977):14–26.

Education

Akam, Noble. "Télé-Niger: La télévision hors de cause." *Afrique Contemporaine,* no. 172 (Oct.–Dec. 1994):134–41.
Allainmat, Y. "Ecoles nomades au Niger." *Encyclopédie Mensuelle d'Outre-Mer,* no. 50 (1954):272–75.

Barbey, Guy "L'Aventure de la télévision scolaire du Niger." *Coopération et Développement,* no. 39 (Jan.–Feb. 1972):22–29; no. 40 (Mar.–Apr. 1972):7–15.

Bellocq, Guy. *Cours sur les institutions politiques de la République du Niger*. Niamey: Centre de Formation Administrative, 1962.

Bosredon, Paul de. "Niamey: Le Centre Culturel franco-nigérien." *France Eurafrique,* no. 200 (Nov. 1968):37–41.

Brierly, T. G. "Radio-Clubs in Niger." *Journal of Administration Overseas* 14, no. 1 (1975):45–47.

Carpenter, Allan, and Janice E. Baker. *Enchantment of Africa*. Chicago: Children's Press, 1976.

Cart, Benoit. "Le cas du Niger et du Sénégal." *Afrique Contemporaine,* no. 172 (Oct.–Dec. 1994):241–59.

Centre Régional de Documentation pour la Tradition Orale. *La Voie d'éducation peul*. Niamey, 1969.

Chéramy, Pierre. "Au Niger les enfants apprennent à lire sur les écrans de la télévision." *France Eurafrique,* no. 193 (Mar. 1968):23–26.

Clair, Andrée. *Les Découvertes d'Alkassoum*. Paris: Editions Farandole, 1962. [School text.]

———. *Dijé*. Paris: Editions Farandole, 1962 [School text.]

———. *Issilim*. Paris: Editions Farandole, 1972. [School text.]

———. *Le Voyage d'Oumarou*. Paris: Editions Bourrelier, 1962 [School text.]

———, and Boubou Hama. *Le Boabab Merveilleux*. Paris: Editions Farandole, 1971. [School text.]

Desalmand, Lucien. *Programmes et Méthodes du Service de l'Alphabétisation au Niger*. Paris: AUDECAM, 1967 [Mimeographed.]

D'Hondt, W., and M. Vandewiele. "Les écoliers nigériens de 7e à 12e ans et le test de l'arbre. *Cahiers de Sociologie Economique et Culturelle,* no. 6 (1987): 41–80.

Diawara, I. "Cultures nigériennes et éducation: Domaine Zarma-Songhay et Hausa." *Présence Africaine,* no. 148 (1988):9–19.

Dickson, A. G. "La formation du citoyen: Une expérience nigérienne." *Education de Base et Education des Adultes,* no. 6 (1954):62–68.

Easton, P. A. *Functional Literacy and Cooperative Education*. Paris: Institut de Recherches et d'Application des Méthodes de Développement, 1972.

Egly, Max. "L'Expérience Nigérienne d'enseignement par télévision." *Nations Nouvelles,* no. 26 (Dec. 1970):7–9.

———. "Télé-Niger, l'école primaire par télévision." *Les Carnets de l'Enfance,* no. 18 (Apr.–June 1972):75–89.

———. "L'Utilisation de la télévision scolaire au Niger, en Côte d'Ivoire et au Sénégal." *International Review of Education* 32, no. 3 (1986):338–46.

Eliou, Marie. "Scolarité primaire et accès au second degré au Niger et au Sénégal." *Tiers-Monde* 11, no. 44 (Oct.–Dec. 1970):733–58.

L'enfance et la jeunesse dans le développement national du Niger. Paris: SEDES, 1966.

Etude du Milieu Africain: Pays du Sahel, le Niger. Paris: EDICEF, 1972.

"Une expérience d'alphabétisation et d'éducation des adultes au Niger." *Nations Nouvelles,* no. 1 (Oct. 1964):6–9.

"Functional Literacy in Niger." *Entente Africaine* (Dec. 1978):42–47.

Garba, Issaka. "Une Centre de réception communautaire dans chacun des 9000 villages." *Europe Outre-Mer,* no. 624 (Jan. 1982):21–23.

Guilhem, Marcel, et al. *Histoire du Niger*. Paris: Ligel, 1965. [Textbook.]

Hama, Boubou. *Education Africaine: Sentences, maximes, proverbes et locutions Zarmas, Songhays, Haoussas, Peuls et Bambaras*. Niamey: 1972.

———. "*Essai d'analyse de l'éducation africaine*. Paris: Présence Africaine, 1968.

———. *Pour une dialogue avec nos jeunes: Démarches pédagogiques*. Niamey, 1972.

———, and Guilhem, Marcel. *Niger, récits historiques*. Paris: Ligel, 1967.

Hentgen, E. F. "Les missions et les fonctions de l'école nationale de la République du Niger." *Cahiers Africains d'Adminstration Publique,* no. 8 (Aug. 1972):169–72.

Hill, C. A. "Sex-Based Differences in Cognitive Processing of Spatial Relations in Bilingual Students in Niger." In R. K. Herbert (ed.), *Patterns in Language, Culture and Society: Subsaharan Africa*. Columbus, Ohio, 1975, pp. 185–98.

Hukill, Mark Alan. "Television Broadcasting for Rural Development in Niger." M.A. thesis, University of Hawaii, 1984.

Hutchison, John P. "Language Policy for Education in Niger." In Nancy Schweda-Nicholson et al. (eds.), *Languages in International Perspective*. Norwood, N.J.: Ablex, 1986, pp. 279–94.

International Labour Office. *Rapport sur l'éducation ouvrière en République du Niger*. Geneva, 1962.

Jarrett, Kevin A. "Dialectes et alphabétisation dans l'écoles." *Journal of West African Languages* 18, no. 2 (1988):105–24.

Kantana, Aljouma. "L'Ecole nomade et ses problèmes." *Niger* (Niamey), no. 19 (Mar. 1973):23–25.

Koley, Glenda Dickison. "Mission Primary School Dilemma: Day or Boarding School for Nationals of the Republic of Niger?" M.A.thesis, Columbia Bible College, 1984.

Leymarie, Philippe. "L'Enseignement télévisée au Niger." *Revue Française d'Etudes Politiques Africaines,* no. 103 (July 1974):55–69.

Lorelle, Yves. "Littératures pour l'oreille. (1) Le Niger procède à l'inventaire de l'oralité." *France Eurafrique,* no. 210 (Oct. 1969):40–42.

Mayer, R. *Die Französische Politik der Cooperation Culturelle et Technique und die Nationale Entwicklung: Niger/Dpt. Maradi.* Hamburg: Helmut Buske, 1973.

Meyer, J. "Une expérience d'alphabétisation et d'éducation des adultes au Niger." *Coopération Pédagogique,* no. 8 (Oct.–Dec. 1964):19–24.

———. "Les radio-clubs du Niger." *Coopération Pédagogique,* no. 7 (July–Sept. 1964):29–34.

Meyer, R. "Die Rolle der lokalen Sprachen im nationalen Entwicklungsprozess in Niger." *Afrika Spectrum* 12, no. 3 (1977):263–73.

Niane, D. T. *Soundjata. Télévision Scolaire du Niger.* Niamey, 1978.

Niger. Ministère de l'Economie Rurale. *Etude d'une réforme de la formation des cadres du développement rural en Niger.* 2 vols., by A. Magnen and N. Plateuw. Paris, 1968.

———. Ministère de l'Education Nationale. *Le Niger, cours de géographie.* Niamey, 1966.

"Niger." In Helen Kitchen (ed.), *The Educated African.* New York: Praeger, 1962.

"Niger." In Martena Sasnett and Inez Sepmeyer, *Educational Systems in Africa.* Berkeley: University of California Press, 1967, pp. 698–704.

"Niger." In *International Yearbook of Education.* Annual. Paris and Geneva: UNESCO and the International Bureau of Education, 1966 +.

Olkes, Cheryl. "Information-Seeking with Mass-Media in the Republic of Niger: An Exploratory Study of Town and Country." Ph.D. diss., University of Texas/Austin, 1978.

Poitou, Daniele. "Intégration et inadoptation sociale de la jeunesse au Niger et au Nigeria." *Psychopathologie Africaine* 19, no. 1 (1983): 33–55.

"Les radio-clubs du Niger." *Afrique* (May 1963):40–43.

"Rapport moral et d'activités des Radio-clubs pour le campagne 1966–67." *Niger* (Niamey), no. 36, (Aug. 28, 1967):2–8.

Rescoussie, P. L. "L'enseignement secondaire dans 18 états francophones d'Afrique et Madagascar." *Afrique Contemporaine,* no. 67 (1973): 11–26.

Salonga, Lydia C. *Niger.* Washington: American Association of Collegiate Registrars and Admissions Officers, 1995.

Sigisbert, Geneviève. "Une expérience originale: L'enseignement télévisuel total." *Europe France Outre-Mer,* no. 503 (Dec. 1971):13–14.

Soubeste, Claude. "L'Association des radio-clubs du Niger." *Coopération et Développement,* no. 35 (Mar.–Apr. 1971):41–42

Tamgak, A. "Les Touaregs du Niger à l'école." *France d'Outre-Mer,* no. 268 (Feb. 1952):37–39.

Taton, Robert. "L'Action dans les domaines de la santé et de l'enseignement." *Europe Outre-Mer,* no. 624 (Jan. 1982).

Triaud, Jean-Louis. "Note sur l'enseignement Franco-Arabe en Niger." *Islam et Sociétés au Sud du Sahara,* no. 2 (1988):155–56.

UNESCO. *World Survey of Education.* 2 vols. Paris, 1958, 1961.

Wilson, Wendy. "Cooperatives as a Vehicle of Adult Education in Africa." *Journal of Negro Education* 56, no. 3 (1987):407–18.

"Yaro vient tous les matins." *Niger* (Niamey), no. 2 (Jan. 1968):45–59.

Scientific Studies

Abadie, Maurice. *Afrique Centrale: La colonie du Niger.* Paris: Société d'Editions Géographiques, Maritimes et Coloniales, 1927.

———. "La colonie du Niger." *Géographie* 47, no. 3/4 (Mar.–Apr. 1927):169–90.

Adam, J. G., N. Echard, and M. Lescot. "Plantes médicinales hausa de l'Ader." *Journal d'Agriculture Tropicale et de Botanique Appliquée* 19, no. 8/9 (Aug.–Sept. 1972):259–399.

Adams, L. J., and G. Tetzloff. "Did Lake Chad Exist Around 18,000 BP?" *Archives for Meteorology, Geophysics and Bioclimatology* (Vienna) 34, no. 3 (1984):299–308.

Adjanohoun, Edouard J. *Médicine Traditionnelle et Pharmacopée: Contribution aux Etudes Ethnobotaniques et Floristiques au Niger.* Paris: Agence de Coopération Culturelle et Technique, 1980.

———, et al. *Contribution aux études ethnobotaniques et floristiques au Niger.* Paris: Agence de Coopération Culturelle et Technique, 1980.

Allan, J. A. (ed.). *The Sahara: Ecological Change and Early History.* London: MENAS Press, 1981.

Atlas du Niger. Paris: Jeune Afrique, 1980.

Aubreville, André. "Les forêts de la colonie du Niger." *Bulletin de le Comité d'Etudes Historiques et Scientifiques de l'AOF* 19, no. 1 (Mar. 1936):1–94.

———. "Mission forestière anglo-française Nigeria-Niger." *Bois et Forêts des Tropiques,* no. 148 (Mar.–Apr. 1973):3–13.

Audoin, J. et al. "Kyste hydatique de la thyroide: Un cas en République du Niger." *Bulletin de la Société de Pathologie Exotique* 81, no. 3 (1988):360–64.

Audry, P. "Etudes de la Pedogénèse." In R. Fauck, *Observations Immediates des Phénomènes Engendrés par les Aléas Climatiques Actuels en Zone Sahélienne.* Paris: ORSTOM, 1974, pp. 47–54.

Bakker-Frijling, M. J. "Orienterend voedingsonderzoek bij jonge kinderen en moeders in Niger." *Voeding* 48, no. 4 (1987):115–18.

Bartha, R. *Futterpflanzen in der Sahelzone Afrika.* Munich: Weltforum Verlag, 1970.

Baumhauer, Roland. "Holozane limnische Akkumulationen im Grossen Erg von Bilma, NE-Niger." In *Geowissenschaftliche Untersuchungen in Afrika*. Würzburg: Universität Institut für Geographie, 1988, pp. 137–48.

———. "Radiocarbondaten aus NE-Niger." In *Geowissenschaftliche Untersuchungen in Afrika*. Würzburg: Universität Institute für Geographie, 1988, pp. 53–70.

———. *Zur jungquartaren Seenentwicklung im Bereich der Stufe von Bilma, NE-Niger*. Würzburg: Institute für Geographie der Würzburg, 1986.

———, and H. Hagedorn. "Problem der Grundwassererscheiessung im Kawar." *Die Erde* 120, no. 1 (1989):11–20.

Belloncle, G. and G. Fournier. *Santé et développement en milieu rural africain. Réflexions sur l'expérience nigérienne*. Paris: IRAM, 1973; Paris: Editions Ouvières, 1975.

Bembelo, Arouna. "La Chèvre rousse et son exploitation au Niger." Thesis, University of Toulouse, 1961.

Bergassoli, Michel. "Scope and Conditions for Improved Use of Food and for Development: The Case of Niger." In Hartmut Schneider, (ed.), *Food Aid for Development*. Paris: OECD, 1978, pp. 69–82.

Bernus, E., and Y. Poncet. *L'Etude Exploratoire du milieu naturel par télédetection*. Paris: ORSTOM, 1981.

Berre, Michel le. *Faune du Sahara I: Poissons, amphibiens, reptiles*. Paris: Lechevalier R. Chabaud, 1989.

Blache, J. *Les Poissons du Bassin du Tchad et du bassin adjacent du Mayo Kebbi*. Paris: ORSTOM, 1964.

Bouchardeau, A., and R. Lefevre. *Monographie du Lac Tchad*. Paris: ORSTOM, 1957.

Boulet, R. *Observations pédologiques dans le Tamesna oriental*. Dakar: ORSTOM, 1966.

Bousquet, Jean. "Influence de la composition chimique de l'Aïr sur le développement des cultures de moisissures." Thesis, University of Paris, 1933; Paris: Les Editions Vega, 1933.

Bowden, P., and J. P. Karche. "Mudplate A-type Magmatism in the Niger-Nigeria Anorogenic Province." In J. Klerx and J. Michot (eds.), *Géologie Africaine*. Tervueren, Belg.: Musée Royale de l'Afrique Centrale, 1984, pp. 167–78.

Brasseur, G. "Le Niger." *Tropiques,* no. 106 (Dec. 1959):6–32.

Bretagne, S., et al. "Répercussions de la schistosomose urinaire sur l'état nutritionnel des populations du Niger." In D. Lemonnier and Y. Ingenbléek (eds.), *Les Manutations dans les Pays du Tiers Monde*. Paris: INSERM, 1986, pp. 357–62.

Brochaye, J. "Le Goruol, République du Niger." Thesis, University of Rouen, 1973.

Brosset, D. "La rose des vents chez les nomades sahariens." *Bulletin du Comité d'Etudes Historiques et Scientifiques de l'AOF* 4 (1929): 666–84.

Brown, W., et al. "An Anorthosite Suite in a Ring-Complex: Crystallization and Emplacement from Abontofok, Aïr, Niger." *Journal of Petrology* 30, no. 6 (1989):1501–40.

Bruneau de Mire, P., and H. Gillet. "Contribution à l'étude de la flore du massif de l'Aïr." *Journal d'Agriculture Tropicale et de Botanique Appliquée* 3, nos. 5–11 (1956):221–47, 422–38, 701–60, 857–86.

Brunengo, J. F., et al. "Iron Deficiency, Pregnancy and Breast-Feeding in the Republic of Niger." *Transactions of the Royal Society of Tropical Medicine and Hygiene* 82, no. 4 (1988):649–50.

Brunet-Moret, Y. *Etude générale des averses exceptionnelles en Afrique occidentale*. Paris: ORSTOM, 1963.

Bugmann, E. "Studienreise des Vereins Schweizerischer Geografiel-ehrer (Niger, Dahomey, Ghana)." *Geographica Helvetica* 27, no. 1 (1972):1–24.

Bui, Elizabeth Nathalie. "Relationships Between Pedology, Geomorphology and Stratigraphy in the Dallol Bosso of Niger, West Africa." Ph.D. diss., Texas A & M University, 1986.

———, and L. P. Wilding. "Pedogenesis and Mineralogy of a Halaquept in Niger, West Africa." *Geoderma* 43, no. 1 (1988):49–64

———, et al. "Geomorphic Features and Associated Iron Oxides of the Dallol Bosso." *Catena* 17, no. 1 (Feb. 1990):41–54.

———. "Using Quartz Grain Size and Shape Analysis to Distinguish Between Aeolian and Fluvial Deposits in the Dallol Bosso of Niger, West Africa." *Earth Surface Processes and Landforms* 14, no. 2 (1989):157–66.

Busche, D. "An Expedition by Geographers to the Southern Sahara." *Universitas* 26, no. 4 (1984):307–14.

———, and B. Sponholtz. "Karsterscheenungen in nichtkarbonitischen Gesteinen der Republik Niger." *Geowissenschaftliche Untersuchungen in Afrika*. Würzburg: Universität Institute für Geographie, 1988, pp. 9–43.

Campbell, David John. "Strategies for Coping with Drought in the Sahel." Ph.D. diss., Clark University, 1977.

Carmouze, J. P., et al. "Contribution à la connaissance du Bassin Tchadien." *Cahiers d'ORSTOM* 6 (1972):103–69.

Castro, R. "Examen de creusets de Maranbet (Niger)." *Bulletin d'IFAN* 36, no. 4 (1974):667–75.

Cenac, A., et al. "Premenstrual Syndrome in Sahelian Africa: A Comparative Study of Four Hundred Literate and Illiterate Women in Niger." *Transactions of the Royal Society of Tropical Medicine and Hygiene* 81, no. 4 (1987):544–47.

Charoy, J. "Dynamique de l'eau dans un type de sol du Goulbi de Maradi au Niger." *Agronomie Tropicale,* no. 10 (Oct. 1974):983–93.

Charre, J. "Le Climat du Niger." Thesis, Université du Grenoble, 1974.

———. "La variabilité du rythme annuel des saisons au Niger." *Revue de Géographie Alpine* 61, no. 3 (1973):411–26.

Chase, Robert G. "Topsoils Collaborative Water Conservation Research in Niger." In Ted J. Davis (ed.), *Development of Rainfed Agriculture Under Arid and Semiarid Conditions.* Washington, D.C.: World Bank, 1988, pp. 291–93.

Chevalier, A. "Les productions végétales du Sahara et des confins Nord et Sud." *Revue de Botanique Appliquée* 12, (1932):699–924.

———, and A. Reznik. "Un sorgho fourrager des régions désertiques du Sahara central." *Revue de Botanique Appliquée* 12 (1932):525–30.

Chudeau, René. "Etudes sur le Sahara et le Soudan." *Annales de Géographie* 17 (1908):34–55.

———. "Etudes sur les dunes sahariennes." *Annales de Géographie* 29 (1920):334–551.

———. "La zone d'inondation du Niger." *Géographie Commerciale* (Paris) 35, no. 9 (Sept. 1913):569–87.

Clair, Andrée. *Niger, Fleuve du Sahel.* Paris: Messidor, 1982.

Contribution à l'étude de l'Aïr. Paris: Larose, 1950.

Cot, M., et al. "Acquisition de l'immunité en zone d'endémie palustre." *Annales de la Société Belge de Médicine Tropicale* 68, no. 1 (1988).

Cozzi, Paolo. "Le principali popolazioni bovine dell'Africa." *Rivista di Agricoltura Subtropicale e Tropicale,* nos. 1–12 (Jan.–Dec. 1973): 24–55.

Dabin, B. *Etude Générale des conditions d'utilisation de sols de la cuvette Tchadienne.* Paris: ORSTOM, 1969.

Daus, S. J., and M. A. Guero. "Remote Sensing Aided Inventory of Fuelwood Volumes in the Sahel Region of West Africa: A Case Study of Five Urban Zones in the Republic of Niger." In M. C. J. Damen et al. (eds.), *Remote Sensing for Resources Development and Environmental Management.* Rotterdam: Balkema, 1986, pp. 403–8.

———, et al. "Development of a Regional Mapping System for the Sahelian Region of West Africa Using Medium-Scale Aerial Photography." In M. C. J. Damen et al. (eds.), *Remote Sensing for Resources Development and Environmental Management.* Rotterdam: Balkema, 1986, pp. 409–14.

De Blij H. J. *A Geography of Subsaharan Africa.* Chicago: Rand McNally, 1964.

Defossez, Michel. "Contribution à l'étude géologique et hydrogéologique de la boucle du Niger." Thesis, Université de Strasbourg, 1958.

Delheure, J. "L'Hyrdraulique traditionnelle à Ouargla." *Fichier Périodique* (Algiers), no. 126 (1975).

Delwaulle, J. C. "Résultats de six ans d'observations sur l'érosion au Niger." *Bois et Forêts des Tropiques,* no. 150 (July–Aug. 1973): 15–36.

———, and A. Roederer. "Le Bois de feu à Niamey." *Bois et Forêts des Tropiques,* no. 152 (Nov.–Dec. 1973):55–60.

Desplagnes, L. *Le Plateau central nigérien.* Paris: Larose, 1907.

Deuson, R. R., and J. H. Sanders. "Cereal Technology Development in the Sahel: Burkina Faso and Niger." *Land Use Policy* 7, no. 3 (1990):195–97.

Develoux, M., et al. "Mycetoma in the Republic of Niger: Clinical Features and Epidemiology." *American Journal of Tropical Medicine and Hygiene* 38, no. 2 (1988):386–90.

Donaint, Pierre. *Les cadres géographiques à travers les langues du Niger. Contribution à la pédagogie de l'étude du milieu.* Paris: Etudes Nigeriénnes no. 37, 1975.

Ducros, Paul. "Mediterranée-Niger." Thesis, University of Paris, 1942; Tourcoing, Fr.: Imprimerie de G. Frere, 1942.

Durand, Alain, et al. "Evolution géomorphologique, stratigraphique et Paléoclimatologique de l'Aïr oriental." *Revue de Géologie Dynamique et de Géographie* 24, no. 1 (1983):47–59.

Durand, J. R., and C. Leveque. *Flore et faune aquatique de l'Afrique sahélo-soudanienne.* Paris: ORSTOM, 1980.

Dussard, B. H. "Copépodes du bassin du Niger." *Bulletin d'IFAN* 43, no. 1/2 (1981).

Echard, Nicole. *Metallurgies africaines.* Paris: Mémoires de la Société des Africanistes, 1983.

Eyraud, Arlette. *Sénégal, Mali, Mauritanie, Niger.* Paris: Hatier, 1975.

Fabrègues, B. Peyre de. *Lexique des noms vernaculaires de plantes du Niger.* 2 vols. Niamey: IEMVT, 1977.

———, and J. P. Lebrun. *Catalogue des plantes vasculaires du Niger.* Maisons-Alfort: IEMVT, 1976.

Faure, H. "Géologie de la cuvette tchadienne." *Cahiers d'ORSTOM* 2, no. 1 (1970).

———. "Une Hypothèse sur la structure du Ténéré." *Comptes Rendus de l'Académie de Sciences* 249, no. 23 (Dec. 9, 1959):2591–93.

Feyler, L. "Sur le trace de la Vallée du Tafassasset au nord du Grand Erg du Ténéré et la probabilité de son prolongement au sud jusqu'à Tchad." *Comptes Rendus de l'Académie de Sciences* 200, no. 9 (Feb. 25, 1935):721–24.

Flitcroft, I. D. "Spatial Aspects of Rainfall and the Water Budget in Semi-Arid West Africa." Ph.D. diss., University of Reading, 1989.

Food and Agriculture Organization. "Projet de développement de la production animale et des ressources en eaux dans l'est du Niger: Etude agrostologique des pâturages de la zone nomade de Zinder." Rome, 1970.

———. Ministère des Colonies. *Documents Scientifiques de la Mission Tilho (1906–1909)*. 3 vols. Paris: Imprimerie Nationale and Larose, 1911–14.

France, Ministère de la Coopération. *Cartographie des pays du Sahel.* Paris, 1976.

———. *Catalogue iconographique des principaux acridiens du Sahel,* by My Hang Launois and Michel Launois. Paris, 1987.

———. *Guide antiacridien du Sahel,* by My Hang Launois, Michel Launois, and Jean-François Duranton. Paris, 1987.

———. Secrétariat d'Etat aux Affaires Etrangères. *Etude sur L'Aménagement du flueve Niger,* by Olivier Gautier. Paris, 1968.

"The French Niger Territority." *Scottish Geographical Magazine* 15, no. 4 (Apr. 1899):186–200.

Frison-Roche, Roger. *Mission Ténéré*. Paris: Arthaud, 1960.

———. *Sahara de l'Aventure*. Paris: Arthaud, 1961.

Frolow, S. "Note sur le climat de Niamey." *Bulletin du Comité d'Etudes Scientifiques et Historiques de l'AOF* (1936):150–87.

Frolow, Vladimir. "Le Niger moyen, étude potamologique." Thesis, 1934.

Funel, Jean Marie. *Politiques d'aménagement hydro-agricole*. Paris: Presses Universitaires de France, 1980.

Garde, G. "Description géologique des régions situées entre le Niger et le Tchad et à l'est et au nord-est du Tchad." Thesis, University of Paris, 1911.

Gauthier-Pilters, H. "Le dromadaire: Fables et réalités." *MIFERMA-Informations,* no. 19 (Dec. 1970):47–52.

Gautier, Olivier. *Etude des possibilités pour la République du Niger d'aménager le fleuve Niger et d'utiliser la voie fluviale*. Paris: Secrétariat d'Etat aux Affaires Etrangères, 1969.

Gavaud, Michel. *Les Grands traits de la pédogenèse au Niger méridional*. Paris: ORSTOM, 1977.

Gentil, P. *Cofins Libyens, lac Tchad, fleuve Niger*. Paris: Lavauzelle, 1946.

Gillet, Hubert, and Bernard Peyre de Fabrègues. "Quelques arbres utiles, en voie de disparition dans le Centre-Est du Niger." *Revue d'Ecologie* 36, no. 3 (1983):465–70.

Gleeson, C. F., and R. Poulin. "Gold Exploration in Niger Using Soils and Termitaria." *Journal of Geochemical Exploration* 31, no. 3 (1989):253–83.

Godana, Bonaya Adhi. *Africa's Shared Water Resources*. London: Pinter, 1985.

Granier, P. *Notes sur l'introduction de technique d'amélioration de la productivité de l'élevage en zone sahélienne*. Maisons-Alfort: IEMVT, 1975.

Greigert, J. *Les Eaux Souterraines de la République du Niger*. 2 vols. Niamey: Direction des Mines et de la Géologie, 1968.

———. *Les formations crétacées et tertiaires du Bassin des Iullemeden*. Paris: BRGM, 1967.

———. *Rapport de Mission géologique au Niger 1948–50*. Dakar: BRGM, 1950.

———, and R. Pougnet. *Essai de description des formations géologiques de la République du Niger*. Paris: Bureau de Recherches Géologiques et Minières, 1967

———, and C. Sauvel. *Modernisation de la zone pastorale nigérienne. Etude Hydrologique*. 2 vols. Paris: BRGM, 1970.

Grove, A. T. "Lake Chad." *Geographical Magazine,* no. 3 (1964): 524–37.

——— (ed.). *The Niger and Its Neighbours: Environmental History and Hydrobiology*. Boston: Balkema, 1985.

Grunert, J. "Klima und Landschaftsentwicklung in Ost-Niger während der Jungpleisentwicklung in Ost-Niger während des Jungpleistozans." In *Geowissenschaftliche Untersuchungen in Afrika*. Würzburg: Universität Institute für Geographie, 1988, pp. 289–304.

———. "Landslides in the Central Sahara: Southwest Libya and East Niger." In V. Gardiner (ed.), *International Geomorphology, 1986: Proceedings of the First International Conference on Geomorphology*. Chichester: Wiley, 1987.

Gschladt, Wolfgang. "Le ronier au Dallol Maouri, Niger." *Bois et Fôret des Tropiques,* no. 145 (Sept.–Oct. 1972):3–16.

Hagedorn, H. "Aolische Abtragungsformen im Massiv von Termit, NE-Niger" In *Geowissenschaftliche Untersuchungen in Afrika*. Würzburg: Universität Institute für Geographie, 1988, pp. 277–87.

Harrison-Church, R. J. *Africa and the Islands*. London: Longmans, 1971.

———. *West Africa*. London: Longmans, 1968.

Hautefeuille, G. "L'Origine des eaux du Kaouar." CHEAM, no. 1538 (1950).

Hutsch, Jonathan Mark. "Geology, Petrology, Structure, and Geochemistry of Anorthositic and Related Rocks Associated with Hypabyssal Ring Complexes, Aïr Massif, Republic of Niger." Ph.D. diss., Princeton University, 1982.

Index, Commission du Fleuve Niger. Niamey: UNESCO, Centre de Documentation, 1972.

Janke, B. "Hydrographische Grundlagen der Bewässerungswirtschaft im Nigertal." *Erdkunde* (Bonn) 30, no. 4 (Dec. 1976):277–86.

Jomini, Patrick Andre. "The Economic Viability of Phosphorus Fertilization in Southwestern Niger: A Dynamic Approach Incorporating Agronomic Principles." Ph.D. diss., Purdue University, 1990.

Justice, C. O., and P. H. Y. Hiernaux. "Monitoring the Grasslands of the Sahel." *International Journal of Remote Sensing* (London) 7, no. 11 (1986):1475–97.

Karabenick, Edmund. "Djerba: A Case Study in the Geography of Isolation." *Journal of Geography* 70, no. 1 (1970):52–57.

Kilian, Conrad. "Expédition 1943 (Aïr et Ténéré)." *Travaux de l'Institut de Recherches Sahariennes* (Algiers) 3 (1945):73–86.

Klotchkoff, J. C. *Le Niger aujourd'hui*. Paris: Jeune Afrique, 1984.

Koechlin, J. *La Flore du Continent Africain*. Paris: UNESCO, 1963.

———. *Les problèmes pastoraux en zone sahélienne: Progamme d'étude des pâturages en République du Niger*. Paris, 1962.

Koster, Stanley Henry. "A Survey of the Vegetation and Ungulate Populations in Park W, Niger." M.S. thesis, Michigan State University, 1982.

Lacrouts, Marcel. "Problèmes de commercialisation du bétail en Afrique." *Revue d'Elevage et Médicine Vétérinaire des Pays Tropicaux,* no. 1 (1969):127–44.

———,and Jean Tyc. *Les ressources animales de la République du Niger; Leur exploitation, perspectives de l'avenir*. Paris: Imprimerie Technography, 1960.

"Lake Chad." In L. C. Beadl (ed.), *The Inland Waters of Tropical Africa*. London: Longman, 1974, pp. 160–74.

Lambert, F. "Contributions à la connaissance hydrologique de la colonie du Niger." *Bulletin du Service des Mines de l'AOF* (1938):29–46.

Lambert, G. *L'Adaptation physiologique et psychologique de l'homme aux conditions de vie désertique*. Paris: Hermann, 1968.

Lambert, R. "Les salines de Tequidda-n-tessoum." *Bulletin du Comité d'Etudes Historiques et Scientifiques de l'AOF* 18, no. 2/3 (Apr.–Sept. 1935):366–71.

———. "La source minérale à Igouloulof." *Bulletin du Comité d'Etudes Historiques et Scientifiques de l'AOF* 19 (1936):237–42.

Laurent, A. "Un bel exploit lyonnais: La mission Berliet-Ténéré-Tchad." *Saharien,* no. 45 (1967):33–43.

LeCoeur, C. "Les 'mapalia' numides et leurs survivance au Sahara." *Hesperis* 24 (1937):29–45.

Lefevre, R. *Etudes d'Ecoulement dans la Massif de l'Aïr*. Paris: ORSTOM, 1960.

Legrand, M., et al. "The Potential of Infrared Satellite Data for the Retrieval of Saharan Dust Optical Depth over Africa." *Journal of Applied Meteorology* 28, no. 4 (1989):309–18.

Leriche, A. "De la médicine au pays de Chinguétti." *Notes Africaines,* no. 27 (1945):7–8.

———. "Santé et Maladie au pays de Chinguétti." *Notes Africaines,* no. 28 (1945):2–4.

Levy-Luxereau, Anne. *Etude Etho-Zoologique du Pays Hausa en République du Niger*. Paris: Société d'Etudes Ethno-botaniques, 1972.

Louarn, François. "Contribution à la modernisation de la médicine itinérante en France Outre-mer et spécialement au Niger." Thesis, University of Paris, 1950.

Louis, S., et al. "Seasonal Changes in Nutritive Values of Rangelands." In J. J. Swift (ed.), *Pastoral Development in Central Niger*. Niamey: Ministry of Rural Deveopment, 1984, pp. 214–23.

Loutan, L. "Nutrition Amongst a Group of Wodaabe (Bororo) Pastoralists in Niger." In A. G. Hill (ed.), *Population, Health and Nutrition in the Sahel*. London: Kegan Paul, 1985.

Macedo, Nilda Guerra de. "Etude géomorphologique des formations sableuses de la vallée moyenne du Niger." Thesis, University of Strasbourg, 1958.

Machens, Eberhard, *Contribution à l'étude des formations du sodacristallin et de la couverture sédementaire de l'Ouest de la République du Niger*. Paris: BRGM, 1973.

———. "Notice explicative sur la carte géologique du Niger occidental." *Bulletin de Service Fédéral des Mines et de la Géologie* (1967).

Mainguet, M. "Carte des degrés de réactivation des manteaux sableux." *Conférence des Nations Unies sur la Désertification* (Sept. 1977).

———, and L. Canon. "Vents et paléovents du Sahara, tentative d'approche paléoclimatique." *Revue de Géographie Physique et de Géologie Dynamique* 18, no. 2/3 (1976):241–54.

Maire, C., and P. Marty. "Etudes sur la flore et la végétation du Sahara central." *Mémoire de la Société d'Histoire Naturelle d'Afrique du Nord* (1933):1–272; (1940):273–433.

Manquet, Monique, et al. "Autochtonie et alloctonie des sables de la zone saharo-sahélienne du Niger." *Revue de Géologie Dynamique et de Géographie Physique* 24, no. 2 (1983):167–73.

Mascianis, Marcel-Paul. "Le précambrien de la partie orientale de la boucle du Niger." Thesis, University of Clermont-Ferrand, 1955.

Mauny, R. "Une belle performance française: La mission Berliet-Ténéré." *Tropiques*, no. 426 (Mar. 1960):10–17.

Mensching, Horst G. *Die Sahelzone: Naturpotential und Probleme: einer Nutzung*. Cologne: Aulis Verlag Deubner, 1986.

Millot, J. "L'Exposition Ténéré-Tchad (Missions Berliet 1958–60)." *Objets et Mondes* 2, no. 2 (Summer 1962):99–106.

Missions Berliet-Ténéré-Tchad: Documents Scientifiques. Paris: Arts et Métiers Graphiques, 1962.

Monod, T. "Les bases d'une division géographique du domaine saharien." *Bulletin d'IFAN* (ser. B) 30, no. 1 (Jan. 1968):269–88.

Morel, A. "Villages et oasis des Monts Bagzan, massif de l'Aïr." *Revue de Géographie* 61, no. 1 (1943):247–66.

———. "Faire renaître le Sahel? Expériences de développement agricole dans le massif de l'Aïr, Niger." *Cultures et Développement* 8, no. 2 (1976):266–86.

———, and Christian Moreau. "Relations entre le modelé et la pétrologie des anorthosites et des roches associés de l'Ofoud." *Revue de Géologie Dynamique et de Géographie Physique* 21, no. 3 (1979) 247–55.

———, et al. "Apport d'un enregistrement *Landsat* à la connaissance géomorphologique et géologique du Massif de l'Ofoud." *Revue de Géomorphologie Dynamique* 32, no. 3 (1983):81–88.

Mortimer, M. J. "The Changing Resources of Sedentary Communities in Aïr, Southern Sahara." *Geographical Review* 62, no. 1 (Jan. 1972): 71–91.

Mouchet, F., et al. "Enquête sur les schistosomoses dans l'arrondissement de Gaya, République du Niger." *Annales de la Société Belge de Médicine Tropicale* 67, no. 1 (1987):23–29.

Munier, P. *Prospection Phenicole en Territoire de République du Niger*. Paris: Institut des Fruits et Agrumes Coloniaux, 1959.

Neumann, K. "Die Bedeutung von Holzkohleuntersuchungen für die Vegetationsgeschichte der Sahara: das Beispiel Fach, Niger." In *Geowissenschaftliche Untersuchungen in Afrika*. Würzburg: Universität Institute für Geographie, 1988, pp. 71–85.

Newby, John E., and John F. Grettenberger. "The Human Dimension in Natural Resource Conservation: A Sahelian Example from Niger." *Environmental Conservation* 13 (Autumn 1986):249–56.

Noel, P. "Pratiques médicales indigènes au Kaouar." *Anthropologie* 30 (1920):551–60.

Olkes, Cheryl. "Information-Seeking with the Mass-Media in the Republic of Niger." Ph.D. diss., University of Texas/Austin, 1978.

Ouattara, Mamadou. "A Study of Two Toposequences of the Dry Valley of Western Niger." Ph.D. diss., Texas A & M University, 1990.

Ousseini, I. "Morphstratigraphie et interprétation des dépôts éoliens entre Sirba et Dargol dans le Moyen Niger." In *Geowissenschaftliche Untersuchungen in Afrika*. Würzburg: Universität Institute für Geographie, 1988, pp. 211–31.

———, and A. Morel. "Utilisation de formation alluviales azotiques pour l'étude des paléoenvironnements du Pleisocène supérieur et de l'Halocène au sud du Sahara: L'exemple da la vallée du fleuve Niger dans le Liptako nigérien." *Bulletin de la Société Géologique de France* 5, no. 1 (1989):85–90.

Over, A. Mead, Jr. "Two Approaches to Projecting the Effect of Scale on the Cost of a Primary Health Program in a Developing Country: Niger." *Présence Africaine,* no. 124 (1982):105–17.

Ozenda, P. *Flore du Sahara*. Paris: CNRS, 1977.

Pales, L., and J. Linhard. *Biologie Comparative des Populations de l'AOF*. Dakar: IFAN, 1951.

Pedrals, Denis-Pierre de. "Le fleuve Niger." *Afrique Contemporaine,* no. 44 (July–Aug. 1969):2–11; no. 45 (Sept.–Oct. 1969):2–9.

Pias, J. "Transgressions et régressions du Lac Tchad à la fin du Tertiaire et au Quaternaire." *Comptes Rendu de l'Académie de Science* 246 (1958):800–803.

Picheral, Henri. *Afrique*. Paris: Edition Lidis, 1973.

Pirard, F. "Géomorphologie du Manga Nigérien." *Bulletin d'IFAN* (ser. A) 28, no. 1 (Jan. 1966):421–25.

Planhol, X. de., and Rognon, P. *Les Zones tropicales arides et subtropicales*. Paris: Armand Colin, 1970.

Poché, R. M. "A Checklist of the Mammals of National Park W." *Nigerian Field* (Ibadan) 41, no. 3 (Sept. 1976):113–15.

———. "Preliminary Census of Wild Ungulates in Parc National du W, Niger." *Nigerian Field* (Ibadan) 40, no. 2 (June 1975):78–88.

———. "Seasonal Distribution and Reproduction in Artiodactyla from Southwestern Niger." *Nigerian Field* (Ibadan) 41, no. 1 (Mar. 1976): 31–40.

Poncet, Yveline. "Avant-projet de l'Atlas du Niger." *Mu Kaara Sani* (Niamey), no. 1 (n.d.):3–8.

———. *Images spatiales et paysages sahéliens*. Paris: ORSTOM, 1986.

———. *Les servitudes pluviométriques au Niger*. Niamey, 1975.

Prescott, J. R. V., and H. P. White. "Sand Formation in the Niger Valley Between Niamey and Bocirem." *Geographical Journal,* no. 126 (1960):200–203.

Prost, A. "Le recensement des cécités dans les savanes de la Boucle du Niger." *Cahiers d'ORSTOM* 19, no. 3 (1983):285–91.

Pullan, R. A. "Recent Geomorphological Evolution of the Chad Basin." *Journal of West African Science Association* (Ibadan) 9 (1964): 115–39.

Quezel, P. "A propos de l'olivier de Laperrine de l'Adrar Gréboun." In H. J. Hugot (ed.), *Mission Berliet-Ténéré-Tchad*. Paris: Arts et Métiers Graphiques, 1962, pp. 313–27.

———. *La Végétation du Sahara*. Stuttgart: Gustav Fischer Verlag, 1965.

Raynaut, C. "Recherches multidisciplinaires sur la région de Maradi." University of Bordeaux, 1980.

Regelsperger, G. "Du Niger au Tchad. La Mission Tilho. Ses Travaux et ses Résultats." *Le Mois Colonial et Maritime* 1 (1909):97–109.

Renaud, G., et al. "Prevalence of Vaginal Schistosomiasis in an Endemic Village in Niger." *Transactions of the Royal Society of Tropical Medicine and Hygiene*. 83, no. 6 (1989).

Riedel, Wolfgang, et al. "Reliefgeschichte und Palaoklima des saharischen Ost-Niger." *Geographische Rundschau* 41, no. 9 (Sept. 1989):493–99.

Rippstein, G., and B. Peyre de Fabrègues. *Modernisation de la zone agrostologique*. Paris: Maisons-Alfort, 1972.

Rodier, J. A. "L'hydrologie des régions sahéliennes et la sécheresse 1968–1973." *Etudes Scientifiques* (June 1975):1–49.

Rousselot, R. "Note sur la faune ornithologique des Cercles de Maradi et de Tanout." *Bulletin d'IFAN* 9, no. 14 (1947):99–137.

Rubon, R. and M. Sacz. *Géographie: Le Niger*. Paris: Istra, 1962.

"Sahel: études sur l'élevage." *Cahiers d'ORSTOM* 11, no. 2 (1974): 115–98.

Scaetta, H., and Conrad Killian. "Observations pédologiques et biologiques sur la latérite fossile, les sols latéritiques et les sols alluviaux de Gao-Bilakolo (Niger)." *Bulletin de la Société de Histoire Naturelle Africaine* 32 (July 1941):225–41.

Schiffers, Heinrich. *Nach der Dürre*. Munich: Weltforum Verlag, 1976.

Schobel, Jürgen. *Ammoniten der Familie Vascoceratidae aus dem Unteren Unterturon des Damergou-Gebietes, Republique du Niger*. Uppsala: Palaeontological Institute of the University of Uppsala, 1975.

Schoeneich, P., and I. Bouzou. "Glissements de terrain dans l'Adar, Niger." In *Geowissenschaftliche Untersuchungen in Afrika*. Würzburg: Universität Institute für Geographie, 1988, pp. 149–65.

Schuh, J. "Kleinformen der Verwitterung am Südrand der Sahara, Republik Niger." In *Geowissenschaftliche Untersuchungen in Afrika*. Würzburg: Universität Institute für Geographie, 1988, pp. 103–18.

Schultz, E., and A. Adamou. "Geographical Investigations on the Fringe of the Sahara." *Universitas* 28, no. 3 (1986):205–16.

Scott-Wendt, John William. "An Evaluation of the Causes of Soil Infertility in Niger." Ph.D. diss., Purdue University, 1989.

Sidikou, M. A. *Géographie du Niger*. Dakar: Nouvelles Editions Africaines, 1976.

Sikes, S. K. *Lake Chad*. London: Methuen, 1972.

Société d'Etudes et de Réalisation Economiques et Sociales dans l'Agriculture. *Eléments de Documentation sur l'Afrique Occidentale,* monograph no. 8. Dakar, 1959.

Société Général des Techniques Hydro-Agricoles. *Etude Hydro-Géologique de la Vallée de Keita*. Paris, 1964.

———. *Etude pédologique de la vallée de la Magya*. Paris, 1964.

Sollod, A. E., et al. "Veterinary Anthropology: Interdisciplinary Methods in Pastoral Systems Research." In J. R. Simpson and P. Evangelou (eds.), *Livestock Development in Subsaharan Africa*. Boulder, Colo.: Westview Press, 1984, pp. 285–302.

Sponholtz, B. "Beobachtungen zur Morphodynamik an Koris des südlichen Air-Vorlandes, Niger." In *Geowissenschaftliche Untersuchungen in Afrika*. Würzburg: Universität Institute für Geographie, 1988, pp. 119– 35.

Soubiran, G., et al. "Approche épidémiologique des affections à virus B et delta au Niger." *Population et Santé Tropicale,* no. 28 (1987):1–4.
Taquet, P. "Dinosaurs of Niger." *Nigerian Field* (Ibadan) (Mar. 1977): 2–10.
———. *Géologie et paléontologie du gisement de Gadoufaoua.* Paris: Editions du CNRS, 1976.
Tchéllé, D., and A. Chamorin. *La Méningite cérébro-spinale au Niger.* Niamey: World Health Organization, n.d.
Thom, D. J. "The City of Maradi: French Influence upon a Hausa Urban Center." *Journal of Geography* 70 (1971):472–82.
———. "The Morphology of Maradi, Niger." *African Urban Notes* 7, no. 1 (1972):26–35.
Thomson, J. T. "Ecological Deterioration: Local-Level Rule-Making and Enforcement Problems in Niger." In M. H. Glantz (ed.), *Desertification: Environmental Degradation in and Around Arid Lands.* Boulder, Colo.: Westview Press, 1977, pp. 57–79.
Thorp, M. G. "Some Aspects of the Geomorphology of the Aïr Mountains, Southern Sahara." *Transactions of the Institute of British Geographers,* no. 47 (Sept. 1969):25–46.
Tilho, J. *Documents Scientifiques de la mission Tilho 1906–09.* Paris: Imprimerie Nationale, 1914.
Touchebeuf de Lussigny, P. *Monographie hydrologique du Lac Tchad.* Paris: ORSTOM, 1969.
Tricart, J. *Rapport de la Mission de reconnaissance géomorphologique de la vallée moyenne du Niger.* Dakar: IFAN, 1965.
Urvoy, Yves. *Les Bassins du Niger.* Paris: Larose, 1942.
———. "La Mekrou et le double-v." *Afrique Française* 39, no. 2 (Feb. 1929):135–40.
———. "Terrasses et changements de climat quaternaires à l'est du Niger." *Annales de Géographie* 44, no. 249 (May 15, 1935):254–63.
Valentine, Christian. *République du Niger: Dynamique de formation et conséquence sur l'économie en eau.* Paris: ORSTOM, 1985.
Vignon, A. "Reconnaissance par engins motorisés du Sahara Nigérien." *Renseignements Coloniaux* (Feb.–Mar. 1934):53, 77, 80; (Apr. 1934): 85–87.
Volkel, J. "Geomorphologische und pedologische Untersuchungen in Dünengebieten der Südsahara und des Sahel der Republik Niger." In *Deutscher Arbeitskreis für Geomorphologie.* Göttingen: E. Goltze, 1987.
———. *Geomorphologische und pedologische Untersuchungen zum jungquarteren Klimawandel in den Dünengebieten Ost-Nigers.* Bonn: Kommission bei F. Dummiler, 1989.
———. "Zum jungquartaren Klimawandel im saharischen und sahelischen Ost-Niger aus bodenkundlicher Sicht." In *Geowissenschaftliche*

Untersuchungen in Afrika. Würzburg: Universität Institute für Geographie, 1988, pp. 255–76.

Wauthier, Magdeleine. "Une exploration au Ténéré." *La Géographie* 64 (1935):32–54.

———, and R. Wauthier. *Connaissance des sables. Du Hoggar au Tchad à travers de Ténéré*. Paris: Plon, 1934.

Weicker, M. "Vieh statt Hirse oder Vieh gegen Hirse: Probleme der Ressourcennutzung und der Nahrungsmittelversorgung bei den Iforas-Tuareg, Niger." *Die Erde* 119, no. 4 (1988):243–51.

White, F. "The Sahel Regional Transition Zone: The Sahara Regional Transition Zone." In *The Vegetation of Africa: A Descriptive Memoir to Accompany UNESCO*. Paris: UNESCO, 1983, pp. 203–15, 216–24.

White, L. P. "The Ancient Erg of Hausaland in Southwestern Niger." *Geographical Journal* 137 (1971):69–73

———. "Brousse Tigrée Patterns in Southern Niger." *Journal of Ecology* 1, no. 58 (1970):549–53.

Williams, M. A. J., et al. "Quaternary Landforms, Sediments, Depositional Environments and Gastropod Isotope Ratios at Adrar Bous, Ténéré, Desert of Niger, South-Central Sahara." In L. E. Frostick and I. Reid (eds.), *Desert Sediments: Ancient and Modern*. Oxford: Blackwell, 1987, pp. 105–25.

Wylie, Bruce Kaile. "Herbaceous Biomass Assessment in the Central Pastoral Zone of the Sahelian Country of Niger, 1986–1988." Ph.D. diss., New Mexico State University, 1991.

Religion

Alexandre, Pierre. "A West African Islamic Movement: Hamalism in French West Africa." In R. Rotberg and A. Mazrui (eds.), *Protest and Power in Black Africa*. New York: Oxford University Press, 1970, pp. 497–512.

Arnaud, R. *L'Islam et la politique musulmane en AOF*. Paris, 1912.

Bastide, Roger. "Réflexions sans titre autour d'une des formes de la spiritualité africaine, polythéisme des Nigériens ou Dahoméens." *Présence Africaine*, no. 17/18 (Feb.–May 1958):9–15.

Besmer, Fremont E. *Horses, Musicians and Gods: The Hausa Cult of Possession*. South Hadley, Mass.: Bergin and Garvey, 1983.

———. "Initiation with the Bori Cult: A Case Study, Ningi Town." *Africa* 47 (1977).

Beyries, J. *Les Confréries musulmanes en Afrique*. Paris: CHEAM, 1948.

———. *L'Islam au Niger*. Paris, CHEAM, 1958.

Biobaku, Saburi, and Muhammad al-Hadj. "The Sudanese Mahdiyya and the Niger-Chad Region." In I. M. Lewis (ed.), *Islam in Tropical Africa*. New York: Oxford University Press, 1966, pp. 425–41.

Broustra-Monfouga, Jacques. "Approche ethnopsychiatrique du phénomène de possession. Le Bori de Konni (Niger), étude comparative." *Journal de la Société des Africanistes* 43, no. 2 (1973):197–220.

Carré, Olivier. *L'Islam et l'Etat dans le Monde d'aujourd'hui.* Paris: Presses Universitaires de France, 1982.

Casajus, Dominique. "La frère, le djinn et le temps qui passe." *Cahiers de Littérature Orale* 12 (1982):15–38. Also in English in *Research in African Literatures* 15, no. 2 (Summer 1984):218–37.

———. *Peau d'âne et autres contes touaregs.* Paris: Harmattan, 1985.

———. "Un salon littéraire chez les Touaregs." *Cahiers de Littérature Orale* ii (1982):177–78.

Cuoq, Joseph. *Histoire de l'Islamisation de l'Afrique de l'Ouest.* Paris: Paul Geuthner, 1984.

Dan-Inna, Chaibou, and J. D. Panel. *Bibliographie de la littérature nigérienne.* Niamey: Imprimerie National du Niger, 1988.

Delafosses, M. "Les confréries musulmanes et maraboutisme dans les pays du Sénégal et du Niger." *Renseignements Coloniaux,* no. 4 (Apr. 5, 1911):81–90.

Deniel, Raymond. *Croyants dans la ville.* Abidjan: INADES, 1982.

Ducroz, Jean Marie. *Les Actes des Premières Chrétiens de Garoul.* Paris: Mission Chrétienne, 1976.

Dutel, René. "L'Animisme des populations islamisées du Moyen Niger (Songhay et Djerma)" *Mémoire du CHEAM* (1946).

Echard, Nicole. "Histoire et phénomène religieuse chez les Asna de l'Ader." *Systèmes de Pensée en Afrique Noire* (1975):63–77.

———. "La pratique religieuse des femmes dans une société d'hommes: Les Haoussas du Niger." *Revue Française de Sociologie* (Oct.–Dec. 1978):551–62.

"Ecrit sur le sable." *Niger* (Niamey), no. 7 (July 1969):40–51.

Erlmann, Veit. *Girkaa: Une cérémonie d'initiation au culte de possession bori des Hausa de la région de Maradi, Niger.* Berlin: Reimer, 1989.

Faulkingham, Ralph H. "The Spirits and Their Cousins: Some Aspects of Beliefs, Rituals, and Social Organization in a Rural Hausa Village in Niger." University of Massachusetts, Department of Anthropology, Research Report no. 15. Amherst, 1975.

Froelich, Jean Claude. "Islam et culture arabe en Afrique au sud du Sahara." *Revue Française d'Etudes Politiques Africaines,* no. 1 (1966): 54–57.

Gibb, H. A. R., and J. H. Kramer. *Shorter Encyclopaedia of Islam.* Ithaca, N.Y.: Cornell University Press, 1953.

Giles, A. *Où en est le Niger musulman?* Paris: CHEAM, 1953.

Gregoire, Emmanuel. "Accumulation marchande et propagation de l'Islam en milieu urbain: Le cas de Maradi, Niger." *Islam et Sociétés au Sud du Sahara* 5 (1991):43–55.

———. "Islam and the Identity of Merchants in Maradi." In Louis Brenner (ed.), *Muslim Identity and Social Change in Subsaharan Africa*. Bloomington: Indiana University Press, 1993, pp. 106–15.

Gruner, Dorothée. "Der Traditionelle Moscheebau am Mittleren Niger." *Paideuma* (Frankfurt), no. 23 (1977):101–40.

Hama, Boubou. "Le culte des ancêtres, quelques tableaux de la vie d'un prêtré de la terre." *Notes Africaines,* no. 31 (July 1946):22.

———. "L'Espirit de la culture sonraie." *Présence Africaine,* no. 14/15 (June–Sept. 1957):149–54.

———. "Note sur les Holé." *Education Africain* (1941–43).

Hautefeuille. "Les origines de l'Islam au Koawar." CHEAM, no. 1654 (1950).

Hunwick, X. J. O. "Religion and State in the Songhay Empire, 1464–1591." In I. M. Lewis (ed.), *Islam in Tropical Africa*. New York: Oxford University Press, 1966, pp. 296–317.

Laizé, M. "Islam dans le Territoire Militaire du Niger." *Bulletin du Comité d'Etudes Historiques et Scientifiques de l'AOF,* no. 2 (Apr.–June 1919):177–83.

Lallemand, Suzanne. *La mangeuse d'âmes: Sorcellerie et famille en Afrique noire*. Paris: Harmattan, 1988.

Lem, A. "Un centre d'islamisation au moyen Niger." *Terre d'Islam,* no. 2 (1943).

Leroux, Henri. "Animisme et Islam dans la subdivision de Maradi (Niger)." *Bulletin d'IFAN* 10, (1948):595–697.

———. "Animisme et Islam dans la subdivision de Maracou (Niger)." Ph.D. diss., University of Paris, 1948.

———. "Survivances animistes dans la subdivision de Maradi." CHEAM, no. 2245 (1953).

Lombard, Jacques. "Les cultes de possession en Afrique Noire et le Bori Hausa." *Psychopathologie Africaine* 3 (1967):419–39.

Loyzance, A. "L'Islam et les survivances de l'animisme dans la subdivision centrale de Niamey." CHEAM, no. 2490 (1953).

Marty, Paul. *Etudes sur l'Islam et les tribus du Sudan*. 4 vols. Paris: Larose, 1920.

———. "L'Islam et les tribus dans la colonie du Niger (ex-Zinder)." *Revue des Etudes Islamiques* 4 (1930):333–432; also Paris: Paul Geuthner, 1931.

Masquelier, Adeline. "Narratives of Power, Images of Wealth: The Ritual Economy of Bori in the Market." In Jean Comaroff and John Comaroff (eds.), *Modernity and Its Discontents*. Chicago: University of Chicago Press, 1993, pp. 3–31.

———. "Ritual Economies, Historical Meditations: The Poetics and Power of Bori Among the Mawri of Niger." Ph.D. diss., University of Chicago, 1993.

Monteil, V. *L'Islam Noire*. Paris: Seuil, 1964.

Moreau, R. L. "Les marabouts de Dori." *Archives de la Sociologie de Religion,* no. 17 (1964):113–34.

Mouradian, A. *La Religion musulmane au Niger*. Paris: Harmattan, 1957.

Nicolaisen, Johannes. "Essai sur la religion et la magie touaregues." *Folk* (Copenhagen), no. 3 (1961):113–62.

Nicolas, Francis. "Etude sur l'Islam, les confréries et les centres maraboutiques chez les twareg du Sud." CHEAM, no. 1537 (1946).

———. "L'Islam, les confréries, chez les Touaregs du Sud." CHEAM, no. 792 (1946).

Nicolas, Guy. "Communautés islamiques et collectivité nationale dans trois Etats d'Afrique Occidentale." *Revue Française d'Histoire d'Outre-Mer* 68, nos. 250–53 (1981):156–94.

———. "Détours d'une conversion collective: Ouverture à l'Islam d'une bastion soudanais de résistance à une guerre Sainte." *Archives de Sciences Sociales des Religions* 24 (1979):48–51.

———. "L'enracinement ethnique de l'Islam au sud du Sahara." *Cahiers d'Etudes Africaines* 18, no. 71 (1981):347–77.

———. "Islam et construction nationale au sud du Sahara." *Revue Française d'Etudes Politiques Africaines,* no. 165/66 (Sept.–Oct. 1979):86–107.

———. "La modèle mobilisateur de 'Jihad' dans les conflits du Soudan central." *Cultures et Développement* 16, no. 3/4 (1984): 583–610.

Nicolas, Jacqueline. "Culpabilité, somatisation et catharsis au sein d'un culte de possession—le Bori Hausa (Niger)." *Psychopathologie Africaine* 9 (1973).

———. *Les 'Juments des Dieux': Rites de possession et condition féminine en pays hausa (Vallée de Maradi, Niger)*. Paris: Etudes Nigeriénnes, no. 21, 1967.

Nicolas-Monfouga, Jacqueline. *Ambivalence et culte de possession. Contribution à l'étude du Bori hausa*. Paris: Anthropos, 1972.

Norris, H. T. *Sufi Mystics of the Niger Desert*. Oxford: Clarendon Press, 1990.

Olodo, Andre K. "On the Geographical Fringe of Islam: The Republic of Niger." *Impact of Science on Society* 26, no. 3 (1976).

Onwuejeogwu, Michael. "The Cult of the Bori Spirits Among the Hausa." In Mary Douglas and Phyllis M. Kalberry (eds.), *Man in Africa*. London: Tavistock, 1969, pp. 279–305.

Palmer, H. R. "Bori Among the Hausa." *Man* 14 (1914):113–17.

Pidoux, C. K. "Aspects psychiatriques de la possession chez les Songhay et les Djerma." Niamey Archives, [1965?].

———. "Les rites de possession en pays Zarma (Niger)." *Comtes Rendus des Séances de L'Institut Français d'Anthropologie* 8 (1954).

"Les pieds sur terre." *Niger* (Niamey), no. 7 (July 1969):24–33.

Pilaszewicz, A. "The Craft of Hausa Oral Praise-Poets." *Artes Populaires* 1, (1983):269–76.

"Les plus jeunes Eglises d'Afrique." *Missi* (Lyons), no. 1 (1972):4–27.

Quechon, M. "Réflexions sur certains aspects du syncrétisme dans l' Islam ouest-africain." *Cahiers d'Etudes Africaines* 11, no. 2 (1971): 206–30.

Rasmussen, Susan Jane. "Accounting for Belief: Causation, Misfortune and Evil in Tuareg Systems of Thought." *Man* 24, no. 1 (1989): 124–44.

———. "Gender and Curing in Ritual and Symbol: Women, Spirit Possession, and Aging Among the Kel Ewey Tuareg (Niger)." Ph.D. diss., Indiana University, 1986.

Raulin, H. "Un aspect historique des rapports de l'Islam et de l'animisme au Niger." *Journal de la Société des Africanistes* 32, no. 2 (1962): 249–74.

Reuke, Ludger. *Die Maguzawa in Nordnigeria*. Bielefeld, 1969.

Rouch, Jean. "Aperçu sur l'animisme sonray." *Notes Africaines,* no. 20 (1943):4–8.

———. *Un chanson de Faran Maka (Niger): La religion et la magie Songhay*. Niger: IRSH, 1983.

———. "Culte des Génies chez les Sonray." *Journal de la Société des Africanistes* 15 (1945):13–32.

———. *La religion et la magie songhay*. Paris: Presses Universitaires de France, 1960.

———. *La religion et la magie songhay*. Brussels: Editions de l'Université de Bruxelles, 1989.

Schmoll, Pamela G. "Black Stomachs, Beautiful Stones: Soul-Eating Among Hausa in Niger." In Jean Comaroff and John Comaroff (eds.), *Modernity and Its Discontents*. Chicago: University of Chicago Press, 1993, pp. 193–220.

Spittler, G. *Herrschaft über Bauern: Staatliche Herrschaft und Islamisch-urbane Kultur in Gobir*. Frankfurt, 1978.

Stoller, Paul. *Embodying Colonial Memories: Spirit Possession, Power and the Hauka in West Africa*. New York: Routledge, 1995.

———. *Fusion of the Worlds: An Ethnography of Possession Among the Songhay of Niger*. Chicago: University of Chicago Press, 1989.

———, and C. Oldes. *In Sorcery's Shadow: A Memoir of Apprenticeship Among the Songhay of Niger*. Chicago: University of Chicago Press, 1987.

Tcheho, I. C. "Gros plan de Ide Oumarou. *Ethiopiques* 2, no. 4 (1984): 56–71.

Tremearne, A. J. N. *The Ban of the Bori Demons and Demon Dancing in West and North Africa*. London: Heath, Cranston and Duseley, 1914.

———. "Bori Beliefs and Ceremonies." *Journal of the Anthropological Institute* 17 (1915):23–68.

———. *Hausa Superstitions and Customs*. London: John Bale, 1913.

Triaud, Jean-Louis. "L'Islam et l'Etat au République du Niger." *Revue Française d'Etudes Politiques Africaines,* no. 192/93 (Dec. 1981–Jan. 1982):9–26; no. 194/95 (Jan.–Feb. 1982):35–48.

———. "Université Islamique du Niger." *Islam et Société au Sud du Sahara,* no. 2, (1988):157–65.

Trimingham, J. S. A. *A History of Islam in West Africa*. Oxford: Clarendon Press, 1962.

———. *Islam in West Africa*. Oxford: Clarendon Press, 1959.

———. "Phases of Islam's Expansion and Islamic Culture Zones in Africa." In I. M. Lewis (ed.), *Islam in Tropical Africa*. London: Oxford University Press, 1966, pp. 127–43.

Vidal, Laurent. *Rituel de possession dans le Sahel*. Paris: Harmattan, 1990.

Weekes, Richard V. (ed.). *Muslim Peoples: A World Ethnographic Survey*. Westport, Conn.: Greenwood Press, 1984.

Zoghby, Samir M. *Islam in Subsaharan Africa: A Partially Annotated Guide*. Washington, D.C.: Library of Congress, 1978.

Literature

Abou Bekrin, Oufa Ould. "El'Omda, poème sur la médicine maure." *Bulletin d'IFAN* 5 (1943):28–66.

Aghali, Zakari, and Jeannine Drouin. *Traditions Touaregues nigeriénnes. Ameroloqis, héros civilisateur pre-islamique, et Aligurran, archetype social*. Paris: Hartmattan, 1979.

Albaka, Moussa, and Dominque Casajus. "Trois poèms touaregs de la région d'Agadez." *Awal: Cahiers d'Etudes Berbères* 4 (1988): 145–63.

Arnott, D. W. "Literature in Fula." In B. W. Andzejewski et al. (eds.), *Literature in African Languages: Theoretical Issues and Sample Surveys*. Cambridge: Cambridge University Press, 1985, pp. 72–96.

Bebnone, Palou. "Kaltouma." *L'Avant Scène,* no. 327 (1965):33–39.

Beik, Janet. "Hausa Theatre in Niger." Ph.D. diss., University of Wisconsin, 1984. Reprint. New York: Garland, 1985.

———. "National Development as a Theme in Current Hausa Drama in

———. "Plays Without Playwrights: Community Creation of Contemporary Hausa Theatre in Niger." In Eileen Julien et al. (eds.), *African Literature in Its Social and Political Dimensions*. Washington, D.C.: Three Continents, 1986, pp. 23–31.

———. "National Development as a Theme in Current Hausa Drama in Niger." *Research in African Literature* 15, no. 1 (Spring 1984):1–24.

Bernus, E., and E. Agg-Albostan ag-Sidiyan. "L'Amour en vert? Poème Touareg." *Journal des Africanistes* 57, no. 1/2 (1987):109–15.

Bisilliat, Jeanne, and Diouldé Laya. *Les zamu ou poèmes sur les noms*. Niamey: CNRS, 1972.

Brandt, Henri. *Nomades du Soleil*. Lausanne: Editions Clairefontaine, 1956.

Brench, A. C. *The Novelist's Inheritance in French Africa: Writers from Senegal to Cameroon*. London: Oxford University Press, 1967.

Calame-Griaule, Geneviève. "Peau d'Anesse." *Cahiers d'Etudes Africaines* 19, no. 3 (1979):501–16.

Casajus, Dominique. "The Brother, the Djinn and the Passing of Time." *Research in African Literatures* 15, no. 2 (1984):217–37.

———. *Peau d'âne et autres contes touaregs*. Paris: Harmattan, 1985.

Charbou, Dan-Inna. "La théâtralité en Pays Hawsa." M.A. thesis, University of Abidjan, 1979.

Chechari, Amar. *Réception de la littérature africaine d'expression française jusqu'en 1970*. Paris: Editions Silex, 1982.

Choupaut, Yves-Marie. "Boubou Hama, dans son roman 'Kotia Nima' réconcilie les hommes de tous les pays avec leur enfance." *France Eurafrique*, no. 222 (Dec. 1970):36–38.

Clair, Andrée, and Boubou Hama. *Founya le vaurien*. Paris: Editions G. P., 1975.

———. *Kangué Izé*. Paris: La Farandole, 1974.

———. *La Savane Enchantée*. Paris: La Farandole, 1972.

"Un conte 'veritable' du Niger." *Afrique* (Sept. 1962):4–5.

Coppe, Claudie, and Adamou Garba. *Contes du Niger*. Paris: Nathan Afrique, 1984.

Dandobi, Mahamane. "L'Aventure d'une chèvre; pièce satirique en 4 tableaux." *Traits d'Union* (Dakar), no. 9 (July–Sept. 1955):76–83.

———. *Kabrin Kabra. Paris,* 1958.

Dann-Inna, C., and J. D. Pennel. *Bibliographie de la littérature nigérienne*. Niamey: Centre Culturel Franco-Nigérien, 1988.

Desenclos, A., A. Clair, and H. Coltrane. "Contes du Niger." *Niger* (Niamey), no. 10 (May 1970):20–62.

"Deux contes de l'Areoua." *Niger* (Niamey), no. 8 (Nov. 1969):60–70.

De Zeltner, Franz. *Contes du Sénégal et du Niger*. Paris: Leroux, 1913.

Diado, Amadou. *Maimou, ou le drame de l'amour*. Niamey: Editions du Niger, 1972.

Douze nouvelles du Niger. Niamey: Centre Culturel Franco-Nigérienne, 1988.

Ducroz, J. M. , and M. C. Charles. "Recherche sur la prosodie soney." *Etudes Linguistiques* (Niamey) 1, no. 1 (1979):50–77.

Ferrand, Gérard. *Anthologie de la poésie nigérienne*. Paris: Centre International de la Pensée et des Arts Français, 1970.

Foucauld, Charles Eugene. *Poésies touaregues*. Paris: Leroux, 1930.

———, and A. de C. Motylinski. *Textes touareg en prose*. Algiers: J. Carbonel, 1922.

Glew, Robert S., and Chaibou Bablé (eds.). *Hausa Folktales from Niger*. Athens: Ohio University Press, 1993.

Grandadam, Sabine, et al. *Neuf nouvelles du Niger*. Niamey: Centre Culturel Franco-Nigérienne, 1983.

Hama, Boubou. *L'Aventure extraordinaire de Bi Kado, fils de noir*. Paris: Présence Africaine, 1971.

———. *Bagouma et Tiegouma*. Paris: Présence Africaine, 1975.

———. *Cet "autre" de l'homme*. Paris: Présence Africaine, 1972.

———. *Contes et légendes du Niger*. 6 vols. Paris: Présence Africaine, 1972–76.

———. *Izegani: L'enfant vert*. Niamey: Centre Culturel Franco-Nigérien, 1990.

———, and Andrée Clair. *Le Baobab merveilleux*. Paris: La Farandole, 1971.

Hassane, Diallo Amadou. *A l'ombre des anciens*. Niamey: Imprimerie Nationale du Niger, 1980.

———. *Moisson de ma jeunesse*. Niamey: Imprimerie National du Niger, 1981.

Hiskett, Mervyn. *A History of Hausa Islamic Verse*. London: School of Oriental and African Studies, 1975.

Issa, Ibrahim. *Grandes eaux noires*. Paris: Les Editions du Scorpion, 1959.

———. *La vie et ses facéties: Poèmes*. Niamey: Imprimerie Nationale du Niger,1974.

"Littérature Nigérienne." Special Issue of *Notre Librairie* (Paris) (1991).

Lorelle, Yves. "Littératures pour l'oreille. (2) Des paroles qui montent au coeur." *France Eurafrique*, no. 212 (Dec. 1969).

Maiga, Boubou Idrissa. *Poésies nigériennes, enfant du Grand et Beau Niger*. Paris: ABC, ___.

Maliki, Angelo. "Kawrital: Texte peul." *Bulletin des Etudes Africaines de l'INALCO* (Paris) 2, no. 4 (1982):101–18.

Malleval, Felix, et al. *Dix nouvelles du Niger*. Niamey: Centre Culturel Franco-Nigérien, 1980.

Mamani, Abdoulaye. *Poèmérides*. Paris: Oswald, 1972.

———. *Sarraounia*. Paris: Harmattan, 1980.

Mariko, Keleteguil. *Sur les rives du fleuve Niger: Contes sahéliens*. Paris: Karthala, 1984.

Mohamadou, Halilou Sabbo. *Abboki, ou l'appel de la côte*. Dakar: Nouvelles Editions Africaines, 1978.

Mounkaila, Fatimata. *Le mythe et l'histoire dans la geste de Zabarkane*. Niamey: CELHTO, 1989.

Muzi, Jean. *Contes des rives du Niger*. Paris: Flammarion, 1986.

Nicolas, Françis. "Folklore twareg: Poésies et chansons de l'Azawarh." *Bulletin d'IFAN* 6. nos. 1–4 (1944):1–459.

———. "Poèmes twaregs." *En Terre d'Islam,* no. 4 (1941):268–76; no. 1 (1942):44–52.

———. "Dictons, proverbes et fables de la 'tamajeq' des Iulemmeden de l'Est." *Anthropos* (1946–49):41–44.

"Niger." In Alain Rouch and Gérard Clavreuil, *Littératures nationales d'écritures française*. Paris: Bandas, 1986.

"Niger." In E. Locha Mateso, *Anthologie de la poésie d'Afrique noire d'expression française*. Paris: Hatier, 1987, pp. 138–46.

Oumarou, Ide. *Gros Plan*. Paris: Nouvelles Editions Africaines, 1978.

———. *Le Représentant*. Abidjan: Nouvelles Editions Africaines, 1984.

Ousmane, Amadou. *15 Ans, ça suffit*. Niamey: Imprimerie Nationale du Niger, 1979.

Outman, Mahamat. *Les Sahels*. Paris: Oswald, 1972.

Paraison, Moustapha Richard. *Une femme qui rêve*. Paris: La Pensée Universelle, 1991.

Penel, J. D., and A. Mailele. *Littérature Nigérienne. Rencontre: Keletiqui Mariko, Mamani Abdoualye, Ide Oumarou, Yenzi Dogo, Hawad.* Niamey: Centre Culturel Franco-Nigérien, 1990.

Petit Soeurs de Jesus. *Contes Touaregues de l'Aïr*. Paris: Société d'Etudes Linguistiques et Anthropologiques de France, 1974.

Poèmes nigériennes, diffusés au cours de la Quinzaine de littérature Africaine au Centre Culturel Franco-Nigérien. Niamey, 1975.

"Poésie Nigérienne." *Niger* (Niamey), no. 11 (1970):9–103.

Prost, A. "Légendes songhay." *Bulletin d'IFAN* 18, no. 1/2 (Jan.–Apr. 1956):188–201.

Pucheu, Jacques. *Contes Haoussa du Niger*. Paris: Karthala, 1982.

"Recueil de contes populaires dans la région de Filingué." *Mu Kaara Sani* (Niamey), no. 2 (n.d.):20–33.

Rodd, Peter M. Rennell. "Translation of Tuareg Poems." *Bulletin of the School of Oriental and African Studies* 5, no. 1 (1928):109–12.

Salifou, André. *Tanimoune*. Paris: Présence Africaine, 1973.

Sauty, Louis. *Le Ténéré*. Paris: René Juliard, 1945.

Say, Bania Mahmadou. *Algaita, trente et un poèmes du Niger*. Niamey: Imprimerie Nationale du Niger, 1980.

———. *Le Voyage d'Hamado*. Abidjan: Nouvelles Editions Africaines, 1981.

Sénones, Marion. "Fables Maures." *Notes Africaines,* no. 83 (July 1959): 85–89.

Seydou, Christiane. "Aspects de la littérature Peul." In Mahdi Adamu and A. H. Kirk-Greene (eds.), *Pastoralists of the African Savanna*. Manchester: Manchester University Press, 1986, pp. 101–12.

———. *Contes et Fables des Veillées*. Paris: Nubia, 1976.

———. "Une légende peule du Niger occidental." *Cahiers des Religions Africaines* (Kinshasa) 6, no. 12 (July 1972):215–33.

———. *Silamaka et Poulori, récit épique peul.* Paris: Armand Colin, 1972.

———. "Panorama de la littérature peule." *Bulletin d'IFAN* 35, no. 1 (Jan. 1973):176–218.

Stephens, Connie Lee. "Relationship of Social Symbols and Narrative Metaphor." Ph.D. diss., University of Wisconsin, 1981.

Souleymane, Yazidou, and Bernard Caron (eds.). *Contes haoussa.* Paris: CILF, 1985.

Tchoumba-Ngouankeu, I. *Autour du Lac Tchad.* Yaoundé: Editions CLE, 1969.

Tersis, Nicole. *La Mare de la Verité, contes et musique zerma.* Yaoundé: Editions CLE, 1977.

———. *En Suivant le calebassier.* Paris: CILF, 1979.

Tilho, J., and M. A. Landeroin. *Grammaire et contes Haoussa.* Paris: Imprimerie Nationale, 1909.

Watta, Oumarou. "The Human Thesis: A Quest for Meaning in African Epic." Ph.D. diss., State University of New York/Buffalo, 1985.

Zoume, Boube. *Les souffles du coeur.* Yaoundé: Editions CLE, 1977.

Linguistics

Abdoulaye, Mahamane L. "Derived Direct Objects in Hausa." *Journal of West African Languages* 21, no. 1 (1991):75–90.

Abraham, Roy C. *Dictionary of the Hausa Language.* London, 1963.

Adam, Yacoudima. *Lexique Kanuri.* Niamey: INDRAP, 1982.

Aghali-Zakara, Mohamed. "Essai de psycholinguistique touaregue." *Bulletin des Etudes Africaines de l'INALCO* (Paris) 6, no. 12 (1986): 5–96.

———. "Enseignement des langues africaines par la télévision: L'expérience nigérienne." *Bulletin des Etudes Africaines de l'INALCO* (Paris) 3, no. 5 (1983):3–13.

———. "L'interaction de systèmes linguistiques et apprentissage d'une langue: Cas du français et du berbère." *Bulletin des Etudes Africaines de l'INALCO* (Paris) 2, no. 3 (1982):13–32.

Alawjely, G. ag. *Awgele temajeq-tefrensist.* Copenhagen: Akademisk Forlag, 1980.

Ardant du Picq, Charles Pierre. *La Langue songhay, dialecte dyerma: Grammaire et lexique français-dyerma et dyerma-français.* Paris: Larose, 1933.

Arnott, D. W. "Fula Language Studies: Present Position and Future Prospects." In Mahdi Adamu and A. H. M. Kirk-Greene (eds.), *Pastoralists of the West African Savanna.* Manchester: Manchester University Press, 1986, pp. 87–100.

———. "Some Features of the Nominal Class System of Fula in Nigeria, Dahomey and Niger." *Afrika und Übersee* 43, no. 4 (Mar. 1960):241–78.

Badejo, B. R. "On the Functional Load of Tone in Kanuri." In M. Lionel Bender (ed.), *Proceedings of the Fourth Nilo-Saharan Conference, 1989*. Hamburg: Buske, 1991.

Bargery, George P. *A Hausa-English and English-Hausa Vocabulary*. London: Oxford University Press, 1951.

Barth, Heinrich. "Vocabulary of the Language of Agadiz." *Journal of the Royal Geographical Society* 21 (1851):169–91.

Basset, André. "Parlers touaregs du Soudan et du Niger." *Bulletin du Comité d'Etudes Historiques et Scientifiques de l'AOF* 18, no. 2/3 (1935):336–52.

Baudin, André, and Waziri Amadou. "Les langues nationales au secours français." *Diagonales* (Apr. 1990).

Bender, M. Lionel (ed.). *Topics in Nilo-Saharan Linguistics*. Hamburg: Buske, 1989.

Bernus, Edmond. "Vocabulaire géographique se référent au corps humain ou animal." *Bulletin des Etudes Africaines de l'INALCO* (Paris) 7, no. 13/14 (1987):173–85.

Bohm, Gerhard. *Die Sprache der Ful: grammatikgeschichtliche Grundlagen und Entwicklung*. Vienna: AFRO-Pub, 1989.

Bulakarima, Umara. "Feature Variation Between Manga and the Central Dialect of Kanuri." *Frankfurter Afrikanische Blätter* 3 (1991):68–77.

Caron, Bernard. "Causatif et extension verbale en haoussa de l'Ader." *Bulletin des Etudes Africaines de l'INALCO* (Paris) 3, no. 5 (1983): 21–41.

———. "Classes verbales et extensions en haoussa de l'Ader." In H. Jungraithmayr and H. Tourneux (eds.), *Etudes Tchadiques*. Paris: Paul Geuthner, 1987, pp. 17–23.

———. *Le haoussa de l'Ader*. Berlin: Reimer, 1991.

———. "Quelques perspectives sur le causatif haoussa fournies par le dialecte de l'Ader." In H. Jungraithmayr and H. Tourneux (eds.), *Etudes Tchadiques*. Paris: Paul Geuthner, 1987, pp. 49–63.

———. "The Verbal System of Ader Hausa." In Zygmunt Frajzyngier (ed.), *Current Progress in Chadic Linguistics*. Philadelphia: Benjamins, 1989, pp. 131–69.

Casajus, Dominique. "Sur l'argot des forgerons touaregs." *Awal: Cahiers d'Etudes Berbères* 5 (1989):124–36.

Cew Sonray. Niamey. Centre Régional de Documentation pour la Tradition Orale, 1970.

Cortade, Jean Marie, and Mouloud Mammeri. *Lexique Français-Touareg dialecte de l'Ahaggar*. Paris: Arts et Métiers, 1967.

———. *Inititation à la langue des Touaregs de l'Aïr*. Agadez: Fraternité Charles de Foucauld, 1968.

Cowan, J. Ronayne, and Russell G. Schuh. *Spoken Hausa*. Ithaca, N.Y.: Spoken Language Service, 1976.

Cyffer, Norbert, and John Hutchinson. *A Dictionary of the Kanuri Language*. Dordrecht, Neth.: Foris Publications, 1990.

Dauzats, André. *Lexique français-peul et peul-français*. Albi, Fr.: Imprimerie Albigeoise, 1952.

De Wolf, P. P. "Further Verbal Extension in Nonaare Fulani." *Afrika und Übersee* 70, no. 1 (1987):61–72.

———. "Verbal extensions in Nonaare Fulani." *Afrika und Übersee* 69, no. 1 (1986):45–60.

Drouin, Jeannine. "A boire et à manger: Hypothèses morpho-sémantiques autour de *imi,* 'bouche' en berbère." *Bulletin des Etudes Africaines de l'INALCO* (Paris) 2, no. 3 (1982):49–56.

———. "Chroniques en touareg dans la presse hebdomadaire nigérienne." *Bulletin des Etudes Africaines de l'INALCO* (Paris) 4, no. 8 (1984):29–40.

———. "Contribution à la toponymie touaregue." *Bulletin des Etudes Africaines de l'INALCO* (Paris) 3, no. 3 (1983):65–83.

———. "De quelques conceptions esthétiques de la parole dans la société touaregue." *Journal des Africanistes* 57, no. 1/2 (1987):77–96.

———. "Inventaire d'une collection de néologismes touaregs liés à l'edition." *Comptes Rendus du Groupe Linguistiques d'Etudes Chamito-Sémitique* (Paris) 24–28 (1988):451–65.

———. "Nouveaux éléments de socio-linguistique touaregue: Un parler méridional nigérien: Le *tameseghalt*." *Comptes Rendus du Groupe Linguistiques d'Etudes Chamito-Sémitique* (Paris) 24–28 (1988): 507–20.

———. "Occurences colorées: 'Noir' et 'blanc' dans la poésie touaregue." *Littérature Orale Arabo-Berbère* 19/20 (1988/89):1–27.

———. "Le parole et le sens, recherche sur quelques contes lexicales chez les Kel Nan." *Littérature Orale Arabo-Berbère,* no. 8 (1977): 56–80.

Ducroz, J. M., and M. C. Charles. *Lexique touareg nigérienne*. Paris: Harmattan, 1992.

———. *Lexique Soney (Songay) Français*. Paris: Harmattan, 1978.

———. "Recherche sur la prosodie soney." *Etudes Linguistiques* (Niamey) 1, no. 1 (1979):50–77.

Dupuis, Yakouba. *Essai de méthode pratique pour l'étude de la langue songoi ou songai*. Paris: Leroux, 1917.

Eguchi, P. K. *An English-Fulfulde Dictionary*. Tokyo: Institute for the Study of Languages and Culture of Asia and Africa, 1986.

Foucauld, Charles Eugene de. *Dictionnaire abrégé touareg-français (dialecte Ahaggar)*. 2 vols. Algiers: Jourdan, 1918.
———. *Dictionnaire touareg-Français*. 4 vols. Paris: Imprimerie Nationale, 1951–52.
Furniss, Graham, and Philip J. Jaggar (eds.). *Studies in Hausa Language and Linguistics*. London: Kegan Paul, 1988.
Gouffe, Claude. "Deux notes grammaticales sur le parler haoussa de Dogondoutchi (République du Niger)." *Afrika und Übersee* 52, no. 1 (Dec. 1968):1–14.
———. "Observations sur le degré causatif dans un parler hausa du Niger: Maradi, Zinder, Tahoua." *Journal of African Languages* 1, no. 2 (1962).
———. "Problèmes de toponymie haoussa: Les noms de villages de la région de Maradi." *Revue Internationale Onomastique* (Paris) 19, no. 2 (June 1967):95–127.
Greenberg, Joseph H. "Arabic Loanwords in Hausa." *Word* (New York) 3, no. 1/2 (1947):86–97.
Guegan, Dominique. "Comparaison d'ensembles—Situation en Haoussa." *Bulletin des Etudes Africaines de l'INALCO* (Paris) 4, no. 8 (1984): 41–59.
Hacquard, A., and Auguste-Victor Dupuis. *Manuel de la langue Songhay parlée de Tombouctou à Say*. Paris: Maisonneuve, 1897.
Homburger, Lilias. *Les préfixes nominaux dans les parlers peul, haoussa et bantous*. Paris: Institut d'Ethnologie, 1929.
Howeidy, A. *Concise Hausa Grammar*. Oxford: Ronald G. Wheatley, 1953.
Hugit, P. *Cours Elémentaire de Hausa*. Paris: Peyronnet, 1953.
Hutchinson, John P. *A Reference Grammar of the Kanuri Language*. Madison: University of Wisconsin African Studies Program, 1981.
Initiation à la langue des Touaregs de l'Aïr. Agadez: Fraternité Charles de Foucauld, 1968.
Jarrett, Kevin A. "Dialectes et alphabétisation dans les écoles Kanuri du Niger." *Journal of West African Languages* 18, no. 2 (Nov. 1988): 105–24.
Jouannet, François. "Catégories de phonèmes socialiques sur une base distributionnelle." *Etudes Linguistiques* 1, no. 1 (1979):105–29.
———. "Prosodie du Kanembou des Ngaldoukon." *Etudes Linguistiques* 1, no. 2 (1979):71–94.
Kaufmann, Paul. *Tuareg-Touareg: ihre sprache in Texten und Dialogen*. Lohn, Switz.: P. Kaufmann, 1990.
Keita, Michel. "Evaulation des impacts et l'évolution du Centre de Formation des Cadres de l'Alphabétisation (C.F.C.A.)." *Mu Kaara Sani* 4, no. 1/2 (1985):1–37.
Kirk-Green, A. H. M., and Yahaya Aliyu. *A Modern Hausa Reader*. London: London University Press, 1966.

Kraft, Charles H. *Hausa*. London: English Universities, 1973.

———. *A Hausa Reader*. Berkeley: University of California Press, 1974.

———. *A Study of Hausa Syntax*. 3 vols. Hartford, Conn.: Seminary Foundation, 1963.

———, and Aboubakar Salisu. *An Introduction to Spoken Hausa*. East Lansing: Michigan State University, 1965.

———, and M. C. Kraft. *Spoken Hausa*. __:__, 1973.

Lacroix, P. F. *"Emghedesie, a Songhay language of Agadez," à travers les documents de Barth*. Paris: CNRS, 1975.

———. "Les langues du Niger." *Synthèses Nigériennes,* no. 1 (Feb. 1968):5–16.

Landeroin, M., and J. Tilho. *Dictionnaire Haoussa*. 2 vols. Paris: Larose, 1910.

———. *Grammaire et contes haoussas*. Paris: Larose, 1909.

Lavergne de Tressan, M. de. *Inventaire linguistique de l'AOF et du Togo*. Dakar: IFAN, 1953.

LeCoeur, Charles. *Dictionnaire Ethnographique Teda procédé d'un lexique français-teda*. Paris: Larose, 1950.

———, and M. LeCoeur. *Grammaire et textes teda-daza*. Dakar: IFAN, 1956.

Luguil, Alphonse. "La corrélation de concomitance en touareg." *Bulletin des Etudes Africaines de l'INALCO* (Paris) 3, no. 6 (1983):77–123.

———. "La phonologie au secours de la grammaire en touareg." *Bulletin de la Société de Linguistique de Paris* 77, no. 1 (1982):341–63.

Lukas, J. *Die Sprache der Tubu in der zentralen Sahara*. Berlin, 1953.

McIntyre, Joseph, and Hilke Meyer-Bahlburg. *Hausa in the Media: A Lexical Guide: Hausa-English-German, English-Hausa, German-Hausa*. Hamburg: Helmut Buske Verlag, 1991.

Maliki, Angelo. "Structures et relations sociales des Wodaabe du Niger." *Bulletin des Etudes Africaines de l'INALCO* (Paris) 2, no. 3 (1982): 115–22.

Manessy, G. "Le Français d'Afrique Noire." *Langue Française,* no. 37 (Feb. 1978):91–105.

Marie, E. *Vocabulaire français-djerma et djerma-français*. 2 vols. Paris: Larose, 1914.

Mohamed, Ghabdouane, and K. G. Prasse. *Poèmes touaregues d'Ayr*. Copenhagen: Museum Tusculman Press, 1990.

Monteil, Charles. "La langue des Bozo: Population des pêcheurs du Niger." *Bulletin du Comité d'Etudes Historiques et Scientifiques de l'AOF* 15, no. 2/3 (Apr.–Sept. 1932):261–399.

Newman, Roxana Ma. *An English-Hausa Dictionary*. New Haven: Yale University Press, 1990.

Nicolai, Robert. "Développement et activités du Département de Linguistique de l'Université de Niamey." *Bulletin de l'AELTA* 4 (Mar. 1981)37–39.

———. *Les Dialectes du Songhay*. Paris: SELAF, 1981.

———. "Les apparentements génétiques du Songhay." In M. Lionel Bender (ed.), *Proceedings of the Fourth Nilo-Saharan Conference, 1989*. Hamburg: Buske, 1991.

———. "Réinterprétation et restructuration en zarma-songhay." *Bulletin d'IFAN* 39, no. 2 (Apr. 1977):432–55.

———. "Le Songhay septentrional: Etudes phonématiques." *Bulletin d'IFAN* 41, no. 3 (July 1979):539–67; 41, no. 4 (Oct. 1979):829–66.

Nicolas, Francis. "Vocabulaires ethnographiques de la Tamajeq des Iullemmeden de l'est." *Anthropos* 52, no. 1/2 (1957):49–64; 52, no. 3/4 (1957):564–80.

Picq, Ardant du. *La langue songhay, dialecte dyerma*. Paris: Larose, 1933.

Pietri, C. *Le Français au Niger*. Paris: Hachette, 1885.

Pilzczikowa, N. "Contribution à l'étude des rapports entre le Haousa et les autres langues du groupe nigéro-tchadien." *Rocznik Orientalistyczny* (Warsaw) 22, no. 2 (1958):76–99.

Prasse, Karl G. "Les conjugations iv et xiii en touareg du Niger." *Etudes Linguistiques* 2, no. 2 (1980):17–28.

———. "Les consonnes palatalisées en Touareg de l'Aïr." *Littérature Orale Arabo-Berbère* 18 (1987):195–200.

Prasse, K. G. *Manuel de Grammaire Touaregue (Tahaggart),* 3 vols. Copenhagen: University of Copenhagen Press, 1972–73.

Prestat, G. *Cours Elémentaire du fulfulbé*. Paris: Peyronnet, 1953.

Prost, André. *La langue songhay et ses dialectes*. Dakar: IFAN, 1956.

———. "Mots mossi empruntés au Songhay." *Bulletin d'IFAN* 28, no. 1/2 (1966):470–75.

———. "Notes sur les Songhay." *Bulletin d'IFAN* 16 (1954):167–213.

Robinson, C. H. *Dictionary of the Hausa Language*. London: Gregg, n.d.

Smirnova, M. A. *The Hausa Language*. London: Routledge and Kegan Paul, 1982.

Sow, Alfa Ibrahim. *Dictionnaire élémentaire fulfulde-français-English Elementary Dictionary*. Niamey: CRDTO, 1971.

Surugue, B. "Schèmes tonals parlés et schèmes tonals chantés." In L. Bouquiaux (ed.), *Théories et méthodes en linguistiques africain*. Paris: Société d'Etudes Linguistiques et Anthropologiques de France, 1976, pp. 103–11.

Taylor, Frank W. *A Fulani-English Phrase Book*. Oxford: Clarendon Press, 1926.

———. *A Fulani-English Dictionary*. Oxford: Clarendon Press, 1932.

———. *Practical Hausa Grammar*. Oxford: Clarendon Press, 1948.

Tersis, Nicole. *Le Dendi: Phonologie, lexique dendi-français*. Paris: Bulletin de SELAF, 1972.

———. "Fréquence des principales formes verbales en Zerma." In L. Bouquiaux (ed.), *Théories et méthodes en linguistiques africain*. France: Société d'Etudes Linguistiques et Anthropologiques de France, 1976, pp. 103–11.

———. *Grammaire Zarma*. Paris: SELAF, 1973.

———. *Le Parler Dendi*. Paris: SELAF, 1968.

———. *Phonologie Zarma*. Paris: SELAF, 1973.

———. *Le Zarma. Etude du parler Djerma de Dosso*. Paris: SELAF, 1972.

Tersis-Surugue, Nicole. *Economie d'un système, unités et relations syntaxiques en Zarma*. Paris: Agence de Coopération Culturelle et Technique, 1981.

Tran, Hong Cam. "Approche socio-linguistique de l'emprunt français en hausa." *Etudes Linguistiques* 2, no. 1 (1980):13–51.

———. "Contribution à l'étude phonétique des nigerismes." *Bulletin de l'AELTA* 2, (Mar. 1981):40–49.

Tuller, Laurice. "Vowel Neutralization in Damagaram Hausa." *Studies in African Linguistics* (Dec. 1981):136–40.

Villiers, A. "Noms vernaculaires de quelques animaux de l'Aïr." *Notes Africaines,* no. 40 (Oct. 1948):23–25.

Waali, Naybi, and Muhammadi Habali. *Kaara Karaatuu*. Niamey: Centre Régional de Documentation pour la Tradition Orale, 1971.

Westermann, Diedrich H. "Ein Beitrag zur Kenntnis des Zarma-Songai am Niger." *Zeitschrift Eingeborenen Sprachen* 11, no. 3 (1921): 188–220.

———, and Margaret Bryan. *The Languages of Africa*. New York: Oxford University Press, 1952.

White, Mary. "Informant Definition in Songhay: Types and Techniques." *Etudes Linguistiques* (Niamey) 2, no. 1 (1980):53–92.

Williamson, Kay. "Songhai Word List (Gao District)." *Research Notes* (Ibadan [Nigeria] University) no. 3 (Dec. 1967):1–34.

Wolff, Ekkehard. "On Tubu Tones." In M. Lionel Bender (ed.), *Proceedings of the Fourth Nilo-Saharan Conference, 1989*. Hamburg: Buske, 1991.

———. "Nationalsprachenpolitik im Niger." *Zeitschrift für Phonetik* 43, no. 4 (1990):484–91.

———, and Soumana Hassana Alidou. "Desegmentation and Tone in Tubu: The Daza Dialect of Tasker." *Journal of West African Languages* 19, no. 2 (1989):67–73.

Yanco, Jennifer J. "Language Attitudes and Bilingualism in Niamey, Niger." *Africana Journal* 14, no. 1 (1983):1–9.

Zaria, Ahmadu Bello."Issues in Hausa Dialectology." Ph.D. diss., Indiana University, 1982.

Arts

Adepegba, C. O. *Decorative Arts of the Fulani Nomads*. Ibadan: Ibadan University Press, 1986.

Anquetil, Jacques. *Côte d'Ivoire, Sénégal, Haute-Volta, Niger*. Paris: ACCT, 1977.

Arkell, A. J. "Some Tuareg Ornaments and Their Connection with India." *Journal of the Royal Anthropological Institute* 65 (July–Dec. 1935):297–306.

Armes, Roy. "Niger." *International Film Guide* (1984):247–48.

"L'Artisanat Touareg." *Balafon* 22 (1971).

"Aspects de l'art haoussa." *Niger* (Niamey), no. 9 (Jan. 1970):29–81.

Aumont, Jacques, and Sylvie Pierre. "Huit fois deux." *Cahiers de Cinéma,* no. 206 (1968).

Beik, Janet. *Hausa Theatre in Niger: A Contemporary Oral Art*. New York: Garland, 1987.

———. "National Development as a Theme in Current Hausa Drama." *Research in African Literatures* 15, no. 1 (1984):1–24.

Bernard, Mariama, and Yves Bernard. "Le cinéma au Niger." *7e Art,* no. 49 (1984):5–7.

Bovin, Mette. "Ethnic Performance in Rural Niger: An aspect of Ethnic Boundry Maintenance." *Folk* 16/17 (1974/75).

Card, Caroline Elizabeth. "Tuareg Music and Social Identity." Ph.D. diss., Indiana University, 1982.

Carey, Margaret. *Beads and Beadwork of West and Central Africa. Buckinghamshire,* Eng.: Shire Publications, 1991.

Casajus, D. "Crafts and Ceremonies: The Inadam in Tuareg Society." In A. Rao (ed.), *The Other Nomads: Peripatetic Minorities in Cross-Cultural Perspective*. Cologne: Bohlau Verlag, 1987.

Cherqui, Halim. "Inoussa Ouesseini: Les films africains trop influencés par le cinéma européen." *Afrique-Asia,* no. 66 (1974):30–32.

Darbois, Dominique, and V. Vasut. *Afrika Tanzt*. Prague: Artia, 1963.

Debrix, Jean René. "La quinzaine nigérienne de cinéma." *Recherche, Pédagogie et Culture,* no. 17/18 (1975):54–55.

Delisse, Louis François. *Enquête sur l'architecture et la décoration murale à Zinder*. Niamey: OAU-CELTHO, 1986.

Demain, H. M., and J. Lugassy. "L'Artisanat rural en Haute-Volta et au Niger." *Bulletin de Chambre du Commerce du Niger,* no. 3 (1964): 1–7.

Diawara, Issoufou. "Moustapha derrière la caméra." *Niger* (Niamey), no. 2 (Jan. 1968):70–75.

Dieterlen, Germaine, and Ziedonis Ligers. "Contributions à l'étude des bijoux touareg." *Journal de la Société des Africanistes* 42, no. 1 (1972):29–54.

Domian, Sergio. *Architecture Soudanaise*. Paris: Harmattan, 1989.
Dudot, B. "Nouvelles notes sur la croix d'Agadès." *Notes Africaines,* no. 111 (July 1966):100–103.
———. "Une production originale de l'artisanat d'Agadez: Les boîtes en peau non tannée dites 'batta.'" *Notes Africaines,* no. 122 (Apr. 1969):55–57.
Dupuis, Annie, and Nicole Echard. "La poterie traditionnelle hausa de l'Ader." *Journal de la Société des Africanistes* 41, no. 1 (1971):7–34.
Dutot, Bernard. "Fabrication des anneaux de bras chez les Touareg au Niger." *Niger* (Niamey), no. 17 (May 1972):31–38.
Emery, Amir. "Hondo's Sarraounia: A Landmark of African Cinema." *New African* (Apr. 1988):40–42.
———. "Musik und Trance: symbolische Aspekte des Bori Besessenheitskultes der Hausa in Maradi." *Africana Marburgensia* 15, no. 1 (1982):3–24. Also in English translation in *Ethnomusicology* 26, no. 1 (Jan. 1982):49–58.
———, and Habou Magagi. "Data on the Sociology of Hausa Musicians in the Valley of Maradi." *Paideuma* (Frankfurt) 27 (1981):63–110.
Etienne-Nugué, Jocelyne, and Mahamane Saley. *Artisants traditionnels en Afrique Noire: Niger*. Paris: Harmattan, 1987.
Foedermayr, Franz. "The Arabian Influence in the Tuareg Music." *African Music* 4, no. 1 (1966/67):25–37.
France. Ministère de la Coopération. *Etude sur certains artisanats ruraux nigériens: Forge, travail du cuir, poterie*. Paris, 1964.
Gabus, J. *Au Sahara, arts et symboles*. Neuchâtel, Switz.: La Bannière, 1958.
Gaudio, Attilio. "Niamey: Africa in a Museum." *Entente Africaine* (July 1979):52–57.
Gruner, Dorothée. *Die Lehm-Moschee am Niger*. Stuttgart: F. Steiner, 1990.
———. "Islamische Tradition oder autochtones Erbe." *Paideuma* (Frankfurt), no. 35 (1989):99–113.
Haberman, Eike. "West African Mud Architecture." *African Arts* (Nov. 1981):44–45.
Habitat Hausa: Dynamique d'une adaptation culturelle. Dakar: ENDA, 1985.
Haffner, Pierre. "Eine nationale Schule: Niger." *Revue pour le Cinéma Français* 27/28 (Nov. 1989):35–46.
———. "Edgar Ray Sugar Robinson, alias Oumarou Ganda dit: Le conteur." *7e Art,* no. 42 (1982):16–19; no. 43 (1981):16–19.
Heathcote, David. *The Arts of the Hausa*. Chicago: University of Chicago Press, 1977.
Hennebelle, Guy. "Le cinéma nigérien, grand vainquer à Ouagadougou." *Afrique Littérature et Artistique,* no. 22 (1972):98–100.

———. "Un moyen métrage nigérien: 'Synapse' de Mustapha Diop." *Afrique-Asie,* no. 87 (1975):87–88.

———. "Un nouveau cinéaste nigérien: Oumarou Ganda de 'Moi un noir' à Cabascabo." *Afrique Littérature et Artistique,* no. 4 (1969): 70–74.

Ilbo, Ousmane. *Le cinéma au Niger*. Brussels: OCIC, 1993.

Imperato, Pascal James. "Blankets and Covers from the Niger Bend." *African Arts* 12, no. 4 (Aug. 1979):38–43.

"Inadan: Artisans of the Sahara." *National Geographic* (Aug. 1979): 282–98.

Katsanies, Iannis. "La politique du zèbre." *Cahiers du Cinéma,* no. 379 (1986):51–52.

Keita, Brigitte, and Susan B. Aradeon. *Habitat Hausa: Dynamique d'une adaptation culturelle*. Dakar: ENDA, 1985.

Kirtley, Michael, and Aubire Kirtley. "Inandan: Artisans of the Sahara." *National Geographic* 156, no. 2 (Aug. 1976):282–98.

Lemaire, Charles. "Le cinéma au Niger." *7e Arts,* no. 49 (1984):5–10.

Lhote, Henri. "Rondes-bosses et broyeur décoré Tassili." *Objets et Mondes* 13, no. 1 (1973):47–52.

———. "La technique de la poterie à Agadez." In *Contribution à L'Etude de l'Aïr*. Paris: Larose, 1950, pp. 507–12.

———. "Technique des potiers de la région de Tessaoua." *Notes Africaines,* no. 153 (Jan. 1977):12–18.

Ligers, Z. *La Sculpture Nigérienne*. Paris: Librarie des Cinq Continents, 1971.

Lorelle, Yves. "De la 'Grande Caravane' à la 'Cure Salée,' des films sur les Touaregs du Niger." *France Eurafrique* no. 217 (June 1970): 22–23.

Malanda, Ange-Séverin. "L'exile et le lointain: Hommage à Oumarou Ganda." *Présence Africaine,* no. 119 (1981):170–75.

Mercier, Paul, and Jean Rouch. *Chants du Dahomey et du Niger*. Paris: GLM, 1950.

Mester de Parajd, Corinne, and Laszio Mester de Parajd. *Regards sur l'habitat traditionnel au Niger*. Nonette, Fr.: Centre de Réalisations d'Etudes et d'Editions Régionales, 1988.

Milburn, Mark. "The Rape of the Agadez Cross: Problem of Typology Among Modern Metal and Stone Pendants of Northern Niger." *Almogaren,* no. 9/10 (1978/79):136–45.

Moughtin, J. C. *Hausa Architecture*. London: Ethnographica, 1985.

"Le Musée de Niamey." *Europe France Outre-Mer,* no. 503 (Dec. 1971):15.

Nagbou, Mustapha. "J'ai dix fleurs à Tashkent." *7e Art,* no. 45 (1982): 10–14.

Niandou, Harouna. "Le cinéma Nigérien." *Nigerama,* no. 3 (1975):5–12.

Nicolas, F. "Poésies et chansons de l'Azawarh." *Bulletin d'IFAN* 6 (1944):1–463.

———. "Dictons, proverbes et fables de la 'tamajeq' des Iullemmeden de l'Est." *Anthropos,* nos. 41–44 (1946–49).

Nikiprowetzky, Tolia. *Les Instruments de musique au Niger*. Paris: ORSTOM, 1964.

———. *Trois Aspects de la Musique Africaine: Mauritanie, Sénégal, Niger*. Paris: Office de Coopération Radiophonique, 1966.

Nourrit, Chantal, and Bill Pruitt. *Musique traditionnelle de l'Afrique Noire*. Paris: Radio-France Internationale, 1985.

ONERSOL. "Niamey." *Mimar* (Singapore) 13 (1984):66–70.

Ousmane, Amadou. "L'Institut nigérien de céramique ou la naissance d'une autre forme de poterie." *Niger* (Niamey), no. 17 (May 1972): 25–29.

Picton, John, and John Mack. *African Textiles: Looms, Weaving and Design*. London: British Museum, 1979.

Prussin, Labelle. "Fulani-Hausa Architecture." *African Arts* 10, no. 1 (Oct. 1976):8–19.

Rauss, Raymond. "L'Art et le récit: Un pont entre deux cultures: à propos du film de Moustapha Diop." *Peuples Noirs: Peuples Africains,* no. 52 (1986):116–26.

Scheinfeigel, Maxime. "Cabascabo: Un film de Oumarou Ganda." *Avant-Scène-Cinéma,* no. 265 (1981):39–50.

Smith, M. G. "The Social Functions and Meaning of Hausa Praise-Singing." *Africa* 27, no. 1 (Jan. 1957):26–43.

Standifer, James A. "The Tuareg: Their Music and Dances." *Black Perspectives in Music* (Cambria Heights) 16, no. 1 (Spring 1988):45–62.

Stoller, Paul. *The Cinematic Griot: The Ethnography of Jean Rouch*. Chicago: University of Chicago Press, 1992.

———. "Sound in Songhay Cultural Experience." *American Ethnologist* 11, no. 3 (Aug. 1984):559–70.

Surugue, B. *Contribution à l'étude de la musique sacrée Zarma-Songhay*. Niamey: INSH, 1972.

Toucet, P. "Young Nation Builds Unique Open-Air Museum." *UNESCO Courier* (Feb. 5, 1975):32–35.

"Towards an African Cinematography." *Entente Africaine* (July 1979): 60–63.

Traore, Bini. "L'Exil d'Oumarou Ganda." *Peuples Noirs: Peuples Africains* no. 23 (1981):54–93.

Urvoy, Yves François. *L'Art dans le territoire du Niger*. Niamey: IFAN, 1955.

Vallées du Niger. Paris: Editions de la Réunion des Musées Nationaux, 1994.

Van Offelen, Marion, and Beckwith, Carol. *Nomads of Niger*. New York: Abrams, 1983.

Vieyra, Paulin Soumarou. "Hommage à Oumarou Ganda: cinéaste nigérien." *Présence Africaine,* no. 119 (1981):165–69.

"Le Wazzou polygame, un film d'Oumarou Ganda." *Jeune Afrique,* no. 591 (1972):60–61.

"Y a-t-il éclipse nigérien?" *Afrique,* no. 33 (1980):43–44.

Tourism and Travel

Allen, Philip M., and Aaron Segal. "Niger." In *The Traveller's Africa.* New York: Hopkinson and Blake, 1973, pp. 577–92.

Béarn, Pierre. *L'Afrique Vivant.* Paris: Arthème Fayard, 1955.

Bennett, Nicholas. *Zigzag to Timbuktu.* London: John Murray, 1963.

Bernus, Edmond, and Hamidou A. Sihidou. *Atlas du Niger.* Paris: Jeune Afrique, 1980.

Boone, Sylvia Ardyn. "Niger: Niamey." In *West African Travels: A Guide to People and Places.* New York: Random House, 1974, pp. 199–213.

Bourget, Henri. *Fascinant Niger.* Boulogne: Delroisse, 1968.

Boy, A. "Lions des environs du Parc National du 'W,' Niger et Haute-Volta." *Bois et Forêts des Tropiques,* no. 86 (Nov.–Dec. 1962):3–118.

Brydon, David. *Africa Overland: A Route and Planning Guide.* Brentford, Eng.: Roger Lescelles, 1991.

Catrisse, Benoit. "Hôtellerie et tourisme." *Afrique Industrie,* no. 203 (Mar. 1980):42–69.

Deriaz, Didier. *Rivage du Desert.* Paris: Harmattan, 1990.

Diawara, Issoufou. "Le musée national du Niger. Une réalisation qui n'a pas fini d'étonner." *France Eurafrique,* no. 184 (May. 1967).

Eitner, Kurt, and Otto Baedeker. *Afrika: West und Zentral Afrika.* Stuttgart: Ernst Klett Verlag, 1971.

Else, David. *Backpackers Africa: A Guide to West and Central Africa for Walkers and Overland Traverllers.* Chalfont St. Peter, Eng.: Bradt Publications, 1990.

Eyraud, Arlette. *Mali. Niger.* Paris: Hatier, 1979.

Gardi, René. *Cram Cram. Erlebnisse rund um die Air-Berge in der südlichen Sahara.* Bern: Benteli Verlag, 1971.

Guide Afrique UTA. Puteaux, Fr.: UTA, 1986.

Guide du Sahara. Paris: Hachette, 1988.

Guid'Ouest Africain. Paris: Diloutremer, 1972

Hallam, W. K. R. "Driving Around the Chad Basin." *Nigerian Field* 31, no. 3 (July 1966):111–18.

Harrington, R. "Unknown Niger." *Travel* (Nov. 9, 1969):46–49.

Helfritz, Hans. *Schwarze Ritter zwischen Niger und Tschad*. Berlin: Safari Verlag, 1958.

Hudgens, Jim, and Richard Trillo. *West Africa: The Rough Guide*. London: Harrap-Columbus, 1990.

Jarry, Isabelle. *Voyage au Ténéré*. Paris: Plon, 1991.

Klobb, A. *Dernier carnet de route*. Paris: Flammarion, 1929?.

Klotchkoff, A. *Le Niger Aujourd'hui*. Paris: Jeune Afrique, 1984.

Lelong, H. *Le Sahara aux cent visages*. Paris: Alsatia, 1948.

Mali, Niger. Paris: Hatier, 1979.

Naylor, Kim. *Discovery Guide to West Africa: The Niger and Gambia River Route*. London: Michael Haag, 1989.

Niger. Ministère de l'Education Nationale. *Guide du Musée National*. 1976.

"Niger." In *Afrika Handbuch*. Hamburg: Übersee-Verlag, 1967, pp. 277–82.

"Niger." In *Le Moniteur du Tourisme Africaine*. Dakar, 1987+.

"Niger." In *Travel Guide to Western and Central Africa*. Paris: UTA French Airlines, 1971+.

"Niger." In *Afrique Occidentale. Guide Poche-Voyage*. Paris: Marcus, 1984.

"Niger." In Susan Blumenthal, *Bright Continent: Africa on a Shoestring*. New York: Anchor Books, 1974, pp. 154–66.

"Niger." In Geoff Crowther, *Africa on a Shoestring*. Hawthorne, Austral.: Lonely Planet Publications, 1989.

"Niger." In Sylvie Glaser, *Guide de Voyageur en Afrique de l'Ouest*. Paris: Ediafric, 1984.

"Niger." In Alex Newton, *West Africa: A Survival Kit,* 2nd ed. Berkeley, Calif: Lonely Planet, 1992, pp. 317–41.

Niger, Guide Touristique. Paris: Delroisse, 1968.

Noblet, Richard. *Au Mali et au Niger*. Paris: Hachette, 1980.

Otto, Dana. *Niger: A Traveler's Handbook*. Maradi: Maradi Interservice Workshop, 1973.

Plossu, Bernard. *The African Desert*. Tucson: University of Arizona Press, 1987.

Regards sur le Niger. Boulogne: Delroisse, 1970.

Rouch, Jean. *Le Niger en Pirogue*. Paris: Fernand Nathan, 1954?

Sahara et Sahel Nigériens. Paris: Guides Bleux Hachette, 1977.

Say, Bania Mahamdou. *Le Niger et ses merveilles*. Saint-Priest, Fr.: Imprimerie Brunaud, 1989.

Schramm, Josef. *Westafrika*. Munich: Verlag Volk und Heimat, n.d.

Seydou, Issoufou. "Propos sur le Tourisme." *Europe Outre-Mer,* no. 554 (Mar. 1976):51–52.

———. "Le tourisme au Niger: Structures d'accueil, movements

touristiques et données statistiques." *Niger* (Niamey), no. 41 (Nov. 13, 1972):4; no. 42 (Nov. 20, 1972):4.

Toucet, P. "Le Musée du Niger à Niamey et le 'village nigérien.' " *Notes Africaines,* no. 87 (July 1960):100–101.

———. "Les richesses du Musée National du Niger." *Coopération et Développement* 25 (May–June 1969):16–20.

The Traveller's Guide to Africa. Chicago: Rand McNally, 1973.

"Tourism in Africa." *Afro-Asian Economic Review,* no. 148/49 (Jan.–Feb. 1972):7–23.

Wauthier, Magdeleine. *Au Péril des Sables.* Neuchâtel, Switz.: Editions de la Baconnière, 1970.

Sources, Reference Works, and Bibliographies

Africa Research Bulletin, ser. A and B (monthly). Exeter, Eng., 1963+.

Africa South of the Sahara. London: Europa Publications, 1971+.

Africa South of the Sahara: Index to Periodical Literature. Washington, D.C.: Library of Congress, Africa and Middle East Division, 1985.

Afrique. Paris: Jeune Afrique, 1968+.

Année Africaine. Paris: Pedone, 1963+.

Année Politique Africaine. Dakar: Société Africaine d'Edition, 1966+.

Asamani, J. O. *Index Africanus: Catalogue of Articles in Western Languages Published from 1885 to 1965.* Stanford, Calif.: Hoover Institution, 1975.

Baier, S. "Archives in Niger." *History in Africa,* no. 1 (1975):155–58.

Ballard, J. A. "Politics and Government in Former French West and Equatorial Africa: A Critical Bibliography." *Journal of Modern African Studies* 3, no. 4 (1965):589–605.

Bederman, Sanford. *Africa: A Bibliography of Geography and Related Disciplines.* Atlanta: Georgia State University Press, 1974.

Beudot, Françoise. *Eléments de Bibliographie sur la sécheresse au Sahel.* 1977. 2nd ed. Paris: OCDE, 1985.

———. *Eléments de Bibliographie sur les pays du Sahel.* Paris: OCDE, 1990.

Biarnes, Pierre, et al. *L'Economie Africaine.* Dakar: Société Africaine d'Edition, 1970.

"Bibliographie." In *Contribution à l'étude de l'Aïr.* Paris: Larose, 1950, pp. 555–62.

Bibliographie de documents et rapports sur les pays du Sahel (1977–1985). Paris: OCDE, 1989.

Bibliographie de documents du CILSS et le Club du Sahel. Paris: OCDE, 1989.

Bibliographie des Travaux en Langue Française sur l'Afrique au Sud du Sahara. Paris: Centre d'Etudes Africaines, 1982.

Bibliographie ethnographique de l'Afrique sud-saharienne. Tevueren: Musée Royal de l'Afrique Centrale, 1966+.

"Bibliographie sommaire de la République du Niger." *Etudes et Documents,* no. 18 (Apr. 1969).

"Bibliographie Toauregue: Langue, culture et société, 1977–1987." In A. Chaker, (ed.), *Etudes Touaregues*. Aix-en-Provence: CNRS, 1990, pp. 92–192.

Blackhurst, Hector (ed.). *Africa Bibliography*. Manchester: Manchester University Press, 1985–89; Edinburgh: Edinburgh University Press, 1990+.

Blake, David, and Carole Travis. *Periodicals from Africa: A Bibliography and Union List of Periodicals Publishers in Africa*. Boston: G. K. Hall, 1984.

Blaudin de Thé, B. *Essai de Bibliographie du Sahara Français et des régions avoisinantes*. Paris: Arts et Métiers Graphiques, 1960.

Carson, P. *Materials for West African History in French Archives*. London: Athlone Press, 1968.

Catalogue Systématique de la Section Afrique, Bibliothèque du Musée de l'Homme. 2 vols. Paris, 1970.

Centre de Développement de l'OCDE. *Sécheresse au Sahel. Selection d'articles de périodiques à partir de Décembre 1972*. Paris, 1974.

Chronologie Politique Africaine. Paris: Fondation Nationale des Sciences Politiques, 1960–70.

CIDA Bibliographie française sur l'Afrique au sud du Sahara. *CARDAN, Bulletin d'Information et de Liaison, études Africaines,* 1970+.

Conover, H. F. *Official Publications of French West Africa, 1946–1958*. Washington, D.C.: Library of Congress, 1960.

Coulibaly, Siaka. *Eléments de bibliographie sur les pays du Sahel*. Paris: OCDE, 1991.

Deutsche Afrika-Gesellschaft. *Afrikanische Köpfe*. Hamburg, 1971.

Deutsches Institut für Afrika Forschung. *Entwicklungsplanuing und Finanzwirtschaft in Westafrika (Frankophon)—ausgewähite neuere Literatur*. Hamburg, 1973.

Dickie, John, and Alan Rake. *Who's Who in Africa*. London: African Buyer and Trader, 1973.

Dictionary of African Biography. London: Melrose Press, 1971.

Documents du Dépôt officiel d'Archives de Fort-Lamy I (Tchad, Cameroun, Nigeria, Niger). N'Djamena: INTSH, 1968.

Donaint, Pierre. "Bibliographie sommaire de la République du Niger d'après le fichier de G. de Beauchêne." *Etudes et Documents* (Niamey), no. 18 (Apr. 1969).

Duignan, Peter. *Handbook of American Resources for African Studies*. Stanford, Calif.: Hoover Institution, 1967.

Economist Intelligence Unit. *Country Profile: Niger, Burkina Faso.* London: The Unit, 1986+.

———. *Country Report: Togo, Niger, Benin, Burkina Faso.* London: The Unit, 1986+.

Ediafric. *L'Afrique Noire de A à Z.* Paris, 1971.

———. *Les 500 Premiers Sociétés.* Paris: 1972.

———. *Les Elites Africaines.* Paris, 1974.

———. *Gouvernements et Cabinets Ministèriels, partis politiques.* Paris, 1961+.

———. *L'Industrie Africaine en 1968.* Paris, 1968.

———. *Momento de l'économie africaine 1970.* Paris, 1970.

———. *Momento Statistique de l'Economie africaine 1969.* Paris, 1969.

———. *Les plans de développement des pays d'Afrique Noire.* Paris, 1972.

———. *Répertoire de la diplomatie Africaine.* Paris, 1972.

———. *Répertoire de l'administration africaine 1969.* Paris, 1969.

Europe France Outre-Mer. Monthly to 1987.

Fondation Nationale des Sciences Politiques. *Afrique au Sud du Sahara: Chronologie bimestrielle,* 1960–70.

Food and Agricultural Organization. *Analytic Bibliography on the Sahel.* Rome, 1974.

France. La Documentation Française. *Bibliographie Sommaire de la République du Niger.* Paris, 1969.

———. Service des Affaires Sahariennes. *Essai de bibliographie du Sahara français et des régions avoisinantes.* 1959. 2nd ed. Paris: Editions Arts et Métiers, 1960.

Fugelstad, Finn. "Archival Research in Niger—Some Practical Hints." *African Research and Documentation* 16/17 (1978):26–27.

Gaignebet, Wanda. *Inventaire des thèses africanistes de langues française.* Paris: CARDAN, 1975, and subsequent intermittent editions.

Gibson, G. D. (ed.). "A Bibliography of Anthropological Bibliographies." *Current Anthropology* 10, no. 5 (1969):527–66.

Gontard, Jean Pierre. "Les priorités de Recherches pour le Développement à moyen et à long terme du Sahel." *Genève-Afrique* 15, no. 1 (1976):99–103.

———, and René V. L. Wadlow. "Research Priorities for Medium and Long-term Development in the Sahel: A Bibliographic Essay." *Genève-Afrique* 14, no. 1 (1975):115–120.

Gorman, G. E., and M. M. Mahoney. *Guide to Current National Bibliographies in the Third World.* Munich: Hans Zell, 1983.

Grandidier, G., and E. Joucla. *Bibliographie Générale des Colonies Françaises.* 2 vols. Paris: Société d'Editions, 1937.

Hall, David (ed.) *International African Bibliography.* Quarterly. London: Mansell, 1971+.

Henige, David P. *Colonial Governors from the Fifteenth Century to the Present*. Madison: University of Wisconsin Press, 1970.

Hertefelt, Marcel d', and Anne-Marie Bouttiaux-Ndiaye. *Bibliographie de l'Afrique sud-saharienne: Sciences humaines et sociales 1986–1987*. Tervueren: Musée Royal de l'Afrique Centrale, 1990.

Hommes et Destins, Travaux et Mémoires de l'Académie des Sciences d'Outre-Mer. Paris, 1975.

Hoover Institution. *U.S. and Canadian Publications and Theses on Africa, 1961–66*. Stanford, Calif.: 1968+.

Hull, Doris (ed.). *A Current Bibliography on African Affairs*. Monthly, Farmingdale, N.Y.: Baywood, 1968+.

Institut Fondamental d'Afrique Noire. *Catalogue des Manuscrits de l'IFAN*. Dakar: IFAN, 1966.

International Africa Institute. *Africa*. 1929+.

International Africa Institute. *Africa Bibliographic Series: West Africa*, Compiled by Ruth Jones. London, 1958.

International Institute for Strategic Studies. *The Military Balance, 1976–77*. London, 1977.

International Labour Office. *Rapport au Gouvernement de la République du Niger*. Geneva, 1970.

Jahn, Janheinz, et al. *Who's Who in African Literture*. Tübingen, Ger., 1972.

Jeune Afrique. Weekly. Paris and Tunis, 1968+.

Joucla, Edmond A. *Bibliographie de l'Afrique occidentale française*. Paris: Société d'Editions Géographiques, Maritimes et Coloniales, 1937.

Journal Officiel de la République du Niger. Niamey, 1958+.

Journal Officiel du Territoire du Niger. Niamey, 1933–58.

Knisser-Weber, Anja. *Zwischen Subsistenz und Marktwirtschaft Haussa-Dorfgemeinschaften*. Hamburg: Institute für Afrikakunde, 1989.

Kohler, Jochen. *Deutsche Dissertationen über Afrika; ein Verzeichnis für die Jahre 1918–59*. Bonn: K. Schroder, 1962.

Legum, Colin (ed.). *Africa: A Handbook of the Continent*. New York: Praeger, 1966.

———. *Africa Contemporary Record*. London and New York: Rex Collings and Africana Publishing Co., 1968–90.

Le Rouvreur, Albert. *Eléments pour un dictionnaire biographique de Tchad et du Niger*. Paris: CNRS, 1978.

Leupen, A. H. A. *Bibliographie des populations Touaregs-Sahara et de Soudan Central*. Leiden: Afrika Studiecentrum, 1979.

Lipschutz, Mark, and R. Kent Rasmussen. *Dictionary of African Historical Biography*. Berkeley: University of California Press, 1986.

La Marche Monthly. Niamey, 1989+.

Marchés Tropicaux et Méditerranéens. Weekly. Paris, 1950+.

Massoni, C., et al. *Liste Bibliographique des Travaux effectués dans le bassin du fleuve Niger par les chercheurs de l'ORSTOM de 1943 à 1968*. Paris: ORSTOM, 1971.

Mauny, Raymond. "Bibliographie de la préhistoire et de la protohistoire de l'Ouest Africain." *Bulletin d'IFAN* 29, no. 3/4 (July–Oct. 1967): 879–917.

———. "Bibliographie du Ténéré et des questions relatives à la mission Berliet-Ténéré." In *Documents Scientifiques, Mission Berliet-Ténéré-Tchad*. Paris: Arts et Métiers, 1962, pp. 365–71.

———. "Contribution à la bibliographie de l'histoire de l'Afrique noire des origines à 1850." *Bulletin d'IFAN* (ser. B) 28, no. 3/4 (1966): 297–965.

Meillassoux, Claude. *Cartes Historiques d'Afrique Occidentale (Sénégal et Haut-Sénégal et Niger, 1802–1899)*. Paris: Musée de l'Homme, 1970.

Mercier, Paul. *Cartes Ethno-Démographiques de l'Ouest Africain*. Dakar: IFAN, 1954.

Meyers Handbuch über Afrika. Mannheim: Bibliographisches Institute, 1962.

Moniot, H. *Bibliographie pratique sur l'Histoire de l'Afrique*. Paris: Institut Pédagogique National, 1963.

Le Moniteur Africain. Weekly. Dakar, 1966+.

Nicolaisen, Johannes. "Bibliography." In idem, *Ecology and Culture of the Pastoral Tuareg*. Copenhagen: National Museum of Copenhagen, 1963, pp. 499–516.

"Niger." In *African Biographies*. Bonn/Bad Godesberg: Friedrich-Ebert Stiftung Research Institute, 1967, 1974.

Niger. Commissariat Général au Développement. Centre de Documentation. *Bibliographie Sommaire de la République du Niger*. Niamey, 1972.

Niger. Ministère du Plan. *Annuaire statistique*. Niamey, 1985+.

"Niger Republic." In L. K. Jakande, *West Africa Annual*. Lagos: John West Publications, 1962+.

Nigerama. Quarterly. Niamey, 1987+.

Oxby, C. "Pastoral Nomads and Development: A Select Annotated Bibliography." International African Institute, 1975.

Painter, T. M. "Rediscovering Sources of Nigerien History: The Dosso Archives." *History in Africa* 12 (1985):375–78.

Personalités Publiques de l'Afrique Centrale. Paris: Ediafric, 1972.

Répertoire des Centres de documentation et bibliothèques. Abidjan: Conseil de l'Entente, Service de Documentation, 1980.

Revue Française d'Etudes Politiques Africaines. Monthly/quarterly. Paris, 1968–1990.

Roch, Jean, et al. "Selective Bibliography on Famine and Drought in the Sahel." *African Environment* 1, no. 2 (1975):94–116.

Roubet, C. "Bibliographie Maghreb-Sahara." *Libyca* (Algiers) 16 (1968): 225–34, and subsequent issues.
Le Sahel (Niamey). Daily. 1960+.
Sahel: A Guide to the Microfiche Collection of Documents and Dissertations. Ann Arbor: University Microfilms International, 1981.
Saix, E. *Cuvette du Lac Tchad: Elément d'une bibliographie*. Paris: Prohuza, 1962.
Salamone, F. A. "The Bibliography on the Hausa." *Africana Journal* 6, no. 2 (1975):99–163.
Salvy, G. "Les fichiers sahariens à Paris." *Afrique et Asie,* no. 62 (1963):58–60.
Scheven, Yvette. *Bibliographies for African Studies, 1970–1986*. London: Hans Zell, 1988.
SCOLMA. *United Kingdom Publications and Theses on Africa*. Cambridge: Heffer, 1963+.
Segal, Ronald. *Political Africa: A Who's Who of Personalities and Parties*. New York: Praeger, 1961.
Seydou, Christiane. *Bibliographie Générale du Monde Peul*. Niamey: INSH, 1977.
Taylor, Sidney (ed.). *The New Africans*. London: Hamlyn, 1967.
"Les travaux scientifiques du Président Boubou Hama." *Mu Kaara Sani* (Niamey), no. 1 (n.d.):40–41.
Urvoy, Yves. "Essai de bibliographie des populations du Soudan central (Colonie du Niger)." *Bulletin du Comité d'Etudes Historiques et Scientifiques de l'AOF* 19, no. 2/3 (1936):243–333.
Van Rensburg, A. P. J. *Contemporary Leaders of Africa*. Cape Town, 1975.
West Africa. Weekly. London. 1919+.
Witherell, Julian W. *French Speaking West Africa: A Guide to Official Publications*. Washington, D.C.: Library of Congress, 1976.
Zamponi, Lynda F. *Niger*. Oxford: Clio Press, 1994.
La Zone Franc en Afrique. Paris: Ediafric, 1981.

About the Author

Samuel Decalo (B. Sc., Ottawa University, M.A. and Ph.D. University of Pennsylvania) is an Israeli citizen, normally resident in the United States. He has taught at various universities including the University of Rhode Island; Graduate Faculty, New School for Social Research; Emory University; and the University of Florida. He has also taught abroad, at the University of Botswana and at the University of the West Indies, and is currently Professor of Political Science at the University of Natal, in Durban, South Africa.

Professor Decalo has conducted extensive research, including multiple fieldwork visits, in some twenty-five African states, mostly in Francophone West and Equatorial Africa. He is the author of thirteen books and sixty articles on Africa and the Middle East. Among these are five of our historical dictionaries; three in the Clio Press series of "World Bibliographies"; the classic book on African civil-military relations (*Coups and Military Rule in Africa,* Yale University Press, 2nd edition 1990); and *Psychoses of Power: African Personal Dictatorships,* which was acclaimed by *Choice* as an "Outstanding Book of 1990." His most recent books, currently in press, are *The Stable Minority: Civilian Rule in Africa* and *Gabon: Under the Shadow of Big Brother*, both to be published in 1997 by Florida Academic Press.